# 11th Workshop on Computational Approaches to Subjectivity, Sentiment and Social Media Analysis (WASSA 2021)

AA001633

Online
19 April 2021

ISBN: 978-1-7138-2973-7

**Printed from e-media with permission by:**

Curran Associates, Inc.
57 Morehouse Lane
Red Hook, NY 12571

**Some format issues inherent in the e-media version may also appear in this print version.**

Copyright© (2021) by the Association for Computational Linguistics
All rights reserved.

Printed with permission by Curran Associates, Inc. (2021)

For permission requests, please contact the Association for Computational Linguistics
at the address below.

Association for Computational Linguistics
209 N. Eighth Street
Stroudsburg, Pennsylvania 18360

Phone: 1-570-476-8006
Fax: 1-570-476-0860

acl@aclweb.org

**Additional copies of this publication are available from:**

Curran Associates, Inc.
57 Morehouse Lane
Red Hook, NY 12571 USA
Phone: 845-758-0400
Fax: 845-758-2633
Email: curran@proceedings.com
Web: www.proceedings.com

EACL 2021

# The Workshop on Computational Approaches to Subjectivity, Sentiment and Social Media Analysis

## Proceedings of the Eleventh Workshop

April 19, 2021
Held online due to the COVID situation

©2021 The Association for Computational Linguistics

# Introduction

After the tenth edition of WASSA in 2019, which came only seven months after WASSA 2018, it was decided to take a one-year break from organising the workshop to give the community some time to breathe... Little did we know what COVID-19 had in mind. 2020 has been a year full of sentiment and emotion, to say the least. The pandemic has dominated the news headlines all around the world and evoked a variety of emotions amongst the general public. Understanding these emotions not only provides insights into the way the public responds to the COVID-19 pandemic in itself and to the media coverage of the disease, but might help to encourage health promotion measures.

Research in automatic subjectivity and sentiment analysis remains a popular research task in the field of computational linguistics with a great application potential. Over the years the problem of dealing with affect in text has evolved, making it a very challenging research area with many research questions that still need to be answered and often requiring interdisciplinary approaches.

The aim of the Eleventh Workshop on Computational Approaches to Subjectivity, Sentiment and Social Media Analysis (WASSA 2021) was to continue the line of the previous editions and bring together researchers working on Subjectivity, Sentiment Analysis, Emotion Detection and Classification and their applications to other NLP or real-world tasks (e.g. public health messaging, fake news, media impact analysis) and researchers working on interdisciplinary aspects of affect computation from text. We also welcomed submissions that specifically tackled sentiment or emotion detection and classification in the context of the COVID-19 pandemic.

Though the timing was rather tight, we decided to also organise a shared task on Predicting Empathy and Emotion in Reaction to News Stories (https://competitions.codalab.org/competitions/28713). This task aimed at developing models which can predict empathy (Track I) and emotion (Track II) based on essays written in reaction to news articles which reported on harm caused to a person, a group, or other situations. Five teams participated in the shared task, with three teams submitting predictions for both tracks. For track I, empathy prediction, four teams submitted a system and the best result obtained was an average Pearson correlation of 0.545. For track II, emotion label prediction, four teams submitted a system and the best result was a macro F-1 of 55.3%.

For the main workshop, we accepted 15 papers as long and another 9 as short papers, leading to a total of 24/32 accepted papers (acceptance rate of 75%). For the shared task we received 6 system description paper submissions, out of which we accepted 5. Thus, in total 29 papers will be presented at the workshop, together with the additional contribution from our invited speaker Lyle Ungar, professor of Computer and Information Science at the University of Pennsylvania.

Accepted papers deal with topics including implicit and explicit sentiment analysis, emotion detection or classification and the detection of hate speech, stance or sarcasm. A large number of papers deal with languages other than English, including multilingual approaches but also work conducted on Italian, Dutch, code-mixed Hindi-English and even less-resourced languages such as Sindhi, Marathi and Arabizi. The dominance of COVID-19 in the headlines did not translate to a high number of COVID-related papers, but we gladly included one paper scrutinising resistance to COVID-19 directives.

This year we also asked the reviewers for recommendations for a best paper award and are thrilled to announce that the paper "Lightweight Models for Multimodal Sequential Data" by Soumya Sourav and Jessica Ouyang wins this year's award.

We would like to thank the EACL 2021 Organizers and Workshop Chairs for their help and support at the different stages of the workshop organisation process. We are also especially grateful to the Program Committee members for the time and effort spent to thoroughly review and assess the papers. Finally, we would like to extend our thanks to our invited speaker – Prof. Lyle Ungar - for accepting the invitation to deliver the keynote talk.

Orphée De Clercq, Alexandra Balahur, João Sedoc, Valentin Barriere, Shabnam Tafreshi, Sven Buechel and Veronique Hoste

WASSA 2021 Chairs

# Keynote talk: Using language to study emotional contagion

**Lyle Ungar**
Computer and Information Science, University of Pennsylvania

**Abstract**
The words people use not only reveal their happiness, anger, depression, and empathy toward others; they also influence the people they communicate with, changing their moods and language. Language thus drives emotional contagion and allows us to measure it. We present case studies in which people experience different amounts of emotional contagion based on two factors: 1) Their empathy style: The words people use on Facebook, when correlated with their scores on empathy-measuring questionnaires, reveal empathy-driven emotional contagion. 2) Their level of depression: SMS messages from cell phones show that although depressed people use more sad, negative, and angry language, the texts they receive only show more anger than texts to non-depressed people, suggesting that anger may be more contagious than sadness.

# Organizers

**Organizers**

Orphée de Clercq – Ghent University, Belgium
Alexandra Balahur – European Commission Joint Research Centre
João Sedoc – New York University, U.S.A
Valentin Barriere – European Commission Joint Research Centre
Shabnam Trafreshi – Georgetown University & IBM, U.S.A.
Sven Buechel – Friedrich Schiller University Jena, Germany
Veronique Hoste – Ghent University, Belgium

**Program Committee**

Liesbeth Allein – European Commission Joint Research Centre
Jeremy Barnes – University Pompeu Fabra, Spain
Sabine Bergler – Concordia University, Canada
Cristina Bosco – University of Torino, Italy
Nicoletta Calzolari – CNR Pisa, Italy
Erik Cambria – Nanyang Technological University, Singapore
Sergio Consoli – European Commission Joint Research Centre
Montse Cuadros – Vicomtech, Spain
Luna De Bruyne – Ghent University, Belgium
Lingjia Deng – Bloomberg, U.S.A.
Antske Fokkens – VU Amsterdam, The Netherlands
Michael Gamon – Microsoft, U.S.A.
Lorenzo Gatti – University of Twente, The Netherlands
Matthias Hartung – Semalytix GmbH, Germany
Dirk Hovy – Bocconi University, Italy
Stefano Maria Iacus – European Commission Joint Research Centre
Carlos A. Iglesias – Universidad Politécnica de Madrid, Spain
Ruben Izquierdo Bevia – Nuance, Spain
Gilles Jacobs – Ghent University, Belgium
Aditya Joshi – Notiv, Australia
Evgeny Kim – University of Stuttgart, Germany
Manfred Klenner – University of Zuerich, Switzerland
Roman Klinger – University of Stuttgart, Germany
Emiel Krahmer – Tilburg University, The Netherlands
Mayank Kulkarni – Bloomberg, U.S.A.
Els Lefever – Ghent University, Belgium
Edison Marrese-Taylor – University of Tokyo, Japan
Saif M. Mohammad – National Research Council Canada, Canada
Karo Moilanen – University of Oxford, U.K.
Guenter Neumann – DFKI, Germany
Malvina Nissim – University of Groningen, The Netherlands
Laura Ana Maria Oberländer – University of Stuttgart, Germany
Constantin Orasan – University of Surrey, U.K.
Sean Papay – University of Stuttgart, Germany
Viviana Patti – University of Torino, Italy

Viktor Pekar – University of Wolverhampton, U.K.
Jose Manuel Perea-Ortega – University of Extremadura, Spain
Barbara Plank – IT University of Copenhagen, Denmark
Daniel Preotiuc-Pietro – Bloomberg, U.S.A.
Paolo Rosso – Technical University of Valencia, Spain
Pranaydeep Singh – Ghent University, Belgium
Josef Steinberger – West Bohemia University Prague, The Czech Republic
Carlo Strapparava – Fondazione Bruno Kessler, Italy
Mike Thelwall – University of Wolverhampton, U.K
Dan Tufis – RACAI, Romania
Cynthia Van Hee – Ghent University, Belgium
Tony Veale – University College Dublin, Ireland
Charles Welch – University of Michigan, U.S.A
Michael Wiegand – Saarland University, Germany
Taras Zagibalov – Brantwatch, U.K.

## Table of Contents

# Conference Program

**Monday, April 19, 2021**

9:00–9:15 *Opening of the WASSA workshop*
Orphée De Clercq

**9:15–11:00 ORAL SESSION 1**

9:15–9:40 *ToxCCIn: Toxic Content Classification with Interpretability*
Tong Xiang, Sean MacAvaney, Eugene Yang and Nazli Goharian

9:40–10:05 *Language that Captivates the Audience: Predicting Affective Ratings of TED Talks in a Multi-Label Classification Task*
Elma Kerz, Yu Qiao and Daniel Wiechmann

10:05–10:30 *Partisanship and Fear are Associated with Resistance to COVID-19 Directives*
Mike Lindow, David DeFranza, Arul Mishra and Himanshu Mishra

10:30–10:45 *Explainable Detection of Sarcasm in Social Media*
Ramya Akula and Ivan Garibay

10:45–11:00 *Emotion Ratings: How Intensity, Annotation Confidence and Agreements are Entangled*
Enrica Troiano, Sebastian Padó and Roman Klinger

**11:00–11:30 *Coffee break***

**11:30–12:50 ORAL SESSION 2**

11:30–11:55 *Disentangling Document Topic and Author Gender in Multiple Languages: Lessons for Adversarial Debiasing*
Erenay Dayanik and Sebastian Padó

11:55–12:20 *Universal Joy A Data Set and Results for Classifying Emotions Across Languages*
Sotiris Lamprinidis, Federico Bianchi, Daniel Hardt and Dirk Hovy

12:20–12:35 *FEEL-IT: Emotion and Sentiment Classification for the Italian Language*
Federico Bianchi, Debora Nozza and Dirk Hovy

**Monday, April 19, 2021 (continued)**

12:35–12:50 *An End-to-End Network for Emotion-Cause Pair Extraction*
Aaditya Singh, Shreeshail Hingane, Saim Wani and Ashutosh Modi

**12:50–13:45** ***Lunch break***

**13:45–14:30 SHARED TASK SESSION**

13:45–14:00 *WASSA 2021 Shared Task: Predicting Empathy and Emotion in Reaction to News Stories*
Shabnam Tafreshi, Orphee De Clercq, Valentin Barriere, Sven Buechel, João Sedoc and Alexandra Balahur

14:00–14:15 *PVG at WASSA 2021: A Multi-Input, Multi-Task, Transformer-Based Architecture for Empathy and Distress Prediction*
Atharva Kulkarni, Sunanda Somwase, Shivam Rajput and Manisha Marathe

14:15–14:30 *WASSA@IITK at WASSA 2021: Multi-task Learning and Transformer Finetuning for Emotion Classification and Empathy Prediction*
Jay Mundra, Rohan Gupta and Sagnik Mukherjee

**14:30–15:30** ***INVITED TALK: Using language to study emotional contagion***
Lyle Ungar

**15:30–15:45** ***Coffee break***

**15:45–16:35 ORAL SESSION 3**

15:45–16:10 *Analyzing Curriculum Learning for Sentiment Analysis along Task Difficulty, Pacing and Visualization Axes*
Anvesh Rao Vijjini, Kaveri Anuranjana and Radhika Mamidi

16:10–16:35 *Lightweight Models for Multimodal Sequential Data*
Soumya Sourav and Jessica Ouyang

**Monday, April 19, 2021 (continued)**

*Me, myself, and ire: Effects of automatic transcription quality on emotion, sarcasm, and personality detection*
John Culnan, Seongjin Park, Meghavarshini Krishnaswamy and Rebecca Sharp

*Emotional RobBERT and Insensitive BERTje: Combining Transformers and Affect Lexica for Dutch Emotion Detection*
Luna De Bruyne, Orphee De Clercq and Veronique Hoste

*EmpNa at WASSA 2021: A Lightweight Model for the Prediction of Empathy, Distress and Emotions from Reactions to News Stories*
Giuseppe Vettigli and Antonio Sorgente

*MilaNLP @ WASSA: Does BERT Feel Sad When You Cry?*
Tommaso Fornaciari, Federico Bianchi, Debora Nozza and Dirk Hovy

*Team Phoenix at WASSA 2021: Emotion Analysis on News Stories with Pre-Trained Language Models*
Yash Butala, Kanishk Singh, Adarsh Kumar and Shrey Shrivastava

**17:45–18:00** ***Best paper award and closing***

# ToxCCIn: Toxic Content Classification with Interpretability

**Tong Xiang** [1] **Sean MacAvaney** [1,2] **Eugene Yang** [1] **Nazli Goharian** [1]
[1] IR Lab, Georgetown University, USA [2] University of Glasgow, UK
tx39@georgetown.edu sean.macavaney@glasgow.ac.uk
eugene@ir.cs.georgetown.edu nazli@ir.cs.georgetown.edu

## Abstract

Despite the recent successes of transformer-based models in terms of effectiveness on a variety of tasks, their decisions often remain opaque to humans. Explanations are particularly important for tasks like offensive language or toxicity detection on social media because a manual appeal process is often in place to dispute automatically flagged content. In this work, we propose a technique to improve the interpretability of these models, based on a simple and powerful assumption: a post is at least as toxic as its most toxic span. We incorporate this assumption into transformer models by scoring a post based on the maximum toxicity of its spans and augmenting the training process to identify correct spans. We find this approach effective and can produce explanations that exceed the quality of those provided by Logistic Regression analysis (often regarded as a highly-interpretable model), according to a human study.

## 1 Introduction

The rapidly increasing usage of social media has made communication easier but also has enabled users to spread questionable content (Matamoros-Fernández, 2017), which sometimes even leads to real-world crimes (Johnson et al., 2019; Committee et al., 2017; Center, 2017). To prevent this type of speech from jeopardizing others' ability to express themselves in online communities, many platforms prohibit content that is considered abusive, hate speech, or more generally, toxic. To enforce such policies, some platforms employ automatic content moderation, which uses machine learning techniques to detect and flag violating content (Djuric et al., 2015; Nobata et al., 2016; MacAvaney et al., 2019).

Leveraging the development of pre-trained language models (Devlin et al., 2019; Liu et al., 2019b) and domain transfer learning (Gururangan et al., 2020; Sotudeh et al., 2020), many models (Wiedemann et al., 2020) achieved high performance on toxicity detection (Zampieri et al., 2020). However, directly deploying such systems could be problematic for the following reasons. Despite being highly effective, one major problem is that the decisions of the systems are largely opaque, i.e., it can be difficult to reason why the model made its decision (Waseem and Hovy, 2016). This interpretability problem is especially apparent when compared to prior models, such as Logistic Regression, that transparently assign scores to each input feature (here, words) that can be used to justify the model's decision. Knowing how one decision is made is important in toxicity detection. On one hand, recent laws such as General Data Protection Regulation[1] highlighted the significance of interpretable models for users; on the other hand, interpretable models can assist online community moderators in reducing their time spent on checking each potentially problematic post. Since the purpose of these explanations is for human consumption, we consider a model to be *interpretable* if it can produce a set of words from the input text that humans would consider a reasonable justification for the model's decision.

In this work, we propose a technique to improve the interpretability of transformer-based models like BERT (Devlin et al., 2019) and ELECTRA (Clark et al., 2020) for the task of toxicity detection in social media posts. We base our technique on a simple and powerful assumption: *A post is at least as toxic as its most toxic span.* In other words, the toxicity of a piece of text should be associated with the most toxic span identified in the text. To this end, we propose using neural multi-task model that is trained on (1) toxicity detection over

[1] https://gdpr-info.eu/



*Proceedings of the 11th Workshop on Computational Approaches to Subjectivity, Sentiment and Social Media Analysis*, pages 1–12
April 19, 2021. ©2021 Association for Computational Linguistics

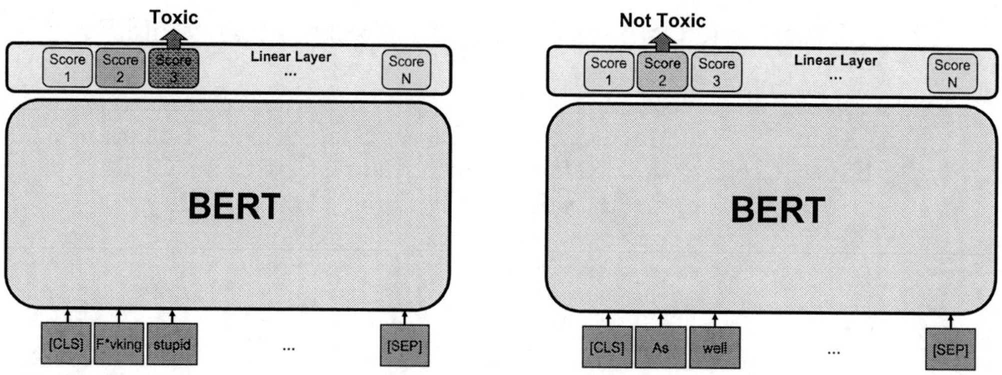


(a) When the input sequence is toxic, the toxicity of the most toxic span is picked to represent the toxicity of the sentence.

(b) When the input sequence is not toxic, none of the spans are toxic, and thus the whole sequence is predicted as non-toxic.

Figure 1: Illustration of our proposed approach. We showcase applying our proposed approach to the transformer-based model, BERT, in this case. In the linear layer, darker color denotes a more toxic span.

the entire piece of text and (2) toxic span detection (i.e., identifying individual tokens in the text that are toxic). Rather than the typical transformer classification approach, our model predicts the toxicity of each individual term in the text and aggregates them via max pooling to predict the toxicity of the entire text (see Fig. 1). Through experiments on the Civil Comment Dataset (Borkan et al., 2019), we find our proposed approach not only improves the classification effectiveness compared to models that are only trained on the classification task, but also helps when transferring the model to a similar task. More importantly, however, the structure of our model inherently generates explanations of the decision by selecting the terms with the highest toxicity scores. We find through a human study that these explanations exceed the quality of those provided by Logistic Regression—a model often regarded as highly interpretable. An error analysis has shown multiple insights into utilizing contextualized models in toxicity detection and lead future directions.

## 2 Related Work

Due to the ubiquity of online conversations, the need for automatic online toxicity detection has become crucial to promote healthy online discussions. Early research relied on surface-level features, e.g., bag-of-words approaches (Warner and Hirschberg, 2012; Waseem and Hovy, 2016; Davidson et al., 2017), and traditional machine learning methods. Although reported to be highly predictive (Schmidt and Wiegand, 2017) and easily interpretable, they suffer from the problem of false positives as the presence of certain patterns could lead to misclassification (Kwok and Wang, 2013). For example, some slurs that frequently appear in African American English are usually picked as strong evidence of toxicity (Xia et al., 2020); these words are indeed innocuous and only confined within the black online community. These features also require such predictive terms to appear in both training and testing set to work effectively. Later on, neural textual representations have shown effectiveness in toxicity detection. Djuric et al. (2015) proposed using sentence-level embedding (Le and Mikolov, 2014) to represent the textual information and has shown great improvement against average over word-level embedding (Nobata et al., 2016). These representations are usually utilized together with either linear classifiers such as Logistic Regression (Djuric et al., 2015), or neural classifiers such as Convolutional Neural Networks (CNN) (Gambäck and Sikdar, 2017) and Long Short-Term Memory Networks (LSTM) (Badjatiya et al., 2017). More recently, large-scale pre-trained language models such as Bidirectional Encoder Representation from Transformer (BERT) (Devlin et al., 2019) have shown great advantages in toxicity detection (Zampieri et al., 2019b, 2020), by learning contextual word embeddings instead of static embeddings.

Despite the fact that systems can achieve astonishing performance on given datasets, they suffer from the problem of lacking interpretability. One way of providing interpretability is to explain predictions (Belinkov and Glass, 2019). For textual data, such explanations could be those sub-strings (i.e., spans) that significantly influence the models' judgments, which were named *rationales* in Zaidan et al. (2007). Zhang et al. (2016) proposed a CNN model that exploits document labels and associated rationales for text classification. On toxicity detection, while most of the works were done focusing on improving the model performances, less attention was paid to interpretability. SemEval-2021 Task 5 provided the Toxic Spans Detection Dataset (TSDD)[2] where each sample is annotated with both post-level label and rationales. Mathew et al. (2020) also provided a hate speech dataset where samples are annotated with rationales and other labels; though they also provided baseline models that can incorporate rationales, these models were built to evaluate the effectiveness of their proposed dataset, and thus cannot be easily transferred to other settings.

## 3 Model

We propose a neural multi-task model that can predict the toxicity and explain its prediction at the same time by providing a set of words that can justify its prediction. In this section, we introduce the assumption that empowers our model with interpretability. Then we present the proposed model's architecture and the multi-task training paradigm.

### 3.1 Assumption

We begin with the following assumption: *A post is at least as toxic as its most toxic span.* This assumption suggests that if there is a word or phrase in a piece of text that is toxic, i.e., with a level of toxicity that is over a certain threshold, the toxicity level of the entire text is certainly over such threshold, and, therefore, should be considered toxic.

This assumption can be formalized as follows. Let $\mathbf{x} = \{x_1, x_2, ..., x_n\}$ denote the input sequence where $n$ is the length of the sequence. Given the input $\mathbf{x}$, we can define $y$ as the toxicity label for the sequence and $\mathbf{y}$ as the toxicity labels for individual token. Let $\mathbf{s} = \{s_1, s_2, ..., s_n\}$ be a model's prediction of toxicity for each token. By our assumption, we apply a max pooling operation over s:

$$\widetilde{s} = \max(\mathbf{s}) \tag{1}$$

where $\widetilde{s}$ represents the predicted toxicity of the entire sequence.

[2]https://sites.google.com/view/toxicspans

We acknowledge that this assumption may not always hold. In some cases, toxicity can be expressed in subtle or implicit ways, such as through sarcasm or metaphor (MacAvaney et al., 2019; Waseem et al., 2017). In such cases, there is often not a clearly identifiable span that is toxic. However, these cases are difficult for any model to identify, and through our experimental results in Section 5, we find that this does not hinder the effectiveness of our model.

### 3.2 Architecture & Methodology

To detect the toxicity and learn the toxic spans at the same time, we propose to use a neural multi-task learning framework (Caruana, 1997). In our settings, we jointly train the model with two related tasks: (1) Toxicity Detection (at the sequence level), and (2) Toxic Span Detection (at the token level). These two tasks share all the parameters in the model. Our approach can be applied to any sequence encoder model (e.g., LSTM or transformer). Given the input sequence $\mathbf{x}$, let the output of the sequence encoder be $\mathbf{H} = \{\mathbf{h_1}, \mathbf{h_2}, ..., \mathbf{h_n}\}$, $\mathbf{H} \in \mathbb{R}^{n \times d}$. Here $\mathbf{h_i} \in \mathbb{R}^d$ denotes the $i$-th hidden state of the final layer, where $d$ denotes the length of the hidden embedding. Unlike what Devlin et al. (2019) do for sequence classification where the linear layer is only stacked on the `[CLS]` token, we place it on top of the whole output sequence $\mathbf{H}$. Let $\mathbf{W} \in \mathbb{R}^{d \times 1}$ denote the parameters of the linear layer, then we have:

$$\mathbf{s} = \mathbf{H} \cdot \mathbf{W} \tag{2}$$

For the classification task, we use $\widetilde{s}$ as the predicted toxicity where $\widetilde{s}$ is calculated following the procedure mentioned in Eq. (1). For the span detection task, we directly leverage the output toxicity sequence s. This setup ensures that the model learns to predict the text as toxic if a span is toxic.

For the purposes of training, let $\mathcal{D}_1$ be the dataset for toxicity detection task, and $\mathcal{D}_2$ be the dataset for toxic spans detection task. We construct the loss of the model $\mathcal{L}$ to be the following:

$$\begin{aligned}\mathcal{L} = \lambda \underbrace{\sum_{(\mathbf{x},y)\in\mathcal{D}_1} \mathcal{L}_C(\mathbf{x}, y)}_{\text{Loss for toxicity detection}} \\ + (1-\lambda) \underbrace{\sum_{(\mathbf{x},\mathbf{y})\in\mathcal{D}_2} \mathcal{L}_S(\mathbf{x}, \mathbf{y})}_{\text{Loss for toxic spans detection}}\end{aligned} \tag{3}$$

where $\mathcal{L}_C$ is the loss for the toxicity detection task and $\mathcal{L}_S$ is the loss for the toxic spans detection task. $\lambda$ denotes a hyperparameter specifying the weight for each task. Here the toxicity detection task is a sequence classification task and the toxic spans detection task is a token classification task. We jointly train the model across tasks in an end-to-end fashion, minimizing the Mean Square Error (MSE) loss for both tasks.

## 4 Experiments

We conduct experiments to answer the following research questions:

**RQ1** Does our aforementioned assumption affect the model's performance at detecting toxic content?

**RQ2** Is our approach applicable to different transformer models?

**RQ3** Does our approach produce models that can generalize to different domains?

**RQ4** Does our model identify spans that improve the interpretability of model decisions?

### 4.1 Data

We primarily train and evaluate our system using the Civil Comment Dataset (CCD) (Borkan et al., 2019). For interpretability, we leverage the Toxic Spans Detection Dataset (TSDD)[2] in a multi-task training paradigm. We also use the Offensive Language Identification Dataset (OLID) (Zampieri et al., 2019a) for the cross-domain evaluation.

**CCD** The CCD (Borkan et al., 2019) is a large-scale dataset with crowd-sourced post-level annotations for toxicity, provided by the Civil Comment platform.[3] Posts that are rude, disrespectful, or unreasonable (Borkan et al., 2019) are considered toxic based on the rating guidelines as published by the Perspective API (Nithum et al., 2017; Wulczyn et al., 2017). Through the platform, crowd-sourced raters were asked to rate comments as "Very Toxic", "Toxic", "Hard to say", or "Not Toxic". A toxicity score between zero and one of a post is the fraction of raters considering it to be toxic. We further cast the scores to binary labels by setting a threshold of 0.5 (i.e., at least half of the raters consider the post toxic). The dataset contains around 1.8 million posts in total, and 8% of them are labeled as toxic.

**TSDD** TSDD[2] is a 10,000-sample subset of CCD, containing only toxic comments, marked up with individual spans that are toxic. Each post is annotated by three annotators. 528 posts have no annotated span since the annotators believe they are toxic as a whole without any explicit span.

**OLID** We use the OLID offensive language dataset (Zampieri et al., 2019b) to examine the domain-transferability. This dataset contains web posts with hierarchical annotation (Waseem et al., 2017). We use its first layer, where the annotations indicate whether the content is offensive (32%) or non-offensive (67%). For our evaluation, we use the official 860-sample OLID test set.

**Curated CCD** For the purpose of training and evaluation, we constructed a 30,000-sample curated CCD by mixing the clear-cut examples with the ambiguous ones, showcased in Table 1. Here, 14,000 samples are used for training and the rest are for testing.

We first sampled 7,000 highly toxic posts (toxicity score greater than 0.8) and 7,000 non-toxic posts (toxicity score less than 0.1) from CCD. Note that 3,000 of the toxic posts sampled were drawn from TSDD, which is still a subset of CDD, for the span annotations. These posts are considered to be *easy* since a great portion of the raters agreed on the judgment.

We further sampled another 8,000 ambiguous posts that have toxicity scores between 0.1 and 0.3 and contain terms that frequently appear in the toxic posts. Terms annotated at least 20 times as part of toxic spans in TSDD are considered frequent, resulting in a list of 62. The top 20 terms are presented in Table 2. We believe that these toxic terms are used in a non-toxic way in these posts, and, therefore, are good adversarial examples for the models to learn from the context instead of memorizing the frequent terms. To maintain an even proportion of toxic and non-toxic posts, we sample an additional 8,000 highly toxic posts.

### 4.2 Implementation

Here, we describe the implementation details of our baselines and the proposed models.

**LR** We use Logistic Regression (LR) classifier with lemmatized uni-gram and bi-gram features and L2 regularization as our baseline for both effectiveness evaluation and interpretability eval-

[3]The platform was shut down by the end of 2017: `https://medium.com/@aja_15265/saying-goodbye-to-civil-comments-41859d3a2b1d`

| Comment | Toxicity | Label |
|---|---|---|
| Like me flagging your comments. | 0 | Non-toxic |
| We need to tax the clueless, irresponsible idiots. | 0.898 | Toxic |
| Don't take the bait of the troll. It's what they want. | 0.167 | Non-toxic |

Table 1: Three samples from Curated CCD. We highlight the toxic spans in the toxic sample with purple underline. We mark the potentially toxic words in the non-toxic sample with pink double underline.

| Word | Freq. ↓ | Word | Freq. ↓ |
|---|---|---|---|
| stupid | 1085 | idiotic | 119 |
| idiot | 572 | ridiculous | 103 |
| idiots | 378 | ass | 102 |
| ignorant | 270 | fools | 100 |
| stupidity | 253 | damn | 100 |
| dumb | 185 | racist | 97 |
| moron | 163 | loser | 91 |
| fool | 163 | morons | 88 |
| pathetic | 145 | hypocrite | 65 |
| crap | 127 | shit | 62 |

Table 2: The 20 most frequent entries of the toxic word list for finding ambiguous non-toxic samples in CCD.

uation. LR is shown to be effective in toxicity detection (Djuric et al., 2015; Waseem and Hovy, 2016) while naturally providing explanations for its predictions if utilized together with bag-of-tokens features. While there are other models that rely on the attention mechanisms to provide various interpretability (Rogers et al., 2020), we choose to use LR instead of them. On the one hand, they usually need postprocessing to perform interpretation, which is less straightforward and intuitive compared to LR; on the other hand, there are still debates about whether attention mechanisms can produce meaningful explanations (Wiegreffe and Pinter, 2019; Jain and Wallace, 2019). For our LR baseline, `NLTK` is used for preprocessing and `scikit-learn` is used for building the classification model.

For the following transformer-based models, we utilize the `transformers` (Wolf et al., 2020) library with Adam (Kingma and Ba, 2015) optimizer. The learning rate is by default set to $2 \times 10^{-5}$ and the number of training epochs is tuned on the validation set. We also utilized the pre-trained BERT-base (Devlin et al., 2019) and ELECTRA-base (Clark et al., 2020) that are available in the Huggingface community. Input sentences are trimmed to a max length of 256 tokens.

**BERT/ELECTRA-CLS** As baselines, we evaluate typical sentence classification (CLS) architectures tuned on only the post-level labels by adding a linear layer on top of the `[CLS]` token. Both BERT and ELECTRA are trained with the cross-entropy loss, which is the default setting in the `transformers` library.

**BERT/ELECTRA-SP** We also evaluate models that are only trained for the span detection (SP) task. It follows the architecture and methodology mentioned in Section 3.2, except only optimizing the toxic spans detection loss $\mathcal{L}_S$. Since only a portion of the samples contains toxic span annotations, the models are only trained on that subset. Beyond the toxic spans detection task, we also evaluate the toxicity detection performance for these models leveraging our proposed assumption, even though these models are not trained for toxicity detection.

**BERT/ELECTRA-MT** Finally, we describe the implementation of our proposed Multi-Task (MT) models. The models are built with the architecture described in Section 3.2 and optimized with the joint loss $\mathcal{L}$ shown in Eq. (3). Since not all the input posts have the labels for toxic spans, the multi-task models are trained by interleaving samples with and without span information. Joint loss $\mathcal{L}$ is calculated for those samples with labels for both tasks; for samples with only post-level labels, we calculate only the classification loss $\mathcal{L}_C$. During training, we interleave the update with each kind of loss to ensure a balance update on the parameters. We specify the hyperparameter $\lambda$ to be 0.5 (i.e., weighting both tasks equally).

## 5 Results on Toxicity Detection

In this section, we answer the first three research questions by presenting and analyzing the classification effectiveness of the proposed models in various settings.

The in-domain toxicity detection performance is

| | Non-Toxic | | | Toxic | | | |
|---|---|---|---|---|---|---|---|
| **Model** | **P** | **R** | **F1** | **P** | **R** | **F1** | **Macro-F1** |
| LR | 0.824 | 0.828 | 0.826 | 0.827 | 0.823 | 0.825 | 0.826 |
| BERT-CLS | 0.944 | 0.674 | 0.786 | 0.746 | 0.960 | 0.840 | 0.813 |
| ELECTRA-CLS | 0.952 | 0.617 | 0.749 | 0.717 | 0.969 | 0.824 | 0.787 |
| BERT-SP | 0.843 | 0.771 | 0.806 | 0.789 | 0.857 | 0.822 | 0.814 |
| ELECTRA-SP | 0.884 | 0.716 | 0.791 | 0.761 | 0.906 | 0.827 | 0.809 |
| BERT-MT | 0.900 | 0.879 | 0.890 | 0.882 | 0.903 | 0.892 | 0.891 |
| ELECTRA-MT | 0.904 | 0.880 | **0.892** | 0.883 | 0.907 | **0.894** | **0.893** |

Table 3: In-domain evaluation results for toxicity classification on the Curated CCD dataset. We report Precision (P), Recall (R), and F1 for each model on all categories. We also report the Macro-F1 for all models. The best F1 performance is indicated in **bold**.

shown in Table 3. Both of our proposed multi-task models BERT-MT and ELECTRA-MT achieve the best performance among all models we evaluated. Models using the `[CLS]` tokens perform the worst among others, even worse than the ones that are only trained on the span detection task. This suggests that the span information is capable of predicting the toxicity of the entire content and combining it with the post-level supervised information further improves the effectiveness. This answers RQ1: our proposed model based on our assumption improves the classification effectiveness. Furthermore, BERT-MT and ELECTRA-MT are equally effective in respect to various evaluation metrics; therefore, we validate RQ2: our approach generalizes to at least two pre-trained transformer models.

Interestingly, LR has the highest precision among the baselines but the lowest recall, suggesting that the model may be relying on high-precision features such as racial slurs. This matches previous observations by MacAvaney et al. (2019).

In a domain transfer setting, i.e., training on CDD and testing on OLID, our approach is competitive with models trained on OLID. In Table 4, both BERT-MT and ELECTRA-MT obtain a competitive 0.77 macro-F1 without training on any example in OLID, even outperforming some leading systems reported on this dataset. Therefore, we confirm that our models remain effective in a domain-transfer setting (RQ3).

### 5.1 Error Analysis

To better understand the limitations of our proposed models, we qualitatively analyze the predictions against the gold labels using BERT-MT.

**False Positives** One major source of false positives comes from treating negative words, usually

| **Model** | **Macro-F1** |
|---|---|
| SVM (Zampieri et al., 2019a) | 0.69 |
| BiLSTM (Zampieri et al., 2019a) | 0.75 |
| BERT-FT (Liu et al., 2019a) | **0.83** |
| BERT-MT (ours, transfer) | 0.77 |
| ELECTRA-MT (ours, transfer) | 0.77 |

Table 4: Evaluation on the OLID. BERT-FT stands for the BERT model fine-tuned on the OLID data. Our system performs competitive in a completely transfer setting (only trained on CCD data). We report Macro-F1 for all models here. The best performance is in **bold**.

adjectives, such as *disgusting*, *lazy*, *incompetent*, as strong signals for toxicity. Also, our proposed models tend to treat certain sub-words that frequently appear in toxic contexts as toxic spans. For example, the sub-word *##nt* of *magnificient* is predicted as toxic (0.979[4]) in the following sentence:

> *Should have had the magnificient Doug Ford stump for Smith....LOL*

This could be attributed to its high frequency in explicitly toxic words such as *ignorant* and *arrogant*.

We also suspect that the model is over-leveraging expression patterns or co-occurrences for toxicity classification. For example:

> *I have never seen a suspect identified as a "brown" man.*

Here, the model misclassifies it as toxic and picks the word *brown* as the most toxic span with a toxicity score of 0.527. We first rule out the possibility that the toxicity comes from the negation

[4]Toxicity score.

by experimentally removing the word *never* from the sentence. We find that the toxicity score of the sentence increases to 0.762 with the word *brown* still as the most toxic span. We then examine by replacing the word *suspect* and keep the rest; when we replace *suspect* with *girl* or *mom*, the toxicity score for *brown* decreases to 0.334 and 0.141 respectively; when changing to *prisoner* or *scammer*, the toxicity score for word *brown* becomes 0.717 and 0.972. Among all the cases that we have experimented with, the word *brown* is consistently the most toxic word in the sentence. It seems that the model is learning the correlation between the noun *suspect* (or any other word positioned here) and the adjective *brown*. Though it might lead to false positives in rare cases, the predictive power that enables this phenomenon could potentially be the reason that our model is doing better in picking unseen words as toxic spans than the LR model since it infers the prediction without leveraging on the lexical information but the syntactic information.

**False Negatives** Some comments are inherently hard for both human and machine classifiers to identify. There are cases where the sentences can reasonably be considered as non-toxic where our model is also predicting as such. For example:

> *Ignore the trolls Sheema......You are great and I always enjoy your pieces.*

> *LOL....I keep hearing Garland never got a hearing blah,blah,blah....It sucks being in the minority....Go win some elections..*

> *When the headline reads "Steve Bannon's porn and meth house"*

In the first and second example, the speaker is not intended to be toxic even with the appearance of the word *trolls* and *sucks*. For the third example, the toxicity lies in the quoted text, which is also not the intention of the speaker. It is debatable that whether our model is indeed making mistakes on these naturally ambiguous comments.

Another major source of false negatives comes from the unawareness of the outside context, e.g., the target of the comment. For example:

> *Degenerate comment.*

> *I'm beginning to think the left lacks the mental capacity to reason.*

| Model | SD-P | SD-R | SD-F1 |
|---|---|---|---|
| LR | 0.111 | 0.195 | 0.120 |
| BERT-SP | 0.836 | 0.798 | 0.792 |
| ELECTRA-SP | 0.840 | 0.807 | **0.798** |
| BERT-MT | 0.837 | 0.785 | 0.784 |
| ELECTRA-MT | 0.842 | 0.788 | 0.789 |

Table 5: Evaluation results on toxic spans detection task. The best performance is **bolded**.

These words/phrases such as *degenerate*, and *lacks the mental capacity to*, which could also be utilized in the neutral descriptions, are used here for expressing toxicity. It is easy for a human to reason out the target mentioned in the sentence and thus be aware of the toxicity raised; this is usually not the case for machine classifiers.

Also, many users intentionally modify the explicitly toxic words (e.g., replacing or removing characters) to obfuscate automatic detection while still keeping their intent clear to human (Djuric et al., 2015), e.g., changing word *idiots* into *I.d.i.o.t.s* or modifying word *asshole* to *a-hole*. Even for advanced transformer models, they still need to learn deeper information or be incorporated with more human supervision to be fully aware of these cases.

## 6 Interpretability

Finally, we examine the interpretability of our models. We first leverage the existing span annotations to evaluate but discovered that they limit our analysis. To overcome the limitation, we further conduct a user study to evaluate the interpretability directly.

### 6.1 Span Detection as Interpretation

We select a balanced 8,000-sample set from the test split of the Curated CCD. Here, non-toxic posts have toxicities between 0 and 0.1 and therefore are all considered to have no toxic spans; toxic samples are all from TSDD. We follow the ad-hoc evaluation metrics which are introduced in Da San Martino et al. (2019) and utilized in SemEval 2021 Task 5[2] – Span Detection Precision (SD-P), Recall (SD-R), and F1 (SD-F1). Due to the nature of the toxicity span detection task where instances span from single tokens to multiple sentences, the ad-hoc evaluation metrics give partial credits to imperfect matches at the character level. Given a post $t$, let the ground truth be a set of character offsets $S_G^t$ and let one certain system $A_i$ return a set of character offsets $S^t_{A_i}$. With the system $A_i$ and ground truth, the SD-P and SP-R on post $t$ are then defined as follow:

$$P^t = \frac{\left|S^t_{A_i} \cap S^t_G\right|}{\left|S^t_{A_i}\right|} \\ R^t = \frac{\left|S^t_{A_i} \cap S^t_G\right|}{\left|S^t_G\right|} \tag{4}$$

With SD-P and SD-R defined, the SD-F1 is also defined:

$$F^t_1 = \frac{2 \cdot P^t \cdot R^t}{P^t + R^t} \tag{5}$$

We report the average values over all samples. The evaluation results are shown in Table 5.

Models trained for the span detection task (*-SP) achieve the highest F1 scores with no surprise. However, our multi-task models provide nearly equal span detection effectiveness with far better performance on toxicity detection (See Table 3). Also, BERT-MT and ELECTRA-MT perform similarly here, further confirming that our approach can be used in various transformer models (RQ2).

We also compared with LR, which is widely considered to be interpretable. The predicted span from the LR model is reconstructed from the bag-of-token features. Features that contribute to the positive score for the sample are considered as the *interpretation* of the model. Our proposed models were shown to strongly outperform LR by a large margin. Note that LR's performance is hindered in this evaluation, as it was not trained for sequence classification (e.g., what CRF would do), despite being considered an interpretable model.

### 6.2 User Study

The labeled toxic spans used for the evaluation in Section 6.1 are not annotated to be the *interpretation* for the toxicity of the post. We argue that it is not sufficient to evaluate the interpretability of prediction along with other known issues in automated evaluation (Manning et al., 2020; Novikova et al., 2017).

Therefore, we select 400 toxic samples from the test split of Curated CCD and 237 offensive samples from the testing set of OLID for the interpretability study. For each sample, three words with the highest predicted score from the models are picked as the explanation and are post-processed to the same form to avoid identifying the models based on the types of token preprocessing. Annotators are asked to annotate for the toxicity (e.g., whether the sample is toxic) of the samples and pick the model with a better explanation. The order and the name of the models are hidden from the annotators to avoid biases. Although ELECTRA-MT and BERT-MT perform comparably in terms of F1, we found that qualitatively BERT-MT is better and therefore picked for the user study.

Despite the subjectivity of the annotation task, the annotators agreed in 78% of the cases. For our quantitative analysis, we use the samples that the annotators agree on. We also filter out 22 samples that both of the annotators considered non-toxic.

| Preference | CCD | OLID | All |
|---|---|---|---|
| LR | 26.5% | 18.8% | 24.0% |
| BERT-MT | 59.4% | 41.6% | 53.7% |
| No Preference | 14.2% | 39.6% | 22.3% |

Table 6: Aggregated human preference during the interpretability experiment for CCD and OLID. We see that the annotators prefer the explanations from the BERT-MT over those from LR by a hefty margin.

On average, our annotators prefer BERT-MT over LR on more than half of the samples. As shown in Table 6, BERT-MT is considered to be more interpretable in both datasets by a wide margin. This result not only suggests that our proposed assumption provides interpretability to transformer models (RQ4) but also better explanations than the widely-known interpretable models.

We now take a closer look at how BERT-MT model's explanations compare to those from LR. Some examples are shown in Table 7. We find that the predictions from BERT-MT are more polarized, while those from LR tend to be neutral. This is because the usage of MSE loss in BERT-MT penalizes values for not being close to 0 or 1; for LR, the L2 regularization penalizes large weight values. It is also worth noting that these models differ in how term scores are aggregated over the post; BERT-MT takes the maximum, whereas LR takes the sum. For analysis, we highlight three cases here:

**When BERT-MT is preferred.** BERT-MT can pick out the toxic spans more accurately by leveraging the context. In comparison, the LR model suffers from picking words based on frequency even with a non-toxic usage, resulting in a bias toward some entities, such as certain groups of people (See example A in Table 7). BERT-MT also takes advantage of the WordPiece tokenization which re-

| # | Model | Example |
|---|---|---|
| A | BERT-MT | red ##neck followers are doing all they can to make america white again . |
| | LR | redneck follower are doing all they can to make america white again . |
| B | BERT-MT | not only is he a liar , he ' s a coward too ! the clown is going down ! |
| | LR | not only is he a liar , he ' s a coward too ! the clown is going down ! |
| C | BERT-MT | wow you ' re un - smart . |
| | LR | wow you ' re un-smart . |
| D | BERT-MT | your constant ability at being an a - hole liar doesn ' t make you great |
| | LR | your constant ability at being an a-hole liar doe n't make you great |

Table 7: Examples for qualitative analysis on interpretability. Here red color indicates toxicity, blue color indicates innocuousness, and white color represents neutral. Darker colors indicate more polarity.

tains the toxic word pieces when users are altering words to avoid censorship; while LR lemmatizes the tokens and resulting in losing this information.

**When LR is preferred.** We observe that LR tends to predict more spans than BERT-MT, leading to higher recall, resulting in more *comprehensive* explanations. Take the example B in Table 7 for instance, the LR is able to pick out the word *coward* and *clown* which are considered to be non-toxic by BERT-MT. We conclude that BERT-MT is more cautious in predicting words as toxic.

**When both models are equal.** We find that both models are doing poorly if the sentence is implicitly toxic. Such indirect toxicity is carried either by negation (Example C in Table 7) or adversarially-modified toxic words (Example D in Table 7). Finally, there are also many cases where both models are doing equally well. This category of samples is generally easier to detect with explicit terms or slurs without ambiguity.

## 7 Conclusion & Future Work

In this paper, we proposed a toxicity detection approach that builds in the interpretability by predicting the toxicity of a piece of text based on the toxicity level of its spans. We showed that our approach is more effective in both in-domain and cross-domain evaluation than baselines that were shown to be effective. By conducting a user study, we further showed that our approach generates better explanations of the classification decisions than what Logistic Regression produces, which is known to be interpretable.

In the future, we plan to extend our current work in several ways. We plan to take the implicit toxicity into consideration to make our assumption more robust. Besides, we will dig more into toxicity detection with long sequences. We also plan to investigate methods that consider more subtle context and actors in the content to better distinguish different usages of the toxic terms.

## Acknowledgements

This work was supported in part by the ARCS Foundation.

## References

Pinkesh Badjatiya, Shashank Gupta, Manish Gupta, and Vasudeva Varma. 2017. Deep learning for hate speech detection in tweets. In *Proceedings of the 26th International Conference on World Wide Web Companion*, WWW '17 Companion, page 759–760, Republic and Canton of Geneva, CHE. International World Wide Web Conferences Steering Committee.

Yonatan Belinkov and James Glass. 2019. Analysis methods in neural language processing: A survey. *Transactions of the Association for Computational Linguistics*, 7:49–72.

Daniel Borkan, Lucas Dixon, Jeffrey Sorensen, Nithum Thain, and Lucy Vasserman. 2019. Nuanced metrics for measuring unintended bias with real data for text classification. In *Companion Proceedings of The 2019 World Wide Web Conference*, WWW '19, page 491–500, New York, NY, USA. Association for Computing Machinery.

Rich Caruana. 1997. Multitask learning. *Machine learning*, 28(1):41–75.

Southern Poverty Law Center. 2017. The year in hate and extremism.

Kevin Clark, Minh-Thang Luong, Quoc V. Le, and Christopher D. Manning. 2020. Electra: Pre-training text encoders as discriminators rather than generators. In *International Conference on Learning Representations*.

Home Affairs Committee et al. 2017. Hate crime: Abuse, hate and extremism online. *Fourteenth Report of Session 2016*, 17.

Giovanni Da San Martino, Seunghak Yu, Alberto Barrón-Cedeño, Rostislav Petrov, and Preslav Nakov. 2019. Fine-grained analysis of propaganda in news article. In *Proceedings of the 2019 Conference on Empirical Methods in Natural Language Processing and the 9th International Joint Conference on Natural Language Processing (EMNLP-IJCNLP)*, pages 5636–5646, Hong Kong, China. Association for Computational Linguistics.

Thomas Davidson, Dana Warmsley, Michael Macy, and Ingmar Weber. 2017. Automated hate speech detection and the problem of offensive language. In *Proceedings of the 11th International AAAI Conference on Web and Social Media*, ICWSM '17, pages 512–515.

Jacob Devlin, Ming-Wei Chang, Kenton Lee, and Kristina Toutanova. 2019. BERT: Pre-training of deep bidirectional transformers for language understanding. In *Proceedings of the 2019 Conference of the North American Chapter of the Association for Computational Linguistics: Human Language Technologies, Volume 1 (Long and Short Papers)*, pages 4171–4186, Minneapolis, Minnesota. Association for Computational Linguistics.

Nemanja Djuric, Jing Zhou, Robin Morris, Mihajlo Grbovic, Vladan Radosavljevic, and Narayan Bhamidipati. 2015. Hate speech detection with comment embeddings. In *Proceedings of the 24th International Conference on World Wide Web*, WWW '15 Companion, page 29–30, New York, NY, USA. Association for Computing Machinery.

Björn Gambäck and Utpal Kumar Sikdar. 2017. Using convolutional neural networks to classify hate-speech. In *Proceedings of the First Workshop on Abusive Language Online*, pages 85–90, Vancouver, BC, Canada. Association for Computational Linguistics.

Suchin Gururangan, Ana Marasović, Swabha Swayamdipta, Kyle Lo, Iz Beltagy, Doug Downey, and Noah A. Smith. 2020. Don't stop pretraining: Adapt language models to domains and tasks. In *Proceedings of the 58th Annual Meeting of the Association for Computational Linguistics*, pages 8342–8360, Online. Association for Computational Linguistics.

Sarthak Jain and Byron C. Wallace. 2019. Attention is not Explanation. In *Proceedings of the 2019 Conference of the North American Chapter of the Association for Computational Linguistics: Human Language Technologies, Volume 1 (Long and Short Papers)*, pages 3543–3556, Minneapolis, Minnesota. Association for Computational Linguistics.

NF Johnson, R Leahy, N Johnson Restrepo, N Velasquez, M Zheng, P Manrique, P Devkota, and Stefan Wuchty. 2019. Hidden resilience and adaptive dynamics of the global online hate ecology. *Nature*, 573(7773):261–265.

Diederik P. Kingma and Jimmy Ba. 2015. Adam: A method for stochastic optimization. In *3rd International Conference on Learning Representations, ICLR 2015, San Diego, CA, USA, May 7-9, 2015, Conference Track Proceedings*.

Irene Kwok and Yuzhou Wang. 2013. Locate the hate: Detecting tweets against blacks. In *Proceedings of the Twenty-Seventh AAAI Conference on Artificial Intelligence*, AAAI'13, page 1621–1622. AAAI Press.

Quoc Le and Tomas Mikolov. 2014. Distributed representations of sentences and documents. In *Proceedings of the 31st International Conference on International Conference on Machine Learning - Volume 32*, ICML'14, page II–1188–II–1196. JMLR.org.

Ping Liu, Wen Li, and Liang Zou. 2019a. NULI at SemEval-2019 task 6: Transfer learning for offensive language detection using bidirectional transformers. In *Proceedings of the 13th International Workshop on Semantic Evaluation*, pages 87–91, Minneapolis, Minnesota, USA. Association for Computational Linguistics.

Yinhan Liu, Myle Ott, Naman Goyal, Jingfei Du, Mandar Joshi, Danqi Chen, Omer Levy, Mike Lewis, Luke Zettlemoyer, and Veselin Stoyanov. 2019b. Roberta: A robustly optimized bert pretraining approach.

Sean MacAvaney, Hao-Ren Yao, Eugene Yang, Katina Russell, Nazli Goharian, and Ophir Frieder. 2019. Hate speech detection: Challenges and solutions. *PLoS ONE*, 14:1–16.

Emma Manning, Shira Wein, and Nathan Schneider. 2020. A human evaluation of AMR-to-English generation systems. In *Proceedings of the 28th International Conference on Computational Linguistics*, pages 4773–4786, Barcelona, Spain (Online). International Committee on Computational Linguistics.

Ariadna Matamoros-Fernández. 2017. Platformed racism: the mediation and circulation of an australian race-based controversy on twitter, facebook and youtube. *Information, Communication & Society*, 20(6):930–946.

Binny Mathew, Punyajoy Saha, Seid Muhie Yimam, Chris Biemann, P. Goyal, and Animesh Mukherjee. 2020. Hatexplain: A benchmark dataset for explainable hate speech detection. *ArXiv*, abs/2012.10289.

Thain Nithum, Dixon Lucas, and Wulczyn Ellery. 2017. Wikipedia talk labels: Toxicity.

Chikashi Nobata, Joel Tetreault, Achint Thomas, Yashar Mehdad, and Yi Chang. 2016. Abusive language detection in online user content. In *Proceedings of the 25th International Conference on World Wide Web*, WWW '16, page 145–153, Republic and Canton of Geneva, CHE. International World Wide Web Conferences Steering Committee.

Jekaterina Novikova, Ondřej Dušek, Amanda Cercas Curry, and Verena Rieser. 2017. Why we need new evaluation metrics for NLG. In *Proceedings of the 2017 Conference on Empirical Methods in Natural Language Processing*, pages 2241–2252, Copenhagen, Denmark. Association for Computational Linguistics.

Anna Rogers, Olga Kovaleva, and Anna Rumshisky. 2020. A primer in BERTology: What we know about how BERT works. *Transactions of the Association for Computational Linguistics*, 8:842–866.

Anna Schmidt and Michael Wiegand. 2017. A survey on hate speech detection using natural language processing. In *Proceedings of the Fifth International Workshop on Natural Language Processing for Social Media*, pages 1–10, Valencia, Spain. Association for Computational Linguistics.

Sajad Sotudeh, Tong Xiang, Hao-Ren Yao, Sean MacAvaney, Eugene Yang, Nazli Goharian, and Ophir Frieder. 2020. GUIR at SemEval-2020 task 12: Domain-tuned contextualized models for offensive language detection. In *Proceedings of the Fourteenth Workshop on Semantic Evaluation*, pages 1555–1561, Barcelona (online). International Committee for Computational Linguistics.

William Warner and Julia Hirschberg. 2012. Detecting hate speech on the world wide web. In *Proceedings of the Second Workshop on Language in Social Media*, pages 19–26, Montréal, Canada. Association for Computational Linguistics.

Zeerak Waseem, Thomas Davidson, Dana Warmsley, and Ingmar Weber. 2017. Understanding abuse: A typology of abusive language detection subtasks. In *Proceedings of the First Workshop on Abusive Language Online*, pages 78–84, Vancouver, BC, Canada. Association for Computational Linguistics.

Zeerak Waseem and Dirk Hovy. 2016. Hateful symbols or hateful people? predictive features for hate speech detection on Twitter. In *Proceedings of the NAACL Student Research Workshop*, pages 88–93, San Diego, California. Association for Computational Linguistics.

Gregor Wiedemann, Seid Muhie Yimam, and Chris Biemann. 2020. UHH-LT at SemEval-2020 task 12: Fine-tuning of pre-trained transformer networks for offensive language detection. In *Proceedings of the Fourteenth Workshop on Semantic Evaluation*, pages 1638–1644, Barcelona (online). International Committee for Computational Linguistics.

Sarah Wiegreffe and Yuval Pinter. 2019. Attention is not not explanation. In *Proceedings of the 2019 Conference on Empirical Methods in Natural Language Processing and the 9th International Joint Conference on Natural Language Processing (EMNLP-IJCNLP)*, pages 11–20, Hong Kong, China. Association for Computational Linguistics.

Thomas Wolf, Lysandre Debut, Victor Sanh, Julien Chaumond, Clement Delangue, Anthony Moi, Pierric Cistac, Tim Rault, Rémi Louf, Morgan Funtowicz, Joe Davison, Sam Shleifer, Patrick von Platen, Clara Ma, Yacine Jernite, Julien Plu, Canwen Xu, Teven Le Scao, Sylvain Gugger, Mariama Drame, Quentin Lhoest, and Alexander M. Rush. 2020. Transformers: State-of-the-art natural language processing. In *Proceedings of the 2020 Conference on Empirical Methods in Natural Language Processing: System Demonstrations*, pages 38–45, Online. Association for Computational Linguistics.

Ellery Wulczyn, Nithum Thain, and Lucas Dixon. 2017. Ex machina: Personal attacks seen at scale. In *Proceedings of the 26th International Conference on World Wide Web*, WWW '17, page 1391–1399, Republic and Canton of Geneva, CHE. International World Wide Web Conferences Steering Committee.

Mengzhou Xia, Anjalie Field, and Yulia Tsvetkov. 2020. Demoting racial bias in hate speech detection. In *Proceedings of the Eighth International Workshop on Natural Language Processing for Social Media*, pages 7–14, Online. Association for Computational Linguistics.

Omar Zaidan, Jason Eisner, and Christine Piatko. 2007. Using "annotator rationales" to improve machine learning for text categorization. In *Human Language Technologies 2007: The Conference of the North American Chapter of the Association for Computational Linguistics; Proceedings of the Main Conference*, pages 260–267, Rochester, New York. Association for Computational Linguistics.

Marcos Zampieri, Shervin Malmasi, Preslav Nakov, Sara Rosenthal, Noura Farra, and Ritesh Kumar. 2019a. Predicting the type and target of offensive posts in social media. In *Proceedings of the 2019 Conference of the North American Chapter of the Association for Computational Linguistics: Human Language Technologies, Volume 1 (Long and Short Papers)*, pages 1415–1420, Minneapolis, Minnesota. Association for Computational Linguistics.

Marcos Zampieri, Shervin Malmasi, Preslav Nakov, Sara Rosenthal, Noura Farra, and Ritesh Kumar. 2019b. SemEval-2019 task 6: Identifying and categorizing offensive language in social media (OffensEval). In *Proceedings of the 13th International Workshop on Semantic Evaluation*, pages 75–86, Minneapolis, Minnesota, USA. Association for Computational Linguistics.

Marcos Zampieri, Preslav Nakov, Sara Rosenthal, Pepa Atanasova, Georgi Karadzhov, Hamdy Mubarak, Leon Derczynski, Zeses Pitenis, and Çağrı Çöltekin. 2020. SemEval-2020 task 12: Multilingual offensive language identification in social media (OffensEval 2020). In *Proceedings of the Fourteenth Workshop on Semantic Evaluation*, pages 1425–1447, Barcelona (online). International Committee for Computational Linguistics.

Ye Zhang, Iain Marshall, and Byron C. Wallace. 2016. Rationale-augmented convolutional neural networks for text classification. In *Proceedings of the 2016 Conference on Empirical Methods in Natural Language Processing*, pages 795–804, Austin, Texas. Association for Computational Linguistics.

# Language that Captivates the Audience: Predicting Affective Ratings of TED Talks in a Multi-Label Classification Task

**Elma Kerz**
RWTH Aachen University

**Yu Qiao**
RWTH Aachen University

**Daniel Wiechmann**
University of Amsterdam

elma.kerz@ifaar.rwth-aachen.de
yu.qiao@rwth-aachen.de
d.wiechmann@uva.nl

## Abstract

The aim of the paper is twofold: (1) to automatically predict the ratings assigned by viewers to 14 categories available for TED talks in a multi-label classification task and (2) to determine what types of features drive classification accuracy for each of the categories. The focus is on features of language usage from five groups pertaining to syntactic complexity, lexical richness, register-based n-gram measures, information-theoretic measures and LIWC-style measures. We show that a Recurrent Neural Network classifier trained exclusively on within-text distributions of such features can reach relatively high levels of overall accuracy (69%) across the 14 categories. We find that features from two groups are strong predictors of the affective ratings across all categories and that there are distinct patterns of language usage for each rating category.

## 1 Introduction

The ability to communicate competently and effectively is key to personal contentment, academic achievement and professional career success. The ability to communicate competently is even found to enhance social relationships (Burleson, 2007; Morreale and Pearson, 2008). In educational and vocational contexts, competent speakers experience more success in sharing their knowledge, ideas and views (De Vries et al., 2010). One of the essential communication skills is that of giving an informative and impactful public speech. The development and mastery of public speaking is recognized as a core communicative competence (Schreiber et al., 2012) and has been incorporated into the educational curricula and standards for both first and second/foreign language (Common Core State Standards Initiative, 2010). Across various assessment grids and evaluation forms, a speech is considered competent and effective when the communicative intention is fulfilled – such as that of informing, persuading or entertaining an audience (and most speeches aim at achieving one or more of these) is achieved – when it is appropriate to the specific communicative context and when it matches the expectations of the audience. Given its central role, it is hardly surprising that research on public speaking has given rise to a vast field, scattered across disciplines using a range of methodological approaches (Backlund and Morreale, 2015). This research has been directed towards understanding the role of both verbal and non-verbal components in the assessment of the multidimensional construct of public speaking competence (Morreale, 2007). In more recent years, there has been a growing interest in automatic assessment of speaking skills. Most studies in this area have primarily focused on the role of auditory and acoustic measures of prosody (such as loudness, voice quality and pitch) and non-verbal cues (such as the use of gestures, eye-contact and posture) in predicting human ratings (see Section 2 on related work for more details).

The present paper contributes to and expands this emerging line of research by modeling public speaking skills in a multi-label classification task on the basis of five groups of features of language usage. More specifically, the aim of the paper is twofold: (1) to automatically predict the affective ratings of public speeches assigned by online viewers across fourteen rating



*Proceedings of the 11th Workshop on Computational Approaches to Subjectivity, Sentiment and Social Media Analysis*, pages 13–24
April 19, 2021. ©2021 Association for Computational Linguistics

categories and (2) to determine what types of features drive classification accuracy in predicting each of the categories. In pursuit of these aims, we use a large open repository of public speaking, TED Talks[1]. TED (Technology, Entertainment and Design) Talks are designed to not exceed the length of 18 minutes and provide succinct and enlightening insights on various topics or ideas that are "worth spreading." Topics presented in these talks range from global warming to what keeps us happy and healthy as we go through life. Most popular TED Talks, such as Brené Brown's "The Power of Vulnerability" has garnered almost 48.000.000 million views. TED presenters are often selected not only on the basis of their expertise on a given topic but also for their ability to effectively and succinctly communicate.

The dataset used in the paper included 2392 public speaking videos aligned with 5.89 million human ratings. Each TED speech is rated in terms of 14 categories: (1) beautiful, (2) confusing, (3) courageous, (4) fascinating, (5) funny, (6) informative, (7) ingenious, (8) inspiring, (9) jaw-dropping, (10) long-winded, (11) obnoxious, (12) OK, (13) persuasive and (14) unconvincing. The speech transcripts were automatically analyzed using CoCoGen, a computational tool that implements a sliding-window technique to compute a series of measurements for a given language feature (contours) that captures the distribution of that feature within a text. A Recurrent Neural Network (RNN) classifier – that exploits the sequential information in those contours – was trained on these distributions to predict 14 rating categories investigated in the paper. The remainder of the paper is organized as follows: Section 2 briefly presents a concise review of related work. Section 3 describes the TED talk corpus we used alongside with viewer ratings. Sections 4 presents the tool used for automated text analysis and the five groups of features used in the paper. Section 5 gives a description of the classification model architecture. Section 6 presents the main results and discusses them. Finally, Section 7 summarizes the main findings reported in the paper and proposes future research directions.

[1]https://www.ted.com/

## 2 Related work

A combined use of automated text analysis of authentic language use in large corpora and machine learning techniques has received increasing interest in recent years. Such an approach has been successfully applied in various classification tasks, including detection of personality, gender, and age in the language of social media (Schwartz et al., 2013), Alzheimer's dementia detection in spontaneous speech (Luz et al., 2020), author identification and/or verification (Khanh and Vorobeva, 2020), fake news detection (Pérez-Rosas et al., 2017), etc. Most closely related to this paper is research focused on predicting human behavioral responses and human subjective/affective ratings/judgements through automated analysis of speaking samples. Several studies have used verbal and non-verbal cues in predicting audience laughter in humorous speeches (Chen and Lee, 2017), human ratings of politicians' speaking performance along multiple dimensions, such as expressiveness, monotonicity and persuasiveness (Scherer et al., 2012) or predicting performance assessments of students' oral presentation (Luzardo et al., 2014). For example, Luzardo et al. (2014) trained a binary classifier to predict the quality of the presentation. The accuracy of the trained binary classifier is 65% and 69% respectively for the features extracted from slides and audio track. In (Pfister and Robinson, 2011), real-time recognition of affective states and its application to the assessment of public speaking skills are proposed by using acoustic features. The skills are predicted with 61-81% accuracy. In another interesting application, (Weninger et al., 2012) analysed 143 online speeches hosted on YouTube to classify an individual as achievers, charismatic speakers, and team players with 72.5% accuracy on unseen data. The most related work to ours is Weninger et al. (2013), which predicted the affective ratings for online TED talks using lexical features, where online viewers assigned 3 out of 14 predefined rating categories that resulted in the affective state invoked in them listening to the talks. Their models reached average recall rates of 74.9 for positive categories (jaw-dropping, funny, courageous, fascinating, inspiring, ingenious, beautiful, informative, persuasive) and 60.3 for neutral or negative ones (OK, confusing, unconvincing, long-winded, obnoxious). In summary, as reviewed above, the available literature on automatic assessment and evaluation of speaking competencies based on human judgments or affective ratings have primarily drawn on audio features (prosody of the speech) and/or visual cues.

## 3 Data

We analysed the TedTalk data gathered on the ted.com website[2]. We crawled the site and obtained every TED Talk transcript and its metadata from 2006 through 2017, which yielded a total of 2668 talks. Viewers on the Internet can vote for three impression-related labels out of the 14 types of labels: beautiful, confusing, courageous, fascinating, funny, informative, ingenious, inspiring, jaw-dropping, longwinded, obnoxious, OK, persuasive, and unconvincing. The labels are not mutually exclusive and users can select up to three labels for each talk. If only a single label is chosen, it is counted three times. All talks that featured more than one speaker as well as talks that centered around music performances were removed. This resulted in a dataset of 2392 TED talks with a total number of views of 4139 million and a total number of 5.89 million ratings (see Table 1). All ratings were normalized per million views to account for differences in the amount of time that talks have been online. All ratings were binarized by their medians, such that each category has a value 1 when the rating of a text in this category was above or equal to the median and 0 if not.

## 4 Automated Text Analysis

The speech transcripts were automatically analyzed using CoCoGen, a computational tool that implements a sliding window technique to calculate within-text distributions of scores for a given language feature (for current applications of the tool in the context of text classification, see (Kerz et al., 2020; Qiao et al., 2020; Ströbel et al., 2020)). Here, in this paper, we employ a total of 119 features derived from multi-disciplinary integrated approaches to language (Christiansen and Chater, 2017) that fall into five categories: (1) measures of syntactic complexity, (2) measures of lexical richness, (3) register-based n-gram frequency measures, (4) information-theoretic measures, and (5) LIWC-style (Linguistic Inquiry and Word Count) measures. The first four categories of features are derived from the literature on language development showing that, in the course of their lifespan, humans learn to produce and understand complex syntactic structures, more sophisticated and diverse vocabulary and informationally denser language (Berman, 2007; Hartshorne and Germine, 2015; Ehret and Szmrecsanyi, 2019; Lu, 2010, 2012; Brysbaert et al., 2019). The inclusion of features in the fourth category is motivated by recent research on language adaptation (Chang et al., 2012) and research that looks at language from the perspective of complex adaptive systems (Beckner et al., 2009; Christiansen and Chater, 2016a) indicating that, based on accumulated language knowledge emerging from lifelong exposure to various types of language inputs, humans learn to adapt their language to meet the functional requirements of different communicative contexts. The fifth group of features is based on insights from many years of research conducted by Pennebaker and colleagues (Pennebaker et al., 2003; Tausczik and Pennebaker, 2010), showing that the words people use in their everyday life provide important psychological cues to their thought processes, emotional states, intentions, and motivations.

In contrast to the standard approach implemented in other software for automated text analysis that relies on aggregate scores representing the average value of a feature in a text, the sliding-window approach employed in CoCoGen tracks the distribution of the feature scores within a text. A sliding window can be conceived of as a window of size $ws$, which is defined by the number of sentences it contains. The window is moved across a text sentence-by-sentence, computing one value per window for a given indicator. The series of measurements generated by CoCoGen captures the progression of language performance within a text for a given indicator and is

[2] https://www.ted.com/

Table 1: Descriptive statistics for TED talk dataset (N=2392 talks); total of 5.89 million ratings from a total of 4162 million views. Descriptive statistics of rating scores are normalized per million views.

| *Meta* | | Mean | SD | Median | Min | Max |
|---|---|---|---|---|---|---|
| Duration (min) | | 13.62 | 5.29 | 14.14 | 2.25 | 44.63 |
| Word Count | | 2044.56 | 885.54 | 2040 | 15 | 5800 |
| Views | | 1730676.52 | 2540236.17 | 1139779.5 | 155895 | 47227110 |
| *Ratings* | N ratings | Mean | SD | Median | Min | Max |
| Inspiring | 1277876 | 534.23 | 1307.69 | 235 | 5 | 24924 |
| Informative | 862945 | 360.76 | 550.77 | 221.5 | 0 | 9787 |
| Fascinating | 758344 | 317.03 | 636.79 | 161.5 | 5 | 14447 |
| Persuasive | 544215 | 227.51 | 476.24 | 101 | 0 | 10704 |
| Beautiful | 444193 | 185.7 | 481.46 | 62 | 0 | 9437 |
| Courageous | 401316 | 167.77 | 437.11 | 53 | 0 | 8668 |
| Funny | 368139 | 153.9 | 603.88 | 20 | 0 | 19645 |
| Ingenious | 360870 | 150.87 | 285.87 | 68 | 0 | 6073 |
| Jaw-dropping | 344204 | 143.9 | 560.84 | 40 | 0 | 14728 |
| OK | 193184 | 80.76 | 90.16 | 55 | 0 | 1341 |
| Unconvincing | 127299 | 53.22 | 93.11 | 27 | 0 | 2194 |
| Longwinded | 78158 | 32.67 | 42.26 | 19 | 0 | 447 |
| Obnoxious | 60440 | 25.27 | 53.55 | 12 | 0 | 1361 |
| Confusing | 49815 | 20.83 | 31.88 | 12 | 0 | 531 |

referred here to as a 'complexity contour'. In general, for a text comprising $n$ sentences, there are $w = n - ws + 1$ windows.[3] CoCoGen uses the Stanford CoreNLP suite (Manning et al., 2014) for performing tokenization, sentence splitting, part-of-speech tagging, lemmatization and syntactic parsing (Probabilistic Context Free Grammar Parser (Klein and Manning, 2003)).

Table 2 provides a concise overview of the features used in this study. The first group consists of 18 features pertaining to syntactic complexity. These features are implemented based on descriptions in Lu (2010) and using the Tregex tree pattern matching tool (Levy and Andrew, 2006) with syntactic parse trees for extracting specific patterns. The second group subsumes 12 features pertaining to lexical richness: five measures of lexical variation, one measure of lexical density, seven measures of lexical sophistication. The operationalizations of these measures follow those described in Lu (2012) and Ströbel (2014). The third group includes 25 n-gram frequency features that are derived from the five register sub-components of the Contemporary Corpus of American English (COCA, (Davies, 2008)): spoken, magazine, fiction, news and academic language[4]. Our frequency-ngram measures differ from those used in the earlier studies reviewed in Section 2. Instead of using only bigrams and trigrams, we extend them to include longer word combinations (four- and five-grams) and use a more nuanced definition to operationalize the usage of such combinations given in equation (1):

$$\text{Norm}_{n,s,r} = \frac{|C_{n,s,r}| \cdot \log \left[\prod_{c \in |C_{n,s,r}|} freq_{n,r}(c)\right]}{|U_{n,s}|} \tag{1}$$

Let $A_{n,s}$ be the list of n-grams ($n \in [1, 5]$) appearing within a sentence $s$, $B_{n,r}$ the list of n-gram appearing in the n-gram frequency list of register $r$ ($r \in \{\text{acad, fic, mag, news, spok}\}$) and $C_{n,s,r} = A_{n,s} \cap B_{n,r}$ the list of n-grams appearing

[3]Given the constraint that there has to be at least one window, a text has to comprise at least as many sentences at the $ws$ is wide $n \geq w$.

[4]The Contemporary Corpus of American English is the largest genre-balanced corpus of American English, which at the time the measures were derived comprised of 560 million words.

Table 2: Overview of the 119 features investigated in the paper

| Feature groups | Number of features | Sub-groups | Example/Description |
|---|---|---|---|
| Syntactic complexity | 18 | Length of production unit<br>Subordination<br>Coordination<br>Particular structures | e.g. Mean length of clause<br>e.g. Clauses per sentences<br>e.g. Coordinate phrases per clause<br>e.g. Complex nominals per clause |
| Lexical richness | 12 | Lexical density<br><br>Lexical diversity<br>Lexical sophistication | The number of lexical words divided by total number of words<br>e.g. Type-token ratio<br>e.g. Words from the New General Service List, see Browne et al. (2013) |
| Register-based | 25 | Spoken ($n \in [1,5]$)<br>Fiction ($n \in [1,5]$)<br>Magazine ($n \in [1,5]$)<br>News ($n \in [1,5]$)<br>Academic ($n \in [1,5]$) | Frequencies of uni-, bi-tri-, four-, five-grams from the five sub-components (genres) of the COCA, see Davies (2008) |
| Information theory | 3 | $\text{Kolmogorov}_{\text{Deflate}}$<br>$\text{Kolmogorov}_{\text{Deflate Syntactic}}$<br>$\text{Kolmogorov}_{\text{Deflate Morphological}}$ | Measures use Deflate algorithm and relate size of compressed file to size of original file |
| LIWC-style | 61 | Linguistic dimensions<br>Psychological processes<br>Relativity<br>Personal concerns | For a comprehensive description of LIWC features, see Pennebaker et al. (2015a) |

both in $s$ and the n-gram frequency list of register $r$. $U_{n,s}$ is defined as the list of unique n-gram in $s$, and $freq_{n,r}(a)$ the frequency of n-gram $a$ according to the n-gram frequency list of register $r$.

A total of 25 measures results from the combination of (a) a 'reference list' containing the top 100,000 most frequent n-grams and their frequencies from one of five register subcomponents of the COCA corpus and (b) the size of the n-gram ($n \in [1, 5]$). The fourth group includes three information-theoretic measures that are based on Kolmogorov complexity. These measures use the Deflate algorithm (Deutsch, 1996) to compress a text and obtain complexity scores by relating the size of the compressed file to the size of the original file (see (Ströbel, 2014) for the operationalization and implementation of these measures).

## 5 Classification Models

We used a Recurrent Neural Network (RNN) classifier, specifically a bidirectional dynamic RNN model with Long Short-term Memory (LSTM) cells. A dynamic RNN was chosen as it can handle sequences of variable length[5]. As shown in Figure 1, the input of the contour-based model is a sequence $X = (x_1, x_2, \ldots, x_l, x_{l+1}, \ldots, x_n)$, where $x_i$, the output of CoCoGen for the $i$th window of a document, is a 119 dimensional vector, $l$ is the length of the sequence, $n \in \mathbb{Z}$ is a number, which is greater or equal to the length of the longest sequence in the dataset and $x_{l+1}, \cdots, x_n$ are padded 0-vectors. The input of the contour-based model is fed into a RNN which consists of 5 bidirectional LSTM layers with 400 hidden units in each cell. To predict the class of a sequence, we concatenate the hidden variable of the last LSTM

[5]The lengths of the feature vector sequences depends on the number of sentences of the texts in our corpus.

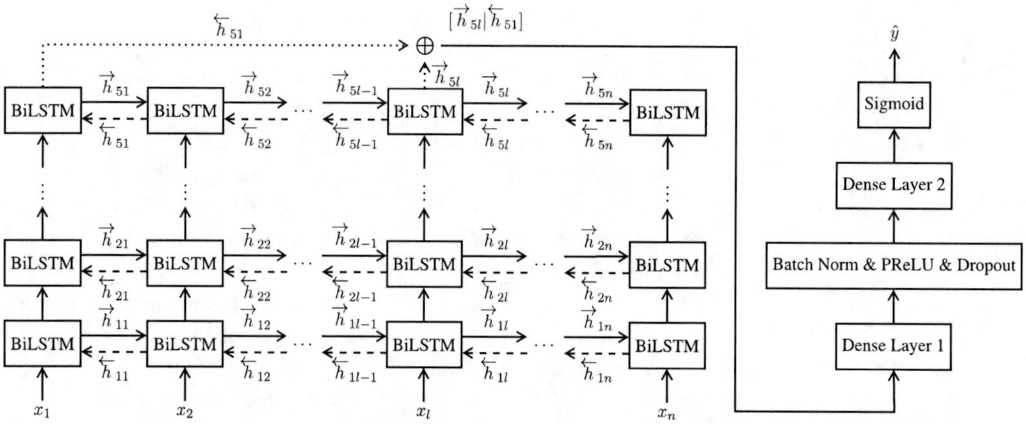


Figure 1: Roll-out of the RNN model based on complexity contours

cell in layer 5 $\overrightarrow{h}_{5l}$, i.e. the hidden variable of $5th$ RNN layer right after the feeding of $x_l$, with hidden variable of the last LSTM cell in the backward direction $\overleftarrow{h}_{51}$. The result vector of concatenation $[\overrightarrow{h}_{5l}|\overleftarrow{h}_{51}]$ is then transformed through a feed-forward neural network. The feed-forward neural-network consists of two fully connected layers (dense layer), whose output dimensions are 400, 14. Between the first and sencond fully connected layer, a Batch Normalization layer, a Parametric Rectifier Linear Unit (PReLU) layer and a dropout layer were added. Before the final output, a sigmoid layer was applied. The dataset was splitted into training and testing sets with a ration of 80:20 and 5-fold cross-validation is applied. As the loss function for training, binary cross entropy was used:

$$\mathcal{L}(\hat{Y}, c) = -\frac{1}{C}\sum_{i=1}^{C}(y_i \log(\hat{y}) + (1-y_i)\log(1-\hat{y}))$$

in which $c = (y_1, y_2, \ldots, y_N), C = 14$ is number of responses and $\hat{Y} = (\hat{y}_1, \hat{y}_2, \ldots, \hat{y}_N)$ is the output vector of the sigmoid layer rounded to closest integer. For optimization, we used Adamax with a learning rate $\eta = 0.0001$. The dropout rate of the RNN layers and the dropout layer is set to 0.5. The minibatch size is 32, which was shown as a reasonable value for modern GPUs (Masters and Luschi, 2018). All models were implemented using PyTorch (Pytorch, 2019).

Our baseline model has the same network architecture as the model described above, but instead of being trained on complexity contours, it was trained on sentence embeddings extracted from the Universal Sentence Encoder (USE) (Cer et al., 2018). USE takes a sentence as input and a 512-dimensional sentence representation as its output. The pretrained USE model we used was obtained from the Tensorflow (TF) Hub website and, according to TF Hub, the model was trained with a deep averaging network (DAN) encoder (Iyyer et al., 2015).

## 6 Results and Discussion

We report the results of multi-label classification with five-fold cross validation. The performance metrics of the RNN classification model (global accuracy, precision, recall and macro F1 scores) are presented in Table 3. The model achieved an average total accuracy of 69% averaged across the 14 rating categories. The highest accuracy was reached for the persuasive category (77%) and lowest for the long-winded category (62%). The results of RNN models trained on each feature set introduced in Section 5 are presented in Table 4. These results revealed that classification accuracy was mainly driven by LIWC-style and ngram-based features: The LIWC set was most predictive for 8/14 rating categories (persuasive, courageous, fascinating, inspiring, funny, ingenious, jaw-dropping and confusing), whereas the n-gram set ranked first in 3/10 rating categories (beautiful, unconvincing, obnoxious). In two rating categories (informative, OK) these two feature sets were equally predictive. Averaged across rating categories, the LIWC-based model achieved slightly better accuracy (+1%) at the cost of using 61 features (36 more features) compared to that of the n-gram based model trained on 25 features. RNN models trained on the lexical and syntactic features both reached 61% classification accuracy. The RNN trained on syntactic features reached the highest accuracy for the long-winded rating category (61%). The classifier based on the three information theoretic features achieved 56% accuracy. The finding that n-gram measures figure prominently in the classification is consistent with a growing body of studies indicating that n-gram measures are good predictors of human judgments/ratings of writing and speaking skills both in first and second language (Christiansen and Arnon, 2017; Garner et al., 2020; Saito, 2020). More generally, the findings are also in support of recent theoretical proposals emphasizing the importance of knowledge of such 'chunks' for human language processing to ameliorate the effects of the 'real-time' constraints on language processing imposed by the limitations of human sensory system and human memory in combination with the continual deluge of language input (cf., Christiansen and Chater, 2016, 2017, for the 'Now-or-Never bottleneck') . The result that LIWC-style features emerged as strong predictors is not surprising since previous research employing these measures has provided valuable insight into psychological processes and behavioral outcomes (Tausczik and Pennebaker, 2010; Pennebaker et al., 2015b). A closer examination of how individual features within each feature-group distinguished between higher-rated and lower-rated TED talks in a given rating category revealed some interesting patterns. For reasons of space, we focus on the results for the seven most frequently selected categories (*persuasive, courageous, fascinating, beautiful, inspiring, informative and funny*) for which classification accuracy was consistently greater than 70%. For each feature, we determined the differences between the group means for each indicator of language use ($M_{\text{higher rated}}$ - $M_{\text{lower rated}}$) for the *persuasive* category. For the *persuasive* rating category, the top LIWC-style features of highly rated talks concern words associated with words related to core drives and needs (*power*) and personal concerns (*risk, money and work*), while words related with perceptual processes (*see, hear, feel*) are associated with talks with lower ratings on the *persuasive* dimension. Highly persuasive talks are further characterized by a stronger reliance on higher frequency n-grams from more formal language registers: the top-five n-gram features associated with highly persuasive talks concern frequent 3-, 4- and 5-grams from the academic register and 3- and 4-grams from the news register. At the same time, frequent n-grams from the fiction register are indicative of lower persuasive talks. Regarding lexical richness, we found that highly-rated talks in the persuasive rating category exhibit high lexical diversity (CTTR, RTTR, NDW) in combination with high word prevalence and low lexical sophistication (NAWL, NGSL, ANC, BNC), indicating that persuasive talks use words that are widely known rather than those that are advanced and infrequent. At the syntactic level, persuasive talks show tendencies towards higher degrees of subordination (e.g. dependent clauses per T-unit) and phrasal complexity (complex nominals per T-unit) and lower degrees of coordination (coordinate phrases per clause). Figure 2 in the appendix shows the frequency with which features of particular types appeared in the top-five most associated (left) or top-five most dissociated features (right).[6] The figure discloses distinct patterns of language usage for particular rating categories: TED talks with high ratings in the categories *beautiful*, *inspiring*, *courageous* and *funny* are characterised by a strong reliance on frequent n-grams from the fiction register, words from the LIWC types *pronoun* and *social*, and relatively higher scores on indicators of lexical sophistication. At the same time, these talks exhibit relatively low proportions of frequent academic n-grams, low lexical diversity and shorter length of production units. Highly rated talks on the

[6]In case a top-five list involved a change in sign only features with positive values (for the associated feature list) or negative values (for the dissociated feature list) were included.

Table 3: Performance statistics of the RNN classifiers aggregated over five crossvalidation runs

| | **Baseline: $\text{RNN}_{\text{USE}}$** | | **RNN model based on complexity contours** | | | | | | | |
|---|---|---|---|---|---|---|---|---|---|---|
| | Acc | SD | Acc | SD | Precision | SD | Recall | SD | F1 | SD |
| Overall | 0.73 | 0.01 | 0.69 | 0.01 | 0.69 | 0.07 | 0.67 | 0.09 | 0.68 | 0.08 |
| Persuasive | 0.80 | 0.02 | 0.77 | 0.03 | 0.77 | 0.07 | 0.80 | 0.07 | 0.78 | 0.07 |
| Courageous | 0.81 | 0.03 | 0.76 | 0.03 | 0.80 | 0.05 | 0.69 | 0.09 | 0.74 | 0.07 |
| Fascinating | 0.82 | 0.03 | 0.75 | 0.03 | 0.75 | 0.06 | 0.78 | 0.06 | 0.76 | 0.06 |
| Beautiful | 0.79 | 0.02 | 0.74 | 0.02 | 0.77 | 0.06 | 0.66 | 0.05 | 0.71 | 0.05 |
| Inspiring | 0.79 | 0.02 | 0.73 | 0.02 | 0.76 | 0.02 | 0.65 | 0.18 | 0.70 | 0.03 |
| Informative | 0.78 | 0.02 | 0.73 | 0.04 | 0.71 | 0.13 | 0.82 | 0.11 | 0.76 | 0.12 |
| Funny | 0.76 | 0.02 | 0.71 | 0.02 | 0.71 | 0.04 | 0.70 | 0.08 | 0.70 | 0.05 |
| Ingenious | 0.77 | 0.02 | 0.70 | 0.02 | 0.68 | 0.04 | 0.75 | 0.05 | 0.71 | 0.05 |
| Jaw-dropping | 0.67 | 0.03 | 0.66 | 0.02 | 0.66 | 0.11 | 0.63 | 0.05 | 0.65 | 0.07 |
| Unconvincing | 0.67 | 0.01 | 0.65 | 0.03 | 0.66 | 0.04 | 0.58 | 0.18 | 0.62 | 0.07 |
| OK | 0.65 | 0.01 | 0.64 | 0.02 | 0.63 | 0.12 | 0.63 | 0.13 | 0.63 | 0.12 |
| Confusing | 0.67 | 0.03 | 0.63 | 0.03 | 0.63 | 0.04 | 0.56 | 0.23 | 0.59 | 0.06 |
| Obnoxious | 0.63 | 0.01 | 0.63 | 0.02 | 0.61 | 0.09 | 0.54 | 0.21 | 0.57 | 0.12 |
| Longwinded | 0.65 | 0.02 | 0.62 | 0.03 | 0.59 | 0.13 | 0.55 | 0.17 | 0.57 | 0.15 |

Table 4: Mean classification accuracy after five-fold cross validation with standard deviations across rating categories and feature-sets.

| | All Features (N = 119) | | LIWC (N=61) | | N-gram (N=25) | | Lexical (N=13) | | Syntactic (N=18) | | Inf. Theo. (N=3) | |
|---|---|---|---|---|---|---|---|---|---|---|---|---|
| Rating category | $M_{Acc}$ | $SD$ | $M_{Acc}$ | $SD$ | $M_{Acc}$ | $SD$ | $M_{Acc}$ | $SD$ | $M_{Acc}$ | $SD$ | $M_{Acc}$ | $SD$ |
| Overall | 0.69 | 0.01 | 0.67 | 0.01 | 0.66 | 0.01 | 0.61 | 0.00 | 0.61 | 0.01 | 0.56 | 0.01 |
| Persuasive | 0.77 | 0.03 | **0.75** | 0.03 | 0.74 | 0.02 | 0.65 | 0.04 | 0.64 | 0.04 | 0.58 | 0.05 |
| Courageous | 0.76 | 0.03 | **0.76** | 0.02 | 0.74 | 0.02 | 0.65 | 0.01 | 0.62 | 0.01 | 0.53 | 0.04 |
| Fascinating | 0.75 | 0.03 | **0.75** | 0.03 | 0.72 | 0.03 | 0.67 | 0.02 | 0.63 | 0.03 | 0.55 | 0.03 |
| Beautiful | 0.74 | 0.02 | 0.71 | 0.01 | **0.73** | 0.01 | 0.63 | 0.02 | 0.63 | 0.03 | 0.56 | 0.04 |
| Inspiring | 0.73 | 0.02 | **0.72** | 0.02 | 0.69 | 0.02 | 0.65 | 0.01 | 0.65 | 0.01 | 0.54 | 0.02 |
| Informative | 0.73 | 0.04 | **0.71** | 0.03 | **0.71** | 0.03 | 0.64 | 0.03 | 0.67 | 0.04 | 0.61 | 0.05 |
| Funny | 0.71 | 0.02 | **0.69** | 0.03 | 0.68 | 0.02 | 0.60 | 0.03 | 0.64 | 0.02 | 0.60 | 0.02 |
| Ingenious | 0.70 | 0.02 | **0.69** | 0.02 | 0.66 | 0.01 | 0.64 | 0.02 | 0.60 | 0.02 | 0.53 | 0.02 |
| Jaw-dropping | 0.66 | 0.02 | **0.62** | 0.03 | 0.57 | 0.02 | 0.59 | 0.02 | 0.60 | 0.03 | 0.57 | 0.05 |
| Unconvincing | 0.65 | 0.03 | 0.60 | 0.01 | **0.61** | 0.03 | 0.57 | 0.02 | 0.56 | 0.04 | 0.53 | 0.05 |
| OK | 0.64 | 0.02 | **0.59** | 0.01 | **0.59** | 0.02 | 0.59 | 0.02 | 0.57 | 0.06 | 0.58 | 0.04 |
| Confusing | 0.63 | 0.03 | **0.60** | 0.02 | 0.58 | 0.02 | 0.56 | 0.02 | 0.57 | 0.02 | 0.51 | 0.02 |
| Obnoxious | 0.63 | 0.02 | 0.58 | 0.02 | **0.61** | 0.01 | 0.56 | 0.01 | 0.54 | 0.03 | 0.54 | 0.03 |
| Longwinded | 0.62 | 0.03 | 0.59 | 0.02 | 0.59 | 0.03 | 0.60 | 0.03 | **0.61** | 0.04 | 0.60 | 0.10 |

*fascinating* and *ingenious* dimensions group together and exhibit higher proportions of n-grams from the spoken register, higher proportions of words from the LIWC *function*-type – notably the personal pronoun *I* and are characterized by higher lexical sophistication. Finally, *persuasive*, *ingenious*, *fascinating* and *inspiring* talks display higher word prevalence score, which estimate the proportion of the population that knows a given word. This result indicates that the inclusion of this newly introduced crowd-sourced language metric (Johns et al., 2020) is a valuable addition to the existing features employed in research on automated assessment of spontaneous speech and calls for the development of additional crowd-sourced language features.

## 7 Conclusion

The ability to communicate competently and efficiently yields innumerable benefits across a range of social areas, including the enjoyment of congenial personal relationships, educational success, career advancement and, more generally, successful participation in the complex communicative environments of the 21st century. Public speaking is the epitome of spoken communication and, at the same time, the most feared form of communication. The paper contributes to the growing body of research that relies on automatic assessment of speaking skills and machine learning to better understand what makes a public speech effective. We performed a multi-label classification task to automatically predict human affective ratings associated with 14 categories on a large dataset of TED Talk speech transcripts. We demonstrated that a Recurrent Neural Network classifier trained exclusively on within-text distributions of 119 language features can reach relatively high levels of accuracy ($> 70\%$) on eight out of fourteen rating categories. We further showed that all rating categories are best predicted by (1) LIWC-style features, which counts words in psychologically meaningful categories, and (2) n-gram frequency measures, which reflect the use of register/genre-specific multiword sequences. Closer analysis of the distributions of particular language features disclosed distinct patterns of language usage for particular rating categories. More generally, the present paper responds to recent calls in the international scientific community of machine learning to use not only black box models but also explainable (white-box) models, since in any given application domain there is a need for both accurate but also understandable models (Rudin, 2019; Loyola-Gonzalez, 2019). In this paper, we have demonstrated in the domain of public speaking that models trained on human interpretable features in combination with deep learning classifiers can compete with black box models based on word embeddings.

## References


Philip M Backlund and Sherwyn P Morreale. 2015. Communication competence: Historical synopsis, definitions, applications, and looking to the future. *Communication competence*, 22:11.

Clay Beckner, Richard Blythe, Joan Bybee, Morten H Christiansen, William Croft, Nick C Ellis, John Holland, Jinyun Ke, Diane Larsen-Freeman, et al. 2009. Language is a complex adaptive system: Position paper. *Language learning*, 59:1–26.

Ruth A Berman. 2007. Developing linguistic knowledge and language use across adolescence. In M. Shatz E. Hoff, editor, *Blackwell handbooks of developmental psychology*, page 347–367. Blackwell Publishing.

Charles Browne et al. 2013. The new general service list: Celebrating 60 years of vocabulary learning. *The Language Teacher*, 37(4):13–16.

Marc Brysbaert, Paweł Mandera, Samantha F McCormick, and Emmanuel Keuleers. 2019. Word prevalence norms for 62,000 english lemmas. *Behavior research methods*, 51(2):467–479.

Brant R Burleson. 2007. Constructivism: A general theory of communication skill. In W. Samter B. B. Whaley, editor, *Explaining communication: Contemporary theories and exemplars*, page 105–128. Lawrence Erlbaum Associates Publishers.

Daniel Cer, Yinfei Yang, Sheng-yi Kong, Nan Hua, Nicole Limtiaco, Rhomni St John, Noah Constant, Mario Guajardo-Cespedes, Steve Yuan, Chris Tar, et al. 2018. Universal sentence encoder. *arXiv preprint arXiv:1803.11175*.

Franklin Chang, Marius Janciauskas, and Hartmut Fitz. 2012. Language adaptation and learning: Getting explicit about implicit learning. *Language and Linguistics Compass*, 6(5):259–278.

Lei Chen and Chong MIn Lee. 2017. Predicting audience's laughter using convolutional neural network. *arXiv preprint arXiv:1702.02584*.

Council of Chief State School Officers & National Governors Association. 2010. Common core state standards for english language arts and literacy in history/social studies, science, and technical subjects.

Morten H Christiansen and Inbal Arnon. 2017. More than words: The role of multiword sequences in language learning and use. *Topics in Cognitive Science*, 9(3):542–551.

Morten H Christiansen and Nick Chater. 2016a. *Creating language: Integrating evolution, acquisition, and processing*. MIT Press.

Morten H Christiansen and Nick Chater. 2016b. The now-or-never bottleneck: A fundamental constraint on language. *Behavioral and Brain Sciences*, 39.

Morten H. Christiansen and Nick Chater. 2017. Towards an integrated science of language. *Nature Human Behaviour*, 1(8).

Mark Davies. 2008. The Corpus of Contemporary American English (COCA): 560 million words, 1990-present.

Reinout E De Vries, Angelique Bakker-Pieper, and Wyneke Oostenveld. 2010. Leadership= communication? the relations of leaders' communication styles with leadership styles, knowledge sharing and leadership outcomes. *Journal of business and psychology*, 25(3):367–380.

Peter Deutsch. 1996. Deflate compressed data format specification version 1.3. *IETF RFC 1951*.

Katharina Ehret and Benedikt Szmrecsanyi. 2019. Compressing learner language: An information-theoretic measure of complexity in sla production data. *Second Language Research*, 35(1):23–45.

James Garner, Scott Crossley, and Kristopher Kyle. 2020. Beginning and intermediate l2 writer's use of n-grams: an association measures study. *International Review of Applied Linguistics in Language Teaching*, 58(1):51–74.

Joshua K Hartshorne and Laura T Germine. 2015. When does cognitive functioning peak? the asynchronous rise and fall of different cognitive abilities across the life span. *Psychological science*, 26(4):433–443.

Mohit Iyyer, Varun Manjunatha, Jordan Boyd-Graber, and Hal Daumé III. 2015. Deep unordered composition rivals syntactic methods for text classification. In *Proceedings of the 53rd annual meeting of the association for computational linguistics and the 7th international joint conference on natural language processing (volume 1: Long papers)*, pages 1681–1691.

Brendan T Johns, Melody Dye, and Michael N Jones. 2020. Estimating the prevalence and diversity of words in written language. *Quarterly Journal of Experimental Psychology*, 73(6):841–855.

Elma Kerz, Yu Qiao, Daniel Wiechmann, and Marcus Ströbel. 2020. Becoming linguistically mature: Modeling english and german children's writing development across school grades. In *Proceedings of the Fifteenth Workshop on Innovative Use of NLP for Building Educational Applications*, pages 65–74.

Bui Khanh and Alisa Vorobeva. 2020. A preliminary performance comparison of machine learning algorithms for web author identification of vietnamese online messages. In *2020 26th Conference of Open Innovations Association (FRUCT)*, pages 166–173. IEEE.

Dan Klein and Christopher D Manning. 2003. Accurate unlexicalized parsing. In *Proceedings of the 41st Annual Meeting on Association for Computational Linguistics-Volume 1*, pages 423–430. Association for Computational Linguistics.

Roger Levy and Galen Andrew. 2006. Tregex and tsurgeon: tools for querying and manipulating tree data structures. In *LREC*, pages 2231–2234. Citeseer.

Octavio Loyola-Gonzalez. 2019. Black-box vs. white-box: Understanding their advantages and weaknesses from a practical point of view. *IEEE Access*, 7:154096–154113.

Xiaofei Lu. 2010. Automatic analysis of syntactic complexity in second language writing. *International Journal of Corpus Linguistics*, 15(4):474–496.

Xiaofei Lu. 2012. The relationship of lexical richness to the quality of ESL learners' oral narratives. *The Modern Language Journal*, 96(2):190–208.

Saturnino Luz, Fasih Haider, Sofia de la Fuente, Davida Fromm, and Brian MacWhinney. 2020. Alzheimer's dementia recognition through spontaneous speech: The adress challenge. *arXiv preprint arXiv:2004.06833*.

Gonzalo Luzardo, Bruno Guamán, Katherine Chiluiza, Jaime Castells, and Xavier Ochoa. 2014. Estimation of presentations skills based on slides and audio features. In *Proceedings of the 2014 acm workshop on multimodal learning analytics workshop and grand challenge*, pages 37–44.

Christopher Manning, Mihai Surdeanu, John Bauer, Jenny Finkel, Steven Bethard, and David McClosky. 2014. The stanford corenlp natural language processing toolkit. In *Proceedings of 52nd annual meeting of the association for computational linguistics: system demonstrations*, pages 55–60.

Dominic Masters and Carlo Luschi. 2018. Revisiting small batch training for deep neural networks. *arXiv preprint arXiv:1804.07612*.

Sherwyn P Morreale. 2007. *The competent speaker speech evaluation form*. National Communication Association.

Sherwyn P Morreale and Judy C Pearson. 2008. Why communication education is important: The centrality of the discipline in the 21st century. *Communication Education*, 57(2):224–240.

James W Pennebaker, R.J. Booth, R.L. Boyd, and M.E Francis. 2015a. *Linguistic inquiry and word count: LIWC 2015. Operator's manual.* Pennebaker Conglomerates.

James W Pennebaker, Ryan L Boyd, Kayla Jordan, and Kate Blackburn. 2015b. The development and psychometric properties of liwc2015. Technical report.

James W Pennebaker, Matthias R Mehl, and Kate G Niederhoffer. 2003. Psychological aspects of natural language use: Our words, our selves. *Annual review of psychology*, 54(1):547–577.

Verónica Pérez-Rosas, Bennett Kleinberg, Alexandra Lefevre, and Rada Mihalcea. 2017. Automatic detection of fake news. *arXiv preprint arXiv:1708.07104*.

Tomas Pfister and Peter Robinson. 2011. Real-time recognition of affective states from nonverbal features of speech and its application for public speaking skill analysis. *IEEE Transactions on Affective Computing*, 2(2):66–78.

Pytorch. 2019. Pytorch: Tensors and dynamic neural networks in python with strong gpu acceleration. `https://github.com/pytorch/pytorch`.

Yu Qiao, Daniel Wiechmann, and Elma Kerz. 2020. A language-based approach to fake news detection through interpretable features and brnn. In *Proceedings of the 3rd International Workshop on Rumours and Deception in Social Media (RDSM)*, pages 14–31.

Cynthia Rudin. 2019. Stop explaining black box machine learning models for high stakes decisions and use interpretable models instead. *Nature Machine Intelligence*, 1(5):206–215.

Kazuya Saito. 2020. Multi-or single-word units? the role of collocation use in comprehensible and contextually appropriate second language speech. *Language Learning*, 70(2):548–588.

Stefan Scherer, Georg Layher, John Kane, Heiko Neumann, and Nick Campbell. 2012. An audiovisual political speech analysis incorporating eye-tracking and perception data. In *LREC*, pages 1114–1120.

Lisa M Schreiber, Gregory D Paul, and Lisa R Shibley. 2012. The development and test of the public speaking competence rubric. *Communication Education*, 61(3):205–233.

H Andrew Schwartz, Johannes C Eichstaedt, Margaret L Kern, Lukasz Dziurzynski, Stephanie M Ramones, Megha Agrawal, Achal Shah, Michal Kosinski, David Stillwell, Martin EP Seligman, et al. 2013. Personality, gender, and age in the language of social media: The open-vocabulary approach. *PloS one*, 8(9):e73791.

Marcus Ströbel. 2014. *Tracking complexity of l2 academic texts: A sliding-window approach.* Master thesis. RWTH Aachen University.

Marcus Ströbel, Elma Kerz, and Daniel Wiechmann. 2020. The relationship between first and second language writing: Investigating the effects of first language complexity on second language complexity in advanced stages of learning. *Language Learning*, 70(3):732–767.

Yla R Tausczik and James W Pennebaker. 2010. The psychological meaning of words: Liwc and computerized text analysis methods. *Journal of language and social psychology*, 29(1):24–54.

Felix Weninger, Jarek Krajewski, Anton Batliner, and Björn Schuller. 2012. The voice of leadership: Models and performances of automatic analysis in online speeches. *IEEE Transactions on Affective Computing*, 3(4):496–508.

Felix Weninger, Pascal Staudt, and Björn Schuller. 2013. Words that fascinate the listener: Predicting affective ratings of on-line lectures. *International Journal of Distance Education Technologies (IJDET)*, 11(2):110–123.

# A Appendix

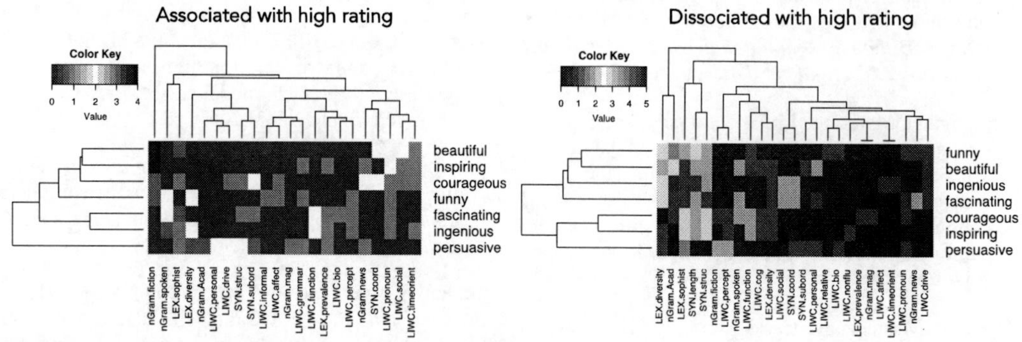


Figure 2: Heatmap of features associated (left; blue indicates higher counts) or dissociated (right, red indicates higher counts) with high ratings on each of the top-seven best predicted rating categories. Dendrograms represent Euclidean distances among rating categories and features respectively.

# Partisanship and Fear are Associated with Resistance to COVID-19 Directives

**Mike Lindow, David DeFranza, Arul Mishra,** and **Himanshu Mishra**
University of Utah
{michael.lindow, david.defranza, arul.mishra, himanshu.mishra}
@eccles.utah.edu

## Abstract

Ideological differences have had a large impact on individual and community response to the COVID-19 pandemic in the United States. Early behavioral research during the pandemic showed that conservatives were less likely to adhere to health directives, which contradicts a body of work suggesting that conservative ideology emphasizes a rule abiding, loss aversion, and prevention focus. We reconcile this contradiction by analyzing semantic content of local press releases, federal press releases, and localized tweets during the first month of the government response to COVID-19 in the United States. Controlling for factors such as COVID-19 confirmed cases and deaths, local economic indicators, and more, we find that online expressions of fear in conservative areas lead to an increase in adherence to public health recommendations concerning COVID-19, and that expressions of fear in government press releases are a significant predictor of expressed fear on Twitter.

## 1 Introduction

Over the last decade, politics in the United States have become increasingly polarized (Balz, 2019; Dimock et al., 2014; Lockhart et al., 2020). This phenomenon is manifest in the increasing politicization of historically non-partisan government agencies (Cooper, 2020; Mulgan, 2007; Peters, 2004), the divide on Ebola preparedness (Nyhan, 2014), and most recently, reactions and responses to the COVID-19 pandemic (Rothwell and Makridis, 2020). A growing body of evidence suggests that, during the pandemic, conservatives in the United States have been less likely to restrict movement during shelter-in-place directives (van Holm et al., 2020; Clinton et al., 2021), less likely to engage in social distancing (Painter and Qiu, 2020), and less likely to search for information about COVID-19 (Barrios and Hochberg, 2020). In addition, conservatives seem more likely to refuse to wear masks, view the pandemic as a hoax, and question or protest against health directives (Van Green and Tyson, 2020).

Though reactance to COVID-19 mitigation efforts among conservatives is well documented, it may have been difficult to predict from existing theory and research. Indeed, a sizeable body of literature suggests that, instead of reacting *against* state-suggested and mandated precautions, conservatives might instead be more inclined to comply than their liberal counterparts (Jost et al., 2003b, 2007; Sales, 1973). Indeed, in previous periods of crisis, conservatives have been more inclined to seek safety (Sales, 1973; Thorisdottir and Jost, 2011). This is associated with an increased likelihood among conservatives to respond to threats in the environment and appeals to fear (Block and Block, 2006; Jost et al., 2003a,b; Oxley et al., 2008; Pliskin et al., 2015).

In other words, both evidence from research and reports from the media suggest that conservatives demonstrate less compliance to COVID-19 directives than liberals while, at the same time, past research suggests conservatives might be more responsive if presented with an objective threat or when consumed by a sense of fear. That said, it is clear the divergent and partisan responses to mitigation efforts which have been observed to date pose a serious threat to communities in the United States (Rothwell and Makridis, 2020). Therefore, in this research we explore what might motivate conservatives to adhere to health directives. Empirically, we utilize community level mobility data to understand changes (or lack thereof) in behavior, analyze millions of tweets and a set of official press releases to measure expressed fear, and seek ways in which public health and other officials might responsibly and effectively apply fear appeals to motivate behavior. Analytically, we first measure



*Proceedings of the 11th Workshop on Computational Approaches to Subjectivity, Sentiment and Social Media Analysis*, pages 25–33
April 19, 2021. ©2021 Association for Computational Linguistics

fear in press releases and tweets using word embeddings and distributed dictionaries, we identify the factors most likely to contribute to expressions of fear with gradient boosted trees, identify the words most common in press releases expressing fear, and explore the associations between expressions of fear and behavior changing with random effects models.

## 2 Background and related work

As stated in the previous section, recent work suggesting increased skepticism and reluctance to adhere to public health directives among conservatives (Barrios and Hochberg, 2020; Iyengar and Massey, 2019; Painter and Qiu, 2020; Rothwell and Makridis, 2020; Van Green and Tyson, 2020) is surprising. Indeed, a long stream of research has found conservatives to be more rule abiding, risk averse, and prevention focused (Jost et al., 2003a, 2007; Sales, 1973). In times of crisis, conservatives are more likely than liberals to seek safety (Sales, 1973; Thorisdottir and Jost, 2011). But given the current tug-of-war between political rhetoric and health risk (Barrios and Hochberg, 2020; Cruwys et al., 2020; Rothgerber et al., 2020; van der Linden et al., 2020) some work suggests conservatives have come to rely more on political identity (van Holm et al., 2020; Allcott et al., 2020; Gadarian et al., 2020; Painter and Qiu, 2020), which could be influenced or exacerbated by conservative officials downplaying the health risks of the coronavirus (Bursztyn et al., 2020; Peters, 2020). One specific attribute commonly associated with a conservative mindset may explain why some have diminished or ignored the importance of COVID-19 health directives. That attribute is fear.

Past research suggests that conservatives, more than liberals, display a reaction to fear in response to threats in the environment (Block and Block, 2006; Jost et al., 2003a,b; Oxley et al., 2008; Pliskin et al., 2015). That is, conservatives have a stronger reaction to threats and new experiences (Oxley et al., 2008) and express stronger emotional reactions to negative outcomes (Joel et al., 2014). Such a response could be driven by a greater need for control over the environment and greater impulse to reduce uncertainty (Jost et al., 2003a). Since conservatives generally respect authority and want the hierarchical structure to remain in place, they are more fearful of change to this structure (Adorno et al., 1950; Jurgert and Duckitt, 2009).

These conflicting streams of research can be reconciled if conservatives who do experience or express fear of coronavirus are more likely to adhere to health directives as compared to conservatives who do not experience fear of coronavirus. Such a pattern would not only explain the response of conservatives to COVID-19 directives and recommendations but would also suggest a path forward for policy makers intent on motivating greater adherence to health directives.

To explore this phenomenon, we utilize two sources of data representing community level expressions of sentiment. First, as a proxy for the attitudes of local and federal officials, we collect press releases. Press releases are a common communication method used to inform a large number of citizens of a problem. Similar to past public health crises, local and federal government offices and agencies have used press releases to communicate official information to the public. Press releases have been used in past research as representations of the overall attitude of government agencies and officials (Fairbanks et al., 2007; Grossman et al., 2020; Lee and Basnyat, 2013; Levi and Stoker, 2000; Mayhew, 1974). Second, to measure the fear expressed by citizens in each community, we collect tweets related to COVID-19.

## 3 Methodology

In this section we first present the press release, Twitter, and behavioral data sets. We then elaborate the method used to measure the degree of fear expressed in text data. Finally, we outline the modeling framework for assessing the factors influencing the expression of fear, the nature of observed communications, and the impact on behavior changes in response to state directives.

### 3.1 Press release data

All data was collected over a 30-day period between February 29, 2020 and March 29, 2020. February 29 was selected as the starting point of observation because the first COVID-related death in the United States was announced on this day (CDC, 2020). We collected press releases from federal government agencies and offices in addition to those from the local governments of the 53 most populous metropolitan areas in the United States. In total, we collected 166 national and 1232 local press releases across all metropolitan areas during the observation period. However, not every local government issued a press release each day. In total, there were 291 observations which included both local and national press releases.

### 3.2 Twitter data

Using the Twitter API, tweets were collected which contained any occurrence (including but not limited to hashtags) of the words *coronavirus*, *covid*, *covid-19*, or *sars-cov2*. Tweets were filtered to include only those from authors whose profile indicated they reside in one of the 53 metropolitan areas. In total, more than two million relevant tweets were collected during the observation period.

### 3.3 Pandemic response data

To measure movement during the pandemic, we utilized mobility data provided by Google, aggregated at the level of the county and collected from individuals who have opted in to location sharing features in Android or Google services (Google, 2020). This data is subset into a variety of location types and represents the percent change in the number of visits and length of stay at each location as compared to an out of period baseline. We calculated the mean value for public locations (retail, grocery and pharmacy, workplaces, and transit stations) as our metric of local movement. County level data was aggregated to the level of the metropolitan area using a population-weighted mean.

To determine the aggregate political identity of the metropolitan area, we collected the results of presidential elections that occurred between 2000 and 2016 (MIT, 2018). Of course, it is possible that communities may have deviated from this baseline since 2016. We encourage future researcher to explore the ways in which community level political identification has changed since 2016. The average votes for Republican and Democrat candidates were calculated. If a metropolitan area cast more votes on average for Republican candidates over this period it was labelled *conservative*, otherwise it was classified as *liberal*. This categorical variable was then dummy coded for analysis. Across the 53 metropolitan areas, 17 were classified as conservative and 36 were classified as liberal.

In addition, we collected control variables including the number of COVID-19 cases and deaths reported for each metropolitan area, for each day, local income and poverty metrics, day of the week, and more. For the sake of parsimony, only variables that had a significant impact on the models are reported and discussed.

### 3.4 Measuring expressed fear

To measure expressed fear in press releases and tweets, we constructed a dictionary to represent the construct. First, we collected 35 common synonyms for the target word *fear*. Next, we extracted a vector representation for each word from a pre-trained language model (Pennington et al., 2014). The cosine similarity between each target-synonym pair was calculated and words were clustered based on these values. Finally, the synonyms forming the tightest cluster around the word *fear* were selected as the construct dictionary. This dictionary consisted of 25 words. Construct vectors were aggregated by taking the sum of individual vectors divided by their Euclidean norm (Garten et al., 2018), resulting in a single construct vector of 200 dimensions. Formally, a construct vector $C$ is calculated as:

$$C = \frac{\sum_{w \in D_R} R(w)}{||\sum_{w \in D_R} R(w)||_2} \quad (1)$$

Where $w$ is a word, $R$ is an embedding representation for $w$, and $D_R$ is the set of words in the construct dictionary representing $C$ (Garten et al., 2018).

Next, press releases and tweets were normalized. Tweets and press release sentences were tokenized into word-grams, made lowercase, and single character words and stop words were removed (Bird et al., 2009; Symeonidis et al., 2018). Then, vectors for tweet and sentence tokens were aggregated as described in equation 1 (Garten et al., 2018; Pennington et al., 2014). Cosine similarity provided a measure of similarity between the construct vector and each aggregated tweet or sentence vector (Caliskan et al., 2017; Garten et al., 2018). Note that the method of aggregation described in equation 1 pre-normalizes the vector representation. As such, similarity $S$ between a construct representation, say for fear, $C_f$, and a given document (e.g., a single tweet), $T_i$, is calculated as the dot product of the respective aggregate vectors:

$$S = C_f \cdot T_i \quad (2)$$

The resulting document-level similarity measures were aggregated to the level of the day and metropolitan area.

### 3.5 Identifying factors influencing fear

To identify the factors most closely associated with increases in expressed fear, we employed gradi-

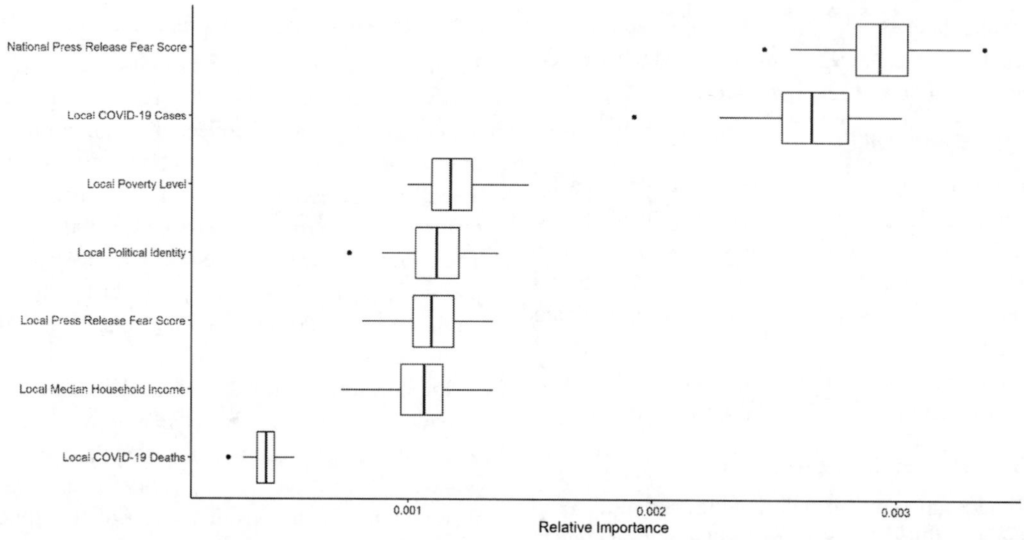


Figure 1: The relative importance of variables for predicting fear expressed in tweets, as determined by the XG-Boost model.

ent boosted trees (Chen and Guestrin, 2016; Friedman, 2001). Gradient boosted decision trees employ a series of shallow trees to predict an outcome variable (Quinlan, 1986). The assumption is that many weak learners will achieve a probably approximately correct (PAC) result (Valiant, 1984). Each tree is evaluated based on the gradient of the error with respect to the prediction via functional gradient descent (Ruder, 2017). Improvements in prediction accuracy for subtrees with a steeper gradient lead to larger overall improvements. Thus, gradient boosted trees result in the identification of variables that have the overall greatest influence on predictive accuracy. The method is amenable to analysis with relatively smaller sample sizes (Zhao and Duangsoithong, 2019), is not impacted by multicolinearity (Ding et al., 2016), and has been used in the past for prediction tasks involving social media in general and tweets in particular (Li et al., 2017; Ong et al., 2017). We implement gradient boosted decision trees via extreme gradient boosting or XGBoost (Chen and Guestrin, 2016).

### 3.6 Press release content analysis

To assess the type of language used in high- versus low-fear press releases, we counted each word in each press release (65,237 total words). Press releases were categorized based on their average cosine similarity (equation 2) with the fear construct (equation 1). Those that were on average more closely associated with fear than the median measure (0.5713) were classified as *high fear* and those below the median were classified as *low fear*. A log-odds ratio was then calculated for each word in each category of high- or low-fear communications, indicating the probability of a word occurring in a press release. Words with a positive (negative) log-odds ratio are more likely to appear in a high (low) fear press release.

### 3.7 Modeling the impact on pandemic response

To model the impact of fear and political identity on pandemic responses, we utilized a random effects model. The data is panel in nature, with individual observations being made each day, for each subject or metropolitan area. Thus, a random effects specification assumes that time invariant variables are uncorrelated with the time varying predictors, which enables an examination of time invariant variables (such as political identity) on the outcome variable (local movement). Errors were clustered at the level of the metropolitan area, allowing us to control for community differences. We used a one-day lag for the expression of fear on Twitter, allowing us to assess the relationship between this expression and subsequent changes in movement behavior. Past work has also used a one-day lag when analyzing tweets (Kaminski, 2016; Li et al., 2017; Zhang et al., 2013) based on evidence that 75% of tweet replies are made within 17 minutes and the majority of twitter users are passive (Ye and Wu, 2013; Romero et al., 2011).

## 4 Analyses

### 4.1 Factors influencing the expression of fear

The gradient boosted model predicts the next period (day) fear expression on Twitter based on the fear expressed in the current period in both local and national press releases, the number of confirmed COVID-19 cases and deaths in the current period, and the majority political identity, poverty rate, and median household income in a metropolitan area. Due to the sparsity in press release data described previously, the current analysis does not distinguish between metropolitan area and instead considers the influence of variables on the expression of fear across the entire data set. The model was trained on 80% of the available data and tested against the remaining 20% holdout sample, resulting in 235 training observations and 56 test observations. Each iteration was cross-validated with 10 folds for the purposes of hyperparameter tuning. After 700 iterations, the best performing model employed a learning rate of 0.025, a max tree depth of two, a minimum child weight of one, and a gamma of zero. The final model improves on the root mean square error (RMSE) of the untuned model from 0.0059 to 0.0055 and increases the $R^2$ value from 0.3388 to 0.3931.

As shown in Figure 1, the most important variable for predicting the amount of fear expressed in tweets was the amount of fear expressed in national press releases the previous day, followed by the number of COVID-19 cases reported for a given metropolitan area on the previous day. The poverty rate, political identity, median household income, and amount of fear expressed in local press releases for each metropolitan area also contributed to the predictive accuracy, though to a lesser degree.

### 4.2 Language used to express fear

In considering the most likely words to appear in high-fear versus low-fear press releases from the local government, it is clear that the former tend to emphasize language directly related to COVID-19 like *fever*, *self-quarantine*, *flu*, *shortness*, *breath*, and *recover* while the latter lacks such a focus and contains words like *tax*, *loan*, *sales*, *bank*, *survey*, *art*, and *cultural* (see Figure 2). Similarly, in national press releases, those with higher expressions of fear are more likely to contain words like *tests*, *CDC*, *testing*, *spread*, *protect*, *support*, and *health*

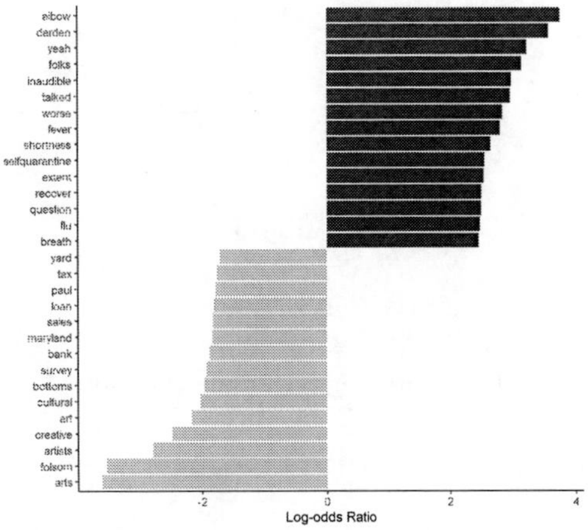


Figure 2: The most likely words to appear in high-fear (log-odds $>$ 0) versus low-fear (log-odds $<$ 0) local press releases.

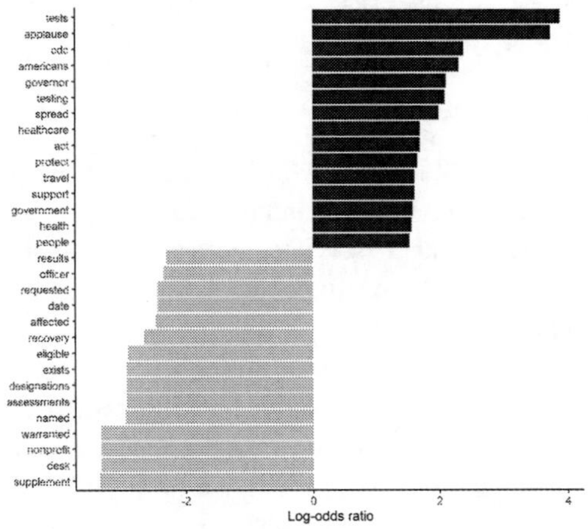


Figure 3: The most likely words to appear in high-fear (log-odds $>$ 0) versus low-fear (log-odds $<$ 0) national press releases.

as opposed to words like *eligible*, *nonprofit*, *office*, *designations*, and *assessments* (see Figure 3).

### 4.3 Relationship with behavior change

Finally, we consider whether an increase in expressed fear is associated with changes in behavior with a random effects model. When the base model is fit, we see both the previous day's fear as expressed on Twitter ($b = 3.578, p < 0.01$) and classification of a community as conservative ($b = 1.880, p < 0.01$) are associated with an increase in movement in public places over the pre-pandemic baseline (see Table 1). Importantly, however, the interaction between conservative identity and the expression of fear is significant and nega-

| | Base Model $b$ $(SE)$ | Covariates Model $b$ $(SE)$ |
|---|---|---|
| Intercept | $-2.113^{***}$ (0.521) | $-1.959^{***}$ (0.507) |
| Confirmed COVID-19 cases | | $-0.0003^{***}$ (0.0001) |
| Confirmed COVID-19 deaths | | $0.005^{***}$ (0.002) |
| Fear expressed on Twitter (lagged 1-day) | $3.578^{***}$ (0.832) | $3.337^{***}$ (0.82) |
| Majority conservative identity | $1.88^{***}$ (0.645) | $1.573^{**}$ (0.623) |
| Expressed fear (lagged 1-day) × Conservative identity | $-2.464^{**}$ (1.048) | |
| $F$ | $19.451^{***}$ | $72.933^{***}$ |
| $R^2$ | 0.013 | 0.045 |

Table 1: Relative changes in movement in public place as compared to an out of sample baseline. For parsimony, only covariates that have a significant influence on the model are included. *Note:* $^{*}p < 0.1$, $^{**}p < 0.05$, $^{***}p < 0.01$.

tive ($b = -2.113, p < 0.01$), suggesting that for majority conservative communities an increase in expressed fear is associated with a subsequent decrease in movement in public places over the baseline.

Similarly, when control variables are added we see both the previous day's fear as expressed on Twitter ($b = 3.337, p < 0.01$) and classification of a community as conservative ($b = 1.573, p = 0.012$) are associated with an increase in movement in public places over the pre-pandemic baseline (see Table 1). Again, the interaction between conservative identity and the expression of fear is significant and negative ($b = -2.464, p = 0.019$), suggesting that for majority conservative communities an increase in expressed fear is associated with a subsequent decrease in movement in public places over the baseline.

## 5 Discussion

Past research suggests that conservatives are more likely to comply with authority (Jost et al., 2003a,b, 2007; Sales, 1973; Thorisdottir and Jost, 2011) and are likely to take preventative measures when they are fearful of a situation (Joel et al., 2014). However, a more recent stream of research argues the opposite (Barrios and Hochberg, 2020; Iyengar and Massey, 2019; Painter and Qiu, 2020; Rothwell and Makridis, 2020; Van Green and Tyson, 2020) including evidence which suggests conservative non-adherence to COVID-19 health directives (Allcott et al., 2020; DeFranza et al., 2020; Gollwitzer et al., 2020). We offer evidence that may help to reconcile this contradiction. The present research suggests that while conservative communities in general ignore public health guidelines, this behavior is not monolithic. Instead, we see an association with the community's expressions of fear when publicly discussing the pandemic and subsequent behaviors. When conservative communities express fear of the pandemic, subsequent movement in public places decreases as compared to pre-pandemic baselines. This is not the case in majority liberal communities, who exhibit no change in behavior in association with expressed fear. Moreover, we see that a dominant antecedent of local expressions of fear in conservative communities is the clear expression of fear from federal agencies and officials. Importantly, increasing confirmed COVID-19 case counts also predicted an increase in the expression of fear among members of majority conservative communities. This finding may be especially helpful in early phases of a pandemic when decisive action is essential.

Taken together, these results suggests that majority conservative communities might benefit from early regular updates from local and federal officials. Because discussions of COVID-19 have become partisan (Allcott et al., 2020), the role of local governments cannot and should not be ignored. It is essential that official communications present details of the current situation clearly and honestly, but also that they emphasize the seriousness and severity of the pandemic (Wood and Schulman, 2021). At the same time, statements that work to diminish perceptions of risk or severity of the pandemic could be a detriment to efforts to manage infection rates in communities. The implications of these results extend beyond COVID-19 and help to inform policy communications at the local and federal level, specifically those targeted at majority conservative communities and for messages which may be unpopular but timely.

## 6 Conclusion

We have presented an analysis of the degree of fear expressed in association with COVID-19 in both official government press releases and by Twitter users in the 53 most populous metropolitan areas in the United States. In doing so, we have identified key factors that influence expressions of fear among members of communities: strong expressions of fear in national communications and increasing confirmed COVID-19 case counts. In addition, we have identified the words most likely to occur in both high- and low- fear official communications. Finally, we have provided evidence that expressions of fear are associated with different prophylactic behaviors in conservative and liberal communities. In the latter, increased expressions of fear are not associated with behavior change. However, in the former, increased expressions of fear are associated with an overall decrease in movement and activity in public spaces.

These results suggest that restricted testing and under-reporting case counts could be detrimental to safe individual behaviors and compliance with public health policy recommendations. Similarly, minimizing the severity or seriousness of COVID-19 poses a particular danger in majority conservative communities. Moving beyond COVID-19 mitigation, the present research emphasizes the importance of timely, relevant, and clear information capable of communicating the authentic seriousness of a situation, especially in majority conservative communities.

## References


Theodor W. Adorno, Else Frenkel-Brunswik, Daniel Levinson, and Nevitt Sanford. 1950. *The authoritarian personality*. Harpers.

Hunt Allcott, Levi Boxell, Jacob Conway, Matthew Gentzkow, Michael Thaler, and David Y. Yang. 2020. Polarization and public health: Partisan differences in social distancing during the coronavirus pandemic. *NBER:w26946*.

Dan Balz. 2019. Americans hate all the partisanship, but they're also more partisan than they were. *Washington Post*.

John M. Barrios and Yael Hochberg. 2020. Risk perception through the lens of politics in the time of the COVID-19 pandemic. *NBER:27008*.

Steven Bird, Ewan Klein, and Edward Loper. 2009. *Natural language processing with Python: Analyzing text with the natural language toolkit*. O'Reilly Media Inc.

Jack Block and Jeanne H. Block. 2006. Nursery school personality and political orientation two decades later. *Journal of Research in Personality*, 40(5):734–749.

Leonardo Bursztyn, Aakaash Rao, Christopher Roth, and David Yanagizawa-Drott. 2020. Misinformation during a pandemic. *University of Chicago, Becker Friedman Institute for Economics Working Paper:2020-44*.

Aylin Caliskan, Joanna J. Bryson, and Arvind Narayanan. 2017. Semantics derived automatically from language corpora contain human-like biases. *Science*, 356(6334):183–186.

CDC. 2020. CDC, Washington State report first COVID-19 death. Technical report, Centers for Disease Control and Prevention.

Tianqi Chen and Carlos Guestrin. 2016. XGBoost: A scalable tree boosting system. In *Proceedings of the 22nd ACM SIGKDD International Conference on Knowledge Discovery and Data Mining*, pages 785—-794. Association for Computing Machinery.

J. Clinton, J. Cohen, J. Lapinski, and M. Trussler. 2021. Partisan pandemic: How partisanship and public health concerns affect individuals' social mobility during covid-19. *Science Advances*, 7(2).

Christopher A. Cooper. 2020. Politicization of the bureaucracy across and within administrative traditions. *International Journal of Public Administration*, pages 1–14.

Tegan Cruwys, Mark Stevens, and Katharine H. Greenaway. 2020. A social identity perspective on COVID-19: Health risk is affected by shared group membership. *British Journal of Social Psychology*, 59(3):584–593.

David DeFranza, Mike Lindow, Kevin Harrison, Arul Mishra, and Himanshu Mishra. 2020. Religion and reactance to COVID-19 mitigation guidelines. *American Psychologist*, Advanced online publication.

Michael Dimock, Jocelyn Kiley, Scott Keeter, and Carroll Doherty. 2014. Political polarization in the American public. Technical report, Pew Research Center.

Chuan Ding, Donggen Wang, Xiaolei Ma, and Haiyling Li. 2016. Predicting short-term subway ridership and prioritizing its influential factors using gradient boosting decision trees. *Sustainability*, 8(11):1100–1116.

Jenille Fairbanks, Kenneth D. Plowman, and Brad L. Rawlins. 2007. Transparency in government communication. *Journal of Public Affairs: An International Journal*, 7(1):23–37.

Jerome H. Friedman. 2001. Greedy function approximation: A gradient boosting machine. *Annals of Statistics*, 29(5):1189–1232.

Shana K. Gadarian, Sata W. Goodman, and Thomas B. Pepinsky. 2020. Partisanship, health behavior and policy attitudes in the early stages of the COVID-19 pandemic. *SSRN:3562796*.

Justin Garten, Joe Hoover, Kate M. Johnson, Reihane Boghrati, Carol Iskiwitch, and Morteza Dehghani. 2018. Dictionaries and distributions: Combining expert knowledge and large scale textual data content analysis. *Behavior Research Methods*, 50(1):344–361.

Anton Gollwitzer, Cameron Martel, William J. Brady, Philip Pärnamets, Isaac G. Freedman, Eric D. Knowles, and Jay J. Van Bavel. 2020. Partisan differences in physical distancing are linked to health outcomes during the COVID-19 pandemic. *Nature Human Behavior*, 4:1186—-1197.

Google. 2020. COVID-19 community mobility report. Technical report, Google.

Guy Grossman, Kim Soojong, Jonah Rexer, and Harsha Thirumurthy. 2020. Political partisanship influences behavioral responses to governor's recommendations for COVID-19 prevention in the United States. *SSRN:3578695*.

Eric Joseph van Holm, Jake Monaghan, Dan C. Shahar, J. P. Messina, and Chris Surprenant. 2020. The impact of political ideology on concern and behavior during COVID-19. *SSRN:3573224*.

Shanto Iyengar and Douglas S. Massey. 2019. Scientific communication in a post-truth society. *Proceedings of the National Academy of Sciences*, 116(16):7656–7661.

Samantha Joel, Caitlin M. Burton, and Jason E. Plaks. 2014. Conservatives anticipate and experience stronger emotional reactions to negative outcomes. *Journal of Personality*, 82(1):32–43.

T. Jost, John, Jack Glaser, Arie W. Kruglanski, and Frank J. Sulloway. 2003a. Exceptions that prove the rule–Using a theory of motivated social cognition to account for ideological incongruities and political anomalies: Reply to Greenberg and Jonas. *Psychological Bulletin*, 129(3):383–393.

T. Jost, John, Jack Glaser, Arie W. Kruglanski, and Frank J. Sulloway. 2003b. Political conservatism as motivated social cognition. *Psychological Bulletin*, 129(3):339–375.

T. Jost, John, Jaime L. Napier, Hulda Thorisdorrit, Samuel D. Gosling, Tibor P. Palfai, and Brian Ostafin. 2007. Are needs to manage uncertainty and threat associated with political conservatism or ideological extremity? *Personality and Social Psychology Bulletin*, 33(7):989–1007.

Philipp Jurgert and John Duckitt. 2009. A motivational model of authoritarianism: Integrating personal and situational determinants. *Political Psychology*, 30(5):693–719.

Jermain Kaminski. 2016. Nowcasting the Bitcoin market with Twitter signals. *ArXiv:1406.7577*.

Seow Ting Lee and Iccha Basnyat. 2013. From press release to news: Mapping the framing of the 2009 H1N1 a influenza pandemic. *Health Communication*, 28(2):119–132.

Margaret Levi and Laura Stoker. 2000. Political trust and trustworthiness. *Annual Review of Political Science*, 3(1):475–507.

Liuwu Li, Runwei Situ, Junyan Gao, Zhenguo Yang, and Wenyin Liu. 2017. A hybrid model combining convolutional neural network with XGBoost for predicting social media popularity. In *Proceedings of the 25th ACM international conference on Multimedia*, pages 1918—-1917. Association for Computing Machinery.

Sander van der Linden, Costas Panagopoulos, and John Kerr. 2020. Coronavirus: New survey shows how Republicans and Democrats are responding differently. *The Conversation*.

Mackenzie Lockhart, Seth J. Hill, Jennifer Merolla, Mindy Romero, and Thad Kousser. 2020. America's electorate is increasingly polarized along partisan lines about voting by mail during the covid-19 crisis. *Proceedings of the National Academy of Sciences*, 117(40):24640–24642.

David R. Mayhew. 1974. *Congress: The electoral connection*. Yale University Press.

MIT. 2018. County presidential election returns 2000-2016. Technical report, MIT Election Data and Science Lab.

Richard Mulgan. 2007. Truth in government and the politicization of public service advice. *Public Administration*, 85(3):569–586.

Brendan Nyhan. 2014. The partisan divide on Ebola preparedness. *The New York Times*.

Veronica Ong, Anneke D. S. Rahmanto, Williem, Derwin Suhartono, Aryo E. Nugroho, Esther W. Andangsari, and Muhamad N. Suprayogi. 2017. Personality prediction based on Twitter information in Bahasa Indonesia. In *Federated Conference on Computer Science and Information Systems (FedCSIS)*, volume 11, pages 367—-372. Annals of Computer Science and Information Systems.

Douglas R. Oxley, Kevin B. Smith, John R. Alford, Matthew V. Hibbing, Jennifer L. Miller, Mario Scalora, and Peter K. Hatemi. 2008. Political attitudes vary with physiological traits. *Science*, 321(5896):1667–1670.

Marcus Painter and Tian Qiu. 2020. Political beliefs affect compliance with COVID-19 social distancing orders. *SSRN:3569098*.

Jeffrey Pennington, Richard Socher, and Christopher Manning. 2014. GloVe: Global vectors for word representation. In *Proceedings of the 2014 Conference on Empirical Methods in Natural Language Processing (EMNLP)*, pages 1532—-1543. Association for Computational Linguistics.

Guy Peters. 2004. Politicization in the united states. In *Politicization of the civil service in comparative perspective*, pages 125–1138. Routledge.

Jeremy W. Peters. 2020. Alarm, denial, blame: The pro-Trump media's coronavirus distortion. *The New York Times*.

Ruthie Pliskin, Gal Sheppes, and Eran Halperin. 2015. Running for your life, in context: Are rightists always less likely to consider fleeing their country when fearing future events? *Journal of Experimental Social Psychology*, 59:90–95.

J. Ross Quinlan. 1986. Induction of decision trees. *Machine Learning*, 1(1):81–106.

Daniel M. Romero, Wojciech Galuba, Sitaram Asur, and Bernardo A. Huberman. 2011. Influence and passivity in social media. In *Machine Learning and Knowledge Discovery in Databases*, pages 18—-33. Joint European Conference on Machine Learning and Knowledge Discovery in Databases.

Hank Rothgerber, Thomas Wilson, Davis Whaley, Daniel L. Rosenfeld, Michael Humphrey, Allison L. Moore, and Allison Bihl. 2020. Politicizing the COVID-19 pandemic: Ideological differences in adherence to social distancing. *PsyArXiv:k23cv*.

Jonathan Rothwell and Chistos Makridis. 2020. Politics is wrecking america's pandemic response. *Brookings*.

Sebastian Ruder. 2017. An overview of gradient descent optimization algorithms. *ArXiv:1609.04747*.

Stephen M. Sales. 1973. Threat as a factor in authoritarianism: an analysis of archival data. *Journal of Personality and Social Psychology*, 28(1):44–57.

Symeon Symeonidis, Dimitrios Effrosynidis, and Avi Arampatzis. 2018. A comparative evaluation of preprocessing techniques and their interactions for twitter sentiment analysis. *Expert Systems with Applications*, 110:298–310.

Hulda Thorisdottir and John T. Jost. 2011. Motivated closed-mindedness mediates the effect of threat on political conservatism. *Political Psychology*, 32(5):785–811.

Leslie G. Valiant. 1984. A theory of the learnable. *Communications of the ACM*, 27(11):1134—-1142.

Ted Van Green and Alec Tyson. 2020. 5 facts about partisan reactions to COVID-19 in the U.S. *Pew Research Center*.

Stacy Wood and Kevin Schulman. 2021. Beyond politics–Promoting COVID-19 vaccination in the United States. *The New England Journal of Medicine*, pages 1–8.

Shaozhi Ye and Felix Wu. 2013. Measuring message propagation and social influence on Twitter. com. *International Journal of Communication Networks and Distributed Systems*, 11(1):59—-76.

Peng Zhang, Xufei Wang, and Baoxin Li. 2013. On predicting Twitter trend: Factors and models. In *Proceedings of the 2013 IEEE/ACM International Conference on Advances in Social Networks Analysis and Mining*, pages 1427—-1429. Association for Computing Machinery.

Yuying Zhao and Rakkrit Duangsoithong. 2019. Empirical analysis using feature selection and bootstrap data for small sample size problems. In *16th International Conference on Electrical Engineering/Electronics, Computer, Telecommunications and Information Technology (ECTI-CON)*, pages 814—-817. Curran Associates.

# Explainable Detection of Sarcasm in Social Media

**Ramya Akula**
University of Central Florida
USA
ramya.akula@knights.ucf.edu

**Ivan Garibay**
University of Central Florida
USA
igaribay@ucf.edu

## Abstract

Sarcasm is a linguistic expression often used to communicate the opposite of what is said, usually something that is very unpleasant with an intention to insult or ridicule. Inherent ambiguity in sarcastic expressions makes sarcasm detection very difficult. In this work, we focus on detecting sarcasm in textual conversations, written in English, from various social networking platforms and online media. To this end, we develop an interpretable deep learning model using multi-head self-attention and gated recurrent units. We show the effectiveness and interpretability of our approach by achieving state-of-the-art results on datasets from social networking platforms, online discussion forum and political dialogues.

## 1 Introduction

Sarcasm is a rhetorical way of expressing dislike or negative emotions using different language constructs, such as exaggeration or ridicule. It is an assortment of mockery and false politeness to intensify hostility without explicitly doing so. In face-to-face conversation, facial expressions, gestures, and tone of the speaker provide cues that help in identifying sarcasm. However, recognizing sarcasm in textual communication is not a trivial task as none of these cues are readily available. With the explosion of internet usage, sarcasm detection in online communications from social networking platforms, discussion forums, and e-commerce websites has become crucial for opinion mining, sentiment analysis, and identifying cyberbullies, online trolls. Thus, developing computational models for automatic detection of sarcasm gathered pace in recent times with multiple studies and collection of new datasets (Ghosh and Veale, 2017; Misra and Arora, 2019; Khodak et al., 2018).

Earlier works on sarcasm detection on texts use lexical (content) and pragmatic (context) cues (Kreuz and Caucci, 2007) such as interjections, punctuation, and sentimental shifts, which are major indicators of sarcasm (Joshi et al., 2015). In these works, the features are hand-crafted which cannot generalize in the presence of informal language and figurative slang widely used in online conversations. With the advent of deep-learning, recent works (Ghosh and Veale, 2017; Ilic et al., 2018; Ghosh et al., 2018; Xiong et al., 2019; Liu et al., 2019), leverage neural networks to learn both lexical and contextual features, eliminating the need for hand-crafted features. In these works, word embeddings are incorporated to train deep convolutional, recurrent, or attention-based neural networks to achieve state-of-the-art results. While deep learning-based approaches achieve impressive performance, they lack interpretability. In this work, we also focus on the interpretability of the model along with its high performance. The main contributions of our work are: a) Propose an interpretable model for sarcasm detection using self-attention. b) Achieve state-of-the-art results on diverse datasets and exhibit the effectiveness of our model with extensive experimentation and ablation studies. c) Exhibit the interpretability of our model by analyzing the learned attention maps.

## 2 Proposed Approach

Our proposed approach consists of five components: Data Pre-processing, Multi-Head Self-Attention, Gated Recurrent Units(GRU), Classification, and Model Interpretability. The architecture of our sarcasm detection model is shown in Figure 1. Data pre-processing involves converting input text to word embeddings, required for training a deep learning model. We employ the pre-trained language model, BERT (Devlin et al., 2019), to extract word embeddings. We use these word embeddings which capture global context as we believe context is essential for detecting sarcasm. These embeddings form the input to our multi-head self-attention module which identifies words in the input text that provide crucial cues for sarcasm. In the next step, the GRU layer aids in learning long-distance relationships among these highlighted words and output a single feature vector encoding the entire sequence. Finally, a fully-connected layer with sigmoid activation is used to get the final classification score.

**Multi-Head Self-Attention** Given a sentence S, we apply a standard tokenizer and use pre-trained models to obtain $D$ dimensional embeddings for individual words in the sentence. These embeddings $S = \{e_1, e_2, ...,$



*Proceedings of the 11th Workshop on Computational Approaches to Subjectivity, Sentiment and Social Media Analysis*, pages 34–39
April 19, 2021. ©2021 Association for Computational Linguistics

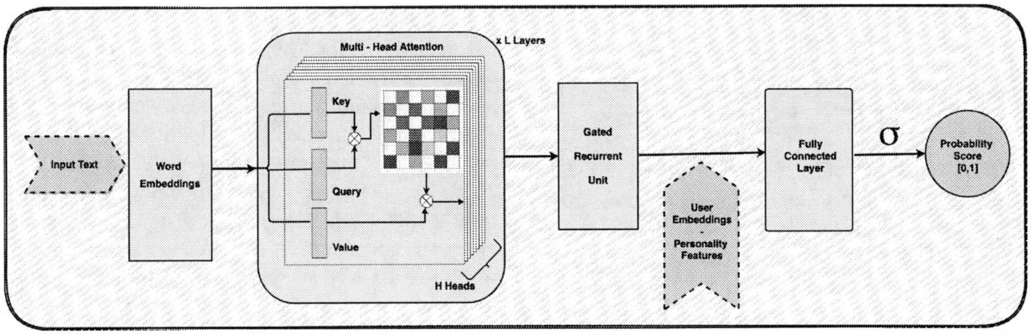


Figure 1: Multi head self-attention architecture for sarcasm detection. Pre-trained word embeddings are extracted for input text and are enhanced by an attention module with $L$ self-attention layers and $H$ heads per layer. Resultant features are passed through a Gated Recurrent Unit and a Feed-forward layer for classification.

$e_N\}$, $S \in \mathbb{R}^{N \times D}$ from the input to our model. To detect sarcasm in sentence S, it is crucial to identify specific words that provide essential cues such as sarcastic connotations and negative emotions. The importance of these cue-words is dependent on multiple factors based on different contexts. In our proposed model we leverage multi-head self-attention to identify these cue-words from the input text. Attention is a mechanism to discover patterns in the input that are crucial for solving the given task. In deep learning, self-attention (Vaswani et al., 2017) is an attention mechanism for sequences, which helps in learning the task-specific relationship between different elements of a given sequence to produce a better sequence representation. In the self-attention module, three linear projections: Key ($K$), Value ($V$), and Query ($Q$) of the given input sequence are generated, where $K, Q, V \in \mathbb{R}^{N \times D}$. Attention-map is computed based on the similarity between $K$, $Q$, and the output of this module $A \in \mathbb{R}^{N \times D}$ is the scaled dot-product between $V$ and the learned softmax attention ($QK^T$). In multi-head self-attention, multiple copies of the self-attention module are used in parallel. Each head captures different relationships between the words in the input text and identify those keywords that aid in classification. In our model, we use a series of multi-head self-attention layers (#$L$) with multiple heads (#$H$) in each layer.

**Gated Recurrent Units** Self-attention finds the words in the text which are important in detecting sarcasm. These words can be close to each other or farther apart in the input text. To learn long-distance relationships between these words, we use GRUs. These units are an improvement over standard recurrent neural networks and are designed to dynamically remember and forget the information flow using Reset ($r_t$) and Update ($z_t$) gates to solve the vanishing gradient problem.

**Classification** A single fully-connected feed-forward layer is used with sigmoid activation to compute the final output. Input to this layer is the feature vector $h_N$ from the GRU module and the output is a probability score $y \in [0, 1]$, where $\hat{y} \in \{0, 1\}$ is the binary label i.e., 1:Sarcasm and 0:No-sarcasm.

**Model Interpretability** Developing models that can explain their predictions is crucial to building trust and faith in deep learning while enabling a wide range of applications with machine intelligence at its backbone. Existing deep learning network architectures such as convolutional and recurrent neural networks are not inherently interpretable and require additional visualization techniques (Zhou et al., 2016; Selvaraju et al., 2017). To avoid this, we in this work employ self-attention which is inherently interpretable and allows identifying elements in the input which are crucial for a given task.

## 3 Experiments

We implement our model in PyTorch (Paszke et al., 2019), a deep-learning framework in Python. To tokenize and extract word embeddings for the input text, we use publicly available resources (Wolf et al., 2019). Specifically, we use tokenizer and pre-trained weights from the "bert-base-uncased" model to convert words to tokens and then convert tokens to word embeddings. The embeddings for the words in the input text are passed through a series of multi-head self-attention layers #$L$ , with multiple heads #$H$ in each of the layers. The output from the self-attention layer is passed through a single bi-directional GRU layer with it's hidden dimension $d = 512$. The 512-dimensional output feature vector from the GRU layer is passed through the fully connected layer to get a 1-dimensional output. A sigmoid activation is applied to the final output and BCE loss is used to compute the loss between the ground truth and the predicted probability score. We use Adam optimizer to train our model with approximately 13 million parameters, using a learning rate of 1e-4, batch size of 64, and dropout set 0.2. We use one NVIDIA Pascal Titan-X with 16GB memory for all our experiments. We set #$H$ = 8 and #$L$ = 3 in all our experiments for all the datasets. Details of these datasets, including the sample counts in train/test splits and the data source, are presented in Table 1.

**Evaluation** We pose Sarcasm Detection as a classification problem, and use Precision, Recall, F1-Score,

| Source | Train | Test | Total |
|---|---|---|---|
| Twitter, 2013 | 1,368 | 588 | 1,956 |
| Dialogues, 2016 | 3754 | 938 | 4,692 |
| Reddit, 2018 | 154,702 | 64,666 | 219,368 |

Table 1: Statistics of datasets used in our experiments. Twitter, 2013 (Riloff et al., 2013), Dialogues, 2016 (Oraby et al., 2016), and Reddit, 2018 (Khodak et al., 2018). These are sourced from varied online platforms including social networks and discussion forums.

and Accuracy as evaluation metrics to test the performance of the trained models. Apart from these standard metrics we also compute Area Under the ROC Curve (AUC score) which is threshold independent.

## 4 Results

We present the results of our experiments on multiple publicly available datasets in this section. Results on the Twitter dataset are presented in Table 2. In Table 4, we present the results on the Reddit SARC 2.0 dataset which is divided into two subsets: Main and Political. In both datasets, our proposed approach outperforms previous methods. To compare our approach with Hazarika et al. (2018), we trained our models with and without the personality features and we show improvement in both the settings. Similar to Hazarika et al. (2018), we use the personality features extracted from a CNN model trained on a multi-label personality detection task using all the comments from a user. These features are appended to the features from the input text before passing them to the final classification layer in the model.

Apart from Twitter and Reddit data, we also experimented with data from one other data source, i.e., Political Dialogues. In Table 3, we present results on the corresponding Sarcasm Corpus V2 Dialogues dataset(Oraby et al., 2016). We use this dataset (Oraby et al., 2016) for the following ablation studies.

**Ablation 1:** We vary the number of self-attention layers and fix the number of heads per layer ($\#H = 8$). From the results of this experiment presented in Table 5, we observe that as the number of self-attention layers increase ($\#L = 0, 1, 3, 5$) the improvement in the performance of the model due to the additional layers saturate. Also, these results show that the proposed multi-head self-attention model achieves a 2% improvement over the baseline model where only a single GRU layer is used without any self-attention layers.

**Ablation 2:** We vary the number of heads per layer with a fixed number of self-attention layers ($\#L = 3$). The results of these experiments are presented Table 6. We observe that the performance of the model also increases with the increase in the number of heads per self-attention layer.

## 5 Model Interpretability

Attention maps from the individual heads of the self-attention layers provide the learned attention weights for each time-step in the input. In our case, each time-step is a word and we visualize the per-word attention weights for sample sentences with and without sarcasm from the SARC 2.0 Main dataset. The model we used for this analysis has 5 attention layers with 8 heads per attention. Figures 2 shows attention analysis (Clark et al., 2019) for sample sentences with and without sarcasm respectively. Each column in these figures corresponds to a single attention layer and attention weights between words in each head are represented using colored edges. The darkness of an edge indicates the strength of the attention weight. CLS and SEP are classifications and separator tokens from BERT.

**Attention Analysis** For a sentence with sarcasm, Figure 2 shows that certain words receive more attention than others. For instance, words such as "just", "again", "totally", "!", have darker edges connecting them with every other word in a sentence. These are the words in the sentence which hint at sarcasm and as expected these receive higher attention than others. Also, note that each cue word is attended by a different head in the first three layers of self-attention. In the final two layers, we observe that the attention is spread out to every word in the sentence indicating redundancy of these layers in the model. Attention weight for a word is computed by first considering the maximum attention it receives across layers and then averaging the weights across multiple-heads in the layer. Finally, the weights for a word are averaged over all the words in the sentence. The stronger the highlight for a word, the higher is the attention weight placed on it by the model while classifying the sentence. Words from the sarcastic sentences with higher weights show that the model can detect sarcastic cues from the sentence. For example, the words "totally", "first", "ever" from the first sentence and "even", "until", "already" from the third sentence. These are the words that exhibit sarcasm in the sentences, which the model can successfully identify. In all the samples which are classified as non-sarcasm, the weights for the individual words are very low in comparison to cue-words from the sarcastic sentences. Our model can predict a high score for sarcastic sentences and low scores for non-sarcastic sentences.

## 6 Conclusion

In this work, we propose a novel multi-head self-attention-based neural network architecture to detect sarcasm in a given sentence. Our proposed approach has 5 components: data pre-processing, multi-head self-attention module, gated recurrent unit module, classification, and model interpretability. Multi-head self-attention is used to highlight the parts of the sentence which provide crucial cues for sarcasm detection. GRUs aid in learning long-distance relationships among these highlighted words in the sentence. The output from this layer is passed through a fully-connected classification layer to get the final classification score. Exper-

| Models | Precision | Recall | F1 | AUC |
|---|---|---|---|---|
| Fracking Sarcasm (Ghosh and Veale, 2016) | 88.3 | 87.9 | 88.1 | - |
| GRNN (Zhang et al., 2016) | 66.3 | 64.7 | 65.4 | - |
| ELMo-BiLSTM (Ilic et al., 2018) | 75.9 | 75.0 | 75.9 | - |
| ELMo-BiLSTM FULL (Ilic et al., 2018) | 77.8 | 73.5 | 75.3 | - |
| ELMo-BiLSTM AUG (Ilic et al., 2018) | 68.4 | 70.8 | 69.4 | - |
| A2Text-Net (Liu et al., 2019) | 91.7 | 91.0 | 90.0 | 97.0 |
| **Our Model** | **97.9** (+ 6.2 ↑) | **99.6** (+ 8.6 ↑) | **98.7** (+ 8.7 ↑) | **99.6** (+ 2.6 ↑) |

Table 2: Results on Twitter dataset (Riloff et al., 2013).

| Models | Precision | Recall | F1 | AUC |
|---|---|---|---|---|
| GRNN (Zhang et al., 2016) | 62.2 | 61.8 | 61.2 | - |
| CNN-LSTM-DNN (Ghosh and Veale, 2016) | 66.1 | 66.7 | 65.7 | - |
| SIARN (Tay et al., 2018) | 72.1 | 71.8 | 71.8 | - |
| MIARN (Tay et al., 2018) | 72.9 | 72.9 | 72.7 | - |
| ELMo-BiLSTM (Ilic et al., 2018) | 74.8 | 74.7 | 74.7 | - |
| ELMo-BiLSTM FULL (Ilic et al., 2018) | 76.0 | 76.0 | 76.0 | - |
| **Our Model** | **77.4** ( + 1.2 ↑) | **77.2** ( + 1.4 ↑) | **77.2** ( + 1.2 ↑) | **0.834** |

Table 3: Results on Sarcasm Corpus V2 Dialogues dataset (Oraby et al., 2016)

| Models | Main | | Political | |
|---|---|---|---|---|
| | Accuracy | F1 | Accuracy | F1 |
| CASCADE (Hazarika et al., 2018) | 77.0 | 77.0 | 74.0 | 75.0 |
| SARC 2.0 (Khodak et al., 2018) | 75.0 | - | 76.0 | - |
| ELMo-BiLSTM (Ilic et al., 2018) | 72.0 | - | 78.0 | - |
| ELMo-BiLSTM FULL (Ilic et al., 2018) | 76.0 | 76.0 | 72.0 | 72.0 |
| **Our Model** | **81.0** ( + 4.0 ↑) | **81.0** ( + 4.0 ↑) | **80.0** ( + 2.0 ↑) | **80.0** ( + 5.0 ↑) |
| CASCADE (w/o personality features) | 68.0 | 66.0 | 68.0 | 70.0 |
| **Our Model (w/o personality features)** | **70.0** ( + 2.0 ↑) | **70.0** ( + 4.0 ↑) | **71.0** ( + 3.0 ↑) | **72.0** ( + 2.0 ↑) |

Table 4: Results on Reddit dataset SARC 2.0 and SARC 2.0 Political (Khodak et al., 2018).

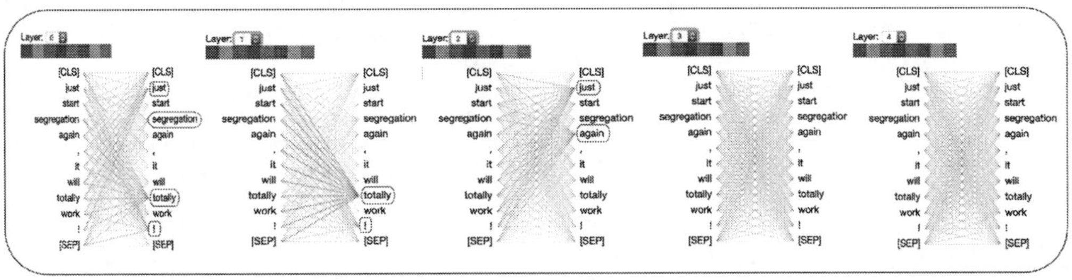


Figure 2: Attention analysis with sample sentence with sarcasm. Words providing cues for sarcasm, highlighted in green, are the words with higher attention weights. The prediction score for this sentence by our model is 0.94.

iments are conducted on two datasets from different data sources and show significant improvement over the state-of-the-art models by all evaluation metrics. Results from ablation studies and analysis of the trained model are presented to show the importance of different components of our model. We analyze the learned attention weights to interpret our trained model and show that it can indeed identify words in the input text which provide cues for sarcasm.

| #*L* - Layers | Precision | Recall | F1 |
|---|---|---|---|
| 0 (GRU only) | 75.6 | 75.6 | 75.6 |
| 1 Layer | 76.2 | 76.1 | 76.1 |
| 3 Layers | 77.4 | 77.2 | 77.2 |
| 5 Layers | 77.6 | 77.6 | 77.6 |

Table 5: Ablation study with varying number of attention layers #*L* and fixed Heads **#*H* = 8** on the Sarcasm Corpus V2 Dialogues dataset (Oraby et al., 2016).

| #*H* - Heads | Precision | Recall | F1 |
|---|---|---|---|
| 1 Head | 74.9 | 74.5 | 74.4 |
| 4 Heads | 76.9 | 76.8 | 76.8 |
| 8 Heads | 77.4 | 77.2 | 77.2 |

Table 6: Ablation study with varying number of Heads #*H* and fixed Layers **#*L* = 3** on the Sarcasm Corpus V2 Dialogues dataset (Oraby et al., 2016).

## References


Kevin Clark, Urvashi Khandelwal, Omer Levy, and Christopher D Manning. 2019. What does bert look at? an analysis of bert's attention. In *Proceedings of the 2019 ACL Workshop BlackboxNLP: Analyzing and Interpreting Neural Networks for NLP*, pages 276–286.

Jacob Devlin, Ming-Wei Chang, Kenton Lee, and Kristina Toutanova. 2019. Bert: Pre-training of deep bidirectional transformers for language understanding. In *Proceedings of the 2019 Conference of NAACL: Human Language Technologies*, pages 4171–4186.

Aniruddha Ghosh and Tony Veale. 2016. Fracking sarcasm using neural network. In *Proceedings of the 7th workshop on computational approaches to subjectivity, sentiment and social media analysis*, pages 161–169.

Aniruddha Ghosh and Tony Veale. 2017. Magnets for sarcasm: making sarcasm detection timely, contextual and very personal. In *Proceedings of the 2017 Conference on EMNLP*, pages 482–491.

Debanjan Ghosh, Alexander R Fabbri, and Smaranda Muresan. 2018. Sarcasm analysis using conversation context. *Computational Linguistics*, pages 755–792.

Devamanyu Hazarika, Soujanya Poria, Sruthi Gorantla, Erik Cambria, Roger Zimmermann, and Rada Mihalcea. 2018. Cascade: Contextual sarcasm detection in online discussion forums. In *Proceedings of the 27th International Conference on Computational Linguistics*, pages 1837–1848.

Suzana Ilic, Edison Marrese-Taylor, Jorge Balazs, and Yutaka Matsuo. 2018. Deep contextualized word representations for detecting sarcasm and irony. In *Proceedings of the 9th Workshop on Computational Approaches to Subjectivity, Sentiment and Social Media Analysis*, pages 2–7.

Aditya Joshi, Vinita Sharma, and Pushpak Bhattacharyya. 2015. Harnessing context incongruity for sarcasm detection. In *Proceedings of the 53rd Annual Meeting of the ACL and the 7th IJCNLP*, pages 757–762.

Mikhail Khodak, Nikunj Saunshi, and Kiran Vodrahalli. 2018. A large self-annotated corpus for sarcasm. In *Proceedings of the Eleventh International Conference on Language Resources and Evaluation (LREC 2018)*.

Roger J Kreuz and Gina M Caucci. 2007. Lexical influences on the perception of sarcasm. In *Proceedings of the Workshop on computational approaches to Figurative Language*, pages 1–4. Association for Computational Linguistics.

Liyuan Liu, Jennifer Lewis Priestley, Yiyun Zhou, Herman E Ray, and Meng Han. 2019. A2text-net: A novel deep neural network for sarcasm detection. In *2019 IEEE First International Conference on Cognitive Machine Intelligence (CogMI)*, pages 118–126. IEEE.

Rishabh Misra and Prahal Arora. 2019. Sarcasm detection using hybrid neural network. *arXiv preprint arXiv:1908.07414*.

Shereen Oraby, Vrindavan Harrison, Lena Reed, Ernesto Hernandez, Ellen Riloff, and Marilyn Walker. 2016. Creating and characterizing a diverse corpus of sarcasm in dialogue. In *Proceedings of the 17th Annual Meeting of the Special Interest Group on Discourse and Dialogue*, pages 31–41.

Adam Paszke, Sam Gross, Francisco Massa, Adam Lerer, James Bradbury, Gregory Chanan, Trevor Killeen, Zeming Lin, Natalia Gimelshein, Luca Antiga, Alban Desmaison, Andreas Kopf, Edward Yang, Zachary DeVito, Martin Raison, Alykhan Tejani, Sasank Chilamkurthy, Benoit Steiner, Lu Fang, Junjie Bai, and Soumith Chintala. 2019. Pytorch: An imperative style, high-performance deep learning library. In *Advances in Neural Information Processing Systems 32*.

Ellen Riloff, Ashequl Qadir, Prafulla Surve, Lalindra De Silva, Nathan Gilbert, and Ruihong Huang. 2013. Sarcasm as contrast between a positive sentiment and negative situation. In *Proceedings of the 2013 Conference on EMNLP*, pages 704–714.

Ramprasaath R Selvaraju, Michael Cogswell, Abhishek Das, Ramakrishna Vedantam, Devi Parikh, and Dhruv Batra. 2017. Grad-cam: Visual explanations from deep networks via gradient-based localization. In *Proceedings of the IEEE international conference on computer vision*, pages 618–626.

Yi Tay, Anh Tuan Luu, Siu Cheung Hui, and Jian Su. 2018. Reasoning with sarcasm by reading in-between. In *Proceedings of the 56th Annual Meeting of the ACL*, pages 1010–1020.

Ashish Vaswani, Noam Shazeer, Niki Parmar, Jakob Uszkoreit, Llion Jones, Aidan N Gomez, Łukasz Kaiser, and Illia Polosukhin. 2017. Attention is all you need. In *Advances in neural information processing systems*, pages 5998–6008.

Thomas Wolf, Lysandre Debut, Victor Sanh, Julien Chaumond, Clement Delangue, Anthony Moi, Pierric Cistac, Tim Rault, R'emi Louf, Morgan Funtowicz, and Jamie Brew. 2019. Huggingface's transformers: State-of-the-art natural language processing. *ArXiv*.

Tao Xiong, Peiran Zhang, Hongbo Zhu, and Yihui Yang. 2019. Sarcasm detection with self-matching networks and low-rank bilinear pooling. In *The World Wide Web Conference*, pages 2115–2124.

Meishan Zhang, Yue Zhang, and Guohong Fu. 2016. Tweet sarcasm detection using deep neural network. In *Proceedings of COLING 2016, The 26th International Conference on Computational Linguistics: Technical Papers*, pages 2449–2460.

Bolei Zhou, Aditya Khosla, Agata Lapedriza, Aude Oliva, and Antonio Torralba. 2016. Learning deep features for discriminative localization. In *Proceedings of the IEEE conference on computer vision and pattern recognition*, pages 2921–2929.

# Emotion Ratings:
# How Intensity, Annotation Confidence and Agreements are Entangled

**Enrica Troiano, Sebastian Padó** and **Roman Klinger**
Institut für Maschinelle Sprachverarbeitung
University of Stuttgart, Germany
{firstname.lastname}@ims.uni-stuttgart.de

## Abstract

When humans judge the affective content of texts, they also implicitly assess the correctness of such judgment, that is, their confidence. We hypothesize that people's (in)confidence that they performed well in an annotation task leads to (dis)agreements among each other. If this is true, confidence may serve as a diagnostic tool for systematic differences in annotations. To probe our assumption, we conduct a study on a subset of the Corpus of Contemporary American English, in which we ask raters to distinguish *neutral* sentences from *emotion*-bearing ones, while scoring the confidence of their answers. Confidence turns out to approximate inter-annotator disagreements. Further, we find that confidence is correlated to emotion intensity: perceiving stronger affect in text prompts annotators to more certain classification performances. This insight is relevant for modelling studies of intensity, as it opens the question wether automatic regressors or classifiers actually predict intensity, or rather human's self-perceived confidence.

## 1 Introduction

A plethora of theories exist on the matter of emotions: the intensity of affective states, their link to cognition, and their arrangement into categories are just a few of the angles from which psychology has tackled this complex phenomenon (Gendron and Feldman Barrett, 2009). Correspondingly, in computational emotion analysis, texts have been associated to values of intensity (Strapparava and Mihalcea, 2007; Mohammad and Bravo-Marquez, 2017), to cognitive components (Hofmann et al., 2020), and discrete classes (Zhang et al., 2018; Zhong et al., 2019, i.a.). In support of these tasks, substantial research effort has been directed to resource construction, which typically relies on the participation of human judges. Yet, emotions are a subjective experience. Their interpretation in text varies across individuals, and this poses a major challenge in emotion analysis: it is hard to reach acceptable levels of inter-annotator agreement (IAA) (Bobicev and Sokolova, 2017; Schuff et al., 2017; Troiano et al., 2019).

On their side, humans (roughly) know how well they can "read" emotions (Realo et al., 2003). They judge the affective content of texts, and at the same time, the correctness of such judgment: in other words, annotators can evaluate their own confidence with respect to their labelling decisions. This hints a possible relation between confidence and IAA. One could expect that annotators are more likely to incur inconsistencies when they feel uncertain about their answers. Hence, it would be interesting to verify if self-assessed confidence approximates inter-annotator disagreements in affect-related annotation tasks. The collection of this type of judgments is not a common practice: past research has found that self-assigned scores of confidence are predictable based on some vocal attributes of emotion speech stimuli (Lausen and Hammerschmidt, 2020), but this has not been done on text, to the best of our knowledge.

Yet another aspect involved in emotion recognition and which, at first sight, relates to confidence, is emotion intensity. It would be intuitive to assume that emotions are recognized with higher confidence if they are expressed with stronger magnitude (e.g., "*The teacher exploded*" > "*He snapped his annoyed temper*", "*sadder*" > "*a bit sad*", "*ecstasy*" > "*joy*"). Still, in the sentence "*We had to cheer him up; later, he was off the ground*", readers have to choose what part of the text to attend to (the challenge that the speakers undertook – not intense, or the effect they had – intense) and be very confident about either choice. Similar counter examples reveal that the link between the perception of emotion intensity and the self-perceived confidence is opaque, and leaves room for exploration.



*Proceedings of the 11th Workshop on Computational Approaches to Subjectivity, Sentiment and Social Media Analysis*, pages 40–49
April 19, 2021. ©2021 Association for Computational Linguistics

In this paper, we experimentally investigate the relationship between three human judgments: about the presence of emotions, about their intensity, and about the confidence of the annotation decision. Leveraging such information, we aim at understanding in what cases annotators differ regarding the judgement that an emotion is expressed. Our first research question is: (RQ1) Are (dis)agreements with respect to the presence of emotions related to confidence? Second, (RQ2) Are judgments of intensity and confidence entangled? We bring these issues together in an annotation study based on emotion recognition, in which self-perceived confidence is a dimension to be rated. Given a subset of the Corpus of Contemporary American English (COCA) (Davies, 2015), raters distinguish emotion-bearing sentences from neutral ones, while quantifying both the intensity of the emotion and their confidence on a Likert scale (Bègue et al., 2018).

We find that confidence can explain systematic differences in decisions of annotators; so does intensity; and impressions on intensity and confidence are correlated. Based on these results, we devise a strategy to leverage the two factors and smoothen out inter-annotator inconsistencies.

## 2 Annotation Setup

**Tasks.** The first step in this study is to collect emotion assessments.[1] We are not interested in which emotion people interpret from text, but rather if they recognize any. Judges read sentences and answer the question: *(*EMO*) Is it Emotional or Neutral?* For the items deemed to express an emotion, we also ask *(*INT*) How strong is it?*, which enables us to obtain ratings about affective strengths on a Likert scale from 1 (not intense) to 3 (very). Lastly, since raters interpret emotions without an immediate first-hand experience, we have them self-evaluate their own judgments on a scale from 1 (unsure) to 3 (certain), in response to the question *(*CONF*) How confident are you about your answer to* EMO*?*

As for EMO, we acknowledge that the emotional content of an utterance can be inferred from many perspectives. It is possible to assess one's own emotion after reading the text, to reconstruct the affective state of the writers who produced it, to guess the reaction that they intended to elicit in the readers, and so on. To avoid confusion, we instruct annotators to consider the presence of an emotion only with respect to their personal viewpoint.

We opt for an in-lab setting. Raters are three female master students aged between 24 and 27, who are proficient in English, and have some annotation experience and background in computational emotion analysis.

**Data.** Corpora that include emotion classes or gradations are tailored on specific domains, like self-reports (Scherer and Wallbott, 1997), tweets (Mohammad, 2018) and newspapers (Strapparava and Mihalcea, 2008). We broaden our focus to multiple genres, and annotate sentences from the 2020 version of COCA[2], which includes unlabelled texts that occurred from 1990 to present in different domains, like blogs, magazines, newspapers, academic texts, spoken interactions, fictions, TV, and movie subtitles.

With a corpus of this size (>1B words), considering all data points would be costly, and randomly selecting them may cause imbalance in the final annotation – i.e., a majority of *neutral* instances. Therefore, we draw a sample biased towards emotional sentences with a combination of rules and classifier-based information. To obtain such a classifier, we fine-tune the pre-trained BERT (Devlin et al., 2019) base-case model on a number of emotion analysis resources[3], adding a classification layer that outputs the labels *emotion* or *neutral*. Having that, we filter academic texts out of COCA for their arguably impartial language, and from each of the other genres, we randomly pick 500 sentences; out of these, we sample 100 sentences balanced by class, i.e., 50 labelled as *neutral* by our classifier, 50 as bearing an *emotion*. Thus, the annotators are shown 700 items, 100 per domain, with a balanced class distribution, according to the classifier.

## 3 Results

To answer our research questions, we first observe annotators' agreements on EMO. The highest Cohen's $\kappa$ (1960) between pairs of human judges was .43 (Table 1a); Fleiss' $\kappa$ (1971) for the three annotators was .34.

At first glance, these numbers appear unsatisfactory. On the one hand, they are due to the skewed class distribution in the annotators' choices.[4] On

[1]The guidelines are in the Appendix. Our data is accessible at `https://www.ims.uni-stuttgart.de/data/emotion-confidence`.

[2]https://www.english-corpora.org/coca/

[3]Details and classifier's performance in Appendix.

[4]With skewed class distribution, chance agreement increases, penalizing the resulting $\kappa$ (Cicchetti and Feinstein, 1990).

| | IAA |
|---|---|
| A1–A2 | .38 |
| A2–A3 | .43 |
| A3–A1 | .30 |

(a) Cohen's $\kappa$ for annotator pairs on EMO.

| | Counts | |
|---|---|---|
| | 1 vs. 2 | 3 vs. 0 |
| E | 138 | 304 |
| N | 170 | 88 |

(b) Counts of *emotion* (E) and *neutral* (N) items for EMO answers, aggregated by agreement (1 vs. 2, 3 vs. 0).

| | CONF | INT |
|---|---|---|
| 1 | −.001 | .04 |
| 2 | .03 | .20 |
| 3 | .39 | .30 |

(c) Fleiss' $\kappa$ on EMO for each value of CONF and INT.

Table 1: Inter-Annotator Agreements.

the other, they can be traced back to the way in which the EMO task was formulated: asking if a text is emotional from the readers' own point of view (e.g., it "describes an event [...] to which *you* would associate an emotion", see Appendix) as opposed, for instance, to the writers', paves the way for more heterogeneous responses.

However, a look at other IAA measures, like the absolute counts of items that were assigned to each label, leads to a more detailed picture. Table 1b breaks down the annotated categories by agreement: column 1 vs. 2 corresponds to the groups of items on which 1 annotator chose a label, while the majority opted for the other; column 3 vs. 0 shows how many times all three annotators agreed. We see that 138 sentences out of 700 were deemed emotionally charged by only 1 person (and hence, were associated to *neutral* by the two others). 2 annotators picked the *emotion* class for 170 sentences, i.e., those which were *neutral* according to just 1 rater. Overall, as the amount of considered judgments increases, so does their intersubjective validity about emotions. This tendency is clear in column 3 vs. 0, which shows that there were more emotional instances with 3 identical labels than those with conflicting ratings. Indeed, perfect agreement was reached for 392 items (304 *emotion* and 88 *neutral*), more than half the data, suggesting that people had a shared understanding.

### 3.1 Confidence Approximates Disagreements (and so does Intensity)

We next focus on the items that received incoherent judgments. Annotators seem to diverge on the presence/absence of emotions in a systematic way. Specifically, their inconsistencies correspond to certain patterns in the ratings of confidence, as well as intensity. Taking pairs of annotators, we see that the one who picks the *emotion* class tends to do that with low confidence.[5] As an example representative of the general trend, on 11 sentences annotator A3 makes the *neutral* choice, while annotator A1 picks *emotion*, but rates such items with confidence 1 (5 sentences), or 2 (6 sentences) – never using the highest degree of confidence. The same holds for intensity: A1 rates 10 of the 11 sentences as having the lowest intensity, and 1 sentence as having intensity 2 – none with the highest intensity value.

Hence, to answer RQ1, the evaluation of intensity and the self-evaluation of confidence underlie disagreements in discrete emotion annotations. Further, they show that different intuitions are not totally incompatible, since the annotator who takes the *emotion* decision does so without being extremely confident, and gauging intensity as rather weak.

We corroborate this finding by looking at a more standard measure of IAA, namely Fleiss' $\kappa$, which turns out to be affected by both CONF and INT. We compute it once more for the answers of EMO, but here we consider to be emotional only the items on which all annotators choose a certain level of confidence or intensity. Table 1c displays $\kappa$ separately for different levels (rows) of CONF and INT. Low values aside, these results inform us that the lower CONF/INT, the more prominent are disagreements. The highest IAA (.39), instead, is achieved for the most confident answers.

**Post-Processing Disagreements.** If systematic differences among annotators can be diagnosed with the help of confidence and intensity, can they also be resolved to some extent? We use the CONF and INT scores as acceptance thresholds for the label *emotion*, so to post-process the EMO decisions of each judge: they turn into *neutral* if the corresponding CONF or INT answer does not reach a certain threshold t. For instance, using INT as thres-

[5]Ratings on disagreements are in Appendix, Table 4.

| | Emo Conf<2 | | Emo Conf<3 | |
|---|---|---|---|---|
| | 1 vs. 2 | 3 vs. 0 | 1 vs. 2 | 3 vs. 0 |
| E | 172 | 187 | 141 | 56 |
| N | 169 | 172 | 73 | 430 |

| | Emo Int<2 | | Emo Int<3 | |
|---|---|---|---|---|
| | 1 vs. 2 | 3 vs. 0 | 1 vs. 2 | 3 vs. 0 |
| E | 165 | 82 | 57 | 7 |
| N | 118 | 335 | 17 | 619 |

Table 2: Counts of labels for subsets of ratings on Emo, post-processed with acceptance thresholds <2 and <3, for both Conf (top) and Int (bottom).

hold, with t<2 all items labeled *emotion* in Emo are kept as such only in case the Int is 2 or more, all the others are mapped to *neutral*.

Agreement counts on the post-processed annotation of Emo are in Table 2. We see, again, that the number of agreed upon items increases by increasing the sets of equal ratings. For instance, 283 sentences received 2 unanimous judgments (column 1 vs. 2, under Emo Int<2), and 417 received 3. In comparison to the original annotation in Table 1b, we can observe a considerable change in the number of items with perfect agreement. While in the raw judgments they were 392, with t<3 they increase to 626. We find a similar pattern when leveraging confidence: with t<2 (low confidence), it is obtained for 359 items, and with t<3 (moderate), perfect agreement increases to 486 items.

This comes at the cost of agreeing on fewer *emotion* sentences (304 before filtering, 7 and 56 after applying the highest threshold to Int and Conf), but it indicates that the better raters agree on intensity or confidence, the more they agree regarding the presence or absence of emotions.

### 3.2 Stronger Intensity, Higher Confidence

Having found that confidence and intensity have a similar relationship to disagreements, we move to analyzing how they link to one another. To address RQ2, we focus on the ratings of the 304 sentences with the unanimous *emotion* judgment. For them, we compute the intra-annotator correlation between the answers to Int and the corresponding ratings of Conf. A Spearman's $\rho$ (Spearman, 1904) of .5 for annotator A1, .58 for A2 and .64 for A3 (p-value <.05 for all) reveals a significant positive correlation between intensity and confidence. This suggests that people believe they correctly classified a text if they also perceived high emotion intensity.

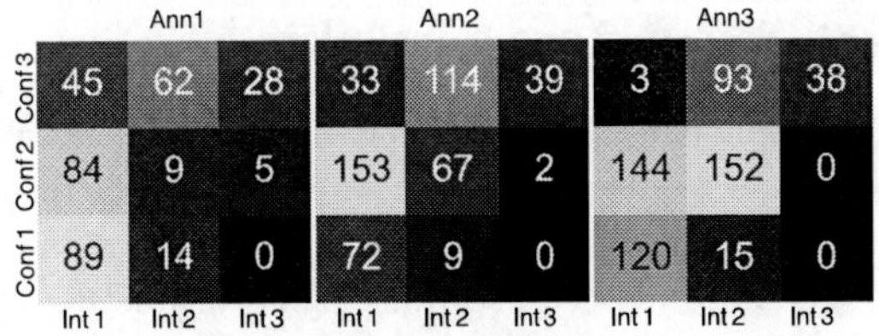


Figure 1: Cross-tabulation of Int and Conf by annotator, for the items that each of them deems emotional.

Figure 1 gives an in-depth account of the Conf-Int relation. It plots the counts of items that were labeled with a certain emotion intensity together with a certain confidence level, separately for each annotator. The columns Int3 tell us that rarely annotators perceive intensity as strong without being extremely confident that the text expresses an emotion. In fact, no instance was rated with the highest intensity and the lowest confidence (Int3-Conf1) at the same time. Conversely, for cases of low intensity, annotators tend to stay low also on the scale of confidence.

**On what do People Agree?** On the 304 sentences considered emotional by all, if the annotators gave the same score to intensity (i.e., perfect agreement is both on Emo and Int), they did not have a total disagreement on confidence (i.e., there are always at least 2 people with the same Conf) and vice versa. This may be a sign of the correlation between the two variables.

Moreover, some items were scored with perfect agreement on all questions. It is the case of sentences like "*I can't believe that you saved my life*", considered, with the highest level of confidence, to convey an emotion of intensity 3, "*Get off my back!*" deemed to have a mild intensity, and "*„You have such an interesting life," she said, after a little small talk*" with intensity 1. While these examples are rated as highly certain (Conf3), there are also sentences on which people agree across all confidence-intensity combinations.[6] None of the instances has Conf1 and Int3, while a number of examples have Conf3 and Int1, indicating that it is harder to be uncertain of a strong emotion than to be sure of a weak one.

[6]A detailed analysis is in Table 5, Appendix.

## 4 Discussion and Conclusion

This annotation investigated if the perceived emotion (class), a perceived feature of emotion (intensity), and self-perception (confidence) are tied together – and can help understand inconsistent annotations. We found that (RQ1) both intensity and confidence account for inter-annotator inconsistencies relative to binary decisions. Adopting confidence as an acceptance threshold showed that higher scores lead to more uniform assessments of emotions; though not a surprising effect of confidence, this also applies to intensity. Moreover, (RQ2) the two variables are correlated, that is, people feel more certain about their emotion recognition performance on items with high intensity.

We acknowledge that our design of EMO naturally incurs the risk of inconsistent answers. However, precisely for the subjective nature of the task, the finding that disagreements decrease with high CONF/INT is interesting in itself: some judgments which are seemingly unsolvable can be explained by certain perceived properties of emotions (intensity) or self-perceived features (confidence).

From these results we can draw some lessons. First, the correlation between confidence and intensity brings relevant implications to all those studies that focus on emotional strength. When asked to evaluate intensity, do people confound that with confidence? Even more, is there a causal relation between the two? As a best practice to put safeguards in their guidelines, experimenters may ask people to tease the two variables apart. Potentially, this issue concerns modelling studies as well: do classifiers for emotion intensity predict such feature, or rather the confidence with which people judge emotions? We provided reasons to look into this further.

Second, confidence turned out to be an important dimension of rating, because it can inform us when the annotators expect to disagree. When judgments diverge, annotators do not deem their intuition credible. Hence, our finding that confidence approximates disagreements means precisely that people themselves predict their performance to differ from that of the others.

Concretely, all this knowledge can come in support of annotation studies. Including confidence as a rating dimension may give an additional source of information about annotators' reliability. This can help experimenters to refine the guidelines in a pre-testing phase: one might want to disentangle cases in which annotators' disagreements are random – signaling a lack of annotators' reliability, and when, instead, they are due to consistently different ways of perceiving and reporting on confidence. In this second case, disagreements may be normalized to an extent, by post-processing the annotation results. For instance, as people seem to agree on the class *emotion* only if they also agree on certain degrees of CONF, there might be some levels of confidence (or intensity) that one filters in/out of the final annotation labels.

A similar strategy may be somewhat restrictive, since it accepts as emotional only those items on which humans' intuition fall above a pre-defined threshold. While we observed agreement on such items, it is possible to adopt more nuanced evaluation approaches and integrate information about intensity or confidence into IAA measures. As an example, disagreements between two raters can be penalized more when the one choosing the *emotion* label does so by perceiving extreme confidence or intensity – even though we provided evidence that these cases are rare. Future work could explore this direction.

In summary, we uphold that disagreements are not necessarily symptomatic of unreliability. This claim has so far not found much attention in emotion annotations, but is in line with a more general body of research dedicated to the reasons and the patterns underlying annotators' disagreements and to the ways in which their intuitions should be aggregated and evaluated (Bayerl and Paul, 2011; Bhardwaj et al., 2010; Qing et al., 2014; Peldszus and Stede, 2013; Plank et al., 2014; Sommerauer et al., 2020, i.a.). The applicability of these ideas to emotions should not come as a surprise — their assessment can derive from perceptive and metaperceptual phenomena (intensity and confidence, for instance). Therefore, if emotion judgments alone might not be sufficient to measure the quality of annotations, they can be enriched and, eventually, explained by the knowledge of such phenomena.

## Acknowledgements

This work was supported by Deutsche Forschungsgemeinschaft (project CEAT, KL 2869/1-2) and the Leibniz WissenschaftsCampus Tübingen "Cognitive Interfaces". We thank Laura Oberländer, Agnieszka Faleńska and the anonymous reviewers for their constructive feedback.

## References


Cecilia Ovesdotter Alm, Dan Roth, and Richard Sproat. 2005. Emotions from text: Machine learning for text-based emotion prediction. In *Proceedings of Human Language Technology Conference and Conference on Empirical Methods in Natural Language Processing*, pages 579–586, Vancouver, British Columbia, Canada. Association for Computational Linguistics.

Petra Saskia Bayerl and Karsten Ingmar Paul. 2011. What determines inter-coder agreement in manual annotations? a meta-analytic investigation. *Computational Linguistics*, 37(4):699–725.

Indrit Bègue, Maarten Vaessen, Jeremy Hofmeister, Marice Pereira, Sophie Schwartz, and Patrik Vuilleumier. 2018. Confidence of emotion expression recognition recruits brain regions outside the face perception network. *Social Cognitive and Affective Neuroscience*, 14(1):81–95.

Vikas Bhardwaj, Rebecca Passonneau, Ansaf Salleb-Aouissi, and Nancy Ide. 2010. Anveshan: A framework for analysis of multiple annotators' labeling behavior. In *Proceedings of the Fourth Linguistic Annotation Workshop*, pages 47–55, Uppsala, Sweden. Association for Computational Linguistics.

Victoria Bobicev and Marina Sokolova. 2017. Inter-annotator agreement in sentiment analysis: Machine learning perspective. In *Proceedings of the International Conference Recent Advances in Natural Language Processing, RANLP 2017*, pages 97–102, Varna, Bulgaria. INCOMA Ltd.

Laura-Ana-Maria Bostan and Roman Klinger. 2018. An analysis of annotated corpora for emotion classification in text. In *Proceedings of the 27th International Conference on Computational Linguistics*, pages 2104–2119, Santa Fe, New Mexico, USA. Association for Computational Linguistics.

Domenic V Cicchetti and Alvan R Feinstein. 1990. High agreement but low kappa: Ii. resolving the paradoxes. *Journal of clinical epidemiology*, 43(6):551–558.

Jacob Cohen. 1960. A coefficient of agreement for nominal scales. *Educational and Psychological Measurement*, 20(1):37–46.

Mark Davies. 2015. Corpus of Contemporary American English (COCA).

Jacob Devlin, Ming-Wei Chang, Kenton Lee, and Kristina Toutanova. 2019. BERT: Pre-training of deep bidirectional transformers for language understanding. In *Proceedings of the 2019 Conference of the North American Chapter of the Association for Computational Linguistics: Human Language Technologies, Volume 1 (Long and Short Papers)*, pages 4171–4186, Minneapolis, Minnesota. Association for Computational Linguistics.

Joseph L. Fleiss. 1971. Measuring nominal scale agreement among many raters. *Psychological bulletin*, 76(5):378–382.

Maria Gendron and Lisa Feldman Barrett. 2009. Reconstructing the past: A century of ideas about emotion in psychology. *Emotion Review*, 1(4):316–339.

Diman Ghazi, Diana Inkpen, and Stan Szpakowicz. 2015. Detecting emotion stimuli in emotion-bearing sentences. In *Computational Linguistics and Intelligent Text Processing*, pages 152–165. Springer International Publishing.

Jan Hofmann, Enrica Troiano, Kai Sassenberg, and Roman Klinger. 2020. Appraisal theories for emotion classification in text. In *Proceedings of the 28th International Conference on Computational Linguistics*, pages 125–138, Barcelona, Spain (Online). International Committee on Computational Linguistics.

Adi Lausen and Kurt Hammerschmidt. 2020. Emotion recognition and confidence ratings predicted by vocal stimulus type and prosodic parameters. *Humanities and Social Sciences Communications*, 7(1):1–17.

Yanran Li, Hui Su, Xiaoyu Shen, Wenjie Li, Ziqiang Cao, and Shuzi Niu. 2017. DailyDialog: A manually labelled multi-turn dialogue dataset. In *Proceedings of the Eighth International Joint Conference on Natural Language Processing (Volume 1: Long Papers)*, pages 986–995, Taipei, Taiwan. Asian Federation of Natural Language Processing.

Vicki Liu, Carmen Banea, and Rada Mihalcea. 2007. Grounded emotions. In *Seventh International Conference on Affective Computing and Intelligent Interaction (ACII 2017)*, pages 477–483. IEEE Computer Society.

Saif Mohammad. 2012. #emotional tweets. In **SEM 2012: The First Joint Conference on Lexical and Computational Semantics – Volume 1: Proceedings of the main conference and the shared task, and Volume 2: Proceedings of the Sixth International Workshop on Semantic Evaluation (SemEval 2012)*, pages 246–255, Montréal, Canada. Association for Computational Linguistics.

Saif Mohammad. 2018. Word affect intensities. In *Proceedings of the Eleventh International Conference on Language Resources and Evaluation (LREC 2018)*, Miyazaki, Japan. European Language Resources Association (ELRA).

Saif Mohammad and Felipe Bravo-Marquez. 2017. WASSA-2017 shared task on emotion intensity. In *Proceedings of the 8th Workshop on Computational Approaches to Subjectivity, Sentiment and Social Media Analysis*, pages 34–49, Copenhagen, Denmark. Association for Computational Linguistics.

Andreas Peldszus and Manfred Stede. 2013. Ranking the annotators: An agreement study on argumentation structure. In *Proceedings of the 7th Linguistic Annotation Workshop and Interoperability with Discourse*, pages 196–204, Sofia, Bulgaria. Association for Computational Linguistics.

Barbara Plank, Dirk Hovy, and Anders Søgaard. 2014. Linguistically debatable or just plain wrong? In *Proceedings of the 52nd Annual Meeting of the Association for Computational Linguistics (Volume 2: Short Papers)*, pages 507–511, Baltimore, Maryland. Association for Computational Linguistics.

Ciyang Qing, Ulle Endriss, Raquel Fernández, and Justin Kruger. 2014. Empirical analysis of aggregation methods for collective annotation. In *Proceedings of COLING 2014, the 25th International Conference on Computational Linguistics: Technical Papers*, pages 1533–1542, Dublin, Ireland. Dublin City University and Association for Computational Linguistics.

Anu Realo, Jüri Allik, Aire Nõlvak, Raivo Valk, Tuuli Ruus, Monika Schmidt, and Tiina Eilola. 2003. Mind-reading ability: Beliefs and performance. *Journal of Research in Personality*, 37(5):420–445.

Klaus R. Scherer and Harald G. Wallbott. 1997. The ISEAR questionnaire and codebook. Geneva Emotion Research Group. https://www.unige.ch/cisa/research/materials-and-online-research/research-material/.

Hendrik Schuff, Jeremy Barnes, Julian Mohme, Sebastian Padó, and Roman Klinger. 2017. Annotation, modelling and analysis of fine-grained emotions on a stance and sentiment detection corpus. In *Proceedings of the 8th Workshop on Computational Approaches to Subjectivity, Sentiment and Social Media Analysis*, pages 13–23, Copenhagen, Denmark. Association for Computational Linguistics.

Pia Sommerauer, Antske Fokkens, and Piek Vossen. 2020. Would you describe a leopard as yellow? evaluating crowd-annotations with justified and informative disagreement. In *Proceedings of the 28th International Conference on Computational Linguistics*, pages 4798–4809, Barcelona, Spain (Online). International Committee on Computational Linguistics.

Charles Spearman. 1904. The proof and measurement of association between two things. *The American Journal of Psychology*, 15(1):71–101.

Carlo Strapparava and Rada Mihalcea. 2007. SemEval-2007 task 14: Affective text. In *Proceedings of the Fourth International Workshop on Semantic Evaluations (SemEval-2007)*, pages 70–74, Prague, Czech Republic. Association for Computational Linguistics.

Carlo Strapparava and Rada Mihalcea. 2008. Learning to identify emotions in text. In *Proceedings of the 2008 ACM symposium on Applied computing*, pages 1556–1560.

Enrica Troiano, Sebastian Padó, and Roman Klinger. 2019. Crowdsourcing and validating event-focused emotion corpora for German and English. In *Proceedings of the 57th Annual Meeting of the Association for Computational Linguistics*, pages 4005–4011, Florence, Italy. Association for Computational Linguistics.

Yuxiang Zhang, Jiamei Fu, Dongyu She, Ying Zhang, Senzhang Wang, and Jufeng Yang. 2018. Text emotion distribution learning via multi-task convolutional neural network. In *Proceedings of the Twenty-Seventh International Joint Conference on Artificial Intelligence, IJCAI-18*, pages 4595–4601. International Joint Conferences on Artificial Intelligence Organization.

Peixiang Zhong, Di Wang, and Chunyan Miao. 2019. Knowledge-enriched transformer for emotion detection in textual conversations. In *Proceedings of the 2019 Conference on Empirical Methods in Natural Language Processing and the 9th International Joint Conference on Natural Language Processing (EMNLP-IJCNLP)*, pages 165–176, Hong Kong, China. Association for Computational Linguistics.

## A Annotation Guidelines

In what follows are the detailed guidelines of the annotation. Q1 corresponds to EMO in the paper, Q2 corresponds to CONF, and Q3 to INT.

In Q1, annotators were required to disregard the emotion that the author of the utterances intended to express or to elicit in others. Their task was to give their immediate, personal impression with respect to the presence of an emotion.

Before annotating the 700 sentences selected from COCA, we observe inter-annotator agreement on a pre-annotation trial. With 70 sentences, Cohen's $\kappa$ for pairs of annotators was found to be satisfactory (.52, .6 and .43) and motivated us to complete the job on the rest of the sentences. The job was completed upon a compensation of 60€.

### A.1 Task Description
### Approx Duration: 3 hours

In this annotation trial, you will assess if texts are emotional or neutral.

**Neutral** sentences are those which

1. bear no affective connotation.

**Emotional** sentences are those which either

2. describe an event, a concept or state of affairs to which you would associate an emotion;

3. have an emotion as a central component of their meaning.

Examples of 1. are:

*I am wearing my mask.*
*She answered her phone.*
*A new deal was established between the parties.*
*The elections are over.*

Examples of 2. are:

*I saw my bestfriend.*
*She was being pretty arrogant to me.*
*A war started in Westeros.*
*The king found an old sausage under his bed.*

Examples of 3. are:

*I am so happy to see you.*
*She was bursting with arrogance.*
*And there she was, desperate for her family.*
*I couldn't stand the catering food, bleark!*

### A.2 Guidelines

You will be shown individual sentences and, for each of them, you will answer 3 questions (**Q1, Q2, Q3**). Go for your immediate reaction to the text – avoid over-assessments.

**Q1** Given a sentence, please ask yourself: **is it emotional (E) or neutral (N)?** Type:

- **N**, if the text does not convey any emotion, like in Examples of 1.;
- **E**, if an emotion could be inferred from the text, like in Examples of 2., or an emotion is a central part of the text, like in Examples of 3.

**Q2** Ask yourself: **how confident am I about my answer to Q1?** Give yourself a rating on a scale from 1 to 3. Indicate if you are

- **1**, not confident at all;
- **2**, confident;
- **3**, sure.

**Q3** This question only applies if you answered 2 or 3 in **Q1**: in case the sentence expresses an emotion, **how strong is such emotion?** Assess the degree of its intensity on a scale from 1 to 3, where

- **1** is mild;
- **2** is intense;
- **3** is very intense.

## B Binary Classification

After data pre-processing step (i.e. exclusion of academic texts and sentences containing words that are masked for copyright reasons), we use a binary classifier as a guide for the selection of sentences from COCA. Using HugginFace[7], we fine-tune the pre-trained BERT base-case model on data for emotion recognition, adding a classification layer that

[7]https://huggingface.co/transformers/

| | P | R | F1 |
|---|---|---|---|
| Emotion | .88 | .84 | .86 |
| Neutral | .89 | .92 | .90 |

Table 3: Binary classification on UED test set.

outputs the labels *emotion* or *neutral*. Data are the resources by Liu et al. (2007), Troiano et al. (2019), Scherer and Wallbott (1997), Alm et al. (2005), Li et al. (2017), Ghazi et al. (2015), Mohammad and Bravo-Marquez (2017), (Mohammad, 2012) and Schuff et al. (2017). We make their format homogeneous with the tool made available by Bostan and Klinger (2018); next, as the labels in the resulting unified emotion data (UED) are not binary, we map *neutral* and *no emotion* instances into *neutral*, and the rest into *emotion*. The total 136891 sentences are then split into train (70%), validation (10%) and test (20%) sets. Classifier's performance is in Table 3.

## C Further Analysis

### C.1 Disagreements

Table 4 reports the distribution of the scores of confidence and intensity for the items where the annotators disagree. This is observed on annotator pairs. A row considers all those items on which either annotators (on the columns) chooses the *emotion* label and the other selects the *neutral* one.

For instance, A1–A2 disagree in total 201 times: on 24 sentences, A1 makes the *emotion* choice, and on 177 sentences it is A2 who picks the class *emotion*. Out of the 24 items, A1 rated 23 as having low intensity and 1 as medium intensity; out of the 177 sentences, 149 are considered of low intensity by A2, 27 as mild, and only 1 as highly intense.

What emerges overall is that people rarely disagree when the *emotion*-leaning annotator has extreme confidence, or perceives very high intensity.

### C.2 Agreements

A manual analysis of the annotations reveals that perfect agreement occurs in the presence of certain patterns. Items unanimously considered emotional often report personal impressions about state of affairs or the speakers' interlocutors (e.g., "*Paris is so sexy*", "*Your expression changed from excited puppy to crestfallen*"), and mostly involve first-hand experiences of the speakers themselves (e.g., "*We'll miss you, but we'll be watching*", "*I'm afraid I don't see anything very beautiful right now*", "*Others helped me and it made a huge difference*"). Instead, sentences that received 3 *neutral* labels seem to be centered on factual statements, like "*Furthermore, the types of materials of manufacture are different*", "*They continue walking*".

One difference between the *emotion* and *neutral* labels is the frequency of agreement, as we found that people concur more on the former – and this invalidates our expectation that, not being given a varied set of affective categories, and not identifying *what* emotion they are judging, people would tend to resort to the neutral choice. Moreover, annotators converge more on one or more on the other label depending on the genre of a text: looking at the distribution of the 304 unanimous *emotions* (magazine: 28 sentences, blogs: 44, news: 27, tv: 67, fiction: 54, spoken: 39, web: 45) and the 88 *neutrals* (magazine: 18 sentences, blogs: 12, news: 22, tv: 4, fiction: 5, spoken: 12, web: 15), we see that people recognize that affect often manifests itself in fictions, for instance, but is rarer in news – the opposite holds for the neutral expressions.

An obvious strategy to recognize emotions would be to find an emotion name in text. But this is not the case. Sentences that contain emotion words considered less emotionally intense than others: the majority of sentences with CONF3-INT2 contain emotion words (e.g.,"*I was sad to leave.*", while those with CONF3-INT3 are related to extremely negative states of mind (e.g.,"*[...] if I could die and bring her back , I would , but I can't , and I have to deal with that now*").

In Table 5, we report some example sentences on which annotators reached perfect agreement across all confidence-intensity combinations, having choosen the label *emotion*. The sentences are extracted from a number of genres in COCA, and are associated to different scores of intensity (INT) and confidence (CONF). Note that there is no instance that elicited a high intensity evaluation (3) and a low confidence (either 2 or 3) in the annotators. Instances of CONF3 and INT1 show that the correlation between confidence and intensity, though intuitive, has counterexamples.

| | A1 | | | | | | A2 | | | | | | A3 | | | | | |
|---|---|---|---|---|---|---|---|---|---|---|---|---|---|---|---|---|---|---|
| | CONF | | | INT | | | CONF | | | INT | | | CONF | | | INT | | |
| | 1 | 2 | 3 | 1 | 2 | 3 | 1 | 2 | 3 | 1 | 2 | 3 | 1 | 2 | 3 | 1 | 2 | 3 |
| A1-A2 | 15 | 8 | 1 | 23 | 1 | 0 | 54 | 95 | 28 | 149 | 27 | 1 | – | – | – | – | – | – |
| A2-A3 | – | – | – | – | – | – | 13 | 25 | 6 | 37 | 7 | 0 | 56 | 61 | 3 | 94 | 26 | 0 |
| A3-A1 | 5 | 6 | 0 | 10 | 1 | 0 | – | – | – | – | – | – | 95 | 128 | 17 | 169 | 70 | 1 |

Table 4: Distribution of INT and CONF for disagreements in the EMO task. For a pair of annotators (rows), disagreements are counted when either annotators (i.e., on the columns) chooses the *emotion* class.

| Text Genre | CONF | INT | Text |
|---|---|---|---|
| Magazine | 1 | 1 | I was always a little wary of Arya and Sansa (who also did a little Stoneheart-style vengeance last year) taking on their mother s role . |
| News | 1 | 1 | You can't stress because you just have no idea what 's going to happen. |
| TV | 1 | 1 | So maybe Willy's hanging around the wawa one night , looking for a party...Yeah . |
| TV | 1 | 2 | Mmm , Lordy , Lordy , Lord have mercy . |
| Web | 1 | 2 | Frost is trying to reconcile impulse with a conscience that needs goals and harbors deep regrets. |
| Magazine | 1 | 2 | Nature always solves her own problems ; and we can go far toward solving our own if we will listen to her teachings and consort with those who love her. |
| Fiction | 2 | 1 | "I'm fine ," he replies absently , eyeing the open book . |
| Web | 2 | 1 | My sister likes her map : ) HI Chery : ) lol I'll take'em where I can get'em ... |
| Magazine | 2 | 1 | Whereas coping well means dealing successfully with problems and setbacks, savoring-glorying in what goes right-is an equally crucial emotional competence. |
| Blogs | 2 | 2 | The soldier talks about child detainees . |
| TV | 2 | 2 | We did n't get to bury the others . |
| TV | 3 | 1 | I bruised my lip . |
| Fiction | 3 | 1 | "You have such an interesting life," she said, after a little small talk |
| Magazine | 3 | 1 | "Chalk is unforgiving, " says Oates . |
| News | 3 | 2 | They looked happy, confident . |
| Blogs | 3 | 2 | I am constantly traveling for my job with DISH , and I hate missing all my shows . |
| Blogs | 3 | 2 | I hope I can work through my feelings and keep his friendship in my life. |
| Web | 3 | 3 | I will completely destroy them and make them an object of horror and scorn , and an everlasting ruin. |
| Spoken | 3 | 3 | "We 're very worried ." |
| Spoken | 3 | 3 | If – if I could die and bring her back , I would , but I can't , and I have to deal with that now. |

Table 5: Sentences on which the annotators reached perfect agreement on EMO, CONF, and INT.

# Disentangling Document Topic and Author Gender in Multiple Languages: Lessons for Adversarial Debiasing

**Erenay Dayanik** and **Sebastian Padó**
IMS, University of Stuttgart
Stuttgart, Germany
{erenay.dayanik, sebastian.pado}@ims.uni-stuttgart.de

## Abstract

Text classification is a central tool in NLP, including social media analysis. However, when the target classes are strongly correlated with other textual attributes, text classification models can pick up "wrong" features, leading to bad generalization and biases. In social media analysis, this problem surfaces for demographic user classes such as language, topic, or gender, which influence how an author writes a text to a substantial extent. Adversarial training has been claimed to mitigate this problem, but a thorough evaluation is missing.

In this paper, we experiment with text classification of the correlated attributes of *document topic* and *author gender*, using a novel multilingual parallel corpus of TED talk transcripts. Our findings are: (a) individual classifiers for topic and author gender are indeed biased; (b) debiasing with adversarial training works for topic, but breaks down for author gender; (c) gender debiasing results differ across languages. We interpret the result in terms of *feature space overlap*, highlighting the role of *linguistic surface realization* of the target classes.

## 1 Introduction

Natural language processing, and machine learning more generally, has recently received a significant deal of criticism because of the frequent presence of *bias* in the predictions, where we define bias as a systematic difference in system performance on one set of instances compared to another. Such biases have been identified in NLP tasks such as word representation (Bolukbasi et al., 2016), textual inference (Rudinger et al., 2017), coreference resolution (Zhao et al., 2018), text classification (Dixon et al., 2018) and emotion intensity prediction (Kiritchenko and Mohammad, 2018).

In text classification tasks, a principal source of such biases are demographic attributes of authors, such as gender, age, or race[1]. The reason is that these attributes shape speakers' language use substantially (Hovy, 2015). NLP models are not only able in principle to pick up such cues, as studies on modeling demographic attributes show (Koppel et al., 2004), but they actually have a motivation to do so whenever some demographic attribute is strongly *correlated* with the model's classification target and therefore supports its recognition. As an example, in social psychology, Gross et al. (1997) report that elderly people experience and express their emotions less intensely than younger people. Therefore, in a corpus of emotional expressions across age groups, it is reasonable for a model that predicts emotion intensity to look out for linguistic cues regarding author age, *even if these cues are not really related to emotion intensity per se*, such as typical markers of youth language ("rad", "fam", "FTW", etc.).

This focus is arguably problematic, though, since it can give rise to a form of *age bias* – namely, overestimating emotion intensity for documents exhibiting youth language. More generally, the bias-inducing role of demographic attributes is dangerous for studies that use texts from a multitude of authors – often gathered from social media – to draw inferences about the authors (Sobkowicz et al., 2012; Cheng et al., 2015). In such studies, demographic biases can lead to erroneous causal attributions (as our case will illustrate).

To counteract the presence of biases in NLP, researchers have devised *debiasing* methods. Due to its general applicability and high effectiveness, adversarial debiasing has become one of the most widely used methods for bias mitigation (Elazar and Goldberg, 2018; Zhang et al., 2018; Arduini et al., 2020). Unfortunately, these advances are not accompanied by an analysis of the prerequisites

[1] A subset of these has specific legal protection in many jurisdictions under the name of *sensitive* or *protected* attributes.



*Proceedings of the 11th Workshop on Computational Approaches to Subjectivity, Sentiment and Social Media Analysis*, pages 50–61
April 19, 2021. ©2021 Association for Computational Linguistics

that need to be satisfied for adversarial training to perform successfully. It has been established empirically is that adversarial training works well for many cases in NLP; nevertheless, we demonstrate that there are relatively simple setups where it can fail. We analyze what factors contribute to the failure.

Concretely, we consider the correlated attributes of document topic (scientific / non-scientific) and author gender on a self-collected multilingual corpus of TED talk transcripts in French, German, Spanish, and Turkish. This setup enables us to observe the interplay between linguistic properties and adversarial debiasing.

Our investigation proceeds in three steps. First, we train independent classifiers for each attribute and evaluate them with regard to overall performance and with regard to the bias they exhibit. In the second step, we apply adversarial debiasing to the predicting of each attribute with respect to the other, and re-evaluate the debiased models. Finally, in the third step we discuss the differences observed in the previous step: (a), both document topic and author gender can be classified reasonably well by independent classifiers, but exhibit considerable bias; (b), author gender bias in topic classifiers can be reduced by adversarial training; however, adversarial debiasing in the opposite direction fails completely; (c) this effect is true for all languages except French. Our interpretation is that the failure of adversarial debiasing is due to the fact that feature space for author gender is *subsumed* the topic feature space for all languages except French, where gender is expressed overtly by morphological cues that can be picked up by the model.

## 2 Related Work

Regarding bias analysis at the representation level, the most important source of bias is arguably formed by corpus-derived embeddings which are used by virtually all current NLP systems. There have been several efforts to investigate the amount of bias within monolingual (Bolukbasi et al., 2016; Caliskan et al., 2017; Garg et al., 2018; Swinger et al., 2019) and multilingual embeddings. (Lauscher and Glavaš, 2019; Zhao et al., 2020). Bias analysis at the system level has investigated a range of applications such as NER (Mehrabi et al., 2020), Machine Translation (Stanovsky et al., 2019), Natural Language Inference (Rudinger et al., 2017), Emotion Intensity Prediction (Kiritchenko and Mohammad, 2018), Coreference Resolution (Rudinger et al., 2018; Zhao et al., 2018) and Text Classification (De-Arteaga et al., 2019).

A number of strategies have been explored for bias mitigation. One common strategy for reducing the bias is to target the representational level again, that is, corpora (Hall Maudslay et al., 2019; Zhao et al., 2018) and word embeddings (Kaneko and Bollegala, 2019; Bolukbasi et al., 2016). Other methods target the model architecture in various ways. For example, Qian et al. (2019) introduce an additional term to be used in loss function of language generation model, seeking to reduce the gender bias exhibited by the model.

A more fundamental idea is to adopt adversarial training (Goodfellow et al., 2014) to other tasks. For instance, Ganin and Lempitsky (2015) adapted adversarial training to the task of domain adaptation by introducing Gradient Reversal Layer (GRL) which acts as an identity function during forward pass and reverses the gradient by multiplying it by a negative scalar during the backward pass. Elazar and Goldberg (2018) apply the idea to the removal of demographic bias; McHardy et al. (2019) remove publication source as a bias variable from a satire detection model. Li et al. (2018) reported that adversarial training with GRL layer can remove unintended bias from the representations of POS tagging and Sentiment analysis models while maintaining task performance. Zhang et al. (2018) show that adversarial training mitigates the bias in word embeddings while maintaining its performance on word analogies task. Finally, Arduini et al. (2020) demonstrate how adversarial learning can be used for debiasing knowledge graph embeddings.

## 3 Dataset

In order to conduct a study on the relationship between topic and author gender in multiple languages, we require a multilingual comparable corpus for which topic and gender information are available. The corpus should be as parallel as possible so that any differences in outcome across languages are not simply due to differences in the evaluation data. Among the available multilingual parallel data sets, arguably the two most prominent ones are WIT$^3$ and OPUS. WIT$^3$ (Cettolo et al., 2012) consists of lecture translations automatically crawled from the TED talks in a variety of languages and was used in the evaluation campaigns

IWSLT 2013 and 2014. OPUS (Tiedemann, 2012) is a collection of data from several sources which provides sentence alignments as well as linguistic markup (for some languages). Unfortunately, neither corpus provides topic or gender labels.

For this reason, we create a new multilingual parallel dataset with these annotations, based on TED talks (`http://ted.com/talks`). A TED talk is a presentation at the TED conference or one of its international partner events. TED talks are limited to a maximum length of 18 minutes and may be on any topic. TED talks are rehearsed talks and at least semi-formal, while still definitely belonging to the category of spoken language. In this regard, they are comparable to the widely used Europarl corpus (Koehn, 2005). The talks are divided according to the languages, topics and posted dates. All original talks are presented in English, but volunteers provide (and double check) translations into other languages. Authors are identified by name.

Checking for which languages the TED webpage provided substantial numbers of transcripts (as of February 2020) led us to select German (DE), Spanish (ES), French (FR) and Turkish (TR) as target languages. We crawled all 1518 TED talks for which transcripts in all four target languages were available. We conducted some preprocessing: we cleaned transcripts by removing extra line breaks, extra spaces, and punctuation marks. Inspired by the work in open-domain Question Answering (Yang et al., 2019), we then segmented the transcripts into a sequence of segments. Rather than using paragraphs or sentences as segments directly, we split articles into segments with the length of 60 words by sliding window as Wang et al. (2019) demonstrated that splitting articles into non-overlapping fixed-length segments leads to better results in Question Answering.

Finally, we annotated the transcripts with topic and author gender information. For topic, we grouped transcripts into two classes according to the community-provided tags. The instances that have either Technology or Science tag were labeled as *SciTech* while the rest was labeled as *Other*. This grouping strategy led to a balanced dataset (53% Science, 47% Other). For author gender, we assume a binary gender classification (male/female) to be compatible with existing datasets (Verhoeven et al., 2016; Pardo et al., 2016). This should not be understood as a rejection of non-binary gender. We manually determine the author's gender information on the basis of gender indicating pronouns such as *he, she, his, her* that are used to refer to the authors in their biographies published in the authors' TED Talks profile or on other websites, keeping only clear cases. The majority gender is male (69%). Table 1 describes the final dataset.[2] The corpus has very similar properties across languages. The main exception is the lower number of words in Turkish which is due to the agglutinative nature of Turkish morphology. For instance, the English sentence with four words "I am at your house." is translated into a single word Turkish sentence "Evinizdeyim."

| # TED Talks | 1518 | | | |
|---|---|---|---|---|
| Author Gender | 1042 (Male) / 476 (Female) | | | |
| Talk Topic | 704 (SciTech) / 814 (Other) | | | |
| | DE | ES | FR | TR |
| # Tokens/doc | 2093 | 2110 | 2280 | 1632 |
| # Sentences/doc | 115 | 110 | 111 | 114 |

Table 1: Statistics of TED multilingual corpora.

| Document Topic | | SciTech | Other |
|---|---|---|---|
| Author Gender | Male | 524 | 518 |
| | Female | 180 | 296 |

Table 2: Topic–gender correlation: Number of documents in TED corpus for each combination

## 4 Experimental Design

Table 2 shows a correlation matrix for the two attributes of topic and author gender in our TED corpus. Indeed, the corpus shows a clear correlation between the two: while male authors are represented about equally in TED for scientific-technological topics and other topics, female authors are underrepresented for scientific-technological topics. As motivated in the Introduction, this situation can lead to the model mistakenly picking up linguistic cues from one attribute to predict the other, leading to systematic biases.

We therefore believe that this corpus can serve as a reasonable case study for correlated document attributes. We proceed as follows:

**Experiment 1:** We learn individual neural models

[2] Code and data are available at `http://www.ims.uni-stuttgart.de/data/ted_wassa21`. This includes the documents we based our gender determination on, along with the list of gendered pronouns we used.

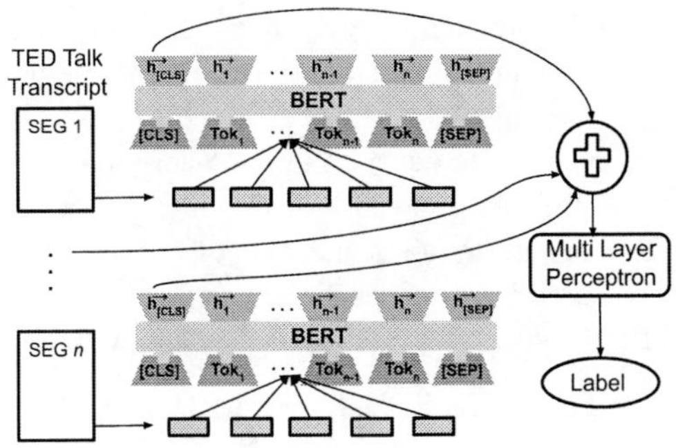


Figure 1: Visualization of classification architecture for topic and author gender

for topic and gender classification. We expect, for each attribute, that predictions are biased regarding the other attribute.

**Experiment 2:** We debias these models by adversarial training. We expect the models to focus better on features that are predictive of the individual attributes, and to show less bias.

We follow Li et al. (2018) and Zhao et al. (2020) by measuring the *amount of bias* in the models as the average difference in classification performance between documents aggregated by author gender (Male vs Female) or aggregated by topic (SciTech vs Other).

## 5 Experiment 1: Simple Classification and Bias Analysis

In our first experiment, we set up neural classification models for the two tasks of topic and gender classification individually and evaluate them for the presence of bias in their predictions.

### 5.1 Method

Figure 1 depicts the model architecture we use for both classification tasks. We use a neural text classifier based on the BERT Transformer (Devlin et al., 2019) with some adjustments. While transformers have shown good performance on many language tasks, most of them can only encode and generate representations for a fixed length token sequence – e.g., BERT implementations are often limited to 512 tokens per sequence. As the average token number per TED talk (cf. Table 1) is much larger. To address this limitation, we encode the input at the paragraph level (cf. Section 3). Specifically, we use the final hidden state corresponding to a special classification token, [CLS], as the representation for the corresponding paragraph. We then obtain the global context vector for the input by summing paragraph representations element-wise. Finally, the global representation of the input is fed through a Multi-Layer Perceptron to a Softmax layer. Our model can be understood as an adaptation of standard transformer classifiers to longer texts.

| Language | Overall | By Gender | | |
|---|---|---|---|---|
| | | Male | Female | Bias |
| DE | 81.2 | 80.0 | 84.0 | 4.0 |
| ES | 80.0 | 79.0 | 82.7 | 3.7 |
| FR | 81.5 | 80.2 | 83.7 | 3.5 |
| TR | 80.2 | 78.7 | 83.0 | 4.3 |
| Majority BL | 37.6 | 33.6 | 47.6 | 14.0 |

Table 3: F1 scores for topic classification (bottom line: majority baseline, identical for all languages)

### 5.2 Topic Classification

We first set up the model for topic classification. We approach it as a document-level binary classification task. The input to the model is the full transcript, and the model labels each transcript either as "SciTech" or "Other".

The topic classification results are shown in Table 3, using weighted $F_1$ score for evaluation. First, we compare the overall performance across languages. A majority baseline performs at 37.6% for all languages, due to the parallel design of the dataset. The neural topic classifiers do substantially better, all showing very similar results around 81% F-Score. Their similar performance may be expected from the parallel nature of the corpus, but it also provides support to our assumption that the texts and transformer models perform comparably across languages. When we break down these results by the other attribute we are interested, namely author gender (Male vs Female), we find that the prediction quality of the topic classifier is an average of 3.6 points lower for male than for female authors. In other words, the topic classifiers show a consistent gender bias across languages, presumably due to the higher-entropy (more equal) topic distribution for male authors (cf. Table 2). While this bias is lower than the bias of a majority baseline (which directly reflects the correlation between the two attributes), it is still substantial and arguably worth mitigating.

| Language | Overall | By Topic | | |
|---|---|---|---|---|
| | | SciTech | Other | Bias |
| DE | 70.8 | 69.0 | 75.0 | 6.0 |
| ES | 72.4 | 69.2 | 75.8 | 6.6 |
| FR | 82.4 | 82.0 | 83.0 | 1.0 |
| TR | 70.4 | 66.0 | 74.8 | 8.8 |
| Majority BL | 57.0 | 64.4 | 50.8 | 13.6 |

Table 4: F1 scores for gender classification (bottom line: majority baseline, identical for all languages)

### 5.3 Author Gender Classification

We now address the opposite task, author gender classification, predicting the labels Male and Female, re-using the model architecture from before.

Table 4 summarizes the results. We see a pattern that differs substantially from topic classification, with much larger cross-lingual differences in performance. The results are again substantially above the 57% baseline. We obtain the best result for French (82%), and the worst for Turkish (70%), with a difference of 12% F-Score. This indicates that gender classification builds much more on language-specific information than topic classification. Arguably, for a word piece-based neural model like BERT, a primary source of evidence on author gender are linguistically marked expressions in the text where the author refers to themselves. Thus, prediction of the author gender should be easiest if a language has a frequent and unambiguous mechanism for *gender marking* (Corbett, 1991; Zmigrod et al., 2019). Table 5 shows a multilingual example where French marks gender inflectionally, while the other languages do not. This is indicative of the general case: The languages that we consider in our experiment provide gender marking to different degrees. At one extreme, French marks most adjectives and many nouns consistently for gender. In contrast, Spanish marks gender only for a subset of the lexicon, and morphologically inconsistently (Harris, 1991); German marks only (some) nouns, and marking is sometimes optional. At the other extreme, Turkish does not mark gender at all.

On this basis, we would expect French to perform best, and lower performance for the other three languages – exactly what we find. However, the performances for TR, DE, and ES are surprisingly close to one another, and substantially above the baseline: on the basis of what information in the texts do these classifiers base their predictions?

| | |
|---|---|
| DE | Genau hier wurde ich geboren und verbrachte die ersten sieben Jahre meines Lebens. |
| ES | Esta es la tierra en la que nací y pasé los primeros siete años de mi vida. |
| FR | Je suis **née** ici même, et j'y ai passé les sept premières années de ma vie. |
| TR | Doğduğum yer burası ve hayatımın ilk yedi yılını burada geçirdim. |

Table 5: Example of inflectional gender marking in different languages (marking only present in French)

| | DE | ES | FR | TR |
|---|---|---|---|---|
| SciTech/Female | 75.0 | 75.8 | 83.0 | 74.4 |

Table 6: F1 scores for gender classification on SciTech talks with a female author.

A look at the size of the biases suggests an explanation: The gender classifiers for DE, ES, and TR make substantial use of *topic* cues, which enables them to proceed to some extent due to the correlations between topic and gender, but also lead to biases of 6–9% (highest for Turkish, consistent with the analysis above). In contrast, the French classifier is least biased, indicating that its text contains enough cues for 'proper' gender classification. We illustrate this in Table 6, where we report results on SciTech documents with female authors, that is, the smallest subcategory in our corpus. We find that the gender classifier for FR significantly outperforms the others, which provides additional evidence that the model relies less on the topic cues for gender classification.

**Summary.** For both tasks, we find that the classification performance shows a bias with respect to the other attribute. The two tasks differ with respect to the cross-lingual component, though: Topic classification works about equally well in all languages. In contrast, author gender classification only works properly in the one language that has consistent linguistic marking of gender, while there is evidence that the other languages fall back on topic features also for this task, which directly leads to biased predictions. These observations motivate experiments into how well these models respond to debiasing.

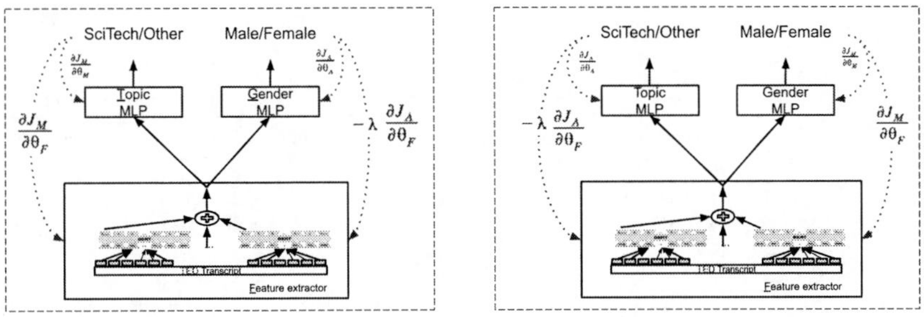


Figure 2: Visualization of debiasing by adversarial training. Left: Adversarial training of topic classifier on author gender, Right: Adversarial training of author gender classifier on topic.

## 6 Experiment 2: Adversarial Debiasing

Let $P$ be some bias attribute (e.g., gender, race, age etc.) that we want our classifier to ignore while learning to solve another task $T$. Adversarial debiasing seeks to achieve this by constraining representations in a way so that representations do not rely on $P$ in any substantial way. To this end, the model is trained to simultaneously predict the correct label for task $T$ ("main component") and to prevent a jointly trained adversary ("adversarial component") from predicting $P$ (McHardy et al., 2019). We define the loss functions of the main ($J_M$) and adversarial ($J_A$) components as follows:

$$J_A = -\mathbb{E}_{(x,y_A)\sim p_{\text{data}}} \log P_{\theta_A \cup \theta_F}(y_A, x) \quad (1)$$

$$J_M = -\mathbb{E}_{(x,y_M)\sim p_{\text{data}}} \log P_{\theta_M \cup \theta_F}(y_M, x) \quad (2)$$

where $\theta_A$, $\theta_M$ are the parameters of adversarial and main components; $y_A$ and $y_M$ are the gold labels for main and adversary tasks. Note that the adversarial and main components share the same feature extractor (i.e., BERT) whose parameters ($\theta_F$) are therefore updated by the gradients coming through the objective functions of both model parts. Let $\lambda$ be the meta-parameter controlling the intensity of the adversarial training and $\eta$ the learning rate. Then the following equations describe update rules for each component in the model:

$$\theta_M := \theta_M - \eta \frac{\partial J_M}{\partial \theta_M} \quad (3)$$

$$\theta_A := \theta_A - \eta \frac{\partial J_A}{\partial \theta_A} \quad (4)$$

$$\theta_F := \theta_F - \eta \left( \frac{\partial J_M}{\partial \theta_F} - \lambda \frac{\partial J_A}{\partial \theta_F} \right) \quad (5)$$

Our application of this training method is shown in Figure 2. We first debias the topic classifier by author gender (left-hand box); then we proceed to debias author gender classifier by topic (right-hand box). For example, to de-bias the topic classification, $J_M$ is the topic loss and $J_A$ the author gender loss; vice versa for author gender de-biasing.

### 6.1 Topic-Debiased Gender Classification

First, we debias topic classification to reduce the gender bias. The left-hand side of Figure 3 compares overall results across a range of values of $\lambda$ between 0 (no adversarial training) and 1 (equal weight of main and adversarial loss). We find that, similar to Experiment 1, the results are essentially identical across languages. Furthermore, the choice of $\lambda$ hardly matters in this interval: adversarial training does not have a major impact on topic classification. We report detailed results for $\lambda$=1 in the right-hand side of Figure 3. The small differences between the Overall results of the Original and Debiased models show that topic classification overall does not lose much by debiasing for gender.[3] The breakdown by gender shows that gender bias is substantially reduced overall. However, there are noticeable differences among languages.

For Spanish and German, we see no overall loss of performance in topic classification, and a substantial reduction in gender bias. For French and Turkish, in contrast, we see a decrease of about 1.5 points in topic classification. Gender bias is reduced for French but hardly for Turkish. This is a somewhat surprising result, given the typological differences between the two languages. Our explanation is that in French, as discussed above, many words are morphologically marked for gender. Due to the correlation between the two attributes, these can be re-used by the topic classifier, but when they are penalized through adversarial training, we see a mild decrease in topic classification accuracy.

[3]See Appendix for performance on the adversarial task.

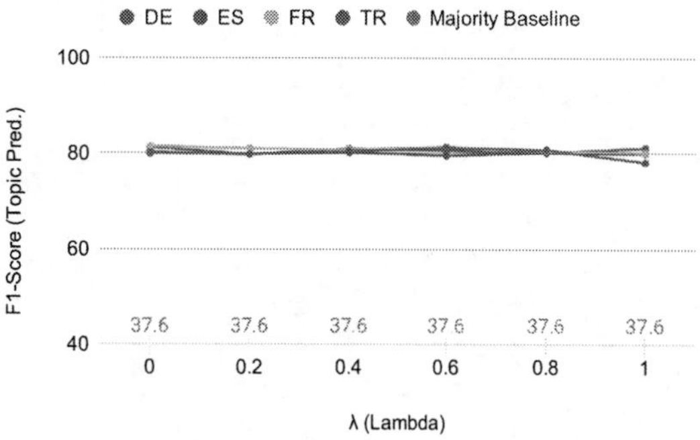


| | Topic classification ($\lambda$ = 1) | | | | | |
|---|---|---|---|---|---|---|
| | Original | | Debiased | | | |
| | Overall | Bias | Overall | Male | Female | Bias |
| DE | 81.2 | 4.0 | 81.2 | 80.8 | 81.2 | **0.4** |
| ES | 80.0 | 3.7 | 80.0 | 79.2 | 81.6 | **2.4** |
| FR | 81.5 | 3.5 | 80.2 | 79.4 | 81.4 | **2.0** |
| TR | 80.2 | 4.2 | 78.4 | 76.8 | 80.7 | **3.9** |

Figure 3: Results for topic classification with adversarial author gender training (F1 scores). Left: Overall results for different $\lambda$ values. Right: Detail results for $\lambda$=1. Original: results from Experiment 1 (cf. Table 3). Lower bias for each language bolded.

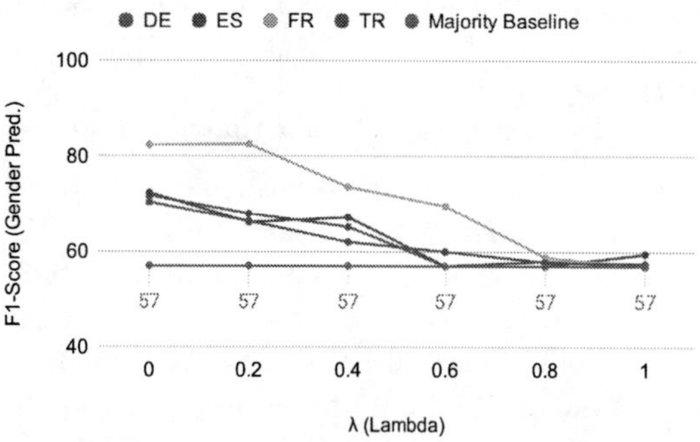


| | Author gender classification ($\lambda$ = 0.2) | | | | | |
|---|---|---|---|---|---|---|
| | Original | | Debiased | | | |
| | Overall | Bias | Overall | SciTech | Other | Bias |
| DE | 70.8 | **6.0** | 68.0 | 63.8 | 72.2 | 8.4 |
| ES | 72.4 | 6.6 | 66.2 | 62.8 | 69.2 | **6.4** |
| FR | 82.4 | 1.0 | 82.6 | 82.6 | 82.6 | **0.0** |
| TR | 70.4 | 8.8 | 66.4 | 64.0 | 68.8 | **4.4** |

Figure 4: Results for author gender classification with adversarial topic training (F1 scores). Left: Overall results for different $\lambda$ values. Right: Detail results for $\lambda$=0.2. Original: results from Experiment 1 (cf. Table 4). Lower bias for each language bolded.

In Turkish, as we have argued in Experiment 1, gender classification depends almost entirely on topic features since there is no linguistic marking of referent gender. Consequently, the adversarial training works against itself to an extent, resulting in a mildly worse topic classification but hardly any decrease in gender bias.

### 6.2 Gender-Debiased Topic Classification

Now we swap the main and adversarial tasks again, debiasing author gender classification with regard to topic. We use the same setup as in Experiment 1.

The results are shown in Figure 4. The left-hand side shows that varying $\lambda$ has a substantial effect this time. If we set $\lambda$ to a value close to 1 – a good choice for gender-debiased topic classification, as we have established in the previous subsection – this leads to a breakdown of the gender classification model. Performance for all languages drops to a F-Score of around 57, the level of the majority baseline (cf. Table 4). Apparently, debiasing author gender classification by adversarial training against topic breaks the author gender classifier for all but small values of $\lambda$.

As in the first experiment, we observe differences among languages: French stands out as the language for which the gender classification 'holds out' the longest for high values of $\lambda$. Its ultimate failure indicates that even for French, gender marking on its own is not strong enough to support the author gender identification task – or at least our models are not powerful enough to pick up on these cues. The other languages, which, as we have argued in Experiment 1, make substantial use of topic cues for gender classification, fail even earlier.

The right-hand side of Figure 4 reports detailed results for $\lambda$=0.2. In line with our analyses above, debiasing works for French but not for the other languages: We find clear decreases in performance (up to 6.2 points, for Spanish), and inconclusive

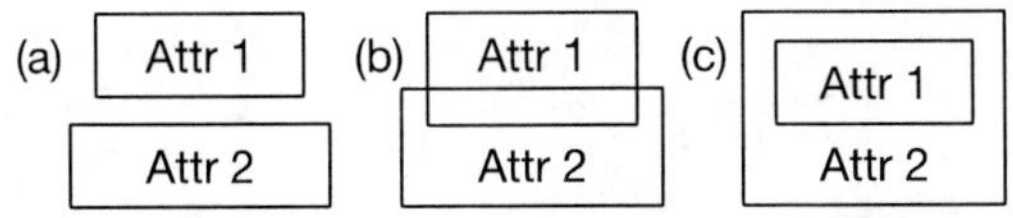


Figure 5: Three cases of latent feature space geometry for two attributes: (a) independent, (b) correlated, (c) subsumed

changes in bias (decrease for Turkish by 4.4 points, increase for German by 1.6 points). While the patterns for these languages are not straightforward to interpret, it seems safe to conclude that topic-debiasing author gender is a failure both with regard to model performance and reduction of bias.

## 7 Discussion

The results of our two experiments show an intriguing asymmetry between the two tasks of topic and author gender classification when debiased for the respective other attribute. Reducing author gender bias in topic classification with adversarial training proceeds as expected, is relatively robust to the choice of $\lambda$ in the interval between 0 and 1, and shows a consistent pattern across languages which can be explained by the properties of the languages involved. In contrast, reducing topic bias in author gender classification relies heavily on $\lambda$, quickly deteriorating to baseline level for large values of $\lambda$, and does not consistently manage to reduce bias in any case. This asymmetry cannot be an artifact of model architecture or data alone, since we use the same model architecture on the same data.

Instead, we believe that these patterns result from an interaction between the representation learning of the model and the information that the model can draw from the data. They can be understood through the *latent feature space* of the final shared layer in our architecture below the two heads (cf. Figure 2), where each class can be characterized by a region of informative features.

Figure 5 shows Venn diagram-style depictions of the three possible cases for a pair of attributes. In the left-hand case, (a), there is no overlap between the latent features of the two attributes. That is, the two attributes are independent of one another, and so is learning. However, this is by definition the case without correlations among attributes that we do not consider. In the center case, (b), there is an intersection between the latent features of the two attributes. The classifiers' use of this overlap potentially creates biases, but adversarial training exactly punishes the use of this region of latent feature space. Thus, debiased classifiers can learn either attribute to the extent that the part of the feature space outside the intersection is still sufficiently informative. The right-hand case, (c), is the limit case when one of the two attributes does not have an independent standing, that is, the informative latent features of attribute 1 are completely contained in the informative feature space of attribute 2. This leads to biases in either classifier just as case (b), but also creates an asymmetry in the effect of adversarial debiasing: Attribute 2 can be debiased by simply 'cutting out' the informative space of attribute 1, but debiasing attribute 1 in the opposite manner results in an empty feature space for attribute 1, and we would expect the classifier to revert to baseline performance.

This set theoretic visualization is a major simplification of the latent feature space in neural models, where the three cases cannot apply categorially — they rather represent different points on a continuum. Nevertheless, the predictions of the subsumption case, (c), match our experimental results well: Assuming that author gender features are included in topic features, we would expect to find successful debiasing of the topic classifier, but breakdown of the debiased author gender classifier. This is exactly the pattern of results that we have observed.

Note that this analysis builds on the behavior of the features of the attributes in the training data, in particular in a representation learning approach like the one we have pursued. In other words, changes of the data – or differences within the data, such as between languages – are expected to influence the outcome. Again, this is what we see: French, due to its consistent morphological marking of gender, is closer to case (b), while the other languages are closer to case (c).

## 8 Conclusion

This paper was concerned with text classification for correlated attributes, which pose an important but often overlooked challenge to model fairness – in particular, as we have argued, in the case of demographic attributes.

We specifically analyzed the relationship between document topic and author gender. We established that topic classifiers exhibit gender bias and author gender classifiers show topic bias; that adversarial debiasing corrects gender bias in topic classification but breaks down in the opposite direction; and that this effect varies by language.

Beyond the concrete study, our contribution is to draw attention to the general question of prerequisites for successful adversarial debiasing, which, to our knowledge, has not received much attention. Our results indicate that when the target attribute and the bias attribute are too strongly correlated – or, indeed, when the target attribute is subsumed by the bias attribute – adversarial debiasing fails: with a small weight on the bias component, no debiasing takes place; with a large weight, target attribute classification deteriorates to baseline level.

Furthermore, we find that the linguistic expression of the attributes matters greatly: the only language for which we achieved satisfactory results was French, due to the consistent morphological marking of gender which can be captured independently of topic (Zmigrod et al., 2019). This highlights the importance of understanding the differences between languages regarding how they encode content (Dubossarsky et al., 2019), and underscores the importance of cross-lingual methods.

In future work, we plan to develop a diagnostic to recognize potentially problematic constellations of correlated attributes and improve debiasing.

## Acknowledgments

Partial funding was provided by Deutsche Forschungsgemeinschaft (DFG) through project MARDY within SPP RATIO. We would like to thank Roman Klinger, Gabriella Lapesa, Vivi Nastase and Michael Roth for valuable comments.

## References

Mario Arduini, Lorenzo Noci, Federico Pirovano, Ce Zhang, Yash Raj Shrestha, and Bibek Paudel. 2020. Adversarial learning for debiasing knowledge graph embeddings. In *Proceedings of the 16th International Workshop on Mining and Learning with Graphs (MLG)*, San Diego, California.

Tolga Bolukbasi, Kai-Wei Chang, James Y Zou, Venkatesh Saligrama, and Adam T Kalai. 2016. Man is to computer programmer as woman is to homemaker? debiasing word embeddings. In *Advances in Neural Information Processing Systems*, volume 29, pages 4349–4357.

Aylin Caliskan, Joanna J Bryson, and Arvind Narayanan. 2017. Semantics derived automatically from language corpora contain human-like biases. *Science*, 356(6334):183–186.

Mauro Cettolo, Christian Girardi, and Marcello Federico. 2012. Wit3: Web inventory of transcribed and translated talks. In *Conference of European Association for Machine Translation*, pages 261–268, Trento, Italy.

Justin Cheng, Cristian Danescu-Niculescu-Mizil, and Jure Leskovec. 2015. Antisocial behavior in online discussion communities. In *Proceedings of the International AAAI Conference on Web and Social Media*, volume 9.

Greville G. Corbett. 1991. *Gender*. Cambridge Textbooks in Linguistics. Cambridge University Press.

Maria De-Arteaga, Alexey Romanov, Hanna Wallach, Jennifer Chayes, Christian Borgs, Alexandra Chouldechova, Sahin Geyik, Krishnaram Kenthapadi, and Adam Tauman Kalai. 2019. Bias in bios: A case study of semantic representation bias in a high-stakes setting. In *Proceedings of the Conference on Fairness, Accountability, and Transparency*, FAT* '19, page 120–128, New York, NY, USA. Association for Computing Machinery.

Jacob Devlin, Ming-Wei Chang, Kenton Lee, and Kristina Toutanova. 2019. BERT: Pre-training of deep bidirectional transformers for language understanding. In *Proceedings of the 2019 Conference of the North American Chapter of the Association for Computational Linguistics: Human Language Technologies, Volume 1 (Long and Short Papers)*, pages 4171–4186, Minneapolis, Minnesota. Association for Computational Linguistics.

Lucas Dixon, John Li, Jeffrey Sorensen, Nithum Thain, and Lucy Vasserman. 2018. Measuring and mitigating unintended bias in text classification. In *Proceedings of the 2018 AAAI/ACM Conference on AI, Ethics, and Society*, AIES '18, page 67–73, New York, NY, USA. Association for Computing Machinery.

Haim Dubossarsky, Arya D. McCarthy, Edoardo Maria Ponti, Ivan Vulić, Ekaterina Vylomova, Yevgeni Berzak, Ryan Cotterell, Manaal Faruqui, Anna Korhonen, and Roi Reichart, editors. 2019. *Proceedings of TyP-NLP: The First Workshop on Typology for Polyglot NLP*. Association for Computational Linguistics, Florence, Italy.

Yanai Elazar and Yoav Goldberg. 2018. Adversarial removal of demographic attributes from text data. In *Proceedings of the 2018 Conference on Empirical Methods in Natural Language Processing*, pages 11–21, Brussels, Belgium. Association for Computational Linguistics.

Yaroslav Ganin and Victor Lempitsky. 2015. Unsupervised domain adaptation by backpropagation. In *Proceedings of the 32nd International Conference on Machine Learning*, volume 37 of *Proceedings of Machine Learning Research*, pages 1180–1189, Lille, France. JMLR.org.

Nikhil Garg, Londa Schiebinger, Dan Jurafsky, and James Zou. 2018. Word embeddings quantify

100 years of gender and ethnic stereotypes. *Proceedings of the National Academy of Sciences*, 115(16):E3635–E3644.

Ian J. Goodfellow, Jean Pouget-Abadie, Mehdi Mirza, Bing Xu, David Warde-Farley, Sherjil Ozair, Aaron Courville, and Yoshua Bengio. 2014. Generative adversarial nets. In *Proceedings of the 27th International Conference on Neural Information Processing Systems - Volume 2*, page 2672–2680, Cambridge, MA, USA. MIT Press.

James J Gross, Laura L Carstensen, Monisha Pasupathi, Jeanne Tsai, Carina Götestam Skorpen, and Angie YC Hsu. 1997. Emotion and aging: Experience, expression, and control. *Psychology and aging*, 12(4):590.

Rowan Hall Maudslay, Hila Gonen, Ryan Cotterell, and Simone Teufel. 2019. It's all in the name: Mitigating gender bias with name-based counterfactual data substitution. In *Proceedings of the 2019 Conference on Empirical Methods in Natural Language Processing and the 9th International Joint Conference on Natural Language Processing (EMNLP-IJCNLP)*, pages 5267–5275, Hong Kong, China. Association for Computational Linguistics.

James W. Harris. 1991. The exponence of gender in spanish. *Linguistic Inquiry*, 22(1):27–62.

Dirk Hovy. 2015. Demographic factors improve classification performance. In *Proceedings of the 53rd Annual Meeting of the Association for Computational Linguistics and the 7th International Joint Conference on Natural Language Processing (Volume 1: Long Papers)*, pages 752–762, Beijing, China. Association for Computational Linguistics.

Masahiro Kaneko and Danushka Bollegala. 2019. Gender-preserving debiasing for pre-trained word embeddings. In *Proceedings of the 57th Annual Meeting of the Association for Computational Linguistics*, pages 1641–1650, Florence, Italy. Association for Computational Linguistics.

Svetlana Kiritchenko and Saif Mohammad. 2018. Examining gender and race bias in two hundred sentiment analysis systems. In *Proceedings of the Seventh Joint Conference on Lexical and Computational Semantics*, pages 43–53, New Orleans, Louisiana. Association for Computational Linguistics.

Philipp Koehn. 2005. Europarl: A Parallel Corpus for Statistical Machine Translation. In *Conference Proceedings: the tenth Machine Translation Summit*, pages 79–86, Phuket, Thailand. AAMT.

Moshe Koppel, Shlomo Argamon, and Anat Rachel Shimoni. 2004. Automatically categorizing written texts by author gender. *Computing Reviews*, 45(1):43.

Anne Lauscher and Goran Glavaš. 2019. Are we consistently biased? multidimensional analysis of biases in distributional word vectors. In *Proceedings of the Eighth Joint Conference on Lexical and Computational Semantics*, pages 85–91, Minneapolis, Minnesota. Association for Computational Linguistics.

Yitong Li, Timothy Baldwin, and Trevor Cohn. 2018. Towards robust and privacy-preserving text representations. In *Proceedings of the 56th Annual Meeting of the Association for Computational Linguistics (Volume 2: Short Papers)*, pages 25–30, Melbourne, Australia. Association for Computational Linguistics.

Robert McHardy, Heike Adel, and Roman Klinger. 2019. Adversarial training for satire detection: Controlling for confounding variables. In *Proceedings of the 2019 Conference of the North American Chapter of the Association for Computational Linguistics: Human Language Technologies, Volume 1 (Long and Short Papers)*, pages 660–665, Minneapolis, Minnesota. Association for Computational Linguistics.

Ninareh Mehrabi, Thamme Gowda, Fred Morstatter, Nanyun Peng, and Aram Galstyan. 2020. Man is to person as woman is to location: Measuring gender bias in named entity recognition. In *Proceedings of the 31st ACM Conference on Hypertext and Social Media*, page 231–232, New York, NY, USA. Association for Computing Machinery.

Francisco Manuel Rangel Pardo, Paolo Rosso, Ben Verhoeven, Walter Daelemans, Martin Potthast, and Benno Stein. 2016. Overview of the 4th author profiling task at PAN 2016: Cross-genre evaluations. In *Working Notes of CLEF 2016 - Conference and Labs of the Evaluation forum, Évora, Portugal, 5-8 September, 2016*, volume 1609 of *CEUR Workshop Proceedings*, pages 750–784. CEUR-WS.org.

Yusu Qian, Urwa Muaz, Ben Zhang, and Jae Won Hyun. 2019. Reducing gender bias in word-level language models with a gender-equalizing loss function. In *Proceedings of the 57th Annual Meeting of the Association for Computational Linguistics: Student Research Workshop*, pages 223–228, Florence, Italy. Association for Computational Linguistics.

Rachel Rudinger, Chandler May, and Benjamin Van Durme. 2017. Social bias in elicited natural language inferences. In *Proceedings of the First ACL Workshop on Ethics in Natural Language Processing*, pages 74–79, Valencia, Spain. Association for Computational Linguistics.

Rachel Rudinger, Jason Naradowsky, Brian Leonard, and Benjamin Van Durme. 2018. Gender bias in coreference resolution. In *Proceedings of the 2018 Conference of the North American Chapter of the Association for Computational Linguistics: Human Language Technologies*, pages 8–14, New Orleans, LA.

Pawel Sobkowicz, Michael Kaschesky, and Guillaume Bouchard. 2012. Opinion mining in social media: Modeling, simulating, and forecasting political opinions in the web. *Government Information Quarterly*, 29(4):470–479. Social Media in Government - Selections from the 12th Annual International Conference on Digital Government Research (dg.o2011).

Gabriel Stanovsky, Noah A. Smith, and Luke Zettlemoyer. 2019. Evaluating gender bias in machine translation. In *Proceedings of the 57th Annual Meeting of the Association for Computational Linguistics*, pages 1679–1684, Florence, Italy. Association for Computational Linguistics.

Nathaniel Swinger, Maria De-Arteaga, Neil Thomas Heffernan IV, Mark DM Leiserson, and Adam Tauman Kalai. 2019. What are the biases in my word embedding? In *Proceedings of the 2019 AAAI/ACM Conference on AI, Ethics, and Society*, AIES '19, page 305–311, New York, NY, USA. Association for Computing Machinery.

Jörg Tiedemann. 2012. Parallel data, tools and interfaces in OPUS. In *Proceedings of the Eighth International Conference on Language Resources and Evaluation (LREC'12)*, pages 2214–2218, Istanbul, Turkey. European Language Resources Association (ELRA).

Ben Verhoeven, Walter Daelemans, and Barbara Plank. 2016. TwiSty: A multilingual twitter stylometry corpus for gender and personality profiling. In *Proceedings of the Tenth International Conference on Language Resources and Evaluation (LREC'16)*, pages 1632–1637, Portorož, Slovenia. European Language Resources Association (ELRA).

Zhiguo Wang, Patrick Ng, Xiaofei Ma, Ramesh Nallapati, and Bing Xiang. 2019. Multi-passage BERT: A globally normalized BERT model for open-domain question answering. In *Proceedings of the 2019 Conference on Empirical Methods in Natural Language Processing and the 9th International Joint Conference on Natural Language Processing (EMNLP-IJCNLP)*, pages 5878–5882, Hong Kong, China. Association for Computational Linguistics.

Wei Yang, Yuqing Xie, Aileen Lin, Xingyu Li, Luchen Tan, Kun Xiong, Ming Li, and Jimmy Lin. 2019. End-to-end open-domain question answering with BERTserini. In *Proceedings of the 2019 Conference of the North American Chapter of the Association for Computational Linguistics (Demonstrations)*, pages 72–77, Minneapolis, Minnesota. Association for Computational Linguistics.

Brian Hu Zhang, Blake Lemoine, and Margaret Mitchell. 2018. Mitigating unwanted biases with adversarial learning. In *Proceedings of the 2018 AAAI/ACM Conference on AI, Ethics, and Society*, AIES '18, page 335–340, New York, NY, USA. Association for Computing Machinery.

Jieyu Zhao, Subhabrata Mukherjee, Saghar Hosseini, Kai-Wei Chang, and Ahmed Hassan Awadallah. 2020. Gender bias in multilingual embeddings and cross-lingual transfer. In *Proceedings of the 58th Annual Meeting of the Association for Computational Linguistics*, pages 2896–2907, Online. Association for Computational Linguistics.

Jieyu Zhao, Tianlu Wang, Mark Yatskar, Vicente Ordonez, and Kai-Wei Chang. 2018. Gender bias in coreference resolution: Evaluation and debiasing methods. In *Proceedings of the 2018 Conference of the North American Chapter of the Association for Computational Linguistics: Human Language Technologies, Volume 2 (Short Papers)*, pages 15–20, New Orleans, Louisiana. Association for Computational Linguistics.

Ran Zmigrod, Sabrina J. Mielke, Hanna Wallach, and Ryan Cotterell. 2019. Counterfactual data augmentation for mitigating gender stereotypes in languages with rich morphology. In *Proceedings of the 57th Annual Meeting of the Association for Computational Linguistics*, pages 1651–1661, Florence, Italy. Association for Computational Linguistics.

# Appendix

## A Training of BERT-based document classifiers

In our experiments, for each language we consider we use a cased BERT variant that was trained specifically for the target language.[4] We use the Adam optimizer with learning rates of 5e-5, $\beta_1$ = 0.9, $\beta_2$ = 0.999, a batch size of 48, a gradient clip threshold of 1.0 and a dropout with p=0.5 on all layers. We train the model for 15 epochs. The Multi Layer Perceptron consists of a single hidden layer with 300 hidden units. We evaluate each classifier using weighted F1-Score which calculate metrics for each label, and find their average weighted by the number of true instances for each label. We repeat every experiment using 5 random train (80%) test (20%) splits and report average of these 5 experiments.

## B Adversarial Debiasing: Performance on adversarial tasks

In addition to majority class classifier and non-adversarial model, we use a third baseline model to analyze how adversarial debiasing effects the model's performance on the adversary task. First, we train feature extractor along with the topic classifier head on the topic classification task. Next, we freeze the weights of the feature extractor and

[4]DE: `https://deepset.ai/german-bert`, ES: `https://github.com/dccuchile/beto`, FR: `https://camembert-model.fr/`, TR: `https://github.com/dbmdz/berts`

| | Overall | |
|---|---|---|
| | Adv | Baseline |
| DE | 39.8 | 67.0 |
| ES | 22.6 | 66.2 |
| FR | 14.0 | 67.6 |
| TR | 22.6 | 69.0 |

Table 7: Gender classification F-scores of gender-debiased topic classifier and baseline model. For main task evaluation, see Figure 3.

| | Overall | |
|---|---|---|
| | Adv | Baseline |
| DE | 34.0 | 74.1 |
| ES | 37.0 | 72.0 |
| FR | 34.6 | 78.2 |
| TR | 32.8 | 69.2 |

Table 8: Topic classification F-scores of topic-debiased gender classifier and baseline model. For main task evaluation, check Figure 4.

train the gender classifier on top of it. Table 7 summarizes the results for gender classification. Significant drop in gender classification performance indicates effectiveness of adversarial training.

As we swapped the main and adversarial tasks, we modify the baseline in the same way too. We start with training the feature extractor and gender classifier head on the topic classification task. Then,we freeze the feature extractor, remove the gender classifier and train the topic classifier on top of freezed feature extractor. Table 8 reports the results on topic classification. Similar to Table 7, adversarial debiasing drops the adversarial task (i.e. topic classification) performance significantly. However, as Figure 4 shows it leads to slight to moderate decrease in gender classification performance and inconclusive changes with regard to topic bias.

# Universal Joy
# A Data Set and Results for Classifying Emotions Across Languages

**Sotiris Lamprinidis**
Copenhagen Business School
sla.msc@cbs.dk

**Federico Bianchi**
Bocconi University
f.bianchi@unibocconi.it

**Daniel Hardt**
Copenhagen Business School
dha.msc@cbs.dk

**Dirk Hovy**
Bocconi University
dirk.hovy@unibocconi.it

## Abstract

While emotions are universal aspects of human psychology, they are expressed differently across different languages and cultures. We introduce a new data set of over 530k anonymized public Facebook posts across 18 languages, labeled with five different emotions. Using multilingual BERT embeddings, we show that emotions can be reliably inferred both within and across languages. Zero-shot learning produces promising results for low-resource languages. Following established theories of basic emotions, we provide a detailed analysis of the possibilities and limits of cross-lingual emotion classification. We find that structural and typological similarity between languages facilitates cross-lingual learning, as well as linguistic diversity of training data. Our results suggest that there are commonalities underlying the expression of emotion in different languages. We publicly release the anonymized data for future research.

## 1 Introduction

Emotions are fundamental to human experience across languages and cultures. The nature of emotions and their linguistic expression is a topic of enduring interest across disciplines such as psychology, linguistics, philosophy, and neuroscience. Emotion researchers have investigated the existence of basic emotions such as anger, fear, disgust, sadness, and happiness (Ekman, 2016), all of which were already described in the 19th century by Darwin ([1872] 1998) and Wundt (1896). Furthermore, Ekman (2016) reports a growing consensus concerning the universality of emotions across languages and cultures. Computational linguistics can help shed light on the way in which emotions are expressed in the languages of the world.

However, most existing research has focused either on English or used very small multilingual data sets. We present a new dataset, **Universal Joy** (UJ), of over 530,000 anonymized public Facebook posts distributed across 18 languages, labeled with five different emotions: anger, anticipation, fear, joy, and sadness. This dataset represents a substantial advance over prior datasets, both in terms of its size and its linguistic diversity. It provides a strong empirical foundation for exploring basic questions about the nature and expression of emotions across the languages of the world. Figure 3 shows the heatmap of relative emotion distribution for each language. In this paper, we use this dataset to explore multilingual emotion classification.

We first perform emotion classification in a **monolingual setting**, i.e., training and testing on a single language. We then expand to a **cross-lingual setting**, i.e., where the training data contains other languages in addition to the test data language. Finally, we test how well we can do in a **zero-shot learning** setting; here the training data does *not* include any data in the language of the test data – a setting particularly relevant for low-resource languages.

Overall, we find consistent effects of cross-lingual learning, which raises several interesting issues: first, it suggests that accurate emotion detection might be possible even for low-resource languages. Accurate models for such languages might be achievable with substantial amounts of training data from high-resource languages like English. More generally, however, we explore *why* cross-lingual learning works, and what linguistic circumstances support or hamper such learning. We explore three main factors: **code-switching**, **typological closeness** of training and test languages, and **linguistic diversity in the training data**.

We hope the richness of this data set opens up exciting future research avenues, and release the models and the complete anonymized dataset at https://github.com/sotlampr/universal-joy.



*Proceedings of the 11th Workshop on Computational Approaches to Subjectivity, Sentiment and Social Media Analysis*, pages 62–75
April 19, 2021. ©2021 Association for Computational Linguistics

**Contributions** 1) We publish a new dataset of over 530k anonymized public Facebook posts in 18 languages, labeled with five basic emotions. 2) We show results for various classification setups, including transfer learning setups like cross-lingual and zero-shot learning. 3) We analyze the sources of cross-lingual learning in depth, including the effect of code-switching, typological closeness, and linguistic diversity.

## 2 Data

The dataset described here is a substantially reorganized and cleaned version of one previously described, but not released Zimmerman et al. (2015). It was collected in October 2014 by searching for public Facebook posts with a Facebook "feelings tag". We did verify publication with the data protection officer of the main institution. For a Data Statement (Bender and Friedman, 2018), see Appendix A.

We remove any duplicates, and classify each instance's language using three methods: `langid`,[1] `cld3`,[2], and `FastText`.[3] We keep only instances where at least two of these methods agree. We manually evaluate 200 randomly selected instances labeled `deu`, `fra`, `eng`, `ita`, and `spa`,[4] and find the average precision of our method is $0.97(\pm 0.04)$.

To anonymize the data, we remove identifying information by replacing names with the special token `[PERSON]`. Where possible (Dutch, English, French, German, Portuguese, Spanish, Italian), we use the `spacy`[5] NER to replace any PERSON entities. For languages without `spacy` support, we either use the Stanford CoreNLP NER tagger (Manning et al., 2014) and replace `PERSON`-tagged words (Chinese), or replace all given names and surnames found in Wiktionary for the respective languages (Bengali, Burmese, Hindi, Indonesian, Khmer, Malay, Romanian, Tagalog, Thai, Vietnamese).

Finally, we perform some additional preprocessing steps to replace any number with `0`, and the Facebook-specific tags *"with [PERSON]"* with the special token `[WITH]`, *"at [LOCATION]"* with the special token `[LOCATION]`, and photos, emails, and URLs with the special tokens `[PHOTO]`, `[EMAIL]`, and `[URL]`, respectively.

Similar to the approach of Zimmerman et al. (2015), we map the 27 initial emotion tags into five labels of basic emotions: anger, anticipation, fear, joy, and sadness (see mapping in Appendix Table 10). We choose this label set for several reasons: first, it is similar to the lists of basic emotions proposed in the psychological literature (Ekman, 2016; Plutchik, 1994). Second, each of the five labels is well-represented in the Facebook data, whereas the original tags are highly imbalanced and often rare. Finally, it is similar to the lists of basic emotions used in recent NLP studies, and facilitates comparison with recent work by e.g., Abdul-Mageed and Ungar (2017).

As training languages, we choose all languages with more than 35 samples for the least frequent emotion (i.e., fear). The size and distribution of emotions for each dataset is presented in table 11.

**Distribution of Languages** There is a wide variety in the amount of data per language, ranging from 284,265 posts for English, the most frequent language, to 869 posts for Bengali (see table 1).

| ISO code | Samples | Language | Family |
|---|---|---|---|
| ben | 869 | Bengali | Indo-European |
| cmn | 4909 | Chinese | Sino-Tibetan |
| deu | 5902 | German | Indo-European |
| eng | 284265 | English | Indo-European |
| fra | 6557 | French | Indo-European |
| hin | 1823 | Hindi | Indo-European |
| ind | 6201 | Indonesian | Austronesian |
| ita | 6709 | Italian | Indo-European |
| khm | 977 | Khmer | Austroasiatic |
| mya | 953 | Burmese | Sino-Tibetan |
| nld | 2201 | Dutch | Indo-European |
| por | 31326 | Portuguese | Indo-European |
| rom | 1940 | Romanian | Indo-European |
| spa | 31326 | Spanish | Indo-European |
| tgl | 4909 | Tagalog | Austronesian |
| tha | 3803 | Thai | Tai-Kadai |
| vie | 3956 | Vietnamese | Austroasiatic |
| zsm | 4908 | Malay | Austronesian |

Table 1: Languages in Universal Joy data set

**Distribution of Emotions per Language** There are significant differences in the prevalence of each

[1] `https://github.com/saffsd/langid.py`

[2] `https://github.com/google/cld3`

[3] `https://fasttext.cc/docs/en/language-identification.html` (Joulin et al., 2016b,a)

[4] Here and in what follows, we use standard ISO language codes, which are given in table 1.

[5] `https://spacy.io`

emotion across languages, as shown in table 2. The relative distributions are shown in Figure 3. Fear is a very rare emotion in all languages, while joy is the most common. Anticipation, the second most frequent class, is especially prevalent in English . There are also differences in joy (more prevalent in Spanish) and sadness (more prevalent in Portuguese).

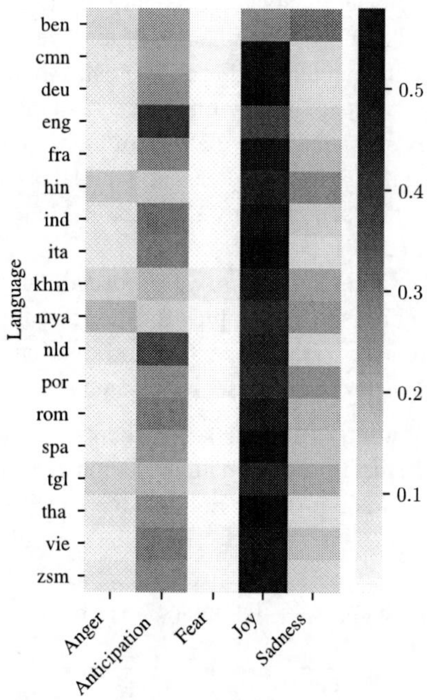


Figure 1: Heatmap of relative emotion distribution per language.

## 2.1 Training Datasets

We create three versions of the dataset for training purposes:

- **Small:** this version includes the five languages with sufficient training data for the least frequent emotion, fear: namely `eng`, `spa`, `por`, `cmn`, `tgl`. This dataset is balanced by language, so that there are 2,947 posts for each language.
- **Large:** this version includes 29,364 posts for each of the three most frequent languages: `eng`, `spa`, `por`. Note that each of these is a superset of the corresponding language in the Small training set.
- **Huge:** this version contains 283,853 posts from the single most frequent language, `eng`.

## 2.2 Test Datasets

For each training language, we create fixed-size development and test sets, stratified by emotion and following a 70:15:15 ratio with respect to the Small version of the dataset. Thus for `eng`, `spa`, `por`, `cmn`, `tgl`, the test and dev sets each consist of 631 posts.

The rest of the languages are combined in a separate test set, labeled *low-resource*. Note that for the purposes of this paper, what we call *low-resource languages* are the thirteen languages with insufficient training data in our corpus. This includes languages such as German and French, which are not, in general, low-resource languages. The low-resource test set for each of these languages simply consists of all the posts in that language. The low-resource sets will allow us to broadly measure zero-shot performance (see Section 4.3).

# 3 Methods

We model the task as a series of binary classification problems, one per emotion, similarly to Mohammad et al. (2018) (this allows for the theoretical case where there are multiple emotions in one instance). We use Logistic Regression and Multilingual BERT as classifiers, to probe for various lexical and syntactic properties of the task.

## 3.1 Logistic Regression Models

We use the `scikit-learn`[6] implementation to extract TFIDF-weighted bag-of-words (BOW) features, and train Logistic Regression **LR** models with L2 regularization ($C = 1.0$) and balanced label loss-weighting. We include BOW features for comparison purposes – in particular, to assess the extent to which cross-lingual effects might arise from code switching or other forms of token overlap across languages. For the **LR** models we use the same tokenization as in 3.2, from the pre-trained multilingual BERT model.

## 3.2 Multilingual BERT

To optimize performance, we use the multilingual BERT (mBERT) model.[7] We follow Devlin et al. (2019) in optimizing the model using a machine with an Intel i9-9940X CPU, 32GB RAM and a NVIDIA Quadro RTX 6000 GPU.

The loss $\mathcal{L}$ is the mean over the individual losses $l \in L$ for each emotion:

[6] `https://scikit-learn.org`

[7] `https://github.com/google-research/bert`

| Language | Anger | Anticipation | Fear | Joy | Sadness | Sum |
|---|---|---|---|---|---|---|
| cmn | **460** | **1094** | **104** | **2666** | 585 | 4909 |
| deu | 425 | **1475** | 8 | **3388** | **606** | 5902 |
| eng | 16842 | **115793** | 3258 | **111211** | **37161** | 284265 |
| fra | 382 | **1788** | 22 | **3222** | 1143 | 6557 |
| ind | 382 | **1841** | 32 | **3077** | 869 | 6201 |
| ita | 472 | **1910** | 20 | **3656** | **651** | 6709 |
| por | 1776 | **8103** | 218 | 13363 | **7866** | 31326 |
| spa | 1795 | **7285** | **150** | **17175** | 4921 | 31326 |
| tgl | **647** | **914** | **159** | 2166 | **1023** | 4909 |
| zsm | 326 | 1344 | 34 | **2566** | 638 | 4908 |
| Sum | 23507 | 141547 | 4005 | 162490 | 55463 | 387012 |

Table 2: Number of samples per language and emotion, for top ten languages, significant outliers at $\alpha = 0.05$ in **bold**, using $\chi^2$ test $\chi^2 = 1780054.57, dof = 36, N = 50, p \ll 0.001$.

$$\mathcal{L} = \sum_{i=1}^{E} L_i(y_i, x)/E$$

$$L_i(y_i; x) = -w_i \left[y_i \log(p(Y_i|\, x)) + (1 - y_i) \log(1 - p(Y_i|\, x)\right]$$

$$p(Y|\, x) = \text{Sigmoid}(\bar{h}(x)W + b)$$

where $E$ is the number of emotions $e \in \mathcal{E}$, $\vec{y} \in \{0, 1\}^E$ is a one-hot vector of the target emotion, $x \in X$ are the input byte-pair pieces, $\bar{h}(x) : X \rightarrow \mathbb{R}^{768}$ is the mean-pooled output of the BERT `[CLS]` token for input $x$, $W_{768 \times E}$ and $\vec{b} \in \mathbb{R}^E$ are learnable parameters, and $P(Y|x)$ is the predicted probability distribution over the emotions.

We use instance weighting to address the high class imbalance. For each emotion, we weight positive class instances as $w_i = N_{e=\neg\mathcal{E}_i}/N_{e=\mathcal{E}_i}$, i.e., the inverse proportion of negative examples to positive examples, averaged for all languages.

We linearly increase the learning rate for half an epoch and then linearly decay it until the end of the training. For the monolingual and zero-shot learning task, we select the model with the highest macro-averaged F1-score across all emotions on the target language development set. For the cross-lingual task, we choose the model with the best average score on all languages.

**Monolingual Classification** The simplest setting is the classification of emotions within one language – that is, the test, development, and training data are all taken from the same language. This provides a strong baseline for cross-lingual work.

**Cross-lingual Classification** In this setting, we test whether knowledge about emotions expressed in one language can be transferred to another language. Here, the training data includes one or more languages in addition to the language of the development and test data. Note that emotion distributions *differ* between languages. This likely affects performance and could be addressed by stratified resampling. However, that presupposes that all languages exhibit the same emotions to the same degree, which is by no means certain. So while sampling would improve performance, it would distort the "natural" distribution, and preclude future analysis of language-specific studies.

**Zero-shot learning** Here the training data does *not* include the language of the development and test sets. We use two versions of zero-shot training: single-language, and multilingual, depending on the number of languages present in the training data. In either case, the size of the training data is the same.

## 4 Results

We treat each emotion as a separate binary task, and compute a macro-average of the F1-scores for each of the six tasks. A random baseline model (table 15 in the Appendix) always predicts the positive class for all emotions, giving an average macro F1-score of around 0.3.

### 4.1 Monolingual English Tests

We evaluate our methods on available data sets for emotion classification in English (Abdul-Mageed and Ungar, 2017; Troiano et al., 2019). We compare performance on the EmoNet test data as well as the English test data from ISEAR (Troiano et al., 2019). In addition, we report performance on the English test data from our Universal Joy dataset. These tests are designed to assess two points: whether our data set is comparable to previously published data, and whether the models we use are performant enough to enable meaningful investigations.

We obtained the EmoNet dataset (Abdul-Mageed and Ungar, 2017) from the authors of the paper. The benchmark shared by the authors contains 80k tweet IDs. However, some of the tweets do not exist anymore, and some contain emotions we are not considering in this work (i.e., *disgust*). Thus, after removal we were left with a test set of around 40K tweets. We were, therefore, unable to reproduce their full setup.

Table 3 shows results on English test data, using the two LR models as well as mBERT on the small, large, and huge training data. For a prediction, we take the output probabilities from EmoNet and use the most probable emotion that is in our set of five emotions.

| Model | Training | Test | | | |
|---|---|---|---|---|---|
| | | UJ | EmoNet | ISEAR | Avg. |
| EmoNet | EmoNet | 0.23 | 0.47 | 0.41 | 0.37 |
| LR | Small | 0.45 | 0.31 | 0.24 | 0.33 |
| | Large | 0.52 | 0.41 | 0.31 | 0.41 |
| | Huge | 0.52 | 0.47 | 0.37 | 0.45 |
| mBERT | Small | 0.46 | 0.40 | 0.48 | 0.45 |
| | Large | 0.58 | 0.48 | 0.46 | 0.51 |
| | Huge | **0.63** | **0.55** | **0.49** | **0.56** |

Table 3: Macro-F1 score for different models on various English datasets.

The results show that using more training data in a LR model or any of the mBERT model improves performance across the board and yields competitive results. We are therefore confident that our data collection and model choices produce meaningful results. But does this performance extend to other test languages than English?

### 4.2 Cross-lingual Tests

We now turn to cross-lingual investigation: table 4 shows results using a variety of training sets with the five test sets from `eng`, `por`, `spa`, `cmn`, and `tgl`. We show results for both LR models and mBERT on monolingual, cross-lingual, and zero-shot Universal Joy data.

In addition to the Small, Large, and Huge training sets described above, we test mBERT on some additional training data combinations. First, we divide Small into Indo-European (Small-IE) and non-Indo-European (Small∼IE). We also combine the Large and Small training datasets from all languages to test whether more diversity balances out more data. This dataset comprises five languages, but only about half as many instances as Huge English.

In general, mBERT models outperform the LR models. Furthermore, the mBERT models frequently show positive cross-lingual effects; that is, training data improves performance even when it is from a language other than the test language. For example, small-mono for `spa` is 0.43, while small-all (including all five languages) is 0.45. Small-all on average is 0.53, while small-mono is 0.51. On the other hand, large-mono (0.57) is better than large-all (0.56). Perhaps cross-lingual improvements are easier to obtain when the monolingual model is weaker.

Using training data based on language families (IE and ∼IE, respectively), indicates typological effects (which we explore further in Sections 5.2 and 5.3). Specifically, training on non-Indo-European languages results in higher performance for `cmn` and `tgl` (though not the highest overall).
Table 5 shows mBERT results for monolingual and zero-shot training. Unsurprisingly, the best results always involve training on the same language as the test language (see diagonal), and more data helps.

Table 6 compares mBERT with the LR models on zero-shot. In particular, we compare single-language zero-shot with multilingual. We see that the multilingual scores are consistently higher than the single-language scores, across all models. This provides evidence for the benefit of diversity in the training data. One reason could be a wider range of ways to express emotions. We will investigate this in more detail in Section 5.

We consistently see cross-lingual learning capabilities with the mBERT models. The zero-shot scores are significantly above the random baseline (paired one-sided t-test): zero-shot vs. random: $t = 4.08, dof = 24, p < 0.001$ monolingual vs. zero-shot: $t = 3.17, dof = 24, p = 0.002$ cross-lingual vs. monolingual: $t = 1.28, dof = 24, p < 0.105$. Zero-shot vs. random and mono-

| Model | Dataset | eng | por | spa | cmn | tgl | Avg |
|---|---|---|---|---|---|---|---|
| LR | Small-mono | 0.45 | 0.48 | 0.41 | 0.46 | **0.59** | 0.48 |
| | Large-mono | 0.52 | 0.50 | 0.46 | | | 0.49 |
| mBERT | Small-mono | 0.46 | 0.48 | 0.43 | **0.67** | 0.53 | 0.51 |
| | Large-mono | 0.58 | 0.59 | 0.55 | | | 0.57 |
| | Huge English | **0.63** | | | | | |
| | Small-all | 0.45 | 0.50 | 0.45 | **0.67** | 0.56 | 0.53 |
| | Small-IE. | 0.49 | 0.52 | 0.44 | 0.41 | 0.32 | 0.44 |
| | Small-∼IE. | 0.46 | 0.38 | 0.36 | 0.66 | 0.56 | 0.48 |
| | Large-all | 0.54 | **0.60** | 0.53 | | | 0.56 |
| | Large-all & Small-all | 0.57 | 0.59 | **0.56** | **0.67** | 0.57 | **0.59** |

Table 4: Macro-F1 results for mono & cross-lingual learning on the Universal Joy data. mBERT and LR models.

lingual vs. zero-shot are significant at Bonferroni-corrected significance level $a = 0.05/3 = 0.0167$. Cross-lingual frequently performs better than monolingual, but with considerable variation.

### 4.3 Zero-shot Learning for Low-Resource Languages

Table 7 shows zero-shot results when testing on the low-resource languages with the Small, Large, Large&Small, and Huge training sets. Small is also split typologically: Small-IE consists only of the Indo-European languages `eng`, `spa`, and `por`, while Small ∼IE consists of the remaining languages in Small, `cmn` and `tgl`. We compare against a monolingual result for each language, using a LR system described in Section 3.1, taking the 10-fold cross-validation average. [8] For Indo-European languages, zero-shot models consistently outperform the monolingual model; furthermore, larger zero-shot models tend to do better, although the linguistically diverse L&S model often does better than the much-larger Huge model (which is only English). The zero-shot models rarely do well with the non-Indo-European languages. This is not surprising, since most of the data in the zero-shot models comes from Indo-European languages.

Below we investigate these results in more detail to assess the factors that facilitate cross-lingual learning.

## 5 Analysis of Cross-lingual Effects

Our results show a wide range of cross-lingual effects. In many cases, they are quite substantial, while in other cases we observe no effect. We believe these differences are due to the linguistic properties of the languages that the models pick up on. Here we examine some of the factors involved in this: code switching, typological closeness, and linguistic diversity. The results can shed light on the similarities and differences in how emotions are expressed in different languages.

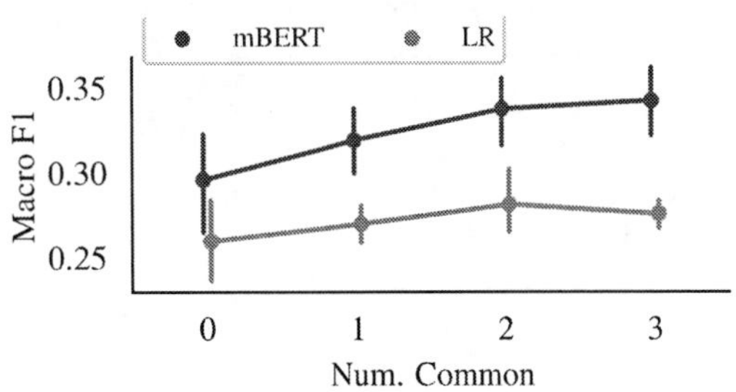


Figure 2: Number of shared WALS features as a function of zero-shot performance for various models.

### 5.1 Code Switching

A post involves code-switching if it combines multiple languages, as in the following:

*"We love you guys ... proud of you.. [PHOTO] jongens heel veel succes vanavond ..!!!!"* (the English translation of the Dutch part is *"guys lots of luck tonight"*)

This post is classified as Dutch, but includes text in English. BoW (bag of word) models are therefore well-suited to take advantage of code switching. This post provides information about both Dutch and English, since there are several tokens in each language associated with the labeled emotion, anticipation. A model could learn here that "love" is associated with anticipation and use this on English test data, even though the training example

[8]For languages that have $k < 10$ instances per any emotion, we do a $k$-fold cross-validation.

| Dataset | Language | eng | por | spa | cmn | tgl |
|---|---|---|---|---|---|---|
| Small | eng | **0.46** | 0.38 | 0.34 | 0.39 | 0.34 |
| | por | 0.44 | **0.48** | 0.38 | 0.38 | 0.31 |
| | spa | 0.34 | 0.39 | **0.43** | 0.34 | 0.31 |
| | cmn | 0.42 | 0.34 | 0.32 | **0.67** | 0.25 |
| | tgl | 0.38 | 0.34 | 0.32 | 0.36 | **0.53** |
| Large | eng | **0.58** | 0.38 | 0.36 | 0.39 | **0.45** |
| | por | 0.42 | **0.59** | 0.38 | **0.40** | 0.44 |
| | spa | 0.42 | 0.44 | **0.55** | 0.38 | 0.31 |

Table 5: mBERT macro-F1 results in mono-lingual setting on two sets of universal joy data. Best result for each training dataset per language in bold.

| Dataset | Method | Model | eng | por | spa | cmn | tgl | Avg |
|---|---|---|---|---|---|---|---|---|
| Small | Zero-shot single-lang avg | LR | 0.26 | 0.24 | 0.24 | 0.17 | 0.22 | 0.23 |
| | | mBERT | 0.40 | 0.36 | 0.34 | 0.37 | 0.30 | 0.35 |
| | Zero-shot multilingual | LR | 0.28 | 0.28 | 0.26 | 0.16 | 0.26 | 0.25 |
| | | mBERT | 0.47 | 0.40 | 0.34 | 0.39 | 0.41 | 0.40 |
| Large | Zero-shot single lang avg | LR | 0.30 | 0.29 | 0.29 | | | 0.29 |
| | | mBERT | 0.42 | 0.41 | 0.37 | | | 0.40 |
| | Zero-shot multilingual | LR | 0.33 | 0.35 | 0.31 | | | 0.33 |
| | | mBERT | 0.45 | 0.45 | 0.39 | | | 0.43 |

Table 6: Macro-F1 results for zero-shot learning with Small and Large training sets. Single lang avg. is based on average results of models for each language other than test language. Multilingual involves a single model with the same amount of training data as single-language, but evenly mixed among the different languages. Results below the random baseline in gray.

is classified as Dutch.

However, observe in table 6 that the BoW models (LR) perform poorly in zero-shot learning. They are near or below baseline, except in the Large multilingual case. mBERT, by contrast, is consistently above the baseline and consistently better than the BoW models. This suggests that code-switching is *not relevant* to the cross-lingual effects we have observed.

### 5.2 Typological Closeness

A natural hypothesis, explored by Singh et al. (2019), is that cross-lingual effects are stronger for typologically close languages; that is, scores are higher when training and test language are closely related. Following Pires et al. (2019), we compute typological closeness as overlap on selected features from the World Atlas of Language Structures (WALS) (Dryer and Haspelmath, 2013). These features are particularly relevant to word order of categories. In Figure 2, we plot for each pair of languages <l1,l2> the number of WALS features[9] shared between l1 and l2 against the zero-shot score obtained when training on l1 and testing on l2. Indeed, more shared features correlate with better performance, especially in mBERT models.

Table 8 shows the correlation between performance and several other measures of similarity between languages, including the number of shared bigrams and emoticons, the shared WALS features, and the proximity in a genealogy tree. Compare the striking positive correlation between shared WALS features and performance (0.27) for the mBERT model, while there is no such correlation for the two LR models, corroborating Figure 2. This suggests that these particular WALS features related to word order, are relevant to abstract features of the mBERT models, while they are irrelevant for the LR models. In contrast, see the flipped correlation

[9] We keep features that all of our languages have annotations for: *81A* (Order of Subject, Object and Verb), *82A* (Order of Subject and Verb), and *83A* (Order of Object and Verb).

| Data | ben | deu | fra | hin | ita | nld | rom | Avg | ind | khm | mya | tha | vie | zsm | Avg |
|---|---|---|---|---|---|---|---|---|---|---|---|---|---|---|---|
| mono | 0.26 | 0.37 | 0.42 | **0.36** | 0.32 | 0.36 | 0.35 | 0.35 | **0.40** | 0.27 | **0.36** | **0.33** | **0.39** | **0.47** | **0.37** |
| S | 0.35 | 0.38 | 0.42 | 0.30 | 0.37 | 0.39 | 0.35 | 0.37 | 0.34 | 0.31 | 0.21 | 0.32 | 0.34 | 0.34 | 0.31 |
| L | 0.34 | 0.37 | 0.42 | 0.29 | 0.37 | 0.40 | **0.38** | 0.37 | 0.35 | 0.32 | 0.29 | **0.33** | 0.37 | 0.37 | 0.34 |
| L&S | **0.38** | 0.38 | **0.44** | 0.30 | **0.38** | 0.40 | 0.37 | **0.38** | 0.35 | 0.32 | 0.28 | 0.32 | 0.38 | 0.37 | 0.34 |
| Huge en | 0.34 | **0.39** | 0.43 | 0.30 | 0.37 | **0.42** | 0.35 | 0.37 | 0.36 | **0.34** | 0.30 | 0.32 | 0.36 | 0.36 | 0.34 |

Indo-European non Indo-European

Table 7: mBERT macro-F1 results for zero-shot learning on low-resource languages in Universal Joy data. Improvements hold mainly for IE languages.

| Model | Bigrams | Emoticons | WALS | Genealogy |
|---|---|---|---|---|
| LR | **0.54** | **0.31** | 0.01 | **0.50** |
| mBERT | 0.18 | **0.41** | **0.27** | **0.57** |

Table 8: Spearman's rank correlation between performance and various language similarity measures. Significant correlations at $\alpha = 0.05$, Bonferroni-corrected for each model, in bold.

of "lexical" features like bigrams and emoticons in the two model types. Genealogical proximity has a high correlation with performance in all models, but again is highest for mBERT.

All this supports the idea, also discussed in (Pires et al., 2019), that mBERT models are sensitive to abstract syntactic features that are shared across languages.

### 5.3 Linguistic Diversity

We find clear evidence that diversity of training languages improves performance. Table 6 shows a clear multilingual advantage in zero-shot learning; for all three models, the multilingual scores are higher than the monolingual scores. In table 7, the last two lines compare a diverse training set of 102k instances (Large&Small) to the more than twice as large Huge English training data (283k). The average results over the 13 low-resource languages of both are identical.

## 6 Related Work

Abdul-Mageed and Ungar (2017) collect tweets based on user-inserted hashtags; the resulting dataset, EmoNet, is similar to ours in that it uses a distant supervision approach. Above we presented results based on the EmoNet dataset and model. The SemEval 2018 Task 1 (Baziotis et al., 2018), involves classification and regression tasks for four emotions: joy, sadness, anger, and fear. The Affect in Tweets Dataset (Mohammad et al., 2018) is a small dataset that includes emotions annotated in multiple languages; it does not involve the cross-linguistic investigation of emotion that is central to the present work. Troiano et al. (2019) describe a small, bilingual emotion dataset, with English and German (ISEAR). Wang et al. (2018) describe a bilingual Chinese-English emotion dataset (NLPCC). We provide results on these datasets in table 9 in the Appendix; it's important to note that these datasets differ in important ways from the Facebook data in our dataset.

## 7 Conclusion

We introduce a new data set of over 530,000 anonymized Facebook posts from 18 languages, labeled with five basic emotions. We show that emotions can be reliably identified, both within and across languages, including zero-shot learning. This suggests substantial opportunities for transferring knowledge from high-resource to low-resource languages. In a detailed investigation of the factors supporting cross-lingual learning, we find evidence for the importance of linguistic diversity of training data as well as syntactic and typological similarities between languages.

These results provide intriguing evidence of deep commonalities in the linguistic expression of emotion across the languages of the world.

## 8 Ethical considerations

Collecting and publishing a data set from social media raises a number of ethical concerns. We have prepared and planned the release of this dataset in close consultation with the Data Protection Officer of the main institution for the publication. The data is completely anonymized, with all identifying information removed. It was collected from public postings on Facebook, accessed using the standard Facebook API for collection of such postings. Based on these considerations, the Data Protection Officer approved our plan to release the dataset, and certified that it complies with GDPR and other relevant requirements. The actual data collection was performed by graduate assistants as part of their studies, and the process involve no manual annotation. We also provide a data statement, to allow future researchers to assess any inherent bias. The primary aim of our study is academic, to understand the interplay between language and emotion.

## References


Muhammad Abdul-Mageed and Lyle Ungar. 2017. EmoNet: Fine-grained emotion detection with gated recurrent neural networks. In *Proceedings of the 55th Annual Meeting of the Association for Computational Linguistics (Volume 1: Long Papers)*, pages 718–728, Vancouver, Canada. Association for Computational Linguistics.

Christos Baziotis, Nikos Athanasiou, Alexandra Chronopoulou, Athanasia Kolovou, Georgios Paraskevopoulos, Nikolaos Ellinas, Shrikanth Narayanan, and Alexandros Potamianos. 2018. NTUA-SLP at Semeval-2018 task 1: Predicting affective content in tweets with deep attentive RNNs and transfer learning. In *Proceedings of the 12th International Workshop on Semantic Evaluation (SemEval-2018)*, pages 245—255.

Emily M. Bender and Batya Friedman. 2018. Data statements for natural language processing: Toward mitigating system bias and enabling better science. *Transactions of the Association for Computational Linguistics*, 6:587–604.

Charles Darwin. [1872] 1998. *The expression of the emotions in man and animals.* Oxford University Press, USA. (Original work published 1872).

Jacob Devlin, Ming-Wei Chang, Kenton Lee, and Kristina Toutanova. 2019. BERT: Pre-training of Deep Bidirectional Transformers for Language Understanding. In *Proceedings of the 2019 Conference of the North American Chapter of the Association for Computational Linguistics: Human Language Technologies, Volume 1 (Long and Short Papers)*, pages 4171–4186.

Matthew S. Dryer and Martin Haspelmath. 2013. WALS online. https://wals.info/.

Paul Ekman. 2016. What scientists who study emotion agree about. *Perspectives on Psychological Science*, 11(1):31–34.

Armand Joulin, Edouard Grave, Piotr Bojanowski, Matthijs Douze, Hérve Jégou, and Tomas Mikolov. 2016a. Fasttext.zip: Compressing text classification models. *arXiv preprint arXiv:1612.03651*.

Armand Joulin, Edouard Grave, Piotr Bojanowski, and Tomas Mikolov. 2016b. Bag of tricks for efficient text classification. *arXiv preprint arXiv:1607.01759*.

Edward Loper and Steven Bird. 2002. Nltk: The natural language toolkit. In *Proceedings of the ACL-02 Workshop on Effective Tools and Methodologies for Teaching Natural Language Processing and Computational Linguistics*, pages 63–70.

Christopher D. Manning, Mihai Surdeanu, John Bauer, Jenny Finkel, Steven J. Bethard, and David McClosky. 2014. The Stanford CoreNLP natural language processing toolkit. In *Association for Computational Linguistics (ACL) System Demonstrations*, pages 55–60.

Saif Mohammad, Felipe Bravo-Marquez, Mohammad Salameh, and Svetlana Kiritchenko. 2018. Semeval-2018 task 1: Affect in tweets. In *Proceedings of the 12th international workshop on semantic evaluation*, pages 1–17.

Telmo Pires, Eva Schlinger, and Dan Garrette. 2019. How multilingual is multilingual bert? *arXiv preprint arXiv:1906.01502*.

Robert Plutchik. 1994. *The psychology and biology of emotion.* HarperCollins College Publishers.

Jasdeep Singh, Bryan McCann, Richard Socher, and Caiming Xiong. 2019. BERT is not an interlingua and the bias of tokenization. In *Proceedings of the 2nd Workshop on Deep Learning Approaches for Low-Resource NLP (DeepLo 2019)*, pages 47–55, Hong Kong, China. Association for Computational Linguistics.

Enrica Troiano, Sebastian Padó, and Roman Klinger. 2019. Crowdsourcing and validating event-focused emotion corpora for German and English. In *Proceedings of the 57th Annual Meeting of the Association for Computational Linguistics*, pages 4005–4011.

Zhongqing Wang, Shoushan Li, Fan Wu, Qingying Sun, and Guodong Zhou. 2018. Overview of nlpcc 2018 shared task 1: Emotion detection in code-switching text. In *CCF International Conference on Natural Language Processing and Chinese Computing*, pages 429–433. Springer.

W. Wundt. 1896. *Grundriss der Psychologie (Outlines of Psychology).* Leipzig: Engelmann.

Christopher Zimmerman, Mari-Klara Stein, Daniel Hardt, and Ravi Vatrapu. 2015. Emergence of things felt: harnessing the semantic space of facebook feeling tags. In *Proceedings of the Thirty Sixth International Conference on Information Systems*.

## A Data Statement

We follow Bender and Friedman (2018) on providing a Data Statement for our corpus, in order to provide a fuller picture of the possibilities and limitations of the data, and to allow future researchers to spot any biases we might have missed.

CURATION RATIONALE We use Facebook postings originally collected in 2014; any identifying information of the authors has been removed by anonymization.

LANGUAGE VARIETY Eighteen different languages, as identified by language classification, therefore presumably mostly standard. Due to the setting (Facebook posts), some non-standard language is likely.

SPEAKER DEMOGRAPHICS Unknown, though gender could be inferred from first names before anonymization. Due to the setting, all authors need to have access to internet, which means a young demographic is likely.

SPEECH SITUATION Facebook posts self-labeled with emotions – i.e., short, written, spontaneous texts written synchronously with a broad audience in mind.

TEXT CHARACTERISTICS Wide range of topics, but confined broadly to emotional issues.

## B Macro-F1 score for the results on other datasets

Results on additional multilingual datasets are given in table 9

## C Datasets

The testing datasets are displayed in table 11.

## D Logistic Regression Results

Table 12 gives monolingual and zero-shot results for the two logistic regression models, Uni-LR an BT-LR. Note that zero-shot results are generally at or below baseline.

## E Code switching & Emoticons

For extracting the bigram types, we remove all punctuation and split the sentences into tokens using `nltk` (Loper and Bird, 2002) `word_tokenizer`. We keep bigrams with more than 5 occurences. For extracting the emoticons/punctuation, we keep only Unicode punctuation characters and use `nltk TweetTokenizer` to split the sentences into tokens. We discard any token consisting of a single character and replace all occurences of more than 3 consecutive punctuation characters with just 3 characters. We keep tokens with more than 5 occurences.

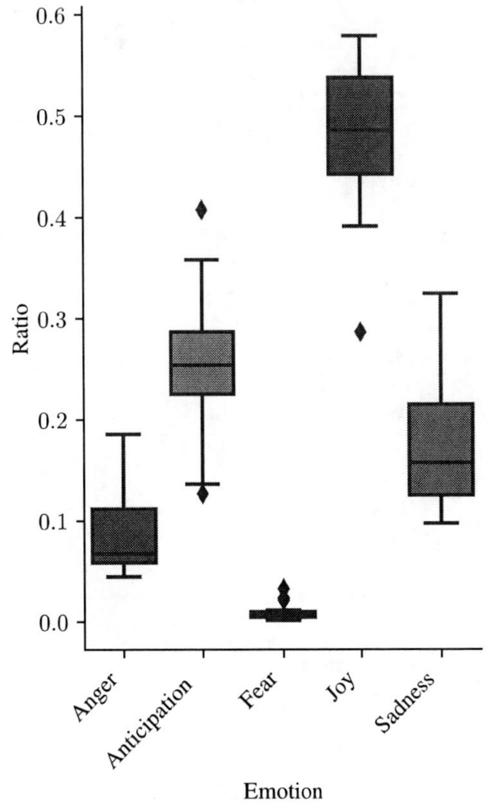


Figure 3: Box plot of emotion ratios over all languages

### E.1 Expanded Results

Tables 16 through 18 give results for mBERT Small models, separated out for the different emotions.

| Dataset | Language(s) | EmoNet | ISEAR eng | ISEAR deu | NLPCC | Avg |
|---|---|---|---|---|---|---|
| baseline | | 0.47 | **0.52** | **0.50** | 0.40 | 0.47 |
| Small | eng | 0.40 | 0.48 | 0.42 | 0.45 | 0.44 |
| | cmn | 0.31 | 0.40 | 0.30 | 0.43 | 0.36 |
| | IE. | 0.36 | 0.46 | 0.40 | 0.40 | 0.41 |
| | ~IE. | 0.37 | 0.46 | 0.38 | 0.42 | 0.41 |
| | all | 0.43 | 0.44 | 0.36 | 0.43 | 0.41 |
| Large | eng | 0.48 | 0.46 | 0.36 | 0.42 | 0.43 |
| | all | 0.46 | 0.43 | 0.31 | 0.41 | 0.40 |
| Large & Small | all | 0.50 | 0.48 | 0.38 | 0.44 | 0.45 |
| Huge | eng | **0.55** | 0.49 | 0.39 | **0.48** | **0.48** |

Table 9: Results on other datasets

| Original Emotion | Mapped Emotion |
|---|---|
| accomplished | |
| amused | |
| angry | anger |
| annoyed | anger |
| awesome | |
| bad | |
| confident | |
| confused | |
| depressed | sadness |
| determined | |
| disappointed | sadness |
| disgusted | |
| down | sadness |
| excited | anticipation |
| fantastic | joy |
| great | joy |
| happy | joy |
| heartbroken | sadness |
| hopeful | anticipation |
| pissed | anger |
| proud | |
| pumped | anticipation |
| sad | sadness |
| scared | fear |
| super | joy |
| wonderful | joy |
| worried | fear |

Table 10: Mapping from Facebook emotion to the 5 basic emotions.

| Dataset | Lang. | Anger | Anticip. | Fear | Joy | Sadness | Total |
|---|---|---|---|---|---|---|---|
| UJ Testing | eng | 58 | 400 | 11 | 384 | 128 | 981 |
| | spa | 56 | 228 | 5 | 538 | 154 | 981 |
| | por | 56 | 254 | 7 | 418 | 246 | 981 |
| | cmn | 92 | 218 | 21 | 533 | 117 | 981 |
| | tgl | 129 | 183 | 32 | 433 | 204 | 981 |
| UJ Low Resource | ben | 120 | 211 | 7 | 249 | 282 | 869 |
| | deu | 425 | 1475 | 8 | 3388 | 606 | 5902 |
| | fra | 382 | 1788 | 22 | 3222 | 1143 | 6557 |
| | hin | 274 | 231 | 8 | 830 | 480 | 1823 |
| | ind | 382 | 1841 | 32 | 3077 | 869 | 6201 |
| | ita | 472 | 1910 | 20 | 3656 | 651 | 6709 |
| | khm | 115 | 158 | 23 | 469 | 212 | 977 |
| | zsm | 326 | 1344 | 34 | 2566 | 638 | 4908 |
| | mya | 177 | 130 | 9 | 412 | 225 | 953 |
| | nld | 150 | 788 | 10 | 981 | 272 | 2201 |
| | rom | 97 | 560 | 8 | 923 | 352 | 1940 |
| | tha | 244 | 938 | 21 | 2202 | 398 | 3803 |
| | vie | 176 | 1137 | 39 | 1982 | 622 | 3956 |

Table 11: Testing Datasets

| Model | Dataset | Language | eng | por | spa | cmn | tgl |
|---|---|---|---|---|---|---|---|
| Uni-LR | Small | eng | 0.40 | 0.30 | 0.25 | 0.30 | 0.29 |
| | | por | 0.28 | 0.48 | 0.31 | 0.25 | 0.27 |
| | | spa | 0.27 | 0.38 | 0.38 | 0.26 | 0.25 |
| | | cmn | 0.32 | 0.25 | 0.26 | 0.43 | 0.28 |
| | | tgl | 0.31 | 0.29 | 0.26 | 0.26 | 0.56 |
| | Large | eng | 0.51 | 0.28 | 0.27 | 0.29 | 0.44 |
| | | por | 0.28 | 0.52 | 0.35 | 0.27 | 0.29 |
| | | spa | 0.32 | 0.37 | 0.47 | 0.31 | 0.29 |
| BT-LR | Small | eng | 0.45 | 0.21 | 0.22 | 0.24 | 0.26 |
| | | por | 0.25 | 0.48 | 0.32 | 0.21 | 0.19 |
| | | spa | 0.24 | 0.32 | 0.41 | 0.15 | 0.21 |
| | | cmn | 0.29 | 0.19 | 0.21 | 0.46 | 0.21 |
| | | tgl | 0.26 | 0.22 | 0.23 | 0.10 | 0.59 |
| | Large | eng | 0.52 | 0.23 | 0.26 | 0.21 | 0.41 |
| | | por | 0.28 | 0.50 | 0.33 | 0.21 | 0.29 |
| | | spa | 0.31 | 0.36 | 0.46 | 0.21 | 0.28 |

Table 12: Macro-F1 results in mono-lingual setting for the Logistic Regression models. Results below the baseline in gray.

| Bigram | # Languages |
|---|---|
| i love | 14 |
| love you | 12 |
| good morning | 9 |
| of the | 9 |
| new year | 9 |
| the best | 8 |
| this is | 8 |
| in the | 8 |
| have a | 8 |
| thank you | 7 |
| happy birthday | 7 |
| so much | 6 |
| coming soon | 6 |
| we are | 6 |
| for the | 6 |
| i am | 6 |
| on the | 5 |
| see you | 5 |
| happy new | 5 |
| a nice | 5 |
| more info | 4 |
| to be | 4 |
| make up | 4 |
| you all | 4 |
| like share | 4 |

Table 13: Prevalence of common bigrams between languages

| Pattern | # Languages |
|---|---|
| !! | 18 |
| !!! | 18 |
| ... | 18 |
| ??? | 18 |
| :) | 18 |
| .. | 18 |
| :D | 17 |
| ?? | 16 |
| :( | 16 |
| *** | 16 |
| !. | 16 |
| ;) | 16 |
| !!!. | 15 |
| :-) | 15 |
| :’( | 15 |
| ). | 15 |
| ...!!! | 15 |
| ,,, | 15 |
| ...! | 14 |
| .( | 14 |
| ” | 14 |
| ,, | 14 |
| ...# | 13 |
| !!. | 13 |
| !... | 13 |

Table 14: Prevalence of common punctuation patterns between languages

| language | anger | anticipation | fear | joy | sadness | avg |
|---|---|---|---|---|---|---|
| eng | 0.11 | 0.58 | 0.02 | 0.56 | 0.23 | 0.30 |
| por | 0.11 | 0.41 | 0.01 | 0.60 | 0.40 | 0.31 |
| spa | 0.11 | 0.38 | 0.01 | 0.71 | 0.27 | 0.3 |
| cmn | 0.17 | 0.36 | 0.04 | 0.70 | 0.21 | 0.3 |
| tgl | 0.23 | 0.31 | 0.06 | 0.61 | 0.34 | 0.31 |
| avg | 0.15 | 0.41 | 0.03 | 0.64 | 0.29 | 0.30 |

Table 15: F1-scores for random baseline.

| language | anger | anticipation | fear | joy | sadness | avg |
|---|---|---|---|---|---|---|
| eng | 0.45 | 0.63 | 0.15 | 0.59 | 0.49 | 0.46 |
| por | 0.39 | 0.54 | 0.13 | 0.66 | 0.68 | 0.48 |
| spa | 0.25 | 0.44 | 0.29 | 0.71 | 0.46 | 0.43 |
| cmn | 0.67 | 0.47 | 0.86 | 0.75 | 0.61 | 0.67 |
| tgl | 0.47 | 0.45 | 0.52 | 0.65 | 0.55 | 0.53 |
| avg | 0.45 | 0.51 | 0.39 | 0.67 | 0.56 | 0.51 |

Table 16: F1-scores for mono-lingual classification.

| language | anger | anticipation | fear | joy | sadness | avg |
|---|---|---|---|---|---|---|
| eng | 0.42 | 0.65 | 0.24 | 0.58 | 0.49 | 0.47 |
| por | 0.28 | 0.54 | 0.00 | 0.61 | 0.55 | 0.4 |
| spa | 0.19 | 0.47 | 0.00 | 0.63 | 0.41 | 0.34 |
| cmn | 0.44 | 0.42 | 0.00 | 0.69 | 0.41 | 0.39 |
| tgl | 0.26 | 0.38 | 0.43 | 0.53 | 0.44 | 0.41 |
| avg | 0.32 | 0.49 | 0.13 | 0.61 | 0.46 | 0.40 |

Table 17: F1-scores for zero-shot multi-lingual classification

| language | anger | anticipation | fear | joy | sadness | avg |
|---|---|---|---|---|---|---|
| eng | 0.43 | 0.66 | 0.07 | 0.56 | 0.54 | 0.45 |
| por | 0.41 | 0.53 | 0.25 | 0.65 | 0.65 | 0.50 |
| spa | 0.33 | 0.49 | 0.18 | 0.72 | 0.53 | 0.45 |
| cmn | 0.63 | 0.47 | 0.89 | 0.77 | 0.62 | 0.67 |
| tgl | 0.51 | 0.45 | 0.65 | 0.64 | 0.57 | 0.56 |
| avg | 0.46 | 0.52 | 0.41 | 0.67 | 0.58 | 0.53 |

Table 18: F1-scores for cross-lingual classification

# FEEL-IT: Emotion and Sentiment Classification for the Italian Language

**Federico Bianchi*** Bocconi University Via Sarfatti 25, 20136 Milan, Italy f.bianchi@unibocconi.it

**Debora Nozza*** Bocconi University Via Sarfatti 25, 20136 Milan, Italy debora.nozza@unibocconi.it

**Dirk Hovy** Bocconi University Via Sarfatti 25, 20136 Milan, Italy dirk.hovy@unibocconi.it

## Abstract

Sentiment analysis is a common task to understand people's reactions online. Still, we often need more nuanced information: is the post negative because the user is angry or because they are sad? An abundance of approaches has been introduced for tackling both tasks. However, at least for Italian, they all treat only one of the tasks at a time. We introduce FEEL-IT, a novel benchmark corpus of Italian Twitter posts annotated with four basic emotions: *anger, fear, joy, sadness*. By collapsing them, we can also do sentiment analysis. We evaluate our corpus on benchmark datasets for both emotion and sentiment classification, obtaining competitive results. We release an open-source Python library, so researchers can use a model trained on FEEL-IT for inferring both sentiments and emotions from Italian text.

## 1 Introduction

Emotions shape our lives and the way we communicate. We can be happy, sad, or angry, and we can let others know of our emotional state through language. Thus, efficiently detecting emotion in text is essential for analyzing people's position towards a topic. Product and service companies frequently use emotion and sentiment data to inform advertising campaigns and measure customer satisfaction (Ahmad et al., 2020). Emotions have a central role in a political campaigns, and political discourse in particular (Huguet Cabot et al., 2020). Emotion and sentiment recognition can also aid in the critical decision-making process of crisis management or emergency scenarios (Stowe et al., 2016; Desai et al., 2020).

| *anger* | *fear* | *joy* | *sadness* | Total |
|---|---|---|---|---|
| 912 | 103 | 728 | 294 | 2037 |

Table 1: FEEL-IT corpus statistics.

Despite the huge interest of the Natural Language Processing community, the majority of benchmark datasets have been proposed for English (Calefato et al., 2017; Abdul-Mageed and Ungar, 2017; Akhtar et al., 2019, inter alia) showing a limited interest for other languages, such as German (Troiano et al., 2019), Chinese (Wang et al., 2018), Spanish (Navas-Loro and Rodríguez-Doncel, 2019), Italian (Barbieri et al., 2016; Sprugnoli, 2020), and multiple languages in shared tasks (Mohammad et al., 2018; Pontiki et al., 2016).a Moreover, they are usually collected either via hashtags and emojis for distant supervision (Abdul-Mageed and Ungar, 2017; Mohammad, 2012; Pak and Paroubek, 2010; Lamprinidis et al., 2021), or via very specific topics (Khanpour and Caragea, 2018; Chang et al., 2018; Nozza et al., 2017). The first causes noisy training data (Bing et al., 2015), the second results in highly domain-specific datasets.

This paper presents FEEL-IT, a novel benchmark corpus of Italian Twitter posts annotated with four basic emotions (Ekman, 1992): *anger, fear, joy, sadness.*[1] To the best of our knowledge, no other Italian dataset with a broad topic and domain coverage for emotion and sentiment classification exists. Beyond releasing benchmark results on FEEL-IT, we evaluate recent neural models trained on our corpus for emotion recognition

*Both authors contributed equally to this research and are ordered alphabetically.

[1]We focus on these emotions because they appear most frequently in text.



*Proceedings of the 11th Workshop on Computational Approaches to Subjectivity, Sentiment and Social Media Analysis*, pages 76–83
April 19, 2021. ©2021 Association for Computational Linguistics

| Example | Emotion |
|---|---|
| Pagliacci ammaestrati dal Grillo parlante di Pinocchio<br>*They are buffoons controlled by Pinocchio's Jiminy Cricket* | *anger* |
| Non ci sto dormendo la notte. #22Agosto #COVID19<br>*This does not make me sleep at night. #22August #COVID19* | *fear* |
| Adoro questa canzone, è una delle mie preferite STREAM ICARUS FALLS<br>*I love this song, it's one of my favourite STREAM ICARUS FALLS* | *joy* |
| I brividi. Come si può spegnere una vita con così tanta facilità? Non ho parole....<br>*I got chills. How can you kill someone so easily? I do not know what to say....* | *sadness* |

Table 2: Examples of FEEL-IT annotations. English translations are reported in italic.

on the MultiEmotions-It dataset (Sprugnoli, 2020). It contains comments on music videos and advertisements posted on YouTube and Facebook. We also test performance on sentiment classification by collapsing positive and negative emotions on the SENTIPOLC16 benchmark dataset (Barbieri et al., 2016). It comprises both general and political topics. The best-performing models are released as part of a Python library to foster and facilitate research on the topic.

**Contributions.** We present FEEL-IT, a new corpus on Italian tweets, annotated with four basic emotions (*anger*, *fear*, *joy*, *sadness*). We demonstrate that we can effectively predict sentiments and emotions in text by training prediction models on this corpus. We release an open-source Python library[2] that researchers can use to classify their text.

## 2 Data Collection and Annotation

We retrieved the data by monitoring trending topics each day between $20^{th}$ August to $12^{th}$ October 2020, using the Twitter API. For each day, we sampled 1000 tweets. This approach allowed us to get data from a range of different topics that span over many weeks.

The two first authors labeled the complete set of posts. Both are native Italian speakers with a strong NLP background. Eventually, the number of annotated tweets that contained an emotion was 2037 tweets (we removed tweets that did not contain any emotion, that is, most of them). This process involves a lot of data that has been discarded, and it is time-consuming, but the upside of it is that the collected tweets are from diverse domains and are high quality.

We computed our inter-rater agreement on a shared set of 220 tweets, annotated both with emotions and with *none* (i.e., no emotion found). We reached an agreement of 0.6 (Krippendorff's Alpha). Once *none* tweets were removed, the agreement on the remaining 68 annotated tweets was 0.8 (Krippendorff's Alpha).

**Corpus Analysis** Table 1 shows the label distribution of the FEEL-IT corpus for the four basic emotions considered. Examples for each class are shown in Table 2.

Similar to other realistic emotion classification datasets (Sprugnoli, 2020; Mohammad et al., 2018; Nozza et al., 2017; Mohammad, 2012), the dataset is imbalanced. The distribution is similar to the SemEval-2018 Task 1 dataset (Mohammad et al., 2018), where anger and joy account for the majority of tweets, and fear is the least frequent emotion.[3]

In FEEL-IT, topics vary both with respect to domains and time. Topic domains ranges from health (*#covid19*, *#mascherina/mask*) to sports (*#F1*, *#Juventus*), from social issues (*#scuola/school*) to TV shows (*#GFvip*, *#pomeriggio5*), from individuals (*#DiMaio*, *#Suarez*) to generic targets (*#negazionisti/negationists*). Each topic is associated with a time range that greatly varies with subject. TV shows are cited when they are broadcast, e.g., *#domenicalive*, literally *Sunday live* is mainly commented on Sunday. Some events, like soccer matches or celebrity birthdays, are mentioned only one day, e.g., the hashtag of the soccer match *#BeneventoInter* appears 371 times, but only the $31^{st}$ September. Tweets related to COVID-19 are present every observed day, with some peaks for specific events (e.g., on the $2^{nd}$ October, we recorded a peak of 132 tweets due to the news of US president Trump testing positive for COVID-19).

## 3 Experiments

We use experimental evaluation to (i) show that our classifier can predict emotions in tweets and (ii)

[2]https://github.com/MilaNLProc/feel-it

[3]Note that in other datasets, joy is the most frequent emotion, because of their focus on music or movies.

that FEEL-IT can also be used to perform sentiment classification with competitive results.

### 3.1 Emotion Classification

We first experiment with emotion recognition in the FEEL-IT dataset. Contextualized representations, such as BERT (Devlin et al., 2019) have obtained a lot of attention due to the great results (Rogers et al., 2021; Nozza et al., 2020) on multiple languages and on different tasks (Scarlini et al., 2020; Mass and Roitman, 2020; Du et al., 2020; Pasini et al., 2020; Peinelt et al., 2020; Bianchi et al., 2021; Nozza et al., 2021, inter alia). In this paper, we use the Italian BERT model UmBERTo trained on Commoncrawl ITA.[4] As the first experimental condition, we fine-tune the UmBERTo model for the task of emotion classification with the considered training data (*UmBERTo-FT*).

As additional experimental frameworks, we use three different approaches to represent tweets: (i) We collect pre-trained UmBERTo representations using average pooling of the last layer (*UmBERTo-PT*); (ii) we use an Italian word2vec model (*W2V*)[5] and create the representation of the tweet as the average of the word embeddings; (iii) we use a *TF-IDF* baseline with bi-grams to represent tweets. To make TF-IDF and W2V as competitive as possible, we apply a pre-processing pipeline to the text: (1) replace URLs and mentions with unique tokens; (2) replace emojis with a description of the emoji (Leonardelli et al., 2020), (3) split hashtags on camel case (#HappyBirthday becomes Happy Birthday); (4) remove punctuation. Given the representations, we use logistic regression with a softmax and with instance-weight balancing for classification. We test the models in a 10-fold cross-validation setting. We use the Most Frequent Class (*MFC*) as the baseline method.

**Results.** Table 3 reports Precision, Recall, F1-score, and Accuracy of the different tested models. First, we see that all the proposed models overcome the MFC baseline. Second, we observe that UmBERTo-FT is the model that obtains the best results in terms of the overall performance metrics.

We can draw further insights from the class-wise F1-score shown in Table 4. As expected, the emotion classes with the most training instances (*joy* and *fear*) are also the ones on which the classifiers perform best. Again, UmBERTo-FT is the model with the highest overall performance.

| Model | P | R | F1 | Acc |
|---|---|---|---|---|
| UmBERTo-FT | **0.72** | **0.73** | **0.71** | **0.82** |
| UmBERTo-PT | 0.64 | 0.67 | 0.65 | 0.76 |
| W2V | 0.57 | 0.62 | 0.58 | 0.76 |
| TF-IDF | **0.72** | 0.60 | 0.64 | 0.74 |
| MFC | 0.11 | 0.25 | 0.15 | 0.45 |

Table 3: Precision (P), Recall (R), F1-score (F1), and Accuracy (Acc) of the cross-validated emotion classification on FEEL-IT.

| Model | *anger* | *fear* | *joy* | *sadness* |
|---|---|---|---|---|
| UmBERTo-FT | **0.88** | **0.51** | **0.87** | **0.60** |
| UmBERTo-PT | 0.85 | 0.38 | 0.86 | 0.51 |
| W2V | 0.80 | 0.31 | 0.76 | 0.42 |
| TF-IDF | 0.80 | **0.51** | 0.80 | 0.46 |

Table 4: F1-score per class of the cross-validated emotion classification on FEEL-IT.

The only emotion for which UmBERTo-FT obtains lower equal to TF-IDF is *fear*. It should be noted that this is the least frequent class in the dataset and, therefore, the more difficult to capture. The different prediction behavior on this class is also why the large difference in precision in Table 3. Indeed, precision for the class *fear* is 0.76 for TF-IDF, 0.55 for UmBERTo-FT, and 0.33 for UmBERTo-PT, while recall is 0.38, 0.52, and 0.53, respectively. This discrepancy means that, while TF-IDF is more cautious on assigning the label *fear*, UmBERTo-FT and UmBERTo-PT have a high number of false positives (see Appendix B for confusion matrices). From a qualitative perspective, we see that many of these false-positive tweets could be associated with *fear*, even if the most prevalent emotion is *anger* or *sadness*. This correspondence indicates that tweet authors tend to communicate their fears by other, less intimate, emotions. Examples are "Siete un branco di egoisti che pensa solo al proprio, fregandosene di mettere a rischio la vita di tutti gli altri" (*You are a bunch of selfish people who only think about themselves, not caring about putting everyone else's life at risk*) and "Ogni giorno compilo il mio excel sulla situazione in Veneto...e ogni giorno lo chiudo pensando Speriamo che domani ci siano dati un po' più incoraggianti" (*Every day I fill an excel file on the situation in Veneto...and every day I close it thinking "Let's hope that tomorrow we are going to have more encouraging data"*).

[4]`https://github.com/musixmatchresearch/umberto`

[5]`http://vectors.nlpl.eu/repository/20/52.zip`, see (Fares et al., 2017)

| | Training data | P | R | F1 | Acc |
|---|---|---|---|---|---|
| FT | SP16 | 0.79 | **0.84** | 0.80 | 0.82 |
| | FEEL-IT | **0.82** | 0.80 | **0.81** | **0.84** |
| | SP16+FEEL-IT | 0.80 | **0.84** | **0.81** | 0.82 |
| PT | SP16 | 0.77 | 0.82 | 0.77 | 0.77 |
| | FEEL-IT | 0.81 | 0.80 | 0.80* | **0.84** |
| | SP16+FEEL-IT | 0.78 | 0.83 | 0.79 | 0.80 |

Table 5: Precision (P), Recall (R), F1-score (F1), and Accuracy (Acc) of sentiment classification on SENTIPOLC16 using UmBERTo-FT and UmBERTo-PT model. We tested the statistical significance of the *F1-score for UmBERTo-PT trained on FEEL-IT showing that it is significantly better than the one trained on SP16 (bootstrap sampling $p < 0.05$).

### 3.2 Sentiment Analysis

We test on SENTIPOLC16 (SP16) (Barbieri et al., 2016) to evaluate the performance of sentiment classification models trained on FEEL-IT. We collapsed the FEEL-IT classes into 2 by mapping *joy* to the *positive* class and *anger*, *fear* and *sadness* into the *negative* class. We use the fine-tuned UmBERTo model (*UmBERTo-FT*) and the logistic regression classifier applied to its representations (*UmBERTo-PT*).

SP16 also comes with a training set. We fit a classifier on this data to see whether it is better to train on FEEL-IT or SP16. Eventually, we also combine the two datasets to see if we can get the best of both worlds. SP16 comprises tweets that could be both positive and negative; in our experiment, we exclude the tweets that were labeled both positive and negative. Thus, SP16 training contains 4154 examples, while the test contains 1050 samples.

**Results.** Table 5 shows the results for the sentiment classification task. They demonstrate that our proposed corpus is useful for sentiment prediction. While FEEL-IT contains roughly half of the tweets that SP16 has, the performance obtained with FEEL-IT on the SP16 test set is the best. Interestingly, using a more sophisticated model (UmBERTo-FT) leads to narrowing the differences between performance. This result confirms that our dataset can 1) be used for sentiment analysis and 2) obtains state-of-the-art performances on the current benchmark for Italian sentiment analysis. Note that the combination between SP16 and FEEL-IT brings good recall, with a slight drop in Precision and F1-score.

| Model | Testing | P | R | F1 | Acc |
|---|---|---|---|---|---|
| UmBERTo-FT | ME | **0.56** | 0.59 | **0.57** | **0.73** |
| UmBERTo-PT | ME | **0.56** | **0.66** | **0.57** | 0.69 |
| MFC | ME | 0.16 | 0.25 | 0.20 | 0.64 |
| UmBERTo-FT | C19 | **0.56** | 0.56 | **0.56** | **0.69** |
| UmBERTo-PT | C19 | 0.53 | 0.53 | 0.50 | 0.60 |
| MFC | C19 | 0.15 | 0.25 | 0.19 | 0.60 |

Table 6: Precision (P), Recall (R), F1-score (F1), and Accuracy (Acc) of emotion recognition on use-cases using UmBERTo model.

## 4 Use-cases: COVID-19 and MultiEmotions-It

To further validate our approach, we showcase the results of emotion recognition models trained on FEEL-IT and tested on two topic-specific datasets: MultiEmotions-It (Sprugnoli, 2020) and a dataset of 662 tweets about COVID-19.

MultiEmotions-It (ME) (Sprugnoli, 2020) is a linguistic resource for Italian which comprises comments of music videos and advertisements posted on YouTube and Facebook. Each text is manually annotated according to four different dimensions: i.e., relatedness, opinion polarity, emotions, and sarcasm. This dataset differs from FEEL-IT both in terms of topic variety and considered social media. Among all the emotion classes considered in ME, we removed the ones not pertaining to our set of emotions. After this process, we are left with 304 comments.

As before, we pick UmBERTo-FT and UmBERTo-PT as our champion models. To give a point of reference, we also show the Most Frequent Class (MFC) baseline results.

**Results.** Table 6 shows that training on FEEL-IT brings stable performance even on datasets from different contexts. Note that the MFC accuracy is high because both datasets contain a wide range of emotions annotated as *anger*.

## 5 Related Work

Different works have explored emotion recognition approaches. However, few of them incorporate text in Italian. Indeed, currently, no general-purpose dataset for emotion recognition has been proposed for the Italian language. However, for Italian, there is a dataset for emotion recognition limited to Youtube and Facebook comments (Sprugnoli, 2020), and one for sentiment analysis SENTIPOLC16 (Barbieri et al., 2016). We used these datasets in the experimental evaluation to show that our model can also perform sentiment prediction.

Regarding other languages, Abdul-Mageed and Ungar (2017) proposes EmoNet, an English emotion dataset that has been collected using a keyword-based approach (e.g., tweets are retrieved using *#happy* as a marker for joy). The authors have obtained high accuracy with this dataset. Alternatevely, we approach the problem annotating manually and without using distant supervision. EmoTxt (Calefato et al., 2017) is an open-source toolkit for emotion prediction supporting prediction for different emotions for the English language: love, joy, surprise, anger, sadness, and fear. Nozza et al. (2017) propose a English corpus of tweets that comprises five different views for each message, i.e. subjective/objective, sentiment polarity, implicit/explicit, irony, emotion. Lamprinidis et al. (2021) introduce a novel dataset that covers multiple languages extracted from Facebook posts. Troiano et al. (2019) introduce a dataset in two languages, English and German, obtained through crowd-sourcing. Interestingly, Akhtar et al. (2019) propose a multi-model architecture that combines visual, auditory, and text information for both emotion and sentiment prediction in English.

## 6 Conclusions

We present FEEL-IT, a new corpus for emotion classification on Italian Twitter data, and release an open-source Python library to run both emotion and sentiment classification. Future work will focus on the extension of this dataset, considering other emotions and languages.

## Acknowledgments

The authors are members of the Data and Marketing Insights research unit in the Bocconi Institute for Data Science and Analysis.

## References

Muhammad Abdul-Mageed and Lyle Ungar. 2017. EmoNet: Fine-grained emotion detection with gated recurrent neural networks. In *Proceedings of the 55th Annual Meeting of the Association for Computational Linguistics (Volume 1: Long Papers)*, pages 718–728, Vancouver, Canada. Association for Computational Linguistics.

Zishan Ahmad, Raghav Jindal, Asif Ekbal, and Pushpak Bhattachharyya. 2020. Borrow from rich cousin: transfer learning for emotion detection using cross lingual embedding. *Expert Systems with Applications*, 139:112851.

Md Shad Akhtar, Dushyant Chauhan, Deepanway Ghosal, Soujanya Poria, Asif Ekbal, and Pushpak Bhattacharyya. 2019. Multi-task learning for multimodal emotion recognition and sentiment analysis. In *Proceedings of the 2019 Conference of the North American Chapter of the Association for Computational Linguistics: Human Language Technologies, Volume 1 (Long and Short Papers)*, pages 370–379, Minneapolis, Minnesota. Association for Computational Linguistics.

Francesco Barbieri, Valerio Basile, Danilo Croce, M. Nissim, N. Novielli, and V. Patti. 2016. Overview of the Evalita 2016 SENTIment POLarity Classification Task. In *CLiC-it/EVALITA*.

Emily M. Bender and Batya Friedman. 2018. Data statements for natural language processing: Toward mitigating system bias and enabling better science. *Transactions of the Association for Computational Linguistics*, 6:587–604.

Federico Bianchi, Silvia Terragni, Dirk Hovy, Debora Nozza, and Elisabetta Fersini. 2021. Cross-lingual Contextualized Topic Models with Zero-shot Learning. In *Proceedings of the Conference of the European Chapter of the Association for Computational Linguistics*.

Lidong Bing, Sneha Chaudhari, Richard Wang, and William Cohen. 2015. Improving distant supervision for information extraction using label propagation through lists. In *Proceedings of the 2015 Conference on Empirical Methods in Natural Language Processing*, pages 524–529, Lisbon, Portugal. Association for Computational Linguistics.

Fabio Calefato, Filippo Lanubile, and Nicole Novielli. 2017. Emotxt: a toolkit for emotion recognition from text. In *Proceedings of the Seventh International Conference on Affective Computing and Intelligent Interaction Workshops and Demos (ACIIW)*, pages 79–80. IEEE.

Serina Chang, Ruiqi Zhong, Ethan Adams, Fei-Tzin Lee, Siddharth Varia, Desmond Patton, William Frey, Chris Kedzie, and Kathy McKeown. 2018. Detecting gang-involved escalation on social media using context. In *Proceedings of the 2018 Conference on Empirical Methods in Natural Language Processing*, pages 46–56, Brussels, Belgium. Association for Computational Linguistics.

Shrey Desai, Cornelia Caragea, and Junyi Jessy Li. 2020. Detecting perceived emotions in hurricane disasters. In *Proceedings of the 58th Annual Meeting of the Association for Computational Linguistics*, pages 5290–5305, Online. Association for Computational Linguistics.

Jacob Devlin, Ming-Wei Chang, Kenton Lee, and Kristina Toutanova. 2019. BERT: Pre-training of deep bidirectional transformers for language understanding. In *Proceedings of the 2019 Conference of the North American Chapter of the Association for Computational Linguistics: Human Language Technologies, Volume 1 (Long and Short Papers)*, pages 4171–4186, Minneapolis, Minnesota. Association for Computational Linguistics.

Chunning Du, Haifeng Sun, Jingyu Wang, Qi Qi, and Jianxin Liao. 2020. Adversarial and domain-aware BERT for cross-domain sentiment analysis. In *Proceedings of the 58th Annual Meeting of the Association for Computational Linguistics*, pages 4019–4028, Online. Association for Computational Linguistics.

Paul Ekman. 1992. An argument for basic emotions. *Cognition and Emotion*, 6(3-4):169–200.

Murhaf Fares, Andrey Kutuzov, Stephan Oepen, and Erik Velldal. 2017. Word vectors, reuse, and replicability: Towards a community repository of large-text resources. In *Proceedings of the 21st Nordic Conference on Computational Linguistics*, pages 271–276, Gothenburg, Sweden. Association for Computational Linguistics.

Pere-Lluís Huguet Cabot, Verna Dankers, David Abadi, Agneta Fischer, and Ekaterina Shutova. 2020. The Pragmatics behind Politics: Modelling Metaphor, Framing and Emotion in Political Discourse. In *Findings of the Association for Computational Linguistics: EMNLP 2020*, pages 4479–4488, Online. Association for Computational Linguistics.

Hamed Khanpour and Cornelia Caragea. 2018. Fine-grained emotion detection in health-related online posts. In *Proceedings of the 2018 Conference on Empirical Methods in Natural Language Processing*, pages 1160–1166, Brussels, Belgium. Association for Computational Linguistics.

Sotiris Lamprinidis, Federico Bianchi, Daniel Hardt, and Dirk Hovy. 2021. Universal Joy: A Data Set and Results for Classifying Emotions Across Languages. In *Proceedings of the Workshop on Computational Approaches to Subjectivity, Sentiment and Social Media Analysis*. Association for Computational Linguistics.

Elisa Leonardelli, Stefano Menini, and Sara Tonelli. 2020. DH-FBK @ haspeede2: Italian hate speech detection via self-training and oversampling. In *Proceedings of the Seventh Evaluation Campaign of Natural Language Processing and Speech Tools for Italian. Final Workshop (EVALITA 2020), Online event, December 17th, 2020*, volume 2765 of *CEUR Workshop Proceedings*. CEUR-WS.org.

Yosi Mass and Haggai Roitman. 2020. Ad-hoc document retrieval using weak-supervision with BERT and GPT2. In *Proceedings of the 2020 Conference on Empirical Methods in Natural Language Processing (EMNLP)*, pages 4191–4197, Online. Association for Computational Linguistics.

Saif Mohammad. 2012. #emotional tweets. In **SEM 2012: The First Joint Conference on Lexical and Computational Semantics – Volume 1: Proceedings of the main conference and the shared task, and Volume 2: Proceedings of the Sixth International Workshop on Semantic Evaluation (SemEval 2012)*, pages 246–255, Montréal, Canada. Association for Computational Linguistics.

Saif Mohammad, Felipe Bravo-Marquez, Mohammad Salameh, and Svetlana Kiritchenko. 2018. Semeval-2018 task 1: Affect in tweets. In *Proceedings of the 12th international workshop on semantic evaluation*, pages 1–17.

María Navas-Loro and Víctor Rodríguez-Doncel. 2019. Spanish corpora for sentiment analysis: a survey. *Language Resources and Evaluation*, pages 1–38.

Debora Nozza, Federico Bianchi, and Dirk Hovy. 2020. What the [MASK]? Making Sense of Language-specific BERT Models. *arXiv preprint arXiv:2003.02912*.

Debora Nozza, Elisabetta Fersini, and Enza Messina. 2017. A multi-view sentiment corpus. In *Proceedings of the 15th Conference of the European Chapter of the Association for Computational Linguistics: Volume 1, Long Papers*, pages 273–280, Valencia, Spain. Association for Computational Linguistics.

Debora Nozza, Pikakshi Manchanda, Elisabetta Fersini, Matteo Palmonari, and Enza Messina. 2021. LearningToAdapt with word embeddings: Domain adaptation of Named Entity Recognition systems. *Information Processing & Management*, 58(3):102537.

Alexander Pak and Patrick Paroubek. 2010. Twitter as a corpus for sentiment analysis and opinion mining. In *Proceedings of the Seventh conference on International Language Resources and Evaluation (LREC'10)*, Valletta, Malta. European Languages Resources Association (ELRA).

Tommaso Pasini, Federico Scozzafava, and Bianca Scarlini. 2020. CluBERT: A cluster-based approach for learning sense distributions in multiple languages. In *Proceedings of the 58th Annual Meeting of the Association for Computational Linguistics*, pages 4008–4018, Online. Association for Computational Linguistics.

Nicole Peinelt, Dong Nguyen, and Maria Liakata. 2020. tBERT: Topic models and BERT joining forces for semantic similarity detection. In *Proceedings of the 58th Annual Meeting of the Association for Computational Linguistics*, pages 7047–7055, Online. Association for Computational Linguistics.

Maria Pontiki, Dimitris Galanis, Haris Papageorgiou, Ion Androutsopoulos, Suresh Manandhar, Mohammad AL-Smadi, Mahmoud Al-Ayyoub, Yanyan Zhao, Bing Qin, Orphée De Clercq, Véronique Hoste, Marianna Apidianaki, Xavier Tannier, Natalia Loukachevitch, Evgeniy Kotelnikov, Nuria Bel, Salud María Jiménez-Zafra, and Gülşen Eryiğit.

2016. SemEval-2016 task 5: Aspect based sentiment analysis. In *Proceedings of the 10th International Workshop on Semantic Evaluation (SemEval-2016)*, pages 19–30, San Diego, California. Association for Computational Linguistics.

Anna Rogers, Olga Kovaleva, and Anna Rumshisky. 2021. A primer in bertology: What we know about how bert works. *Transactions of the Association for Computational Linguistics*, 8:842–866.

Bianca Scarlini, Tommaso Pasini, and Roberto Navigli. 2020. With more contexts comes better performance: Contextualized sense embeddings for all-round word sense disambiguation. In *Proceedings of the 2020 Conference on Empirical Methods in Natural Language Processing (EMNLP)*, pages 3528–3539, Online. Association for Computational Linguistics.

Rachele Sprugnoli. 2020. Multiemotions-it: a new dataset for opinion polarity and emotion analysis for italian. In *Proceedings of the Seventh Italian Conference on Computational Linguistics, CLiC-it 2020, Bologna, Italy, March 1-3, 2021*, volume 2769 of *CEUR Workshop Proceedings*. CEUR-WS.org.

Kevin Stowe, Michael J. Paul, Martha Palmer, Leysia Palen, and Kenneth Anderson. 2016. Identifying and categorizing disaster-related tweets. In *Proceedings of The Fourth International Workshop on Natural Language Processing for Social Media*, pages 1–6, Austin, TX, USA. Association for Computational Linguistics.

Enrica Troiano, Sebastian Padó, and Roman Klinger. 2019. Crowdsourcing and validating event-focused emotion corpora for German and English. In *Proceedings of the 57th Annual Meeting of the Association for Computational Linguistics*, pages 4005–4011.

Zhongqing Wang, Shoushan Li, Fan Wu, Qingying Sun, and Guodong Zhou. 2018. Overview of nlpcc 2018 shared task 1: Emotion detection in code-switching text. In *CCF International Conference on Natural Language Processing and Chinese Computing*, pages 429–433. Springer.

## A Data Statement

We follow Bender and Friedman (2018) on providing a Data Statement for the proposed FEEL-IT corpus.

Data has been annotated by two native Italian speakers, age group in 25-35, both with experience in computational linguistics. The data we share is not sensitive to personal information, as it does not contain information about individuals. Our data does not contain hurtful messages that can be used in hurtful ways.

## B Additional results

As follows, we show the confusion matrices for UmBERTo-FT (Figure 1), UmBERTo-PT (Figure 2) and TF-IDF (Figure 3) representation models for the experiments in emotion recognition task with 10-fold cross validation on FEEL-IT.

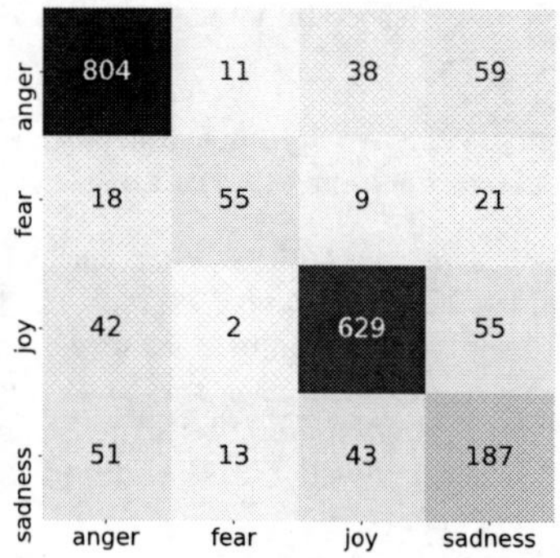


Figure 1: Confusion matrix of UmBERTo-FT predictions of cross-validated emotion classification on FEEL-IT.

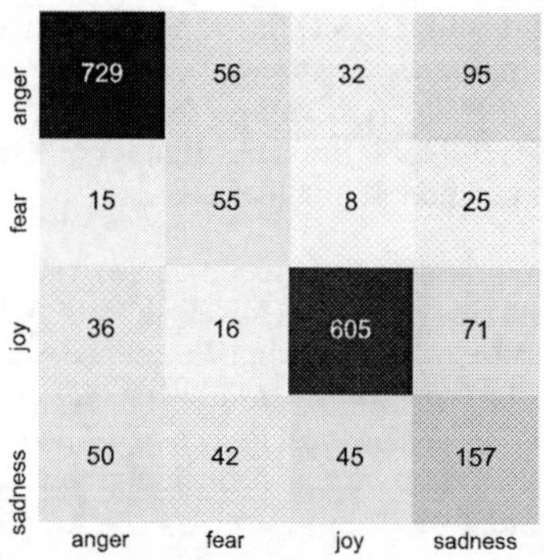


Figure 2: Confusion matrix of UmBERTo-PT predictions of cross-validated emotion classification on FEEL-IT.

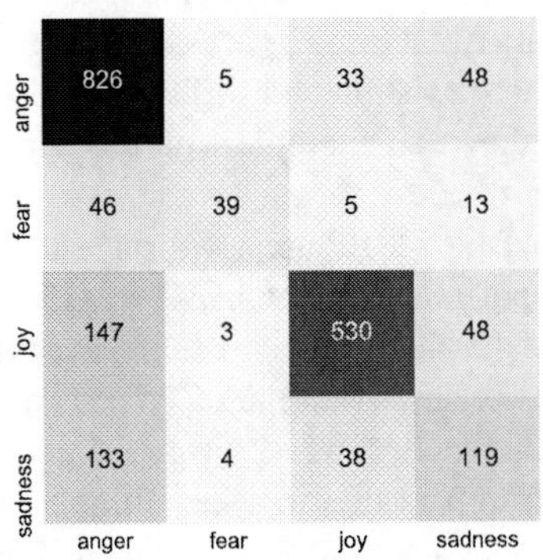


Figure 3: Confusion matrix of TF-IDF predictions of cross-validated emotion classification on FEEL-IT.

# An End-to-End Network for Emotion-Cause Pair Extraction

**Aaditya Singh**[*†] **Shreeshail Hingane**[†] **Saim Wani**[†] **Ashutosh Modi**
Indian Institute of Technology Kanpur (IIT Kanpur)
{aadisin, shreessh, saim}@iitk.ac.in
ashutoshm@cse.iitk.ac.in

## Abstract

The task of Emotion-Cause Pair Extraction (ECPE) aims to extract all potential clause-pairs of emotions and their corresponding causes in a document. Unlike the more well-studied task of Emotion Cause Extraction (ECE), ECPE does not require the emotion clauses to be provided as annotations. Previous works on ECPE have either followed a multi-stage approach where emotion extraction, cause extraction, and pairing are done independently or use complex architectures to resolve its limitations. In this paper, we propose an end-to-end model for the ECPE task. Due to the unavailability of an English language ECPE corpus, we adapt the NTCIR-13 ECE corpus and establish a baseline for the ECPE task on this dataset. On this dataset, the proposed method produces significant performance improvements ($\sim 6.5\%$ increase in F1 score) over the multi-stage approach and achieves comparable performance to the state of the art methods.

## 1 Introduction

There have been several works on emotions prediction from the text (Alswaidan and Menai, 2020; Witon et al., 2018) as well as generating emotion oriented texts (Ghosh et al., 2017; Colombo et al., 2019; Modi et al., 2020; Goswamy et al., 2020). However, recently the focus has also shifted to finding out the underlying cause(s) that lead to the emotion expressed in the text. In this respect, Gui et al. (2016) proposed the Emotion Cause Extraction (ECE), a task aimed at detecting the cause behind a given emotion annotation. The task is defined as a clause level classification problem. The text is divided at the clause level and the task is to detect the clause containing the cause, given the clause containing the emotion. However, the applicability of models solving the ECE problem is limited by the fact that emotion annotations are required at test time. More recently, Xia and Ding (2019) introduced the Emotion-Cause Pair Extraction (ECPE) task i.e. extracting all possible emotion-cause clause pairs in a document with no emotion annotations. Thus, ECPE opens up avenues for applications of real-time sentiment-cause analysis in tweets and product reviews. ECPE builds on the existing and well studied ECE task. Figure 1 shows an example with ground truth annotations.

Xia and Ding (2019) use a two-stage architecture to extract potential emotion-cause clauses. In Stage 1, the model extracts a set of emotion clauses and a set of cause clauses (not mutually exclusive) from the document. In Stage 2, it performs emotion-cause pairing and filtering, i.e. eliminating pairs that the model predicts as an invalid emotion-cause pair. However, this fails to fully capture the mutual dependence between emotion and cause clauses since clause extraction happens in isolation from the pairing step. Thus, the model is never optimized using the overall task as the objective. Also, certain emotion clauses are likely not to be detected without the corresponding cause clauses as the context for that emotion. Recent methods such as Ding et al. (2020a) and Ding et al. (2020b) use complex encoder and classifier architectures to resolve these limitations of the multi-stage method.

In this paper, we propose an end-to-end model to explicitly demonstrate the effectiveness of joint training on the ECPE task. The proposed model attempts to take into account the mutual interdependence between emotion and cause clauses. Based on the benchmark English-language corpus used in the ECE task of the NTCIR-13 workshop (Gao et al., 2017), we evaluate our approach on this dataset after adapting it for the ECPE task. We demonstrate that the proposed approach works sig-

[*] Currently affiliated with IBM Research
[†] Authors equally contributed



*Proceedings of the 11th Workshop on Computational Approaches to Subjectivity, Sentiment and Social Media Analysis*, pages 84–91
April 19, 2021. ©2021 Association for Computational Linguistics

| | |
|---|---|
| `Clause 1:` | Adele arrived at her apartment late in the afternoon after a long day of work. |
| `Clause 2:` | She was still furious with her husband for not remembering her 40th birthday. |
| `Clause 3:` | As soon as she unlocked the door, she gasped with surprise; |
| `Clause 4:` | Mikhael and Harriet had organized a huge party for her. |

Figure 1: An example document. The above example contains two emotion-cause pairs. Clause 2 is an emotion clause (*furious*) and is also the corresponding cause clause (*for not remembering her 40th birthday*). Clause 3 is an emotion clause (*surprise*) and Clause 4 is its corresponding cause clause (*organized a huge party for her*).

nificantly better than the multi-stage method and achieves comparable performance to the state of the art methods. We also show that when used for the ECE task by providing ground truth emotion annotations, our model beats the state of the art performance of ECE models on the introduced corpus. We provide the dataset and implementations of our models via GitHub[1].

## 2 Related Work

The problem of Emotion Cause Extraction (ECE) has been studied extensively over the past decade. ECE was initially proposed as a word-level sequence detection problem in Lee et al. (2010). Attempts to solve this task focused on either classical machine learning techniques (Ghazi et al., 2015), or on rule-based methods (Neviarouskaya and Aono, 2013; Gao et al., 2015). Subsequently, the problem was reframed as a clause-level classification problem (Chen et al., 2010) and the Chinese-language dataset introduced by Gui et al. (2016) has since become the benchmark dataset for ECE and the task has been an active area of research (Xia et al., 2019; Gui et al., 2017; Yu et al., 2019; Li et al., 2018, 2019; Fan et al., 2019).

However, the main limitation of ECE remains that it requires emotion annotations even during test time, which severely limits the applicability of ECE models. To address this, Xia and Ding (2019) introduced a new task called emotion-cause pair extraction (ECPE), which extracts both emotion and its cause without requiring the emotion annotation. They demonstrated the results of their two-stage architecture on the benchmark Chinese language ECE corpus (Gui et al., 2016). Following their work, several works have been proposed to address the limitations of the two-stage architecture (Ding et al. (2020a), Ding et al. (2020b), Fan et al. (2020), Yuan et al. (2020), Cheng et al. (2020), Chen et al. (2020)) . In order to explore the corpus further and to encourage future work from a broader community, we use an English language ECE corpus. (see section 5).

## 3 Task Definition

Formally, a document consists of text that is segmented into an ordered set of clauses D $= [c_1, c_2, ..., c_d]$ and the ECPE task aims to extract a set of emotion-cause pairs P $= \{..., (c_i, c_j), ...\}$ $(c_i, c_j \in$ D), where $c_i$ is an emotion clause and $c_j$ is the corresponding cause clause. In the ECE task, we are additionally given the annotations of emotion clauses and the goal is to detect (one or more) clauses containing the cause for each emotion clause.

## 4 Approach

We propose an end-to-end emotion cause pairs extraction model (Figure 2), henceforth referred to as $\texttt{E2E-PExt}_{\texttt{E}}$ (refer to section 6 for the naming convention). The model takes an entire document as its input and computes, for each ordered pair of clauses $(c_i, c_j)$, the probability of being a potential emotion-cause pair. To facilitate the learning of suitable clause representations required for this *primary* task, we train the model on two other *auxiliary* tasks: Emotion Detection and Cause Detection.

We propose a hierarchical architecture. Word level representations are used to obtain clausal representations (vi BiLSTM) and clause level representations are further *contextualized* using another BiLSTM network. The resulting contextualized clause representations are then used for the classification task. Let $\mathbf{w}_i^j$ represent the vector representation of the $j^{th}$ word in the $i^{th}$ clause. Each clause $\mathbf{c}_i$ in the document $d$ is passed through a *word-level* encoder (BiLSTM + Attention (Bahdanau et al., 2015)) to obtain the clause representation $\mathbf{s}_i$. The clause embeddings are then fed into two separate *clause-level* encoders (`Emotion-Encoder` and `Cause-Encoder`) each of which corresponds, respectively, to the two auxiliary tasks. The purpose of the clause-level encoders is to help learn

[1] `https://github.com/Aaditya-Singh/E2E-ECPE`

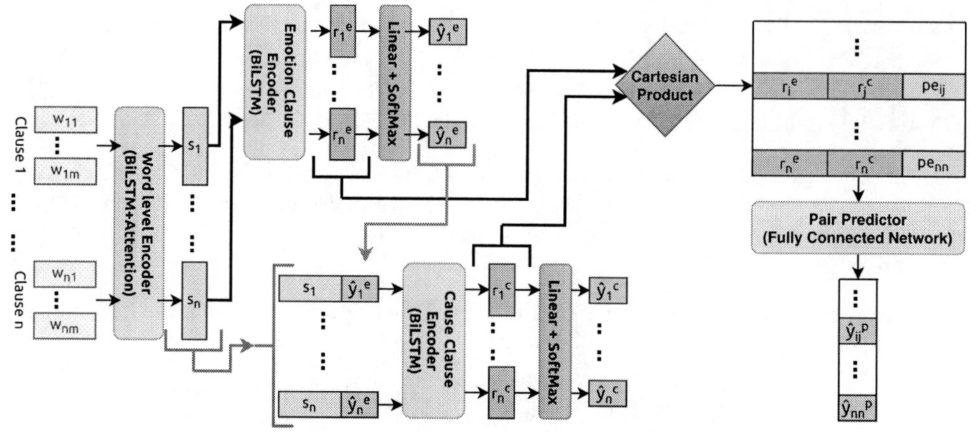

Figure 2: End-to-End network (E2E-PExt$_E$)

*contextualized* clause representations by incorporating context from the neighboring clauses in the document. For each clause $c_i$, we obtain its contextualized representations $\mathbf{r}_i^e$ and $\mathbf{r}_i^c$ by passing it through a BiLSTM network.

For the clause $c_i$, its contextual representations $\mathbf{r}_i^e$ and $\mathbf{r}_i^c$ are then used to predict whether the clause is an emotion-clause and a cause-clause respectively, i.e.,

$$\hat{\mathbf{y}}_i^e = \text{softmax}(\mathbf{W}^e * \mathbf{r}_i^e + \mathbf{b}^e); \quad (1)$$

$$\hat{\mathbf{y}}_i^c = \text{softmax}(\mathbf{W}^c * \mathbf{r}_i^c + \mathbf{b}^c) \quad (2)$$

As observed by Xia and Ding (2019), we also noticed that performance on the two auxiliary tasks could be improved if done in an interactive manner rather than independently. Hence, the `Cause-Encoder` also makes use of the corresponding emotion-detection prediction $\mathbf{y}_i^e$, when generating $\mathbf{r}_i^c$ (Figure 2).

For the primary task, every ordered pair $(c_i, c_j)$ is represented by concatenating $\mathbf{r}_i^e$, $\mathbf{r}_j^c$ and $\mathbf{pe}_{ij}$, wherein $\mathbf{pe}_{ij}$ is the positional embedding vector representing the relative positioning between the two clauses $i, j$ in the document (Shaw et al., 2018).

The primary task is solved by passing this pair-representation through a fully-connected neural network to get the pair-predictions.

$$\mathbf{r}_{ij}^p = [\mathbf{r}_i^e \oplus \mathbf{r}_j^c \oplus \mathbf{pe}_{ij}]; \quad (3)$$

$$\mathbf{h}_{ij}^p = \text{ReLU}(\mathbf{W}^{p_1} * \mathbf{r}_{ij}^p + \mathbf{b}^{p_1}); \quad (4)$$

$$\hat{\mathbf{y}}_{ij}^p = \text{softmax}(\mathbf{W}^{p_2} * \mathbf{h}_{ij}^p + \mathbf{b}^{p_2}) \quad (5)$$

To train the end-to-end model, loss function is set as the weighted sum of loss on the primary task as well as the two auxiliary tasks i.e. $L^{\text{total}} = \lambda_c * L^c + \lambda_e * L^e + \lambda_p * L^p$, where $L^e$, $L^c$, and $L^p$ are cross-entropy errors for emotion, cause and pair predictions respectively. Further, $L^p = L^{pos} + loss\_weight * L^{neg}$, where $L^{pos}$ and $L^{neg}$ are the errors attributed to positive and negative examples respectively. We use hyperparameter $loss\_weight$ to scale down $L^{neg}$, since there are far more negative examples than positive ones in the primary pairing task.

## 5 Corpus/Data Description

We adapt an existing Emotion-Cause Extraction (ECE) (Fan et al., 2019; Li et al., 2019) corpus for evaluating our proposed models (as well as the architectures proposed in previous work). The corpus was introduced in the NTCIR-13 Workshop (Gao et al., 2017) for the ECE challenge.

The corpus consists of 2843 documents taken from several English novels. Each document is annotated with the following information: i) emotion-cause pairs present in the document, that is, the set of emotion clauses and their corresponding cause clauses; ii) emotion category of each clause; and iii) the keyword within the clause denoting the labeled emotion. We do not use the emotion category or the keyword during training of either ECE or ECPE tasks only the emotion-cause pairs are used. At test time, none of the annotations are used for the ECPE task. For ECE task, emotion annotation is provided at test time and the model predicts the corresponding cause clauses. 80%-10%-10% splits are used for training, validation and testing. 10 such randomly generated splits are used to get statistically significant results, and the average results are reported.

| | Emotion Extraction | | | Cause Extraction | | | Pair Extraction | | |
|---|---|---|---|---|---|---|---|---|---|
| | Precision | Recall | F1 Score | Precision | Recall | F1 Score | Precision | Recall | F1 Score |
| `ECPE 2-stage` (Xia and Ding, 2019) | 67.41 | 71.60 | 69.40 | 60.39 | 47.34 | 53.01 | 46.94 | 41.02 | 43.67 |
| `ECPE-2D(BERT)` (Ding et al., 2020a) | 74.35 | 69.68 | 71.89 | 64.91 | 53.53 | 58.55 | 60.49 | 43.84 | 50.73 |
| `ECPE-MLL(ISML-6)` (Ding et al., 2020b) | 75.46 | 69.96 | 72.55 | 63.50 | 59.19 | 61.10 | 59.26 | 45.30 | 51.21 |
| `E2E-PExt`$_E$ (Ours) | 71.63 | 67.49 | 69.43 | 66.36 | 43.75 | 52.26 | 51.34 | 49.29 | 50.17 |
| `RHNN` (Fan et al., 2019) | - | - | - | - | - | - | 69.01 | 52.67 | 59.75 |
| `E2E-CExt` (Ours) | - | - | - | - | - | - | 65.21 | 66.18 | **65.63** |

Table 1: Experimental results comparing our models with the already existing benchmarks. The top half compares our model for ECPE (`E2E-PExt`$_E$) against the existing benchmarks. The bottom half compares existing ECE benchmark on this dataset against our model (`E2E-CExt`). Note that the Pair Extraction task in ECPE with true-emotion provided reduces to the Cause Extraction task of ECE. The results on `RHNN` and `E2E-CExt` are only for the primary task, since in the ECE setting, there are no auxiliary tasks. The evaluation metrics are same as the ones used in previous works.

## 6 Experiments and Results

**Naming Scheme for Model Variants:**
`E2E`: End to End.
`PExt/CExt/EExt`: Pair Extraction/ Cause Extraction/ Emotion Extraction.
Subscript `E/C`: represents how the auxiliary tasks are solved interactively (emotion predictions used for cause detection or vice versa).

For the purpose of evaluation on our dataset, we reproduced the two-stage model: `ECPE 2-stage` (Xia and Ding, 2019). We also adapted two models that achieve state of the art performance on the ECPE task: `ECPE-2D(BERT)` (Ding et al., 2020a) and `ECPE-MLL(ISML-6)` (Ding et al., 2020b) and compared them against our model: `E2E-PExt`$_E$. The model is trained for 15 epochs using Adam optimizer (Kingma and Ba, 2014). The learning rate and batch size were set to 0.005 and 32 respectively. Model weights and biases were initialized by sampling from a uniform distribution U$(-0.10, 0.10)$. GloVe word embeddings (Pennington et al., 2014) of 200 dimension are used. For regularization, we set the dropout rate to 0.8 for word embeddings and L2 weight decay of 1e-5 over softmax parameters. We set $\lambda_c : \lambda_e : \lambda_p = 1 : 1 : 2.5$. The values chosen through grid search on the hyperparameter space reflect the higher importance of the primary pair detection task compared to the auxiliary tasks. To obtain better positional embeddings which encode the relative positioning between clauses, we trained randomly initialized embeddings after setting the clipping distance (Shaw et al., 2018) to 10 all clauses that have a distance of 10 or more between them have the same positional embedding.

We use the same evaluation metrics (precision, recall and F1-score), as used in the past work on ECE and ECPE tasks. Following Xia and Ding (2019), the metric definitions are defined as:

$$P = \frac{\#correct\_pairs}{\#proposed\_pairs}$$
$$R = \frac{\#correct\_pairs}{\#annotated\_pairs}$$
$$F1 = \frac{2 * P * R}{P + R}$$

where,

$\#proposed\_pairs$ = no. of emotion-cause pairs predicted by model
$\#correct\_pairs$ = number of emotion-cause pairs predicted *correctly* by the model
$\#annotated\_pairs$ = total number of actual emotion-cause pairs in the data

$P, R, F1$ for the two auxiliary classification tasks (emotion-detection and cause-detection) have the usual definition (see Gui et al. (2016)).

The results are summarized in Table 1. Our model `E2E-PExt`$_E$ outperforms `ECPE 2-stage` on the task of emotion-cause pair extraction by a significant margin of 6.5%. This explicitly demonstrates that an end-to-end model works much better since it leverages the mutual dependence between the emotion and cause clauses. As shown in Table 1, our model achieves comparable performance to the highly parameterized and complex models `ECPE-2D(BERT)` and `ECPE-MLL(ISML-6)` (which either leverage a pre-trained BERT (Devlin et al., 2019) and 2D Transformer (Vaswani et al., 2017) or iterative BiLSTM encoder). To further demonstrate this point, we compare the number of trainable parameters across models in Table 2.

| Method | Trainable parameters |
|---|---|
| `E2E-PExt`$_E$ | 790,257 |
| `ECPE-2D(BERT)` | 1,064,886 |
| `ECPE-MLL(ISML-6)` | 6,370,452 |

Table 2: Comparison of trainable parameters of our model (`E2E-PExt`$_E$) with the state-of-the-art models (`ECPE-2D(BERT)` and `ECPE-MLL(ISML-6)`). We achieve comparable performance with these models with fewer parameters and simpler architecture.

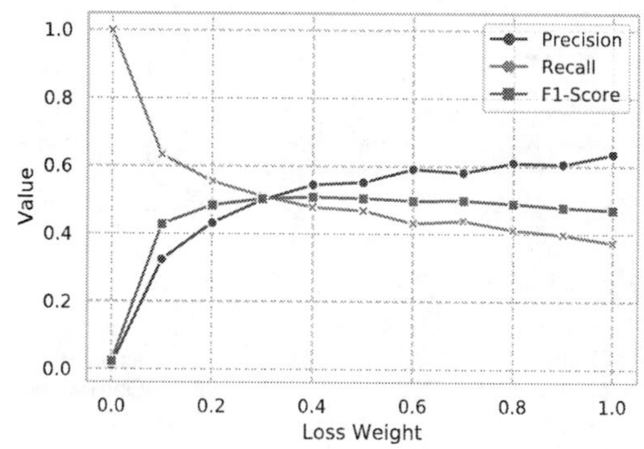


Figure 3: Precision, Recall and F1 Score as a function of weight assigned to negative examples.

We also evaluate our model on the ECE task. For this, we use a variant of `E2E-PExt`$_E$ i.e. `E2E-CExt`, so that it utilizes the emotion annotations. Specifically, we incorporate the knowledge of emotion annotations by incorporating them into the `Cause-Encoder` as well as the `Pair-Prediction-Module` and show that this improves performance in both the primary pair prediction task as well as the auxiliary cause detection task (appendix section A). `E2E-CExt` outperforms the state of the art model `RHNN`: (Fan et al., 2019) on the ECE task. This is indicative of the generalization capability of our model and further demonstrates that performance on ECPE can be enhanced with improvements in the quality of emotion predictions.

### 6.1 Ablation Experiments

We analyzed the effect of different components of the model on performance via ablation experiments. We present some notable results below. More results are presented in the Appendix.

**Positional Embeddings:** For finding the extent to which positional embeddings affect the performance, we train `E2E-PExt`$_E$ without positional embeddings. This resulted in a slight drop in validation F1 score from 51.34 to 50.74, which suggests that the network is robust to withstanding the loss of distance information at the clause-level.

**Loss Weighting:** To handle the problem of data imbalance, we varied loss weight. We observed (Figure 3) that assigning less weight to the negative examples leads to more predicted positives, and hence a better recall but worse precision.

## 7 Conclusion

In this paper, we demonstrated that a simple end-to-end model can achieve competitive performance on the ECPE task by leveraging the inherent correlation between emotions and their causes and optimizing directly on the overall objective. We also showed that a variant of our model which further uses emotion annotations, outperforms the previously best performing model on the ECE task, thereby showing its applicability to variety of related tasks involving emotion analysis. In future, we plan on developing a larger benchmark English-language dataset for the ECPE task. We plan to explore other model-architectures which we expect will help us learn richer representations for causality detection in clause-pairs.

## References


Nourah Alswaidan and Mohamed El Bachir Menai. 2020. A survey of state-of-the-art approaches for emotion recognition in text. *Knowledge and Information Systems*, pages 1–51.

Dzmitry Bahdanau, Kyunghyun Cho, and Yoshua Bengio. 2015. Neural machine translation by jointly learning to align and translate. In *3rd International Conference on Learning Representations, ICLR 2015*.

Xinhong Chen, Qing Li, and Jianping Wang. 2020. A unified sequence labeling model for emotion cause pair extraction. In *Proceedings of the 28th International Conference on Computational Linguistics*, pages 208–218.

Ying Chen, Sophia Yat Mei Lee, Shoushan Li, and Chu-Ren Huang. 2010. Emotion cause detection with linguistic constructions. In *Proceedings of the 23rd International Conference on Computational Linguistics (Coling 2010)*, pages 179–187.

Zifeng Cheng, Zhiwei Jiang, Yafeng Yin, Hua Yu, and Qing Gu. 2020. A symmetric local search network for emotion-cause pair extraction. In *Proceedings of the 28th International Conference on Computational Linguistics*, pages 139–149.

Pierre Colombo, Wojciech Witon, Ashutosh Modi, James Kennedy, and Mubbasir Kapadia. 2019.

Affect-driven dialog generation. In *Proceedings of the 2019 Conference of the North American Chapter of the Association for Computational Linguistics: Human Language Technologies, Volume 1 (Long and Short Papers)*, pages 3734–3743, Minneapolis, Minnesota. Association for Computational Linguistics.

Jacob Devlin, Ming-Wei Chang, Kenton Lee, and Kristina Toutanova. 2019. BERT: Pre-training of deep bidirectional transformers for language understanding. In *Proceedings of the 2019 Conference of the North American Chapter of the Association for Computational Linguistics: Human Language Technologies, Volume 1 (Long and Short Papers)*, pages 4171–4186, Minneapolis, Minnesota. Association for Computational Linguistics.

Zixiang Ding, Rui Xia, and Jianfei Yu. 2020a. Ecpe-2d: Emotion-cause pair extraction based on joint two-dimensional representation, interaction and prediction. In *Proceedings of the 58th Annual Meeting of the Association for Computational Linguistics*, pages 3161–3170.

Zixiang Ding, Rui Xia, and Jianfei Yu. 2020b. End-to-end emotion-cause pair extraction based on sliding window multi-label learning. In *Proceedings of the 2020 Conference on Empirical Methods in Natural Language Processing (EMNLP)*, pages 3574–3583.

Chuang Fan, Hongyu Yan, Jiachen Du, Lin Gui, Lidong Bing, Min Yang, Ruifeng Xu, and Ruibin Mao. 2019. A knowledge regularized hierarchical approach for emotion cause analysis. In *Proceedings of the 2019 Conference on Empirical Methods in Natural Language Processing and the 9th International Joint Conference on Natural Language Processing (EMNLP-IJCNLP)*, pages 5614–5624, Hong Kong, China. Association for Computational Linguistics.

Chuang Fan, Chaofa Yuan, Jiachen Du, Lin Gui, Min Yang, and Ruifeng Xu. 2020. Transition-based directed graph construction for emotion-cause pair extraction. In *Proceedings of the 58th Annual Meeting of the Association for Computational Linguistics*, pages 3707–3717.

Kai Gao, Hua Xu, and Jiushuo Wang. 2015. A rule-based approach to emotion cause detection for chinese micro-blogs. *Expert Syst. Appl.*, 42(9):45174528.

Qinghong Gao, Gui Lin, Yulan He, Jiannan Hu, Qin Lu, Ruifeng Xu, and Kam-Fai Wong. 2017. Overview of ntcir-13 eca task. In *Proceedings of the NTCIR-13 Conference*.

Diman Ghazi, Diana Inkpen, and Stan Szpakowicz. 2015. Detecting emotion stimuli in emotion-bearing sentences. In *International Conference on Intelligent Text Processing and Computational Linguistics*, pages 152–165. Springer.

Sayan Ghosh, Mathieu Chollet, Eugene Laksana, Louis-Philippe Morency, and Stefan Scherer. 2017. Affect-lm: A neural language model for customizable affective text generation. *arXiv preprint arXiv:1704.06851*.

Tushar Goswamy, Ishika Singh, Ahsan Barkati, and Ashutosh Modi. 2020. Adapting a language model for controlled affective text generation. In *Proceedings of the 28th International Conference on Computational Linguistics*, pages 2787–2801, Barcelona, Spain (Online). International Committee on Computational Linguistics.

Lin Gui, Jiannan Hu, Yulan He, Ruifeng Xu, Qin Lu, and Jiachen Du. 2017. A question answering approach for emotion cause extraction. In *Proceedings of the 2017 Conference on Empirical Methods in Natural Language Processing*, pages 1593–1602, Copenhagen, Denmark. Association for Computational Linguistics.

Lin Gui, Dongyin Wu, Ruifeng Xu, Qin Lu, and Yu Zhou. 2016. Event-driven emotion cause extraction with corpus construction. In *Proceedings of the 2016 Conference on Empirical Methods in Natural Language Processing*, pages 1639–1649, Austin, Texas. Association for Computational Linguistics.

Diederik P Kingma and Jimmy Ba. 2014. Adam: A method for stochastic optimization. *arXiv preprint arXiv:1412.6980*.

Sophia Yat Mei Lee, Ying Chen, and Chu-Ren Huang. 2010. A text-driven rule-based system for emotion cause detection. In *Proceedings of the NAACL HLT 2010 Workshop on Computational Approaches to Analysis and Generation of Emotion in Text*, pages 45–53, Los Angeles, CA. Association for Computational Linguistics.

Xiangju Li, Shi Feng, Daling Wang, and Yifei Zhang. 2019. Context-aware emotion cause analysis with multi-attention-based neural network. *Knowl. Based Syst.*, 174:205–218.

Xiangju Li, Kaisong Song, Shi Feng, Daling Wang, and Yifei Zhang. 2018. A co-attention neural network model for emotion cause analysis with emotional context awareness. In *Proceedings of the 2018 Conference on Empirical Methods in Natural Language Processing*, pages 4752–4757, Brussels, Belgium. Association for Computational Linguistics.

Ashutosh Modi, Mubbasir Kapadia, Douglas A. Fidaleo, James R. Kennedy, Wojciech Witon, and Pierre Colombo. 2020. Affect-driven dialog generation. *US Patent 10,818,312*.

Alena Neviarouskaya and Masaki Aono. 2013. Extracting causes of emotions from text. In *Proceedings of the Sixth International Joint Conference on Natural Language Processing*, pages 932–936.

Jeffrey Pennington, Richard Socher, and Christopher D Manning. 2014. Glove: Global vectors for word representation. In *Proceedings of the 2014 conference on empirical methods in natural language processing (EMNLP)*, pages 1532–1543.

Peter Shaw, Jakob Uszkoreit, and Ashish Vaswani. 2018. Self-attention with relative position representations. In *Proceedings of the 2018 Conference of the North American Chapter of the Association for Computational Linguistics: Human Language Technologies, Volume 2 (Short Papers)*, pages 464–468.

Ashish Vaswani, Noam Shazeer, Niki Parmar, Jakob Uszkoreit, Llion Jones, Aidan N Gomez, Łukasz Kaiser, and Illia Polosukhin. 2017. Attention is all you need. In *Advances in neural information processing systems*, pages 5998–6008.

Wojciech Witon, Pierre Colombo, Ashutosh Modi, and Mubbasir Kapadia. 2018. Disney at IEST 2018: Predicting emotions using an ensemble. In *Proceedings of the 9th Workshop on Computational Approaches to Subjectivity, Sentiment and Social Media Analysis*, pages 248–253, Brussels, Belgium. Association for Computational Linguistics.

Rui Xia and Zixiang Ding. 2019. Emotion-cause pair extraction: A new task to emotion analysis in texts. In *Proceedings of the 57th Annual Meeting of the Association for Computational Linguistics*, pages 1003–1012, Florence, Italy. Association for Computational Linguistics.

Rui Xia, Mengran Zhang, and Zixiang Ding. 2019. Rthn: a rnn-transformer hierarchical network for emotion cause extraction. In *Proceedings of the 28th International Joint Conference on Artificial Intelligence*, pages 5285–5291. AAAI Press.

X. Yu, W. Rong, Z. Zhang, Y. Ouyang, and Z. Xiong. 2019. Multiple level hierarchical network-based clause selection for emotion cause extraction. *IEEE Access*, 7:9071–9079.

Chaofa Yuan, Chuang Fan, Jianzhu Bao, and Ruifeng Xu. 2020. Emotion-cause pair extraction as sequence labeling based on a novel tagging scheme. In *Proceedings of the 2020 Conference on Empirical Methods in Natural Language Processing (EMNLP)*, pages 3568–3573.

# Appendix

## A Model Variants

We present a variant of `E2E-PExt`$_{\mathrm{E}}$ called `E2E-PExt`$_{\mathrm{C}}$ (Figure 4). Here, we feed the clause embeddings $\mathbf{s}_i$ into a clause-level BiLSTM to obtain context-aware clause encodings $\mathbf{r}_i^c$ which is fed into a softmax layer to obtain cause predictions $\mathbf{y}_i^c$. We concatenate the cause predictions with the clause embeddings, $\mathbf{s}_i \oplus \mathbf{y}_i^c$, and feed them into another clause-level BiLSTM to obtain emotion representations $\mathbf{r}_i^e$, which are fed into another softmax layer to obtain the emotion predictions $\mathbf{y}_i^e$. The pair prediction network remains the same as described for `E2E-PExt`$_{\mathrm{E}}$. For finding the extent to which emotion labels can help in improving pair predictions, we present a variant of `E2E-PExt`$_{\mathrm{E}}$ called `E2E-CExt`. We use the true emotion labels instead of emotion predictions $\mathbf{y}_i^e$ to obtain the context-aware clause encodings $\mathbf{r}_i^c$. We also concatenate them with the input of pair-prediction network $\mathbf{r}_i^e \oplus \mathbf{r}_j^c \oplus \mathbf{pe}_{ij}$ to make full use of the additional knowledge of emotion labels. Similarly, the corresponding variant of `E2E-PExt`$_{\mathrm{C}}$ which utilizes true cause labels is called `E2E-EExt`. The results of model variation are shown in Table 3. Here, the pair prediction network consists of a single fully connected layer. After comparing the performance of `E2E-PExt`$_{\mathrm{C}}$ and `E2E-EExt` we conclude that huge improvements in performance can be achieved if the quality of cause predictions is improved.

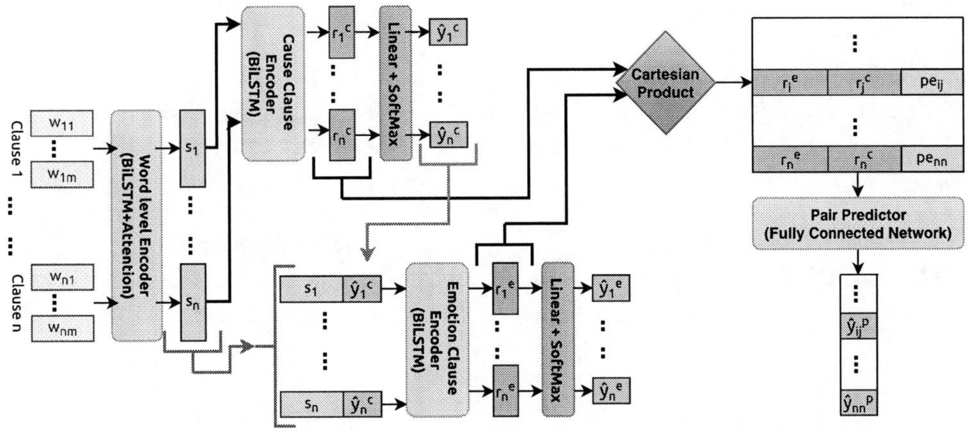


Figure 4: End-to-End network variant ($\texttt{E2E-PExt}_{\texttt{C}}$)

| | Emotion Extraction | | | Cause Extraction | | | Pair Extraction | | |
|---|---|---|---|---|---|---|---|---|---|
| | Precision | Recall | F1 Score | Precision | Recall | F1 Score | Precision | Recall | F1 Score |
| $\texttt{E2E-PExt}_{\texttt{C}}$ | 71.70 | 66.77 | 69.10 | 63.75 | 42.50 | 50.42 | 48.88 | 48.22 | 48.37 |
| E2E-EExt | 81.74 | 71.95 | 76.47 | 100.00 | 100.00 | 100.00 | 74.17 | 78.63 | 76.30 |

Table 3: Results of Model variants using precision, recall, and F1-score on the ECPE task and the two sub-tasks.

# WASSA 2021 Shared Task: Predicting Empathy and Emotion in Reaction to News Stories

**Shabnam Tafreshi**
Georgetown University
st1093@georgetown.edu

**Orphée De Clercq**
LT3, Ghent University
orphee.declercq@ugent.be

**Valentin Barriere**
European Commission Joint Research Centre
Valentin.BARRIERE@ec.europa.eu

**João Sedoc**
New York University
jsedoc@stern.nyu.edu

**Sven Buechel**
Friedrich Schiller University Jena
sven.buechel@uni-jena.de

**Alexandra Balahur**
European Commission Joint Research Centre
alexandra.balahur@ec.europa.eu

## Abstract

This paper presents the results that were obtained from the WASSA 2021 shared task on predicting empathy and emotions. The participants were given access to a dataset comprising empathic reactions to news stories where harm is done to a person, group, or other. These reactions consist of essays, Batson empathic concern, and personal distress scores, and the dataset was further extended with news articles, person-level demographic information (age, gender, ethnicity, income, education level), and personality information. Additionally, emotion labels, namely Ekman's six basic emotions, were added to the essays at both the document and sentence level. Participation was encouraged in two tracks: predicting empathy and predicting emotion categories. In total five teams participated in the shared task. We summarize the methods and resources used by the participating teams.

## 1 Introduction

It is important to be able to analyze empathy and emotion in natural languages. Emotion classification in natural languages has been studied over two decades and many applications successfully used emotion as their major components. Empathy utterances can be emotional, therefore, examining emotion in text-based empathy possibly has a major impact on predicting empathy. Analyzing text-based empathy and emotion have different applications; empathy is a crucial component in applications such as empathic AI agents, effective gesturing of robots, and mental health, emotion has natural language applications such as commerce, public health, and disaster management. In this paper, we present the WASSA 2021 Shared Task: Predicting Empathy and Emotion in Reaction to News Stories. This shared task included two individual tasks where teams develop models to predict emotions and empathy in essays in which people expressed their empathy and distress in reaction to news articles in which an individual, group of people or nature was harmed. Additionally, the dataset also included the demographic information of the authors of the essays such as age, gender, ethnicity, income, and education level, and personality information (details of the collection of the dataset is provided in section 3). Optionally, we suggested that the teams could also use emotion labels when modeling empathy to learn more about the impact of emotions on empathy. The shared task consisted of two tracks:

1. Predicting Empathy (EMP): the formulation of this track is to predict the Batson empathic concern ("feeling for someone") and personal distress ("suffering with someone") using the essay, personality information, demographic information, and emotion.

2. Emotion Label Prediction (EMO): the formulation of this track is to predict emotion tags



*Proceedings of the 11th Workshop on Computational Approaches to Subjectivity, Sentiment and Social Media Analysis*, pages 92–104
April 19, 2021. ©2021 Association for Computational Linguistics

(sadness, joy, disgust, surprise, anger, or fear), taken from Ekman's six basic emotions (Ekman, 1971), plus *no-emotion* tag for essays. In this setting personality and demographic information as well as empathy and distress scores were also made available and optional to use.

For both tasks, an identical train-dev-test split was provided. The dataset consists of essays that were collected from participants, who had read disturbing news articles about a person, a group of people, or painful situations. Empathy, distress, demographic, and personality information was taken from the original work by Buechel et al. (2018). They used Batson's Empathic Concern – Personal Distress Scale (Batson et al., 1987), i.e, rating 6 items for empathy (i.e., warm, tender, sympathetic, softhearted, moved, compassionate) and 8 items for distress (i.e., worried, upset, troubled, perturbed, grieved, disturbed, alarmed, distressed) using a 7-point scale for each of these items (detailed information can be found in the Appendix section of the original paper). Regarding emotion, all data was annotated with the six basic Ekman emotions (sadness, joy, disgust, surprise, anger, or fear).
Five teams participated in this shared task, three participated in both tracks, and each time one additional team participated in either the EMP or EMO track. During the evaluation phase, every team was allowed to submit their results until a certain deadline, after which the final submission was taken into consideration for the ranking. The best result for the empathy prediction track was an average Pearson correlation of 0.545 and the best macro F1-score for the emotion track amounted to 55%.

All tasks were designed in CodaLab [1] and the teams were allowed to submit one official result during evaluation phase and several ones during the training phase.

In the remainder of this paper we first review related work (Section 2), after which we introduce the dataset used for both tracks (Section 3). The shared task is presented in Section 4 and the official results in Section 5. A discussion of the different systems participating in both tracks is presented in Section 6 and we conclude our work in Section 7.

[1] Task descriptions, datasets, and results are designed in CodaLab `https://competitions.codalab.org/competitions/28713`

## 2 Related Work

Emotion has been studied for two decades and a large body of works have provided insights and remarkable findings. In contrast, detecting and predicting empathy and distress in text is a growing field and there is little work on the correlation and relatedness of emotion, empathy, and distress. This shared task is designed to study the modeling of empathy and distress and the correlation among them. In the literature empathy is considered towards negative events, however, recent studies suggest that people's joyful emotions towards positive events can be termed as *positive empathy* (Morelli et al., 2015). The psychological theory distinguishes two separate constructs for distress and empathy; distress is a self-focused, negative affective state (*suffering with someone*), and empathy is a warm, tender, and compassionate state (*feeling for someone*). To quantify empathy and distress, studies present different approaches, the most popular one is Batson's Empathic Concern – Personal Distress Scale (Batson et al., 1987), which is used to obtain empathy and distress scores for each essay in this dataset. To annotate emotions in text, classical studies in NLP suggest categorical tagsets, and most studies are focused on basic emotion models that are suggested by psychological emotion models. The most popular ones are the Ekman 6 basic emotions (Ekman, 1971), the Plutchik 8 basic emotions (Plutchik, 1984), and 4 basic emotions (Frijda, 1988). We opted for the Ekman emotions, because this model is well adopted in different downstream NLP tasks of which emotion is a component, and it is most suited to the dataset we aim to study in this shared task.

### 2.1 Emotions

Crowdsourcing annotations have become a popular way to acquire human judgments. Collecting categorical annotations for emotions is among the tasks that has been designed successfully in crowdsourcing platforms (Mohammad and Turney, 2013; Mohammad et al., 2014; Abdul-Mageed and Ungar, 2017; Mohammad et al., 2018; Tafreshi and Diab, 2018; Bostan et al., 2019). Example of such platforms are Amazon Mechanical Turk or Figure Eight (previously known as Crowdflower). There are several SemEval shared tasks that have successfully been developed for Affect computing and emotion classification (Strapparava and Mihalcea, 2007; Mohammad and Bravo-Marquez,

2017; Mohammad et al., 2018; Chatterjee et al., 2019; Sharma et al., 2020), in which, several approaches, methods, resources, and features have been developed by the participants. These works mainly focused on supervised machine learning approaches with different ways of designing features (traditional feature engineering) to feature representations using word2vec embedding models (Mikolov et al., 2013), contextualized word embeddings (Peters et al., 2018) and pretrained language models from transformers (Devlin et al., 2018).

### 2.2 Empathy and Distress

Prior work on modeling text-based empathy focused on the empathetic concern which is to share others' emotions in the conversations Litvak et al. (2016); Fung et al. (2016); Xiao et al. (2015, 2016); Gibson et al. (2016) modeled empathy based on the ability of a therapist to adapt to the emotions of their clients; Zhou and Jurgens (2020) quantified empathy in condolences in social media using appraisal theory.

## 3 Data Collection and Annotation

In this section, we present how the dataset that was used for this shared task has been collected and annotated. The starting point was the dataset as described in (Buechel et al., 2018). This dataset comprises both news articles and essays, we provide a brief description of both below.[2]

**News article collection** We used the same news articles in Buechel et al. (2018) in which there is major or minor harm inflicted to an individual, group of people, or other by either a person, group of people, political organization, or nature. The stories were specifically selected by Buechel et al. (2018) to evoke varying degrees of empathy among readers.

**Essay collection** The corpus acquisition was set up as a crowdsourcing task on `MTurk.com` pointing to a `Qualtrics.com` questionnaire. The participants completed background measures on demographics and personality and then proceeded to the main part of the survey where they read a random selection of five of the news articles. After reading each of the articles, participants were asked to rate their level of empathy and distress before describing their thoughts and feelings about it in writing. From this initial dataset, the training data was extracted for the shared task. For the development and test dataset, an additional 805 essays were added to the dataset, these were written in response to the same news articles by an additional 161 participants using the same AMT setting as described above. The test and development datasets were both new collections. Since each message is annotated by only one rater, its author, typical measures of inter-rater agreement are not applicable. Instead, we compute split-half reliability (SHR), a standard approach in psychology (Cronbach, 1947). SHR is computed by splitting the ratings for the individual scale items (e.g., *warm*, *tender*, etc. for empathy) of all participants randomly into two groups, averaging the individual item ratings for each group and participant, and then measuring the correlation between both groups. This process is repeated 100 times with random splits, before again averaging the results. Doing so for empathy and distress, we find very high SHR values of r=.875 and .924, for the training set and value of r=.872 and .928 for test+dev set for empathy and distress respectively.

### 3.1 Emotion Annotation Process

In a next phase, all essays were further enriched with the 6 basic Ekman emotion labels at the essay level in order to find out whether certain basic emotions are more correlated with empathy and distress. To this purpose the emotion labels were first predicted automatically and then manually verified.

For the automatic prediction two different NN models were applied to generate predictions at the essay level. The models were 1) a Gated RNN with attention mechanism which is trained with multigenre corpus, i.e., news, tweets, blog posts, (Tafreshi, 2021) (chapter 5), 2) *fine-tuned* RoBERTa model (Liu et al., 2019) on the GoEmotions dataset (Demszky et al., 2020).

For the manual verification another Amazon Mechanical Turk task was set up for which annotators with the highest AMT quality rating were recruited. For each essay the turkers were provided with the two automatically predicted labels. If they did not indicate one of these labels as correct, they had to choose the correct label from a tagset including the 6 basic Ekman emotions (sadness, joy, disgust, surprise, anger, or fear) or assign the label *no-emotion*. Some instances were ambiguous, which means that neither of the machines' labels nor the two annotators were agreeing on the same tag. We excluded

[2]For more details we refer the reader to the original paper of Buechel et al. (2018).

these essays, and a PhD candidate in NLP further annotated these instances and selected the most related tag. Results obtained from this post annotation step completed the annotation procedure, thus, we acquired gold emotion labels for each essay.

The distribution of the emotion tags per data split split is illustrated in Table 1.

As anticipated, the majority of the essays have the emotion tag *sadness*. Moreover, we observe an even distribution of the emotion tags *disgust, fear*, and *anger*, and a small number of *joy*, which seems somewhat counter-intuitive given the nature of the essays. After inspecting a small sample of the latter, we found that in these instances the authors of the essays were suggesting actions to improve the situation, in some cases, these essays also contained political views. This could explain the positive emotion that was assigned by the turkers.

## 4 Shared Task

We setup both empathy and emotion label predictions in CodaLab. We describe each task separately, the objectives and the metadata that we provided for each task, the data split, resources, and evaluation metric.

### 4.1 Empathy Prediction (EMP)

The formulation of this task is to predict Batson empathic concern ("feeling for someone") and personal distress ("suffering with someone") scores using the essay. Each empathy score is a real value between 0 and 7. Given the essay and empathy score, participants suppose to predict the empathy score for each essay. We provided personality and demographic information for each essay as well as emotion labels. The demographic information consists of: gender, education, race, age, and income. To code personality information the Big 5 personality traits were provided, also known as the OCEAN model (Gosling et al., 2003) and the Interpersonal Reactivity Index (Davis, 1980). In the OCEAN model, the theory identifies five factors (e.g., openness to experience, conscientiousness, extraversion, agreeableness and neuroticism). The Interpersonal Reactivity Index (IRI) is a measurement tool for the multi-dimensional assessment of empathy. The four subscales are: Perspective Taking, Fantasy, Empathic Concern and Personal Distress.

Both personality and demographic information were provided by a real value from 0 to 7. Besides, we provided emotion labels, from Ekman's six basic emotions (sadness, joy, disgust, surprise, anger, or fear) for each essay.

### 4.2 Emotion Label Prediction (EMO)

The formulation of this task is to predict emotion labels for essays. Given the essay and emotion label X, the task is to predict emotion label X per essay. The same set of metadata that we described in section 4.1 were also provided for each essay in this task. Participants optionally could use this information as features to predict emotion labels.

### 4.3 Training, Development, and Test Sets

Table 2 represents the train, development, and test splits. Participants were able to add the development set to the training set and submit systems trained on both. Training and development sets with gold labels for empathy, distress, demographic, and personality information were available at the beginning of the competition. For the first two weeks of the competition automatic emotion labels were provided, after which the gold-labeled emotions were made available. The test set was made available to the participants at the beginning of the evaluation period.

### 4.4 Resources and Systems Restrictions

Participants were allowed to use any lexical resources (e.g., emotion or empathy dictionaries) of their choice, any training data besides the one we provided, or any off-the-shelf emotion or empathy models they could access. We did not put any restriction in this shared task nor did we suggest any baseline models. These are the first generated results for this task setup.

### 4.5 Systems Evaluation

The organizers published an evaluation script that calculates Pearson correlation for the predictions of the empathy prediction task and precision, recall, and F1 measure for each emotion class as well as the micro and macro average for the emotion label prediction task.

Pearson coefficient is the linear correlations between two variables, and it produces scores from -1 (perfectly inversely correlated) to 1 (perfectly correlated). A score of 0 indicates no correlation. The official competition metric for the empathy prediction task (EMP) is the average of the two Pearson correlations. The official competition metric for the emotion evaluation is the macro F1-score, which is the harmonic mean between precision and recall.

| | joy | sadness | disgust | fear | anger | surprise | no-emo |
|---|---|---|---|---|---|---|---|
| **Train** | 82 | 647 | 149 | 194 | 349 | 164 | 275 |
| **Dev** | 14 | 98 | 12 | 31 | 76 | 14 | 25 |
| **Test** | 33 | 177 | 28 | 70 | 122 | 40 | 55 |
| **Total** | 129 | 922 | 189 | 295 | 547 | 218 | 355 |

Table 1: Distribution of emotion labels in the datasets.

| **Dataset Split** | | | |
|---|---|---|---|
| Train | Dev | Test | Total |
| 1860 | 270 | 525 | 2655 |

Table 2: Train, dev and test set splits.

| **Abs. diff** | **Empathy** | | **Distress** | |
|---|---|---|---|---|
| 0-1 | 206 | (39.2%) | 237 | (45.14%) |
| 1-2 | 194 | (37.0%) | 165 | (31.43%) |
| 2-3 | 105 | (20.0%) | 102 | (19.43%) |
| 3-4 | 17 | (3.2%) | 20 | (3.81%) |
| 4-5 | 3 | (0.6%) | 1 | (0.19%) |

Table 4: Absolute difference in score between predicted and gold for both the empathy and distress scores of the best-performing system (expressed in number of instances and percentagewise).

## 5 Results and Discussion

### 5.1 Empathy Prediction (EMP)

Table 3 shows the main results of the track on empathy (Emp) and distress (Dis) prediction. Four teams submitted results and the best scoring system is the one of *PVG* (averaged $r$ = .545). If we examine the results for the empathy and distress prediction separately, we observe that for empathy, team WASSA@IITK scored best ($r$ = .558), whereas for distress *PVG* obtained the best result ($r$ = .574).

| **Team** | **Emp** | **Dis** | **Avg** |
|---|---|---|---|
| PVG | 0.517 | **0.574** | **0.545** |
| EmpNa | 0.516 | 0.554 | 0.536 |
| WASSA@IITK | **0.558** | 0.507 | 0.533 |
| Team Phoenix | 0.358 | 0.476 | 0.417 |

Table 3: Results of the teams participating in the EMP track (Pearson correlations).

To compare, in Buechel et al. (2018) the best-performing system, a CNN, obtained $r$=.404 for empathy and $r$=.444 for distress. Of course these results were achieved only on the training set using ten-fold cross validation experiments.

In Table 4 the absolute difference between the predicted and gold empathy and distress scores by the best-performing system (*PVG*) are presented. It can be observed that the majority of predicted Batson emphatic concern and distress instances only differ in between zero or one point from the gold scores, i.e. 39% and 45%, respectively. For both labels the maximum difference amounts to 4-5 points and this in only a very few cases, 3 instances for empathy and 1 instance for distress.

### 5.2 Emotion Label Prediction (EMO)

The results of the track on emotion label prediction are presented in Table 5. Four teams submitted results and the best scoring system is the one of *WASSA@IITK* (indicated in bold, 55% Macro F1), largely outperforming the runner-up *Team Phoenix* (50%).

| **Team** | **P** | **R** | **F1** | **Acc** |
|---|---|---|---|---|
| WASSA@IITK | **0.57** | **0.55** | **0.55** | **0.62** |
| Team Phoenix | 0.55 | 0.48 | 0.50 | 0.59 |
| MilaNLP | 0.55 | 0.47 | 0.49 | 0.58 |
| EmpNa | 0.32 | 0.31 | 0.31 | 0.40 |

Table 5: Results of the teams participating in the EMO track (macro-averaged precision (P), recall (R), F1-score (F1) and accuracy (Acc)).

Given that the labels in the datasets were not equally distributed (see Table 1), we also have a look at the accuracy, which equals the micro-averaged F-1 score. Again, the result by *WASSA@IITK* outperforms the second team, 62% versus 59%, though with a less outspoken margin.

To get more insight we also provide a breakdown of the macro-averaged results by emotion class in Table 6. As expected sadness and especially anger are predicted with the highest performance by most systems. For anger, the F1-score ranges from 59% to 77%, even though this label was not the most frequently occurring one in the training and development data (Table 1). In the same vein, the classification of disgust also seems better than expected given its limited number of training instances. For all emotion labels team *WASSA@IITK* outperforms the others, except for the label fear, though the difference is only marginal (45 instead of 44% F1). Please recall that besides the 6 Ekman emotions label, the systems could also predict a seventh category "no-emotion". The macro F1 scores for predicting this particular label were 67, 64, 63, and 40%, respectively.

### 5.3 Error Analysis

#### 5.3.1 Empathy prediction

We had a closer look at those instances that were predicted with a difference in score of between 4 and 5 by the best-performing system, you can find the actual essays in Appendix A.

For empathy there were three such instances: in the first one (essay 1) the gold score was 7 and the predicted one 2.470, which is actually a pretty strange error as this describes a really typical high empathy - high distress essay. For the other two instances, the predicted empathy scores were very high (5.428 and 5.272) compared to the gold one (1). In essay 2 the low empathy score seems obvious for a human reader, but aside from "whining" there are few markers without deeper understanding, making this a challenging example for automatic prediction. Moreover, we observe that a few questions are being raised by the author in the essay, and questions are often associated with high empathy. Upon first inspection we would have expected higher empathy given the text in essay 3. Initially, we thought this was a bad annotation, but upon second reading it seems to be a rare case of very low empathy and high distress.

For distress there was one instance with a high discrepancy between the predicted (5.347) and gold (1.25) score. If we consider essay 4 we observe that there is no self-focus language at all. So a low distress score does make sense here. Nonetheless this is not a typical low distress response since there is some empathy expressed.

Considering essays 3 and 4 we can state that these exhibit high distress/low empathy and vice versa low distress/ mild empathy. It is possible that models have difficulty in scenarios where there is empathy with a lack of distress and vice versa.

#### 5.3.2 Emotion label prediction

Table 7 presents the confusion matrix of the top-performing team on the test data. It can be observed that the top three occurring labels in the training data, sadness (Sa) – anger (A) – no-emotion (No) – are accurately classified most frequently and that anger and fear are most often confused with sadness, whereas the same goes for sadness being classified as anger.

Assigning an emotion label at the document level is not a trivial task as certain sentences within an essay may exhibit different emotions or sentiment. In Appendix B we present for every possible label a first essay (i) which was correctly classified by all four participating systems and a second one (ii) where most systems assigned the wrong label.

Looking at the correctly classified essays, we observe that in these essays many emotional words and phrases are being used and that there is not much discrepancy of emotions between the sentences. The same cannot be said for the erroneously classified essays, there we clearly observe that often many emotions are being presented within the same essay.

In the meantime all essays have also been labeled with emotions at the sentence level using the same annotation procedure as described in Section 3, this dataset will also be made available for research purposes.

## 6 Empathy and Emotion Systems

A total of 5 teams participated in the shared tasks with 3 teams participating in both tracks. In this section, we provide a summary of the machine learning models, features, resources, and lexicons that were used by the teams.

### 6.1 Machine Learning Architectures

All systems follow supervised machine learning models for empathy prediction and emotion classification (Table 8). Most teams built systems using pre-trained transformer language models, which were fine-tuned or from which features from different layers were extracted. Linear Regression and logistic regression with feature engineering and the CNN model were proposed by one team.

### 6.2 Features and Resources

Detection and classification of emotion in text is challenging because marking textual emotional cues is difficult. Emotion model performance has been always improved when lexical features (e.g., emotion, sentiment, subjectivity, etc.), emotion-specific embedding, or different emotional datasets

| Team | Joy | | | Sadness | | | Disgust | | | Fear | | | Anger | | | Surprise | | |
|---|---|---|---|---|---|---|---|---|---|---|---|---|---|---|---|---|---|---|
| | P | R | F1 | P | R | F1 | P | R | F1 | P | R | F1 | P | R | F1 | P | R | F1 |
| WASSA@IITK | **40** | **53** | **46** | 72 | **55** | **63** | **70** | **42** | **52** | 46 | 42 | 44 | **74** | 80 | **77** | 36 | **50** | **42** |
| Team Phoenix | 35 | 45 | 40 | 67 | 37 | 48 | 57 | 38 | 45 | **52** | 40 | **45** | 67 | **83** | 74 | **48** | 33 | 39 |
| MilaNLP | 34 | 38 | 36 | **77** | 31 | 44 | 58 | 38 | 46 | 34 | 48 | 40 | 73 | 81 | 76 | **48** | 33 | 39 |
| EmpNa | 23 | 28 | 25 | 31 | 25 | 28 | 28 | 30 | 29 | 30 | 28 | 29 | 60 | 59 | 59 | 10 | 15 | 12 |

Table 6: Breakdown EMO labels (MACRO)

| Gold EMO labels | Predicted EMO labels | | | | | | |
|---|---|---|---|---|---|---|---|
| | No | J | Sa | D | F | A | Su |
| No | 23 | 2 | 7 | 0 | 4 | 9 | 10 |
| J | 4 | 18 | 6 | 0 | 1 | 2 | 2 |
| Sa | 7 | 0 | 141 | 8 | 5 | 13 | 3 |
| D | 3 | 0 | 4 | 14 | 0 | 7 | 0 |
| F | 7 | 3 | 14 | 4 | 29 | 5 | 8 |
| A | 5 | 1 | 13 | 12 | 1 | 81 | 9 |
| Su | 1 | 1 | 8 | 1 | 2 | 6 | 21 |

Table 7: Confusion matrix best performing team on EMO

were augmented and used (Mohammad et al., 2018) to represent an emotion. Similar to emotion, predicting text-based empathy is challenging as well, and using lexical features, and external resources have an impact on empathy model performance. As such, it is quite common to use different resources and design different features in emotion and empathy models. As part of the dataset we provided to teams, we include personality, demographic, and categorical emotions as additional features for both emotion and empathy tasks. Teams were allowed to use any external resources or design any features of their choice and use them in their models. Table 9 summarizes the features and extra resources that teams used to build their models.

### 6.3 Lexicons

The presence of emotion and empathic words are the first cues for a piece of text to be emotional or empathic, therefore, it is beneficial to use emotion/empathy lexicons to extract those words and create features. Table 10 summarizes the lexicons that were employed by the different teams.

### 6.4 Top three systems in EMP track

**PVG** The best performing system in predicting empathy was *PVG*. The team developed a multi-task, multi-view system. To design the multi-views the team used the information provided in the dataset in the form of an empathy bin. This feature divides essays with empathy from the ones with low empathy based on a threshold empathy score (this threshold is 4). In the multi-task model, the tasks are predicting empathy scores and classifying empathy and emotion. The primary task is to predict empathy, thus emotion and empathy classifications are considered auxiliary (secondary) tasks. The machine learning algorithm has a NN architecture that consists of an embedding layer, a max-pooling layer, and a fully connected layer. To represent contextual features, they used RoBERTA-base (Liu et al., 2019). Further, the demographic and personality information was concatenated and used as features. For the distress system, in addition to the previously mentioned feature representations, the NRC emotion intensity (Mohammad, 2018a) and NRC VAD (Mohammad, 2017) lexicons were also used.

**EmpNa** The team developed a linear regression model and built the features representing the text as n-grams and adding a set of characteristics extracted from a handcrafted set of lexicons (AFINN, QWN, SenticNet, etc). The lexical n-gram features consisted of uni-gram, bi-gram, and tri-grams. They defined a threshold to select words with higher frequency (80% for empathy and 70% for distress). These lexical features were concatenated with all the scores extracted from the different lexicons, plus the personality and demographic information that was provided in this shared task as extra features. They used this feature to represent contextual features per essay as information for a linear regression model to predict empathy and distress. They selected two baseline model: a CNN model as described in (Buechel et al., 2018) and a model relying solely on n-grams. Their results suggest that combining all features (lexical, demographic, and personality features) yields the best result.

**WASSA@IITK** This team built a multi-task model using a transformer architecture, then they

**Machine Learning Algorithms**

| ML Algorithm | # of team | Emp System | Emo System |
|---|---|---|---|
| RoBERTa base | 2 | ✓ | ✓ |
| RoBERTa Large | 2 | ✓ | ✓ |
| ELECTRA base | 1 | ✓ | ✓ |
| ELECTRA Large | 1 | ✓ | ✓ |
| Alberta Large | 1 | ✓ | ✓ |
| BERT Large (uncased) | 1 | | ✓ |
| BERT base | 1 | ✓ | ✓ |
| ALBERT-base-v2 | 1 | ✓ | ✓ |
| T5 base | 1 | ✓ | ✓ |
| T5 finetuned | 1 | ✓ | ✓ |
| Pegasus-xsum | 1 | ✓ | ✓ |
| CNN | 1 | | ✓ |
| Linear Regression | 1 | ✓ | |
| Logistic Regression | 1 | | ✓ |

Table 8: Machine learning algorithms used by the different teams. We listed all the models that teams reported in their results.

**Features and Resources**

| Features | # of team | Emp System | Emo System |
|---|---|---|---|
| *n-gram* | 1 | ✓ | ✓ |
| Transformer embeddings | 1 | | |
| [CLS] token from Transformer model | 2 | ✓ | ✓ |
| Word embedding (*fasttext*) | 1 | ✓ | |
| Affect/emotion/empathy lexicons | 1 | ✓ | ✓ |
| Personality information | 3 | ✓ | ✓ |
| Demographic infromation | 3 | ✓ | ✓ |
| External dataset | 1 | | ✓ |

Table 9: Features and resources that are used by different teams. We listed all the features and resources that teams reported in their results.

*fine-tuned* this model for empathy and distress with the Mean Squared Error loss function. In their multi-task model, they jointly learned empathy and distress. The pre-trained language model they used was the ELECTRA large model (Clark et al., 2020) with two dense layers on top of it, one responsible for Empathy and another for Distress. MSE loss was used, adding the loss for Empathy and Distress and jointly training the architecture end to end on that total loss. The same approach was tried out with the RoBERTa model (Liu et al., 2019). Finally, they built an Ensemble model consisting of multi-task RoBERTA and Vanilla ALBERTA. For distress prediction they used an ensemble of two models, both being multi-task ELECTRA models (Clark et al., 2020) with different performance on the dev set.

### 6.5 Top three systems in EMO track

**WASSA@IITK** The best performing system in emotion classification was *WASSA@IITK*. The team developed multiple systems by fine-tuning several pre-trained transformer language models on the dataset that was provided for the shared task, which they augmented with the GoEmotions dataset (Demszky et al., 2020). The transformer models that were employed were ELECTRA base and large (Clark et al., 2020), and RoBERTA base and large (Liu et al., 2019). Eventually, the models' outputs were averaged or summed into ensembles and the results of these ensemble models were used for the shared task. The best-performing system was an ensemble model consisting of a combination of two ELECTRA base and one ELECTRA large.

**Empathic or Emotion Lexicons**

| Lexicons | # of team | Emp System | Emo System |
|---|---|---|---|
| NRC *EmoLex* (Mohammad and Turney, 2010) | 1 | | ✓ |
| NRC intensity (Mohammad, 2018c) | 1 | | ✓ |
| NRC valence (Mohammad, 2018b) | 1 | | ✓ |
| Opinion Lexicon (Hu and Liu, 2004) | 1 | ✓ | ✓ |
| AFINN (Nielsen, 2011) | 1 | ✓ | ✓ |
| General Inquirer lexicon (Inquirer, 1966) | 1 | ✓ | ✓ |
| Sentiment140 Lexicon (Mohammad et al., 2013) | 1 | ✓ | ✓ |
| +/-Effect Lexicon (Choi and Wiebe, 2014) | 1 | ✓ | ✓ |
| QWN (San Vicente et al., 2014) | 1 | ✓ | ✓ |
| Twitter (Speriosu et al., 2011) | 1 | ✓ | ✓ |
| SenticNet (Cambria et al., 2010) | 1 | ✓ | ✓ |
| Affective rating (Warriner et al., 2013) | 1 | ✓ | ✓ |
| Empath Lexicon (Fast et al., 2016) | 1 | ✓ | |

Table 10: Empathic or Emotion Lexicons that are used by different teams. We listed all the lexicons that teams reported in their results.

**Team Phoenix** This team fine-tuned a T5 or Text-to-Text Transfer Transformer model (Raffel et al., 2019) using the emotion recognition dataset (Saravia et al., 2018) to predict categorical emotion labels. They used features extracted ([CLS] token) from transformer models such as BERT base, ALBERT-base-v2, Pegasus-xsum, and T5-base, however, fine-tuning yielded the best result by a large margin.

**MilaNLP** Several multi-inputs models were constructed by this team, a combination of essay text, demographic, and personality information, and a number of multi-task learning models, where they learned categorical emotion as one task and empathy and distress as another task. The model architecture was NN, where contextualized features were extracted from BERT large-uncased. The best model was a two inputs model which was the combination of contextualized features and gender. The worst results they reported were the output of the multi-task model with four inputs: contextual features, and gender, income, and Interpersonal Reactivity Index (personality information).

## 7 Conclusions

In this paper we presented the shared task on empathy and emotion prediction of essays that were written in response to news stories to which five teams participated. Based on the analysis of the systems we can conclude that fine-tuning a transformer language model or relying on features extracted from transformer models along with jointly learning related tasks can lead to a robust modeling of empathy, distress, and emotion. Despite the strenght of these strong contextualized features, we also observed that task-specific lexical features extracted from emotion, sentiment, opinion, and empathy lexicons can still create a significant impact on empathy, distress, and emotion models. Furthermore, the top-performing emotion models used external datasets to further fine-tune the language models, which indicates that data augmentation is important when modeling emotion, even if the text genre is different from the genre of the task at hand. Finally, using demographic and personality information as features revealed a significant impact on empathy, distress, and emotion models. Particularly, joint modeling of distress and empathy coupled with those features yielded the best results for most of the top-ranked systems that were developed as part of this shared task.

## Acknowledgments

This work was partially supported by the Amazon AWS Cloud Credits for Research program, João Sedoc's Microsoft Dissertation Grant and JRC's Exploratory Research Activity. Given the short time period in which the shared task was organized, we want to thank everyone who participated in this task.

## References


Muhammad Abdul-Mageed and Lyle Ungar. 2017. Emonet: Fine-grained emotion detection with gated recurrent neural networks. In *Proceedings of the 55th Annual Meeting of the Association for Computational Linguistics (Volume 1: Long Papers)*, volume 1, pages 718–728.

C Daniel Batson, Jim Fultz, and Patricia A Schoenrade. 1987. Distress and empathy: Two qualitatively distinct vicarious emotions with different motivational consequences. *Journal of personality*, 55(1):19–39.

Laura Bostan, Evgeny Kim, and Roman Klinger. 2019. Goodnewseveryone: A corpus of news headlines annotated with emotions, semantic roles, and reader perception. *arXiv preprint arXiv:1912.03184.*

Sven Buechel, Anneke Buffone, Barry Slaff, Lyle Ungar, and João Sedoc. 2018. Modeling empathy and distress in reaction to news stories. In *Proceedings of the 2018 Conference on Empirical Methods in Natural Language Processing*, pages 4758–4765.

Erik Cambria, Robert Speer, Catherine Havasi, and Amir Hussain. 2010. Senticnet: A publicly available semantic resource for opinion mining. In *AAAI fall symposium: commonsense knowledge*, volume 10. Citeseer.

Ankush Chatterjee, Kedhar Nath Narahari, Meghana Joshi, and Puneet Agrawal. 2019. SemEval-2019 task 3: EmoContext contextual emotion detection in text. In *Proceedings of the 13th International Workshop on Semantic Evaluation*, pages 39–48, Minneapolis, Minnesota, USA. Association for Computational Linguistics.

Yoonjung Choi and Janyce Wiebe. 2014. +/-effectwordnet: Sense-level lexicon acquisition for opinion inference. In *Proceedings of the 2014 Conference on Empirical Methods in Natural Language Processing (EMNLP)*, pages 1181–1191.

Kevin Clark, Minh-Thang Luong, Quoc V. Le, and Christopher D. Manning. 2020. Pre-training transformers as energy-based cloze models. In *EMNLP*.

Lee J Cronbach. 1947. Test "reliability": Its meaning and determination. *Psychometrika*, 12(1):1–16.

Mark H Davis. 1980. *Interpersonal Reactivity Index*. Edwin Mellen Press.

Dorottya Demszky, Dana Movshovitz-Attias, Jeongwoo Ko, Alan Cowen, Gaurav Nemade, and Sujith Ravi. 2020. Goemotions: A dataset of fine-grained emotions. *arXiv preprint arXiv:2005.00547.*

Jacob Devlin, Ming-Wei Chang, Kenton Lee, and Kristina Toutanova. 2018. Bert: Pre-training of deep bidirectional transformers for language understanding. *arXiv preprint arXiv:1810.04805.*

Paul Ekman. 1971. Universals and cultural differences in facial expressions of emotion. In *Nebraska symposium on motivation*. University of Nebraska Press.

Ethan Fast, Binbin Chen, and Michael S Bernstein. 2016. Empath: Understanding topic signals in large-scale text. In *Proceedings of the 2016 CHI conference on human factors in computing systems*, pages 4647–4657.

Nico H Frijda. 1988. The laws of emotion. *American psychologist*, 43(5):349.

Pascale Fung, Dario Bertero, Yan Wan, Anik Dey, Ricky Ho Yin Chan, Farhad Bin Siddique, Yang Yang, Chien-Sheng Wu, and Ruixi Lin. 2016. Towards empathetic human-robot interactions. In *International Conference on Intelligent Text Processing and Computational Linguistics*, pages 173–193. Springer.

James Gibson, Dogan Can, Bo Xiao, Zac E Imel, David C Atkins, Panayiotis Georgiou, and Shrikanth Narayanan. 2016. A deep learning approach to modeling empathy in addiction counseling. *Commitment*, 111:21.

Samuel D Gosling, Peter J Rentfrow, and Williams B Swann Jr. 2003. A very brief measure of the big-five personality domains. *Journal of Research in Personality*, 37:504–528.

Minqing Hu and Bing Liu. 2004. Mining and summarizing customer reviews. In *Proceedings of the tenth ACM SIGKDD international conference on Knowledge discovery and data mining*, pages 168–177.

General Inquirer. 1966. A computer approach to content analysis. *Cambridge, MA*.

Marina Litvak, Jahna Otterbacher, Chee Siang Ang, and David Atkins. 2016. Social and linguistic behavior and its correlation to trait empathy. In *Proceedings of the Workshop on Computational Modeling of People's Opinions, Personality, and Emotions in Social Media (PEOPLES)*, pages 128–137.

Yinhan Liu, Myle Ott, Naman Goyal, Jingfei Du, Mandar Joshi, Danqi Chen, Omer Levy, Mike Lewis, Luke Zettlemoyer, and Veselin Stoyanov. 2019. Roberta: A robustly optimized bert pretraining approach. *arXiv preprint arXiv:1907.11692.*

Tomas Mikolov, Kai Chen, Greg Corrado, and Jeffrey Dean. 2013. Efficient estimation of word representations in vector space. *arXiv preprint arXiv:1301.3781.*

Saif Mohammad. 2018a. Obtaining reliable human ratings of valence, arousal, and dominance for 20,000 English words. In *Proceedings of the 56th Annual Meeting of the Association for Computational Linguistics (Volume 1: Long Papers)*, pages 174–184, Melbourne, Australia. Association for Computational Linguistics.

Saif Mohammad, Felipe Bravo-Marquez, Mohammad Salameh, and Svetlana Kiritchenko. 2018. Semeval-2018 task 1: Affect in tweets. In *Proceedings of the 12th international workshop on semantic evaluation*, pages 1–17.

Saif Mohammad and Peter Turney. 2010. Emotions evoked by common words and phrases: Using mechanical turk to create an emotion lexicon. In *Proceedings of the NAACL HLT 2010 workshop on computational approaches to analysis and generation of emotion in text*, pages 26–34.

Saif Mohammad, Xiaodan Zhu, and Joel Martin. 2014. Semantic role labeling of emotions in tweets. In *Proceedings of the 5th Workshop on Computational Approaches to Subjectivity, Sentiment and Social Media Analysis*, pages 32–41.

Saif M Mohammad. 2017. Word affect intensities. *arXiv preprint arXiv:1704.08798*.

Saif M. Mohammad. 2018b. Obtaining reliable human ratings of valence, arousal, and dominance for 20,000 english words. In *Proceedings of The Annual Conference of the Association for Computational Linguistics (ACL)*, Melbourne, Australia.

Saif M. Mohammad. 2018c. Word affect intensities. In *Proceedings of the 11th Edition of the Language Resources and Evaluation Conference (LREC-2018)*, Miyazaki, Japan.

Saif M Mohammad and Felipe Bravo-Marquez. 2017. Wassa-2017 shared task on emotion intensity. *arXiv preprint arXiv:1708.03700*.

Saif M Mohammad, Svetlana Kiritchenko, and Xiaodan Zhu. 2013. Nrc-canada: Building the state-of-the-art in sentiment analysis of tweets. *arXiv preprint arXiv:1308.6242*.

Saif M. Mohammad and Peter D. Turney. 2013. Crowdsourcing a word-emotion association lexicon. *Computational Intelligence*, pages 436–465.

Sylvia A Morelli, Matthew D Lieberman, and Jamil Zaki. 2015. The emerging study of positive empathy. *Social and Personality Psychology Compass*, 9(2):57–68.

Finn Årup Nielsen. 2011. A new anew: Evaluation of a word list for sentiment analysis in microblogs. *arXiv preprint arXiv:1103.2903*.

Matthew E. Peters, Mark Neumann, Mohit Iyyer, Matt Gardner, Christopher Clark, Kenton Lee, and Luke Zettlemoyer. 2018. Deep contextualized word representations. In *Proc. of NAACL*.

Robert Plutchik. 1984. Emotions: A general psychoevolutionary theory. *Approaches to emotion*, 1984:197–219.

Colin Raffel, Noam Shazeer, Adam Roberts, Katherine Lee, Sharan Narang, Michael Matena, Yanqi Zhou, Wei Li, and Peter J Liu. 2019. Exploring the limits of transfer learning with a unified text-to-text transformer. *arXiv preprint arXiv:1910.10683*.

Inaki San Vicente, Rodrigo Agerri, and German Rigau. 2014. Simple, robust and (almost) unsupervised generation of polarity lexicons for multiple languages. In *Proceedings of the 14th Conference of the European Chapter of the Association for Computational Linguistics*, pages 88–97.

Elvis Saravia, Hsien-Chi Toby Liu, Yen-Hao Huang, Junlin Wu, and Yi-Shin Chen. 2018. Carer: Contextualized affect representations for emotion recognition. In *Proceedings of the 2018 Conference on Empirical Methods in Natural Language Processing*, pages 3687–3697.

Chhavi Sharma, Deepesh Bhageria, William Scott, Srinivas PYKL, Amitava Das, Tanmoy Chakraborty, Viswanath Pulabaigari, and Bjorn Gamback. 2020. Semeval-2020 task 8: Memotion analysis– the visuo-lingual metaphor! *arXiv preprint arXiv:2008.03781*.

Michael Speriosu, Nikita Sudan, Sid Upadhyay, and Jason Baldridge. 2011. Twitter polarity classification with label propagation over lexical links and the follower graph. In *Proceedings of the First workshop on Unsupervised Learning in NLP*, pages 53–63.

Carlo Strapparava and Rada Mihalcea. 2007. Semeval-2007 task 14: Affective text. In *Proceedings of the Fourth International Workshop on Semantic Evaluations (SemEval-2007)*, pages 70–74.

Shabnam Tafreshi. 2021. *Cross-Genre, Cross-Lingual, and Low-Resource Emotion Classification*. Ph.D. thesis, The George Washington University.

Shabnam Tafreshi and Mona Diab. 2018. Sentence and clause level emotion annotation, detection, and classification in a multi-genre corpus. In *Proceedings of the Eleventh International Conference on Language Resources and Evaluation (LREC 2018)*.

Amy Beth Warriner, Victor Kuperman, and Marc Brysbaert. 2013. Norms of valence, arousal, and dominance for 13,915 english lemmas. *Behavior research methods*, 45(4):1191–1207.

Bo Xiao, Chewei Huang, Zac E Imel, David C Atkins, Panayiotis Georgiou, and Shrikanth S Narayanan. 2016. A technology prototype system for rating therapist empathy from audio recordings in addiction counseling. *PeerJ Computer Science*, 2:e59.

Bo Xiao, Zac E Imel, Panayiotis G Georgiou, David C Atkins, and Shrikanth S Narayanan. 2015. " rate my therapist": automated detection of empathy in drug and alcohol counseling via speech and language processing. *PloS one*, 10(12):e0143055.

Naitian Zhou and David Jurgens. 2020. Condolences and empathy in online communities. In *Proceedings of the 2020 Conference on Empirical Methods in Natural Language Processing (EMNLP)*, pages 609–626.

## Appendices

### A Examples Track I (EMP)

Below examples are shown of four essays that received an erroneous empathy or distress label by the best-performing system. This is discussed in Section 5.3.

*Essay 1*: This just totally breaks my heart. I'm not one to get emotional you know that. But reading about kids in the foster care system and how messed up they come out its just heart breaking. Kids that no one cared enough about to change their ways is what it is. It's heartbreaking. Why have kids if this is the kind of parent you are going to be? Kids didn't have a shot straight from the start. (Gold Emp: 7, Predicted Emp: 2.470)

*Essay 2*: Can you tell we live in the age of Me! Me! Me! Now we have obese and trans people whining that their special needs are not being met. Are medical device companies supposed to design machines extra large for the few morbidly obese people in the world? Won't that make them more expensive and make them take up more space and raise costs for everyone? Should doctors be expected to learn even more than the incredible amount they already have to learn just for morbidly obese patients? Same thing goes for the "trans" patients. We seem to be living in a world where the small minority of people with special circumstances want the world to cater to them at the expense of everyone else's time, effort and money. (Gold Emp: 1, Predicted Emp: 5.428)

*Essay 3*: I understand that businesses need to worry about profits. But It really angers me when governments and companies throw away lives in order to protect their bottom line. When people riot and chaos breaks out, it is always for a reason. It is up to the government and our police forces to protect the everyday citizens, not take their lives to protect their own. It angers me so much, all the needless violence and lives lost for no good reason. (Gold Emp: 1, Predicted Emp: 5.272)

*Essay 4*: This article was about the crisis in Syria that is currently going on. Families are struggling with no end in sight. It's horrible conditions over there and impossible to get themselves out. Elderly people who have been retired and worked for so long, are faced with the horrible scenario of fighting for every little bit of resources they can find. Younger families don't have a supply of anything to fall back on. They fearful they will die at any moment. (Gold Dis: 1.25, Predicted Dis: 5.347)

### B Examples Track II (EMO)

Below examples are shown of essays that received one of the seven labels and for each label we present one essay that was correctly classified by all teams (i) and one that was misclassified by most systems (ii). This is discussed in closer detail in Section 5.3.

**Joy**: (i) Connecting with people is just always good for me personally, It's a matter of finding people with similar desires. That person who hasn't seen you in six month may be your "true friend" in an abstract sense, and even be very loyal and dependable in an emergency. But if you're bored on the weekends and want someone to hang out with you regularly ... just go find some more friends. Don't try to guilt your old friends that are busy or have different interests into changing their social habits to match yours. You can have old friends and new friends. We just have so much in common in what we can do and I just really think that's awesome.
(ii) I believe we all have someone in our lives suffering from PTSD, whether we know it or not. I know it takes quite a lot of courage and strength (and persistence) to get PTSD diagnosed and treated. Please know that you're loved and supported. Any way I can help get the word I will, I just need the messaging. (Predicted as: sadness, sadness, no-emo, surprise).

**Sadness**: (i) Hello Friend, i am writing to you as regards an article i read and i will also like to let you how i felt about the article. I was really sad and gutted by what transpired in the article. It was about an inmate with the name Richardson. Richardson normally stay alone in his cell room, but on this day another inmate was brought to him to start living with Richardson in his cell room the nickname of the Cell room mate was The prophet which has previous record of assaulting about 20 other inmate. This also lead to the assault of Richardson which really mad me sad.
(ii) Hey man, I just read this article about smokers and cancer and stuff and I think you should have a look. I know you like to smoke but I think you should try to cut back a bit. I don't want you to

end up with cancer man. The risk is really high and I care about you dude. I think we're too young to have to start worrying about cancer and death and stuff man. (Predicted: fear, anger, no-emo, no-emo).

**Disgust**: (i) This is kinda of disgusting that the Royal Carribean workers were taunting a passenger for being gay. However, is that any reason for the passenger to kill himself? Either way, the Cruise line is at fault and should be sued by the dead guys husband because they didn't do what they could in order ot save the man once he went overboard.
(ii) You know, our city has this odour to it sometimes. When I was a kid, we would be congested in traffic just trying to get to the beach for hours on end, burning up in 80 degree heat in a tiny beater car, but yeah, you don't feel choked. You definitely feel like the city isn't cleanly. I have better scents from my socks sometimes. (Predicted: no-emo, sadness, anger, sadness).

**Fear**: (i) So there are these flesh-eating bacteria that kills 25 percent of people. You can be enjoying your day and you can go some time without knowing what is attacking you. We have to be more vigilant with our bodies and get tested in order to prevent such things to happen to us. It could be scary thinking you're okay but you can be under attack by such a bacteria.
(ii) I just read an article concerning the repatriation of somalia's by the Kenyan government. Apparently thee a quite of few somalian refugees who fled their country and Kenya is attempting to repatriate them. It sounds like a very significant and challenging undertaking requiring tremendous amounts of resources. Hopefully the efforts will be successful and the families involved won't be adversely affected. (Predicted:no-emo, joy, no-emo, anger).

**Anger**: (i) We need more training for police. Police shouldn't be getting killed in the line of duty. It's not fair to their families because people are stupid and can't follow the law. People need to stop being so selfish and we need to make it less easy to obtain guns if people didn't have such easy access to them there wouldn't be so many deaths overall.
(ii) If only the republican party could get their act together. I'm not a republican, but some of this article really tells the tale of how republican are trying to deal with the currant president and the lack of confidence practically most of what female republican voters are feeling concerning everything that's happening today. You need to read this, a lot of this article is really interesting! (Predicted: joy, surprise, no-emo, sadness).

**Surprise**: (i) The article is so shocking. I had heard a little about it before but I had no idea that it was so drastic. And now I am not surprised about how the weather has been so screwy for the past few years. It doesn't seem like there is anything that we can do about it though. So I feel kind of helpless about that.
(ii) Is this what we have come to beaten a boy for stealing food something that he really needed he must of been hungry why else would he steal it something should be done in cases like this and the people that did it need the same jungle justice to happen to them also where is people hearts when they do things like this. (Predicted: anger, anger, no-emo, disgust).

**No-emo**: (i) More todlers and preschooler are over dozing on opiods as shown in a recentt research. the analyzed data show that kids admittted in hospitals for opiods poisoning and it focused on 13000 records of patients aged beween 1 and 19. Possible increase on prescribed pain killers show reail sales of the drug increased by four times.
(ii) I think as a parent you will find this very interesting. There is a study from Denmark that people who take the pill . That can be concerning for people that take the pill for health reasons and also to keep from having unnecessary pregnancy. I think that is really a cause from concern. I think that the pill is something that a lot of people take but if they know about the side effect of it with the depression they may not want to take it. I think that it can cause concern because of the things that will happen after they do not take the pill. There is a risk of pregnancy and that can cause issues down the road. I think that we need to research it further and see how we can turn it around and make it positive. I think you should really read this and tell me what you think about it. (Predicted: fear, surprise, no-emo, sadness).

# PVG at WASSA 2021: A Multi-Input, Multi-Task, Transformer-Based Architecture for Empathy and Distress Prediction

**Atharva Kulkarni**[1], **Sunanda Somwase**[1], **Shivam Rajput**[1], and **Manisha Marathe**[2]

[1, 2]Department of Computer Engineering, PVG's College of Engineering and Technology, affiliated to Savitribai Phule Pune University, India.

[1]{atharva.j.kulkarni1998, sunandasomwase, shivamraje43}@gmail.com

[2] mvm_comp@pvgcoet.ac.in

## Abstract

Active research pertaining to the affective phenomenon of empathy and distress is invaluable for improving human-machine interaction. Predicting intensities of such complex emotions from textual data is difficult, as these constructs are deeply rooted in the psychological theory. Consequently, for better prediction, it becomes imperative to take into account ancillary factors such as the psychological test scores, demographic features, underlying latent primitive emotions, along with the text's undertone and its psychological complexity. This paper proffers team PVG's solution to the WASSA 2021 Shared Task on Predicting Empathy and Emotion in Reaction to News Stories. Leveraging the textual data, demographic features, psychological test score, and the intrinsic interdependencies of primitive emotions and empathy, we propose a multi-input, multi-task framework for the task of empathy score prediction. Here, the empathy score prediction is considered the primary task, while emotion and empathy classification are considered secondary auxiliary tasks. For the distress score prediction task, the system is further boosted by the addition of lexical features. Our submission ranked $1^{st}$ based on the average correlation (0.545) as well as the distress correlation (0.574), and $2^{nd}$ for the empathy Pearson correlation (0.517).

## 1 Introduction

In recent years, substantial progress has been made in the NLP domain, with sentiment analysis and emotion identification at its core. The advent of attention-based models and complex deep learning architectures has led to substantial headways in sentiment/ emotion classification and their intensity prediction. However, the studies addressing the prediction of affective phenomenons of empathy and distress have been relatively limited. Factors such as lack of large-scale quality labeled datasets, the weak notion of the constructs themselves, and inter-disciplinary dependencies have hindered the progress. The WASSA 2021 Shared Task on Predicting Empathy and Emotion in Reaction to News Stories (Tafreshi et al., 2021) provides a quality, gold-standard dataset of the empathic reactions to news stories to predict Batson's empathic concern and personal distress scores.

Empathy, as defined by Davis (1983), is considered as "reactions of one individual to the observed experiences of another." It is more succinctly summarized by Levenson and Ruef (1992) in three key components, "(a) knowing what another person is feeling (cognitive), (b) feeling what another person is feeling (emotional), and (c) responding compassionately to another person's distress (behavioral)." Distress, on the other hand, as delineated by Dowling (2018), is "a strong aversive and self-oriented response to the suffering of others, accompanied by the desire to withdraw from a situation in order to protect oneself from excessive negative feelings." Empathy and distress are multifaceted interactional processes that are not always self-evident and often depend on the text's undertone. Moreover, along with the textual data, multiple psychological and demographic features also play a vital role in determining these complex emotions. Evidence by Fabi et al. (2019) suggests that empathy and distress are not independent of the basic emotions (happiness, sadness, disgust, fear, surprise, and anger) the subject feels during a given scenario. This appositeness of the primitive emotions with empathy and distress can be aptly exploited using a multi-task learning approach.

Multi-task learning has led to successes in many applications of NLP such as machine translation (McCann et al., 2017), speech recognition (Arık et al., 2017), representation learning (Hashimoto et al., 2017), semantic parsing (Peng et al., 2017), and information retrieval (Liu et al., 2015) to name



*Proceedings of the 11th Workshop on Computational Approaches to Subjectivity, Sentiment and Social Media Analysis*, pages 105–111
April 19, 2021. ©2021 Association for Computational Linguistics

a few. NLP literature (Standley et al., 2020) suggests that under specific circumstances and with well-crafted tasks, multi-task learning frameworks can often aid models to achieve state-of-the-art performances. Standley et al. (2020) further asserts that seemingly related tasks can often have similar underlying dynamics. With the same intuition, Deep et al. (2020) designed a multi-task learning model for sentiment classification and their corresponding intensity predictions. Building on these findings, we propose a multi-input, multi-task, transformer-based architecture for the prediction of empathy and distress scores. The multi-input nature of the framework aggregates information from textual, categorical, and numeric data to generate robust representations for the regression task at hand. Exploiting the latent interdependencies between primitive emotions and empathy/ distress, we formulate the multi-task learning problem as a combination of classification and regression. The model simultaneously classifies the text into its correct basic emotion, detects if it exhibits high empathy/ distress, and accordingly predicts its appropriate empathy/ distress intensity score according to Batson's scale (Batson et al., 1987). This multi-input, multi-task learning paradigm is further bolstered with the addition of NRC Emotion Intensity Lexicons (Mohammad, 2018b); NRC Valence, Arousal, and Dominance Lexicons (Mohammad, 2018a); and relevant features from Empath (Fast et al., 2016). Moreover, our proposed models have less than 110k trainable parameters and are still able to achieve relatively high Pearson's correlation of 0.517 and 0.574 for empathy and distress, respectively, and 0.545 for average correlation, outperforming other teams.

## 2 Related Work

Over the last few years, earnest endeavours have been made in the NLP community to analyze empathy and distress. Earlier work in empathy mostly addressed the presence or absence of empathy in spoken dialogue (Gibson et al., 2015; Alam et al., 2016; Fung et al., 2016; Pérez-Rosas et al., 2017; Alam et al., 2018). For text-based empathy prediction, Buechel et al. (2018) laid a firm foundation for predicting Batson's empathic concern and personal distress scores in reaction to news articles. They present the first publicly available gold-standard dataset for text-based empathy and distress prediction. Sharma et al. (2020) contemplated a computational approach for understanding empathy in text-based health support. They developed a multi-task RoBERTa-based bi-encoder paradigm for identifying empathy in conversations and extracting rationales underlying its predictions. Wagner (2020) analysed the linguistic undertones for empathy present in avid fiction readers.

Computational work done for predicting distress is relatively modest. Shapira et al. (2020) analysed textual data to examine associations between linguistic features and clients distress during psychotherapy. They combined linguistic features like positive and negative emotion words with psychological measures like Outcome Questionnaire-45 (Lambert et al., 2004) and Outcome Rating Scale(Miller, 2003). Zhou and Jurgens (2020) studied the affiliation between distress, condolence, and empathy in online support groups using nested regression models.

| Dataset | Datapoints |
|---|---|
| Train | 1860 |
| Development | 270 |
| Test | 525 |

Table 1: Data distribution.

## 3 Data Description

The WASSA 2021 Shared Task (Tafreshi et al., 2021) provides an extended dataset to the one compiled by Buechel et al. (2018). The dataset has a total of 14 features spanning textual, categorical, and numeric data types. Essays represent the subject's empathic reactions to news stories he/she has read. The demographic features of gender, race, education, and the essay's gold-standard emotion label cover the categorical input features. The numeric features include the subject's age and income, followed by personality traits scores (conscientiousness, openness, extraversion, agreeableness, stability) and interpersonal reactivity index (IRI) scores (fantasy, perspective taking, empathetic concern, personal distress). The train-development-test split of the dataset is illustrated in Table 1.

## 4 Proposed Methodology

In this section, we posit two multi-task learning frameworks for empathy and distress score prediction. They are elucidated in detail as follows:

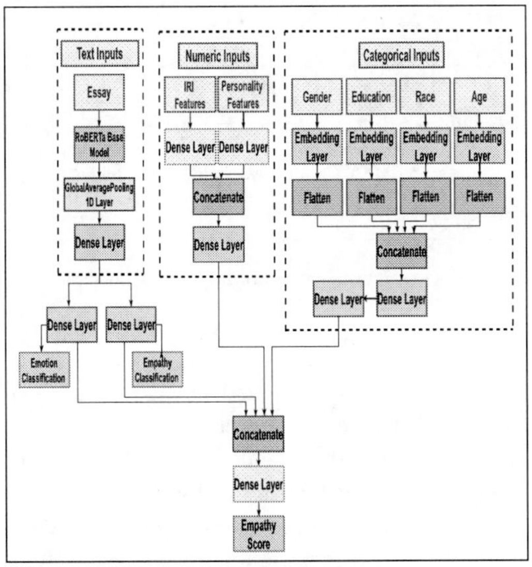


Figure 1: System architecture for empathy score prediction. The Dense layers in red have an $\ell^2$ kernel regularization applied to them.

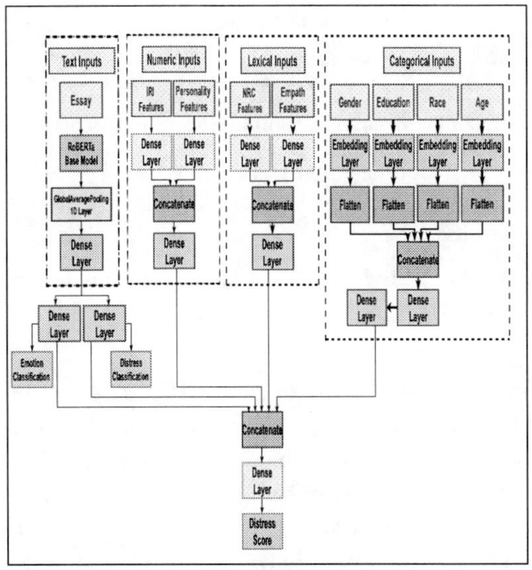


Figure 2: System architecture for distress score prediction. The Dense layers in red have an $\ell^2$ kernel regularization applied to them.

### 4.1 Empathy Score Prediction

Figure 1 depicts the system architecture for empathy score prediction. We formulate the task of empathy score prediction as a multi-input, multi-task learning problem. The proposed multi-task learning framework aims to leverage the empathy bin [1] and the text's emotion to predict its empathy score. Here, the empathy score prediction is treated as the primary task, whereas emotion and empathy classification are considered secondary auxiliary tasks. The multi-input, multi-task nature of the framework efficiently fuses the diverse set of information (textual, categorical, and numeric) provided in the dataset to generate robust representations for empathy score prediction.

For the task of empathy and emotion classification, we make use of the pre-trained RoBERTa base model (Liu et al., 2019). The contextualized representations generated by RoBERTa help extract the context-aware information and capture the undertone of the text better than standard deep learning models. For each word in the essay, we extract the default pre-trained embeddings from the last hidden layer of RoBERTa. The 768-dimensional word embeddings are averaged to generate essay-level representations, followed by a hidden layer (128 units) for dimensionality reduction. The model further branches into two parallel fully-connected layers (16 units each), which form the task-specific layers for empathy and emotion classification, respectively. Let $T_1$ and $T_2$ denote the generated task-specific representations for empathy and emotion classification, respectively, of dimension $d_1$. Finally, a classification layer (binary classification for empathy and multi-class classification for emotion) is added to each of the task-specific layers.

To incorporate the demographic information encoded in the categorical variables, we make use of entity embeddings (Guo and Berkhahn, 2016). Formally, entity embeddings are domain-specific multi-dimensional representations of categorical variables, automatically learned by a neural network when trained on a particular task. For each of the demographic features (gender, education, race, and age[2]), 3-dimensional entity embeddings are generated. All the resultant embeddings are flattened, concatenated, and passed through two fully-connected layers (32 and 16 units, respectively), generating a layer having relevant information from each categorical input. Let this representation be denoted as $C$ of dimension $d_2$.

The numeric inputs of the personality and the

[1] empathy bin is a feature given in the training dataset, where its value is 1 if empathy score greater than or equal to 4.0, and 0 if empathy score is less than 4.0. Thus, an essay exhibits high empathy if its empathy bin is 1 and exhibits low empathy if its empathy bin is 0. The same analogy is true for distress bin.

[2] In the dataset age is given as a numeric input. We split it into intervals of below 25, 26-40, 41-60, and 61 and above.

| | Correlation with empathy score | Correlation with distress score |
|---|---|---|
| **NRC features** | sadness (0.19), fear (0.12), arousal (0.11), joy (0.11), valence (0.11), dominance (0.10) | fear (0.22), sadness (0.20), disgust (0.15), arousal (0.15), anger (0.15), dominance (0.12) |
| **Empath features** | domestic_work (0.15), death (0.14), home (0.12), sadness (0.12), suffering (0.11), help (0.11), party (0.11), family (0.10), shame (0.10), celebration (0.10), leisure (0.9), negative_emotion (0.9), air_travel (0.8), violence (0.8), pain (0.7) | suffering (0.16), death (0.15), torment (0.13), hate (0.11), negative_emotion (0.10), sadness (0.10), aggression (0.09), fight (0.09), help (0.09), pain (0.08), kill (0.08), horror (0.08), violence (0.08), war (0.08), ugliness (0.7) |

Table 2: Selected NRC and Empath features and their pearson's correlation with training data's empathy and distress score.

Interpersonal Reactivity Index (IRI) scores are incorporated in the model by passing them individually through a single hidden layer (8 units). The results are concatenated and further passed on to a fully-connected layer (32 units) to generate their combined representations. Let this representation be denoted as $N$ of dimension $d_3$.

The task-specific layers for empathy and emotion classification and the representations generated by the final hidden layer of the entity embeddings and the numeric psychological score inputs are concatenated as given in equation 1 to generate the final representation $F_1$ for empathy score prediction.

$$F_1 = [T_1; T_2; C; N] \in \mathbb{R}^{d_1+d_2+d_3} \quad (1)$$

It is further passed to another hidden layer (16 units). Thus, this layer contains the compressed information from different knowledge views of the input data. A final regression layer is added for the empathy score prediction task. The multi-input, multi-task model is trained end-to-end with the objective loss calculated as the sum of the loss for each of the three tasks.

### 4.2 Distress Score Prediction

Figure 2 depicts the system architecture for distress score prediction. The distress score prediction model is the same as that of the empathy score prediction model, but with the addition of handcrafted lexical features. We use 6 NRC Emotion Intensity Lexicons (Mohammad, 2018b); 2 NRC Valence, Arousal, and Dominance Lexicons (Mohammad, 2018a); and 15 features from Empath (Fast et al., 2016) as stated in Table 2. These features are chosen as they exhibit a high Pearson correlation with the training data. For each essay, the respective NRC and Empath score is calculated as the sum of each word's score in the essay. The NRC lexicons and Empath features are passed to a single hidden layer (8 and 16 units for NRC and Empath, respectively.) independently before concatenation. The resultant representation is further passed through another hidden layer (48 units). Let this representation be denoted by $L$ of dimension $d_4$. It is concatenated with the final layer representations from other inputs to generate the final representation $F_2$ for distress score prediction, as given by equation 2.

$$F_2 = [T_1; T_2; C; N; L] \in \mathbb{R}^{d_1+d_2+d_3+d_4} \quad (2)$$

## 5 Experimental Setup

### 5.1 Data Preparation

We applied standard text cleaning steps for each essay in the dataset, such as removing the punctuations, special characters, digits, single characters, multiple spaces, and accented words. The essays are further normalized by removing wordplay, replacing acronyms with full forms, and expanding contractions [3].

Each essay is tokenized and padded to a maximum length of 200 tokens. Longer essays are truncated. Each Empath feature is converted into its percentage value. For distress score prediction, the numeric features, NRC lexicon scores, and Empath features are standardized by removing the mean and scaling to unit variance before being passed to the model.

### 5.2 Parameter Setting and Training Environment

Given the small amount of data, the weights of the RoBERTa layers were freezed and not updated during the training. The multi-task model is trained end-to-end using the Adam optimizer (Kingma and Ba, 2014) with a learning rate of $1 \times 10^{-3}$ and a batch size of 32. We used Hyperbolic Tangent

[3] https://pypi.org/project/pycontractions/

| Model Name | Empathy Train | Empathy Dev | Distress Train | Distress Dev |
|---|---|---|---|---|
| Plain RoBERTa model | 0.56 | 0.47 | 0.56 | 0.41 |
| Plain multi-input model | 0.64 | 0.50 | 0.64 | 0.49 |
| **Multi-input, multi-task model** | **0.74** | **0.57** | 0.66 | 0.53 |
| **Multi-input, multi-task model+ NRC + Empath** | 0.64 | 0.54 | **0.66** | **0.56** |

Table 3: Performance comparison of various models as per Pearson's correlation ($p < 0.05$).

(tanh) activation for all the hidden layers as it performed better than ReLU activation and its other variants. The model is trained for 200 epochs with early stopping applied if the validation loss does not improve after 20 epochs. Furthermore, the learning rate is reduced by a factor of 0.2 if validation loss does not decline after ten successive epochs. The model with the best validation loss is selected. $\ell^2$ kernel regularizer of $5 \times 10^{-4}$ applied to certain hidden layers as shown in Figures 1 and 2. A dropout of probability 0.2 is applied after the average pooling of contextual RoBERTa embeddings. Our code is available at our GitHub repository.[4]

## 6 Results and Discussion

The performance comparison of the various models on the validation data is reported in Table 3. As illustrated in the Table 3, we compare the performances of a RoBERTa based regression model, a multi-input model (text + categorical + numeric); a multi-input (text + categorical + numeric), multi-task model; and a multi-input (text + categorical + numeric), multi-task model with added lexical features (NRC + Empath). The systems submitted by our team are highlighted in Table 3. It is evident from Table 3 that the addition of categorical and numeric input features leads to an appreciable improvement in the models performance. This further attests that the demographic features and the psychological scores contribute valuable information for predicting scores of complex emotions like empathy and distress. The performance is further improved by adopting a multi-task approach, thus, reinstating our belief in the interdependencies between the primitive emotions and the complex emotions of empathy and distress. The addition of lexical features, however, leads to an improvement for distress prediction but a decrease in performance for empathy prediction. This may be explained by the theories in the affective neuroscience literature, wherein empathy is considered a neocortex emotion, describing it as an emotional, cognitive, and behavioral process. Thus, ones empathic quotient is reflected in how one expresses ones feelings and the undertone of it, rather than the mere words one uses. Moreover, as stated by Sedoc et al. (2020) in their work, there exist no clear set of lexicons that can accurately distinguish empathy from self-focused distress. Another reason for the decrease in the performance for empathy score prediction may be attributed to the fact that the Empath features for empathy, as reported in Table 2 lack some interpretability from a human perspective. Empath features such as *domestic work, party, celebration, leisure,* and *air travel* are not innately empathic categories and perhaps show high correlation due to corpus-based topical bias. The Empath features for distress, on the other hand, seem quite relevant and thus, might explain the increase in performance for distress prediction. We encourage further research in this direction.

[4]`https://github.com/mr-atharva-kulkarni/WASSA-2021-Shared-Task`

## 7 Conclusion and Future Work

In this work, we propose a multi-input, multi-task, transformer-based architecture to predict Batson's empathic concern and personal distress scores. Leveraging the dependency between the basic emotions and empathy/ distress, as well as incorporating textual, categorical, and numeric data, our proposed model generates robust representations for the regression task at hand. The addition of certain lexical features further improves the model's performance for distress score prediction. Our submission ranked $1^{st}$ based on average correlation (0.545) as well as distress correlation (0.574), and $2^{nd}$ for empathy Pearson correlation (0.517) on the test data. As for the future work of this research, a weighted loss scheme could be employed to enhance the results. From a psychological and linguistic standpoint, features such as part-of-speech tags, syntax parse tree, and the text's subjectivity and polarity scores could also be exploited.

## References

F. Alam, M. Danieli, and G. Riccardi. 2016. Can we detect speakers' empathy?: A real-life case study. In *2016 7th IEEE International Conference on Cognitive Infocommunications (CogInfoCom)*, pages 000059–000064.

Firoj Alam, Morena Danieli, and Giuseppe Riccardi. 2018. Annotating and modeling empathy in spoken conversations. *Comput. Speech Lang.*, 50(C):4061.

Sercan Ö. Arık, Mike Chrzanowski, Adam Coates, Gregory Diamos, Andrew Gibiansky, Yongguo Kang, Xian Li, John Miller, Andrew Ng, Jonathan Raiman, Shubho Sengupta, and Mohammad Shoeybi. 2017. Deep voice: Real-time neural text-to-speech. In *Proceedings of the 34th International Conference on Machine Learning*, volume 70 of *Proceedings of Machine Learning Research*, pages 195–204, International Convention Centre, Sydney, Australia. PMLR.

C Daniel Batson, Jim Fultz, and Patricia A Schoenrade. 1987. Distress and empathy: Two qualitatively distinct vicarious emotions with different motivational consequences. *Journal of personality*, 55(1):19–39.

Sven Buechel, Anneke Buffone, Barry Slaff, Lyle Ungar, and João Sedoc. 2018. Modeling empathy and distress in reaction to news stories. In *Proceedings of the 2018 Conference on Empirical Methods in Natural Language Processing*, pages 4758–4765, Brussels, Belgium. Association for Computational Linguistics.

Mark H Davis. 1983. The effects of dispositional empathy on emotional reactions and helping: A multidimensional approach. *Journal of personality*, 51(2):167–184.

Kumar Shikhar Deep, Md Shad Akhtar, Asif Ekbal, and Pushpak Bhattacharyya. 2020. Related tasks can share! a multi-task framework for affective language. *arXiv preprint arXiv:2002.02154*.

Trisha Dowling. 2018. Compassion does not fatigue! *The Canadian Veterinary Journal*, 59(7):749.

Sarah Fabi, Lydia Anna Weber, and Hartmut Leuthold. 2019. Empathic concern and personal distress depend on situational but not dispositional factors. *PLoS ONE*, 14(11):e0225102.

Ethan Fast, Binbin Chen, and Michael S. Bernstein. 2016. Empath: Understanding topic signals in large-scale text. In *Proceedings of the 2016 CHI Conference on Human Factors in Computing Systems*, CHI '16, page 46474657, New York, NY, USA. Association for Computing Machinery.

Pascale Fung, Anik Dey, Farhad Bin Siddique, Ruixi Lin, Yang Yang, Yan Wan, and Ho Yin Ricky Chan. 2016. Zara the Supergirl: An empathetic personality recognition system. In *Proceedings of the 2016 Conference of the North American Chapter of the Association for Computational Linguistics: Demonstrations*, pages 87–91, San Diego, California. Association for Computational Linguistics.

James Gibson, Nikolaos Malandrakis, Francisco Romero, David C Atkins, and Shrikanth S Narayanan. 2015. Predicting therapist empathy in motivational interviews using language features inspired by psycholinguistic norms. In *Sixteenth annual conference of the international speech communication association*.

Cheng Guo and Felix Berkhahn. 2016. Entity embeddings of categorical variables.

Kazuma Hashimoto, Caiming Xiong, Yoshimasa Tsuruoka, and Richard Socher. 2017. A joint many-task model: Growing a neural network for multiple NLP tasks. In *Proceedings of the 2017 Conference on Empirical Methods in Natural Language Processing*, pages 1923–1933, Copenhagen, Denmark. Association for Computational Linguistics.

Diederik P Kingma and Jimmy Ba. 2014. Adam: A method for stochastic optimization. *arXiv preprint arXiv:1412.6980*.

Michael J Lambert, Ann T Gregersen, and Gary M Burlingame. 2004. The outcome questionnaire-45. *The use of psychological testing for treatment planning and outcomes assessment: Instruments for adults*.

Robert W Levenson and Anna M Ruef. 1992. Empathy: a physiological substrate. *Journal of personality and social psychology*, 63(2):234.

Xiaodong Liu, Jianfeng Gao, Xiaodong He, Li Deng, Kevin Duh, and Ye-yi Wang. 2015. Representation learning using multi-task deep neural networks for semantic classification and information retrieval. In *Proceedings of the 2015 Conference of the North American Chapter of the Association for Computational Linguistics: Human Language Technologies*, pages 912–921, Denver, Colorado. Association for Computational Linguistics.

Yinhan Liu, Myle Ott, Naman Goyal, Jingfei Du, Mandar Joshi, Danqi Chen, Omer Levy, Mike Lewis, Luke Zettlemoyer, and Veselin Stoyanov. 2019. Roberta: A robustly optimized bert pretraining approach. *arXiv preprint arXiv:1907.11692*.

Bryan McCann, James Bradbury, Caiming Xiong, and Richard Socher. 2017. Learned in translation: Contextualized word vectors. In *Proceedings of the 31st International Conference on Neural Information Processing Systems*, NIPS'17, page 62976308, Red Hook, NY, USA. Curran Associates Inc.

Scott D Miller. 2003. The outcome rating scale: A preliminary study of the reliability, validity, and feasibility of a brief visual analog measure. *Journal of brief Therapy*, 2(2):91–100.

Saif Mohammad. 2018a. Obtaining reliable human ratings of valence, arousal, and dominance for 20,000 English words. In *Proceedings of the 56th Annual Meeting of the Association for Computational Linguistics (Volume 1: Long Papers)*, pages 174–184, Melbourne, Australia. Association for Computational Linguistics.

Saif Mohammad. 2018b. Word affect intensities. In *Proceedings of the Eleventh International Conference on Language Resources and Evaluation (LREC 2018)*, Miyazaki, Japan. European Language Resources Association (ELRA).

Hao Peng, Sam Thomson, and Noah A. Smith. 2017. Deep multitask learning for semantic dependency parsing. In *Proceedings of the 55th Annual Meeting of the Association for Computational Linguistics (Volume 1: Long Papers)*, pages 2037–2048, Vancouver, Canada. Association for Computational Linguistics.

Verónica Pérez-Rosas, Rada Mihalcea, Kenneth Resnicow, Satinder Singh, and Lawrence An. 2017. Understanding and predicting empathic behavior in counseling therapy. In *Proceedings of the 55th Annual Meeting of the Association for Computational Linguistics (Volume 1: Long Papers)*, pages 1426–1435, Vancouver, Canada. Association for Computational Linguistics.

João Sedoc, Sven Buechel, Yehonathan Nachmany, Anneke Buffone, and Lyle Ungar. 2020. Learning word ratings for empathy and distress from document-level user responses. In *Proceedings of the 12th Language Resources and Evaluation Conference*, pages 1664–1673, Marseille, France. European Language Resources Association.

Natalie Shapira, Gal Lazarus, Yoav Goldberg, Eva Gilboa-Schechtman, Rivka Tuval-Mashiach, Daniel Juravski, and Dana Atzil-Slonim. 2020. Using computerized text analysis to examine associations between linguistic features and clients distress during psychotherapy. *Journal of counseling psychology*.

Ashish Sharma, Adam Miner, David Atkins, and Tim Althoff. 2020. A computational approach to understanding empathy expressed in text-based mental health support. In *Proceedings of the 2020 Conference on Empirical Methods in Natural Language Processing (EMNLP)*, pages 5263–5276, Online. Association for Computational Linguistics.

Trevor Standley, Amir Zamir, Dawn Chen, Leonidas Guibas, Jitendra Malik, and Silvio Savarese. 2020. Which tasks should be learned together in multi-task learning? In *Proceedings of the 37th International Conference on Machine Learning*, volume 119 of *Proceedings of Machine Learning Research*, pages 9120–9132. PMLR.

Shabnam Tafreshi, Orphée De Clercq, Valentin Barriere, Sven Buechel, João Sedoc, and Alexandra Balahur. 2021. WASSA2021 Shared Task: Predicting Empathy and Emotion in Reaction to News Stories. In *Proceedings of the Eleventh Workshop on Computational Approaches to Subjectivity, Sentiment and Social Media Analysis*. Association for Computational Linguistics.

Rachel Wagner. 2020. *It's not what you say, it's how you say it: a linguistic analysis of empathy in fiction readers*. Ph.D. thesis, Rutgers University-Camden Graduate School.

Naitian Zhou and David Jurgens. 2020. Condolence and empathy in online communities. In *Proceedings of the 2020 Conference on Empirical Methods in Natural Language Processing (EMNLP)*, pages 609–626, Online. Association for Computational Linguistics.

# WASSA@IITK at WASSA 2021: Multi-task Learning and Transformer Finetuning for Emotion Classification and Empathy Prediction

**Jay Mundra*** **Rohan Gupta*** **Sagnik Mukherjee***
Indian Institute of Technology Kanpur (IIT Kanpur)
{jaym, rohangpt, sagnikm}@iitk.ac.in

## Abstract

This paper describes our contribution to the WASSA 2021 shared task on Empathy Prediction and Emotion Classification. The broad goal of this task was to model an empathy score, a distress score and the overall level of emotion of an essay written in response to a newspaper article associated with harm to someone. We have used the ELECTRA model abundantly and also advanced deep learning approaches like multi-task learning. Additionally, we also leveraged standard machine learning techniques like ensembling. Our system achieves a Pearson Correlation Coefficient of **0.533** on sub-task I and a macro F1 score of **0.5528** on sub-task II. We ranked $\mathbf{1}^{st}$ in Emotion Classification sub-task and $\mathbf{3}^{rd}$ in Empathy Prediction sub-task.

## 1 Introduction

With the growing interest in human-computer interface, machines still lag in having and understanding emotions. Emotions are considered a trait of a living being and are often used to list differences between machines and living beings. Human emotions such as empathy are hard to describe even for humans, and a consensus is hard to be reached. The inherent knowledge humans have for these emotions is hard to pass on to machines, and hence this task is challenging. That is also probably the reason why the prior work in this area is really limited. Although there has been some research done by Xiao et al. (2012), Gibson et al. (2015) and Khanpour et al. (2017), they have some significant limitations, such as the oversimplified notion of empathy and unavailability of these corpora in the public domain. Sedoc et al. (2020) investigated the utility of Mixed-Level Feed Forward Network and also created an empathy lexicon.

Another problem in the affect domain is that of emotion classification of textual data. Klinger et al. (2018) presented an analysis of many datasets for this task. These datasets vary in size, origin and taxonomy. The most frequent emotion taxonomy used is that proposed by Ekman (1992) - identifying anger, disgust, fear, joy, sadness and surprise as the 6 emotion categories. Demszky et al. (2020) presented a dataset obtained from Reddit comments and tagged according to 27 fine-grained emotion categories identified by them. They also present a baseline obtained by fine-tuning a BERT-base (Devlin et al., 2019) model on their dataset.

In the WASSA 2021 Shared Task (Tafreshi et al., 2021) there are two major sub-tasks addressing the issues of empathy and distress prediction and emotion classification.

**Track I: Empathy Prediction -** the objective is to model the empathy concern as well as the personal distress at the essay level. This is a regression task.

**Track II: Emotion Prediction -** the objective is to predict the overall emotion of the essay. The labels are categorical, and it is a classification task.

In our approach, we have used transformer-based language models, primarily ELECTRA (Clark et al., 2020). We also experimented across different forms of multi-task learning, keeping ELECTRA at the base and having several feedforward layers on top of it, responsible for different tasks. It was also observed that various ensembling techniques worked pretty well for the tasks and improved the scores due to a better bias-variance trade-off.

## 2 Dataset

For this task, an extended version of the dataset by Buechel et al. (2018) was used, as per the official release from the task organizers.

The dataset contained 1860 data points for training where each data point was a tuple of the following - the essay, an empathy score, a distress score, age

* Authors equally contributed to this work.



*Proceedings of the 11th Workshop on Computational Approaches to Subjectivity, Sentiment and Social Media Analysis*, pages 112–116
April 19, 2021. ©2021 Association for Computational Linguistics

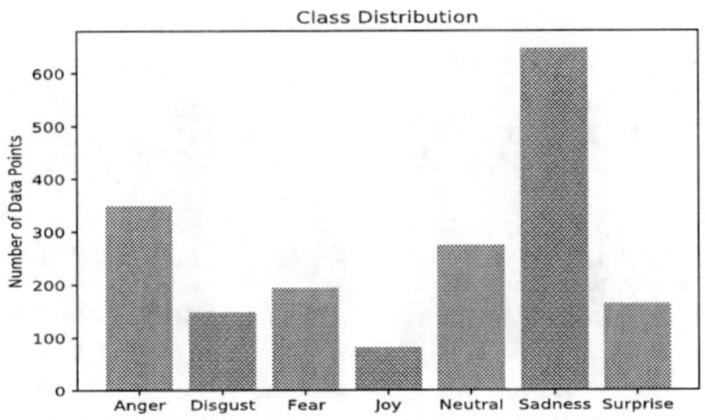


Figure 1: Frequency of classes in the dataset

and income of the annotator (demographic factors), overall emotion of the essay and various metrics denoting the personality of the respondent. The empathy and distress scores were in the range $(1, 7)$, and they were annotated with a 7-point scale. The validation and test sets had 270 and 525 data points, respectively. The emotion classes used in the task are closely related to the emotion classes discussed in Ekman (1992).

For this task, the volume of data was insufficient for finetuning large language models like ELECTRA. To overcome this, we experimented with data augmentation; in particular, we used the Ekman grouped data for emotion classification provided in the GoEmotions dataset (Demszky et al., 2020). The pros and cons of this methodology will be discussed in Section 3.2.2

## 3 System Description

### 3.1 Empathy Prediction

We propose two separate approaches for this task.

#### 3.1.1 Transformer finetuning

The first approach is based on finetuning an ELECTRA large model separately for empathy and distress with the Mean Squared Error (MSE) loss function. The ELECTRA parameters were kept trainable, and it was finetuned with a single feed-forward layer on top of it. We experimented with the number of linear layers and the number of hidden neurons and chose a single layer since it yielded the best validation score. We shall refer to this approach as the Vanilla ELECTRA method.

#### 3.1.2 Finetuning with Multi-task learning

Multi-task learning has recently caught a lot of interest in the NLP community (Liu et al. (2019a), Worsham and Kalita (2020)). The objectives, namely empathy and personal distress, are seemingly closely related, and hence a multi-task learning setup was used, jointly modelling them. We used an ELECTRA-large with two dense layers on top of it, one responsible for Empathy and another for Distress. Like the previous approach, MSE loss was used, adding the loss for Empathy and Distress and jointly training the architecture end to end on that total loss.

The same approach was tried out with the RoBERTa (Liu et al., 2019b) model.

#### 3.1.3 Final Ensemble

For the empathy prediction task, the final system was an ensemble of two models - Roberta multi-task model and Vanilla ELECTRA model.

For the distress prediction task, the final system was an ensemble of two models, both being ELECTRA models trained with multi-task loss, with different performances on the development set. We finally submitted an ensemble of two models for each task - Empathy prediction, and Distress prediction.

For all these ensembling, a simple average of the output across the trained models was taken.

### 3.2 Emotion Classification

#### 3.2.1 Transformer finetuning

In this approach the ELECTRA model was finetuned. The [CLS] token was passed through a single linear layer to produce a vector of size 7, representing class probabilities (or scores). We trained using the cross entropy loss function.

As per our observations these models were sensitive to initialisation. The validation accuracy scores varied significantly across different seed values. Hence, the models were trained several times, and the snapshots with best validation scores were saved.

#### 3.2.2 Data Augmentation

The Figure 1 clearly shows that there was a heavy class imbalance in the dataset provided by the organizers, 'joy' being the least represented class (since the data collected is related to harm done to someone). Class imbalance is a standard problem faced by the machine learning community in classification problems (Longadge and Dongre (2013), Haixiang et al. (2017)). To address this issue, the dataset was augmented with the GoEmotions dataset (Demszky et al., 2020), since the class labels of the Ekman variant of it was exactly the same. However, this dataset was different from ours because the

| Method | Val Macro F1 |
|---|---|
| + aug | 0.6042 |
| - aug | 0.561 |

Table 1: Variation of validation macro F1 scores with and without the data augmentation technique for classification task for the ELECTRA base model ('+ aug' means data augmentation has been used and '- aug' means otherwise.)

essays' length was significantly lesser for GoEmotions dataset than our task dataset. Hence the appropriate number of data points to be sampled was an important hyperparameter. Too much sampling would make the distribution of the train data very different from the distribution of validation and test data, and would cause the model to eventually fail to generalise.

The augmentation scheme was different across different components of the final ensemble. While an ELECTRA base was finetuned on a class balanced dataset of total 2800 samples represented by BA (Balanced Augmentation) in Table 2, another ELECTRA base was finetuned with randomly chosen 1000 samples represented by RA (Random Augmentation) in Table 2. Same augmentation scheme was followed on ELECTRA Large and RoBERTa. We also trained an ALBERT (Lan et al., 2019) model on the BA augmented data. The intuition behind using multiple transformer models was to have different "strength" of different models.

### 3.2.3 Final Ensemble

We created two ensemble models for this task by summing the probability scores of the models involved in ensemble. The final systems submitted for this task were two ensembles. The ensembling technique was to take sum or average across class scores and then selecting the class with the highest score. One of them (Ensemble 1 in table 2) was an ensemble of two ELECTRA base models and one ELECTRA large model (model 1, 2, 3 in the table 2) that were trained on different augmentation schemes.

The second ensemble (Ensemble 2 in table 2) is the ensemble of the first 7 models shown in Table 2 comprising of 2 ELECTRA base, 2 ELECTRA large, 2 RoBERTa, and an ALBERT trained using the methods outlined in the previous subsection.

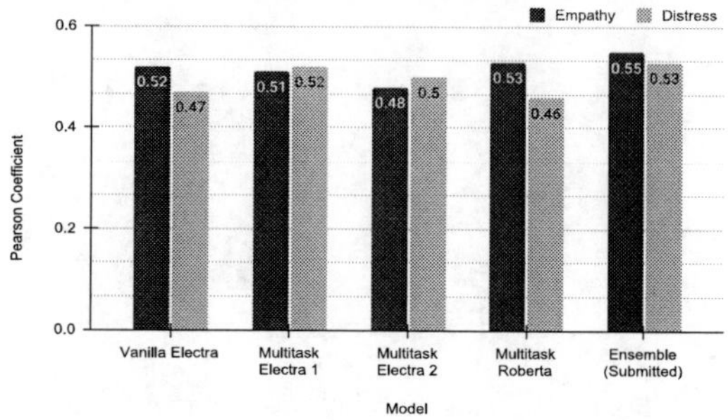


Figure 2: Pearson's Correlation Coefficient of Sub-task I on dev data

| Model | Macro F1 | Accuracy |
|---|---|---|
| ELECTRA base (RA) | 0.604 | **69.25** |
| ELECTRA base (BA) | **0.608** | 67.77 |
| ELECTRA Large (RA) | 0.582 | 68.51 |
| ELECTRA Large (BA) | 0.585 | 66.29 |
| RoBERTa Large (RA) | 0.588 | 67.03 |
| RoBERTa Large (BA) | 0.583 | 66.29 |
| ALBERT Large (BA) | 0.595 | 68.51 |
| Ensemble 1* | 0.64 | 71.11 |
| Ensemble 2 | **0.65** | **72.59** |

Table 2: Accuracy and macro-F1 scores on emotion classification on the dev data. * - Submitted model

## 4 Experimental Setup

For all tasks the learning rate was set to $10^{-5}$, and the models were trained using AdamW (Loshchilov and Hutter, 2017) as optimizer. The parameters for AdamW were $\beta = (0.9, 0.99)$, $\epsilon = 10^{-6}$, weight_decay = 0. Batch size was set to 16 for the Section 3.1.1 approach, and set to 8 for Section 3.1.2 and Section 3.2.1 with the shuffle parameter set to True on pytorch dataloader. A single Tesla V100-SXM2-16GB GPU was used for the finetuning experiments. The GPUs were available on the Google Colab platform.

The ELECTRA and RoBERTa were used off the shelf from the HuggingFace library (Wolf et al., 2020).

## 5 Results

The results on the empathy prediction sub-task and the distress prediction sub-task on the development set can be found in Figure 2. Also presented in the figure is the performance of the ensemble models that we submitted for evaluation. On the test data, the ensembles achieved a pearson correlation

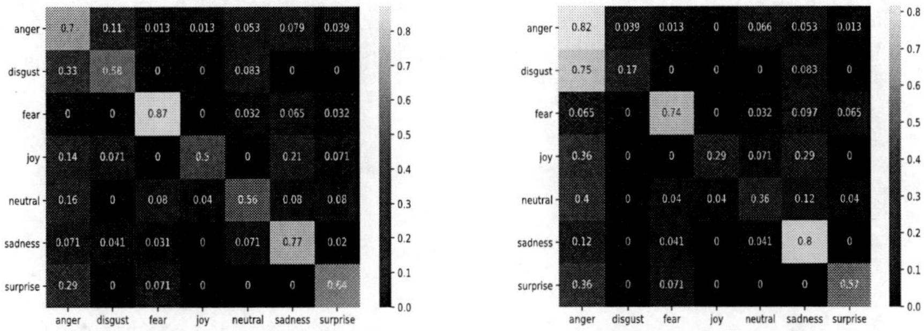


(a) Final Submission (b) Electra base without augmentation

Figure 3: Confusion matrix (normalized) for the emotion classification task on the dev data

coefficient of **0.558** and **0.507** on the Empathy prediction, and Distress prediction respectively. This amounts to an average score of **0.533** which ranks us $3^{rd}$ in this sub-task.

In Table 1, we present a result on the development set with and without using balanced data augmentation (BA) using GoEmotions for the ELECTRA base model. As we expected, the data augmentation helped improve performance of the model. The results for the various EMO models on the development set are available in Table 2. We also list the performance of two final ensembles in the table. On the test data, the Ensemble 1 and Ensemble 2 achieved a macro F1 score of **0.5528** and **0.588** respectively. We submitted Ensemble 1 as our final submission in the evaluation phase, as we were allowed only one submission. We ranked $1^{st}$ in this sub-task.

## 6 Error Analysis

It was observed that the training was highly sensitive to the initialization of the models. These include the initializations of the weight vectors of the feed-forward layers, and the ordering and organization of the batches fed to the model. Across different seeds the models' scores varied significantly. This is in line with the analysis done by Dodge et al. (2020) for transformer based models on the GLUE Benchmark (Wang et al., 2018). The high variability in performance can be observed Fig 2 . The Multi-task ELECTRA model performed differently on different runs, and we list two such runs for each Empathy Prediction and Distress Prediction.

The confusion matrix in Figure 3 shows that while the submitted system performed extremely well on the fear class, it underperformed a bit on joy and neutral, the performance on joy being very low. A point worth noting might be that the only 'positive' human emotion here is joy, and all the others are negative emotions and are often hard to distinguish by humans. A fare share of data points have been labeled as sadness and anger while they actually belong to the class joy. We also present, for comparison, the confusion matrix of the ELECTRA base model trained on non-augmented data. This model performed much worse on all emotions except sadness and anger; the model being very prone to predict the emotion as anger. The good performance of this model on sadness could be because of high number of samples from the that class in training data. The tendency to predict anger correlates with the fact that anger is the 2nd most frequent label in the training data. From this comparison, we can say data augmentation helped us achieve a more balanced performance with respect to all emotions, in particular bringing down the tendency to predict anger as the emotion, and improving performance for all other emotion classes which had less training data.

## 7 Conclusion

This paper describes our submission to the WASSA 2021 shared task, where we have leveraged off the shelf transformer models pre-trained on huge corpora in the English language. The intuition for keeping these models was to exploit the huge information they already possess. In the evaluation phase our systems ranked 1st in track II and 3rd in track I.

## References


Sven Buechel, Anneke Buffone, Barry Slaff, Lyle Ungar, and João Sedoc. 2018. Modeling empathy and distress in reaction to news stories. In *Proceedings of the 2018 Conference on Empirical Methods in Natural Language Processing*, pages 4758–4765, Brussels, Belgium. Association for Computational Linguistics.

Kevin Clark, Minh-Thang Luong, Quoc V. Le, and Christopher D. Manning. 2020. Electra: Pre-training text encoders as discriminators rather than generators.

Dorottya Demszky, Dana Movshovitz-Attias, Jeongwoo Ko, Alan Cowen, Gaurav Nemade, and Sujith Ravi. 2020. Goemotions: A dataset of fine-grained emotions.

Jacob Devlin, Ming-Wei Chang, Kenton Lee, and Kristina Toutanova. 2019. Bert: Pre-training of deep bidirectional transformers for language understanding.

Jesse Dodge, Gabriel Ilharco, Roy Schwartz, Ali Farhadi, Hannaneh Hajishirzi, and Noah Smith. 2020. Fine-tuning pretrained language models: Weight initializations, data orders, and early stopping. *arXiv preprint arXiv:2002.06305*.

Paul Ekman. 1992. An argument for basic emotions. *Cognition and Emotion*, 6(3-4):169–200.

James Gibson, Nikos Malandrakis, Francisco Romero, David C. Atkins, and Shrikanth S. Narayanan. 2015. Predicting therapist empathy in motivational interviews using language features inspired by psycholinguistic norms. In *INTERSPEECH*.

Guo Haixiang, Li Yijing, Jennifer Shang, Gu Mingyun, Huang Yuanyue, and Gong Bing. 2017. Learning from class-imbalanced data. *Expert Syst. Appl.*, 73(C):220–239.

Hamed Khanpour, Cornelia Caragea, and Prakhar Biyani. 2017. Identifying empathetic messages in online health communities. In *Proceedings of the Eighth International Joint Conference on Natural Language Processing (Volume 2: Short Papers)*, pages 246–251, Taipei, Taiwan. Asian Federation of Natural Language Processing.

Roman Klinger et al. 2018. An analysis of annotated corpora for emotion classification in text. In *Proceedings of the 27th International Conference on Computational Linguistics*, pages 2104–2119.

Zhenzhong Lan, Mingda Chen, Sebastian Goodman, Kevin Gimpel, Piyush Sharma, and Radu Soricut. 2019. Albert: A lite bert for self-supervised learning of language representations. *arXiv preprint arXiv:1909.11942*.

Xiaodong Liu, Pengcheng He, Weizhu Chen, and Jianfeng Gao. 2019a. Multi-task deep neural networks for natural language understanding. In *Proceedings of the 57th Annual Meeting of the Association for Computational Linguistics*, pages 4487–4496, Florence, Italy. Association for Computational Linguistics.

Yinhan Liu, Myle Ott, Naman Goyal, Jingfei Du, Mandar Joshi, Danqi Chen, Omer Levy, Mike Lewis, Luke Zettlemoyer, and Veselin Stoyanov. 2019b. Roberta: A robustly optimized bert pretraining approach. *arXiv preprint arXiv:1907.11692*.

Rushi Longadge and Snehalata Dongre. 2013. Class imbalance problem in data mining review.

Ilya Loshchilov and Frank Hutter. 2017. Decoupled weight decay regularization. *arXiv preprint arXiv:1711.05101*.

João Sedoc, Sven Buechel, Yehonathan Nachmany, Anneke Buffone, and Lyle Ungar. 2020. Learning word ratings for empathy and distress from document-level user responses.

Shabnam Tafreshi, Orphée De Clercq, Valentin Barriere, Sven Buechel, João Sedoc, and Alexandra Balahur. 2021. WASSA2021 Shared Task: Predicting Empathy and Emotion in Reaction to News Stories. In *Proceedings of the Eleventh Workshop on Computational Approaches to Subjectivity, Sentiment and Social Media Analysis*. Association for Computational Linguistics.

Alex Wang, Amanpreet Singh, Julian Michael, Felix Hill, Omer Levy, and Samuel R Bowman. 2018. Glue: A multi-task benchmark and analysis platform for natural language understanding. *arXiv preprint arXiv:1804.07461*.

Thomas Wolf, Lysandre Debut, Victor Sanh, Julien Chaumond, Clement Delangue, Anthony Moi, Pierric Cistac, Tim Rault, Rémi Louf, Morgan Funtowicz, Joe Davison, Sam Shleifer, Patrick von Platen, Clara Ma, Yacine Jernite, Julien Plu, Canwen Xu, Teven Le Scao, Sylvain Gugger, Mariama Drame, Quentin Lhoest, and Alexander M. Rush. 2020. Huggingface's transformers: State-of-the-art natural language processing.

Joseph Worsham and Jugal Kalita. 2020. Multi-task learning for natural language processing in the 2020s: Where are we going? *Pattern Recognition Letters*, 136:120–126.

B. Xiao, D. Can, P. G. Georgiou, D. Atkins, and S. S. Narayanan. 2012. Analyzing the language of therapist empathy in motivational interview based psychotherapy. In *Proceedings of The 2012 Asia Pacific Signal and Information Processing Association Annual Summit and Conference*, pages 1–4.

# Analyzing Curriculum Learning for Sentiment Analysis along Task Difficulty, Pacing and Visualization Axes

**Anvesh Rao Vijjini*** **Kaveri Anuranjana*** **Radhika Mamidi**

International Institute of Information Technology - Hyderabad
{vijjinianvesh.rao,kaveri.anuranjana}@research.iiit.ac.in
radhika.mamidi@iiit.ac.in

## Abstract

While Curriculum Learning (CL) has recently gained traction in Natural language Processing Tasks, it is still not adequately analyzed. Previous works only show their effectiveness but fail short to explain and interpret the internal workings fully. In this paper, we analyze curriculum learning in sentiment analysis along multiple axes. Some of these axes have been proposed by earlier works that need more in-depth study. Such analysis requires understanding where curriculum learning works and where it does not. Our axes of analysis include Task difficulty on CL, comparing CL pacing techniques, and qualitative analysis by visualizing the movement of attention scores in the model as curriculum phases progress. We find that curriculum learning works best for difficult tasks and may even lead to a decrement in performance for tasks with higher performance without curriculum learning. We see that One-Pass curriculum strategies suffer from catastrophic forgetting and attention movement visualization within curriculum pacing. This shows that curriculum learning breaks down the challenging main task into easier sub-tasks solved sequentially.

## 1 Introduction

Learning in humans has always been a systematic approach of handling the fundamentals first and then learning incrementally harder concepts. Cognitive Science has established that this leads to a clearer, robust understanding and the most efficient learning (Krueger and Dayan, 2009; Avrahami et al., 1997). Indeed, something similar can be applied while training neural networks. (Bengio et al., 2009) show that Curriculum Learning (CL) - sampling data based on increasing order of difficulty leads to quicker generalization. (Weinshall et al., 2018) also demonstrate that CL increases the rate of convergence at the beginning of training. Their CL strategy involved sorting the training data based on transfer learning from another network trained on a larger dataset. The idea of reordering samples has been explored in various approaches. In this paper, we evaluate the "easiness" with a network and train the samples on another network. Hence, even in our case, we shall pick easier points regarding a target hypothesis then train another network that optimizes its current hypothesis. This idea has been suggested by previous works as well. (Hacohen and Weinshall, 2019; Weinshall et al., 2018).

(Cirik et al., 2016) proposed Baby Steps and One Pass curriculum techniques using sentence length as a curriculum strategy for training LSTM (Hochreiter and Schmidhuber, 1997) on Sentiment Analysis. A tree-structured curriculum ordering based on semantic similarity is proposed by (Han and Myaeng, 2017). (Rao et al., 2020) propose an auxiliary network that is first trained on the dataset and used to calculate difficulty scores for the curriculum order.

CL is also used in NLP within tasks such as Question Answering (Sachan and Xing, 2016, 2018) and NLG for Answer Generation (Liu et al., 2018). For Sentiment Analysis, (Cirik et al., 2016) propose a strategy derived from sentence length, where smaller sentences are considered easier and are provided first. (Han and Myaeng, 2017) provide a tree-structured curriculum based on semantic similarity between new samples and samples already trained. (Tsvetkov et al., 2016) suggest a curriculum based on handcrafted semantic, linguistic, syntactic features for word representation learning.

Some of these works (Cirik et al., 2016; Han and Myaeng, 2017; Rao et al., 2020) have suggested that Baby Steps performs better than One Pass. We

*The authors contributed equally to the work.



*Proceedings of the 11th Workshop on Computational Approaches to Subjectivity, Sentiment and Social Media Analysis*, pages 117–128
April 19, 2021. ©2021 Association for Computational Linguistics

perform experiments using both techniques. While the idea of curriculum remains the same across these works, the strategy itself to decide sample ordering is often diverse.

## 2 Axis I: Curriculum Learning: One Pass and Baby Steps

While Curriculum Learning as defined by (Bengio et al., 2009) is not constrained by a strict description, later related works (Cirik et al., 2016; Han and Myaeng, 2017; Spitkovsky et al., 2010; Rao et al., 2020) make distinctions between Baby Steps curriculum and One-Pass curriculum. Most of these previous works have also shown the dominance of Baby Steps over One-Pass. Baby Steps and One Pass curriculum can be defined as follows. For every sentence $s_i \in D$, its sentiment is described as $y_i \in \{0, 1, 2, 3, 4\}$, where $i \in \{1, 2...n\}$ for $n$ data points in $D$. For a model $f_w$, its prediction based on $s_i$ will be $f_w(s_i)$. Loss $L$ is defined on the model prediction and actual output as $L(y_i, f_w(s_i))$ and Cost defining the task as $C(D, f_w)$ as

$$\sum_{\forall i} \frac{1}{n} L(y_i, f_w(s_i)) \quad (1)$$

Here, curriculum strategy $S(s_i)$ defines an "easiness"/"difficulty" quotient of sample $s_i$. Furthermore, One Pass makes distinct, mutually exclusive sets of the training data and trains on each one of these sets one by one. This makes it faster as compared to Baby Steps, where data cumulatively increases in each pass. This implies that the model is trained on previous data and the additional harder data.

To analyze the two methods for executing CL we choose two curriculum strategies (difficulty scoring function). Furthermore, we also experiment with an individual setting explained in following sections.

### 2.1 Dataset

Following previous works in curriculum-driven sentiment analysis (Cirik et al., 2016; Han and Myaeng, 2017; Tsvetkov et al., 2016; Rao et al., 2020) We use the Stanford Sentiment Treebank (SST) dataset (Socher et al., 2013). Unlike most sentiment analysis datasets with binary labels, SST is for a 5-class classification consisting of 8544/1101/2210 samples in train, development, and test set. We use this standard split with reported results averaged over 5 turns.

### 2.2 Model Details: BERT

We use the popular transformer model BERT(Devlin et al., 2019) for our experiments due to how ubiquitous it is across natural language processing tasks. Bidirectional Encoder Representations from Transformers (BERT) is a masked language model trained on large corpora. A sentence is added with a special token (CLS) at the beginning and is passed into the pre-trained BERT model. It tokenizes the sentence with a maximum length of 512 and outputs a contextual representation for each of the tokenized words. There are variants of pre-trained BERT depending upon the hyper-parameters of the model. BERT-Base Uncased consists of 12 transformer encoders, and output from each token is a 768 dimension embedding. We apply a softmax layer over the first token position (CLS) output by the BERT model for sentiment analysis.

### 2.3 Curriculum Strategies

#### 2.3.1 Auxiliary Model Strategy

Auxiliary Model Strategy is based on previous works (Weinshall et al., 2018; Hacohen and Weinshall, 2019; Rao et al., 2020) which propose a difficulty scoring function, transfer learned from an another network. We first train an auxiliary model $Aux$ for sentiment analysis on the same dataset. This $Aux$ model architecture will be the same as the model finally used for CL. This allows us to find out which training samples are actually difficult. We learn what samples are the most difficult to classify and what are the easiest from this model. For all training samples of $D$, we define the curriculum score as follows:

$$S(s_i) = \sum_{j}^{c} (Aux(s_i)^j - y_i^j)^2 \quad (2)$$

where $Aux(s_i)^j$ is the prediction of auxiliary model $Aux$ on sentence $s_i$, $j$ is the iterator over the number of classes $c = 5$. In essence, we find the mean squared error between the prediction and the sentence's true labels. If $S(s_i)$ is high, it implies the sentence is hard to classify, and if less, then the sentence is easy. Because the features were trained on an auxiliary model from BERT features, we get an easiness-difficulty score purely from the perspective of sentiment analysis. Section A gives

Our dataset has 5 labels.
https://nlp.stanford.edu/sentiment/

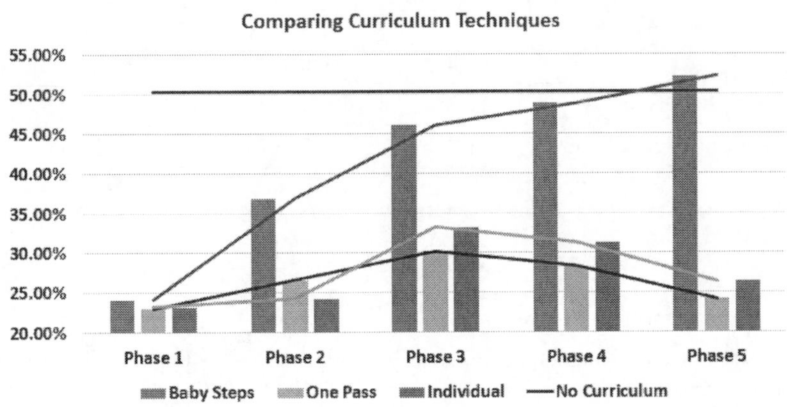


Figure 1: Performance comparison shows weakness of One Pass.

some examples of difficult and easy samples according to this curriculum.

#### 2.3.2 Sentence Length

This simple strategy tells that architectures, especially LSTM find it difficult to classify longer sentences. Hence, longer sentences are difficult and should be ordered later. Conversely, shorter sentence lengths are easier and should be trained first. This strategy is prevalent and has not only been used in sentiment analysis (Cirik et al., 2016) but also in dependency parsing (Spitkovsky et al., 2010). This is why it becomes a strong comparison metric, especially to evaluate the distinction between One Pass and Baby Steps.

#### 2.3.3 Individual

In this strategy, we report accuracy on the test set when trained on $D_1$,$D_2$, and so on individually. This is by no means a curriculum strategy since no model ever sees the complete training data. The Individual experiment can be thought of as One Pass, but the weights are reset after every training phase.

### 2.4 Results and Discussion

Table 1 and Figure 1 give us an insight into what is happening with One Pass. Firstly, Table 1 clearly shows that One Pass underperforms both No curriculum and Baby Steps for both the Curriculum Strategies. This is in line with previous experiments as well (Cirik et al., 2016; Han and Myaeng, 2017; Rao et al., 2020). One Pass is less time-consuming since it only observes a sample once, unlike Baby Steps which repeatedly sees samples from the previous and the current phase. Furthermore, we see that auxiliary outperforms sentence length. Finally, Figure 1 illustrates the reason for One Pass's weakness. We observe that on successive phases, One Pass closely follows the curve of the proposed Individual experiment. However, unlike One Pass, Individual has no memory of samples at previous stages. This shows that in every phase of One Pass, the model forgets the previous stage samples and effectively behaves like Individual, hence catastrophically forgetting previous phases. Furthermore, this is especially a major issue for the myriad of methods involving the Language Model pre-training and downstream tasks fine-tuning Paradigm. Language Model backed transformers (Vaswani et al., 2017) are now ubiquitous for tasks across Natural Language Understanding (Devlin et al., 2019; Liu et al., 2019; Yang et al., 2019; Lan et al., 2020; Raffel et al., 2020; Choudhary et al., 2020). These architectures are trained in a language model task first, followed by fine-tuning on the downstream task. In this regard, they are similar to the One Pass strategy since they successively train on disjoint datasets. Hence, problems with One Pass, such as catastrophic forgetting, are likely to occur with these architectures as well. Additionally, while Baby Steps addresses the catastrophic forgetting in One Pass, it will be harder to address catastrophic forgetting in Language Models. The downstream task objective in the CL setting is different from the Language Model objective making joint training harder, unlike Baby Steps.

(Cirik et al., 2016) have done on CL SST as well. However, our numbers do not match because they use the much larger phrase dataset.

| Model | Curriculum Strategies | | |
|---|---|---|---|
| | Baby Steps | One Pass | No Curriculum |
| Auxiliary Strategy | 52.3 | **24.15** | 50.03 |
| Sentence Length Strategy | 51.2 | **23.64** | 50.03 |

Table 1: Accuracy scores in percentage of the two curriculums across Baby Steps and One Pass as compared to no curriculum on the SST5 dataset.

#### 2.4.1 Visualizing Catastrophic Forgetting

To visualize Catastrophic Forgetting, Figure 2 plots the BERT model's performance. The figure illustrates the corresponding match or mismatch between model prediction and ground truth rather than just the model prediction. In this figure, the correctness of model prediction across all test samples is illustrated for every phase of the One Pass and Baby Steps methods. The samples are vertically stacked along the $y$-axis in an order based on the number of phases sample missclassified in. The consecutive phases of the curriculum training are indicated on the $x$-axis.. A darker color (value of "0") indicates miss-classification, and brighter or lighter color (value of "1") indicates that the sample is correctly classified. Note that the classification task itself is not a binary task but a multi-class classification problem. For SST5, this is a five-class classification task. Figure 2 edifies the following points.

- **Easy and Hard Samples**: In both the figures, some sections are always dark or always light in color. The difficulty of certain samples is consistent irrespective of model training. The accuracy is actually determined by the samples with intermediate difficulty whose prediction can fluctuate as the model observes more data encounters.
- **Memory in Baby Steps**: The figure for Baby Steps shows the model fairly remembering well the concepts it is trained on. Here, once the model prediction is corrected, it mostly stays corrected. Hence, implying a "memory" in the model.
- **Catastrophic Forgetting in One Pass** Contrary to Baby Steps, One Pass heavily suffers from catastrophic forgetting, which is observed every time the color of a sample changes from lighter to darker. In One Pass, in successive phases, the model makes more correct predictions in new regions. However, at the same time, samples become darker in the regions earlier it was lighter in. Model performance decreases to the lowest in the final stages because the model is the farthest from all previous learning phases at this point.
- **Visualizing Test Performance**: This visualization is done on the unseen test set. Our above hypotheses are still natural to understand if visualized on the train set. However, the samples in the visualization are always unseen during the training. This implies that the model forgets or remembers training samples in the corresponding phases and the associated concepts as well.

## 3 Axis II: Curriculum Learning only helps Difficult tasks

(Hacohen and Weinshall, 2019) and (Xu et al., 2020) propose that CL might help tasks which are harder than easier. They observe that for tasks which have low performance, the difference in performance caused due to introducing a curriculum training is more than the tasks which have a higher performance without curriculum. We call this the Task Difficulty Hypothesis.

(Hacohen and Weinshall, 2019) perform an image classification experiment where they experiment with enabling curriculum on the CIFAR dataset(Krizhevsky et al., 2009) with 100 classes(CIFAR-100) and 10 classes(CIFAR-10) as two separate experiments. They use VGG network(Simonyan and Zisserman, 2014) as the common neural network for these experiments. Naturally, they report performance of CIFAR 10 in the range of 90 to 100% (hence, an *easy* task) and CIFAR-10 in the range pf 60 to 70 % (hence, a *hard* task). On addition of a curriculum training to these datasets, they observe that the increment

As discussed earlier, we take $k = 5$; hence we end up with 5 phases on the $x$-axis.

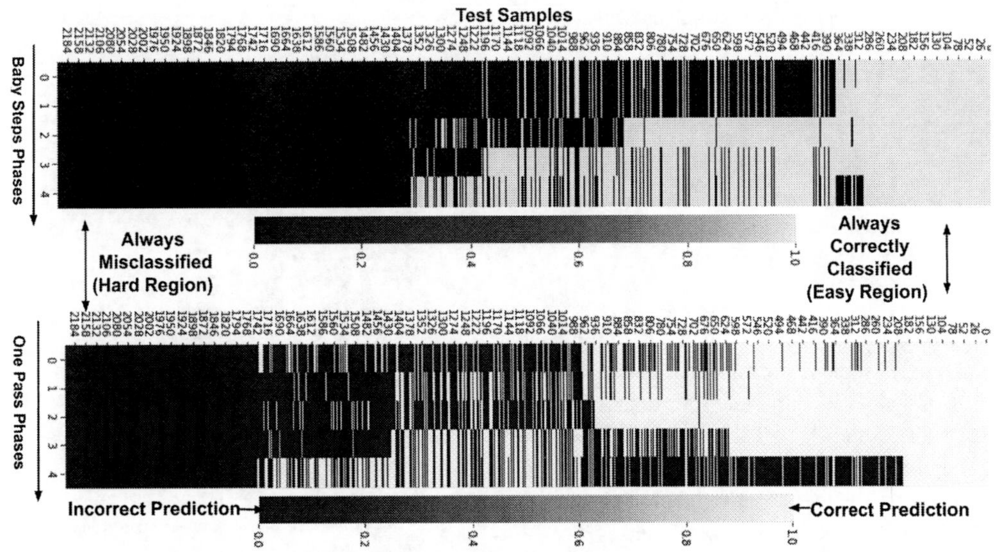


Figure 2: Catastrophic Forgetting in One Pass Visualized. In the above images, the model performance on each individual test set sample is illustrated across all curriculum phases. These phases correspond with how much data the model has observed so far.

in performance on CIFAR-100 is almost twice the increment in performance on CIFAR-10 while using the same network VGG-net for training. They argue that this might be because in easier tasks such as CIFAR-10, there are already enough easy samples observed during training without CL, and hence improvement caused by CL is subdued.

(Xu et al., 2020) enable their CL across the range of tasks in GLUE(Wang et al., 2018). GLUE encompasses a wide range of tasks in natural language understanding, with varying performances. For example a task such as RTE or CoLA is considered harder than SST-2 or QNLI. The BERT(Devlin et al., 2019) model's performance for the same are 70.1, 60.5, 94.9, 91.1 respectively .

We built our experiments upon these works. Proposed work is different from (Hacohen and Weinshall, 2019) in the way that our work focuses on sentiment analysis in NLP, whereas (Hacohen and Weinshall, 2019) experimented strictly with image processing tasks. Furthermore, since the apparent relation between task difficulty and improvement due to CL wasn't the main focus of the work, the experimentation wasn't enough to fully establish the correlation. While (Xu et al., 2020) perform experiments within the purview of NLU and Text Classification, the experiments themselves are not consistent across dataset and the nature of task. Specifically, we believe it's hard to conclude from experiments on tasks as disparate as Linguistic Acceptability(Warstadt et al., 2019) and Sentiment Analysis(Socher et al., 2013) to establish the relationship between CL and task difficulty. Such an experiment inadvertently raises more questions whether the difference of improvement due to CL is due to the nature of tasks (Sentiment Identification as opposed to Linguistical soundness detection) or the nature of the dataset being different (sentence lengths or vocabulary). We eschew this concern by performing experiment within the same task (Sentiment Analysis), and the same dataset (SST-5), instead we introduce change in task difficulty by using the fine grained labels provided by this dataset. This experimental setup will be explained in more detailed in the following sections.

### 3.1 Dataset

To ensure no effect of nature of task or dataset on our experiments, we utilize just a single dataset but under different conditions and sampling to simulate difficulty. All these meta-datas are generated using the SST-5 (Socher et al., 2013) dataset. It is important to note that we do not use the phrase data for training which is why our scores may fall short of earlier reported performances of BERT on SST5 and SST derived datasets (Devlin et al., 2019; Liu et al., 2019; Xu et al., 2020). The fine-grained 5 classes of this dataset enable us to create easier

As reported in the original paper (Devlin et al., 2019)

https://nlp.stanford.edu/sentiment/

|  | With Curriculum | No Curriculum | Difference |
|---|---|---|---|
| SST-2 | 89.95 | 91.11 | − 1.6 |
| SST-3 | 75.47 | 75.52 | − 0.05 |
| SST-4 | 62.04 | 61.72 | + 0.32 |
| SST-5 | 52.3 | 50.03 | + 2.0 |

Table 2: Accuracy scores in percentage on all the created meta-data with and without curriculum. Results are obtained by averaging over 5 runs.

variants of the same dataset without any significant change in the problem statement definition and the dataset statistics. We generate four datasets from SST5: SST-2, SST-3, SST-4 and SST-5 itself. In SST-3 and SST-5 neutral label is preserved, otherwise dropped. The two negative labels and the two positive labels are clubbed in SST-3 and SST-2.

In each of the SST-$x$ dataset, the train, test and dev sets are all converted accordingly. The model in all cases is strictly trained on the train data with development as validation and results are reported on test set. This way the comparison can be fair since dataset specific effects on the hypothesis would not be pertinent.

Humans are likely to observe sentiment polarity of a natural language sentence on a continuous scale rather than distinct classes. Hence, it makes natural sense that making a distinction between, Very Positive and Positive is a harder task than just making a distinction between positive and negative.

### 3.2 Curriculum Training

We use the Auxiliary Model Strategy (Section 2.3.1) coupled with Baby Steps (Section 2) as our curriculum training technique and BERT as the model architecture. We use Baby Steps (Cirik et al., 2016) as the curriculum pacing since we observed it to have best performance.

### 3.3 Results and Discussions

Our Experiments are illustrated in figure 3 and table 2. Following are the major points to be noted

- **Number of classes is detrimental to model performance** We observe that in both with curriculum and No curriculum settings, model performance varies tremendously between SST-5 and SST-2. This is also evident in previous works which have shown performance ranges on SST to lie in the ranges of 45-50% (Cirik et al., 2016) for a 5 class problem and in the order of 90%(Lan et al., 2020; Devlin

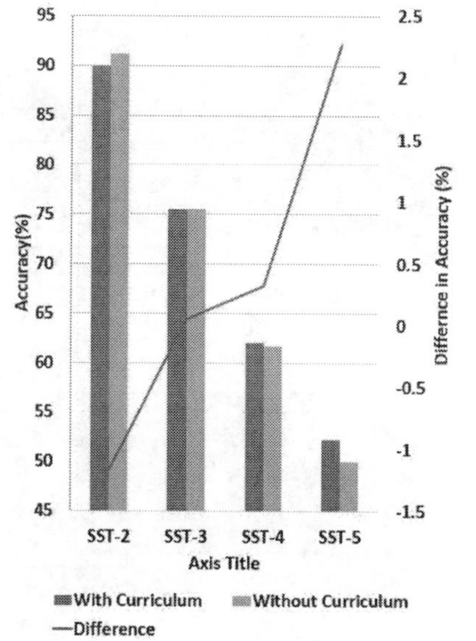


Figure 3: Accuracy scores in percentage on all the created meta-data with and without curriculum. The difference has been plotted on the secondary y-axis (Right)

et al., 2019; Xu et al., 2020) for a binary class problem. Furthermore, it is interesting to note that the performance gap between SST-$i$ and SST-$i+1$ decreases as number of classes increase. This implies while adding classes makes the task harder, the hardness is less relevant if already many classes.

- **Curriculum has adverse effects on high performing models** The most striking point to be observed is that curriculum actually does not help in certain cases. In SST-2 and SST-3, the model is already performing quite well with accuracy of 91.11 and 75.52 respectively In these cases the model observes a decrements= of 1.6 and 0.05 % respectively due to CL. The performance on SST-2 is in line with previous work (Xu et al., 2020) who also observe a slight decrement to no increment in this dataset for their own curriculum technique. Tasks which are having performance are in essence, possessing higher number of easier samples than tougher tasks. In such a condition, A model observing these easy samples again and again (as we saw earlier in Baby Steps), might lead to overfitting. We believe this to be the reason behind then apparent performance degradation.

- **Curriculum has positive effects on low per-**

**forming models** Despite low performance on SST-2, the resourcefulness of CL is felt in SST-5 and SST-4 where there is a positive difference. These tasks are harder in nature with No Curriculum performance below 65%, and CL is able to improve the scores significantly with an average of $+1.16\%$. As we saw in previous section, Hard samples are catastrophically forgotten all the time, hence training on these samples again and again will lead to an improvement. Unlike SST-2 and SST-3 which have a huge proportion of easy samples, Hard tasks according have harder samples and hence instead repeated training in a systematic ordering would not have an adverse effect.

Furthermore, (Xu et al., 2020) suggest a similar reasoning for the Task Difficulty hypothesis. They suggest that when learning without curriculum, in the case of harder tasks, the model is confounded and overwhelmed by the presence of hard samples. Hence, laying out the training where the model observes easier samples first is natural to improve performance. However, this reasoning does not explain well why there is an apparent decrement of performance for CL on high performing tasks.

## 4 Axis III: Attention Movement Visualization

Visualization of Attention (Vaswani et al., 2017) is an important and popular visualization method for interpreting the prediction in these models. Previous works such as (Clark et al., 2019) have visualized attentions to identify where does BERT look. (Vaswani et al., 2017) also show in attention visualization that various heads of the transformer look at various linguistic details. In this section we use attention visualization to qualitatively analyze and explain how the model's focus on the sentence changes as the various stages (when model encounters new and harder data) of CL progresses.

It is important to note that BERT has $N$ layers and $H$ heads. Within each of these $N$x$H$ heads there lies a $T$x$T$ self attention from each input time stamp to every other time stamp. Where $T$ is the maximum sentence length. Thereby, there are a total of $N$x$H$ 2D $T$x$T$ Attention visualizations observed in BERT.

### 4.1 Experiments

To particularly identify how focus of the BERT model changes across multiple stages or phases of the curriculum, we devise an attention movement visualization. We define Attention Movement index as

$$M(i,h,n) = A(i,h,n) - A(i-1,h,n) \quad \forall i \in \{1,2,3..c\} \tag{3}$$

where $M$ is the proposed Movement index, $A(i,h,n)$ is the Attention visualization of the $h^{th}$ head of $n_{th}$ layer after training $i^{th}$ phase of curriculum training and $c$ is the total number of phases in the curriculum training. We can see that a positive $M(i)$ indicates that across subsequent stages of the curriculum, the model has added attention or increased focus in the area.

Conversely, a negative $M(i)$ indicates that after completing phase $i$ model has decided to attend to certain area or region lesser than before the phase's training. Essentially the Movement indicates relative change in attention rather than attention itself. This is significant because, unlike typical visualization where we observe a singular model in isolation, here we are attempting to analyze how the model behaves in subsequent stages of the training in a curriculum fashion and furthermore, how this change effects the prediction label.

Additionally, a point to note is that while previous works such as (Clark et al., 2019) establish that BERT's distinct heads attend on linguistic notions of syntax among other linguistic ideas, we do not visualize these attention heads themselves. In this experiment, we are looking for an overall perspective into where there is a positive or negative change in the attention focus rather than understanding the individual linguistic nuances of individual heads. For this reason we further propose an Averaged Movement index as follows:

$$M_{avg}(i) = \sum_{h=2,n=2}^{H,N} M(i,h,n) \tag{4}$$

where, $M_{avg}(i)$ is Averaged Movement index across all heads and layers after the $i_{th}$ curriculum training phase. $h$ and $i$ are iterators $h$ and $n$ are iterators over the total number of heads $H$ and total number of layers $N$ in the BERT Transformer. Total number of curriculum phases are $c$. Since, $M$ is a difference between subsequent phases, there are a total of $c-1$ Average Movement index visualizations of size $TxT$.

Other experimental details such as dataset, curriculum strategy, baby steps, model are all same

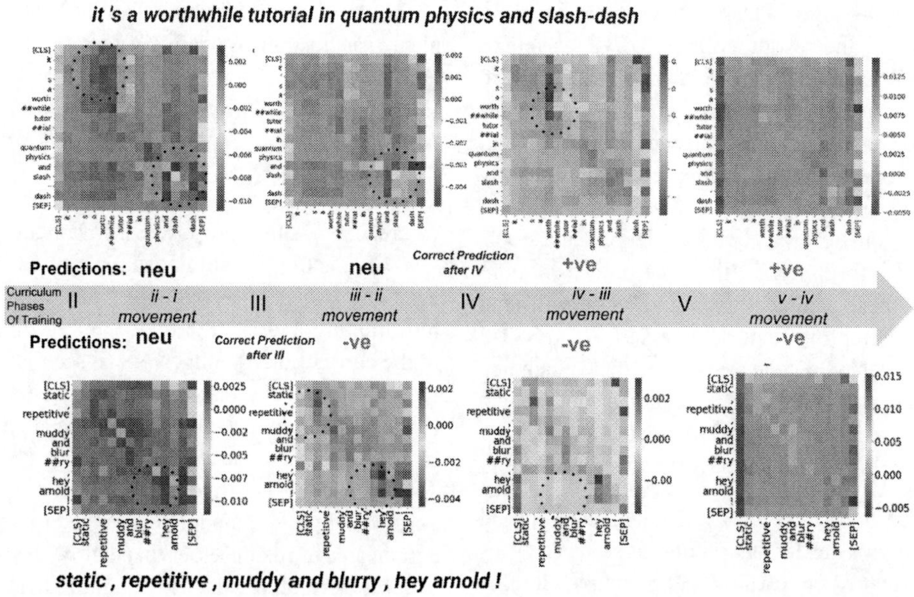


Figure 4: Attention Movement Index ($M_{avg}(i)$) visualization for the first and second sentence. The matrices show how model's focus changes for the input sentence between the phases. Blue color implies attention was added during phase transition while red implies attention diminished for those words.

as of the experiments explained in Section 3. To recapitulate, we use SST-5 dataset with Auxiliary Model Technique in Baby Steps training procedure. The $c$ in Baby Steps training is 5 in our experiments.

## 4.2 Results and Discussions

Figures 4 gives examples for $M_{avg}$ scores for three sentences. There are a total five phases in our training and hence total four $M_{avg}$ scores per sentence with each score being $TxT$ in attention size with $T$ as maximum sentence length. In these images, a blue color implies there was a addition of attention or focus in the region and red or a negative value implies there was a negation in the model's focus on the area. Almost no color or white color indicates no change in attention in the region. The movement index visualizations is shown along the direction of the arrow. All the following examples are from the Testing set, after the curriculum training, the intermediate phase wise models were extracted and made to predict on the individual test sentences. Furthermore, please note that for each of the $TxT$ attentions, y-axis denotes the input positions and x-axis denotes the output positions of the self attention. Our analysis can be listed for each sentence as follows:

- In this sentence (True Label: Negative), *"static , repetitive , muddy and blurry , hey arnold !"* the model predicts incorrectly in the beginning and continues to mislabel until the third phase of training. We observe that on finishing the third phase of the training the movement index (2nd image from top), shows a motion of higher focus on "static repetitive muddy" (and lower focus from redundant words. While in the first and second phase when the model observed just a sample of easy data, the movement of attention wasn't in any direction that could help the classification. The motion in third phase however shows the addition of focus on words which could help the model classify the sentence as negative. Furthermore, until the last phase we also see an addition of focus to the terms "hey arnold !", this could model's way of focusing on some neutral words to avoid predicting Very Negative as opposed to Negative. Essentially, CL has divided up the task of predicting sentiment into multiple sections where the model first learnt the neutrality from "hey arnold" followed by focusing the polarity terms to predict just negative. This makes the prediction easier and hence effective than no curriculum.

- In this sentence (True Label: Positive), *"it 's a worthwhile tutorial in quantum physics and slash-dash"* the model predicts incorrectly until model's completion of Phase four training. In phases two and three we see that model is adding weight to some neutral words such as "it ' s a" and "slash-dash", hence ends up predicting neutral which is an incorrect prediction. However, After observing phase four samples, model finally increases attention to the actual polarity indicating words in the sentence "worthwhile". and hence shifts prediction appropriately to Positive. There is a possibility that since "worthwhile" does not exist in BERT's vocabulary it might have found it hard to map the word to positive polarity until enough training data was observed by the model in subsequent phases.

In all the above examples, there is a common pattern, which is that CL spreads out the sentiment prediction process. Training on initial easier samples rules out whether prediction is correct.

## 5 Conclusion

In this paper we conduct experiments to analyze CL. We first hypothesize the failure of One Pass for Curriculum learning in text classification. We conduct an Individual non curriculum experiment, to show that One Pass heavily suffers with catastrophic forgetting. Unless this forgetting is tackled, One Pass will continue to under perform even no curriculum settings. Then, we analyze CL along Task Difficulty Hypothesis to establish firmly that CL only helps when coupled with difficult tasks. The scope of improvement may diminish or even be negative for tasks which are already easy. Finally we propose movement visualizations to analyse CL. We observe that for hard examples, CL breaks down the task into multiple phases. These phases in a way rule out certain sections of the sentence for sentiment prediction first, such that when the model encounters harder data in later phases, it is clear on what not to focus on. Furthermore, after both the experiments, we can conclude that the reason CL might be deleterious to performance in easier tasks could be because in these tasks, multiple phases are unnecessary. If the model prediction was already correct in the first couple of phases, then further phases may only move the prediction away hence leading to poor performance.

## References


Judith Avrahami, Yaakov Kareev, Yonatan Bogot, Ruth Caspi, Salomka Dunaevsky, and Sharon Lerner. 1997. Teaching by examples: Implications for the process of category acquisition. *The Quarterly Journal of Experimental Psychology Section A*, 50(3):586–606.

Yoshua Bengio, Jérôme Louradour, Ronan Collobert, and Jason Weston. 2009. Curriculum learning. In *Proceedings of the 26th annual international conference on machine learning*, pages 41–48. ACM.

Nurendra Choudhary, Nikhil Rao, Sumeet Katariya, Karthik Subbian, and Chandan K Reddy. 2020. Self-supervised hyperboloid representations from logical queries over knowledge graphs. *arXiv preprint arXiv:2012.13023*.

Volkan Cirik, Eduard Hovy, and Louis-Philippe Morency. 2016. Visualizing and understanding curriculum learning for long short-term memory networks. *arXiv preprint arXiv:1611.06204*.

Kevin Clark, Urvashi Khandelwal, Omer Levy, and Christopher D Manning. 2019. What does bert look at? an analysis of bert's attention. In *Proceedings of the 2019 ACL Workshop BlackboxNLP: Analyzing and Interpreting Neural Networks for NLP*, pages 276–286.

Jacob Devlin, Ming-Wei Chang, Kenton Lee, and Kristina Toutanova. 2019. Bert: Pre-training of deep bidirectional transformers for language understanding. In *Proceedings of the 2019 Conference of the North American Chapter of the Association for Computational Linguistics: Human Language Technologies, Volume 1 (Long and Short Papers)*, pages 4171–4186.

Guy Hacohen and Daphna Weinshall. 2019. On the power of curriculum learning in training deep networks. In *International Conference on Machine Learning*, pages 2535–2544. PMLR.

Sanggyu Han and Sung-Hyon Myaeng. 2017. Tree-structured curriculum learning based on semantic similarity of text. In *2017 16th IEEE International Conference on Machine Learning and Applications (ICMLA)*, pages 971–976. IEEE.

Sepp Hochreiter and Jürgen Schmidhuber. 1997. Long short-term memory. *Neural computation*, 9(8):1735–1780.

Alex Krizhevsky, Geoffrey Hinton, et al. 2009. Learning multiple layers of features from tiny images.

Kai A Krueger and Peter Dayan. 2009. Flexible shaping: How learning in small steps helps. *Cognition*, 110(3):380–394.

Zhenzhong Lan, Mingda Chen, Sebastian Goodman, Kevin Gimpel, Piyush Sharma, and Radu Soricut. 2020. Albert: A lite bert for self-supervised learning of language representations. In *International Conference on Learning Representations*.

Cao Liu, Shizhu He, Kang Liu, and Jun Zhao. 2018. Curriculum learning for natural answer generation. In *IJCAI*, pages 4223–4229.

Yinhan Liu, Myle Ott, Naman Goyal, Jingfei Du, Mandar Joshi, Danqi Chen, Omer Levy, Mike Lewis, Luke Zettlemoyer, and Veselin Stoyanov. 2019. Roberta: A robustly optimized bert pretraining approach. *arXiv preprint arXiv:1907.11692*.

Colin Raffel, Noam Shazeer, Adam Roberts, Katherine Lee, Sharan Narang, Michael Matena, Yanqi Zhou, Wei Li, and Peter J Liu. 2020. Exploring the limits of transfer learning with a unified text-to-text transformer. *Journal of Machine Learning Research*, 21:1–67.

Vijjini Anvesh Rao, Kaveri Anuranjana, and Radhika Mamidi. 2020. A sentiwordnet strategy for curriculum learning in sentiment analysis. In *International Conference on Applications of Natural Language to Information Systems*, pages 170–178. Springer.

Mrinmaya Sachan and Eric Xing. 2016. Easy questions first? a case study on curriculum learning for question answering. In *Proceedings of the 54th Annual Meeting of the Association for Computational Linguistics (Volume 1: Long Papers)*, volume 1, pages 453–463.

Mrinmaya Sachan and Eric Xing. 2018. Self-training for jointly learning to ask and answer questions. In *Proceedings of the 2018 Conference of the North American Chapter of the Association for Computational Linguistics: Human Language Technologies, Volume 1 (Long Papers)*, pages 629–640.

Karen Simonyan and Andrew Zisserman. 2014. Very deep convolutional networks for large-scale image recognition. *arXiv preprint arXiv:1409.1556*.

Richard Socher, Alex Perelygin, Jean Wu, Jason Chuang, Christopher D Manning, Andrew Ng, and Christopher Potts. 2013. Recursive deep models for semantic compositionality over a sentiment treebank. In *Proceedings of the 2013 conference on empirical methods in natural language processing*, pages 1631–1642.

Valentin I Spitkovsky, Hiyan Alshawi, and Daniel Jurafsky. 2010. From baby steps to leapfrog: How less is more in unsupervised dependency parsing. In *Human Language Technologies: The 2010 Annual Conference of the North American Chapter of the Association for Computational Linguistics*, pages 751–759. Association for Computational Linguistics.

Yulia Tsvetkov, Manaal Faruqui, Wang Ling, Brian MacWhinney, and Chris Dyer. 2016. Learning the curriculum with bayesian optimization for task-specific word representation learning. In *Proceedings of the 54th Annual Meeting of the Association for Computational Linguistics (Volume 1: Long Papers)*, pages 130–139.

Ashish Vaswani, Noam Shazeer, Niki Parmar, Jakob Uszkoreit, Llion Jones, Aidan N Gomez, Łukasz Kaiser, and Illia Polosukhin. 2017. Attention is all you need. In *Advances in neural information processing systems*, pages 5998–6008.

Alex Wang, Amanpreet Singh, Julian Michael, Felix Hill, Omer Levy, and Samuel Bowman. 2018. Glue: A multi-task benchmark and analysis platform for natural language understanding. In *Proceedings of the 2018 EMNLP Workshop BlackboxNLP: Analyzing and Interpreting Neural Networks for NLP*, pages 353–355.

Alex Warstadt, Amanpreet Singh, and Samuel R Bowman. 2019. Neural network acceptability judgments. *Transactions of the Association for Computational Linguistics*, 7:625–641.

Daphna Weinshall, Gad Cohen, and Dan Amir. 2018. Curriculum learning by transfer learning: Theory and experiments with deep networks. In *International Conference on Machine Learning*, pages 5238–5246. PMLR.

Benfeng Xu, Licheng Zhang, Zhendong Mao, Quan Wang, Hongtao Xie, and Yongdong Zhang. 2020. Curriculum learning for natural language understanding. In *Proceedings of the 58th Annual Meeting of the Association for Computational Linguistics*, pages 6095–6104.

Zhilin Yang, Zihang Dai, Yiming Yang, Jaime Carbonell, Russ R Salakhutdinov, and Quoc V Le. 2019. Xlnet: Generalized autoregressive pretraining for language understanding. In *Advances in neural information processing systems*, pages 5754–5764.

## A Difficult and Easy samples according to the Auxiliary Strategy

Table 3 shows some examples of difficult ad easy samples according to the Auxiliary Model Curriculum Strategy explained in section 2.3.1. As we can observe, this curriculum is effective because it considers a sample as difficult in similar ways to a human discerning the sentiment as well.

## B Additional Explanation for Attention Movement Visualization

In the sentence from figure 5 (True Label: Negative) *"if this dud had been made in the '70s , it would have been called the hills have antlers and played for about three weeks in drive-ins ."*, the model predicts incorrectly until the fourth phase. After the second phase, the model predicts Positive by increasing focus on parts of the sentence such as "the hills" and "played for" which could have a slight positive (as opposed to very positive) connotation in a movie review context. After the third

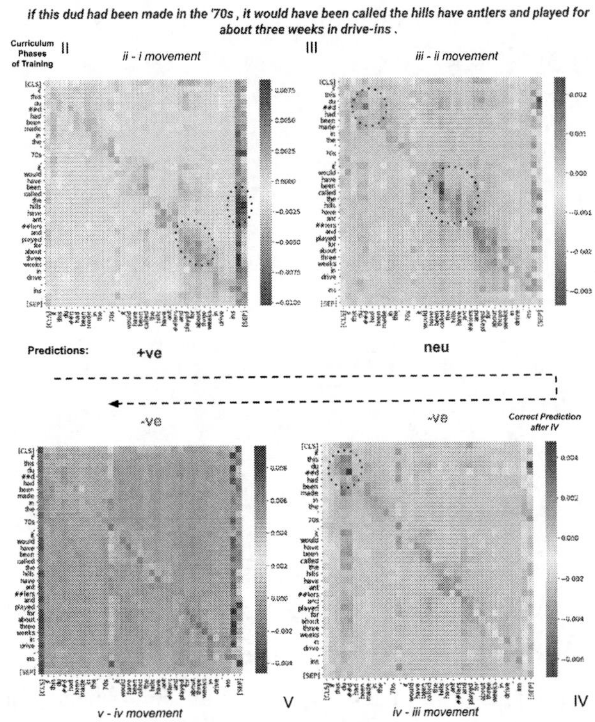


Figure 5: Attention Movement Index Visualizations for the sentence. The matrices show how model's focus changes for the input sentence between the phases. Blue color implies attention was added during phase transition while red implies attention diminished for those words.

phase, the motion is more towards "the hills" and "dud" which have neutral and negative connotation respectively leading to an overall sentiment of Neural. Finally, after the fourth phase, the movement is most towards the only strongly negative word "dud". Like the previous example, "dud" is not part of BERT's vocabulary and the only reason the model choose to increase its attention here must be because it already explored other regions of the sentence in previous phases. Hence, without this specific ordering, model would have lower probability of focusing on the broken subwords "*du - ##d*".

In all the examples, there is a common pattern, that curriculum learning spreads out the sentiment prediction process. Training on initial easier samples rules out incorrect predictions from parts of the sentence which do not contribute to the sentiment. This helps in later phases when model receives information to focus on right segment of the sentence. In this stage, the model would be more confident in its prediction since other regions of the sentence were already explored and excluded from the prediction process. In essence, CL debases the probability of incorrect prediction by revealing the right data at the right time in the spread out curriculum form of training.

| Label | Example |
|---|---|
| Easy | 1. meeting , even exceeding expectations , it 's the best sequel since the empire strikes back ... a majestic achievement , an epic of astonishing grandeur and surprising emotional depth . |
| (from first 50 samples) | 2. the most wondrous love story in years , it is a great film . |
| | 3. one of the best looking and stylish animated movies in quite a while ... |
| Hard | 1. if the predictability of bland comfort food appeals to you , then the film is a pleasant enough dish . |
| (from last 50 samples) | 2. it is a testament of quiet endurance , of common concern , of reconciled survival .' |
| | 3. this movie is so bad , that it 's almost worth seeing because it 's so bad .' |

Table 3: Examples of Difficult and Easy samples according to the Auxiliary Model Strategy

# Lightweight Models for Multimodal Sequential Data

**Soumya Sourav**
The University of Texas at Dallas
sxs180011@utdallas.edu

**Dr. Jessica Ouyang**
The University of Texas at Dallas
jessica.ouyang@utdallas.edu

## Abstract

Human language encompasses more than just text; it also conveys emotions through tone and gestures. We present a case study of three simple and efficient Transformer-based architectures for predicting sentiment and emotion in multimodal data. The *Late Fusion* model merges unimodal features to create a multimodal feature sequence, the *Round Robin* model iteratively combines bimodal features using cross-modal attention, and the *Hybrid Fusion* model combines trimodal and unimodal features together to form a final feature sequence for predicting sentiment. Our experiments show that our small models are effective and outperform the publicly released versions of much larger, state-of-the-art multimodal sentiment analysis systems.

## 1 Introduction

Language is composed of three different modalities: text, audio, and video. These three modalities together make it easier for humans to convey emotion and sentiment. Thus, a machine learning model for sentiment analysis needs to learn the features and interactions of all three modalities. For example, a frown in the video can alter the emotion expressed in the text transcript, or audio intensity can help determine if a speaker is getting agitated.

Multimodal learning has recently received a good deal of attention from the natural language processing community [Sun et al., 2016, Chen et al., 2018, Liu et al., 2018, Pham et al., 2019]. The Transformer network [Vaswani et al., 2017], with its self-attention modules, has achieved strong performance in multimodal learning; attention provides a natural way to model the relationship between pairs of modalities.

In this work we investigate three small, lightweight, Transformer-based architectures for multimodal sentiment analysis and emotion recognition. Our first model is an implementation of the *Late Fusion* model commonly used as a baseline system, which assigns individual Transformer blocks to each of the three modalities for feature extraction and then combines these unimodal features to learn cross-modal interactions. The second model is an implementation of the *Round Robin* approach; the model generates bimodal features by using cross-modal attention to combine pairs of modalities, one pair at a time. Our last model is a *Hybrid* of the early and late fusion schemes. This model merges the features extracted using a late fusion pipeline, as well as those from an early fusion pipeline, where the three modalities are concatenated and passed through a single Transformer block for feature extraction;.

We present experiments using these three models on three multimodal datasets: IEMOCAP [Busso et al., 2008], an emotion recognition dataset, and CMU-MOSI [Zadeh et al., 2016] and CMU-MOSEI [Zadeh et al., 2018b], two multimodal sentiment analysis datasets. Our results show that our small models are competitive with state-of-the-art models that use much more complex architectures.

Our main contributions are as follows:

- We present three lightweight architectures for multimodal sentiment analysis that achieve comparable results to much larger, state-of-the-art models.
- We analyze the effect of removing or simplifying components of state-of-the-art multimodal architectures.
- We conduct experiments on small training sets, demonstrating the ability of our lightweight architectures to leverage limited training data and computational resources.



*Proceedings of the 11th Workshop on Computational Approaches to Subjectivity, Sentiment and Social Media Analysis*, pages 129–137
April 19, 2021. ©2021 Association for Computational Linguistics

## 2 Related Work

We do not give an exhaustive list of prior work in multimodal sentiment analysis, but focus on recent neural approaches that achieved state-of-the-art performance at their times of publication.

### 2.1 Recurrent Network Approaches

The Memory Fusion Network (MFN) of Zadeh et al. [2018a] uses a separate LSTM to encode each of the three modalities and then uses attention to model cross-modal interactions for different combinations of modalities. The Recurrent Attended Variation Embedding Network (RAVEN) of Wang et al. [2019] encodes the audio and video features using two recurrent neural networks; these features are combined with the textual input using cross-modal attention in a Gated Modality Mixing Network. The Multi-Attention Recurrent Network (MARN) of Zadeh et al. [2018c] is an LSTM-based architecture that stores representations of each of the three modalities, which are then combined using a multi-attention block. Finally, the Multimodal Cyclic Translation Network (MCTN) of Pham et al. [2019] produces multimodal features by translating one modality into another, learning a joint encoding in that direction, and then back-translating to learn a joint encoding in the other direction.

### 2.2 Transformer Network Approaches

The Transformer network [Vaswani et al., 2017] has been used widely in neural machine translation [Tubay and Costa-jussà, 2018, Edunov et al., 2018, Xia et al., 2019, Devlin et al., 2019] and has proven effective for sentiment analysis and emotion recognition. However, existing architectures are very dense compared to our three lightweight models.

The Multimodal Transformer (MuLT) of Tsai et al. [2019] modifies the Transformer block to compute cross-modal attention for two modalities at a time. It combines modalities in directed pairs, using a total of six Transformers, whose outputs are then merged into a single multimodal representation. Unlike other works, MuLT is able to handle cases where the three modalities are not aligned at the word level; it learns soft alignments via the cross-modal attention weights for each pair of modalities. The model works well in the unaligned case, and in the aligned case, it gives state of the art performance the *Happy* emotion in IEMOCAP.

The Factorized Multimodal Transformer (FMT) of Zadeh et al. [2019] introduces Factorized Multimodal Self-Attention (FSM) modules, which compute self-attention over unimodal, bimodal, and trimodal inputs in parallel. FMT gives state of the art performance in the word-aligned case on CMU-MOSI and on the *Sad*, *Angry*, and *Neutral* emotions in IEMOCAP. We use FMT, along with the word-aligned version of MuLT, as baselines for comparison in our experiments.

### 2.3 Canonical Correlation Approach

The Interaction Canonical Correlation Network (ICCN) [Sun et al., 2020] implements Deep Canonical Correlation Analysis (DCCA) [Andrew et al., 2013] to extract bimodal features from the outer product matrix of a pair of modalities. Sun et al. use two pairs, text with audio and text with video; these "text-based audio" and "text-based video" features are concatenated with purely textual features to form a multimodal embedding for sentiment analysis. ICCN gives state-of-the-art performance on CMU-MOSEI and on the *Sad* emotion in IEMOCAP.

## 3 Models

### 3.1 Input Alignment

We use $T$, $A$, and $V$, to represent the three modalities: text, audio, and video, respectively. Following the notation in [Tsai et al., 2019] and [Zadeh et al., 2019], we denote the input as

$$X_{T,A,V} = \{x_T, x_A, x_V\}$$

where

$$x_i = [x_{t,i}] \text{ for } i \in [T, A, V] \text{ and } t \in [1, \tau]$$

and $\tau$ is the length of the input sentence.

Each of the three modalities has its own low-level features, such as the Mel spectrogram for audio or facial landmarks for video. These features are extracted at different sampling rates — one set of features per word or character for text, per millisecond for audio, and per frame for video — and thus the input sequences for the three modalities are often different. A five-thousand-millisecond audio sequence, for example, may be only a three-word sequence from a textual perspective and a 50-frame sequence from a video perspective.

We align the audio and video to the text using the timestamps provided in the text transcripts. The set of audio or video samples that correspond to a

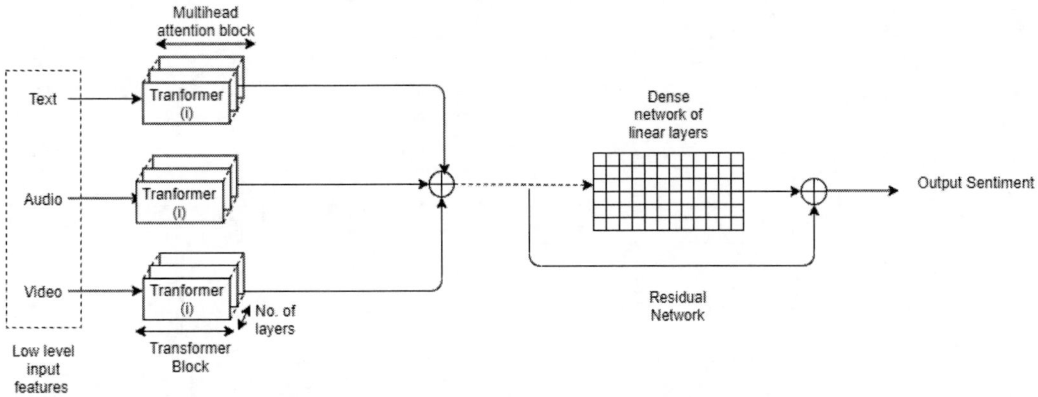


Figure 1: Architecture of our *Late Fusion* model. Unimodal Transformers process each modality separately; the outputs of these Transformers are summed and passed through a residual network of linear layers to produce the final prediction.

word in the transcript are combined using a series of 1D convolutional layers:

$$\bar{X}_{\{T,A,V\}} = conv1D\left(X_{\{T,A,V\}}\right) \in R^d$$

where $d$ is a common feature dimension size. This procedure ensures that the input sequence length is the same across modalities.

### 3.2 Transformer Blocks

Our three lightweight architectures are comprised of Transformer blocks [Vaswani et al., 2017], which are non-recurrent neural networks that can process sequential data. It consists of alternating attention and linear layers. The attention block of a Transformer uses multi-head attention, where each head computes scaled dot product attention:

$$\begin{aligned} \text{attn}(Q,K,V) &= \text{softmax}\left(\frac{QK^T}{\sqrt{d_k}}\right)V \\ \text{head}_i &= \text{attn}\left(QW_i^Q, KW_i^K, VW_i^V\right) \\ \text{multi}(Q,K,V) &= [\text{head}_1; \ldots; \text{head}_h]W^O \end{aligned}$$

where $Q$, $K$, $V$ represent the query, key and value; $d_k$ is the key dimension size; $W_i^Q$, $W_i^K$, $W_i^V$ are learned projection matrices for head $i$; and $W^O$ is a learned projection matrix for the attention block.

In addition, Vaswani et al. note that positional encodings must be added to Transformer input because there is no sequential information present in the Transformer itself:

$$\begin{aligned} PE_{(\text{pos},2i)} &= sin(\text{pos}/10000^{2i/d_{model}}) \\ PE_{(\text{pos},2i+1)} &= cos(\text{pos}/10000^{2i/d_{model}}) \end{aligned}$$

$$\hat{X} = \bar{X} + PE$$

### 3.3 Three Multimodal Architectures

Figure 1 shows our *Late Fusion* architecture. Three unimodal Transformers learn high-level features from the low-level input features of each modality. The outputs of these unimodal Transformers are then merged together using a simple summation, rather than the merge layer used in previous work [Tsai et al., 2019], and passed to a residual network of linear layers [Xie et al., 2017] for sentiment prediction.

Figure 2 shows our *Round Robin* architecture, which is a simplification of MuTL [Tsai et al., 2019]. Three cross-modal Transformers learn bimodal feaatures for ordered pairs of modalities, where the query is one modality and the key/value is the other. We use only three pairs — text query and audio key/value, audio query and video key/value, and video query and text key/value — with bimodal information flowing in only one direction; in contrast, MuLT uses six pairs of cross-modal Transformers, with information flowing in both directions. MuLT also uses three Transformers, one for each modality, to merge the two pairs sharing that modality as key/value; our pairwise features are simply concatenated and passed to the output residual network.

Figure 3 shows our *Hybrid Fusion* architecture, which uses both an early fusion approach that concatenates the inputs and passes them to a single Transformer to learn trimodal features, as well as a late fusion approach that passes each modality through a separate Transformer to learn unimodal features. The trimodal and unimodal features are concatenated together and merged using a layer of Gated Recurrent Units [Liang et al., 2018].

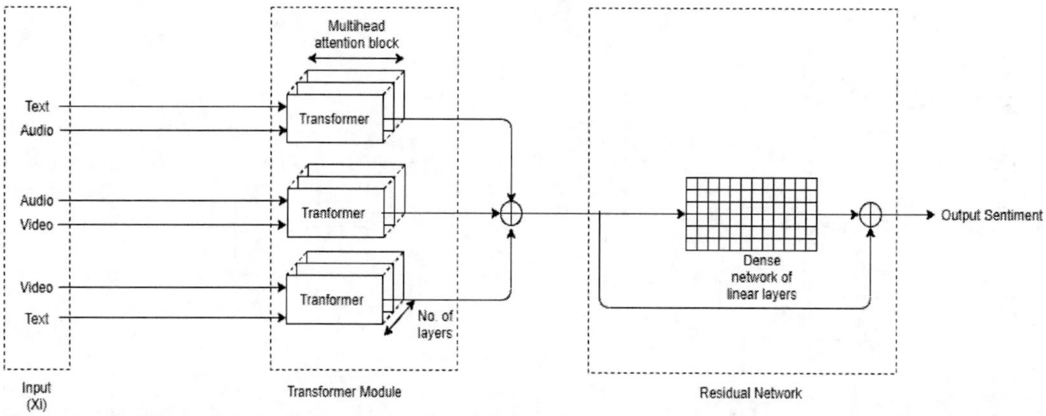


Figure 2: Architecture of our *Round Robin* model. Modalities are combined in a round-robin fashion via thrree cross-modal Transformers, one for each ordered pair of modalities: $[T, A]$, $[A, V]$, $[V, T]$. The outputs of these cross-modal Transformers are concatenated and passed through a residual network of linear layers to produce the final prediction.

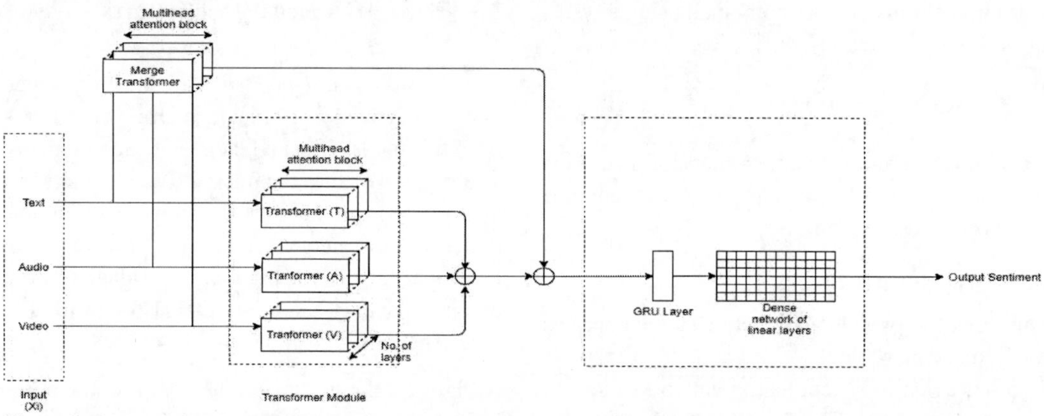


Figure 3: Architecture of our *Hybrid Fusion* model. All three modalities are passed through an early fusion Transformer to produce trimodal features; in parallel, they are individually passed to separate Transformers to produce unimodal features. All features are then concatenated and passed through a GRU and a residual network of linear layers to produce the final prediction.

## 4 Experiments

We train our models on a single NVIDIA K80 GPU. We tune hyperparameter values for our model using the validation sets provided by our evaluation datasets; we achieve the best validation performance using 8 attention blocks per Transformer, each with 5 attention heads, and a hidden size was set to 40. The dropout rate was set to 0.15; the best learning rate for IEMOCAP was 0.02, while for CMU-MOSI and CMU-MOSEI it was 0.01, with batch sizes of 32, 128, and 40, respectively.

### 4.1 Datasets

**IEMOCAP** [Busso et al., 2008] consists of video recordings of 151 conversation sessions (dialogues), totaling around 6k verbal interactions. This dataset is intended for multilabel emotion classification; we evaluate on the four labeled emotions (*Happy*, *Sad*, *Angry*, and *Neutral*) used in previous work [Wang et al., 2019]; also following previous work, we report binary accuracy and F1 score as the evaluation metrics on this dataset.

**CMU-MOSI** [Zadeh et al., 2016] is a sentiment analysis dataset of 2199 short monologues labeled in the range $[-3, 3]$, with $-3$ being strongly negative and $+3$ being strongly positive. Following previous work, we report seven-class and binary accuracy, F1 score, mean absolute error, and correlation with human judgments.

**CMU-MOSEI** [Zadeh et al., 2018b] is a sentiment and emotion analysis dataset of 23K movie reviews from YouTube. As with CMU-MOSI, it is labeled in the range of $[-3, 3]$, and its evaluation metrics are the same as in CMU-MOSI.

### 4.2 Features and Alignment

**Text Features:** For word-level textual features we use the pretrained, 300-dimensional, Common Crawl GloVe embeddings [Pennington et al., 2014].

**Audio Features:** We use Neurospeech [Orozco-Arroyave et al., 2018] to extract 74 low-level audio

| Model | Happy | | Sad | | Angry | | Neutral | |
|---|---|---|---|---|---|---|---|---|
| Metric | BA | F1 | BA | F1 | BA | F1 | BA | F1 |
| MARN [Zadeh et al., 2018b] | 86.7 | 83.6 | 82.0 | 81.2 | 84.6 | 84.2 | 66.8 | 65.9 |
| MFN [Zadeh et al., 2018a] | 86.5 | 84.0 | 83.5 | 82.1 | 85.0 | 83.7 | 69.6 | 69.2 |
| RAVEN [Wang et al., 2019] | 87.3 | 85.8 | 83.4 | 83.1 | 87.3 | 86.7 | 69.7 | 69.3 |
| MCTN [Pham et al., 2019] | 84.9 | 83.1 | 80.5 | 79.6 | 79.7 | 80.4 | 62.3 | 57.0 |
| ICCN [Sun et al., 2020] | 87.4 | 84.7 | **88.6** | **88.0** | 86.3 | 85.9 | 69.7 | 68.5 |
| MuLT [Tsai et al., 2019] | **90.7** | **88.6** | 86.7 | 86.0 | 87.4 | 87.0 | **72.4** | 70.7 |
| MuLT* | 84.7 | 83.5 | 84.5 | 84.1 | 84.9 | 84.7 | 70.4 | 70.7 |
| FMT [Zadeh et al., 2019] | **88.8** | **87.2** | **88.0** | **87.7** | **89.7** | **89.5** | **74.0** | **73.8** |
| FMT* | 85.6 | 85.1 | 84.1 | 83.8 | 87.9 | 88.2 | 70.6 | 70.4 |
| *Late Fusion* | 87.7 | 86.8 | 87.3 | 86.8 | 87.9 | 87.0 | 72.0 | 71.5 |
| *Round Robin* | 87.5 | 84.9 | 85.2 | 84.4 | 87.4 | 87.5 | 70.0 | 69.4 |
| *Hybrid Fusion* | 88.0 | 86.0 | 86.9 | 86.2 | 89.0 | 89.0 | 71.0 | 71.5 |

Table 1: Emotion recognition results on IEMOCAP. The metrics are binary (one vs all) accuracy and the F1 score for each of the four emotions. * indicates results from open source code. **Bold** indicates scores higher than that of our model.

| Model | $ACC_7$ | $ACC_2$ | F1 | MAE | Corr |
|---|---|---|---|---|---|
| MARN | - | 77.1 | 77.0 | 0.97 | 0.63 |
| MFN | - | 77.4 | 77.3 | 0.97 | 0.63 |
| RAVEN | 33.2 | 78.0 | 76.6 | 0.92 | 0.69 |
| MCTN | 35.6 | 79.3 | 79.1 | 0.91 | 0.68 |
| ICCN | 39.0 | 83.1 | **83.0** | **0.86** | **0.71** |
| MuLT | 40.0 | 83.0 | **82.8** | **0.87** | **0.70** |
| MuLT* | 30.7 | 77.5 | 76.9 | 1.04 | 0.66 |
| FMT | - | 83.5 | **83.5** | **0.84** | **0.74** |
| FMT* | - | 78.3 | 77.8 | **0.91** | **0.70** |
| *Late Fusion* | 40.2 | **83.6** | 80.0 | 0.92 | 0.69 |
| *Round Robin* | 39.3 | 78.1 | 76.7 | 0.96 | 0.68 |
| *Hybrid Fusion* | **40.6** | 82.1 | 79.9 | 0.94 | 0.69 |

Table 2: Sentiment analysis results on CMU-MOSI. $ACC_7$ was not reported by some baselines. The metrics are seven-way and binary accuracy, F1 score, mean absolute error, and correlation with human judgments. All metrics are better when higher, except for mean absolute error.

| Model | $ACC_7$ | $ACC_2$ | F1 | MAE | Corr |
|---|---|---|---|---|---|
| MFN | 45.0 | 76.9 | 77.0 | 0.71 | 0.54 |
| RAVEN | 50.0 | 79.1 | 79.5 | 0.61 | 0.66 |
| MCTN | 49.6 | 79.8 | 80.6 | 0.61 | 0.67 |
| ICCN | 51.6 | **84.2** | **84.2** | **0.57** | **0.71** |
| MuLT | 51.8 | **82.5** | **82.3** | **0.58** | **0.70** |
| MuLT* | 48.9 | 80.7 | **80.9** | 0.63 | 0.65 |
| *Late Fusion* | **52.3** | 80.7 | 80.7 | 0.61 | 0.69 |
| *Round Robin* | 51.4 | 80.6 | 79.9 | 0.62 | 0.66 |
| *Hybrid Fusion* | 51.9 | 80.6 | 80.5 | 0.61 | 0.68 |

Table 3: Sentiment analysis results on CMU-MOSEI. The metrics used are the same as in Table 2.

features, including Mel-frequency cepstral coefficients and transformations thereof, as well as harmonic, percussive, and glottal source parameters. We also use COVERAP [Degottex et al., 2014] to extract pitch tracking and voiced/unvoiced sloping parameters, peak slope parameters, and maximum dispersion quotients.

**Video Features:** We extract 35 facial units using Facet [iMotions, 2017], as well as 35 facial action units and 30 facial landmark and gaze features using OpenFace [Baltrusaitis et al., 2018].

### 4.3 Baseline Models

We compare our results with the state-of-the-art Multimodal Transformer (MuLT)[1] [Tsai et al., 2019] and Factorized Multimodal Transformer (FMT) [Zadeh et al., 2019], as well as Memory Fusion Network (MFN) [Zadeh et al., 2018a], Recurrent Attended Variation Embedding Network (RAVEN) [Wang et al., 2019], Multi-Attention Recurrent Network (MARN) [Zadeh et al., 2018c], and Multimodal Cyclic Translation Network (MCTN) [Pham et al., 2019]. These systems are described in Section 2; all attained state of the art on at least one of the evaluation datasets at their times of publication, and all use a similar feature set to our work.

## 5 Results and Discussion

We present the results of our model compared to the reported results of our baseline models in Tables 1, 2, and 3. The best-performing MuLT and FMT models are extremely dense, with around 15 and 77 million parameters, respectively. In contrast, our models have between 7-9 million trainable parameters, depending on the architecture; despite using about half as many parameters as MuLT, we see that our models produce comparable results.

We perform fairly well on IEMOCAP, which has around 2717 training samples; we achieve scores around 1-2% below the best-performing model, FMT. On the tiny CMU-MOSI dataset, which has just 1284 training samples, our *Hybrid Fusion* and

[1]We use the aligned version of MuLT for fair comparison with models that obligatorily use word alignments.

| | IEMOCAP | | CMU-MOSI | | CMU-MOSEI | |
|---|---|---|---|---|---|---|
| Model | Time (min) | Mem use (%) | Time (min) | Mem. use (%) | Time (min) | Mem. use (%) |
| MuLT* | 8.1 | 24.2 | 7.4 | 20.0 | 58.6 | 59.1 |
| FMT* | 55.2 | 28.0 | 151.1 | 26.5 | - | - |
| *Late Fusion* | 1.8 | 22.1 | 1.3 | 22.0 | 14.9 | 48.0 |
| *Round Robin* | 1.7 | 22.7 | 2.7 | 19.0 | 15.8 | 45.0 |
| *Hybrid Fusion* | 2.5 | 23.0 | 1.4 | 20.0 | 21.3 | 54.0 |

Table 4: Comparison of training time and memory use among MuLT*, FMT*, and our models.

| Model | Happy | | Sad | | Angry | | Neutral | |
|---|---|---|---|---|---|---|---|---|
| Metric | BA | F1 | BA | F1 | BA | F1 | BA | F1 |
| MuLT* | 82.6 | 81.5 | 79.4 | **80.7** | 78.3 | 78.9 | 60.1 | 60.7 |
| FMT* | 82.1 | 81.2 | 80.2 | **80.9** | 80.0 | **81.7** | 60.5 | 60.2 |
| *Late Fusion* | 84.1 | **82.4** | 80.3 | 76.5 | **81.0** | 79.4 | 61.6 | 61.2 |
| *Round Robin* | 85.2 | 81.2 | 79.9 | 77.2 | 79.0 | 76.6 | 63.2 | 58.1 |
| *Hybrid Fusion* | **85.5** | 80.7 | **80.8** | 79.9 | **81.0** | 80.8 | **64.7** | **63.5** |

Table 5: Results on the reduced IEMOCAP dataset of 1284 training samples. The metrics used are the same as in Table 1.

| Model | Happy | | Sad | | Angry | | Neutral | |
|---|---|---|---|---|---|---|---|---|
| Metric | BA | F1 | BA | F1 | BA | F1 | BA | F1 |
| Unimodal [T] | 86.4 | 84.0 | 82.7 | 78.5 | 81.6 | 78.3 | 67.9 | 65.9 |
| Unimodal [A] | 85.9 | 79.0 | 82.2 | 81.5 | 85.9 | 85.9 | 62.8 | 60.5 |
| Unimodal [V] | 85.1 | 81.0 | 79.1 | 70.4 | 75.6 | 74.1 | 58.8 | 56.3 |
| Bimodal [T,A] | 84.5 | 82.6 | 84.8 | 84.1 | 85.8 | 86.1 | 68.9 | 67.2 |
| Bimodal [T,V] | 85.3 | 85.1 | 80.1 | 80.7 | 84.2 | 83.5 | 66.4 | 65.4 |
| Bimodal [V,A] | 86.8 | 82.9 | 81.4 | 77.9 | 86.4 | 86.1 | 62.5 | 62.6 |
| *Late Fusion* [T,A,V] | 87.7 | 86.8 | 87.3 | 86.8 | 87.9 | 87.0 | 72.0 | 71.5 |

Table 6: Ablation results on IEMOCAP for our *Late Fusion* model.

| Model | Happy | | Sad | | Angry | | Neutral | |
|---|---|---|---|---|---|---|---|---|
| Metric | BA | F1 | BA | F1 | BA | F1 | BA | F1 |
| Bimodal [T,A] | 85.2 | 82.9 | 82.9 | 83.9 | 86.2 | 86.4 | 70.2 | 69.5 |
| Bimodal [T,V] | 86.4 | 83.9 | 79.3 | 77.4 | 81.4 | 81.4 | 65.1 | 65.0 |
| Bimodal [V,A] | 86.4 | 82.5 | 79.6 | 78.6 | 85.6 | 85.2 | 63.1 | 62.7 |
| *Round Robin* [T,A,V] | 87.5 | 84.9 | 85.2 | 87.4 | 87.5 | 86.8 | 70.0 | 69.4 |

Table 7: Ablation results on IEMOCAP for our *Round Robin* model.

*Late Fusion* models give state of the art results on seven-way and binary accuracy, respectively.

The CMU-MOSEI dataset is much larger than IEMOCAP and CMU-MOSI, with close to 16265 training samples. Our models perform the weakest on this dataset, falling short of the state of the art models by around 2-3%, suggesting that our models may be too small to learn the entire distribution. Neither MARN [Zadeh et al., 2018c] nor FMT [Zadeh et al., 2019] reports results on CMU-MOSEI, so they are omitted from Table 3.

We also experiment with the open source code available for MuLT and FMT (denoted by *). Using the hyperparameter settings provided[2], we were nevertheless unable to match those systems' reported performance, possibly due to differences resulting from random initialization. In training MuLT* and FMT*, we observe that the models are overfitting, with a mean difference of 15-20% between the train and test accuracy; in contrast, the largest train-test accuracy difference among our three models is only about 10%. The smaller number of parameters in our model reduces the risk of overfitting on smaller datasets, while still achieving good performance on larger datasets.

### 5.1 Analysis of Lightweight Architectures

We compare the training time and memory footprint of our models with MuLT* and FMT* in Table 4[3]. All models are trained on a single NVIDIA K80 GPU with 24GB of memory. We train for 30 epochs on IEMOCAP, 100 on CMU-MOSI and 40

[2]Batch size for FMT* is not given; we use 20, the default.

[3]FMT* does not provide hyperparameter settings for CMU-MOSEI, so those results are omitted.

| Model | Happy | | Sad | | Angry | | Neutral | |
|---|---|---|---|---|---|---|---|---|
| Metric | BA | F1 | BA | F1 | BA | F1 | BA | F1 |
| Bimodal early [T,A] | 84.8 | 83.1 | 82.8 | 81.3 | 85.1 | 86.2 | 68.6 | 68.7 |
| Bimodal early [T,V] | 86.2 | 83.6 | 80.3 | 80.7 | 85.6 | 84.8 | 67.8 | 67.7 |
| Bimodal early [V,A] | 83.9 | 86.2 | 84.1 | 84.2 | 84.8 | 85.1 | 70.0 | 68.5 |
| *Hybrid Fusion* [T,A,V] | 88.0 | 86.0 | 86.9 | 86.2 | 89.0 | 89.0 | 71.0 | 71.5 |
| Bimodal late [T,A] | 87.0 | 85.1 | 85.0 | 84.9 | 86.7 | 86.9 | 70.3 | 68.8 |
| Bimodal late [T,V] | 86.2 | 83.8 | 83.7 | 83.5 | 85.6 | 85.8 | 67.8 | 66.9 |
| Bimodal late [V,A] | 85.7 | 83.2 | 81.1 | 82.0 | 86.8 | 86.9 | 69.9 | 67.6 |

Table 8: Ablation results on IEMOCAP for our *Hybrid Fusion* model: bimodal early fusion with trimodal late fusion (top) and trimodal early fusion with bimodal late fusion (bottom).

| Model | Happy | | Sad | | Angry | | Neutral | |
|---|---|---|---|---|---|---|---|---|
| Metric | BA | F1 | BA | F1 | BA | F1 | BA | F1 |
| MuLT | **90.7** | **88.6** | **86.7** | **86.0** | **87.4** | 87.0 | **72.4** | **70.7** |
| MuLT* | 84.7 | 83.5 | 84.5 | 84.1 | 84.85 | 84.7 | 70.4 | **70.7** |
| *Round Robin* $[T \rightarrow A \rightarrow V]$ | 87.5 | 84.9 | 85.2 | 84.4 | **87.4** | **87.5** | 70.0 | 69.4 |
| *Round Robin* $[V \rightarrow A \rightarrow T]$ | 83.0 | 81.8 | 82.2 | 83.7 | 85.9 | 82.7 | 68.2 | 68.3 |

Table 9: Results on IEMOCAP for our *Round Robin* model, comparing information flow in each direction, alongside MuLT and MuLT*, which capture information flowing in both directions.

on CMU-MOSEI (the number of epochs needed for MuLT to converge, as reported by Tsai et al. [2019]).

On the smallest dataset, CMU-MOSI, training MuLT* took just over seven minutes, while FMT* took 2.5 hours. Our models train in under three minutes and outperform both MuLT* and FMT*, and this difference in training speed holds for CMU-MOSI and CMU-MOSEI as well. Thus our model, available in the supplementary materials[4], is the fastest and best-performing multimodal sentiment system currently available for public use.

We also conduct experiments on a substantially reduced IEMOCAP training subset of 1284 samples, matching the size of CMU-MOSI, which we create by randomly sampling from the full IEMOCAP training set. Table 5 shows the results of our models, as well as MuLT* and FMT*, retrained on this smaller IEMOCAP training set, and evaluated on the full IEMOCAP test set. We see that our models, with their smaller numbers of parameters, are better able to learn from limited training data than are state-of-the-art models with double or more the number of trainable parameters.

### 5.2 Analysis of Architecture Components

We perform ablation experiments on our models using the IEMOCAP dataset; ablation results for CMU-MOSI and CMU-MOSEI are omitted due to space constraints, but exhibit similar trends. Table 6 presents the results of modality ablation on the simplest *Late Fusion* model; it clearly shows that unimodal and bimodal models are unable to match the performance of a full multimodal model. This demonstrates the importance of considering all modalities when analyzing spoken language, since some of the emotions or sentiment may be dependent more on the audio or the visual actions of the speaker, rather than the text.

Examining the unimodal results, we see that the Text modality is the most informative for predicting *Happy, Sad*, and *Neutral*, while Audio is the most informative for *Angry*. However, the bimodal results do not always match the unimodal results. The best-performing bimodal model for *Happy* is [V,A], despite Video being the worst-performing single modality, and [T,A] is the worst-performing bimodal model, despite both Text and Audio outperforming Video individually. Considering the other three emotions, we see that the best bimodal model varies between [T,A] and [V,A], with [T,V] generally performing the worst.

Table 7 shows the results of modality ablation on the *Round Robin* model; as the architecture does not support unimodal experiments, only bimodal results are shown. Comparing Table 6 to Table 7, we see that the cross-modal Transformers of the full *Round Robin* model are outperformed by the full *Late Fusion* model. However, the relative performance among modality pairs is consistent across Tables 6 and 7.

Finally, Table 8 shows the results of modality ablation on the *Hybrid Fusion* model, where we

[4]We will release it online after the anonymity period.

compare the relative contributions of the early fusion and late fusion halves of the architecture. The top of the table shows the results of reducing the early fusion half to only two modalities while retaining all three modalities in the late fusion half, and the bottom shows the results of reducing the late fusion half to two modalities while retaining all three in the early fusion half; in both sets of experiments, the overall model has access to all three modalities, but only through either the early fusion path or the late fusion path.

Surprisingly, although standalone early fusion models are outperformed by standalone late fusion models [Tsai et al., 2019], we find that a hybrid model containing a full, trimodal early fusion half is more robust to modality ablation in its late fusion half than a model with a full late fusion half is to an ablated early fusion half. Our results in this experiment also show greater variability among modality pairs. The [T,A] combination, which gave the best performance in the *Late Fusion* and *Round Robin* experiments, remains the strongest modality pair for the full early fusion, bimodal late fusion model. In contrast, for the bimodal early fusion, full late fusion model, [T,A] is outperformed by one of the two Video-based modality pairs, [T,V] or [V,A], on each of the four emotions, suggesting that the performance gap of early versus late fusion differs across modalities.

### 5.2.1 Order of Modalities in Round Robin

The effect of direction on our *Round Robin* model is shown in Table 9; this experiment shows the impact of the direction of information flow across modalities within the model. Comparing our results to those of MuLT and MuLT*, we see that capturing information flow in one direction, text to audio to video and back to text, is enough for a model to give good predictions, without requiring the additional overhead of handling both directions. We can also see that the direction does matter; the performance of the Round Robin model with information flowing in the opposite direction, from video to audio to text and back to video, is relatively poor. These results suggest that the interactions between pairs of modalities are directed.

## 6 Conclusion

We have presented three lightweight architectures for multimodal sentiment analysis and emotion recognition. The *Late Fusion* model merges unimodal features, the *Round Robin* model iteratively combines bimodal features, and the *Hybrid Early-Late Fusion* model combines early-fusion trimodal and late-fusion unimodal features. Our proposed models are much smaller in size compared to existing state-of-the-art models; they are able to attain new state-of-the-art scores on the CMU-MOSI and CMU-MOSEI datasets on two metrics, while remaining competitive on the others. Further, our experiments analyzing the relative contribution of modalities and architecture components in our models suggest new directions for developing multimodal systems. We hope that our simple architectures for sentiment and emotion detection, currently the fastest and best-performing publicly available system, as well as the insights revealed in our experimental results, can be useful for further research in the field.

## References


G. Andrew, R. Arora, J. Bilmes, and Karen Livescu. Deep canonical correlation analysis. In *ICML*, 2013.

Tadas Baltrusaitis, Amir Zadeh, Yao Chong Lim, and Louis-Philippe Morency. Openface 2.0: Facial behavior analysis toolkit. *2018 13th IEEE International Conference on Automatic Face Gesture Recognition (FG 2018)*, pages 59–66, 2018.

Carlos Busso, Murtaza Bulut, Chi-Chun Lee, Abe Kazemzadeh, Emily Mower Provost, Samuel Kim, Jeannette N. Chang, Sungbok Lee, and Shrikanth S. Narayanan. Iemocap: interactive emotional dyadic motion capture database. *Language Resources and Evaluation*, 42:335–359, 2008.

Mia Xu Chen, Orhan Firat, Ankur Bapna, Melvin Johnson, Wolfgang Macherey, George Foster, Llion Jones, Niki Parmar, Michael Schuster, Zhi-Feng Chen, Yonghui Wu, and Macduff Hughes. The best of both worlds: Combining recent advances in neural machine translation. In *ACL*, 2018.

Gilles Degottex, John Kane, Thomas Drugman, Tuomo Raitio, and Stefan Scherer. Covarep — a collaborative voice analysis repository for speech technologies. *2014 IEEE International Conference on Acoustics, Speech and Signal Processing (ICASSP)*, pages 960–964, 2014.

Jacob Devlin, Ming-Wei Chang, Kenton Lee, and Kristina Toutanova. Bert: Pre-training of deep bidirectional transformers for language understanding. *ArXiv*, abs/1810.04805, 2019.

Sergey Edunov, Myle Ott, Michael Auli, and David Grangier. Understanding back-translation at scale. In *EMNLP*, 2018.

iMotions. Facial expression analysis, 2017. URL `https://rb.gy/hkrcc4`.

Paul Pu Liang, Ziyin Liu, Amir Zadeh, and Louis-Philippe Morency. Multimodal language analysis with recurrent multistage fusion. *EMNLP*, 2018.

Zhun Liu, Ying Shen, Varun Bharadhwaj Lakshminarasimhan, Paul Pu Liang, Amir Zadeh, and Louis-Philippe Morency. Efficient low-rank multimodal fusion with modality-specific factors. In *ACL*, 2018.

Juan R. Orozco-Arroyave, Juan Camilo Vasquez-Correa, Jesus Francisco Vargas-Bonilla, Raman Arora, Najim Dehak, Phani S. Nidadavolu, Heidi Christensen, Frank Rudzicz, Maria Yancheva, Hamid R. Chinaei, Alyssa Vann, Nikolai Vogler, Tobias Bocklet, Milos Cernak, Julius Hannink, and Elmar Noth. Neurospeech: An open-source software for parkinson's speech analysis. *Digital Signal Process.*, 77:207–221, 2018.

Jeffrey Pennington, Richard Socher, and Christopher D. Manning. Glove: Global vectors for word representation. In *EMNLP*, 2014.

Hai Pham, Paul Pu Liang, Thomas Manzini, Louis-Philippe Morency, and Barnabas Poczos. Found in translation: Learning robust joint representations by cyclic translations between modalities. In *AAAI*, 2019.

Felix Sun, David F. Harwath, and James R. Glass. Look, listen, and decode: Multimodal speech recognition with images. *2016 IEEE Spoken Language Technology Workshop (SLT)*, pages 573–578, 2016.

Zhongkai Sun, P. Sarma, W. Sethares, and Yingyu Liang. Learning relationships between text, audio, and video via deep canonical correlation for multimodal language analysis. *ArXiv*, abs/1911.05544, 2020.

Yao-Hung Hubert Tsai, Shaojie Bai, Paul Pu Liang, J. Zico Kolter, Louis-Philippe Morency, and Ruslan Salakhutdinov. Multimodal transformer for unaligned multimodal language sequences. *Proceedings of the conference. Association for Computational Linguistics. Meeting*, 2019:6558–6569, 2019. version 2.

Brian Tubay and Marta R. Costa-jussà. Neural machine translation with the transformer and multi-source romance languages for the biomedical wmt 2018 task. In *WMT*, 2018.

Ashish Vaswani, Noam Shazeer, Niki Parmar, Jakob Uszkoreit, Llion Jones, Aidan N Gomez, Łukasz Kaiser, and Illia Polosukhin. Attention is all you need. In *Advances in neural information processing systems*, pages 5998–6008, 2017.

Yansen Wang, Ying Shen, Zhun Liu, Paul Pu Liang, Amir Zadeh, and Louis-Philippe Morency. Words can shift: Dynamically adjusting word representations using nonverbal behaviors. *Proceedings of the AAAI Conference on Artificial Intelligence. AAAI Conference on Artificial Intelligence*, 33 1:7216–7223, 2019.

Yingce Xia, Tianyu He, Xu Tan, Fei Tian, Di He, and Tao Qin. Tied transformers: Neural machine translation with shared encoder and decoder. In *AAAI*, 2019.

Saining Xie, Ross B. Girshick, Piotr Dollár, Zhuowen Tu, and Kaiming He. Aggregated residual transformations for deep neural networks. *2017 IEEE Conference on Computer Vision and Pattern Recognition (CVPR)*, pages 5987–5995, 2017.

Amir Zadeh, Rowan Zellers, Eli Pincus, and Louis-Philippe Morency. Multimodal sentiment intensity analysis in videos: Facial gestures and verbal messages. *IEEE Intelligent Systems*, 31:82–88, 2016.

Amir Zadeh, Paul Pu Liang, Navonil Mazumder, Soujanya Poria, Erik Cambria, and Louis-Philippe Morency. Memory fusion network for multi-view sequential learning. In *AAAI*, 2018a. version 1.

Amir Zadeh, Paul Pu Liang, Soujanya Poria, Erik Cambria, and Louis-Philippe Morency. Multimodal language analysis in the wild: Cmu-mosei dataset and interpretable dynamic fusion graph. In *ACL*, 2018b.

Amir Zadeh, Paul Pu Liang, Soujanya Poria, Prateek Vij, Erik Cambria, and Louis-Philippe Morency. Multi-attention recurrent network for human communication comprehension. *Proceedings of the ... AAAI Conference on Artificial Intelligence. AAAI Conference on Artificial Intelligence*, 2018:5642–5649, 2018c. version 2.

Amir Zadeh, Chengfeng Mao, Kelly Shi, Yiwei Zhang, Paul Pu Liang, Soujanya Poria, and Louis-Philippe Morency. Factorized multimodal transformer for multimodal sequential learning. *ArXiv*, abs/1911.09826, 2019.

# Exploring Implicit Sentiment Evoked by Fine-grained News Events

**Cynthia Van Hee, Orphée De Clercq and Véronique Hoste**
LT[3], Language and Translation Technology Team
Department of Translation, Interpreting and Communication, Ghent University
Ghent, Belgium
firstname.lastname@ugent.be

## Abstract

We investigate the feasibility of defining sentiment evoked by fine-grained news events. Our research question is based on the premise that methods for detecting implicit sentiment in news can be a key driver of content diversity, which is one way to mitigate the detrimental effects of filter bubbles that recommenders based on collaborative filtering may produce. Our experiments are based on 1,735 news articles from major Flemish newspapers that were manually annotated, with high agreement, for implicit sentiment. While lexical resources prove insufficient for sentiment analysis in this data genre, our results demonstrate that machine learning models based on SVM and BERT are able to automatically infer the implicit sentiment evoked by news events.

## 1 Introduction

Why do we read the news that we read and how are news articles received by their audiences? Both research questions are important in the domains of news personalization, framing theory and sentiment and emotion analysis, among others. Digitization and globalization have profoundly changed the media ecology (Mitchelstein and Boczkowski, 2009; Deuze, 2003). There is an increasing trend to consume news via the internet (54%, as opposed to 22% consuming print media[1]), and more specifically via newspaper websites, smartphone apps, social media, etc.

This (partial) shift to online news consumption assigns much more responsibility to citizens, who select from a wide variety of news sources, distributors and topics. Recommendation algorithms do part of the work by filtering, out of the extensive offer of information, news that sparks citizens' interest. Most commonly, such algorithms apply collaborative filtering, which is based on users' past reading behaviour and similar interests in their network. A detrimental side effect of this interplay between algorithms and user behaviour, especially on social media platforms, is that it may lead to a less diverse news consumption, a phenomenon often referred to as the 'filter bubble' (Parser, 2013).

A game changer in this respect are algorithms that use content diversity as the key driver for personalized news recommendation. To date, however, content-based filtering is largely based on topic clustering and keyword matching (Adnan et al., 2014; Liu et al., 2010) without considering semantic information including sentiment and controversy. The present study is part of the #NewsDNA project which aims to investigate and develop a news recommendation algorithm that is driven by content-based diversity[2]. However, before implementing this type of diversity into a recommender, we need to be able to automatically derive sentiment from newswire text. To this end, we explore whether news events evoke implicit sentiment in the reader and, if so, whether this implicit sentiment can be derived automatically using lexicon-based and machine learning techniques. We focus on text spans that describe hard news events (i.e. covering important topics in the public debate, such as politics, finance and economics, war and crime, as well as international news (Shoemaker and Cohen, 2005; Patterson, 2000; Tuchman, 1973)).

This paper is the first initiative to model the semantics of written editorial content (devoid of topic restrictions), where fine-grained news events' implicit sentiment is examined manually, and where attempts are made to model this sentiment automatically. Besides presenting a novel dataset for implicit sentiment detection in news texts, we aim

[1] Figures from the yearly imec.digimeter report (Vandendriessche and De Marez, 2019), publishing recent information about media and technology use in Flanders.

[2] https://www.ugent.be/mict/en/research/newsdna.



*Proceedings of the 11th Workshop on Computational Approaches to Subjectivity, Sentiment and Social Media Analysis*, pages 138–148
April 19, 2021. ©2021 Association for Computational Linguistics

to answer the following research question:

- *Can we automatically detect the implicit sentiment evoked by fine-grained news events?*

## 2 Related Research

While sentiment and emotion analysis have a long history in review analysis and recommendation applications using user-generated content, one of the first studies on subjectivity analysis focused on newswire text (Bruce and Wiebe, 1999). This work, among others, has inspired researchers to apply similar techniques to other data genres, and with the rise of Web 2.0, user-generated content (UGC) quickly became widely investigated, and the main genre under consideration for sentiment research. Compared to the high number of sentiment prediction pipelines that have been established for UGC analysis (Li and Hovy, 2017), not a great deal of research has been done into sentiment analysis at a fine-grained (i.e. below the sentence) level, sentiment analysis in factual data, multi-modal data or in figurative language like irony and humour, etc. (Mohammad, 2017). With this paper, we aim to tackle two of the above-mentioned challenges simultaneously by predicting implicit sentiment evoked by fine-grained (factual) news events.

Sentiment analysis has a broader application range than detecting explicit sentiment clues in subjective texts. Objective utterances can express sentiment as well, be it indirectly by either specific language use (i.e. words that activate emotional values), or by the sentiment certain events evoke through cultural or personal emotional connection. This distinction brings up the terminological confusion around *sentiment* and *opinion*. As pointed out by Liu (2015), the difference between the two is quite subtle, but dictionary definitions of both terms indicate that opinions represent a person's concrete view, whereas sentiments are more of a person's feeling. Although both are not completely independent of one another, it is worthwhile to mention this distinction so as to have a good understanding of the related research.

Implicit sentiment can thus be analyzed from the author's perspective (i.e. implicit opinions), as well as from the reader's (i.e. implicit sentiment). Research on implied opinions is prevalent in research areas such as electoral politics (e.g. Bansal and Srivastava, 2018; Chiu and Hsu, 2018), political viewpoints and argumentation mining (e.g. Chen et al., 2010) and stock market predictions (e.g. Khedr et al., 2017), but it is also gaining research interest in typical UGC analysis, for instance to detect irony and sarcasm (e.g. Van Hee et al., 2018), and for analyzing newswire text.

Looking at the mere impact of news events on their audiences without having readers' reactions at hand, the focus of this research lies on detecting implicit sentiment rather than implied opinions. Irrespective of potential framing, when consuming news, readers may infer a positive or negative impression of an event or topic based on world knowledge, cultural background, historical context or even personal experiences. Such text spans are known as "statements or phrases that describe positive or negative factual information about something without conveying a private state" (Wilson, 2008, p. 2741). Later, Toprak et al. (2010) coined the term 'polar facts' to refer to such statements. In what follows, we discuss some seminal studies on sentiment analysis in factual text from both the author's and readers' perspectives.

### 2.1 Implicit sentiment analysis from the author's perspective

Balahur et al. (2010) performed sentiment analysis on quotations in English newswire text. They defined the sentiment of named entities in quotations by applying sentiment lexicons to varying context windows inside the quotes. Jiang et al. (2017) combined a clustering algorithm with lexicon-based sentiment analysis using SentiWordNet (Baccianella et al., 2010) at the sentence level to distinguish between positive and negative attitudes from UK news sources towards climate change-related topics. A similar methodology was applied by Burscher et al. (2016) to analyze the framing of the topic of nuclear power in English news articles. They found that within the frame of nuclear accidents or waste, articles were much more negative compared to articles that focused on the effects of nuclear power on climate change, or its economic aspects.

Nozza et al. (2017) presented a multi-view corpus enriched with different variations of sentiment annotations; including objective versus subjective labels, implicit versus explicit sentiment, emotion categories, irony annotations, and so on. While the study presents clear definitions of the categories, the accompanying corpus examples are rather confusing (e.g. with "Tonight @CinemaX #SuicideSquad!! Come to see #HarleyQuinn :)" as an example of an objective text and "I went out the cinema after 15 minutes #suicidesquad" as an example of an implied opinion). Low inter-rater agreement scores also confirm the difficulty to distinguish between implicit and explicit opinions. Chen and Chen (2016) explored implicit aspect-based sentiment analysis in Chinese hotel reviews following the premise that implicit opinion expressions are located nearby explicit opinions. Fang et al. (2020) proposed an aspect-based approach to implicit opinion analysis of Chinese car reviews. They applied similarity metrics and clustering algorithms to extract and categorize feature expressions and aggregated their implicit sentiment based on pointwise mutual information (PMI).

### 2.2 Implicit sentiment analysis from the readers' perspective

Henley et al. (2002) investigated framing effects on violence perception in news reporting of homophobic attacks. Apart from investigating author's perceptions, they performed a manual content analysis to investigate readers' viewpoints regarding the framing of events. It was shown that, for instance, more homophobic newspapers reported on violence against gay people more vaguely compared to violence against straight people, as a result of which the former incidents were perceived less harmful. Conversely, more neutral newspapers were found to report on all types of violence in the same manner. In 2007, a shared task was set up by Strapparava and Mihalcea (2007) focusing on valence and emotion classification of English newspaper headlines. The SemEval-2015 task on implicit sentiment detection of events (Russo et al., 2015) focused on predicting whether structured events (i.e. newspaper sentences containing the pattern "I—we + [verbal/nominal keyword]") are considered pleasant or unpleasant.

While most work has been done on English data, similar approaches to detect sentiment and emotions in news from the readers' perspective have been applied to Czech (Burget et al., 2011), Chinese (Lin et al., 2008) and Dutch (Atteveldt et al., 2008). Related research has also focused on sentiment analysis of named entities in news (Godbole et al., 2007) and sentiment analysis for fake news detection (Kula et al., 2020; Bhutani et al., 2019).

Most similar to the present research is the work by Atteveldt et al. (2008), who classify implicit sentiment evoked by Dutch news on national political elections with a classification accuracy of 0.56 $F_1$-score. To the best of our knowledge, they are the first to perform such sentiment classification at a more fine-grained level (i.e. considering entity relations, evaluations and performances), as opposed to the document or sentence level. However, their approach is limited in that only specific event structures are considered, and that the data are collected within one well-defined domain, i.e. political elections. Given that the ultimate goal of the present research is to detect sentiment in any kind of hard news, our corpus is not restricted to political events, but encompasses a wide variety of news topics. In addition, we aim to not only detect positively or negatively evoked sentiment, but also consider 'neutral' and 'conflict' as sentiment labels (see Table 4).

## 3 Corpus Construction

Striving for diversification driven by content analysis, our research focus is on fine-grained news events (see Section 1), and more specifically the implicit sentiment they evoke in the reader. In the following paragraphs, we zoom in on the data collection and annotation process and present the results of inter-rater-agreement experiments.

### 3.1 Data Collection and Preparation

We collected a large set of Dutch news articles from major Flemish newspapers published in 2017 and 2018[3]. As mentioned before, our focus was on collecting hard news. Moreover, all articles were reduced to the title and lead, which include the most relevant information as defined by the inverted-pyramid structure applied in journalism.

A first step in the annotation process involved the identification of text spans that present news events. This was done as part of an important effort to create a new Dutch dataset in this research area by Colruyt et al. (2020). Once identified, all news events were subsequently annotated for implicit sentiment (see Section 3.3.1). Since identifying the sentiment that is evoked by an isolated chunk of text is quite an arduous task, all events were presented to the annotators in their original context, being the news articles' titles and leads. In total, 1,735 articles were annotated with fine-grained news events and their implicit sentiment, as well as the sentiment triggers.

[3]The data were provided as JSON files by Mediahuis, a media company that publishes national and regional newspapers in Belgium, the Netherlands and Ireland.

### 3.2 Data Annotation

All annotations were executed in the web-based annotation tool WebAnno (Eckart de Castilho et al., 2016) and by making use of a novel annotation scheme for implicit sentiment evoked by news events (Van Hee et al., 2021). To sum up, news events are pieces of text that describe an event, situation or description that is newsworthy, i.e. that caused the reporter to write the article. In the first step of the annotation process, the annotators indicated the implicit sentiment evoked by each event (e.g. *in 2040 stevige opwarming aarde [EN: in 2040 robust increase in global warming]*). All events were assigned a sentiment label out of the following: 'positive', 'negative', 'neutral' and 'conflict'. Where 'positive' and 'negative' were used to mark events evoking a positive and negative sentiment in the reader, the 'neutral' label was used when no specific sentiment was elicited.

As the reception and evaluation of news events may largely depend on personal factors (e.g. sociocultural and historical background), we provided the annotators with an extra guideline stating that annotations should be made from a European/Western viewpoint. The annotators were instructed to use 'conflict' labels sparingly, and only in cases where an event's implicit sentiment was ambiguous or depended too heavily on the annotator's personal interests, background, ideology, etc.

Once an event was assigned a non-neutral sentiment, the annotators marked all words or word groups that are indicative of this sentiment. In the annotation scheme, such text spans are referred to as 'sentiment triggers', which have either a 'positive', 'negative', or 'conflict' sentiment and can be flagged as ironic if the annotator judges irony is involved. The challenge in annotating sentiment triggers resides in the fact that these are, given the data genre, no explicit subjectivity markers, but rather *polar facts* (see Section 2). Figure 1 shows an annotation example where events are linked to their sentiment triggers. Importantly, sentiment triggers can be, but are not necessarily, part of the event span and they can be non-consecutive spans.

### 3.3 Inter-annotator Agreement

An inter-annotator agreement study was conducted on a subset of the corpus to verify the consistency of sentiment annotations across the annotators and hence to substantiate the feasibility of annotating implicit sentiment evoked by newswire text. Forty randomly selected documents were reserved for this experiment, which were annotated by three annotators, independently from one another. The annotations were carried out after briefing and training the annotators for the task and before the remainder of the corpus was labeled so as to allow the guidelines to be revised or clarified where deemed necessary.

#### 3.3.1 Implicit Sentiment of News Events

| | **Pos** | **Neg** | **Neu** | **Conf** | **Total** |
|---|---|---|---|---|---|
| *Rater 1* | 22 | 93 | 51 | 5 | 171 |
| *Rater 2* | 33 | 106 | 23 | 9 | 171 |
| *Rater 3* | 28 | 93 | 49 | 1 | 171 |
| *Average* | 27.67 | 97.33 | 41 | 5 | 171 |

Table 1: Event distribution by rater and sentiment.

Tables 1 and 2 present the data distribution statistics and inter-rater agreement scores, respectively. It is clear from Table 1 that most events in the IAA set evoked a negative implicit sentiment. More specifically, on average 97 out of 171 of the events or 57% were attributed a negative sentiment and 28 or 16% a positive one. On average, 5 events, or 3% of the events, were attributed the 'conflict' label, meaning that the event's evoked sentiment depended too heavily on its broader context or on the annotator's personal viewpoints. The above reveals that more than 3 in 4 news events in the corpus evoke a sentiment in the reader and can hence be considered *polar facts*. By contrast, on average 41 or 24% of the events were annotated as neutral.

Inter-rater agreement scores were calculated using the cloud-based version of AgreeStat360[4], a software package for advanced statistical analysis of agreement among multiple raters (Gwet, 2014). The software allows to calculate the Krippendorff's Alpha (Krippendorff, 2011) with all of its weights and coefficients, including Fleiss' Kappa (Fleiss, 1971), used for multiple raters' agreement calculation and AC1 (Gwet, 2014), which is a variation of Kappa that corrects an expected agreement in skewed data distributions that is artificially high.

Table 2 presents agreement scores between the three raters in terms of defining individual news events' evoked sentiment. All metrics considered and following the interpreting guidelines by Landis and Koch (1977), we can conclude that the annotations show a high level of agreement.

[4]http://agreestat360.com.

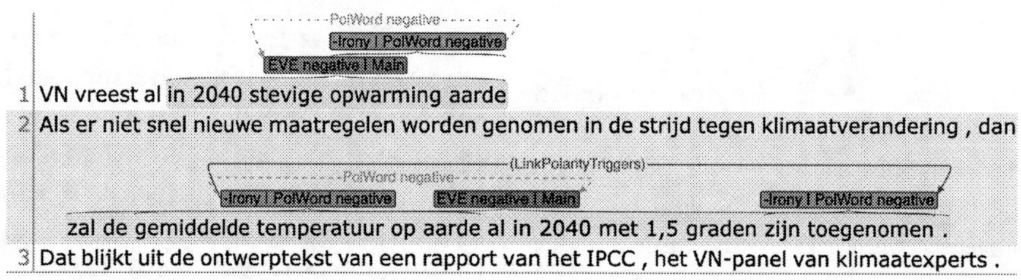


Figure 1: Pre-annotated events *"in 2040 robust increase in global warming"* and *"by 2040 the average temperature on earth will have risen by 1.5 degree"* are linked to their sentiment triggers *"robust increase in global warming"* and *"average temperature on earth" + "will have risen"*.

| Method | Coeff | StdErr | 95% C.I. | P-Value |
|---|---|---|---|---|
| AC 1 | 0.77 | 0.03 | (0.71,0.83) | 0.00e+00 |
| Fleiss' Kappa | 0.69 | 0.04 | (0.62,0.76) | 0.00e+00 |
| Krippendorff's Alpha | 0.69 | 0.04 | (0.62,0.76) | 0.00e+00 |
| Percent Agreement | 0.82 | 0.02 | (0.77,0.86) | 0.00e+00 |

Table 2: Inter-rater agreement coefficients for implicit sentiment annotation of news events.

### 3.3.2 Sentiment Triggers

Apart from annotating implicit sentiment evoked by news events, the annotators also marked in the same sentence all sentiment triggers that influenced their decision. Given the data genre, identifying such words was expected to be difficult because this depends on (i) the amount of context available and (ii) the extent to which an event has an intrinsic sentiment that humans are aware of by context or world knowledge.

No specific guidelines were defined for the annotation of sentiment triggers; they could be single words or phrases of any type of syntactic structure. Annotators were, however, asked to select the minimal word span. Calculating inter-rater agreement for sentiment triggers requires a strategy to align the text spans between the different annotators. Matching text spans between two outputs (whether they are human annotations or system predictions) is a familiar challenge in sentiment annotation and detection tasks, and especially known in the field of aspect-based sentiment analysis. Depending on the importance of exact span overlap, text spans can be evaluated by searching for an exact or a relaxed match at the start and ending token boundaries. In Lee and Sun (2019), an exact match imposes a 100% overlap between two text spans, whereas a relaxed match imposes that 1) either side of the boundaries is matched with at least one token or 2) at least one token overlaps between the spans.

As no detailed guidelines were provided for the syntactic composition of sentiment triggers, an exact span match evaluation would affect the inter-rater agreement too negatively. In fact, we looked at the 100% overlap ratio for sentiment triggers when annotated for a specific event and found that (one or more) sentiment trigger(s) were annotated for 148 events. For 38 events (26%), all annotators indicated the exact same sentiment triggers. For 12 events (8%), half of the sentiment triggers were identical amongst the three annotators. For 92 events (62%), there were no exact matches. For the remaining 6 events (4%), 1 out of 3 or 4 sentiment triggers were annotated by all three raters.

Partial matches were not taken into account for the above statistics. In a second and more detailed examination, we considered two annotations to match if at least one character index between the two text spans overlapped, regardless of matching boundaries. Table 3 shows these agreement results as $F_1$-scores per annotator pair, where the first rater mentioned served as the gold standard for the evaluation. As can be deduced from this table, with an average $F_1$-score of 0.72 over all events, the inter-rater agreement for sentiment triggers is quite high. It means that out of 10 sentiment triggers annotated by the gold standard 7 are also found by a second, independent rater.

| | Raters 2 and 1 | Raters 2 and 3 | Raters 3 and 1 |
|---|---|---|---|
| $F_1$-score | 0.72 | 0.74 | 0.70 |
| Average | | 0.72 | |

Table 3: Inter-rater scores for sentiment trigger annotation amongst three annotator pairs.

## 4 Corpus analysis and experiments

In the following paragraphs, we thoroughly investigate our research question by analyzing the full corpus and conducting experiments to examine whether detecting implicit sentiment evoked by news events is a feasible task.

### 4.1 Annotating Implicit Sentiment in News

Table 4 reveals the sentiment distribution in the full corpus, which contains 7,652 news events in total. We observe that, comparable to the results of the inter-rater experiment (see Section 3.3), most events have a negative sentiment or are considered neutral. Only 1 in 10 news events evokes a positive sentiment, and 4% were considered ambiguous.

| | Event sentiment | | | |
|---|---|---|---|---|
| | Pos | Neg | Neu | Conf |
| **# events** | 849 | 3,699 | 2,789 | 315 |
| **Percentage** | 11% | 48% | 36% | 4% |

Table 4: Event sentiment distribution in the full corpus.

A qualitative, manual analysis of the annotations was performed to gain more insights into the differences between neutral and non-neutral news events. This analysis revealed that words that occur more frequently in neutral events compared to positive and negative events are topical words that occur frequently in the news bulletin, like 'government', 'minister', 'European' and 'American'. Neutral events also more often contain time indicators such as 'Monday', 'last week', 'today' and verbs expressing locutionary acts (e.g. 'said', 'asks', 'communicated'), compared to non-neutral events. Negative events more often contain nouns and adjectives like 'murder', 'attack', 'shooting', 'war', 'famine', and verbs including 'judging', 'arrested' and 'wounded' than positive and neutral events. The noun 'increase' also occurs most frequently in negative events, mostly associated with terms like 'tension' or terms related to addiction and disease. Frequently occurring terms in positive events are more difficult to pinpoint at the word level, but it is observed that words like 'solution', 'approved' and 'new' occur more frequently in positive events compared to negative and neutral ones. An analysis of the conflict events revealed that often, these mention highly topical nouns and named entities like 'Brexit' (56 out of 315 events), 'Trump' (24/315), 'Catalonia' (23/315), 'referendum' (16/315), 'Jerusalem' (12/315) and 'nuclear exit' (10/315). These are all examples of concepts that evoke ambivalent feelings depending on the reader and on the broader context, hence the events they occur in were labeled as 'conflict'.

An analysis of the sentiment triggers (underlined in the examples) showed that they are mostly (>99% of the cases) included inside the event span, as shown in example 1. Interestingly, sentiment triggers outside of the event span (example 2) are often part of a subjective statement by the author or a quotation.

(1) [Brother of the presumed Giant of the Brabant Killers provides investigators with new tips]$_{event}$.

(2) [The billion-dollar takeover of 21st Century Fox]$_{event}$ creates a new major power.

### 4.2 Automatically Predicting Implicit Sentiment in News

Having a news article corpus in place, in which annotators differentiated between neutral events and events that evoke a particular sentiment, we were able to investigate the feasibility of implicit sentiment detection. Filtering out the doubles lead to an experimental corpus of 7,425 events, which was split in a training partition of 6,683 events and a test set of 742 events. The label distributions in both sets remained the same as in Table 4.

#### 4.2.1 Lexicon-based Approach to Event Sentiment Detection

We first explored the effectiveness of two lexicon-based approaches to automatically determine implicit sentiment in news events. For the first approach, we relied on four sentiment lexicons for Dutch, including the Pattern lexicon (De Smedt and Daelemans, 2012) composed of 3,223 qualitative adjectives, an in-house sentiment lexicon with size $n$= 434 composed of manual review annotations, the Duoman lexicon (Jijkoun and Hofmann, 2009) composed of 8,757 wordforms and the NRC Hashtag Lexicon (Mohammad and Turney, 2013) including 13,683 entries[5]. All lexicons were manually checked to filter irrelevant entries. The order in which these lexicons were consulted was determined by preliminary experiments (i.e. when a word had no match in the Pattern lexicon, the next step was to consult the in-house lexicon, next Duoman and finally NRC).

For the second approach, we used SenticNet (Cambria and Hussain, 2015), an automatically constructed semantic knowledge resource based on common sense knowledge from the Open Mind Common Sense initiative (Singh et al., 2002) and

[5]The original lexicon of 14,182 unigrams, which had been automatically translated to Dutch, was manually filtered by a Translation student.

GECKA (Cambria et al., 2015), combined with affective knowledge from WordNet-Affect (Strapparava and Valitutti, 2004). SenticNet entries provide sentiment information for concepts of varying $n$-gram length, such as "accomplish goal", "celebrate special occasion", "be on cloud nine", etc. We considered it a potentially valuable resource for our task as it is not restricted to explicit sentiment terms, which are probably hard to find in newswire text. For our experiments, we made use of the SenticNet 5 API (Cambria et al., 2018), which returns sentiment values for the concepts it receives.

Table 5 presents the results of the lexicon-based sentiment analysis approaches. Overall, the scores are low, with a top $F_1$ score of 0.47 obtained with the four combined lexicons that outperformed SenticNet with 16%. Looking at the performance per class, we can conclude that the results are clearly better for the negative and neutral instances. Intuitively, we expected SenticNet to be better suited for the task, given the data genre and SenticNet's inclusion of implicit polar concepts. However, there are several hypotheses as to why it was outperformed by the other lexicons. Firstly, a qualitative analysis revealed that the coverage largely differs, with on average 3 or more matches per event for the regular lexicons, and only 1 for SenticNet. Secondly, all entries in the combined lexicons were manually verified, either by the authors of the lexica or by the authors of this paper, unlike SenticNet's entries, which are automatically collected from a small annotated seed set. Thirdly, as SenticNet contains concepts rather than words, all text needed to be pre-processed using a concept parser (Rajagopal et al., 2013)[6]. As such a parser is currently unavailable for Dutch, we decided to translate all events to English using Google Translate[7]. Automatic translation, however, means that some of the semantics may be lost, which may have affected the results of this approach.

#### 4.2.2 Machine Learning Approach to Event Polarity Detection

Using machine learning, we investigated a feature-based and end-to-end architecture. For the feature-based approach, we applied Support Vector Machines using the LibSVM library (Chang and Lin, 2011). For the latter approach, we applied two state-of-the-art transformer-based architectures for Dutch, i.e. BERTje (Vries et al., 2019) and RobBERT (Delobelle et al., 2020). While both models are based on the BERT architecture originally released for English (Devlin et al., 2019), they were each pre-trained on different corpora. BERTje is pre-trained on a 12 GB Dutch corpus composed of different genres, including books, social media data, Wikipedia and -especially relevant for our task- newswire text. By contrast, RobBERT is based on the Dutch section of the OSCAR corpus (Ortiz Suárez et al., 2019), a 39 GB large subcorpus of the Common Crawl corpus[8], the largest web crawl corpus available. Although the latter is pre-trained on much more data, we expect BERTje to be better suited for the current task.

SVM parameter settings for the classifier and feature extraction were simultaneously optimized using a grid search in a nested cross-validation setup. For the classification algorithm, we varied the kernel type, cost and $gamma$ parameters and tested equal versus balanced class weighting. Regarding feature engineering, we varied the $n$-gram length and type (i.e. words versus characters and uni-/bi-/trigrams) and tested with a maximum feature threshold (i.e. None; 5,000; 10,000; 20,000). In both transformer setups, 3 epochs were defined with preliminary experiments. However, actual training did not even require that many epochs, as from epoch 1 (BERTje) and 2 (RobBERT) onwards, validation loss surpassed training loss, which may suggest overfitting. For all classifiers, the parameter settings and feature combinations that yielded the best results in the cross-validation experiments were used to train the final model that was subsequently applied to the held-out test set[9].

The results (Table 6) reveal that all three classifiers perform in a similar way, especially when considering the weight-averaged $F_1$ scores. Ranging between $F_1 = 0.69$ and 0.72, the scores clearly outperform the combined sentiment lexicons approach and the majority baseline (predicting the negative class only). The SVM classifier seems to handle the underrepresented classes 'positive' and 'conflict' better than RobBERT and BERTje.

We also conducted a qualitative analysis, the results of which are presented in Table 7. Predictions for the first event suggest that the SVM predic-

[6]https://github.com/SenticNet/concept-parser.

[7]Translations done on 22/09/2020.

[8]https://commoncrawl.org/

[9]Best SVM parameters and features: linear kernel with cost $C$=10; balanced class weighting; 45,973 uni- and bigram word $n$-grams without threshold. Best settings for BERT: dropout: 0; sequence length: 128; learning rate (Adam): 5e-05; batch size 64; number of epochs: 3.

| Classifier | Performance held-out test set: Accuracy | Macro-avg $F_1$ | Weight.-avg $F_1$ | Performance per class: $F_1$Pos | $F_1$Neg | $F_1$Neu | $F_1$Conf |
|---|---|---|---|---|---|---|---|
| Pattern+in-house +Duoman+NRC | **0.44** | **0.33** | **0.47** | **0.28** | **0.58** | **0.40** | 0.04 |
| SenticNet | 0.26 | 0.21 | 0.31 | 0.15 | 0.45 | 0.20 | 0.04 |

Table 5: Scores obtained by the lexicon-based approaches on the held-out test set ($n$= 742).

| Classifier | Performance held-out test set: Accuracy | Macro-avg $F_1$ | Weight.-avg $F_1$ | Performance per class: $F_1$Pos | $F_1$Neg | $F_1$Neu | $F_1$Conf |
|---|---|---|---|---|---|---|---|
| SVM | 0.69 | **0.61** | 0.69 | **0.49** | 0.76 | 0.65 | **0.53** |
| RobBERT | 0.72 | 0.60 | **0.72** | 0.48 | 0.80 | 0.70 | 0.43 |
| BERTje | **0.74** | 0.54 | **0.72** | 0.48 | **0.81** | **0.71** | 0.15 |
| Majority baseline | 0.50 | 0.17 | 0.33 | 0.00 | 0.66 | 0.00 | 0.00 |

Table 6: Scores obtained by the machine learning approach on the held-out test set ($n$= 742).

| Gold | Event | SVM | BERTje | RobBERT |
|---|---|---|---|---|
| negative | *In the night of July 14th, the day of national celebration, and after the country's World Cup win, 845 vehicles went up in flames.* | positive | negative | negative |
| conflict | *a speech Trump gave to the NRA gun lobby* | negative | neutral | neutral |
| negative | *in Antwerp they currently remain cautious* | positive | positive | positive |
| negative | *an inferno* | negative | neutral | negative |
| positive | *a deal* | negative | neutral | positive |

Table 7: Qualitative analysis examples: gold label, event text and predictions by SVM, BERTje and RobBERT.

tion might be triggered by the positive words in the event, whereas they do not influence the predictions of the BERT models. The second example shows the difficulty of nested events, i.e. "RNA gun lobby" which is annotated as "conflict", but is nested inside the neutral event "a speech Trump gave (...)". Here as well, the SVM seems rather triggered by purely lexical items. The third example demonstrates the importance of context for accurate sentiment prediction at a more fine-grained level. The event's context is a proposition to make two Belgian ports work more closely together, which is welcomed by one party, but not by the port of Antwerp. The last two events ("een inferno" and "een deal" in Dutch) are examples of correct predictions by RobBERT while the predictions by BERTje are incorrect. An explanation could be that the web crawl data RobBERT is trained on is more likely to contain English terms, unlike the cleaner corpus at the basis of BERTje. Lastly, while some events are extensive in terms of context (example 1), others are more constrained, which complicates their prediction.

## 5 Conclusion and Future Work

With this paper, we investigated the detection of implicit sentiment evoked by Dutch newswire text. While related research approaches the task mainly at the document or sentence level using lexicon-based methods, we focused on fine-grained events below the sentence level and experimented with lexicon-based approaches and machine learning. For the latter, we compared the performance of SVMs, which have proven successful in sentiment analysis tasks, with two transformer-based models. Our results demonstrate that the machine learning approach performs accurately with a top $F_1$ score of 0.72 and shows a considerable improvement over the majority baseline. The experiments also demonstrate that machine learning clearly outperforms the lexicon-based approach, even when extensive (implicit) sentiment lexicons are used. Furthermore, we created and manually annotated a Dutch corpus of news events and were able to show high inter-rater agreement for event sentiment and sentiment span annotations. In future research, it will be interesting to explore whether additional context, including named entities and co-referring events, inside and across sentence boundaries, can improve implicit sentiment detection further.

## Acknowledgments

We thank Siel Debouver and Annaïs Airapetian for their invaluable contribution to the corpus annotation and Bram Vanroy for his code contribution. This research was funded by the Special Research Fund of Ghent University and supported by #News-DNA.

## References


Md Adnan, Mohammed Chowdury, Iftifar Taz, Tauqir Ahmed, and Mohammad Rahman. 2014. Content based news recommendation system based on fuzzy logic. In *International Conference on Informatics, Electronics and Vision (ICIEV 2014)*, pages 1–6.

Wouter Atteveldt, Jan Kleinnijenhuis, Nel Ruigrok, and Stefan Schlobach. 2008. Good news or bad news? conducting sentiment analysis on dutch text to distinguish between positive and negative relations. *Journal of Information Technology & Politics*, 5:73–94.

Stefano Baccianella, Andrea Esuli, and Fabrizio Sebastiani. 2010. Sentiwordnet 3.0: An enhanced lexical resource for sentiment analysis and opinion mining. In *Proceedings of the Seventh International Conference on Language Resources and Evaluation (LREC'10)*, Valletta, Malta. ELRA.

Alexandra Balahur, Raf Steinberger, Mijail Kabadjov, Vanni Zavarella, Erik van der Goot, Matina Halkia, Bruno Pouliquen, and Jenya Belyaeva. 2010. Sentiment analysis in the news. In *Proceedings of the Seventh International Conference on Language Resources and Evaluation (LREC'10)*, Valletta, Malta. ELRA.

Barkha Bansal and Sangeet Srivastava. 2018. On predicting elections with hybrid topic based sentiment analysis of tweets. *Procedia Computer Science*, 135:346 – 353. The 3rd International Conference on Computer Science and Computational Intelligence (ICCSCI 2018) : Empowering Smart Technology in Digital Era for a Better Life.

Bhavika Bhutani, Neha Rastogi, Priyanshu Sehgal, and Archana Purwar. 2019. Fake news detection using sentiment analysis. In *2019 Twelfth International Conference on Contemporary Computing (IC3)*, pages 1–5.

Rebecca F. Bruce and Janyce M. Wiebe. 1999. Recognizing subjectivity: A case study of manual tagging. *Natural Language Engineering*, 5:187–205.

Radim Burget, Jan Karasek, and Zdeněk Smékal. 2011. Recognition of emotions in czech newspaper headlines. *Radioengineering*, 20:39–47.

Bjorn Burscher, R. Vliegenthart, and C. D. Vreese. 2016. Frames beyond words. *Social Science Computer Review*, 34:530–545.

Erik Cambria and Amir Hussain. 2015. *Sentic Computing: A Common-Sense-Based Framework for Concept-Level Sentiment Analysis*, 1st edition. Springer Publishing Company, Incorporated.

Erik Cambria, Soujanya Poria, Devamanyu Hazarika, and Kenneth Kwok. 2018. Senticnet 5: Discovering conceptual primitives for sentiment analysis by means of context embeddings. In *Thirty-Second AAAI Conference on Artificial Intelligence*.

Erik Cambria, Dheeraj Rajagopal, Kenneth Kwok, and Jose Sepulveda. 2015. Gecka: Game engine for commonsense knowledge acquisition. In *Proceedings of the Twenty-Eighth International Florida Artificial Intelligence Research Society Conference*.

Richard Eckart de Castilho, Éva Mújdricza-Maydt, Seid Muhie Yimam, Silvana Hartmann, Iryna Gurevych, Anette Frank, and Chris Biemann. 2016. A web-based tool for the integrated annotation of semantic and syntactic structures. In *Proceedings of the Workshop on Language Technology Resources and Tools for Digital Humanities (LT4DH)*, pages 76–84, Osaka, Japan. The COLING 2016 Organizing Committee.

Chih-Chung Chang and Chih-Jen Lin. 2011. Libsvm: A library for support vector machines. *ACM Transactions on Intelligent Systems and Technology Journal*, 2(3).

Bi Chen, Leilei Zhu, Daniel Kifer, and Dongwon Lee. 2010. What is an opinion about? exploring political standpoints using opinion scoring model. In *Proceedings of the Twenty-Fourth AAAI Conference on Artificial Intelligence*, AAAI'10, page 1007–1012. AAAI Press.

Huan-Yuan Chen and Hsin-Hsi Chen. 2016. Implicit polarity and implicit aspect recognition in opinion mining. pages 20–25.

Shu-I Chiu and Kuo-Wei Hsu. 2018. Predicting political tendency of posts on facebook. In *Proceedings of the 2018 7th International Conference on Software and Computer Applications*, ICSCA 2018, page 110–114, New York, NY, USA. Association for Computing Machinery.

Camiel Colruyt, Orphée De Clercq, and Véronique Hoste. 2020. EventDNA: a dataset for Dutch news event extraction as a basis for news diversification. Manuscript under review.

Tom De Smedt and Walter Daelemans. 2012. "vreselijk mooi!" (terribly beautiful): A subjectivity lexicon for Dutch adjectives. In *Proceedings of the Eighth International Conference on Language Resources and Evaluation (LREC'12)*, pages 3568–3572, Istanbul, Turkey. ELRA.

Pieter Delobelle, Thomas Winters, and Bettina Berendt. 2020. Robbert: a dutch roberta-based language model.

Mark Deuze. 2003. The web and its journalisms: Considering the consequences of different types of newsmedia online. *New Media & Society*, 5(2):203–230.

Jacob Devlin, Ming-Wei Chang, Kenton Lee, and Kristina Toutanova. 2019. Bert: Pre-training of deep bidirectional transformers for language understanding. In *Proceedings of the 2019 Conference of the North American Chapter of the Association for Computational Linguistics: Human Language Technologies, Volume 1 (Long and Short Papers)*, pages 4171–4186, Minneapolis, Minnesota. ACL.

Zhao Fang, Qiang Zhang, Xiaoan Tang, Anning Wang, and Claude Baron. 2020. An implicit opinion analysis model based on feature-based implicit opinion patterns. *Artificial Intelligence Review*, 53:4547–4574.

Joseph L. Fleiss. 1971. Measuring nominal scale agreement among many raters. *Psychological bulletin*, 76(5):378—382.

Namrata Godbole, Manjunath Srinivasaiah, and Steven Skiena. 2007. Large-scale sentiment analysis for news and blogs. In *ICWSM 2007 - International Conference on Weblogs and Social Media.*

Kilem L. Gwet. 2014. *Handbook of Inter-Rater Reliability (Fourth Edition), The Definitive Guide to Measuring the Extent of Agreement Among Raters.* Advanced Analytics, LLC, Gaithersburg, USA.

Nancy M. Henley, Michelle D. Miller, Jo Anne Beazley, Diane N. Nguyen, Dana Kaminsky, and Robert Sanders. 2002. Frequency and specificity of referents to violence in news reports of anti-gay attacks. *Discourse & Society*, 13(1):75–104.

Ye Jiang, Xingyi Song, Jackie Harrison, Shaun Quegan, and Diana Maynard. 2017. Comparing attitudes to climate change in the media using sentiment analysis based on Latent Dirichlet Allocation. In *Proceedings of the 2017 EMNLP Workshop: Natural Language Processing meets Journalism*, pages 25–30, Copenhagen, Denmark. ACL.

Valentin Jijkoun and Katja Hofmann. 2009. Generating a non-english subjectivity lexicon: Relations that matter. In *Proceedings of the 12th Conference of the European Chapter of the Association for Computational Linguistics*, EACL'09, page 398–405, USA. ACL.

Ayman Khedr, S.E. Salama, and Nagwa Yaseen. 2017. Predicting stock market behavior using data mining technique and news sentiment analysis. *International Journal of Intelligent Systems and Applications*, 9:22–30.

Klaus Krippendorff. 2011. Computing krippendorff's alpha-reliability. Online: https://repository.upenn.edu/asc_papers/43/.

Sebastian Kula, Michał Choraś, Rafał Kozik, Paweł Ksieniewicz, and Michał Woźniak. 2020. Sentiment analysis for fake news detection by means of neural networks. In *Computational Science (ICCS 2020)*, pages 653–666, Cham, Switzerland. Springer International Publishing.

Richard J. Landis and Gary G. Koch. 1977. The measurement of observer agreement for categorical data. *Biometrics*, 33(1):159–174.

Grace E. Lee and Aixin Sun. 2019. A study on agreement in pico span annotations. In *Proceedings of the 42nd International ACM SIGIR Conference on Research and Development in Information Retrieval*, SIGIR'19, page 1149–1152, New York, NY, USA. ACM.

Jiwei Li and Eduard Hovy. 2017. Reflections on sentiment/opinion analysis. In Erik Cambria, Das Dipankar, Sivaji Bandyopadhyay, and Antonio Feraco, editors, *A Practical Guide to Sentiment Analysis*, chapter 3, pages 41–61. Springer International Publishing AG, Cham, Switzerland.

K.H.-Y Lin, Changhua Yang, and Hsin-Hsi Chen. 2008. Emotion classification of online news articles from the reader's perspective. In *2008 IEEE/WIC/ACM International Conference on Web Intelligence and Intelligent Agent Technology*, volume 1, pages 220–226.

Bing Liu. 2015. *Sentiment analysis: mining opinions, sentiments, and emotions*, 1st edition. New York: Cambridge University Press.

Jiahui Liu, Peter Dolan, and Elin Rønby Pedersen. 2010. Personalized news recommendation based on click behavior. In *Proceedings of the 15th International Conference on Intelligent User Interfaces*, IUI '10, page 31–40, New York, NY, USA. ACM.

Eugenia Mitchelstein and Pablo Boczkowski. 2009. Between tradition and change: A review of recent research on online news production. *Journalism*, 10(5):562–586.

Saif Mohammad. 2017. Challenges in sentiment analysis. In Erik Cambria, Das Dipankar, Sivaji Bandyopadhyay, and Antonio Feraco, editors, *A Practical Guide to Sentiment Analysis*, chapter 4, pages 61–85. Springer International Publishing AG, Cham, Switzerland.

Saif M. Mohammad and Peter D. Turney. 2013. Crowdsourcing a word-emotion association lexicon. *Computational Intelligence*, 29(3):436–465.

Debora Nozza, Elisabetta Fersini, and Enza Messina. 2017. A multi-view sentiment corpus. In *Proceedings of the 15th Conference of the European Chapter of the Association for Computational Linguistics: Volume 1, Long Papers*, pages 273–280, Valencia, Spain. Association for Computational Linguistics.

Pedro Javier Ortiz Suárez, Benoît Sagot, and Laurent Romary. 2019. Asynchronous pipelines for processing huge corpora on medium to low resource infrastructures. In *Proceedings of the Workshop on Challenges in the Management of Large Corpora (CMLC-7)*, pages 9–16, Mannheim. Leibniz-Institut für Deutsche Sprache.

Eli Parser. 2013. *The Filter Bubble: What The Internet Is Hiding From You.* Penguin Books Limited, London, England.

Thomas E. Patterson. 2000. *Doing Well and Doing Good: How Soft News Are Shrinking the News Audience and Weakening Democracy.* Harvard University Press, Cambridge, MA.

Dheeraj Rajagopal, Erik Cambria, Daniel Olsher, and Kenneth Kwok. 2013. A graph-based approach to commonsense concept extraction and semantic similarity detection. In *WWW 2013 Companion - Proceedings of the 22nd International Conference on World Wide Web*, pages 565–570.

Irene Russo, Tommaso Caselli, and Carlo Strapparava. 2015. SemEval-2015 task 9: CLIPEval implicit polarity of events. In *Proceedings of the 9th International Workshop on Semantic Evaluation (SemEval 2015)*, pages 443–450, Denver, Colorado. Association for Computational Linguistics.

Pamela Shoemaker and Akiba Cohen. 2005. News around the world: Content, practitioners, and the public. *News Around the World: Content, Practitioners, and the Public*, pages 1–409.

Push Singh, Thomas Lin, Erik T. Mueller, Grace Lim, Travell Perkins, and Wan Li Zhu. 2002. Open mind common sense: Knowledge acquisition from the general public. In *On the Move to Meaningful Internet Systems 2002: CoopIS, DOA, and ODBASE*, pages 1223–1237, Berlin, Heidelberg. Springer Berlin Heidelberg.

Carlo Strapparava and Rada Mihalcea. 2007. SemEval-2007 task 14: Affective text. In *Proceedings of the Fourth International Workshop on Semantic Evaluations (SemEval-2007)*, pages 70–74, Prague, Czech Republic. ACL.

Carlo Strapparava and Alessandro Valitutti. 2004. Wordnet affect: an affective extension of wordnet. In *Proceedings of the Fourth International Conference on Language Resources and Evaluation (LREC'04)*, Lisbon, Portugal. ELRA.

Cigdem Toprak, Niklas Jakob, and Iryna Gurevych. 2010. Sentence and expression level annotation of opinions in user-generated discourse. In *Proceedings of the 48th Annual Meeting of the Association for Computational Linguistics*, pages 575–584, Uppsala, Sweden. ACL.

Gaye Tuchman. 1973. Making news by doing work: Routinizing the unexpected. *American journal of Sociology*, 79(1):110–131.

Cynthia Van Hee, Orphée De Clercq, and Véronique Hoste. 2021. Guidelines for annotating implicit sentiment evoked by fine-grained news events (version 1.0). Technical report, LT3, Faculty of Arts, Humanities and Law, Ghent University (Ghent, Belgium).

Cynthia Van Hee, Els Lefever, and Veronique Hoste. 2018. We usually don't like going to the dentist : using common sense to detect irony on twitter. *Computational Linguistics*, 44(4):793–832.

Karel Vandendriessche and Lieven De Marez. 2019. imec.digimeter 2019: Measuring digital media trends in flanders. Online: https://www.imec.be/nl/expertises/imec-digimeter/digimeter-2019.

Wietse de Vries, Andreas van Cranenburgh, Arianna Bisazza, Tommaso Caselli, Gertjan van Noord, and Malvina Nissim. 2019. BERTje: A Dutch BERT Model. *arXiv:1912.09582 [cs]*.

Theresa Wilson. 2008. Annotating subjective content in meetings. In *Proceedings of the Sixth International Conference on Language Resources and Evaluation (LREC'08)*, pages 2738–2745, Marrakech, Morocco. ELRA.

# Exploring Stylometric and Emotion-Based Features for Multilingual Cross-Domain Hate Speech Detection


**Ilia Markov**
CLIPS Research Center
University of Antwerp, Belgium
ilia.markov@uantwerpen.be

**Nikola Ljubešić**
Dept. of Language Technologies
Jožef Stefan Institute, Slovenia
nikola.ljubesic@ijs.si

**Darja Fišer**
Faculty of Arts
University of Ljubljana, Slovenia
darja.fiser@ff.uni-lj.si

**Walter Daelemans**
CLIPS Research Center
University of Antwerp, Belgium
walter.daelemans@uantwerpen.be



## Abstract

In this paper, we describe experiments designed to evaluate the impact of stylometric and emotion-based features on hate speech detection: the task of classifying textual content into hate or non-hate speech classes. Our experiments are conducted for three languages – English, Slovene, and Dutch – both in in-domain and cross-domain setups, and aim to investigate hate speech using features that model two linguistic phenomena: the writing style of hateful social media content operationalized as function word usage on the one hand, and emotion expression in hateful messages on the other hand. The results of experiments with features that model different combinations of these phenomena support our hypothesis that stylometric and emotion-based features are robust indicators of hate speech. Their contribution remains persistent with respect to domain and language variation. We show that the combination of features that model the targeted phenomena outperforms words and character n-gram features under cross-domain conditions, and provides a significant boost to deep learning models, which currently obtain the best results, when combined with them in an ensemble.


## 1 Introduction

Hate speech is commonly defined as communication that disparages a person or a group on the basis of some characteristic such as race, color, ethnicity, gender, sexual orientation, nationality, religion, or other characteristics (Nockleby, 2000). The exact definition of hate speech, however, remains a disputed topic, as it is a subjective and multi-interpretable concept (Waseem et al., 2017; Poletto et al., 2020).

The lack of a consensus on its definition poses a challenge to hate speech annotation. Annotating hateful content remains prone to personal bias and is culture-dependent, which often results in low inter-annotator agreement and therefore scarcity of high quality training data for developing supervised hate speech detection systems (Ross et al., 2016; Waseem, 2016; Sap et al., 2019).

Hate speech online presents additional challenges for natural language processing (NLP): offensive vocabulary and keywords evolve fast due to their relatedness with the hate speech triggering events (Florio et al., 2020), moreover, users may adapt their lexical choices as a countermeasure against identification or introduce minor misspellings to bypass filtering systems (Berger and Perez, 2006; Vidgen et al., 2019). Therefore, we intend to investigate more abstract features, less susceptible to specific vocabulary, topic or corpus bias, which we examine in in-domain and cross-domain settings: training and testing on social media datasets belonging to same/different domains, for three languages: English, Slovene, and Dutch.

Our hypothesis is that the style and emotional dimension of hateful textual content may provide useful cues for its detection. We investigate this through a binary hate speech classification task using features that model such information, i.e., function words and emotion-based features. The latter are operationalized in terms of the types of emotions expressed and the frequency of emotion-conveying words in the data.

Function word usage is one of the most important and revealing aspects of style in written language, as shown by numerous studies in stylometric analysis for authorship attribution (Grieve, 2007; Kestemont, 2014; Markov et al., 2018). While stylometric characteristics have been implicitly included in some hate speech detection studies (e.g., in bag-of-words or character-level models),



*Proceedings of the 11th Workshop on Computational Approaches to Subjectivity, Sentiment and Social Media Analysis*, pages 149–159
April 19, 2021. ©2021 Association for Computational Linguistics

their impact on the task has not been studied. We propose the hypothesis that stylometric characteristics of hateful writing are distinctive enough to contribute to the hate speech detection task. In other words, hate speech acts as a specific text type with an associated writing style.

On the other hand, we are motivated by psychological and sociological studies, which correlate toxic behaviour online with the emotional profile of the user (Kokkinos and Kipritsi, 2012). However, unlike previous research that used sentiment information for detecting unacceptable content (Davidson et al., 2017; Dani et al., 2017; Van Hee et al., 2018; Brassard-Gourdeau and Khoury, 2019), we test whether we are able to capture some of these phenomena by going beyond the sentiment level (positive / negative / neutral) to a more fine-grained emotion level.

We compare the performance of stylometric and emotion-based features with commonly used features for hate speech detection: words, character n-grams, and their combination, and with more recent deep learning models that currently provide the state-of-the-art results for the hate speech detection task (Mandl et al., 2019; Basile et al., 2019): convolutional neural networks (CNN), long short-term memory networks (LSTM), and bidirectional encoder representations from transformers (BERT). The results of these experiments indicate that the combination of stylometric and emotion-based features performs better than words and character n-grams under cross-domain conditions, and allows to further improve the results of deep learning models when combined with them in an ensemble.

In summary, the contributions of the research presented here are the following: (i) evaluating the contribution of stylometric and emotion-based features to hate speech detection, (ii) examining how robust and persistent their contribution is with respect to domain and language variation, (iii) comparing their performance with commonly used features for the hate speech detection task: words and character n-grams, and with the state-of-the-art deep learning models.

## 2 Methodology

### 2.1 Datasets

To investigate the role of stylometric and emotion information in the hate speech detection task, we conducted experiments on several recent social media datasets in hate speech detection research.

#### 2.1.1 In-domain datasets

**FRENK** (Ljubešić et al., 2019) The FRENK dataset consists of Facebook comments in English and Slovene covering LGBT and migrant topics. The dataset was manually annotated for fine-grained types of socially unacceptable discourse (e.g., violence, offensiveness, threat). We used the coarse-grained (binary) hate speech classes: hate speech or non-hate speech messages, selecting the messages for which more than four out of eight annotators agreed upon the class. The detailed description of the dataset collection and annotation procedures can be found in (Ljubešić et al., 2019).

**LiLaH** The LiLaH dataset consists of Facebook comments on LGBT and migrant topics in Dutch. The dataset was collected using the same procedure and annotated following the same annotation guidelines as the FRENK dataset by two trained annotators and one expert annotator. For the binary classes used in this paper, the Percent Agreement for two annotators equals 78.7% and Cohen's Kappa 0.56, which corresponds to an inter-annotator agreement halfway between "fair" and "good" (Fleiss, 1981).

The statistics of the datasets used are shown in Table 1. We used training and test partitions splitting the datasets by post boundaries in order to avoid comments from the same discussion thread to appear in both training and test sets, that is, to avoid within-post bias. The partitions were performed in such a way that the distribution of hate ('1') and non-hate speech ('0') classes is as balanced as possible, while the proportion of 80% training and 20% test messages for the addressed languages is preserved.

The balanced subsets of the datasets, in terms of the number of messages for each of the languages, were used for 10-fold cross-validation experiments in order to provide a fair comparison across the targeted languages (the maximum number of available hate and non-hate speech examples across the three languages was selected; marked with '*' in Table 1), while the merged training and test partitions were used as training sets for the cross-domain experiments in order to provide more examples for training the supervised models described further in the paper.

#### 2.1.2 Cross-domain datasets

For cross-domain experiments, we merged the training and test splits of the FRENK and LiLaH

| Dataset | Label | Training | | Test | | Training & test | | Balanced | |
|---|---|---|---|---|---|---|---|---|---|
| | | # mes | % | # mes | % | # mes | % | # mes | % |
| | '1' | 2,848 | 35.9 | 744 | 35.5 | 3,592* | 35.8 | 3,500 | 46.7 |
| **English (FRENK)** | '0' | 5,091 | 64.1 | 1,351 | 64.5 | 6,442 | 64.2 | 4,000 | 53.3 |
| | Total | **7,939** | (79.1) | **2,095** | (20.9) | **10,034** | (100) | **7,500** | |
| | '1' | 3,506 | 52.0 | 882 | 51.8 | 4,388 | 51.9 | 3,500 | 46.7 |
| **Slovene (FRENK)** | '0' | 3,238 | 48.0 | 821 | 48.2 | 4,059* | 48.1 | 4,000 | 53.3 |
| | Total | **6,744** | (79.8) | **1,703** | (20.2) | **8,447** | (100) | **7,500** | |
| | '1' | 3,753 | 43.8 | 949 | 44.0 | 4,702 | 43.8 | 3,500 | 46.7 |
| **Dutch (LiLaH)** | '0' | 4,821 | 56.2 | 1,209 | 56.0 | 6,030 | 56.2 | 4,000 | 53.3 |
| | Total | **8,574** | (79.9) | **2,158** | (20.1) | **10,732** | (100) | **7,500** | |

Table 1: Statistics of the datasets used for in-domain experiments.

datasets (see Table 1) and used it as training data, while the following social media datasets belonging to other domains were used as test sets.

**HASOC** (Mandl et al., 2019) We used the training subset in English of the HASOC-2019 (Hate Speech and Offensive Content Identification in Indo-European Languages) shared task dataset. It contains Twitter and Facebook messages covering various topics (e.g., Brexit, cricket).

**Ask.fm** (Van Hee et al., 2015). We used the Dutch cyberbullying dataset, which contains 85,485 posts from the social networking website Ask.fm annotated with fine-grained cyberbullying categories (e.g., general insult, sexual harassment, sexism, racism). We selected the same number of positive and negative messages as for English in order to provide a fair comparison between the two languages.

The statistics of the datasets used as test sets for the cross-domain experiments is shown in Table 2.[1]

| Dataset | Label | # mes | % |
|---|---|---|---|
| | '1' | 2,261 | 38.6 |
| **English (HASOC)** | '0' | 3,591 | 61.4 |
| | Total | **5,852** | |
| | '1' | 2,261 | 38.6 |
| **Dutch (Ask.fm)** | '0' | 3,591 | 61.4 |
| | Total | **5,852** | |

Table 2: Statistics of the datasets used for the cross-domain experiments as test sets.

## 2.2 Experiment setup

We performed tokenization, lemmatization, and POS tagging using the StanfordNLP library (Qi et al., 2018) for all the languages addressed in this work, removing metadata and URL mentions in preprocessing. We used the sets of features described below, a term frequency (tf) weighting scheme and the liblinear scikit-learn (Pedregosa et al., 2011) implementation of Support Vector Machines (SVM) with optimized parameters for classification (we selected the optimal liblinear classifier parameters: penalty parameter (C), loss function (loss), and tolerance for stopping criteria (tol) based on grid search). The effectiveness of SVM has been shown by numerous experiments on hate speech detection (Fortuna and Nunes, 2018; Basile et al., 2019).

We used a CNN model (Kim, 2014) to learn discriminative word-level features with the following architecture: first, an embedding layer transforms sparse vectors into dense vector representations. To process the word embeddings, we used a convolutional layer (kernel size: 3) followed by a global max pooling layer. Then, a dense layer with a ReLU activation is applied, followed by a dropout of 0.6, and finally, a dense layer with a sigmoid activation to make the prediction for the binary classification. We used an LSTM model (Hochreiter and Schmidhuber, 1997), which takes a sequence of words as input and aims at capturing long-term dependencies. We processed the sequence of word embeddings with a unidirectional LSTM layer with 300 units, followed by a dropout of 0.4, and a dense layer with a sigmoid activation for predictions. The multilingual BERT model (BERT-base, multilingual cased (Devlin et al., 2019)) was used for all the languages addressed in this work. The implementation was done in PyTorch (Paszke et al., 2019) using the simple transformers library.[2] Deep learning models currently achieve the state-of-the-art results for the hate speech detection task, which are in 80%–90% F1-score range in in-domain set-

[1]For Slovene, we did not find an annotated dataset belonging to a different hate speech domain.

[2]https://simpletransformers.ai/

tings, depending on the languages being considered, amount of data, etc. (Mandl et al., 2019; Basile et al., 2019; Zampieri et al., 2020).

We report the results in terms of precision, recall, and F1-score (macro-averaged). Note that we used similar settings, tools, and models, i.e., size of the training and test data, StanfordNLP for tokenization, lemmatization, and POS tagging, multilingual BERT models, in order to provide a fair comparison across the different languages covered in the paper.

### 2.3 Features

The experiments we report were designed to investigate and quantify the impact of stylometric information, modeled through function word usage, and emotion-based features on hate speech detection. While representations of documents through word/character n-grams provide good results for detecting abusive language (Nobata et al., 2016; Van Hee et al., 2018), these features cover – and at the same time obscure – a wide range of phenomena, and therefore, it is not clear what the impact is of subsets of these features representing specific linguistic information. Moreover, these features include content words and are susceptible to topic, genre, and domain bias, which often results in overfitting the data. Because of this we abstract away from domain-dependent content word patterns and use more abstract POS n-gram features, to which we add stylometric features (function words) and emotion-based features, to evaluate their impact on the hate speech detection task.

**Part-of-speech (POS)** POS features capture the morpho-syntactic patterns in a text, and are indicative of hate speech, especially when used in combination with other types of features (Warner and Hirschberg, 2012; Robinson et al., 2018). POS tags were obtained with the Stanford POS Tagger (Toutanova et al., 2003). We used the same 17 universal POS tags for the three languages and built n-grams from this representation with n = 1–3.

**Stylometric features** Function words (FW) are considered one of the most important stylometric feature types (Kestemont, 2014). They clarify the relationships between the content-carrying elements of a sentence, and introduce syntactic structures like verbal complements, relative clauses, and questions (Smith and Witten, 1993). With respect to emotion features, FW can appear as quantifiers, intensifiers (e.g., very good) or modify the emotion expressed in other ways. We used linguistically-defined FW, that is, words belonging to the closed syntactic classes.[3] FW are incorporated into the POS representation, as shown in Table 3.

**Emotion-based features** To encode emotion information in our data, we used the 14,182 emotion words and their associations with eight emotions (anger, fear, anticipation, trust, surprise, sadness, joy, and disgust) and two sentiments (negative and positive) from the NRC emotion lexicon (Mohammad and Turney, 2013). We used the LiLaH emotion lexicon for Slovene and Dutch (Ljubešić et al., 2020; Daelemans et al., 2020), which contains manual translations of the NRC emotion lexicon entries. The emotion information was modeled through (i) incorporating emotion-conveying words into the POS & FW representation, as shown in Table 3, (ii) counting the number of such words in a message (count), and (iii) using the emotion associations of the emotion words in a message. These features were used to encode the types of emotions in a message and to capture how high-emotional or low-emotional a message is.

Consider the following English comment from our data belonging to the hate speech class: *Mental illness on parade*. Table 3 shows an example of the representation of this message through the features described above. From the POS & FW & emotion word representations, n-grams (n = 1–3) are built.[4] The count of emotionally-charged words and the emotion associations were added as additional feature vectors.

| phrase | *Mental illness on parade* |
|---|---|
| POS | ADJ NOUN ADP NOUN |
| POS & FW | ADJ NOUN on NOUN |
| POS & FW & emo. words | ADJ illness on parade |
| POS & FW & emo. words & count | ADJ illness on parade & 2 |
| POS & FW & emo. features | ADJ illness on parade & 2 & fear sadness surprise ... |

Table 3: Example of features used.

## 3 Results and Discussion

The main goal of this paper is to identify and analyze specific linguistic phenomena with respect to their role in hate speech detection. In particular,

[3] https://universaldependencies.org/u/pos/

[4] Representing the messages in the following way provided higher 10-fold cross-validation results than combining separate feature vectors (0.8%–1.2% depending on the language).

we focused on function word usage (as an expression of style of the hateful content) and emotion (as personality and psychological state indicators with respect to the usage of emotion terms in written messages).

First, we perform a separate analysis of the contribution of the phenomena we target, and then compare the performance of combining features that encode these phenomena with the commonly used features for the hate speech detection task: words, character n-grams, and their combination (tf weighting scheme and the liblinear SVM classifier with optimized parameters), and with more recent deep learning models that achieve state-of-the-art results for hate speech detection (Mandl et al., 2019; Basile et al., 2019): CNN, LSTM, and BERT (see Section 2.2).

Sections 3.1 and 3.2 show the results of these experiments in in-domain and cross-domain settings, respectively.

### 3.1 In-domain experiments

**10-fold cross-validation** First, we analyze the features that capture the phenomena we target in isolation and in combination on the balanced subsets of the datasets (see Table 1) for 10-fold cross-validation results. The results of these experiments, presented in Table 4, are compared with words (BoW), character 1–3-grams (char), and their combination. We also present the results when all the feature sets are combined. As a reference point we provide the random baseline (stratified strategy).

The results of the experiments presented in Table 4 indicate that stylometric features indeed contribute to the hate speech detection task, as evidenced by their positive impact to the POS representation for all the considered languages (POS & FW representation). Likewise, emotion-conveying words (POS & FW & emotion words), the count of such words in a message (POS & FW & emo words & count) and ten features that correspond to the type of emotions being conveyed (POS & FW & emo words & emo feats) further contribute to the results. While their performance in isolation is moderate, higher results are achieved when features representing each of these phenomena are combined, indicating that they are complementary for the hate speech detection task (this representation is marked in bold and in the remainder of this paper referred to as 'our' approach). Feature importance analysis revealed that negative emotion words, such as 'disgusting', 'sick', 'invasion', are the most indicative features in our model.

We also note that words (BoW) and character n-gram features perform well in in-domain conditions and achieve higher results than our approach. While words are the best unique features for English, the combination of words and character n-grams shows the highest results for Slovene and Dutch. This may be related to the fact that Slovene and Dutch are morphologically richer languages than English, as character n-grams are able to capture morphological affixes.

When stylometric and emotion features are combined with words and character n-grams, the best results are obtained for English and Slovene. For the Dutch language, the combination of words and character n-grams performs very well in in-domain settings, as confirmed by the additional experiments we present further in the paper. It is also interesting to note that for the English language adding the combination of BoW and character n-grams to our approach provides a higher boost than adding BoW features only, the best unique feature type for this language.

**Train-test partitions** Next, we present the results when splitting the training and test sets by post boundaries in order to avoid within-post bias, as described in Section 2.1. In this scenario, we additionally compare the performance of stylometric, emotion, and BoW and character n-gram features with more recent deep learning models: CNN, LSTM, and BERT. The results for these experiments are shown in Table 5.

The results presented in Table 5 indicate that splitting the data by post boundaries is a more challenging scenario, as evidenced by the drop in performance for the BoW approach for all the languages. Nonetheless, the trends observed in the 10-fold cross-validation experiments remain consistent: stylometric and emotion-based features provide substantial improvements when added to the POS representation, while the gap in performance when compared to BoW and character n-grams is smaller for all the languages but Dutch. For the Dutch language, character n-grams provide higher results than in the 10-fold cross-validation experiments, and higher boost when combined with BoW. The combination of character n-grams and BoW for this language shows even higher results than BERT: the best deep learning model across the three languages. For all the targeted languages, adding BoW

| Features | English | | | | Slovene | | | | Dutch | | | |
|---|---|---|---|---|---|---|---|---|---|---|---|---|
| | Prec. | Rec. | F1-score | # feats | Prec. | Rec. | F1-score | # feats | Prec. | Rec. | F1-score | # feats |
| Random baseline | 52.0 | 52.0 | 52.0 | – | 52.0 | 52.0 | 52.0 | – | 52.0 | 52.0 | 52.0 | – |
| BoW | 80.2 | 79.2 | **79.3** (± 1.0) | 15,091 | 72.5 | 71.3 | 71.3 (± 1.6) | 29,898 | 74.4 | 73.2 | 73.3 (± 1.6) | 18,043 |
| Character 1–3-grams (char) | 78.3 | 77.5 | 77.6 (± 0.7) | 19,030 | 74.1 | 73.5 | 73.5 (± 1.7) | 18,648 | 74.1 | 73.2 | 73.3 (± 1.1) | 17,165 |
| BoW & char | 79.1 | 78.3 | 78.5 (± 0.6) | 34,121 | 74.6 | 74.0 | **74.1** (± 1.6) | 48,546 | 74.8 | 74.0 | **74.1** (± 1.2) | 35,208 |
| Function words (FW) | 65.0 | 62.2 | 61.2 (± 1.6) | 745 | 63.1 | 61.4 | 60.6 (± 2.2) | 1,207 | 65.4 | 62.7 | 61.8 (± 1.7) | 988 |
| Emotion words | 74.0 | 72.1 | 72.1 (± 1.6) | 2,376 | 66.8 | 65.1 | 64.7 (± 1.9) | 2,451 | 69.2 | 67.3 | 67.1 (± 1.8) | 2038 |
| POS 1–3-grams (POS) | 64.6 | 63.5 | 63.2 (± 1.7) | 3,423 | 61.6 | 60.5 | 60.0 (± 1.9) | 3,417 | 65.5 | 64.3 | 64.0 (± 1.2) | 3,055 |
| POS & FW (1–3-grams) | 69.1 | 67.6 | 67.4 (± 1.7) | 36,463 | 65.0 | 63.8 | 63.5 (± 1.8) | 47,027 | 68.1 | 66.9 | 66.7 (± 1.4) | 45,561 |
| POS & FW & emotion words | 74.9 | 73.9 | 74.0 (± 1.4) | 105,400 | 67.7 | 66.9 | 66.9 (± 1.3) | 117,265 | 70.4 | 69.8 | 69.8 (± 1.2) | 109,169 |
| POS & FW & emo words & count | 75.2 | 74.4 | 74.5 (± 1.4) | 105,401 | 68.4 | 67.7 | 67.7 (± 1.0) | 117,266 | 70.3 | 69.8 | 69.9 (± 1.4) | 109,170 |
| **POS & FW & emo features (emo)** | 75.3 | 74.5 | 74.6 (± 1.4) | 105,411 | 68.9 | 68.2 | 68.3 (± 1.4) | 117,276 | 71.1 | 70.6 | 70.6 (± 1.2) | 109,180 |
| POS & FW & emo & BoW | 79.2 | 78.7 | 78.8 (± 1.0) | 120,502 | 72.7 | 72.1 | 72.2 (± 1.7) | 147,174 | 73.4 | 72.9 | 73.0 (± 2.2) | 127,223 |
| POS & FW & emo & char | 79.6 | 78.9 | 79.0 (± 1.0) | 124,441 | 75.3 | 74.8 | 74.8 (± 1.1) | 135,924 | 73.2 | 73.0 | 73.0 (± 1.5) | 126,345 |
| POS & FW & emo & BoW & char | 80.1 | 79.4 | **79.6** (± 0.9) | 139,532 | 75.7 | 75.1 | **75.2** (± 1.4) | 165,822 | 73.8 | 73.5 | **73.6** (± 1.7) | 144,388 |

Table 4: Performance of the features explored in isolation and in combination on the balanced subsets of the datasets under 10-fold cross-validation. The results for bag-of-words (BoW), character 1–3-grams (char), and their combination with each other and with the stylometric and emotion-based features (emo) as well as the number of features for each experiment (# feats) are also provided.

| Model | English | | | Slovene | | | Dutch | | |
|---|---|---|---|---|---|---|---|---|---|
| | Precision | Recall | F1-score | Precision | Recall | F1-score | Precision | Recall | F1-score |
| Random baseline | 50.7 | 50.7 | 50.7 | 50.9 | 50.9 | 50.9 | 48.3 | 48.3 | 48.3 |
| (1) BoW | 71.0 | 70.8 | 70.9 | 68.5 | 68.5 | 68.5 | 72.0 | 70.9 | 71.1 |
| (2) Char 1–3-grams | 69.0 | 69.2 | 69.1 | 72.1 | 72.1 | 72.1 | 74.5 | 73.4 | 73.7 |
| (3) BoW & char | 70.6 | 70.6 | 70.6 | 72.4 | 72.4 | 72.4 | 75.0 | 74.4 | **74.6** |
| (4) CNN | 73.4 | 73.6 | 73.5 | 67.7 | 67.7 | 67.7 | 72.6 | 72.9 | 72.5 |
| (5) LSTM | 71.0 | 69.9 | 70.4 | 68.5 | 67.3 | 67.1 | 70.5 | 70.5 | 70.5 |
| (6) BERT | 74.9 | 74.6 | **74.8** | 73.0 | 72.9 | **72.9** | 74.3 | 74.1 | 74.2 |
| (7) POS | 57.3 | 57.0 | 57.1 | 63.2 | 63.1 | 62.8 | 63.9 | 62.9 | 62.9 |
| (8) POS & FW | 64.3 | 63.6 | 63.8 | 63.5 | 63.4 | 63.1 | 70.2 | 67.7 | 67.8 |
| (9) **POS & FW & emo** | 70.9 | 69.9 | 70.3 | 68.0 | 68.0 | 67.8 | 73.1 | 70.6 | 70.8 |
| (10) POS & FW & emo & BoW & char | 74.4 | 73.7 | **74.0** | 74.3 | 74.3 | **74.3** | 75.1 | 74.5 | **74.7** |

Table 5: In-domain results (training-test splits by post boundaries).

and character n-grams to our approach further improves the results, outperforming BoW, character n-grams, and their combination, and achieving competitive results with the deep learning models.

Having confirmed that due to stylometric choices and emotion expression we can distinguish the hateful messages in in-domain settings, we proceed with a cross-domain analysis of the targeted phenomena.

### 3.2 Cross-domain experiments

In this section, we evaluate the robustness of stylometric and emotion-based features under cross-domain conditions: training and testing on out-of-domain social media datasets described in Section 2.1. Cross-domain scalability is essential to identify features of online hate speech that generalize well across domains. Table 6 presents the results for the cross-domain experiments.

The results in Table 6 show that using out-of-domain data for testing leads to a drop in performance for all the models. The drop for the English language is much higher than for Dutch, despite that for English we used a dataset annotated for the same task (hate speech detection) and for a different task, cyberbullying detection, for Dutch.[5] The descriptive analysis showed that the Jaccard similarity coefficient (Jaccard, 1901) for the cross-domain training and test sets is 20.6% for English and 12.4% for Dutch, which implies that a large part of the training and test vocabularies do not overlap.

[5]We also tested the robustness of cross-domain settings by experimenting with other subsets for Dutch, e.g., balanced class distribution, more examples, as well as with other English datasets, achieving similar results with the same trends.

| Model | English | | | | Dutch | | | |
|---|---|---|---|---|---|---|---|---|
| | Precision | Recall | F1-score | F1 drop | Precision | Recall | F1-score | F1 drop |
| Random baseline | 49.2 | 49.3 | 49.2 | – | 50.7 | 50.7 | 50.6 | – |
| (1) BoW | 60.5 | 57.4 | 56.6 | 14.3 | 71.6 | 65.9 | 66.3 | 4.8 |
| (2) Char 1–3-grams | 55.8 | 56.1 | 55.1 | 14.0 | 72.3 | 66.0 | 66.3 | 7.4 |
| (3) BoW & char | 56.5 | 56.8 | 55.6 | 14.9 | 73.7 | 67.4 | 67.8 | 6.8 |
| (4) CNN | 58.7 | 58.2 | 58.3 | 15.2 | 72.3 | 70.0 | **70.6** | 1.9 |
| (5) LSTM | 57.5 | 57.5 | 57.5 | 12.9 | 71.7 | 66.6 | 67.1 | 3.4 |
| (6) BERT | 59.3 | 59.8 | **59.1** | 15.7 | 74.0 | 69.5 | 70.2 | 4.0 |
| (7) POS | 52.9 | 52.5 | 52.0 | 5.1 | 65.9 | 60.6 | 60.0 | 2.9 |
| (8) POS & FW | 55.2 | 54.5 | 54.2 | 9.6 | 69.7 | 63.6 | 63.5 | 4.3 |
| **(9) POS & FW & emo** | 59.1 | 57.8 | 57.7 | 12.6 | 73.1 | 68.8 | **69.5** | 1.3 |
| (10) POS & FW & emo & BoW & char | 58.1 | 58.5 | **57.9** | 16.1 | 73.8 | 68.6 | 69.3 | 5.4 |
| Ensemble (4 & 6 & 9) | 60.7 | 60.1 | **60.2*** | 16.5 | 77.1 | 71.6 | **72.5*** | 2.9 |

Table 6: Cross-domain results (testing on out-of-domain datasets). The F1 drop column reports the drop in F1 points for each model when compared to the in-domain experiments. Statistically significant gains of the ensemble model over the best deep learning models (BERT or CNN) according to McNemar's statistical significance test (McNemar, 1947) with $\alpha < 0.05$ are marked with '*'.

Therefore, the asymmetric drop in performance across the two languages cannot be explained by lexical overlap. The lower drop for Dutch may be related to the relative non-complexity of the cyberbullying content. An analogous effect was observed in (Emmery et al., 2020), where a similar behaviour is reported when training on toxic messages and using Ask.fm as out-of-domain test set, and which is also evidenced by the high precision scores obtained for the models used in this paper when testing on the Dutch cyberbullying data.

We note that, similarly to the in-domain experiments, stylometric and emotion-based features provide substantial improvements when combined with the POS representation. Being more abstract features, they cope well with domain variation and show a lower drop in cross-domain conditions when compared to the baseline models. This indicates that the features that capture the targeted phenomena are robust and portable across social media domains.

Words and character n-gram features, on the contrary, show a high drop in cross-domain settings and provide marginal improvement for English and no improvement for Dutch when combined with our approach. For the Dutch language, stylometric and emotion-based features partly compensate for the loss in performance brought by words and character n-grams under cross-corpus conditions. We can also observe that our approach outperforms commonly used features for the hate speech detection task: words, character n-grams, and their combination both for English and Dutch.

The deep learning models provide high results in cross-domain settings. Combining our approach with the best performing deep learning models: CNN and BERT, using a hard majority-voting ensemble, significantly improves the results when compared to the performance of CNN and BERT in isolation (according to McNemar's statistical significance test (McNemar, 1947) with $\alpha < 0.05$) and achieves the highest cross-domain results for the both languages. We conclude that this significant improvement is brought by the ability of our approach to capture the style of hateful content and the emotional peculiarities present in hateful messages, which are hard to encode by deep learning models on relatively small datasets. A detailed analysis presented below provides deeper insights into the nature of these improvements.

### 3.3 Error analysis

In this section, we report on a manual error analysis performed on the difference in the output of the BERT model (the best-performing deep learning model in our experiments) and the stylometry-emotion-based approach (POS & FW & emo, 'our' model) by inspecting hate speech instances that were correctly identified by one model but not by the other. We perform the analysis on the Slovene in-domain dataset and the English cross-domain dataset. We inspect 50 random misclassified hate speech instances per dataset (in-domain vs. cross-domain) and the model correctly identifying hate

| Type | Element | In-domain Style-emo (%) | In-domain BERT (%) | Cross-domain Style-emo (%) | Cross-domain BERT (%) |
|---|---|---|---|---|---|
| explicit | violence | 4 | 22 | 0 | 4 |
| | insult | 26 | 40 | 40 | 34 |
| | swearword | 2 | 2 | 4 | 50 |
| implicit | violence | 4 | 4 | 4 | 0 |
| | argument | 10 | 6 | 0 | 0 |
| | accusation | 0 | 0 | 24 | 2 |
| | othering | 20 | 10 | 0 | 0 |
| other | quotation | 2 | 2 | 0 | 0 |
| | multilingual | 0 | 0 | 4 | 0 |
| | unclear | 32 | 16 | 24 | 10 |

Table 7: Distribution of correctly classified hate speech instances by one model and not by the other, with respect to the type and element of hate speech, in in-domain and cross-domain settings.

speech (BERT vs. our). Our error analysis is based on annotating each instance with the type of hate speech (explicit vs. implicit), the element of hate speech (call to violence, insult, swearword, argument, accusation, and othering) and, where relevant, the reason why it was undetected (informal expression, unconventional spelling, foreign language, creative language, metaphorical language, unconventional tokenization). In Table 7, we present the quantitative results of this manual analysis, reporting for each model and dataset the distribution of correctly classified hate speech instances, the other model failing on these instances, given the type and element of hate speech.

On the first level of the type of hate speech, where we discriminate between explicit and implicit hate speech, both in the in-domain and the cross-domain settings, we observed that BERT is better at identifying explicit cases of hate speech (overall 72% of instances correctly identified by BERT but not by the stylometry-emotion-based approach vs. 32% of instances correctly identified by the stylometry-emotion-based approach but not by BERT on the in-domain dataset, on the cross-domain dataset this relation being 84% vs. 44%), while the stylometry-emotion-based approach deals better with implicit instances of hate speech (34% vs. 20% in-domain; 28% vs. 2% cross-domain).

The results for the hate speech elements reflect the difference between the in-domain and the cross-domain datasets. For the explicit cases of hate speech, in both datasets insults tend to be the dominant elements caught by one model but not by the other, while the in-domain dataset contains much more calls to violence, and swearing prevails in the cross-domain dataset. For the explicit cases of hate speech, arguments and othering strategies were most frequently misclassified in the in-domain dataset, while accusations were the most frequent issues in the cross-domain dataset. These differences can be followed back to the differences in the medium mostly containing Facebook discussions in the in-domain case, which are more discursive and implicit and Twitter messages in the cross-domain case, which are much shorter and direct.

We also performed a closer inspection of insults and swearwords, which are lexical categories and should in principle be simple to identify via means of supervised machine learning, but were missed because they were highly informal, non-canonically spelled or tokenized, taken from foreign languages, incomplete or idiosyncratic. Another type of undetected insults were words from the general vocabulary from topics such as animals, hygiene, intelligence, etc. that were used metaphorically or with a distinctly negative connotation.

For the category of misclassifications by one model but not by the other, where the reason for not detecting the element of hate speech was unclear, we observed a trend that our approach is prevailing in that category both for the in-domain and the cross-domain settings. Furthermore, we observed that these instances were rather long, which brought us to question whether there is a consistent difference in the length of instance given which model correctly classified the hate speech instance. The analysis of the median length in characters for hate speech instances correctly classified by one model but not by the other for all the languages both in the in-domain and cross-domain settings revealed that there is a drastic tendency for the longer instances to be correctly identified by our approach, while BERT performs better on shorter instances. The only deviation from this trend is the cross-domain Dutch dataset where the instances are overall very short.

We conclude that the stylometry-emotion-based approach performs better on less explicit and longer instances of hate speech, while it lags behind BERT on capturing the more explicit cases.

## 4 Conclusions

The goal of this work was to evaluate and quantify the role of stylometric and emotion-based features in the hate speech detection task. We showed that stylometric and emotional dimensions of hateful content provide useful cues for its detection, as evidenced by the positive impact of stylometric and emotion-based features in various in-domain experiments for all the considered languages. Their contribution remains persistent with respect to domain variations. Under cross-domain conditions, our approach that combines features that capture the targeted phenomena performs better than commonly used features for hate speech detection such as words, character n-grams, and their combination. Finally, we showed that in cross-domain settings our approach that incorporates stylometric and emotion-based features significantly contributes to the recent deep learning models when combined through a majority-voting ensemble, which allows to achieve the highest results for the languages addressed in this work. A manual error analysis showed that this improvement is brought by the ability of stylometric and emotion-based features to capture implicit and longer instances of hate speech. The consistent and substantial improvement in hate speech detection brought by including stylometric and emotion-based features in the different setups and for different languages explored indicates that their usage is a robust indicator of the hateful content.

The importance of stylometric features points in the direction of the existence of a linguistic register for hate speech messages with specific stylistic properties and a negative emotional load. Focusing on these features in text representation leads to more cross-domain robustness.

## Acknowledgments

This work has been supported by the Slovenian Research Agency and the Flemish Research Foundation through the bilateral research project ARRS N6-0099 and FWO G070619N "The linguistic landscape of hate speech on social media", the Slovenian Research Agency research core funding No. P6-0411 "Language resources and technologies for Slovene language", and the European Union's Rights, Equality and Citizenship Programme (2014-2020) project IMSyPP (grant no. 875263).

## References

Valerio Basile, Cristina Bosco, Elisabetta Fersini, Debora Nozza, Viviana Patti, Francisco Manuel Rangel Pardo, Paolo Rosso, and Manuela Sanguinetti. 2019. SemEval-2019 task 5: Multilingual detection of hate speech against immigrants and women in Twitter. In *Proceedings of the 13th International Workshop on Semantic Evaluation*, pages 54–63, Minneapolis, Minnesota, USA. ACL.

JM Berger and Heather Perez. 2006. The Islamic State's diminishing returns on Twitter: How suspensions are limiting the social networks of English-speaking ISIS supporters. Technical report, George Washington University.

Eloi Brassard-Gourdeau and Richard Khoury. 2019. Subversive toxicity detection using sentiment information. In *Proceedings of the Third Workshop on Abusive Language Online*, pages 1–10, Florence, Italy. ACL.

Walter Daelemans, Darja Fišer, Jasmin Franza, Denis Kranjčić, Jens Lemmens, Nikola Ljubešić, Ilia Markov, and Damjan Popič. 2020. The LiLaH Emotion Lexicon of Croatian, Dutch and Slovene. Slovenian language resource repository CLARIN.SI.

Harsh Dani, Jundong Li, and Huan Liu. 2017. Sentiment informed cyberbullying detection in social media. In *Proceedings of the European Conference on Machine Learning and Knowledge Discovery in Databases*, pages 52–67, Skopje, Macedonia. Springer.

Thomas Davidson, Dana Warmsley, Michael Macy, and Ingmar Weber. 2017. Automated hate speech detection and the problem of offensive language. *CoRR*, abs/1703.04009.

Jacob Devlin, Ming-Wei Chang, Kenton Lee, and Kristina Toutanova. 2019. BERT: Pre-training of deep bidirectional transformers for language understanding. In *Proceedings of the 2019 Conference of the North American Chapter of the Association for Computational Linguistics: Human Language Technologies)*, pages 4171–4186, Minneapolis, MN, USA. ACL.

Chris Emmery, Ben Verhoeven, Guy De Pauw, Gilles Jacobs, Cynthia Van Hee, Els Lefever, Bart Desmet, Véronique Hoste, and Walter Daelemans. 2020. Current limitations in cyberbullying detection: On evaluation criteria, reproducibility, and data scarcity. *Language Resources and Evaluation.*

Joseph Fleiss. 1981. *Statistical methods for rates and proportions*, 2nd edition. New York: John Wiley, Heidelberg, Germany.

Komal Florio, Valerio Basile, Marco Polignano, Pierpaolo Basile, and Viviana Patti. 2020. Time of your hate: The challenge of time in hate speech detection on social media. *Applied Sciences*, 10(12):4180.

Paula Fortuna and Sérgio Nunes. 2018. A survey on automatic detection of hate speech in text. *ACM Computing Surveys*, 51(4):1–30.

Jack Grieve. 2007. Quantitative Authorship Attribution: An Evaluation of Techniques. *Digital Scholarship in the Humanities*, 22(3):251–270.

Sepp Hochreiter and Jürgen Schmidhuber. 1997. Long short-term memory. *Neural Computation*, 9(8):1735–1780.

Paul Jaccard. 1901. Étude comparative de la distribution florale dans une portion des Alpes et des Jura. *Bulletin de la Société vaudoise des sciences naturelles*, 37:547–579.

Mike Kestemont. 2014. Function words in authorship attribution. From black magic to theory? In *Proceedings of the 3rd Workshop on Computational Linguistics for Literature*, pages 59–66, Gothenburg, Sweden. ACL.

Yoon Kim. 2014. Convolutional neural networks for sentence classification. In *Proceedings of the 2014 Conference on Empirical Methods in Natural Language Processing*, pages 1746–1751, Doha, Qatar. ACL.

Constantinos Kokkinos and Eirini Kipritsi. 2012. The relationship between bullying, victimization, trait emotional intelligence, self-efficacy and empathy among preadolescents. *Social Psychology of Education*, 15(1):41–58.

Nikola Ljubešić, Darja Fišer, and Tomaž Erjavec. 2019. The FRENK datasets of socially unacceptable discourse in Slovene and English. In *Proceedings of the 22nd International Conference on Text, Speech, and Dialogue*, pages 103–114, Ljubljana, Slovenia. Springer.

Nikola Ljubešić, Ilia Markov, Darja Fišer, and Walter Daelemans. 2020. The LiLaH emotion lexicon of Croatian, Dutch and Slovene. In *Proceedings of the Third Workshop on Computational Modeling of People's Opinions, Personality, and Emotions in Social Media*, pages 153–157, Barcelona, Spain (Online). ACL.

Thomas Mandl, Sandip Modha, Prasenjit Majumder, Daksh Patel, Mohana Dave, Chintak Mandlia, and Aditya Patel. 2019. Overview of the HASOC track at FIRE 2019: Hate speech and offensive content identification in Indo-European languages. In *Proceedings of the 11th Forum for Information Retrieval Evaluation*, page 14–17, New York, NY, USA. ACM.

Ilia Markov, Efstathios Stamatatos, and Grigori Sidorov. 2018. Improving cross-topic authorship attribution: The role of pre-processing. In *Proceedings of the 18th International Conference on Computational Linguistics and Intelligent Text Processing*, volume 10762, pages 289–302, Budapest, Hungary. Springer.

Quinn McNemar. 1947. Note on the sampling error of the difference between correlated proportions or percentages. *Psychometrika*, 12(2):153–157.

Saif Mohammad and Peter Turney. 2013. Crowdsourcing a word-emotion association lexicon. *Computational Intelligence*, 29:436–465.

Chikashi Nobata, Joel Tetreault, Achint Thomas, Yashar Mehdad, and Yi Chang. 2016. Abusive language detection in online user content. In *Proceedings of the 25th International Conference on World Wide Web*, pages 145–153, Switzerland. IW3C2.

John Nockleby. 2000. Hate speech. *Encyclopedia of the American Constitution*, pages 1277–1279.

Adam Paszke, Sam Gross, Francisco Massa, Adam Lerer, James Bradbury, Gregory Chanan, Trevor Killeen, Zeming Lin, Natalia Gimelshein, Luca Antiga, Alban Desmaison, Andreas Kopf, Edward Yang, Zachary DeVito, Martin Raison, Alykhan Tejani, Sasank Chilamkurthy, Benoit Steiner, Lu Fang, Junjie Bai, and Soumith Chintala. 2019. Pytorch: An imperative style, high-performance deep learning library. In *Advances in Neural Information Processing Systems 32*, pages 8026–8037. Curran Associates, Inc.

Fabian Pedregosa, Gaël Varoquaux, Alexandre Gramfort, Vincent Michel, Bertrand Thirion, Olivier Grisel, Mathieu Blondel, Peter Prettenhofer, Ron Weiss, Vincent Dubourg, Jake Vanderplas, Alexandre Passos, David Cournapeau, Matthieu Brucher, Matthieu Perrot, and Édouard Duchesnay. 2011. Scikit-learn: Machine learning in Python. *Journal of Machine Learning Research*, 12:2825–2830.

Fabio Poletto, Valerio Basile, Manuela Sanguinetti, Cristina Bosco, and Viviana Patti. 2020. Resources and benchmark corpora for hate speech detection: a systematic review. *Language Resources and Evaluation*.

Peng Qi, Timothy Dozat, Yuhao Zhang, and Christopher Manning. 2018. Universal dependency parsing from scratch. In *Proceedings of the CoNLL 2018 Shared Task: Multilingual Parsing from Raw Text to Universal Dependencies*, pages 160–170, Brussels, Belgium. ACL.

David Robinson, Ziqi Zhang, and Jonathan Tepper. 2018. Hate speech detection on Twitter: Feature engineering v.s. feature selection. In *Proceedings of the Satellite Events of the 15th Extended Semantic Web Conference*, pages 46–49, Heraklion, Greece. Springer.

Björn Ross, Michael Rist, Guillermo Carbonell, Ben Cabrera, Nils Kurowsky, and Michael Wojatzki. 2016. Measuring the reliability of hate speech annotations: The case of the European refugee crisis. In *Proceedings of the 3rd Workshop on Natural Language Processing for Computer-Mediated Communication*, pages 6–9, Bochum, Germany. Ruhr-Universität Bochum.

Maarten Sap, Dallas Card, Saadia Gabriel, Yejin Choi, and Noah A. Smith. 2019. The risk of racial bias in hate speech detection. In *Proceedings of the 57th Annual Meeting of the Association for Computational Linguistics*, pages 1668–1678, Florence, Italy. ACL.

Tony Smith and Ian Witten. 1993. Language inference from function words. Technical Report 93/3, Department of Computer Science, University of Waikato. Computer Science Working Papers.

Kristina Toutanova, Dan Klein, Christopher Manning, and Yoram Singer. 2003. Feature-rich part-of-speech tagging with a cyclic dependency network. In *Proceedings of the 2003 Human Language Technology Conference of the North American Chapter of the Association for Computational Linguistics*, pages 252–259, Edmonton, Canada. ACL.

Cynthia Van Hee, Gilles Jacobs, Chris Emmery, Bart Desmet, Els Lefever, Ben Verhoeven, Guy De Pauw, Walter Daelemans, and Véronique Hostel. 2018. Automatic detection of cyberbullying in social media text. *PLoS ONE*, 13(10).

Cynthia Van Hee, Els Lefever, Ben Verhoeven, Julie Mennes, Bart Desmet, Guy De Pauw, Walter Daelemans, and Veronique Hoste. 2015. Detection and fine-grained classification of cyberbullying events. In *Proceedings of the International Conference Recent Advances in Natural Language Processing*, pages 672–680, Hissar, Bulgaria. INCOMA.

Bertie Vidgen, Alex Harris, Dong Nguyen, Rebekah Tromble, Scott Hale, and Helen Margetts. 2019. Challenges and frontiers in abusive content detection. In *Proceedings of the Third Workshop on Abusive Language Online*, pages 80–93, Florence, Italy. ACL.

William Warner and Julia Hirschberg. 2012. Detecting hate speech on the world wide web. In *Proceedings of the Second Workshop on Language in Social Media*, pages 19–26, Montréal, Canada. ACL.

Zeerak Waseem. 2016. Are you a racist or am I seeing things? Annotator influence on hate speech detection on Twitter. In *Proceedings of the First Workshop on NLP and Computational Social Science*, pages 138–142, Austin, TX, USA. ACL.

Zeerak Waseem, Thomas Davidson, Dana Warmsley, and Ingmar Weber. 2017. Understanding abuse: A typology of abusive language detection subtasks. In *Proceedings of the First Workshop on Abusive Language Online*, pages 78–84, Vancouver, Canada. ACL.

Marcos Zampieri, Preslav Nakov, Sara Rosenthal, Pepa Atanasova, Georgi Karadzhov, Hamdy Mubarak, Leon Derczynski, Zeses Pitenis, and Çağrı Çöltekin. 2020. Semeval-2020 task 12: Multilingual offensive language identification in social media (offenseval 2020). *CoRR*, abs/2006.07235.

# Emotion-Aware, Emotion-Agnostic, or Automatic: Corpus Creation Strategies to Obtain Cognitive Event Appraisal Annotations

**Jan Hofmann, Enrica Troiano,** and **Roman Klinger**
Institut für Maschinelle Sprachverarbeitung, University of Stuttgart, Germany
{jan.hofmann,enrica.troiano,roman.klinger}@ims.uni-stuttgart.de

## Abstract

Appraisal theories explain how the cognitive evaluation of an event leads to a particular emotion. In contrast to theories of basic emotions or affect (valence/arousal), this theory has not received a lot of attention in natural language processing. Yet, in psychology it has been proven powerful: Smith and Ellsworth (1985) showed that the appraisal dimensions *attention*, *certainty*, *anticipated effort*, *pleasantness*, *responsibility/control* and *situational control* discriminate between (at least) 15 emotion classes. We study different annotation strategies for these dimensions, based on the event-focused enISEAR corpus (Troiano et al., 2019). We analyze two manual annotation settings: (1) showing the text to annotate while masking the experienced emotion label; (2) revealing the emotion associated with the text. Setting 2 enables the annotators to develop a more realistic intuition of the described event, while Setting 1 is a more standard annotation procedure, purely relying on text. We evaluate these strategies in two ways: by measuring inter-annotator agreement and by fine-tuning RoBERTa to predict appraisal variables. Our results show that knowledge of the emotion increases annotators' reliability. Further, we evaluate a purely automatic rule-based labeling strategy (inferring appraisal from annotated emotion classes). Training on automatically assigned labels leads to a competitive performance of our classifier, even when tested on manual annotations. This is an indicator that it might be possible to automatically create appraisal corpora for every domain for which emotion corpora already exist.

## 1 Introduction

Automatically detecting emotions in written texts consists of mapping textual units, like documents, paragraphs, or sentences, to a predefined set of emotions. Common sets of classes used for this purpose rely on psychological theories such as those proposed by Ekman (1992) (*anger*, *disgust*, *fear*, *joy*, *sadness*, *surprise*) or Plutchik (2001). These theories are based on the assumption that there is a restricted number of emotions that have prototypical realizations. However, not all sets of emotions are appropriate for every domain. For instance, Dittrich and Zepf (2019) argue that some of the basic emotions are too strong for measuring how people feel when driving a car and, based on that, Cevher et al. (2019) resort to *joy*, *annoyance* (instead of *anger*), *insecurity* (instead of *fear*), *boredom*, and *relaxation* to classify in-car utterances. Haider et al. (2020) model the emotional perception of poetry and opt for the categories *beauty/joy*, *sadness*, *uneasiness*, *vitality*, *awe/sublime*, *suspense*, *humor*, *nostalgia*, and *annoyance*, following the definition of aesthetic emotions (Schindler et al., 2017; Menninghaus et al., 2019). Demszky et al. (2020) define a taxonomy of emotions, reaching a high coverage while maintaining inter-class relations.

An alternative to the use of categorical variables are the so-called "dimensional" approaches. The most popular of them models affective experiences along the variables of dominance, valence, and arousal (Russell and Mehrabian, 1977, VAD). Feldman Barrett (2006, 2017) theorizes that emotions are interpretations of continuous affective states experiencers find themselves in. Still, as Smith and Ellsworth (1985) note, not all emotions can be distinguished based on valence and arousal. One might argue that predicting three continuous variables instead of a richer set of categories is a simplification and can be limiting for downstream applications of emotion analysis models.

Smith and Ellsworth (1985) particularly argue that the VAD model does not capture all relevant aspects of an emotion in the context of an event. In a *fight or flight* situation (Cannon, 1929), for instance, the decision to take one of these two actions



*Proceedings of the 11th Workshop on Computational Approaches to Subjectivity, Sentiment and Social Media Analysis*, pages 160–170
April 19, 2021. ©2021 Association for Computational Linguistics

| Emotion | Appraisals | Text |
|---|---|---|
| Joy | Attention, Certainty, Pleasant, Sit. Ctrl. | I felt ... when I knew that I was going back to Florida a year earlier than I thought I would. |
| Disgust | Attention, Certainty, Effort, Sit. Ctrl. | I felt ... when my kitten was sick and I had to clean it up. |
| Fear | Attention, Effort, Sit. Ctrl. | I felt ... when I was having a hard attach. |
| Guilt | Attention, Certainty, Effort, Respons., Control | I felt ... when I went on holiday and left our cat behind. |
| Sadness | Attention, Certainty, Sit. Ctrl. | I felt ... when I found out one of my favourite shops had shut down. |

Table 1: Examples from the corpus of Hofmann et al. (2020).

is mostly made based on the effort that the emotion experiencer anticipates, but this is not represented by VAD. Therefore, Smith and Ellsworth (1985) propose a dimensional approach with the appraisal variables of how pleasant an event is (*pleasantness*, likely to be associated with *joy*, but unlikely to appear with *disgust*), how much effort an event can be expected to cause (*anticipated effort*, likely to be high when *anger* or *fear* is experienced), how certain the experiencer is in a specific situation (*certainty*, low, e.g., in the context of *hope* or *surprise*), how much attention is devoted to the event (*attention*, likely to be low, e.g., in the case of *boredom* or *disgust*), how much responsibility the experiencer of the emotion has for what has happened (*self-other responsibility/control*, high for feeling *guilt* or *pride*), and how much the experiencer feels to be controlled by the situation (*situational control*, high in *anger*).

As the cognitive appraisal is a fundamental subcomponent of emotions, we deem that appraisal dimensions are useful to perform emotion recognition, and that even the prediction of appraisals themselves can contribute to computational approaches to affective states. These appraisal dimensions have only recently found application in automatic emotion analysis in text: Hofmann et al. (2020) re-annotated a corpus of 1001 English emotional event descriptions (Troiano et al., 2019) for which the experienced emotion has been disclosed by the author of the description (Table 1 shows examples from their corpus). Their annotation is designed as a preliminary step for inferring discrete emotion categories. In contrast, we argue *that the prediction of appraisal dimensions is in itself valuable*. This intuition has an impact on our annotation strategy. While Hofmann et al. (2020) did not show any emotion label to the annotators, thus avoiding information leaks, we hypothesize that knowing such emotion helps understanding how the described events were originally appraised by their experiencers: at times, properly annotating appraisals as a third party might be unfeasible without having prior access to emotions.

We test this by comparing three annotation procedures: (1) we give the annotator access only to the text but not to its emotion label; (2) we give the annotator access to the text and the emotion, and evaluate if this additional information has an impact on annotation reliability and performance of a pretrained transformer-based classifier fine-tuned on these data; and (3) we automatically infer the appraisal dimensions from existing emotion annotations, investigating the hypothesis that manual annotation might not be necessary.

Our main contributions are that we show that (a) appraisal annotation is more reliable when annotators have access to the emotion label of the original experiencer, hence, *the event description itself does not carry sufficient information for annotation*. That also means that annotating appraisals for corpora in which the original emotion is not available might be particularly challenging. (b) Automatic, rule-based annotation of appraisals that leverages emotion labels is a viable alternative to human annotation, and therefore, appraisal corpora can automatically be created for domains for which emotion corpora are already available.

Our classifier further constitutes a novel state of the art for appraisal prediction on the data by Hofmann et al. (2020). The data is available at https://www.ims.uni-stuttgart.de/data/appraisalemotion.

## 2 Related Work

### 2.1 Resources for Emotion Analysis

There is a wealth of literature in psychology surrounding emotions, specifically regarding the way they are elicited, their universal validity, their number and stereotypical expressions, and their function (Scherer, 2000; Gendron and Feldman Barrett, 2009). The two prominent traditions which have dominated the field of emotion classification in natural language processing are discrete and dimensional models (Kim and Klinger, 2019).

Next to the creation of lexicons for emotion analysis (Pennebaker et al., 2001; Strapparava and Valitutti, 2004; Mohammad et al., 2013; Mohammad, 2018, i.a.), the annotation of text corpora received substantial attention (Bostan and Klinger, 2018). They vary across emotion categories and domains, with discrete classes being dominating – some exceptions focused on valence and arousal annotations are Buechel and Hahn (2017), Preoţiuc-Pietro et al. (2016), and Yu et al. (2016). For instance, the ISEAR study by Scherer and Wallbott (1994) led to self-reports of emotionally connotated events. Its creators aimed at understanding what aspects of emotions are universal and which are relative to culture. It was built by asking students to recall an emotion-inducing event and to describe it.

Other efforts focused more on creating corpora specifically for emotion analysis in NLP. Troiano et al. (2019) built enISEAR and deISEAR, whose 1001 event-descriptions were collected via crowdsourcing, with a questionnaire inspired by ISEAR, both in English and in German. TEC (Mohammad, 2012), another popular resource, is bigger in size ($\approx$21k instances), contains tweets and was automatically annotated with hashtags. The Blogs corpus by Aman and Szpakowicz (2007) has sentence-level annotations for 5205 texts, annotated by multiple raters. While ISEAR, enISEAR and deISEAR are focused on describing specific emotion-inducing events, the Blogs corpus and TEC are more general.

This is also the set of corpora that we use in our study (a more comprehensive resource overview was made available by Hakak et al. (2017) and Bostan and Klinger (2018)).

### 2.2 Appraisal Theories

A richer perspective on emotions and their experience than affect models or fundamental emotion sets is provided by appraisal models (Scherer, 2009b), which did not receive a lot of attention from the NLP community so far. Appraisals are immediate evaluations of situations which guide the emotion felt by the experiencer (Scherer, 2009a). More precisely, an emotion is a synchronized change in five organismic subsystems (i.e., cognitive, peripheral efference, motivational, motor expression and subjective feeling) in response to the evaluation of a stimulus event important to an individual. Emotion states can be distinguished on the basis of their accompanying appraisals. For instance, fear emerges when an event is appraised as unforeseen and disagreeable, a frightening event is one appraised as an unforeseen, unpleasant, and contrary to one's goal (Mortillaro et al., 2012). The cognitive part of the emotion is the one guiding the evaluation of the stimulus along different dimensions. According to Scherer et al. (2001), they are relevance (i.e., the pleasantness of the event, and its relevance for one's goals), implication (i.e., its potential consequences), coping potential (i.e., one's ability to adjust to or control the situation) and normative significance (i.e. its congruity to one's values and beliefs). On a similar vein, Smith and Ellsworth (1985) argue that six cognitive appraisal dimensions can differentiate emotional experiences, as there is a relationship between the way situations are appraised along such dimensions and the experienced emotion. They are *pleasantness*, *anticipated effort*, *certainty*, *attention*, *responsibility/control* and *situational control*. We use their model to explore appraisals in text.

## 3 Experimental Setting

### 3.1 Annotation Guidelines

We adhere to the annotation guidelines and the appraisal dimensions of Hofmann et al. (2020), splitting the original *situational control* from Smith and Ellsworth (1985) into *control* and *circumstance*. Our judges take binary decisions with respect to seven appraisal dimensions. We ask them the following questions:

"Most probably, at the time when the event happened, the writer… …wanted to devote further attention to the event (*Attention*) ; …was certain about what was happening (*Certainty*) ; …had to expend mental or physical effort to deal with the situation (*Effort*) ; …found that the event was pleasant (*Pleasantness*) ; …was responsible for the situation (*Responsibility*) ; …found that he/she was in control of the situation (*Control*) ; …found that the event could not have been changed or influenced by anyone (*Circumstance*)."

### 3.2 Experiment 1: Manual Annotation

To annotate the appraisal dimensions, judges need to make assumptions about the experienced situation. We believe this is possible, at times, purely from the textual description that needs to be judged. Other times, knowing which emotion a person developed might be necessary to understand how the overall experience was originally appraised.

To analyze this assumption and measure the importance of emotion labels to reliably assign appraisal dimensions, we build our experiment on top of the English enISEAR corpus by Troiano et al. (2019). Its authors asked workers on a crowdsourcing platform to complete sentences like "I felt [emotion name], when/that/because...", where [emotion name] is replaced by a concrete emotion. In a later annotation round, other annotators had to infer the emotion of the text, and for this reason the creators of the corpus replaced emotion words with "...". The resulting 1001 instances of enISEAR are labeled by the experiencers of the emotion themselves and have masked emotion words in the text.

We use these data to perform two annotation experiments on 210 instances, randomly sampled from enISEAR and stratified by emotion. Two annotators judge all of these instances in two different settings. Setting 1, EMOHIDE, replicates the study by Hofmann et al. (2020): the emotion label is not available to the annotator. In Setting 2, EMOVIS, the emotion is presented along with the text. The two rounds of annotations (first EMOHIDE, later EMOVIS which makes the emotion available) were distantiated by six months, to avoid a bias by recalling the previous round. We evaluate the reliability of the annotation via inter-annotator agreement with Cohen's $\kappa$ (1960), under the hypothesis that having knowledge of the emotion leads to more reliable human annotations.

**Computational Modelling.** One of the annotators annotated the full 1001 instances twice, that is, for the EMOHIDE and the EMOVIS approaches as a basis to evaluate how well the realization of the appraisal concepts in the corpus can be modelled automatically. As we expect the annotations EMOVIS to be more reliable, we also expect the model to perform better.[1]

We use RoBERTa (Liu et al., 2019) with the abstraction layer for tensorflow as provided by ktrain (Maiya, 2020), and choose the number of epochs to be 5, based on the appraisal prediction and emotion classification tasks in the data by Hofmann et al. (2020) (which we annotate in this paper). Only minor differences in performance can be seen between epochs 4–7. We keep this number of epochs fixed across all experiments and all other parameters at their default. The batch size is 5. More concretely, we opt for a 3×10-fold cross-validation setting, use the RoBERTa-base model in all experiments except for those on the German deISEAR (in the next Experiment 2), where we use XLM-R (Conneau et al., 2020).

[1]We acknowledge that model performance on an annotated corpus can only to some degree be used to assess data quality. However, in combination with our inter-annotator agreement assessments, it serves as an indicator of the amount of noise.

| Emotion | Attention | Certainty | Effort | Pleasant | Resp/Contr. | Sit. Control |
|---|---|---|---|---|---|---|
| Anger | 1 | 1 | 1 | 0 | 0 | 0 |
| Disgust | 0 | 1 | 1 | 0 | 0 | 0 |
| Fear | 1 | 0 | 1 | 0 | 0 | 1 |
| Guilt | 0 | 1 | 1 | 0 | 1 | 0 |
| Joy | 1 | 1 | 0 | 1 | 1 | 0 |
| Sadness | 0 | 1 | 0 | 0 | 0 | 1 |
| Shame | 0 | 0 | 1 | 0 | 1 | 0 |
| Surprise | 1 | 0 | 0 | 1 | 0 | 1 |

Table 2: Discretized associations between appraisal dimensions and emotion categories, following Smith and Ellsworth (1985), as we use them for automatic annotation in Exp. 2.

### 3.3 Experiment 2: Automatic Annotation

As Smith and Ellsworth (1985) showed, appraisal dimensions are sufficient to discriminate emotion categories: this is knowledge which we can make use of, and we can leverage their findings to automatically assign discrete appraisal labels to enISEAR (see Table 2) in a rule-based manner. For comparability to the manual annotation setup, we opt for discrete labels which we infer from the continuous principle component analysis values from the original paper.

The question to be answered is if this rule-based annotation actually represents the same concepts as the manual annotation. To answer this, we compare the automatic annotation (AUTOAPPR) with both annotations that have been performed manually (EMOHIDE, EMOVIS). Further, we train a model to predict these automatic annotations and evaluate on the manually annotated labels.

Since the automatic method relies on emotion labels, we expect its annotations to be more similar to EMOVIS, where the annotators also have access to this information. For the same reason, we also assume that the model trained on automatically annotated labels performs better on EMOVIS than on EMOHIDE. Finding that models trained on labels assigned in such rule-based manner show comparable performance to manual annotations (when tested on manual annotations) would suggest that

| | Inter Annotator Agreement | | | RoBERTa Modelling | | | | | | |
|---|---|---|---|---|---|---|---|---|---|---|
| | EMOVIS | EMOHIDE | | EMOVIS | | | EMOHIDE | | | |
| Appraisal | $\kappa$ | $\kappa$ | $\Delta$ | P | R | $F_1$ | P | R | $F_1$ | $\Delta F_1$ |
| Attentional Activity | .55 | .30 | +.25 | .79 | .84 | .82 | .84 | .88 | .86 | −.04 |
| Certainty | .71 | .43 | +.28 | .94 | .97 | .96 | .81 | .93 | .87 | +.09 |
| Anticipated Effort | .44 | .38 | +.06 | .77 | .83 | .80 | .66 | .58 | .62 | +.18 |
| Pleasantness | .93 | .87 | +.06 | .92 | .94 | .93 | .91 | .92 | .92 | +.01 |
| Responsibility | .80 | .64 | +.16 | .85 | .79 | .82 | .83 | .81 | .82 | ±.00 |
| Control | .66 | .71 | −.05 | .64 | .49 | .56 | .74 | .68 | .71 | −.15 |
| Circumstance | .65 | .54 | +.11 | .80 | .72 | .76 | .76 | .74 | .75 | +.01 |
| Macro ∅ | .68 | .55 | +.13 | .82 | .80 | .80 | .79 | .79 | .79 | +.01 |
| Micro ∅ | | | | .84 | .85 | .84 | .80 | .81 | .81 | +.03 |

Table 3: Experiment 1: Cohen's $\kappa$ between annotators on EMOVIS and EMOHIDE and modelling experiments. The model is separately trained and tested on EMOVIS and EMOHIDE.

the latter might not be necessary to obtain appraisal prediction models.

In this automatic setup, we merge *responsibility* and *control*. While they are divided in the manually annotated corpora, this separation is not available in the results by Smith and Ellsworth (1985). This affects the comparability of the averages of performance measures between Exp. 1 and 2.

Further, under the assumption that automatic annotation shows competitive results on the manually annotated corpus enISEAR, we extend this analysis to other resources for corpus generalization. In addition to enISEAR, we use the original ISEAR dataset (Scherer and Wallbott, 1994), the German event corpus deISEAR (Troiano et al., 2019) and, as resources without focus on events, the Twitter Emotion Corpus (TEC) (Mohammad, 2012) and the Blogs corpus (Aman and Szpakowicz, 2007). Since these corpora are not manually annotated for appraisals, we only evaluate on automatic appraisal annotations.

## 4 Results

### 4.1 Experiment 1: Manual Annotation

**Inter-Annotator Agreement.** In Experiment 1, we compare the reliability of the annotation with and without access to the emotion label. We show the inter-annotator agreement results in Table 3. As we hypothesized, the agreement on EMOVIS is clearly higher than on EMOHIDE, with .68 in comparison to .55 $\kappa$. The highest agreement increase is observed for *attention* (+.25) and *certainty* (+.28), followed by *responsibility* (+.16). The only decrease in agreement, for *control*, is comparably small (−.05).

Figure 1 (and Table 9 in the Appendix) shows the distribution of emotions for the different appraisal dimensions: for most dimensions, the annotation becomes more clearly connected to emotions with its availability, with *certainty* and *anticipated effort* being exceptions: here, the number of instances of a set of emotion classes partially increases. This confirms that knowledge of the emotion "denoises" the annotation.

**Modelling.** Table 3 also reports the prediction performance on appraisal classes using RoBERTa. We observe that the performances on EMOVIS are higher than on EMOHIDE (+.03pp on micro $F_1$, .01 on macro $F_1$). This is in line with our assumptions, but the improvement is actually lower than we expected, given the more substantial difference in inter-annotator agreement. However, for *certainty* (+.09) and *anticipated effort* (+.18), the change is substantial. *Attentional Activity*, which shows a high increase in agreement, has a small decrease in modelling performance (−.04). *Control*, which does not improve in agreement, has a considerable loss in prediction performance (−.15).

From this experiment, we conclude that the annotation is more reliable with access to the emotion: this reflects on the modelling results, and it does so to different extents for different emotions.

### 4.2 Experiment 2: Automatic Annotation

**Inter-Annotator Agreement.** We now evaluate the rule-based annotation procedure, in which appraisal classes are purely assigned by the automatic procedure, shown in Table 2.

The agreement between the rule-based annotation AUTOAPPR and both manual annotations is shown in Table 4. As expected, we observe a higher agreement with EMOVIS. Again, the differences

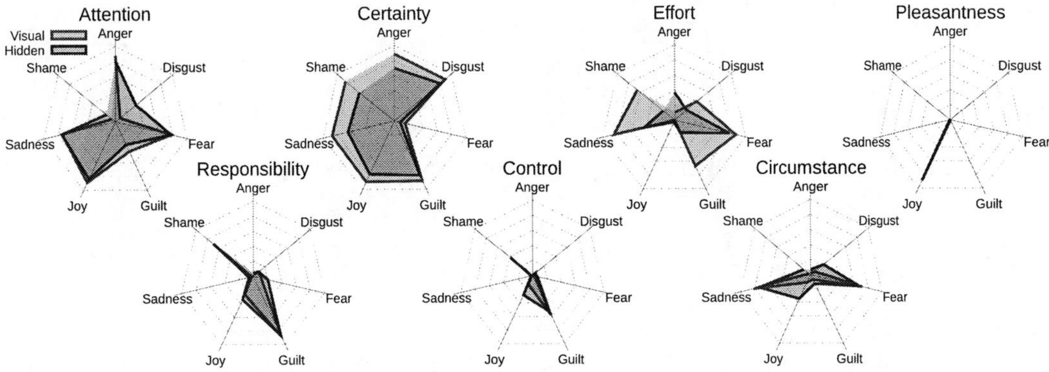


Figure 1: Frequency distribution of appraisals across emotions for EMOVIS (Visual) and EMOHIDE (Hidden).

| | Agreement to AUTOAPPR, $\kappa$ | | | | Modelling: RoBERTa trained on AUTOAPPR | | | | | | | | |
|---|---|---|---|---|---|---|---|---|---|---|---|---|---|
| | EMOVIS | | EMOHIDE | | EMOVIS | | | EMOHIDE | | | AUTOAPPR | | |
| Appraisal | A1 | A2 | A1 | A2 | P | R | $F_1$ | P | R | $F_1$ | P | R | $F_1$ |
| Attentional Activity | .47 | .63 | .33 | .48 | .85 | .59 | .70 | .88 | .59 | .71 | .86 | .85 | .85 |
| Certainty | .35 | .53 | .50 | .51 | .97 | .81 | .88 | .81 | .83 | .82 | .88 | .90 | .89 |
| Anticipated Effort | .31 | .08 | .19 | .16 | .61 | .77 | .68 | .39 | .79 | .52 | .95 | .96 | .96 |
| Pleasantness | .93 | 1.00 | .91 | .96 | .90 | .93 | .92 | .91 | .95 | .93 | .96 | .94 | .95 |
| Responsibility/Control | .39 | .63 | .39 | .59 | .66 | .81 | .72 | .74 | .78 | .76 | .91 | .89 | .90 |
| Situational Control | .44 | .64 | .34 | .59 | .77 | .74 | .75 | .78 | .59 | .67 | .84 | .83 | .84 |
| Macro ∅ | .48 | .58 | .44 | .54 | .79 | .77 | .78 | .75 | .75 | .74 | .90 | .89 | .90 |
| Micro ∅ | | | | | .78 | .75 | .77 | .70 | .73 | .72 | .90 | .90 | .90 |

Table 4: Experiment 2 Main Results: Cohen's $\kappa$ between annotators of EMOHIDE/EMOVIS and AUTOAPPR, on the subset of 210 instances from enISEAR. The classifier is trained on the full set of 1001 instances annotated automatically (AUTOAPPR) and evaluated on all other annotations (cross-validation splits remain the same).

are not equally distributed across emotions and they resemble the changes in the other experiments, but agreement is lower between AUTOAPPR and the manual annotations than between the latters, suggesting that the automatic process does not lead to the same conceptual annotation[2].

**Modelling.** To answer the question how well one model trained on rule-based annotations performs on manual annotations, we test the model three times: on EMOVIS, EMOHIDE, and AUTOAPPR. The right side of Table 4 reports the results. Note that *responsibility* and *control* have been merged, as explained in the experimental setting.

We see that the highest macro average $F_1$ is non-surprisingly achieved when testing on AUTOAPPR (.90$F_1$). When testing the same model on EMOVIS, the performance drops by 12pp (.78$F_1$), but is still substantially higher than for the corpus in which the emotions were not available to the annotators (.72$F_1$). Note that the performance of .78$F_1$ (EMOVIS) and .74$F_1$ (EMOHIDE) are not too different from the model trained on manually annotated data, with .80$F_1$ and .79$F_1$. We therefore conclude that automatically labeling a corpus with appraisal dimensions leads to a meaningful model.

**Corpus Generalization.** Finally, we apply the automatic labeling procedure to other emotion corpora. Results are in Table 5.

Given the different nature of the domains and languages (German vs. English – deISEAR/enISEAR; tweets vs. blog texts – TEC vs. Blogs), these numbers cannot be directly compared, but we can observe that they are comparably high, similar to the other experiments. We carefully infer (without having compared the prediction on these corpora to manual annotations) that this is an indicator that automatic annotation of appraisal dimensions also works across different corpora and languages.

[2]These labels could be compared to humans' only on EMOVIS, which turned out more reliable. We also consider EMOHIDE because it represents standard emotion annotation procedures, where judges assess texts without further information.

| Appraisal | deISEAR P | R | $F_1$ | ISEAR P | R | $F_1$ | TEC P | R | $F_1$ | Blogs P | R | $F_1$ |
|---|---|---|---|---|---|---|---|---|---|---|---|---|
| Attentional Activity | 79 | 68 | 73 | 83 | 82 | 83 | 90 | 91 | 91 | 94 | 94 | 94 |
| Certainty | 79 | 90 | 84 | 89 | 92 | 90 | 87 | 89 | 88 | 97 | 97 | 97 |
| Anticipated Effort | 88 | 93 | 91 | 94 | 95 | 94 | 74 | 68 | 71 | 91 | 93 | 92 |
| Pleasantness | 80 | 69 | 77 | 91 | 90 | 91 | 85 | 86 | 86 | 97 | 97 | 97 |
| Responsibility/Control | 80 | 69 | 74 | 88 | 85 | 86 | 79 | 79 | 79 | 94 | 96 | 95 |
| Situational Control | 73 | 69 | 71 | 83 | 81 | 82 | 79 | 79 | 79 | 88 | 86 | 87 |
| Macro ∅ | 81 | 76 | 78 | 88 | 87 | 88 | 82 | 82 | 82 | 94 | 94 | 94 |
| Micro ∅ | 82 | 81 | 81 | 89 | 89 | 89 | 84 | 84 | 84 | 94 | 95 | 94 |

Table 5: Experiment 2, Generalization to other corpora. All results are averages across 3×10 cross validations. Note that the last three columns from Table 4 correspond to the same setting as it is in here.

### 4.3 Model Performance Notes and Comparison to Original Data Annotation

The data that we use was made available to support appraisal-based research in emotion analysis. It consists of the same instances we annotated in Hofmann et al. (2020). However, in this previous work, each instance was judged by three annotators, who did not have access to the emotion labels of the texts, and the experiments have been performed on labels obtained with the majority vote of the annotators. Instead, for the current experiments, the labels by only one annotator on all instances have been used. Therefore, the experiments of the two papers are not strictly comparable. In addition, Hofmann et al. (2020) adopted a CNN-based classifier. Brief, there are two sources for non-comparability in our experiments: different label sets and different models. We aimed at leveraging a more state-of-the-art transformer-based model, but at the same time, we needed different label sets to better understand the appraisal annotation processes.

For transparency reasons, we show the performance of our RoBERTA model on the original labels against the results by Hofmann et al. (2020). Table 6 compares the two studies with respect to appraisals and Table 7 with respect to emotion predictions. The emotion recognition models consist of a text-based model (T→E), a pipeline that first predicts the appraisal and then classifies the emotion without access to text with a two-layer dense neural network (T→A, A→E). To measure the complementarity of these two settings, a third model is an oracle ensemble (T→A→E + T→E) which accepts a prediction as true positive if one of the two models provides the correct prediction.

On this original data set by Hofmann et al. (2020), our model constitutes a new state of the art. The micro-averaged appraisal prediction with

| Appraisal | CNN P | R | $F_1$ | RoBERTa P | R | $F_1$ |
|---|---|---|---|---|---|---|
| Attention | 81 | 84 | 82 | 86 | 90 | 88 |
| Certainty | 84 | 86 | 85 | 87 | 94 | 91 |
| Effort | 68 | 68 | 68 | 79 | 77 | 78 |
| Pleasantness | 79 | 63 | 70 | 92 | 92 | 92 |
| Responsibility | 74 | 68 | 71 | 86 | 85 | 85 |
| Control | 63 | 49 | 55 | 81 | 73 | 77 |
| Circumstance | 65 | 58 | 61 | 74 | 69 | 71 |
| Macro ∅ | 73 | 68 | 70 | 83 | 83 | 83 |
| Micro ∅ | 77 | 74 | 75 | 84 | 85 | 85 |

Table 6: RoBERTA model performance on predicting appraisals on the original data by Hofmann et al. (2020), compared to their CNN results.

RoBERTa is 10pp higher than the original CNN-based model; the emotion classification has similar improvements, and the overall relation between the model configurations remains comparable.

## 5 Qualitative Analysis

To better understand how revealing emotions affects the annotations in Experiment 1, we provide some concrete examples. Table 8 reports instances from enISEAR. We show for *which appraisal variables the agreement changes*, by marking the appraisal with + or −. For instance, −*attention* means that the annotators came to disagree on that appraisal dimension when the emotion was uncovered, while +*pleasantness* indicates that they came to agree thanks to the knowledge of the emotion label. Note that + does not mean that the dimension was marked as 1 by both annotators. The examples are sorted by the sum of changes in agreement.

In Example (1) an event is described in a way which leaves open if there is *responsibility*, *pleasantness*, *anticipated effort*, and even if the experiencer is entirely certain about what is happening.

| | T→E | | | | | | T→A,A→E | | | | | | T→A→E + T→E | | | | | |
|---|---|---|---|---|---|---|---|---|---|---|---|---|---|---|---|---|---|---|
| | CNN | | | RoBERTa | | | CNN | | | RoBERTa | | | CNN | | | RoBERTa | | |
| Emotion | P | R | $F_1$ | P | R | $F_1$ | P | R | $F_1$ | P | R | $F_1$ | P | R | $F_1$ | P | R | $F_1$ |
| Anger | 51 | 52 | 52 | 62 | 62 | 62 | 34 | 62 | 44 | 44 | 72 | 54 | 66 | 81 | 73 | 72 | 85 | 78 |
| Disgust | 65 | 63 | 64 | 70 | 71 | 71 | 59 | 34 | 43 | 65 | 38 | 48 | 78 | 68 | 73 | 86 | 74 | 80 |
| Fear | 69 | 71 | 70 | 80 | 82 | 81 | 55 | 55 | 55 | 65 | 76 | 70 | 76 | 77 | 77 | 85 | 92 | 88 |
| Guilt | 47 | 42 | 44 | 60 | 60 | 60 | 38 | 50 | 43 | 50 | 68 | 58 | 60 | 63 | 62 | 72 | 80 | 76 |
| Joy | 74 | 80 | 77 | 92 | 96 | 94 | 77 | 69 | 72 | 92 | 95 | 93 | 79 | 80 | 80 | 94 | 98 | 96 |
| Sadness | 69 | 67 | 68 | 82 | 81 | 81 | 58 | 40 | 47 | 74 | 55 | 63 | 74 | 70 | 72 | 87 | 84 | 86 |
| Shame | 44 | 45 | 45 | 57 | 54 | 55 | 36 | 24 | 29 | 51 | 23 | 32 | 58 | 51 | 54 | 77 | 59 | 67 |
| Macro ∅ | 60 | 60 | 60 | 72 | 72 | 72 | 51 | 48 | 48 | 63 | 61 | 60 | 70 | 70 | 70 | 82 | 82 | 82 |
| Micro ∅ | | | 60 | | | 72 | | | 48 | | | 61 | | | 70 | | | 82 |

Table 7: Comparison of the CNN (Hofmann et al., 2020) and our RoBERTa model on the Text-to-Emotion baseline (T→E), the pipeline experiment (T→A,A→E) and the oracle ensemble experiment (T→A→E + T→E). These experiments follow the model configurations by Hofmann et al. (2020).

| ID | Score | Emotion | Aggr. Change | Input Text |
|---|---|---|---|---|
| 1 | +4 | Fear | +e +p +r +ci | I felt … when I was abseiling down a cliff-face. |
| 2 | +3 | Joy | +ce +r +ci | I felt … when I got a new job. |
| 3 | ±0 | Guilt | | I felt ... when I participated in gossip at work. |
| 4 | −2 | Shame | −a −ce −r +ci | I felt … when I found out that my daughter had been having a difficult time and I didn't realise straight away what she was going through. |
| 5 | −2 | Anger | −a −e | I felt … when we were charged by a care home for the three months after my father had died, even though we had emptied his room the day after his death. |
| 6 | −3 | Fear | −a −ce −r | I felt … when cycling home after a long ride one evening, unaware how dark it had become, and thus relying on some very weak led lights that I'd never tested in complete darkness - I could barely see ten feet ahead of me. |

Table 8: Examples of differences between annotations with masked and visible emotion labels. + and − indicate the agreement and the disagreement on a specific dimension which is reached after making the emotion visible. The score is the sum of agreement changes, either improvements (+1 for each dimension) or degradation (−1). a: *attention*, ce: *certainty*, e: *anticipated effort*, p: *pleasantness*, r: *responsibility*, ci: *circumstance*.

With the knowledge that the emotion is fear, it becomes clear that the situation does involve *anticipated effort*, is not *pleasant*, and that *circumstance* is not likely. The annotators also agree here that there is *responsibility* involved, which is likely an interpretation based on world-knowledge.

In the situation of getting a new job (Example (2)), knowing the emotion adds agreement regarding certainty, which is in line with added agreement that the person was responsible. Example (3) is an instance in which the situation was already entirely clear without knowing the emotion – the experiencer participated in gossip. That is a certain, non-pleasurable situation (when recognizing this) which is under their own control. Knowledge that guilt has been experienced does not add anything.

Example (4) shows that complex situations cause more disagreement in annotations which are not necessarily resolved by knowing the emotion. The described event is about a negative emotion felt because the experiencer did not recognize the bad mood of the daughter. Annotators come to disagree about *attention*, *certainty* and *responsibility*.

Example (5) describes another situation in which a negative event is discussed. Knowledge of the emotion puts a clear focus away from the sad part of the description (father dying) and puts it on something that causes anger. However, this shift does not resolve appraisal disagreements but indeed adds on top of them, with *attention* and *anticipated effort*.

Finally, Example (6) is another long description with annotators' focus on different aspects, one on the darkness (hence, no *responsibility*), the other on the cycling (*responsibility*). Here, knowledge of the emotion does not change the interpretability of the event. However, it informs on which part of the described situation the original author focused on.

These examples show that EmoVis helps solve ambiguities when events can be associated to multiple emotions, other times it helps people give more weight to specific portions of texts. In the first case agreement tends to be reached more easily.

## 6 Conclusion & Future Work

We analyzed how to build corpora of text annotated with appraisal variables and we evaluated how well such concepts can be modelled. By doing so, we brought together emotion analysis and a strand of emotion research in psychology which has received little attention from the computational linguistics community. We propose that in addition to well-established approaches to emotion analysis, like affect-oriented dimensional approaches or classification into predefined emotion inventories, psychological models of appraisals will be considered in future emotion-based studies, particularly those relying on event-oriented resources.

The use of appraisals is interesting from a *theoretical perspective*: motivated by psychology, we leveraged the cognitive mechanisms underlying emotions, thus accounting for many complex patterns in which humans appraise an event and emotionally react to it. In this light, it is interesting in itself that our annotators were able to empathically reconstruct the event appraisals experienced by others, even without knowing their emotion.

From a *practical perspective*, appraisal annotations are less prone to being poorly chosen for particular domains, in comparison to regular emotion classes, as the actual feeling develops based on the cognitive evaluation of an event. We also have shown that event descriptions alone might not be sufficient to properly annotate the hypothetical appraisal of the experiencer (which is, however, also an issue with traditional emotion analysis annotations and models – we cannot look into the feeler, we deal with private states). This shows and is presumably the reason that additional context (e.g., the emotion label) is required.

Some implications for future research and developments follow: ideally, appraisal (and emotion) annotations should stem directly from the experiencer. This is not doable in many NLP settings. For instance, when analyzing literature, it is impossible to ask fictional characters for their current event appraisal. However, we presume that settings on social media might be realistic, for instance by probing appropriate distant labeling methods, e.g., a careful choice of hashtags. If this is unfeasible, because text authors do not disclose their appraisals, the available emotion labels still represent a valuable source of information: as we have shown, they can guide the interpretation of the described events, and hence, the way in which these are post-assigned appraisal dimensions.

Finally, we provided evidence that even if a model is trained on automatically obtained appraisal labels, it is still capable of substantial performance. Therefore, we conclude that more corpora with appraisal dimensions from different languages and domains should be created from scratch. In the meantime, one can build on top of the rich set of available emotion corpora and automatically create appraisal-annotated resources out of them.

## Acknowledgements

This work was supported by Deutsche Forschungsgemeinschaft (projects SEAT, KL 2869/1-1 and CEAT, KL 2869/1-2) and has partially been conducted within the Leibniz WissenschaftsCampus Tübingen "Cognitive Interfaces". We thank Kai Sassenberg and Laura Oberländer for inspiration and fruitful discussions.

## References

Saima Aman and Stan Szpakowicz. 2007. Identifying expressions of emotion in text. In *Text, Speech and Dialogue*, pages 196–205, Berlin, Heidelberg. Springer Berlin Heidelberg.

Laura-Ana-Maria Bostan and Roman Klinger. 2018. An analysis of annotated corpora for emotion classification in text. In *Proceedings of the 27th International Conference on Computational Linguistics*, pages 2104–2119, Santa Fe, New Mexico, USA. Association for Computational Linguistics.

Sven Buechel and Udo Hahn. 2017. EmoBank: Studying the impact of annotation perspective and representation format on dimensional emotion analysis. In *Proceedings of the 15th Conference of the European Chapter of the Association for Computational Linguistics: Volume 2, Short Papers*, pages 578–585, Valencia, Spain. Association for Computational Linguistics.

Walter B. Cannon. 1929. *Bodily changes in pain, hunger, fear, and rage*. Appleton-Century, New York, US.

Deniz Cevher, Sebastian Zepf, and Roman Klinger. 2019. Towards multimodal emotion recognition in german speech events in cars using transfer learning. In *Proceedings of the 15th Conference on Natural Language Processing (KONVENS 2019): Long Papers*, pages 79–90, Erlangen, Germany. German Society for Computational Linguistics & Language Technology.

Jacob Cohen. 1960. A coefficient of agreement for nominal scales. *Educational and Psychological Measurement*, 20(1):37–46.

Alexis Conneau, Kartikay Khandelwal, Naman Goyal, Vishrav Chaudhary, Guillaume Wenzek, Francisco Guzmán, Edouard Grave, Myle Ott, Luke Zettlemoyer, and Veselin Stoyanov. 2020. Unsupervised cross-lingual representation learning at scale. In *Proceedings of the 58th Annual Meeting of the Association for Computational Linguistics*, pages 8440–8451, Online. Association for Computational Linguistics.

Dorottya Demszky, Dana Movshovitz-Attias, Jeongwoo Ko, Alan Cowen, Gaurav Nemade, and Sujith Ravi. 2020. GoEmotions: A dataset of fine-grained emotions. In *Proceedings of the 58th Annual Meeting of the Association for Computational Linguistics*, pages 4040–4054, Online. Association for Computational Linguistics.

Monique Dittrich and Sebastian Zepf. 2019. Exploring the validity of methods to track emotions behind the wheel. In *Persuasive Technology: Development of Persuasive and Behavior Change Support Systems*, pages 115–127, Cham. Springer International Publishing.

Paul Ekman. 1992. An argument for basic emotions. *Cognition & emotion*, 6(3-4):169–200.

Lisa Feldman Barrett. 2006. Solving the emotion paradox: categorization and the experience of emotion. *Personality and Social Psychology Review*, 10(1):20–46.

Lisa Feldman Barrett. 2017. *How Emotions Are Made*. Houghton Mifflin Harcourt, New York, USA.

Maria Gendron and Lisa Feldman Barrett. 2009. Reconstructing the past: A century of ideas about emotion in psychology. *Emotion review*, 1(4):316–339.

Thomas Haider, Steffen Eger, Evgeny Kim, Roman Klinger, and Winfried Menninghaus. 2020. PO-EMO: Conceptualization, annotation, and modeling of aesthetic emotions in German and English poetry. In *Proceedings of The 12th Language Resources and Evaluation Conference*, pages 1652–1663, Marseille, France. European Language Resources Association.

Nida Manzoor Hakak, Mohsin Mohd, Mahira Kirmani, and Mudasir Mohd. 2017. Emotion analysis: A survey. In *2017 International Conference on Computer, Communications and Electronics (Comptelix)*, pages 397–402.

Jan Hofmann, Enrica Troiano, Kai Sassenberg, and Roman Klinger. 2020. Appraisal theories for emotion classification in text.

Evgeny Kim and Roman Klinger. 2019. A survey on sentiment and emotion analysis for computational literary studies. *Zeitschrift fuer Digitale Geisteswissenschaften*, 4.

Yinhan Liu, Myle Ott, Naman Goyal, Jingfei Du, Mandar Joshi, Danqi Chen, Omer Levy, Mike Lewis, Luke Zettlemoyer, and Veselin Stoyanov. 2019. RoBERTa: A robustly optimized bert pretraining approach. *ArXiv*, abs/1907.11692.

Arun S. Maiya. 2020. ktrain: A low-code library for augmented machine learning.

Winfried Menninghaus, Valentin Wagner, Eugen Wassiliwizky, Ines Schindler, Julian Hanich, Thomas Jacobsen, and Stefan Koelsch. 2019. What are aesthetic emotions? *Psychological review*, 126(2):171.

Saif Mohammad. 2012. #emotional tweets. In **SEM 2012: The First Joint Conference on Lexical and Computational Semantics – Volume 1: Proceedings of the main conference and the shared task, and Volume 2: Proceedings of the Sixth International Workshop on Semantic Evaluation (SemEval 2012)*, pages 246–255, Montréal, Canada. Association for Computational Linguistics.

Saif Mohammad. 2018. Obtaining reliable human ratings of valence, arousal, and dominance for 20,000 English words. In *Proceedings of the 56th Annual Meeting of the Association for Computational Linguistics (Volume 1: Long Papers)*, pages 174–184, Melbourne, Australia. Association for Computational Linguistics.

Saif Mohammad, Svetlana Kiritchenko, and Xiaodan Zhu. 2013. NRC-canada: Building the state-of-the-art in sentiment analysis of tweets. In *Second Joint Conference on Lexical and Computational Semantics (*SEM), Volume 2: Proceedings of the Seventh International Workshop on Semantic Evaluation (SemEval 2013)*, pages 321–327, Atlanta, Georgia, USA. Association for Computational Linguistics.

Marcello Mortillaro, Ben Meuleman, and Klaus R. Scherer. 2012. Advocating a componential appraisal model to guide emotion recognition. *International Journal of Synthetic Emotions (IJSE)*, 3(1):18–32.

James W. Pennebaker, Martha E. Francis, and Roger J. Booth. 2001. Linguistic inquiry and word count: LIWC 2001. *Mahway: Lawrence Erlbaum Associates*, 71:2001.

Robert Plutchik. 2001. The nature of emotions. *American Scientist*, 89(4):344–350.

Daniel Preoţiuc-Pietro, H. Andrew Schwartz, Gregory Park, Johannes Eichstaedt, Margaret Kern, Lyle Ungar, and Elisabeth Shulman. 2016. Modelling valence and arousal in Facebook posts. In *Proceedings of the 7th Workshop on Computational Approaches to Subjectivity, Sentiment and Social Media Analysis*, pages 9–15, San Diego, California. Association for Computational Linguistics.

James A. Russell and Albert Mehrabian. 1977. Evidence for a three-factor theory of emotions. *Journal of research in Personality*, 11(3):273–294.

Klaus R. Scherer. 2000. Psychological models of emotion. In *The neuropsychology of emotion.*, Series in affective science., pages 137–162. Oxford University Press, New York, NY, US.

Klaus R Scherer. 2009a. The dynamic architecture of emotion: Evidence for the component process model. *Cognition and emotion*, 23(7):1307–1351.

Klaus R. Scherer. 2009b. Emotions are emergent processes: they require a dynamic computational architecture. *Philosophical transactions of the Royal Society of London. Series B, Biological sciences*, 364(1535):3459–3474. Publisher: The Royal Society.

Klaus R. Scherer, Angela Schorr, and Tom Johnstone. 2001. *Appraisal processes in emotion: Theory, methods, research.* Oxford University Press.

Klaus R. Scherer and Harald G. Wallbott. 1994. Evidence for universality and cultural variation of differential emotion response patterning. *Journal of personality and social psychology*, 66(2):310.

Ines Schindler, Georg Hosoya, Winfried Menninghaus, Ursula Beermann, Valentin Wagner, Michael Eid, and Klaus R. Scherer. 2017. Measuring aesthetic emotions: A review of the literature and a new assessment tool. *PloS one*, 12(6):e0178899.

Craig A. Smith and Phoebe C. Ellsworth. 1985. Patterns of cognitive appraisal in emotion. *Journal of Personality and Social Psychology*, 48(4):813–838.

Carlo Strapparava and Alessandro Valitutti. 2004. WordNet affect: an affective extension of WordNet. In *Proceedings of the Fourth International Conference on Language Resources and Evaluation (LREC'04)*, Lisbon, Portugal. European Language Resources Association (ELRA).

Enrica Troiano, Sebastian Padó, and Roman Klinger. 2019. Crowdsourcing and validating event-focused emotion corpora for German and English. In *Proceedings of the 57th Annual Meeting of the Association for Computational Linguistics*, pages 4005–4011, Florence, Italy. Association for Computational Linguistics.

Liang-Chih Yu, Lung-Hao Lee, Shuai Hao, Jin Wang, Yunchao He, Jun Hu, K. Robert Lai, and Xuejie Zhang. 2016. Building Chinese affective resources in valence-arousal dimensions. In *Proceedings of the 2016 Conference of the North American Chapter of the Association for Computational Linguistics: Human Language Technologies*, pages 540–545, San Diego, California. Association for Computational Linguistics.

# A Corpus Statistics for Manual Annotations of enISEAR

Table 9 shows the corpus statistics for the manually annotated corpora. In particular, it depicts how the availability of the emotion to the annotators influences the distribution of appraisal labels. The same numbers are also shown in a comparative manner in Figure 1. For most appraisal dimensions, the annotations are more specific, narrower, across the counts for emotions and mostly manifest in a lower number of those. An exception is *certainty*, which shows higher counts for all emotions, and *anticipated effort*, which receives higher counts for shame, sadness, fear, and guilt, but not for anger.

| | | Appraisal Dimension | | | | | | |
|---|---|---|---|---|---|---|---|---|
| | Emotion | Attention | Certainty | Effort | Pleasant | Respons. | Control | Circum. |
| enISEAR EmoVis | Anger | 141 | 143 | 17 | 0 | 4 | 1 | 3 |
| | Disgust | 13 | 143 | 65 | 0 | 14 | 8 | 11 |
| | Fear | 126 | 24 | 139 | 0 | 18 | 4 | 115 |
| | Guilt | 70 | 141 | 108 | 0 | 141 | 93 | 11 |
| | Joy | 143 | 143 | 0 | 143 | 43 | 21 | 18 |
| | Sadness | 120 | 141 | 136 | 0 | 4 | 2 | 132 |
| | Shame | 10 | 137 | 105 | 0 | 113 | 23 | 4 |
| | Total | 623 | 872 | 570 | 143 | 337 | 152 | 294 |
| enISEAR EmoHide | Anger | 130 | 113 | 60 | 0 | 8 | 1 | 11 |
| | Disgust | 58 | 129 | 35 | 1 | 16 | 7 | 35 |
| | Fear | 126 | 13 | 125 | 0 | 33 | 11 | 108 |
| | Guilt | 54 | 128 | 29 | 1 | 139 | 85 | 21 |
| | Joy | 134 | 125 | 4 | 139 | 55 | 46 | 56 |
| | Sadness | 121 | 105 | 69 | 1 | 10 | 3 | 119 |
| | Shame | 25 | 98 | 33 | 1 | 113 | 62 | 18 |
| | Total | 648 | 711 | 355 | 143 | 374 | 215 | 368 |

Table 9: Manual Annotation: Instance counts across emotions and appraisal annotations.

# Hate Towards the Political Opponent: A Twitter Corpus Study of the 2020 US Elections on the Basis of Offensive Speech and Stance Detection

**Lara Grimminger** and **Roman Klinger**
Institut für Maschinelle Sprachverarbeitung, University of Stuttgart
Pfaffenwaldring 5b, 70569 Stuttgart, Germany
{lara.grimminger,roman.klinger}@ims.uni-stuttgart.de

## Abstract

The 2020 US Elections have been, more than ever before, characterized by social media campaigns and mutual accusations. We investigate in this paper if this manifests also in online communication of the supporters of the candidates Biden and Trump, by uttering hateful and offensive communication. We formulate an annotation task, in which we join the tasks of hateful/offensive speech detection and stance detection, and annotate 3000 Tweets from the campaign period, if they express a particular stance towards a candidate. Next to the established classes of *favorable* and *against*, we add *mixed* and *neutral* stances and also annotate if a candidate is mentioned without an opinion expression. Further, we annotate if the tweet is written in an offensive style. This enables us to analyze if supporters of Joe Biden and the Democratic Party communicate differently than supporters of Donald Trump and the Republican Party. A BERT baseline classifier shows that the detection if somebody is a supporter of a candidate can be performed with high quality (.89 $F_1$ for Trump and .91 $F_1$ for Biden), while the detection that somebody expresses to be against a candidate is more challenging (.79 $F_1$ and .64 $F_1$, respectively). The automatic detection of hate/offensive speech remains challenging (with .53 $F_1$). Our corpus is publicly available and constitutes a novel resource for computational modelling of offensive language under consideration of stances.

## 1 Introduction

Social media are indispensable to political campaigns ever since Barack Obama used them so successfully in 2008 (Tumasjan et al., 2010). Twitter in particular is a much-frequented form of communication with monthly 330 million active users (Clement, 2019). The microblogging platform was credited to have played a key role in Donald Trump's rise to power (Stolee and Caton, 2018). As Twitter enables users to express their opinions about topics and targets, the insights gained from detecting stance in political tweets can help monitor the voting base.

In addition to the heated election of Trump in 2016, the world has also seen an increase of hate speech (Gao and Huang, 2017). Defined as "any communication that disparages a target group of people based on some characteristic such as race, colour, ethnicity, gender, sexual orientation, nationality, religion, or other characteristic" (Nockelby, 2000), hate speech is considered "a particular form of offensive language" (Warner and Hirschberg, 2012). However, some authors also conflate hateful and offensive speech and define hate speech as explicitly or implicitly degrading a person or group (Gao and Huang, 2017). Over the years, the use of hate speech in social media has increased (de Gibert et al., 2018). Consequently, there is a growing need for approaches that detect hate speech automatically (Gao and Huang, 2017).

From the perspective of natural language processing (NLP), the combination of political stance and hate speech detection provides promising classification tasks, namely determining the attitude a text displays towards a pre-determined target and the presence of hateful and offensive speech. In contrast to prior work on stance detection (Somasundaran and Wiebe, 2010; Mohammad et al., 2016, i.a.), we not only annotate if a text is *favorable*, *against* or does not mention the target at all (*neither*), but include whether the text of the tweet displays a *mixed* (both favorable and against) or *neutral* stance towards the targets. With this formulation we are also able to mark tweets that mention a target without taking a clear stance. To annotate hateful and offensive tweets, we follow the def-

This paper contains offensive language.



*Proceedings of the 11th Workshop on Computational Approaches to Subjectivity, Sentiment and Social Media Analysis*, pages 171–180
April 19, 2021. ©2021 Association for Computational Linguistics

inition of Gao and Huang (2017) and adapt our guidelines to political discourse.

Our contributions are the following:

- We publish a Twitter-corpus that is annotated both for stance and hate speech detection. We make this corpus of 3000 Tweets publicly available at https://www.ims.uni-stuttgart.de/data/stance_hof_us2020.

- Based on a manual analysis of these annotations, our results suggest that Tweets that express a stance against Biden contain more hate speech than those against Trump.

- Our baseline classification experiments show that the detection of the stance that somebody is in-favor of a candidate performs better than that somebody is against a candidate. Further, the detection of hate/offensive speech on this corpus remains challenging.

## 2 Related Work

### 2.1 Hate Speech and Offensive Language

In early work on hate speech detection, Spertus (1997) described various approaches to detect abusive and hostile messages occurring during online communication. More recent work also considered cyberbullying (Dinakar et al., 2012) and focused on the use of stereotypes in harmful messages (Warner and Hirschberg, 2012). Most of the existing hate speech detection models are supervised learning approaches. Davidson et al. (2017) created a data set by collecting tweets that contained hate speech keywords from a crowd-sourced hate speech lexicon. They then categorized these tweets into hate speech, offensive language, and neither. Mandl et al. (2019) sampled their data from Twitter and partially from Facebook and experimented with binary as well as more fine-grained multi-class classifications. Their results suggest that systems based on deep neural networks performed best.

Waseem and Hovy (2016) used a feature-based approach to explore several feature types. Burnap and Williams (2014) collected hateful tweets related to the murder of Drummer Lee Rigby in 2013. The authors examined different classification methods with various features including n-grams, restricted n-grams, typed dependencies, and hateful terms. Schmidt and Wiegand (2017) outlined that the lack of a benchmark data set based on a commonly accepted definition of hate speech is challenging. Roß et al. (2016) found that there is low agreement among users when identifying hateful messages.

For the SemEval 2019 Task 5, Basile et al. (2019) proposed two hate speech detection tasks on Spanish and English tweets which contained hateful messages against women and immigrants. Next to a binary classification, participating systems had to extract further features in harmful messages such as target identification. None of the submissions for the more fine-grained classification task in English could outperform the baseline of the task organizers. In case of Spanish, the best results were achieved by a linear-kernel SVM. The authors found that it was harder to detect further features than the presence of hate speech. The recent shared task on offensive language identification organized by Zampieri et al. (2020) was featured in five languages. For a more detailed overview, we refer to the surveys by Mladenović et al. (2021); Fortuna and Nunes (2018); Schmidt and Wiegand (2017).

In contrast to this previous work, we provide data for a specific recent use case, and predefine two targets of interest to be analyzed.

### 2.2 Stance Detection

Related work on stance detection includes stance detection on congressional debates (Thomas et al., 2006), online forums (Somasundaran and Wiebe, 2010), Twitter (Mohammad et al., 2016, 2017; Aker et al., 2017; Küçük and Can, 2018; Lozhnikov et al., 2020) and comments on news (Lozhnikov et al., 2020). Thomas et al. (2006) used a corpus of speeches from the US Congress and modeled their support/oppose towards a proposed legislation task. Somasundaran and Wiebe (2010) conducted experiments with sentiment and arguing expressions and used features based on modal verbs and sentiments for stance classification. For the SemEval 2016 Task 6 organized by Mohammad et al. (2016), stance was detected from tweets. The task contained two stance detection subtasks for supervised and weakly supervised settings. In both classification tasks, tweet-target pairs needed to be classified as either Favor, Against or Neither. The baseline of the task organizers outperformed all systems' results that were submitted by task participants.

In hope that sentiment features would have the same effect on stance detection as they have on sentiment prediction, Mohammad et al. (2017) concurrently annotated a set of tweets for both stance and sentiment. Although sentiment labels proved to be beneficial for stance detection, they were not sufficient. Instead of a target-specific stance classification, Aker et al. (2017) described an open stance classification approach to identify rumors on Twitter. The authors experimented with different classifiers and task-specific features which measured the level of confidence in a tweet. With the additional features, their approach outperformed state-of-the-art results on two benchmark sets.

In addition to this previous work, we opted for a more fine-grained stance detection and not only annotated *favor*, *against* and *neither* towards a target but also whether the stance of the text was *mixed* or *neutral*. Further, we combine stance detection with hate/offensive speech detection.

## 3 Corpus

### 3.1 Data Collection

Our goal is on the one side to create a new Twitter data set that combines stance and hate/offensive speech detection in the political domain. On the other side, we create this corpus to investigate the question how hate/offensive speech is distributed among different stances.

We used the Twitter API v 1.1. to fetch tweets for 6 weeks leading to the presidential election, on the election day and for 1 week after the election. As search terms, we use the mention of the presidential and vice presidential candidates and the outsider West; the mention of hashtags that show a voter's alignment such as the campaign slogans of the candidate websites, and further nicknames of the candidates. The list of search terms is: #Trump2020, #TrumpPence2020, #Biden2020, #BidenHarris2020, #Kanye2020, #MAGA2020, #BattleForTheSoulOfTheNation, #2020Vision, #VoteRed2020, #VoteBlue2020, Trump, Pence, Biden, Harris, Kanye, President, Sleepy Joe, Slow Joe, Phony Kamala, Monster Kamala.

After removing duplicate tweets, the final corpus consists of 382.210 tweets. From these, there are 220.941 that contain Trump related hashtags and mentions, 230.629 tweets that carry hashtags and mentions associated with Biden and 1.412 tweets with hashtags and mentions related to Kanye West.

| | Stance | | | |
|---|---|---|---|---|
| Iteration | Trump | Biden | West | HOF |
| 1 A1+A2 | 0.83 | 0.81 | 0.00 | −0.02 |
| 2 A1+A2 | 0.78 | 0.78 | 0.75 | 0.42 |
| 3 A1+A2 | 0.81 | 0.88 | 0.00 | 0.73 |
| 4 A2+A3 | 0.61 | 0.76 | 0.75 | 0.62 |

Table 1: Cohen's $\kappa$ for stance and hate/offensive speech (HOF).

### 3.2 Annotation

#### 3.2.1 Annotation Task

From the 382.210 tweets, we sampled 3000 tweets for annotation. Given the text of a tweet, we rated the stance towards the targets Trump, Biden, and West in the text. The detected stance can be from one of the following labels:

- *Favor*: Text argues in favor of the target
- *Against*: Text argues against the target
- *Neither*: Target is not mentioned; neither implicitly nor explicitly
- *Mixed*: Text mentions positive as well as negative aspects about the target
- *Neutral*: Text states facts or recites quotes; unclear, whether text holds any position towards the target.

The default value shown in the annotation environment is *Neither*.

The text was further annotated as being hateful and non-hateful. We did not separate if a group or a single person was targeted by hateful language. Further, we adapted the guidelines on hate speech annotation to be able to react to name-calling and down talking of the political opponent. Thus, we rated expressions such as "Dementia Joe" and "DonTheCon" as hateful/offensive (HOF).

#### 3.2.2 Annotation Procedure

To evaluate the annotation guidelines (which we make available together with the data) we perform multiple annotation iterations with three annotators. Annotator 1 is a 22 year old male undergraduate student of computational linguistics who speaks German, English, Catalan, and Spanish. Annotator 2 is a 26 year old female undergraduate student of computational linguistics who speaks German

| Class | HOF | ¬HOF | $\sum$ | %HOF |
|---|---|---|---|---|
| Favor | 101 | 679 | 780 | 12.9 |
| Against | 156 | 686 | 842 | 18.5 |
| Neither | 76 | 941 | 1017 | 7.5 |
| Mixed | 1 | 19 | 20 | 5.0 |
| Neutral | 18 | 323 | 341 | 5.3 |
| Total | 352 | 2648 | 3000 | 11.7 |

Table 2: Distribution of tweets about target Trump

| Class | HOF | ¬HOF | $\sum$ | %HOF |
|---|---|---|---|---|
| Favor | 141 | 1095 | 1236 | 11.4 |
| Against | 108 | 296 | 404 | 26.7 |
| Neither | 87 | 900 | 987 | 8.8 |
| Mixed | 6 | 41 | 47 | 12.8 |
| Neutral | 10 | 316 | 326 | 3.1 |
| Total | 352 | 2648 | 3000 | 11.7 |

Table 3: Distribution of tweets about target Biden

and English. Annotator 3 is a 29 year old female graduate student of computational linguistics who speaks German and English. Annotator 1 and 2 annotated 300 tweets in three iterations with 100 tweets per iteration. After each iteration, the annotators discussed the tweets they rated differently and complemented the existing guidelines. Finally, Annotator 2 and 3 annotated 100 tweets with the improved guidelines to check whether the rules are clear and understandable, especially if read for the first time.

Table 1 shows the result of Cohen's $\kappa$ of each iteration. In the first iteration, the agreement for HOF is purely random ($-0.02\kappa$), the stance annotations show acceptable agreement ($.83$, $.81\kappa$, respectively for Trump and Biden). West has not been mentioned in any of the 100 tweets. In a group discussion to identify the reasons for the substantial lack of agreement for HOF, we developed guidelines which described hateful and offensive speech in more detail and added further examples to our guidelines. We particularly stressed to annotate name-calling as hateful and offensive. This showed success in a second iteration with $.42\kappa$ for HOF agreement. The scores for Trump and Biden decreased slightly but still represented substantial agreement. We carried out another group discussion to discuss tweets where Annotator 1 and 2 chose different classes. We particularly refined the guidelines for class *Neutral mentions* and included offensive and hateful abbreviations such as "POS" ("piece of shit") and "BS" ("bullshit") which have been missed before. This led to a HOF agreement of $.73\kappa$, while the stance agreement remained on similar levels (.81, .88).

As a concluding step, Annotator 2 and 3 rated 100 tweets. The annotators were provided with the guidelines established during the iterations between Annotator 1 and 2. Table 1 shows that the inter-annotator agreement for HOF is 0.62, for target Trump 0.61, for target Biden 0.76 and for target West 0.75. These scores indicate substantial agreement between Annotator 2 and 3 based on comprehensive guidelines. The final annotation of the overall data set has been performed by Annotator 2.

## 4 Results

### 4.1 Corpus Statistics

We now analyze the corpus for the targets Trump and Biden to answer the question if supporters of Trump (and Pence) use more hateful and offensive speech than supporters of Biden (and Harris). Tables 2 and 3 show the distribution of the classes *Favor, Against, Neither, Mixed, Neutral mentions* and how often each class was labeled as HOF or Non-HOF (¬HOF).

The data set is unbalanced: only 11.7% of the tweets are hateful/offensive. Furthermore, there are more tweets labeled as *Favor, Against*, and *Neither* than *Mixed*, or *Neutral mentions* for target Trump. In case of target Biden, more tweets are labeled as *Favor* and as *Neither* than as *Against, Mixed*, or *Neutral mentions*. In total, there were only 9 tweets about Kanye West in the annotated data set, which is why we do not present statistics about him.

**Did Trump supporters use more hateful and offensive speech than supporters of Biden?** A comparison of Tables 2 and 3 suggests that supporters of team Trump use slightly more often harmful and offensive speech with 12.9% than supporters of team Biden, with 11.4%. This indicates that Trump supporters use more hateful speech than supporters of Biden, yet, this difference is only minor. This is arguable a result of the aspect that HOF is also often expressed without naming the target explicitly. Furthermore, given the fact that we added offensive nicknames such as "Sleepy Joe" to our search terms, this result is biased.

By means of pointwise mutual information we identified the top 10 words that are unlikely to

| HOF | Against Trump | Against Biden |
|---|---|---|
| fuck | #biden2020 | #trump2020 |
| disgusting | #bidenharris2020 | @seanhannity |
| idiots | #trumptaxreturns | hunter |
| bitch | taxes | creepy |
| fat | #vote | top |
| bullshit | very | sleepy |
| vs | gop | radical |
| idiot | pence | evidence |
| #covidiot | vote. | leading |
| sleepy | thinks | across |

Table 4: Results of the pointwise mutual information calculation

| | Target Trump | | | Target Biden | | |
|---|---|---|---|---|---|---|
| Class | P | R | $F_1$ | P | R | $F_1$ |
| Against | .77 | .81 | .79 | .67 | .62 | .64 |
| Favor | .88 | .90 | .89 | .90 | .93 | .91 |
| Mixed | .00 | .00 | .00 | .00 | .00 | .00 |
| Neither | .95 | .95 | .95 | .93 | .99 | .96 |
| Neutral | .58 | .49 | .53 | .59 | .58 | .59 |

Table 5: Precision, Recall, and $F_1$ of stance detection baseline for targets Trump and Biden

occur in a tweet labeled as Non-Hateful. As Table 4 shows, these words are offensive and promote hate. This list also mirrors the limitations of our search terms as the adjective "sleepy" is part of the top 10.

Likewise, we identified the top 10 words that are unlikely to appear in a tweet labeled as *Favor* towards Trump and thus, argue against him. Next to hashtags that express a political preference for Biden, the top 10 list contains words that refer to Trump's taxes and a demand to vote. Similarly, the top 10 words that are unlikely to occur in a tweet labeled as *Favor*ing Biden and therefore express the stance *Against* him, consist of adjectives Trump mocked him with (creepy, sleepy) as well as a reference to his son Hunter.

**Who is more targeted by hateful and offensive speech, Biden and the Democratic party or Trump and the Republican Party?** We note that 26.7% of the tweets against target Biden contain hateful/offensive language, whereas only 18.5% of the tweets against target Trump are hateful/offensive. Thus, our results suggest that Biden and the Democratic Party are more often targets of hateful and offensive tweets than Trump and the Republican Party.

However, from this analysis we cannot draw that the offensive stems from supporters of the other party. Due to the limitations in our search terms we also note that there might be an unknown correlation of the search terms to HOF which we cannot entirely avoid. Further, these results should be interpreted with a grain of salt, given that the sampling procedure of the Twitter API is not entirely transparent.

### 4.2 Stance Classification Experiments

Next to the goal to better understand the distribution of hate/offensive speech during the election in 2020, the data set constitutes an interesting resource valuable for the development of automatic detection systems. To support such development, we provide results of a baseline classifier. We used the pretrained BERT base model[1] (Devlin et al., 2019) and its TensorFlow implementation provided by HuggingFace[2] (Wolf et al., 2020). Our data set was divided into 80% for training and 20% for testing.

Each model was trained with a batch size of 16, a learning rate (Adam) of $5 \cdot 10^{-5}$, a decay of 0.01, a maximal sentence length of 100 and a validation split of 0.2. Further, we set the number of epochs to 10 and saved the best model on the validation set for testing.

Table 5 shows the results for stance detection prediction. We observe that not all classes can be predicted equally well. The two best predicted classes for Trump are *Neither* and *Favor* with a $F_1$ score of 0.95 and 0.89, respectively. These scores are followed by class *Against* with a $F_1$ score of 0.79. However, our model had difficulties to correctly predict the class *Neutral*, with a more limited precision and recall (.58 and .49). The class *Mixed* could not be predicted at all.

These results only partially resemble for the target Biden: The classes *Neither* and *Favor* have the highest $F_1$ score with 0.96 and 0.91, respectively. In contrast to target Trump, the performance of our model to predict the class *Against* is much lower (.64 $F_1$). The $F_1$ score of class *Neutral* is low again with .59 and class *Mixed* could not be predicted. We conclude that stance can be detected from tweets. Yet, our results suggest that it

[1]https://huggingface.co/bert-base-uncased

[2]https://github.com/huggingface/transformers

| Train data | | Class | Davidson P | Davidson R | Davidson $F_1$ | Mandl P | Mandl R | Mandl $F_1$ | Ours P | Ours R | Ours $F_1$ |
|---|---|---|---|---|---|---|---|---|---|---|---|
| | | | **Test data** | | | | | | | | |
| Davidson | | HOF | .98 | .98 | .98 | .34 | .55 | .42 | .08 | .75 | .14 |
| Davidson | | Non-HOF | .89 | .88 | .88 | .48 | .28 | .36 | .71 | .07 | .12 |
| Mandl | | HOF | .61 | .24 | .35 | .66 | .48 | .56 | .20 | .53 | .29 |
| Mandl | | Non-HOF | .06 | .22 | .09 | .70 | .83 | .76 | .94 | .77 | .85 |
| Ours | | HOF | .52 | .16 | .25 | .52 | .60 | .56 | .52 | .54 | .53 |
| Ours | | Non-HOF | .06 | .25 | .09 | .70 | .62 | .66 | .95 | .94 | .95 |

Table 6: F1 scores of the hate speech detection baseline model trained and tested on different corpora

is more challenging to predict fine-grained stance classes such as *Mixed* and *Neutral mentions* than the classes *Favor, Against* and *Neither*. This result is, at least partially, a consequence of the data distribution. The *Mixed* label has very few instances (20+47); the *Neutral* label is the second most seldomly annotated class, though it is substantially more frequent (341+326).

### 4.3 Cross-Corpus Hate Speech Detection Experiments

Similar to the stance detection baseline results, we now report results of a classifier (configured the same as the one in Section 4.2). To obtain an understanding how challenging the prediction is on our corpus, and how different the concept of hate/offensive speech is from existing resources, we perform this analysis across a set of corpora, as well as inside of each corpus.

To that end, we chose the following hate speech/offensive speech corpora:

1. Data Set 1 by Davidson et al. (2017).
   This corpus contains 24.783 tweets, categorized into into hateful, offensive, and neither. In our study, we we only use two classes, hateful/offensive and non-hateful. Therefore, we conflate the two classes, hateful and offensive, into one. We randomly split their data, available at https://github.com/t-davidson/hate-speech-and-offensive-language, into 80% for training and 20% for testing.

2. Data Set 2 by Mandl et al. (2019).
   In this study, the authors conducted three classification experiments including a binary one, where 5.852 posts from Twitter and Facebook were classified into hate speech and non-offensive (Sub-task A). From their multi-lingual resource, we only need the English subset. We use the training data available at https://hasocfire.github.io/hasoc/2019/dataset.html and perform a 80/20% train/test split.

Table 6 shows the results for all combinations of training on the data by Davidson et al. (2017), Mandl et al. (2019), and ours (presented in this paper). When we only look at the results of the model when trained and tested on subcorpora from the same original source, we observe that there are some noteworthy differences. The recognition of HOF on the data by Davidson et al. (2017) shows a high .98 $F_1$ (note that this result cannot be compared to their original results, because we conflate two classes). Training and testing our baseline model on the data by Mandl et al. (2019) shows .56 $F_1$ but with a particularly limited recall. On our corpus, given that it is the smallest one, the model performs still comparably well with .53 $F_1$. Precision and recall values are more balanced for the other corpora than for Mandl et al. (2019). Note that these results are comparably low in comparison to other previously published classification approaches. However, they allow for a comparison of the performances between the different corpora. We particularly observe that the data set size seems to have an impact on the predictive performance.

When we move to a comparison of models trained on one corpus and tested on another, we see that the subcorpora created for a binary classifica-

| Target | Pred | Gold | Text |
|---|---|---|---|
| Trump | A | A | TWO HUNDRED THOUSAND PEOPLE HAVE DIED OF #COVID19 UNDER Trump's WATCH. IT DID NOT HAVE TO BE LIKE THIS. #BidenHarris2020 will take steps to make us safe. Trump is happy to let us burn, and so he is a #weakloser #VoteBidenHarrisToSaveAmerica #RepublicansForBiden |
| Trump | F | F | Trump is making all types of economic/peace deals. While Democrats are creating mobs tearing down historical statutes and destroying WHOLE cities. It is a NO brainer on who to vote for in 2020. Trump builds! Democrats DESTROY! #Trump2020. #Trump2020LandslideVictory |
| Trump | A | F | President Trump please don't let this son of a bitch crazy creepy pedophile motherfucker of Joe Biden and his brown paper bag bitch of Kamala Harris win this election do not let them win. |
| Trump | F | A | #Trump2020? Wish full recovery to see him ask forgiveness to the country for his incompetence and lack of respect for the American people during Covid-19 crisis.#VictoryRoad to #Biden/Harris |
| Biden | A | A | Joe Biden is a weak weak man in many ways. Jimmy Carter by half. 1/2 of America literally can't stand Kamala today. Women will hate on her viciously. Enjoy the shit sandwich. |
| Biden | F | F | Kamala was my first choice, but I agree at this moment in time. Joe Biden is the right choice. We are lucky that he is willing to continue to serve our country. When I voted for Biden/Harris I felt good, I felt hopeful, I know this is the right team to recover our country/democracy |
| Biden | A | F | @KamalaHarris @JoeBiden Dominate and Annihilate trump, Joe aka 46 #BidenHarris2020 #WinningTeam #PresidentialDebate #TrumpTaxReturns #TrumpHatesOurMilitary #TrumpKnew #TrumpLiedPeopleDied GO JOE |
| Biden | F | A | While we are here, this type of BS is what Kamala Harris and Joe Biden call "science". |

Table 7: Examples of correct and incorrect predictions of favor (F) and against (A) stance in the tweets.

tion experiment yield better results. The imbalance of labels caused by the conflation of two classes on the data by Davidson et al. (2017) led to weak predictions on the other subcorpora.

Therefore, we conclude that the concept of hate/offensive speech between these different resources is not fully comparable, be it due to different instances, settings or annotators. The development of models that generalize across domains, corpora, and annotation guidelines is challenging.

### 4.4 Analysis

We now take a closer look at the tweets and their predicted classes to explore why tweets have been misclassified. We show examples in Table 7 for stance classification.

Our model performed well when predicting the class *Favor* for both targets. The examples in Table 7 show a common pattern, namely that tweets being in favor of the respective target praise target's achievements and contain words of support such as *builds, vote* and *right choice*. Additionally, users often complement their tweets with target-related hashtags, including *Trump2020, Trump2020LandslideVictory* and *Biden/Harris* to stress their political preference. However, these hashtags can be misleading as they not always express support of the candidate. The 4th example contains the hashtag *#Trump2020* and was therefore predicted to be in favor of Trump, while it actually argues against him. In the 5th example, the irony expressed by the quotation marks placed around the word *science* and the offensive expression *BS* for "bullshit" were not detected.

Supporters of both candidates verbally attack each other over who to vote for and use hashtags and expressions to make the opposite side look poorly. Looking at tweets incorrectly labeled as *Against*, we see that in case of target Trump the string of insults addressing Biden and Harris possi-

| Pred | Gold | Text |
|---|---|---|
| HOF | HOF | Two Kamala Harris staffers have covid-19. Let's hope at least one of them has been recently sniffed by Creepy Joe. |
| HOF | ¬HOF | He's a badass!!! #Trump2020 #Suckit #Winning |
| ¬HOF | HOF | The democrats are literally the nazis. If they pack the courts and pass the 25th amendment Joe Biden and Kamala Harris will be in the exact same place that hindenburg and hitler were in. The 25th amendment is almost the same exact law hitler got passed in order to take power. |

Table 8: Examples of correct and incorrect predictions for hateful and offensive speech in the tweets.

bly confused our baseline and led to a misclassification of the tweet. Turning to Biden, the sentence *Joe aka 46* was not detected to be positive and supportive.

We also show a set of examples for hate/offensive speech detection in Table 8. As the first tweet exemplifies, tweets correctly predicted as HOF often contain one or more hate and offensive key words, e.g. *Creepy Joe.* The first example also wishes Joe Biden to fall ill with Covid-19.

However, although the 2nd example seems to contain offensive words such as *"badass"* and *"Suckit"*, it is not meant in a hateful way. On the contrary, this tweet uses slang to express admiration and support.

The 3rd example clearly is hateful, comparing the Democratic Party to the Nazis and the position of Biden and Harris to Hindenburg and Hitler. However, apparently the word Nazis is not sufficient to communicate hate speech, while the other signals in this tweet are presumably infrequent in the corpus as well. These are interesting examples which show that hate/offensive speech detection requires at times world knowledge and common-sense reasoning (which BERT is arguable only capable of to a very limited extent).

### 4.5 Discussion

The results in Table 5 show that the disproportion among the classes *Against, Favor, Neither, Mixed* and *Neutral mentions* seen in Tables 2 and 3 are presumably influencing the performance. The classes *Mixed* and *Neutral mentions* contain less tweets than the other classes. Consequently, the model did not have the same amount of training data for these two classes and tweets that should be categorized as *Neither* or *Neutral* were misclassified. In addition to *Mixed* and *Neutral mentions*, the class *Against* of target Biden is also outweighed by the dominant classes *Favor* and *Neither* (see Table 3).

When looking at the distribution of hateful and offensive and non-hateful tweets, we see that our data set contains more non-hateful tweets. As a result, the classification is biased. While Davidson et al. (2017) created their data set with keywords from a hate speech lexicon and Mandl et al. (2019) sampled their data with hashtags and keywords for which hate speech can be expected, our data was collected by using, but not limited to, offensive and hateful mentions. Thus, our hate speech data is more imbalanced but provides interesting insights into how people talk politics on Twitter. We assume that our corpus exhibits a more realistic distribution of hate/offensive speech for a particular topic than a subset of already existing resources.

There may be some possible limitations in this study. Using Twitter as data source provides challenges, because tweets contain noise, spelling mistakes and incomplete sentences. Further, the specified search criteria mentioned above might have had an effect on the results. Next to the nicknames Trump uses for his opponents, most of the keywords used to collect tweets refer to political candidates. Mentions of the respective political parties such as "Democrats", "Republicans" etc. were not included in the search. Yet, during the annotation we realized that it was not possible to differentiate the candidates from their respective parties. Hence, tweets were annotated for political parties and candidates inferring from hashtags such as "#VoteBlue2020" that the tweeter argues in favor of Joe Biden.

## 5 Conclusion and Future Work

In this paper, we have investigated stance detection on political tweets and whether or not supporters of Trump use more hate speech than supporters of Biden (not significantly). We found that manual annotation is possible with acceptable agreement scores, and that automatic stance detection towards political candidates and parties is possible with good performance.

The limitations of this study are twofold – on the one side, future work might want to consider to add the nicknames of all main candidates and explicitly include social media posts about the party, not only about the candidate, as we found a separation is often difficult. Further, we did not perform extensive hyperparameter optimization in our neural approach.

We suggest that future work invests in developing computational models that work across corpora and are able to adapt to domain and time-specific as well as societal and situational expressions of hate and offensive language. This is required, as our corpus shows that some references to offensive content are realized by domain-specific and societal expressions.

This might be realized by combining offensive language detection and stance detection in a joint multi-task learning approach, potentially including other aspects like personality traits or specific emotions. We assume that such concepts can benefit from representations in joint models.

## Acknowledgements

This project has been partially funded by Deutsche Forschungsgemeinschaft (projects SEAT, KL 2869/1-1 and CEAT, KL 2869/1-2). We thank Anne Kreuter and Miquel Luján for fruitful discussions.

## References

Ahmet Aker, Leon Derczynski, and Kalina Bontcheva. 2017. Simple open stance classification for rumour analysis. In *Proceedings of the International Conference Recent Advances in Natural Language Processing, RANLP 2017*, pages 31–39, Varna, Bulgaria.

Valerio Basile, Cristina Bosco, Elisabetta Fersini, Debora Nozza, Viviana Patti, Francisco Manuel Rangel Pardo, Paolo Rosso, and Manuela Sanguinetti. 2019. SemEval-2019 task 5: Multilingual detection of hate speech against immigrants and women in Twitter. In *Proceedings of the 13th International Workshop on Semantic Evaluation*, pages 54–63, Minneapolis, Minnesota, USA. Association for Computational Linguistics.

Peter Burnap and Matthew Williams. 2014. Hate speech, machine classification and statistical modelling of information flows on twitter: interpretation and communication for policy decision making. In *Internet, Policy and Politics*, Oxford, United Kingdom.

Jessica Clement. 2019. Twitter: monthly active users worldwide. https://www.statista.com/statistics/282087/number-of-monthly-active-twitter-users/.

Thomas Davidson, Dana Warmsley, Michael W. Macy, and Ingmar Weber. 2017. Automated hate speech detection and the problem of offensive language. In *Proceedings of the Eleventh International Conference on Web and Social Media, ICWSM*, pages 512–515, Montréal, Québec, Canada. AAAI Press.

Jacob Devlin, Ming-Wei Chang, Kenton Lee, and Kristina Toutanova. 2019. BERT: Pre-training of deep bidirectional transformers for language understanding. In *Proceedings of the 2019 Conference of the North American Chapter of the Association for Computational Linguistics: Human Language Technologies, Volume 1 (Long and Short Papers)*, pages 4171–4186, Minneapolis, Minnesota. Association for Computational Linguistics.

Karthik Dinakar, Birago Jones, Catherine Havasi, Henry Lieberman, and Rosalind Picard. 2012. Common sense reasoning for detection, prevention, and mitigation of cyberbullying. *ACM Trans. Interact. Intell. Syst.*, 2(3).

Paula Fortuna and Sérgio Nunes. 2018. A survey on automatic detection of hate speech in text. *ACM Comput. Surv.*, 51(4).

Lei Gao and Ruihong Huang. 2017. Detecting online hate speech using context aware models. In *Proceedings of the International Conference Recent Advances in Natural Language Processing, RANLP 2017*, pages 260–266, Varna, Bulgaria. INCOMA Ltd.

Ona de Gibert, Naiara Perez, Aitor García-Pablos, and Montse Cuadros. 2018. Hate speech dataset from a white supremacy forum. In *Proceedings of the 2nd Workshop on Abusive Language Online (ALW2)*, pages 11–20, Brussels, Belgium. Association for Computational Linguistics.

Dilek Küçük and Fazli Can. 2018. Stance detection on tweets: An SVM-based approach. *CoRR*, abs/1803.08910.

Nikita Lozhnikov, Leon Derczynski, and Manuel Mazzara. 2020. Stance prediction for russian: Data and analysis. In *Proceedings of 6th International Conference in Software Engineering for Defence Applications*, pages 176–186, Cham. Springer International Publishing.

Thomas Mandl, Sandip Modha, Prasenjit Majumder, Daksh Patel, Mohana Dave, Chintak Mandlia, and Aditya Patel. 2019. Overview of the HASOC track at FIRE 2019: Hate speech and offensive content identification in indo-european languages. In *Proceedings of the 11th Forum for Information Retrieval Evaluation*, FIRE '19, page 14–17, New

York, NY, USA. Association for Computing Machinery.

Miljana Mladenović, Vera Ošmjanski, and Staša Vujičić Stanković. 2021. Cyber-aggression, cyberbullying, and cyber-grooming: A survey and research challenges. *ACM Comput. Surv.*, 54(1).

Saif Mohammad, Svetlana Kiritchenko, Parinaz Sobhani, Xiaodan Zhu, and Colin Cherry. 2016. SemEval-2016 task 6: Detecting stance in tweets. In *Proceedings of the 10th International Workshop on Semantic Evaluation (SemEval-2016)*, pages 31–41, San Diego, California. Association for Computational Linguistics.

Saif M. Mohammad, Parinaz Sobhani, and Svetlana Kiritchenko. 2017. Stance and sentiment in tweets. *ACM Trans. Internet Technol.*, 17(3).

John T. Nockelby. 2000. Hate speech. *Encyclopedia of the American Constitution*, 3:1277–1279.

Björn Roß, Michael Rist, Guillermo Carbonell, Benjamin Cabrera, Nils Kurowsky, and Michael Maximilian Wojatzki. 2016. Measuring the reliability of hate speech annotations: The case of the european refugee crisis. https://duepublico2.uni-due.de/receive/duepublico_mods_00042132.

Anna Schmidt and Michael Wiegand. 2017. A survey on hate speech detection using natural language processing. In *Proceedings of the Fifth International Workshop on Natural Language Processing for Social Media*, pages 1–10, Valencia, Spain. Association for Computational Linguistics.

Swapna Somasundaran and Janyce Wiebe. 2010. Recognizing stances in ideological on-line debates. In *Proceedings of the NAACL HLT 2010 Workshop on Computational Approaches to Analysis and Generation of Emotion in Text*, pages 116–124, Los Angeles, CA. Association for Computational Linguistics.

Ellen Spertus. 1997. Smokey: Automatic recognition of hostile messages. In *Proceedings of the Fourteenth National Conference on Artificial Intelligence and Ninth Conference on Innovative Applications of Artificial Intelligence*, AAAI'97/IAAI'97, page 1058–1065. AAAI Press.

Galen Stolee and Steve Caton. 2018. Twitter, trump, and the base: A shift to a new form of presidential talk? *Signs and Society*, 6:147–165.

Matt Thomas, Bo Pang, and Lillian Lee. 2006. Get out the vote: Determining support or opposition from congressional floor-debate transcripts. In *Proceedings of the 2006 Conference on Empirical Methods in Natural Language Processing*, pages 327–335, Sydney, Australia. Association for Computational Linguistics.

Andranik Tumasjan, Timm Sprenger, Philipp Sandner, and Isabell Welpe. 2010. Predicting elections with twitter: What 140 characters reveal about political sentiment. In *Fourth International AAAI Conference on Weblogs and Social Media*, pages 178–185.

William Warner and Julia Hirschberg. 2012. Detecting hate speech on the world wide web. In *Proceedings of the Second Workshop on Language in Social Media*, pages 19–26, Montréal, Canada. Association for Computational Linguistics.

Zeerak Waseem and Dirk Hovy. 2016. Hateful symbols or hateful people? predictive features for hate speech detection on Twitter. In *Proceedings of the NAACL Student Research Workshop*, pages 88–93, San Diego, California. Association for Computational Linguistics.

Thomas Wolf, Lysandre Debut, Victor Sanh, Julien Chaumond, Clement Delangue, Anthony Moi, Pierric Cistac, Tim Rault, Rémi Louf, Morgan Funtowicz, Joe Davison, Sam Shleifer, Patrick von Platen, Clara Ma, Yacine Jernite, Julien Plu, Canwen Xu, Teven Le Scao, Sylvain Gugger, Mariama Drame, Quentin Lhoest, and Alexander M. Rush. 2020. Transformers: State-of-the-art natural language processing. In *Proceedings of the 2020 Conference on Empirical Methods in Natural Language Processing: System Demonstrations*, pages 38–45, Online. Association for Computational Linguistics.

Marcos Zampieri, Preslav Nakov, Sara Rosenthal, Pepa Atanasova, Georgi Karadzhov, Hamdy Mubarak, Leon Derczynski, Zeses Pitenis, and Çağrı Çöltekin. 2020. SemEval-2020 task 12: Multilingual offensive language identification in social media (OffensEval 2020). In *Proceedings of the Fourteenth Workshop on Semantic Evaluation*, pages 1425–1447, Barcelona (online). International Committee for Computational Linguistics.

# Synthetic Examples Improve Cross-Target Generalization: A Study on Stance Detection on a Twitter Corpus

**Costanza Conforti[1], Jakob Berndt[2], Mohammad Taher Pilehvar[1,3], Chryssi Giannitsarou[2], Flavio Toxvaerd[2], Nigel Collier[1]**

[1] Language Technology Lab, University of Cambridge
[2] Faculty of Economics, University of Cambridge
[3] Tehran Institute for Advanced Studies, Iran

{cc918, jb2088}@cam.ac.uk

## Abstract

Cross-target generalization is a known problem in stance detection (SD), where systems tend to perform poorly when exposed to targets unseen during training. Given that data annotation is expensive and time-consuming, finding ways to leverage abundant unlabeled in-domain data can offer great benefits. In this paper, we apply a weakly supervised framework to enhance cross-target generalization through synthetically annotated data. We focus on Twitter SD and show experimentally that integrating synthetic data is helpful for cross-target generalization, leading to significant improvements in performance, with gains in $F_1$ scores ranging from $+3.4$ to $+5.1$.

## 1 Introduction

Stance Detection (SD) is a widely investigated task (Mohammad et al., 2017), which constitutes an important component of many complex NLP problems, ranging from fake news detection to rumour verification (Vlachos and Riedel, 2014; Baly et al., 2018; Zubiaga et al., 2018b). Since from early works (Agrawal et al.), research on SD focused on user-generated content, ranging from blogs and commenting sections on websites (Hercig et al.), to Reddit or Facebook posts (Klenner et al.) and, above all, Twitter data (Inkpen et al., 2017; Zubiaga et al., 2018a).

Recently, Conforti et al. (2020) released Will-They-Won't-They (WT–WT), a very large corpus of stance-annotated tweets discussing five US mergers and acquisitions (M&A) operations spanning over two industries: healthcare and entertainment. M&A is a general term that refers to the process in which the ownership of companies are transferred. Such process has many stages that range from informal talks to the closing of a deal, and discussions may not be publicly disclosed until a formal agreement is signed (Bruner and Perella, 2004): in this sense, the analysis of the evolution of opinions and concerns expressed by users about a possible M&A operation, from early stage discussion to the signing of the merger (or its rejection), is a process similar to rumor verification, a widely studied field (Zubiaga et al., 2018a). Interestingly, Conforti et al. (2020) observed a consistent drop in performance when a system trained on mergers in one industry is tested on data discussing a merger in a different industry. Such a performance drop when testing conditions deviate from training conditions is a known problem in Stance Detection (SD) (Aker et al.).

In this paper, we investigate the impact of using synthetically annotated data to improve zero-shot cross-target generalization in Twitter SD:
(1) We investigate a weakly supervised framework for SD, which integrates synthetically annotated data to improve performance on new targets; as to our knowledge, we are the first to use synthetically annotated data for SD;
(2) We test our framework on Twitter SD and prove that it successfully improves cross-target generalization on new, unseen targets;
(3) We extend the WT–WT corpus with additional annotated tweets discussing M&A operations in one additional domain, which we release for future research on cross-target generalization[1].

## 2 Cross-Target Generalization with Synthetically Annotated Samples

Given an in-domain (ID) test set and a gold out-of-domain (OOD) train set, we augment the corpus with synthetically labeled ID data (Figure 1):

1. We train a SD system on the gold OOD data.
2. We crawl for a large amount of unlabeled ID data and label it with the system trained in 1, obtaining silver, synthetically annotated data.

[1] https://github.com/cambridge-wtwt/



*Proceedings of the 11th Workshop on Computational Approaches to Subjectivity, Sentiment and Social Media Analysis*, pages 181–187
April 19, 2021. ©2021 Association for Computational Linguistics

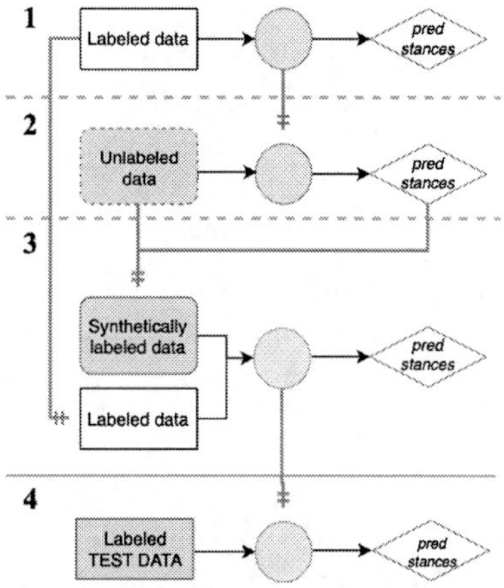


Figure 1: Pipeline of the framework. Rectangular boxes: gold annotations; cornered boxes: unlabeled/synthetic annotations; green lines: elements which are passed from different stages of the pipeline.

3. We train a new system on both gold OOD and synthetic ID data: in this way, the system is exposed to a gold signal from the OOD data and to a noisy but ID signal from silver data.
4. We predict the ID test data with the system trained in 3.

**Comparison with previous work on Data Augmentation and Domain Adaptation.**
Note that this framework differs from data augmentation (DAug) strategies adopted to supply for small training data, like in question answering (Kafle et al.), machine translation (Fadaee et al.) distillation (Tang et al., 2019), or for adversarial sample generation (Jia and Liang, 2017). Such techniques, inspired by DAug in speech recognition and computer vision (Chatfield et al., 2014), work by deformating gold samples to generate new artificial samples (for example, by random token masking, or POS- or semantics-based token replacement). Our approach differs in a number of aspects:

1. In DAug the goal is to enlarge a set of initial ID data; here, we assume we don't have *any* ID training data, but only OOD;
2. For this reason, while DAug helps to cope with data sparsity, our approach is also useful for domain shifts;
3. In DAug, sample generation might introduce two kinds of noise: it can lead to mismatches between the new samples and the associated labels, and also produce ungrammatical samples; in our approach, the system is always exposed to well-structured input: the only noise are potential errors in synthetic labeling.

Our approach fits into the broad family of weakly- and semi-supervised frameworks which have been adopted to tackle domain adaptation (DAda) problems (Søgaard, 2013). In recent literature, such methods have been applied with mixed success to many tasks, ranging from named entity recognition (Fries et al., 2017) to relation extraction (Mintz et al., 2009), tagging (Plank et al., 2014), parsing (McClosky et al., 2010), and sentiment analysis (Blitzer et al., 2007; Ruder and Plank, 2018; Ratner et al., 2020). In this paper, we propose to apply weakly supervision to SD, by adopting the extremely simple and inexpensive framework described above.

## 3 Related Work on Stance Detection

SD is a widely investigated field in NLP. Starting from Mohammad et al. (2017), research in SD focused on the analysis of Twitter posts. Another research direction explored the classification of Twitter users with respect to given topics, like political independence (Darwish et al., 2019). Work on other types of user-generated data includes SD on parenting blogs (Skeppstedt et al., 2017), political posts on newspapers websites (Hanselowski et al., 2018), posts on online debate forums on various topics (Hasan and Ng, 2014) and posts on wordpress blogs (Simaki et al., 2017). SD has been also integrated into Fake News Detection (Pomerleau and Rao, 2017) and constitutes an important step in the rumor verification pipeline (Zubiaga et al., 2018b): in this framework, popular shared tasks focused on SD of rumorous tweets (Gorrell et al., 2018) and Reddit posts (Gorrell et al., 2018). These works analyze tweets in a tree-shaped stream (Zubiaga et al., 2015). Note that SD constitutes a related but different task than sentiment analysis (Mohammad et al., 2017): the latter focuses on the *polarity* expressed w.r.t. a topic, while the former aims to determine the text's *orientation* w.r.t. the topic. Consider the following tweet:

*#Cancer patients will suffer if CVSHealth buys Aetna CVS #PBM has resulted in delays in therapy, switches, etc all documented. Terrible!*

The sentiment of the tweet w.r.t. the target is *negative*: the user believes that the merger would harm patients; however, its stance is *comment*, as it is

| M&A | buyer | target | industry | crawl start-end dates | | samples | outcome | labels |
|---|---|---|---|---|---|---|---|---|
| ABT_STJ | Abbott Lab. | St. Jude | pharma | 15/11/15 | 05/02/17 | 756 | success | no |
| AVGO_QCOM | Broadcom | Qualcomm | broadband | 01/02/16 | 01/07/19 | 7,211 | failure | no |
| BMY_CELG | B-M-S | Celgene | pharma | 04/03/17 | 01/07/19 | 3,940 | tbd | no |
| CHTR_TWC | Charter Com | Time W. Cable | broadband | 01/01/14 | 30/06/16 | 4,248 | success | no |
| CLN_HUN | Clariant | Huntsman | chemicals | 01/01/17 | 30/11/17 | 836 | failure | no |
| CMCSA_TWC | Comcast | Time W. Cable | broadband | 01/04/13 | 01/01/14 | 23,672 | failure | no |
| CTL_LVLT | CenturyLink | Level 3 | technology | 01/04/16 | 30/11/17 | 1,524 | success | no |
| DELL_EMC | Dell | EMC | technology | 11/06/14 | 29/03/17 | 7,978 | success | no |
| HAL_BHGE | Halliburton | Baker Hughes | oil industry | 01/12/13 | 06/05/17 | 6,386 | failure | no |
| IBM_RHT | IBM | Red Hat | technology | 01/03/18 | 31/08/19 | 16,106 | success | no |
| MDT_COV | Medtronic | Covidien | pharma | 01/05/14 | 31/03/19 | 5,608 | success | no |
| MSFT_LNKD | Microsoft | LinkedIn | technology | 16/01/16 | 06/01/17 | 15,107 | success | no |
| TMUS_S | T-Mobile | Sprint | broadband | 01/04/17 | 31/08/19 | 24,559 | success | no |
| VIAB_CBS | Viacom | CBS Corp | entertainment | 01/09/16 | 10/12/19 | 12,934 | success | no |
| WATS_AGN | Actavis | Allergan | pharma | 01/09/12 | 30/04/15 | 2,740 | success | no |
| WATS_WCRX | Actavis | Warner Chilcott | pharma | 01/04/13 | 31/12/13 | 613 | success | no |
| AET_HUM$^{\star}$ | Aethna | Humana | healthcare | 01/09/14 | 23/01/17 | 7,829 | failure | yes |
| ANTM_CI$^{\star}$ | Anthem | Cigna | healthcare | 01/04/14 | 28/04/17 | 11,021 | failure | yes |
| CVS_AET$^{\star}$ | CVS Health | Aetna | healthcare | 15/02/17 | 17/12/18 | 11,517 | success | yes |
| CI_ESRX$^{\diamond\star}$ | Cigna | Express Scripts | healthcare | 27/05/17 | 17/09/18 | 2,511 | success | yes |
| DIS_FOXA$^{\diamond\star}$ | Disney | 21 Century Fox | entertainment | 09/07/17 | 18/04/18 | 18,428 | success | yes |
| UTX_COL$^{\diamond}$ | United Tech. | Rockwell Col. | conglomerate | 23/12/16 | 04/09/17 | 535 | success | yes |

Table 1: M&A operations considered in this work. Operations before the horizontal line are unlabeled. Operations followed by: $\star$ are part of the WT–WT corpus; $\diamond$ are used for testing. Note that some companies (WATS, AETNA and CI) appear in different operations.

not stating that the merger is going to happen or to be rejected, but is talking about its consequences.

## 4 Experimental Setup

**Data.** We consider the following data (Table 1-2):

- *Annotated data.* The WT–WT corpus constitutes our primary source of labeled data, which we extend with gold-annotated tweets discussing a merger in the defense industry, following the same procedure as in Conforti et al. (2020). Each {`tweet, merger`} sample is annotated with a label from *support, comment, refute* and *unrelated*, which expresses its stance w.r.t the likelihood of the merger to happen.
- *Unlabeled data.* We crawl for 16 additional mergers, obtaining 134,922 unlabeled tweets.

We consider 3 healthcare mergers as gold train data (AET_HUM, ANTM_CI, CVS_AET) and 3 test sets: CI_ESRX (healthcare, ID), DIS_FOXA (entertainment, OOD) and UTX_COL (defense, OOD).

**Models and Hyperparameters.** We employ a multi-layer perceptron (MLP) classifier, which takes as input the concatenation of the tweet's and the target's TF-IDF representations and their cosine similarity. This simple model achieved good results on SD (Riedel et al., 2017) and is relatively stable over parameter selection. Hyperparameters used are listed in Table 6 (Appendix B) for replication.

**Synthetic Label Generation.** We train a system on the gold train set (total 30,367 samples). We use early stopping with a patience of 5 over the

| | | Sup | Rel | Com | Unr |
|---|---|---|---|---|---|
| **Train Set** | – | 14.52 | 11.87 | 37.43 | 36.16 |
| **Test Sets** | | | | | |
| CI_ESRX | S | 30.39 | 10.55 | 37.24 | 21.82 |
| DIS_FOXA | S | 7.67 | 2.05 | 46.09 | 42.91 |
| UTX_COL | S | 36.99 | 7.30 | 18.13 | 44.13 |
| **Synthetic Data** | | | | | |
| ABT_STJ | S | 12.70 | 1.06 | 8.73 | 77.51 |
| AVGO_QCOM | F | 9.22 | 7.79 | 23.58 | 59.41 |
| BMY_CELG | T | 7.67 | 1.68 | 26.45 | 46.20 |
| CHTR_TWC | S | 9.37 | 1.15 | 10.92 | 78.55 |
| CLN_HUN | F | 9.69 | 7.54 | 13.64 | 69.13 |
| CMCSA_TWC | F | 4.27 | 3.30 | 19.07 | 73.35 |
| CTL_LVLT | S | 9.25 | 0.79 | 20.28 | 69.69 |
| DELL_EMC | S | 7.65 | 1.42 | 28.92 | 62.02 |
| HAL_BHGE | F | 7.62 | 8.75 | 21.77 | 61.68 |
| IBM_RHT | S | 4.20 | 0.21 | 12.97 | 82.62 |
| MDT_COV | S | 7.99 | 0.64 | 14.30 | 77.07 |
| MSFT_LNKD | S | 2.68 | 1.22 | 18.66 | 77.43 |
| TMUS_S | S | 4.91 | 4.83 | 19.54 | 70.73 |
| VIAB_CBS | S | 4.67 | 1.72 | 21.75 | 71.86 |
| WATS_AGN | S | 12.37 | 0.55 | 10.88 | 76.20 |
| WATS_WCRX | S | 20.23 | 2.12 | 11.42 | 66.23 |

Table 2: Label distribution of: the training set, the test sets and the synthetically labeled data. The second column reports the merger's outcome (*Success/Fail/Tbd*). See Appendix A for a complete list of companies.

| | dataset | synth data | prec | rec | $F_1$ | acc | SUP | REF | COM | UNR |
|---|---|---|---|---|---|---|---|---|---|---|
| health *ID* | CI_ESRX | *none* | **56.80** | **54.19** | **54.99** | **59.52** | **71.17** | **37.70** | **62.48** | 45.39 |
| | CI_ESRX | *related merger* | 52.24 | 51.81 | 52.12 | 56.59 | 63.52 | 28.57 | 53.82 | 61.03 |
| | CI_ESRX | *succeeded merger* | 52.05 | 49.60 | 49.50 | 55.64 | 62.41 | 18.65 | 53.69 | 63.65 |
| | CI_ESRX | *all merger* | 53.94 | 50.94 | 50.94 | 56.59 | 63.25 | 21.83 | 53.95 | **64.74** |
| entertain *OOD* | DIS_FOXA | *none* | 39.61 | 35.10 | 34.55 | 55.34 | **83.36** | 7.41 | 14.43 | 34.85 |
| | DIS_FOXA | *related merger* | 39.34 | **37.93** | **37.69** | 55.56 | 60.38 | **15.87** | **17.12** | 59.33 |
| | DIS_FOXA | *succeeded merger* | 38.80 | 35.55 | 35.92 | 54.75 | 46.86 | 6.61 | 16.34 | **72.39** |
| | DIS_FOXA | *all merger* | **40.99** | 36.16 | 36.95 | **57.42** | 54.99 | 6.35 | 12.87 | 70.44 |
| defense *OOD* | UTX_COL | *none* | 35.18 | 27.16 | 21.91 | 44.02 | 8.08 | 0.00 | **8.54** | 92.00 |
| | UTX_COL | *related merger* | **46.91** | **38.98** | **24.09** | 45.54 | 15.15 | 0.00 | 6.53 | 94.22 |
| | UTX_COL | *succeeded mergers* | 41.68 | 29.19 | 23.99 | **45.73** | **16.16** | 0.00 | 5.03 | **95.56** |
| | UTX_COL | *all merger* | 37.62 | 28.52 | 23.67 | 44.97 | 14.14 | 0.00 | 7.04 | 92.89 |

Table 3: Results of SD on the three test sets (one ID and two OOD), when selecting synthetic data of different types; as recommended when dealing with unbalanced class distribution (Hanselowski et al., 2018), we report on macro-averaged precision, recall and $F_1$ score; the last four columns report on single label accuracy.

| | dataset | synth data | prec | rec | $F_1$ | acc | SUP | REF | COM | UNR |
|---|---|---|---|---|---|---|---|---|---|---|
| *entertainment (out of domain)* | DIS_FOXA | *none* | 39.61 | 35.10 | 34.55 | 55.34 | **83.36** | 7.41 | 14.43 | 34.85 |
| | DIS_FOXA | UNR | 39.33 | 33.27 | 32.52 | **58.35** | 63.60 | 1.06 | 3.04 | 63.91 |
| | DIS_FOXA | COM-UNR | 40.28 | 34.79 | 34.33 | 55.15 | 47.39 | 12.17 | 5.09 | **74.49** |
| | DIS_FOXA | COM | 37.06 | 34.24 | 33.28 | 54.75 | 50.82 | 11.09 | 4.17 | 70.06 |
| | DIS_FOXA | SUP-REF-COM | 37.08 | 34.40 | 35.98 | 56.97 | 76.54 | 8.47 | 4.24 | 57.36 |
| | DIS_FOXA | SUP-REF | **40.79** | 35.42 | 35.18 | 58.42 | 60.47 | 8.47 | 4.53 | 68.23 |
| | DIS_FOXA | *all stances* | 39.34 | **37.93** | **37.69** | 55.56 | 60.38 | **15.87** | **17.12** | 59.33 |
| *defense (out of domain)* | UTX_COL | *none* | 35.18 | 27.16 | 21.91 | 44.02 | 8.08 | 0.00 | 8.54 | 92.00 |
| | UTX_COL | UNR | **45.38** | 28.27 | 22.00 | 44.97 | 13.13 | 0.00 | 3.52 | **96.44** |
| | UTX_COL | COM-UNR | 36.93 | 28.30 | 23.21 | 44.21 | 16.16 | 0.00 | 5.03 | 92.00 |
| | UTX_COL | COM | 41.42 | **30.94** | **27.04** | **47.06** | **22.22** | 0.00 | **9.55** | 92.00 |
| | UTX_COL | SUP-REF-COM | 34.48 | 28.14 | 23.24 | 43.45 | 18.18 | 0.00 | 5.03 | 89.33 |
| | UTX_COL | SUP-REF | 39.91 | 29.04 | 24.46 | 45.35 | 16.16 | 0.00 | 7.54 | 92.44 |
| | UTX_COL | *all stances* | 40.99 | 28.84 | 25.87 | 45.73 | 20.20 | 0.00 | 8.40 | 91.11 |

Table 4: Results of SD on the OOD test sets, selecting synthetic data annotated with different stances ($3^{rd}$ col).

heldout data. The system achieved an $F_1$ score of 78.33 on the heldout data. Then, the unlabeled data is annotated using the trained system. The predicted label distribution reflects the actual merger output (Table 2). Refer to Table 5 (Appendix A) for qualitative examples of correctly and wrongly synthetically annotated samples.

## 5 Experiments and Discussion

**Baseline.** Table 3 reports on results without using any synthetic data. As expected, we observe a notable gap in generalization performance between the ID healthcare test set and the OOD test sets.

**Experiment I.** To understand the impact of including different types of synthetic data during training, we consider three settings:

(1) *related mergers*: adding synthetic data from mergers which are ID w.r.t. the considered test set (we select ID mergers for each test set according to similarities between industries, see Appendix A);

(2) *succeeded mergers*: adding data from mergers which were successful: such mergers tend to better match the distribution of the test mergers, as all of them succeeded;

(3) *all mergers*: adding data from all synthetically annotated mergers: this last setting was implemented to test whether synthetically annotated data, even if not perfectly ID w.r.t. the testset, could have a positive regularization function beyond DA (as hypothesized by Sennrich et al. (2016) in the context of Machine Translation).

For experiments, we randomly add synthetic samples with a proportion of 50% w.r.t. the train set size; to account for uncertainty, we use sample weighting for synthetic samples: *sup*, *ref* and *com* are weighted 0.6, while *unr* are weighted 0.2 (after qualitative analysis, we found them to be noisier).

Results in Table 3 show that adding synthetic samples leads to improvements in generalization over OOD test sets in all considered settings (up to $+3.4$ in $F_1$ score for FOXA_DIS and up to $+5.1$ for UTX_COL; note that results on UTX_COL without synthetic data were significantly lower than on FOXA_DIS). This is in line with previous results on semi-supervised learning investigating other tasks, such as sentiment analysis (Blitzer et al., 2007) or text categorization (Ando and Zhang, 2005). Interestingly, synthetic samples didn't bring any improvement to the ID test set; moreover, best results overall were obtained with the *related merger* setting: this seems to indicate that synthetic data act as a powerful domain adaptation technique rather than as a regularizer alone, this is in line with findings in Machine Translation (Edunov et al., 2018).

**Experiment II.** We consider the best performing setting, *related mergers*, and perform a second set of experiments to understand the impact of adding synthetic samples belonging to different stances; we consider: only *unr*; only *com*; only *unr+com*; *sup+ref+com*; *sup+ref*; and finally adding samples from all stances. Differences in performance

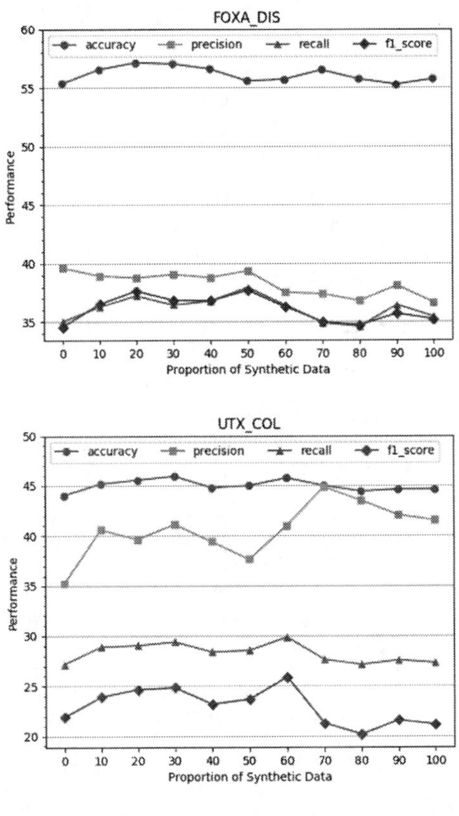


Figure 2: Performance of models trained on different amounts of synthetic data (percentage with respect to the train set size).

between settings are negligible (Table 4). Concerning single labels, synthetic samples had the most significant impact on *unr* not only for OOD testsets (up to $+39.7$ in accuracy for FOXA_DIS and $+4.5$ for UTX_COL), but even for ID ($+18.44$).

**Experiment III.** We run a final set of experiments to investigate the relation between performance and the amount of synthetic data considered. For both operations (Figure 2), we observe that improvements in $F_1$ score are supported by a rise in recall which reaches a pleateau around 30% and, for UTX_COL, in precision.

## 6 Conclusions and Future Work

We investigated an inexpensive framework to integrate unlabeled ID data to improve cross-target SD. We studied Twitter SD and showed, through a comprehensive set of experiments, that it is a promising strategy. We reserve to study its applicability to other domains in future work.

## Acknowledgments


We thank the anonymous reviewers for their efforts and for the constructive suggestions. We gratefully acknowledge funding from the Keynes Fund, University of Cambridge (grant no. JHOQ). CC is grateful to NERC DREAM CDT (grant no. 1945246) for partially funding this work. CG and FT are thankful to the Cambridge Endowment for Research in Finance (CERF).


## References


Rakesh Agrawal, Sridhar Rajagopalan, Ramakrishnan Srikant, and Yirong Xu. Mining newsgroups using networks arising from social behavior. In *Proceedings of WWW 2003*. ACM.

Ahmet Aker, Arkaitz Zubiaga, Kalina Bontcheva, Anna Kolliakou, Rob Procter, and Maria Liakata. Stance classification in out-of-domain rumours: A case study around mental health disorders. In *Social Informatics - 9th International Conference*.

Rie Kubota Ando and Tong Zhang. 2005. A framework for learning predictive structures from multiple tasks and unlabeled data. *Journal of Machine Learning Research*, 6:1817–1853.

Ramy Baly, Mitra Mohtarami, James R. Glass, Lluís Màrquez, Alessandro Moschitti, and Preslav Nakov. 2018. Integrating stance detection and fact checking in a unified corpus. In *Proceedings of NAACL 2018*.

John Blitzer, Mark Dredze, and Fernando Pereira. 2007. Biographies, bollywood, boom-boxes and blenders: Domain adaptation for sentiment classification. In *Proceedings of ACL 2007*.

Robert F Bruner and Joseph R Perella. 2004. *Applied mergers and acquisitions*, volume 173. John Wiley & Sons.

Ken Chatfield, Karen Simonyan, Andrea Vedaldi, and Andrew Zisserman. 2014. Return of the devil in the details: Delving deep into convolutional nets. In *BMVC 2014*. BMVA Press.

Costanza Conforti, Jakob Berndt, Mohammad Taher Pilehvar, Chryssi Giannitsarou, Flavio Toxvaerd, and Nigel Collier. 2020. Will-they-won't-they: A very large dataset for stance detection on twitter. In *Proceedings of ACL 2020*.

Kareem Darwish, Peter Stefanov, Michaël J. Aupetit, and Preslav Nakov. 2019. Unsupervised user stance detection on twitter. *CoRR*, abs/1904.02000.

Sergey Edunov, Myle Ott, Michael Auli, and David Grangier. 2018. Understanding back-translation at scale. In *Proceedings of EMNLP 2018*.

Marzieh Fadaee, Arianna Bisazza, and Christof Monz. Data augmentation for low-resource neural machine translation. In *Proceedings of ACL 2017*.

Jason A. Fries, Sen Wu, Alexander Ratner, and Christopher Ré. 2017. Swellshark: A generative model for biomedical named entity recognition without labeled data. *CoRR*, abs/1704.06360.

Genevieve Gorrell, Kalina Bontcheva, Leon Derczynski, Elena Kochkina, Maria Liakata, and Arkaitz Zubiaga. 2018. Rumoureval 2019: Determining rumour veracity and support for rumours. *CoRR*, abs/1809.06683.

Andreas Hanselowski, Avinesh P., Benjamin Schiller, Felix Caspelherr, Debanjan Chaudhuri, Christian M. Meyer, and Iryna Gurevych. 2018. A retrospective analysis of the fake news challenge stance-detection task. In *Proceedings of COLING 2018*.

Kazi Saidul Hasan and Vincent Ng. 2014. Why are you taking this stance? identifying and classifying reasons in ideological debates. In *Proceedings of EMNLP 2014*, pages 751–762.

Tomáš Hercig, Peter Krejzl, Barbora Hourová, Josef Steinberger, and Ladislav Lenc. Detecting stance in czech news commentaries. In *Proceedings of SloNLP 2017*.

Diana Inkpen, Xiaodan Zhu, and Parinaz Sobhani. 2017. A dataset for multi-target stance detection. In *Proceedings of EACL 2017*, pages 551–557. Association for Computational Linguistics.

Robin Jia and Percy Liang. 2017. Adversarial examples for evaluating reading comprehension systems. In *Proceedings of EMNLP 2017*, pages 2021–2031, Copenhagen, Denmark. Association for Computational Linguistics.

Kushal Kafle, Mohammed A. Yousefhussien, and Christopher Kanan. Data augmentation for visual question answering. In *Proceedings of INLG 2017*.

Manfred Klenner, Don Tuggener, and Simon Clematide. Stance detection in facebook posts of a german right-wing party. In *Proceedings of LSDSem@EACL 2017*.

David McClosky, Eugene Charniak, and Mark Johnson. When is self-training effective for parsing? In *Proceedings of COLING2008*.

David McClosky, Eugene Charniak, and Mark Johnson. 2010. Automatic domain adaptation for parsing. In *Proceedings of NAACL-HLT 2010*.

Mike Mintz, Steven Bills, Rion Snow, and Daniel Jurafsky. 2009. Distant supervision for relation extraction without labeled data. In *Proceedings of ACL 2009*. The Association for Computer Linguistics.

Saif M. Mohammad, Parinaz Sobhani, and Svetlana Kiritchenko. 2017. Stance and sentiment in tweets. *ACM Trans. Internet Techn.*, 17(3):26:1–26:23.

Barbara Plank, Dirk Hovy, Ryan T. McDonald, and Anders Søgaard. 2014. Adapting taggers to twitter with not-so-distant supervision. In *Proceedings of COLING 2014*.

Dean Pomerleau and Delip Rao. 2017. Fake news challenge.

Alexander Ratner, Stephen H. Bach, Henry R. Ehrenberg, Jason A. Fries, Sen Wu, and Christopher Ré. 2020. Snorkel: rapid training data creation with weak supervision. *VLDB J.*

Benjamin Riedel, Isabelle Augenstein, Georgios P. Spithourakis, and Sebastian Riedel. 2017. A simple but tough-to-beat baseline for the fake news challenge stance detection task. *CoRR*, abs/1707.03264.

Sebastian Ruder and Barbara Plank. 2018. Strong baselines for neural semi-supervised learning under domain shift. In *Proceedings of ACL 2018*.

Rico Sennrich, Barry Haddow, and Alexandra Birch. 2016. Improving neural machine translation models with monolingual data. In *Proceedings of ACL 2016*.

Vasiliki Simaki, Carita Paradis, Maria Skeppstedt, Magnus Sahlgren, Kostiantyn Kucher, and Andreas Kerren. 2017. Annotating speaker stance in discourse: the brexit blog corpus. *Corpus Linguistics and Linguistic Theory*.

Maria Skeppstedt, Andreas Kerren, and Manfred Stede. 2017. Automatic detection of stance towards vaccination in online discussion forums. In *Proceedings of DDDSM@IJCNLP 2017*, pages 1–8.

Anders Søgaard. 2013. *Semi-Supervised Learning and Domain Adaptation in Natural Language Processing*. Synthesis Lectures on Human Language Technologies. Morgan & Claypool Publishers.

Raphael Tang, Yao Lu, Linqing Liu, Lili Mou, Olga Vechtomova, and Jimmy Lin. 2019. Distilling task-specific knowledge from BERT into simple neural networks. *CoRR*, abs/1903.12136.

Andreas Vlachos and Sebastian Riedel. 2014. Fact checking: Task definition and dataset construction. In *Proceedings of the Workshop on Language Technologies and Computational Social Science@ACL 2014*. Association for Computational Linguistics.

Arkaitz Zubiaga, Ahmet Aker, Kalina Bontcheva, Maria Liakata, and Rob Procter. 2018a. Detection and resolution of rumours in social media: A survey. *ACM Comput. Surv.*, 51(2):32:1–32:36.

Arkaitz Zubiaga, Geraldine Wong Sak Hoi, Maria Liakata, Rob Procter, and Peter Tolmie. 2015. Analysing how people orient to and spread rumours in social media by looking at conversational threads. *CoRR*, abs/1511.07487.

Arkaitz Zubiaga, Elena Kochkina, Maria Liakata, Rob Procter, Michal Lukasik, Kalina Bontcheva, Trevor Cohn, and Isabelle Augenstein. 2018b. Discourse-aware rumour stance classification in social media using sequential classifiers. *Inf. Process. Manage.*, 54(2):273–290.

## Appendix A: Details on Data

Table 5 reports examples of correctly and wrongly synthetically labeled samples.

## Appendix B: Details on Modeling

For each test set, we include synthetically annotated tweets from a number of related mergers. Related mergers have been manually selected by an expert in the Economics domain, based on industry similarity.

- CI_ESRX (health): TMUS_S, VIAB_CBS, BMY_CELG, MSFT_LNKD, MDT_COV, IBM_RHT
- DIS_FOXA (entertainment): TMUS_S, VIAB_CBS, CMCSA_TWC, MSFT_LNKD, IBM_RHT, CHTR_TWC, MDT_COV, BMY_CELG, DELL_EMC
- UTX_COL (defense): TMUS_S, MDT_COV, VIAB_CBS, CHTR_TWC, MSFT_LNKD, BMY_CELG, CMCSA_TWC, CTL_LVLT

**Preprocessing.** We perform the following steps on all tweets: lowercasing, tokenization; digits/URL normalization; stripping of the # sign from hashtags; normalization of low-frequency users.

**Hyperparameters Specifications** Hyperparameters are reported in Table 6. When possible, we follow Riedel et al. (2017) for parameter selection. Note that we perform minimal parameter tuning: the goal of this paper is to investigate the efficacy of synthetically annotated data for SD, independently from the chosen architecture.

| | |
|---|---|
| batch size | 32 |
| epochs | 70 |
| optimizer | *Adam* ($\lambda = 0.001$) |
| BoW vocabulary size | 3000 |
| dense hidden layer size | 100 |
| hidden layer dropout | 0.2 |

Table 6: Network hyperparameters

**Computing Infrastructure.** We run experiments on an NVIDIA GeForce GTX 1080 GPU.

**Evaluation Specifications.** We use the sklearn's implementation of macro-averaged precision, recall and $F_1$ score.

| M&A | correct | predicted | tweet text |
|---|---|---|---|
| IBM_RHT | support | support | *IBM Completes Red Hat Deal the Largest Software Acquisition Ever <URL>via Barronsonline* |
| AVGO_QCOM | refute | refute | *EU's $1.2-Billion Fine Against Qualcomm Might Complicate Broadcom's Bid <URL>* |
| MSFT_LNKD | comment | comment | *Bill Gates believes #Microsoft Can Make #LinkedIn as Successful as #Facebook <URL>$MSFT $LNKD $FB* |
| DELL_EMC | unrelated | unrelated | *Synnex reaches agreement with Dell for Canadian distribution <url >* |
| DELL_EMC | comment | support | *The largest tech deal in history is like mating elephants? Really. #dellemc <URL>* |
| IBM_RHT | comment | unrelated | *IBM and Red Hat Explained #ibm – <URL>* |
| MDT_COV | support | refute | *Medtronic's proposed $43B acquisition of Covidien has cleared all anti-trust hurdles worldwide <URL>* |
| MSFT_LNKD | comment | unrelated | *How Microsofts bid for LinkedIn sets a standard for every business to copy <URL>* |
| DELL_EMC | support | unrelated | *Dell to acquire EMC in $67 billion record tech deal <URL>#CloudComputing* |
| MDT_COV | support | comment | *Medtronic is still in on Covidien buyout — MassDevice <URL>* |

Table 5: Examples of correctly and wrongly synthetically annotated tweets.

# Creating and Evaluating Resources for Sentiment Analysis in the Low-resource Language: Sindhi

**Wazir Ali**[1] **Naveed Ali**[1] **Yong Dai**[1] **Jay Kumar**[1]

**Saifullah Tumrani**[1] **Zenglin Xu**[1,2]

[1]University of Electronic Science and Technology of China, Chengdu 611731, China

[2]Harbin Institute of Technology, Shenzhen, Nanshan 510085, China

{aliwazirjam,zenglin}@gmail.com

## Abstract

In this paper, we develop Sindhi subjective lexicon using a merger of existing English resources: NRC lexicon, list of opinion words, SentiWordNet, Sindhi-English bilingual dictionary, and collection of Sindhi modifiers. The positive or negative sentiment score is assigned to each Sindhi opinion word. Afterwards, we determine the coverage of the proposed lexicon with subjectivity analysis. Moreover, we crawl multi-domain tweet corpus of news, sports, and finance. The crawled corpus is annotated by experienced annotators using the Doccano text annotation tool. The sentiment annotated corpus is evaluated by employing support vector machine (SVM), recurrent neural network (RNN) variants, and convolutional neural network (CNN).

## 1 Introduction

The exponential growth in the online professional and user-generated textual data (Akhtar et al., 2016), including blog posts, news headlines, product, and book reviews, led to the growth of the sentiment analysis task. The required essential resources for the classification of such opinionated text are the polarity assigned sentiment lexicon (Asghar et al., 2019) and sentiment annotated corpora (Ekbal et al., 2020). Sophisticated research efforts have been employed for English sentiment analysis (Joshi et al., 2017; Hussein, 2018). In the result, a number of resources are available including opinion words (Hu and Liu, 2004), subjective lexicon (Wilson et al., 2005), SentiWordNet (SWN) (Esuli and Sebastiani, 2006; Baccianella et al., 2010), NRC lexicon (Mohammad and Turney, 2010). The sentiment annotated corpora including financial news (FN) (Takala et al., 2014), sports tweets (ST) (Yu and Wang, 2015), tweet dataset (Thelwall et al., 2012), and more recently a multi-domain corpora (Ekbal et al., 2020). Among these resources the SWN has been widely used for the construction of sentiment lexicon for low-resource languages including Urdu (Asghar et al., 2019), Turkish (Dehkharghani et al., 2016), and Hindi (Bakliwal et al., 2012).

Sindhi is an Indo-Aryan language, spoken by more than 75 million (Motlani, 2016) people. Presently, it is being written in two main scripts of Persian-Arabic and Devanagari (Jamro, 2017). However, Persian-Arabic is a popular and standard script (Ali et al., 2020). It is widely used in online communication, mainly in the Sindh province of Pakistan and some regions of India (Ali et al., 2019). The generated content on social media contains rich information about the interests of individuals. Thus, the modeling of such information is essential to analyze where people's opinions are conveyed. The low-resource Sindhi language lacks the primary resources for content analysis, such as polarity assigned lexicon and sentiment annotated corpora.

In this paper, we create Sindhi subjective lexicon using existing English resources. Moreover, due to the scarcity of sentiment annotated corpora, we crawl and annotate news headline (NH) tweets, sports tweets (ST), and FN tweets, respectively. Three native annotators performed the annotation using Doccano (Nakayama et al., 2018) text annotation tool with 79.3% inter-annotator agreement. To the best of our knowledge, both datasets[1] are the first benchmark for Sindhi sentiment analysis (SSA). Furthermore, we develop strong baselines of SVM (Cortes and Vapnik, 1995), CNN (Dos Santos and Gatti, 2014) and RNN variants of long-short-term memory (LSTM) (Hochreiter and Schmidhuber, 1997), bidirectional long-short-term memory (BiLSTM) (Schuster and Paliwal, 1997) for the evaluation purpose.

[1]The resources can be found at https://github.com/AliWazir/SdSenti-lexicon



*Proceedings of the 11th Workshop on Computational Approaches to Subjectivity, Sentiment and Social Media Analysis*, pages 188–194
April 19, 2021. ©2021 Association for Computational Linguistics

## 2 Related Work

The development of polarity assigned sentiment lexicon have largely been investigated for the rich-resource English language, such as Bing Liu's lexicon (Hu and Liu, 2004), SentiWordNet (SWN) (Esuli and Sebastiani, 2006), SWN 3.0 (Baccianella et al., 2010), and NRC lexicon (Mohammad and Turney, 2010). These resources have been widely used to create a sentiment lexicon for low-resource languages, mainly by translating the terms into the target languages. The human annotators assigned polarity score to create the sentiment lexicon for South Asian languages such as Hindi (Bakliwal et al., 2012), Bengali, Telugu (Das and Bandyopadhyay, 2010), Tamil (Kannan et al., 2016), Persian (Amiri et al., 2015), Urdu (Asghar et al., 2019), Panjabi (Kaur and Gupta, 2014), and Sinhala (Medagoda et al., 2015). Bakliwal et al. (2012) proposed a graph-based WordNet-based approach to develop subjective lexicon by using synonym and antonym relations. Das and Bandyopadhyay (2010) opted multiple methods such as, dictionary-based, corpus-based or generative approach, and WordNet-based for the construction of sentiment lexicon for Indian languages. Various resources and tools including Bing Liu's lexicon, SWN, subjectivity lexicon (Wilson et al., 2005), AFINN-111 lexicon (Nielsen, 2011), and Google translate (Amiri et al., 2015) are utilized to develop sentiment lexicon for Persian language. A word-level translation scheme (Asghar et al., 2019) is proposed to construct Urdu lexicon using English resources including Bing Liu's lexicon, SWN 3.0, and English to Urdu bilingual dictionary. Medagoda et al. (2015) proposed sentiment lexicon for low-resource Sinhala Language by using SWN 3.0 using word-level translation scheme. As we mentioned earlier, Sindhi stands among the low-resource languages because lack the subjective lexicon and sentiment annotated corpus except a recently Ali and Wagan 6842 part-of-speech tagged lexicon. Hence, their lexicon lack a sentiment intensity score. Thus, we propose Sindhi subjective lexicons using a merger of existing English resources. Moreover, we also crawl multi-domain NH, FT, and ST tweets and annotate them using Doccano (Nakayama et al., 2018) text annotation tool.

Many sentiment-annotated corpora have also been created for English in multiple domains, such as news, sports, finance, and products. Shamma et al. (2009) created tweet dataset by crawling U.S. presidential debate in multiple sentiment classes. Blitzer et al. (2007) proposed sentiment dataset on product reviews, electronics, and kitchen appliances obtained from Amazon.com. (Thelwall et al., 2012) manually annotated tweet dataset with $+ve$ and $-ve$ sentiments. The annotation of financial blogs and news domain (O'Hare et al., 2009; Malo et al., 2013; Takala et al., 2014) have also been investigated at a large scale. Yu and Wang (2015) proposed a dataset by crawling sports tweets from Twitter using search API. More recently, Ekbal et al. (2020) proposed multi-domain tweet corpora, annotated with three sentiment classes. Review shows that Sindhi lacks the subjective lexicon as well as sentiment annotated corpora for its supervised sentiment analysis that we consider.

## 3 Development of Subjective Lexicon

We construct Sindhi subjective lexicon by depicting the sentiment polarity score of all English opinion words using bilingual English to Sindhi dictionary[2]. The construction steps are described as follows:

### 3.1 Used Resources

To create the Sindhi subjective lexicon, we merge the list of Bing Liu's opinion words and the NRC lexicon. Afterwards, sentiment polarity is assigned using SWN 3.0 and translated to Sindhi using a bilingual dictionary.

- **NRC lexicon** is the list of English opinion words associated with basic emotions of fear, anger, sadness, disgust, surprise, and joy, etc. The lexicon include 2,312 $+ve$ and 3,324 $-ve$ words.

- **Bing Liu's lexicon** are general purpose English sentiment lexicon consists of 2,036 $+ve$ 4,814 $-ve$ words.

- **SentiWordNet 3.0** contains 117,659 English WordNet synset. Each term is associated with a numerical opinion score ranging between $[0.0, 1]$ to indicate the sentiment strength into $+ve$, $-ve$, or neutral classes.

- **Sindhi modifiers** increase or decrease sentiment strength of opinion words. Thus, we collect 173 Sindhi modifiers and assigned polarity using SWN 3.0 as well as human judgment. We manually assign the score to modifiers (see Table

[2] http://dic.sindhila.edu.pk/

5) in case of the unavailability of English translation of Sindhi modifiers in SWN 3.0 dataset.

- **English-Sindhi dictionary** is used to translate each English opinion word to the corresponding Sindhi word using comprehensive online English to Sindhi dictionary. If a bilingual dictionary returns more than one meaning of an opinion word, then the first or exact meaning is chosen by ignoring less common meanings.

### 3.2 Scoring Mechanism

We merge Bing Liu's, NRC lexicon and remove duplicates to develop a list of opinion lexicon. Each word from the list is looked up into SWN 3.0 to assign a polarity score. We choose the maximum polarity score of a retrieved word, such as we select $-0.778$ among all the synset of a word *heinous* in SWN (see Table 1). Afterwards, Sindhi translation is looked up in English to Sindhi dictionary. If a bilingual dictionary returns more than one meaning of a word, then the first or exact meaning (see Table 2) is chosen by ignoring less common or poetic meanings. An example of few constructed Sindhi subjective unigram and bigram terms is given in Table 3 and Table 4, respectively. Moreover, the sentiment score to Sindhi modifiers is assigned using SWN 3.0 and with decision making by assigning $+ve$ and $-ve$ polarity. Four native experienced annotators assigned polarity scores to the opinion lexicon and translated them into Sindhi. The overall inter-annotator agreement of 84.7% is achieved.

| SenseID | Synsets | Pos | Neg | Neu |
|---|---|---|---|---|
| 02514380 | heinous#1 | 0.222 | 0.778 | 0.00 |

Table 1: An example of a word *heinous* (synset ID-02514380) in SWN 3.0 with two polarity scores.

| Term | Synsets | Polarity score |
|---|---|---|
| Heinous | #1 سنگين 2#مڪروھ 3#ڪِريل | سنگين#1\|-0.778 |

Table 2: An example of a translated English word *heinous* to its equivalent Sindhi word by choosing the first meaning.

## 4 Development of Sentiment-annotated Corpus

Our main contributions include: a) The construction of polarity assigned Sindhi subjective lexicon using a merger of existing English resources. b) The acquisition of multi-domain NH, ST, FN tweet corpus and annotation for SSA using Doccano text annotation tool. c) The coverage of the proposed lexicon is determined with a subjectivity analysis test, and the sentiment annotated corpus is evaluated by employing SVM, LSTM, BiLSTM, and CNN models.

| Term | Sense ID | English Translation | Polarity Score |
|---|---|---|---|
| سٺو | 01123148 | Good | 0.75 |
| محفوظ | 02550868 | Save | 0.50 |
| بدلو | 01153486 | Revenge | -0.50 |
| شرم | 02547225 | Shame | -0.625 |
| پريشاني | 02460502 | True | 0.50 |
| تيزاب | 1460752 | Acid | -0.25 |
| ٿڌ | 01251128 | Cold | -0.75 |

Table 3: List of few unigrams in the proposed Sindhi subjective lexicon. The *Sense ID* represents a WordNet (3.0) synset.

| Terms | Sense ID | English Translation | Polarity Score |
|---|---|---|---|
| نا معلوم | 00028672 | Unacknowledged | -0.625 |
| غير منظم | 00641944 | Unmannered | -0.625 |
| نا اميد | 01229020 | Hopeless | -0.75 |
| مقابلو ڪندڙ | 00007990 | Resistant | -0.5 |
| ڦيريءَ بابت | 02708232 | Cyclic | 0.5 |
| انصاف ڪرڻ | 05615373 | Judiciousness | 0.875 |
| نا اهلي | 05648953 | Inefficiency | -0.50 |
| تعريف جوڳو | 02585545 | Praiseworthy | 0.625 |

Table 4: List of few bigrams in proposed Sindhi subjective lexicon. The *Sense ID* represents a WordNet (3.0) synset.

### 4.1 Data Acquisition

Due to the scarcity of corpus in multiple domains with gold annotations, we crawl the data from twitter using search API[3] and use web-scrapy[4,5] to collect the NH, ST, and FN headlines, tweets for sentiment annotation[6] text (see Table 7). The NH and ST tweets reflect the events, people's opinions, and their feelings about the events. The FN tweets contain people's opinions about inflation,

[3]https://twitter.com/search-advanced?f=live

[4]https://github.com/scrapy/scrapy

[5]List of few resources..
https://twitter.com/sindhtvnews247
https://twitter.com/awamiawazsindhi
https://www.pahenjiakhbar.com/categories/ trade
http://wichaar.com/news/202/ Finance & Business
http://wichaar.com/news/208/sports

[6]Corpus is crawled between December 11, 2019 to February 15, 2020

| Term | Roman Transliteration | Polarity Score |
|---|---|---|
| گھٽ | Ghatt | -0.50 |
| نا | Na | -0.50 |
| بي | Bey | -0.375 |
| اڻ | Annh | -0.25 |
| تمام | Tamam | 0.5 |
| انتهائي | Intihayi | 0.75 |

Table 5: List of few $+ve$, $-ve$ Sindhi modifiers.

| Lexicon | Positive | Negative |
|---|---|---|
| Unigrams | 3,986 | 7,562 |
| Bigrams | 179 | 269 |
| Total | 4,165 | 7,831 |

Table 6: Statistics of the proposed Sindhi subjective lexicon including modifiers.

the economy, capital expenditures, etc.

| Dom | Tws | Sent | Pos | Neg | Neu |
|---|---|---|---|---|---|
| NH | 2,096 | 3,534 | 1,134 | 1,141 | 1,259 |
| ST | 2,187 | 3,217 | 1,073 | 1,076 | 1,068 |
| FN | 1,754 | 2,853 | 953 | 952 | 948 |
| Total | 6,037 | 9,604 | 3,160 | 3,169 | 3,275 |

Table 7: Statistics of the preprocessed crawled corpus. The Dom, Tws, Sent, denote domain, tweets, and sentences. While Pos, Neg, Neu represent positive, negative, and neutral classes of the annotated sentences.

### 4.2 Data Preprocessing

We design a preprocessing pipeline for the filtration of unwanted data in the crawled tweets to get the desirable text for annotation, which consists of: a) Removal of unwanted punctuation marks from the start and end of the tweets. b) Filtration of noisy data such as special characters, non-Sindhi words, HTML tags, emails, and URLs. c) Normalization, removal of duplicates, multiple white spaces, and tweets that only contain user mentions. We also remove sentences containing more than 80 words and less than the length of 5 words.

### 4.3 Data Annotation

We use Doccano (Nakayama et al., 2018) text annotation tool for sentiment annotations of tweets into $+ve$, $-ve$, and neutral classes using crawled corpus (see Table 7). It is an open-source annotation tool for sequence labeling and sentiment analysis. The annotation is performed by three expert native annotators, keeping in view the sentiment ambiguities (Mohammad, 2016) in expressions such as success or failure, ridiculous expressions differing multiple entities, rhetorical questions, and requests are particularly challenging for the sentiment annotation. The overall inter annotation agreement (Cohen, 1960) of 79.3% shows the acceptable quality of the proposed dataset.

## 5 Evaluation

We determine the coverage of the proposed lexicon with subjectivity analysis (Asghar et al., 2019). The sentiment annotated corpus is evaluated by employing SVM, LSTM, BiLSTM, and CNN models.

### 5.1 Experimental Setup

The SVM, LSTM, BiLSTM, and CNN models are employed to evaluate the annotated dataset after combining all the domains. We filter stop words (Ali et al., 2019) and conduct the experiments, where the dataset was split into training, validation, and test sets. The results are reported in macro precision (P), recall (R), and F-value (F) for the average of the 10-fold runs along with accuracy (Kim, 2014) over the testing fold.

#### 5.1.1 Representation Learning

A neural network requires word embedding (or sentence embedding) as an input to the network, i.e., a vector representation of each word or sentence. The tweets, books and news corpus (2174K tokens) (Ali et al., 2019) are converted into word representations before training neural models. The pretrained sub-word based representation learning has the ability to encode the structure of words (Bojanowski et al., 2017) at character-level by sharing the character n-gram representations across words. In that way, the representation for each word is made of the sum of those character n-grams. We obtain contextual representations by concatenating the sentence representations obtained through both $\overrightarrow{h}$ and $\overleftarrow{h}$ of BiLSTM hidden layers and residual connection (Jiang et al., 2019).

#### 5.1.2 Support Vector Machine

We Employ SVM (Cortes and Vapnik, 1995) as an initial baseline for opinion extraction in each domain. The input features include N-gram tokens $(N = 1, 2, 3)$, character N-grams $(N = 2, 3, 4, 5)$ and proposed lexicons to extract the features.

#### 5.1.3 Deep Neural Models

We employ LSTM, BiLSTM, and CNN models for the evaluation of our proposed dataset. The LSTM, BiLSTM networks can learn long-term dependencies. They contain input, forget, and output gates, which determine how much information should be lost and how much information should be added to memory. The BiLSTM network has the ability to encode past (left) and future (right) contexts in two separate forward and backward hidden states. Then both hidden states are concatenated for the final output. Moreover, the CNN consists of a representation layer, two convolutional layers, a pooling layer, and a fully connected layer.

#### 5.1.4 Training Methodology

For the training of neural models for sentence type classification, all the sentences of each domain are used. The LSTM contains 300 hidden layers, and BiLSTM has 300 forward and 300 backward hidden layers, the concatenation of both resulted in 600 layers. A dense layer follows each hidden unit. We project input features by utilizing the dense layer. We employ 0.25% dropout in the fully connected LSTM, BiLSTM layers and 0.50% for CNN (Srivastava et al., 2014) and Adam optimizer (Kingma and Ba, 2015) with learning rate of 0.001%. All the neural models are implemented using TenserFlow (Abadi et al., 2016) deep learning framework on GTX 1080-TITAN GPU.

## 6 Results and Analysis

To assess the coverage of the proposed lexicon, the subjectivity analysis experiment is conducted to classify the sentences as subjective or objective. The sentence is classified as subjective if it contains one or more subjective word(s), otherwise classified as an objective in the absence of subjective word(s). The classification results of each domain are depicted in Table 8. Afterwards, all the domains are combined for sentence-level classification using supervised classifiers of SVM, LSTM, BiLSTM, and CNN, respectively. The overall performance of the SVM and neural models is presented in Table 9. The SVM is the weakest baseline classifier. It yields an accuracy of 67.86% with 68.00% precision, 69.00% recall, and 68.00% F1-value. The LSTM network shows better results than SVM by outputting 81.42% precision, 82.59% recall, 81.76% F-value, and 79.83% accuracy. The BiLSTM yields the best F-value of 83.11% and accuracy of 82.37%, respectively. The performance of the CNN network is very close to BiLSTM with precision 83.26%, recall 82.67%, F1-value 82.54%, and accuracy 81.68%.

| Domain | P(%) | R(%) | F(%) |
|---|---|---|---|
| NH | 75.28 | 74.65 | 73.89 |
| ST | 76.52 | 75.84 | 75.24 |
| FN | 75.33 | 75.69 | 74.61 |

Table 8: Results of subjectivity analysis.

| Model | P(%) | R(%) | F(%) | A(%) |
|---|---|---|---|---|
| SVM | 68.00 | 69.00 | 68.00 | 67.86 |
| LSTM | 81.42 | 82.59 | 81.76 | 79.83 |
| BiLSTM | **83.70** | **84.37** | **83.11** | **82.37** |
| CNN | **83.26** | 82.67 | 82.54 | 81.68 |

Table 9: The evaluation results based on supervised classifiers. The bold results reflect best performance.

The results demonstrate that the BiLSTM and CNN yield better results than SVM and LSTM. However, the BiLSTM network surpasses SVM, LSTM as well as CNN models.

## 7 Conclusion and Future Work

In this paper, we propose Sindhi subjective lexicon using various resources and sentiment annotated corpus, which serves as a benchmark for future expansions. The SVM and deep neural models are exploited for evaluation purposes. We achieve notable F-value and accuracy of 83.11%, 82.37% with the BiLSTM network. In the future, the proposed lexicon can be expanded using a corpus-based approach to capture language-specific words. Also, it can be used as a seed list, and the corpus can be tagged on the basis of the seed list. Moreover, the proposed lexicon consists of positive and negative classes, so a five-point scale can replace this classification in the future.

## Acknowledgments

We would like to thank the anonymous reviewers for the helpful discussions and suggestions. This work was funded by the National Key R&D Program of China (No. 2018YFB1005100 & No. 2018YFB1005104).

## References


Martin Abadi, Paul Barham, Jianmin Chen, Zhifeng Chen, Andy Davis, Jeffrey Dean, Matthieu Devin, Sanjay Ghemawat, Geoffrey Irving, Michael Isard, et al. 2016. Tensorflow: A system for large-scale machine learning. In *12th Symposium on Operating Systems Design and Implementation*, pages 265–283.

Md Shad Akhtar, Asif Ekbal, and Pushpak Bhattacharyya. 2016. Aspect based sentiment analysis in hindi: resource creation and evaluation. In *Proceedings of the Tenth International Conference on Language Resources and Evaluation*, pages 2703–2709.

Mazhar Ali and Asim Imdad Wagan. Sentiment summerization and analysis of Sindhi text. *International Journal of Advanced Computer Science and Applications*.

Wazir Ali, Jay Kumar, Junyu Lu, and Zenglin Xu. 2019. Word embedding based new corpus for low-resourced language: Sindhi. *arXiv preprint arXiv:1911.12579*.

Wazir Ali, Jay Kumar, Zenglin Xu, Congjian Luo, Junyu Lu, Junming Shao, Rajesh Kumar, and Yazhou Ren. 2020. A subword guided neural word segmentation model for sindhi. *arXiv preprint arXiv:2012.15079*.

Fatemeh Amiri, Simon Scerri, and Mohammadhassan Khodashahi. 2015. Lexicon-based sentiment analysis for Persian text. In *Proceedings of the International Conference Recent Advances in Natural Language Processing*, pages 9–16.

Muhammad Zubair Asghar, Anum Sattar, Aurangzeb Khan, Amjad Ali, Fazal Masud Kundi, and Shakeel Ahmad. 2019. Creating sentiment lexicon for sentiment analysis in Urdu: The case of a resource-poor language. *Expert Systems*.

Stefano Baccianella, Andrea Esuli, and Fabrizio Sebastiani. 2010. Sentiwordnet 3.0: An enhanced lexical resource for sentiment analysis and opinion mining. In *Proceedings of the International Conference on Language Resources and Evaluation*.

Akshat Bakliwal, Piyush Arora, and Vasudeva Varma. 2012. Hindi subjective lexicon: A lexical resource for Hindi polarity classification. In *Proceedings of the Eight International Conference on Language Resources and Evaluation*, pages 1189–1196.

John Blitzer, Mark Dredze, and Fernando Pereira. 2007. Biographies, bollywood, boom-boxes and blenders: Domain adaptation for sentiment classification. In *Proceedings of the 45th annual meeting of the association of computational linguistics*, pages 440–447.

Piotr Bojanowski, Edouard Grave, Armand Joulin, and Tomas Mikolov. 2017. Enriching word vectors with subword information. *Transactions of the Association for Computational Linguistics*, 5:135–146.

Jacob Cohen. 1960. A coefficient of agreement for nominal scales. *Educational and psychological measurement*, 20(1):37–46.

Corinna Cortes and Vladimir Vapnik. 1995. Support-vector networks. *Machine learning*, 20(3):273–297.

Amitava Das and Sivaji Bandyopadhyay. 2010. SentiWordNet for Indian languages. In *Proceedings of the Eighth Workshop on Asian Language Resouces*, pages 56–63.

Rahim Dehkharghani, Yucel Saygin, Berrin Yanikoglu, and Kemal Oflazer. 2016. SentiTurkNet: a Turkish polarity lexicon for sentiment analysis. *Language Resources and Evaluation*, 50(3):667–685.

Cicero Dos Santos and Maira Gatti. 2014. Deep convolutional neural networks for sentiment analysis of short texts. In *25th International Conference on Computational Linguistics*, pages 69–78.

Asif Ekbal, Pushpak Bhattacharyya, Shikha Srivastava, Alka Kumar, Tista Saha, et al. 2020. Multi-domain tweet corpora for sentiment analysis: Resource creation and evaluation. In *Proceedings of The 12th Language Resources and Evaluation Conference*, pages 5046–5054.

Andrea Esuli and Fabrizio Sebastiani. 2006. SENTIWORDNET: A publicly available lexical resource for opinion mining. In *Proceedings of the Fifth International Conference on Language Resources and Evaluation*, pages 417–422.

Sepp Hochreiter and Jürgen Schmidhuber. 1997. Long short-term memory. *Neural computation*, 9(8):1735–1780.

Minqing Hu and Bing Liu. 2004. Mining and summarizing customer reviews. In *Proceedings of the tenth ACM SIGKDD international conference on Knowledge discovery and data mining*, pages 168–177.

Doaa Mohey El-Din Mohamed Hussein. 2018. A survey on sentiment analysis challenges. *Journal of King Saud University-Engineering Sciences*, 30(4):330–338.

Wazir Ali Jamro. 2017. Sindhi language processing: A survey. In *International Conference on Innovations in Electrical Engineering and Computational Technologies*, pages 1–8.

Qingnan Jiang, Lei Chen, Ruifeng Xu, Xiang Ao, and Min Yang. 2019. A challenge dataset and effective models for aspect-based sentiment analysis. In *Conference on Empirical Methods in Natural Language Processing and the 9th International Joint Conference on Natural Language Processing*, pages 6281–6286.

Aditya Joshi, Pushpak Bhattacharyya, and Sagar Ahire. 2017. Sentiment resources: Lexicons and datasets. In *A Practical Guide to Sentiment Analysis*, pages 85–106. Springer.

Abishek Kannan, Gaurav Mohanty, and Radhika Mamidi. 2016. Towards building a SentiWordNet for Tamil. In *Proceedings of the 13th International Conference on Natural Language Processing*, pages 30–35.

Amandeep Kaur and Vishal Gupta. 2014. Proposed algorithm of sentiment analysis for Punjabi text. *Journal of Emerging Technologies in Web Intelligence*, 6(2):180–183.

Yoon Kim. 2014. Convolutional neural networks for sentence classification. In *Proceedings of the 2014 Conference on Empirical Methods in Natural Language Processing*, pages 1746–1751.

Diederik P. Kingma and Jimmy Ba. 2015. Adam: A method for stochastic optimization. In *International Conference on Learning Representations*.

Pekka Malo, Ankur Sinha, Pyry Takala, Oskar Ahlgren, and Iivari Lappalainen. 2013. Learning the roles of directional expressions and domain concepts in financial news analysis. In *IEEE International Conference on Data Mining Workshops*, pages 945–954.

Nishantha Medagoda, Subana Shanmuganathan, and Jacqueline Whalley. 2015. Sentiment lexicon construction using sentiwordnet 3.0. In *International Conference on Natural Computation*, pages 802–807.

Saif Mohammad. 2016. A practical guide to sentiment annotation: Challenges and solutions. In *Proceedings of the 7th Workshop on Computational Approaches to Subjectivity, Sentiment and Social Media Analysis*, pages 174–179.

Saif Mohammad and Peter Turney. 2010. Emotions evoked by common words and phrases: Using mechanical turk to create an emotion lexicon. In *workshop on computational approaches to analysis and generation of emotion in text*, pages 26–34.

Raveesh Motlani. 2016. Developing language technology tools and resources for a resource-poor language: Sindhi. In *Proceedings of the NAACL Student Research Workshop*, pages 51–58.

Hiroki Nakayama, Takahiro Kubo, Junya Kamura, Yasufumi Taniguchi, and Xu Liang. 2018. doccano: Text annotation tool for human. Software available from https://github.com/doccano/doccano.

Finn Årup Nielsen. 2011. A new anew: Evaluation of a word list for sentiment analysis in microblogs. In *Workshop on'Making Sense of Microposts: Big things come in small packages*, pages 93–98.

Neil O'Hare, Michael Davy, Adam Bermingham, Paul Ferguson, Páraic Sheridan, Cathal Gurrin, and Alan F Smeaton. 2009. Topic-dependent sentiment analysis of financial blogs. In *Proceedings of the 1st international CIKM workshop on Topic-sentiment analysis for mass opinion*, pages 9–16.

Mike Schuster and Kuldip K Paliwal. 1997. Bidirectional recurrent neural networks. *IEEE transactions on Signal Processing*, 45(11):2673–2681.

David A Shamma, Lyndon Kennedy, and Elizabeth F Churchill. 2009. Tweet the debates: understanding community annotation of uncollected sources. In *Proceedings of the first SIGMM workshop on Social media*, pages 3–10.

Nitish Srivastava, Geoffrey Hinton, Alex Krizhevsky, Ilya Sutskever, and Ruslan Salakhutdinov. 2014. Dropout: a simple way to prevent neural networks from overfitting. *The journal of machine learning research*, 15(1):1929–1958.

Pyry Takala, Pekka Malo, Ankur Sinha, and Oskar Ahlgren. 2014. Gold-standard for topic-specific sentiment analysis of economic texts. In *Proceedings of the Ninth International Conference on Language Resources and Evaluation*, volume 2014, pages 2152–2157.

Mike Thelwall, Kevan Buckley, and Georgios Paltoglou. 2012. Sentiment strength detection for the social web. *Journal of the American Society for Information Science and Technology*, 63(1):163–173.

Theresa Wilson, Paul Hoffmann, Swapna Somasundaran, Jason Kessler, Janyce Wiebe, Yejin Choi, Claire Cardie, Ellen Riloff, and Siddharth Patwardhan. 2005. Opinionfinder: A system for subjectivity analysis. In *HLT/EMNLP*, pages 34–35. The Association for Computational Linguistics.

Yang Yu and Xiao Wang. 2015. World cup 2014 in the twitter world: A big data analysis of sentiments in us sports fans tweets. *Computers in Human Behavior*, 48:392–400.

# Towards Emotion Recognition in Hindi-English Code-Mixed Data: A Transformer Based Approach

**Anshul Wadhawan and Akshita Aggarwal**
Department of Computer Engineering
Netaji Subhas University of Technology
Dwarka, New Delhi
{anshulw, akshitaa}.co.16@nsit.net.in

## Abstract

In the last few years, emotion detection in social-media text has become a popular problem due to its wide ranging application in better understanding the consumers, in psychology, in aiding human interaction with computers, designing smart systems etc. Because of the availability of huge amounts of data from social-media, which is regularly used for expressing sentiments and opinions, this problem has garnered great attention. In this paper, we present a Hinglish dataset labelled for emotion detection. We highlight a deep learning based approach for detecting emotions in Hindi-English code mixed tweets, using bilingual word embeddings derived from FastText and Word2Vec approaches, as well as transformer based models. We experiment with various deep learning models, including CNNs, LSTMs, Bi-directional LSTMs (with and without attention), along with transformers like BERT, RoBERTa, and ALBERT. The transformer based BERT model outperforms all other models giving the best performance with an accuracy of 71.43%.

## 1 Introduction

With the growth of social networking sites like Facebook and Twitter, humans have started communicating online much more than ever before. This leads to the generation of huge amounts of textual data which introduces interesting challenges in the domain of NLP. Automatic detection of various linguistic expressions like irony, hate, sarcasm, aggression etc. is being widely explored. Another problem that has drawn keen interest of NLP researchers is detecting emotions of a human via the texts they have produced. In order to aid human-computer interaction, determining the emotions via texts becomes significant (Greaves et al., 2009). There are multiple ways of detecting emotions, including but not limited to speech (Schmitt et al., 2016), facial expressions recognition (Ko, 2018) and text-based approaches.

Text-based emotion detection is based on the assumption that when a person is happy, they would use positive words. Likewise, when they are angry, frustrated or upset, negative emotions will be depicted by a certain kind of words carrying negative connotation. Contrary to popular belief, emotions are not only significant in human creativity, but they also play an instrumental part in making rational decisions. With the rise of artificial intelligence and increased focus on human-computer interaction, smart machines that will communicate naturally and intelligently with humans, need to recognize their emotions effectively. Affective computing has emerged as an exciting field with recent focus on emotion detection (Picard, 2000).

Most of earlier work has been carried out on a mono-lingual dataset due to easy availability of a large corpus of annotated data (Chen et al., 2010; Canales and Martínez-Barco, 2014). However, in multilingual cultures, use of multiple languages while exchanging information on social media is quite common. Studies show that as many as 314.9 million people in India are bilingual[1]. This leads to the issue of code-mixing and code-switching especially while communicating on social media platforms like Twitter, Facebook and Reddit (Gupta et al., 2016; Mónica et al., 2009). Code-mixing occurs when lexicons and grammatical features of multiple languages are used in the same sentence (Poplack and Walker, 2003; Auer and Wei, 2007; 10, 2009). The major issue in dealing with code-mixed problems is the absence of sufficiently annotated datasets (Nguyen and Dogruoz, 2013).

In this paper, we present our findings on one of the most challenging problems in the domain of Natural Language Processing, 'emotion detection'.

[1] https://en.wikipedia.org/wiki/Multilingualism_in_India



*Proceedings of the 11th Workshop on Computational Approaches to Subjectivity, Sentiment and Social Media Analysis*, pages 195–202
April 19, 2021. ©2021 Association for Computational Linguistics

While a lot of work has been carried out for the English language (Aman and Szpakowicz, 2007), the domain of Hindi-English code-mixed texts remains relatively new and not much explored. We present an annotated Hindi-English code-mixed dataset of 150k tweets for addressing this issue and for enabling future researchers to contribute to this domain. Our aim in this paper is to compare multiple deep learning models including CNNs, LSTMs, Bi-directional LSTMs (with and without attention) with the aid of bilingual self-trained word embeddings on a code-mixed dataset, along with transformer based models like BERT, RoBERTa, and ALBERT.

The paper is organized as follows – Section 2 details about the background and related work in this domain. Section 3 enumerates the methodology we used to perform the experiments including data annotation, pre-processing, embeddings and models used. Section 4 lists down the experimental settings to replicate the work done. Section 5 contains details of the results obtained and section 6 consists of conclusions drawn from the results.

## 2 Related Work

With the huge growth of micro-blogging platforms like Facebook and Twitter, there has been an increased interest in detecting sentiments and emotions in large text corpus (Kouloumpis et al., 2011; Pak and Paroubek, 2010). In initial work aimed at emotion detection in textual data, experiments have been carried out with text-based emotion classification in fairy tales for kids on the lines of basic emotions (Alm et al., 2005; Ekman, 1992). In another related work (Liu et al., 2003), the authors work on real-world knowledge bases highlighting human's natural reactions towards various situations, aimed at identifying emotions at the sentence-level. With the increase of non-native English speakers on social media, sentiment analysis on regional languages and code-mixed data has gained momentum.

A pivotal work of sentiment analysis in Hindi corpus was done, where the authors were successful in extracting sentiment lexons from HindiWordNet and were able to achieve an accuracy of 87% in the domain of movie (Joshi et al., 2010). In a detailed analysis of data of English-Hindi bilingual users on Facebook, it was shown that 17.2% of all posts, which accounted for around one-fourth of the words in their dataset, revealed some form of code-mixing (Bali et al., 2014). Sub-word level LSTM architecture for performing sentiment analysis was introduced on Hindi-English code-mixed dataset (Prabhu et al., 2016). Experiments were conducted with supervised learning (SVM) on a Hindi-English code-mixed corpus for emotion detection (Vijay et al., 2018).

## 3 Proposed Methodology

This section describes the series of steps that constitute the methodology proposed, including detailed descriptions of dataset creation, annotation, preprocessing, embeddings, and the deep learning models.

### 3.1 Dataset Creation

The dataset annotated by paper (Vijay et al., 2018) contains 2866 tweets. This data being insufficient for doing any meaningful work with deep learning due to the issue of overfitting, we created a self-annotated class-balanced dataset using TwitterScraper API[2] with relevant search tags like #happy, #sad, #angry, #fear, #disgust, #wow along with some commonly used hindi words to obtain Hinglish data.

### 3.2 Dataset Annotation and Analysis

We scraped around 250k tweets for analysis. After dropping the noisy instances containing unknown characters, we filtered the dataset down to a class balanced corpus of 150k tweets. The tweets were annotated with six standard emotions, including, happiness, sadness, anger, fear, disgust and surprise (Ekman, 1992). The hashtags which were used as searching criteria for scraping the tweets, were used for annotation. All examples which were fetched using hashtags like #yayy were marked to have a positive happiness label. This process was repeated for all the 6 emotions under consideration. The number of tweets per class is depicted in Table 1. Initially, embeddings were trained on just Hinglish tweets, however, English tweets were added later because of excess of hindi words in Hinglish tweets, causing a lack of English specific words. The labelled emotion detection dataset along with the deep learning classification models is made available online[3] to

[2] https://github.com/taspinar/twitterscraper

[3] https://github.com/anshulwadhawan/emotion_detection

| Emotion | Number of instances |
|---|---|
| Happiness | 25869 |
| Sadness | 20931 |
| Anger | 28705 |
| Fear | 18981 |
| Disgust | 35667 |
| Surprise | 18935 |
| Total sentences | 149088 |

Table 1: Tweet count per class

promote additional research.

Examples of some annotated data :

TWEET: Great darshan today at siddhi vinayak along wid aarti!! #happiness @dollydas261 @vishal71182 @vishalbti ..

TRANSLATION: Had a great experience in Siddhi Vinayak Temple, along with the ceremonies #happiness

EMOTION: Happy

TWEET : Jindagi me Maut sabse bada loss nahi, sabse bada loss tab hota hai jab Do logo ke jinda rehte hue unke beech aapsi riste toot jaye.#Sad :(

TRANSLATION: The biggest loss in life is not death. The biggest loss is banishment of relations between loved ones even when alive.

EMOTION: Sad

### 3.3 Data Preprocessing

We preprocessed the scraped data by retaining only Hinglish tweets while removing tweets in pure English and Devanagari. We also removed rare words (words having occurrence of less than 10 in the entire dataset), mentions, '#' symbols, URLs, punctuations and keywords used for scraping (like happy, sad, etc.) in order to feed our models with cleaner data.

### 3.4 Creation of Hindi-English Bi-lingual Word Embeddings

This being a multi-label text classification problem, it is required that the text be first converted to a form understandable by the various machine learning algorithms. Word embeddings are numerical representation of words. Specifically, word embeddings are vector representations of words that are learned in an unsupervised manner where their relative similarities are directly related to their semantic similarity (Mandelbaum and Shalev, 2016). Due to unavailability of pre-trained Hindi-English bilingual word embeddings, we created our own embeddings by scrapping 427k Hinglish tweets and 300k English tweets using TwitterScrapper API. Processing was carried out by removing pure English and pure Devanagari tweets along with rare words, hashtags and mentions for obtaining better training results. We chose 2 types of word embeddings for our problem, each of which was trained on two kinds of datasets, after processing (removing hashtags, user mentions, URLs, punctuations and keywords used for scraping), one which had only Hinglish tweets, the other which had a mix of English and Hinglish tweets. In order to get the right co-relation between the words of the two languages, we experimented with a mixture of Hinglish and English tweets.

**Word2Vec**: In this kind of embedding, words are converted to vector representations where words having common context are placed in vicinity amidst the vector space (Mikolov et al., 2013). Taking a huge corpus of words as input, it generates a vector space with each word being assigned a unique vector value in that space. Since the available Word2Vec embeddings are pre-trained on English datasets only, we trained our embeddings on custom Hindi-English code-mixed dataset, to obtain the desired code-mixed embeddings.

**FastText**: FastText is a modification to the Word2Vec embeddings that was developed by Facebook in 2016 (Joulin et al., 2017). FastText assumes a word to be composed of character n-grams (Bojanowski et al., 2017) and hence breaks a given word into various sub-words (Example: light, li, ig, igt, gt) unlike word2vec which feeds individual words to the network. The training session of a FastText model involves learning of weights for not only the whole word, but also for each of the character n-grams. Unlike Word2vec, it can not only approximate rare words but also give representation of words not present in the corpus, as now it is highly possible that some of their n-grams are present in other words. This is particularly useful for messages on social networks where multiple representations are used for similar words (like pyar, pyaar, pyaaar).

### 3.5 Deep Learning Models

We introduce seven deep learning based models for solving the task of emotion detection in textual

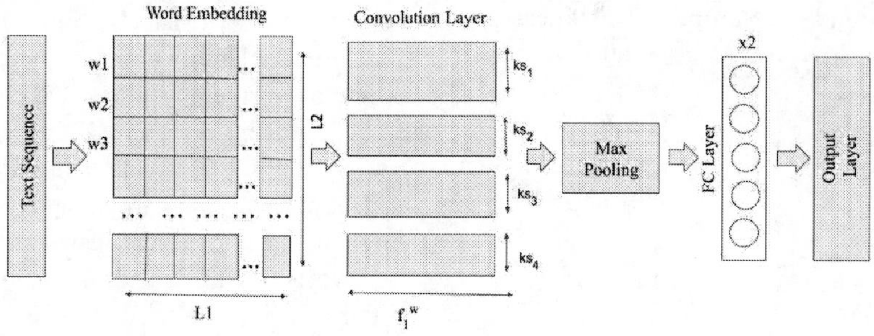


Figure 1: CNN model architecture

code-mixed data. The models proposed are CNN, LSTM, Bi-directional LSTM, attention based Bi-directional LSTM and transformer based models like BERT, RoBERTa and ALBERT. We trained FastText and Word2vec word representations on two types of data, one which solely consisted of hinglish text, the other which was a mixture of hinglish and english text. These embeddings were then used to predict the emotion of the tweet by serving as input to all the proposed models except the transformer based models.

### 3.5.1 Convolutional Neural Networks (CNNs)

CNNs have been proven to be successful for multi class classification problems, where images are provided as inputs (Ezat et al., 2020). In our case, word embeddings are given as input, from which features are extracted and final classification is performed. The network architecture we employed has been depicted in Fig. 2. Embedding layer serves as the first layer, which is used to transfer the word vector representations of select words in the tweet under consideration, to the model structure. Four convolutional layers in parallel receive the output of the embedding layer, followed by a global max pooling layer, upon which dropout is applied. Three dense fully connected layers follow in which the last layer is responsible for classification. Application of dropout led to better convergence and decreased difference in the training and validation accuracies.

### 3.5.2 Recurrent Neural Networks (RNNs)

The context in which a word is used, determines the meaning of the word, which in-turn may play a significant role in determining the overall sentiment of the sentence. For example,

Sentence 1 : There are multiple kinds of human beings in this huge world.

Sentence 2 : She is very generous and kind-hearted.

The context in which the word 'kind' is used, is different in both the sentences, thus the word carries different meanings in different scenarios. RNNs are helpful in modelling the context of a word, by having unique ways to capture the context of words using the surrounding words.

**Long Short-Term Memory (LSTM)**: LSTMs have been shown to capture the relevant context for words (Tran et al., 2017) as well as address the issue of vanishing gradients (Hochreiter and Schmidhuber, 1997). The words which precede a particular

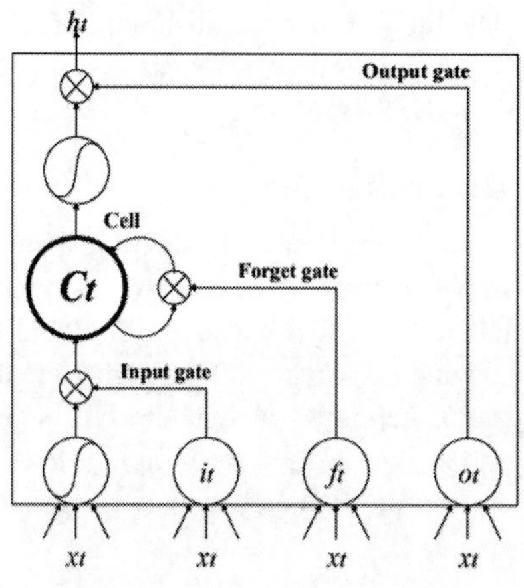


Figure 2: LSTM block structure

word, determine the context of the word. LSTMs inculcate memory cells in the network which serve to record the meaning of words that occurred previously. In order to model this scenario, an LSTM based network is constructed. In our model, an embedding layer, followed by an LSTM layer, further followed by 2 fully connected layers constitute the network. The last layer, consisting of 6 neurons, is responsible for the classification of the tweet's emotion.

**Bi-directional LSTM**: Bi-directional LSTMs have been proven successful in capturing the context for text classification tasks (Wang et al., 2016). The words that precede as well as follow a particular word, determine the context of the word under consideration. Thus, memory cells must exist in both directions in order to maintain the track of words that surround a particular word. This is achieved by appending 2 LSTM layers to the embedding layer, whose concatenated output ($\overrightarrow{h_T}$, $\overleftarrow{h_1}$) is flattened and fed to 2 fully connected (FC) layers. The last layer carries out classification, as is done in all other proposed models.

**Attention based Bi-directional LSTM**: The technique of attention is based on learning the words which contribute the most towards the overall emotion of the sentence, and filtering out the words which contribute the least, i.e. noise. Attention based BiLSTM differs in the manner of concatenation of states, which is fed to the fully connected (FC) layers. Apart from using concatenated $\{\overrightarrow{h_T}, \overleftarrow{h_1}\}$ ($\overrightarrow{h_T}$ denoting forward directed final hidden state representation, $\overleftarrow{h_1}$ denoting backward directed first hidden state representation) as inputs to the fully connected layers, attention based BiLSTMs also take into consideration the weighted summation of all time steps ($\overrightarrow{h_t}$, $\overleftarrow{h_t}$). Hence, all hidden states serve as inputs to the 2 dense fully connected layers, out of which the final layer performs the classification.

#### 3.5.3 Transformer Based Models

**BERT (bert-base-uncased)**: (Devlin et al., 2018) Being a bidirectional transformer based model pretrained on a large Wikipedia and Toronto Book Corpus, BERT makes use of a combination of objectives which are meant for the next sentence prediction and masked language modeling tasks. **RoBERTa (roberta-base)**: (Liu et al., 2019) With some modifications to the parameters of BERT, i.e. changing key hyperparameters, removing the next sentence prediction objective, and training with larger learning rate and batch size values, RoBERTa is built on top of BERT. **ALBERT (albert-base-v2)**: (Lan et al., 2019) Trying to increase the training speed and decrease the memory utilization of BERT, ALBERT is another variation of BERT which repeats layers which are split among groups and splits the embedding matrix into two.

| Parameter | Value |
|---|---|
| **Embedding Training** | |
| Embedding Size | 300 |
| Window Length | 10 |
| Sampling Polarity | Negative |
| **CNN Training** | |
| Dropout | 0.5 |
| Stride | 1 |
| #Kernels | 200 |
| $ks_1$ | 3 |
| $ks_2$ | 6 |
| $ks_3$ | 9 |
| $ks_4$ | 12 |
| **RNN Training** | |
| #LSTM Units | 150 |
| Input State Dropout | 0.2 |
| Recurrent State Dropout | 0.2 |
| **Transformers Fine Tuning** | |
| Learning Rate | 1e-5 |
| Epsilon (Adam optimizer) | 1e-8 |
| Maximum Sequence Length | 256 |
| Batch Size | 3 |
| #Epochs | 5 |

Table 2: Parameter Values

## 4 Experimental Settings

A split of ten percent was made on the total training dataset and the model was trained for a total of 20 epochs. At each epoch, we saved the model checkpoints, and particularly used that checkpoint which was saved before the model begins to overfit to calculate the metrics on the ten percent test dataset split.

Different hyper parameters are involved for the task of training embeddings as well as the models. After working with several optimizers, loss functions and activation functions, the adam optimizer with categorical cross entropy loss function produced the best results for all stated deep learning models. We used relu activation function for all the layers except the output layer, which has sigmoid activation function. We evaluated the performance of CNN models with different values for kernel sizes, activation functions, number of kernels, dropouts, strides and optimizers.

We use pre-trained models like bert-base-uncased, roberta-base, and albert-base-v2, to fine tune the transformer based models on our dataset.

| DL Models | Hinglish Data | | Hinglish + English Data | |
|---|---|---|---|---|
| | Word2Vec | FastText | Word2Vec | FastText |
| CNN | 62.22 | 62.24 | 63.00 | 62.52 |
| LSTM | 63.83 | 63.69 | 64.04 | 64.59 |
| Bi-LSTM | 64.80 | 66.02 | 65.32 | 66.37 |
| Bi-LSTM attention | 66.65 | 67.34 | 67.44 | 68.29 |
| BERT | **71.43** | | | |
| RoBERTa | 70.06 | | | |
| ALBERT | 66.22 | | | |

Table 3: Accuracy of Deep Learning Models

Hugging-face[4] API was used to fine tune all the transformer based models. Table 2 denotes the hyperparameter combinations used in the training of embeddings, CNN, RNN and fine tuning transformer based models.

## 5 Results

Using all features, (Vijay et al., 2018) show that the baseline model i.e. the SVM classifier with RBF kernel, presented an accuracy of 58.2%, when dealing with the same emotion labels as we deal with in this paper. In the domain of emotion detection in Hindi-English code-mixed data, as far as we know, we are the first to compare transformer based models and word representations. In table 4, the results of CNN, RNN based models for both Word2Vec and FastText based word representations, along with those of transformer based models have been presented. All proposed deep learning models yield better results than state-of-the-art models which deal with these six emotion labels. The best accuracy of 71.43% is achieved with BERT, as expected. All models utilizing embeddings trained on Hinglish plus English data, perform better than those using embeddings trained on Hinglish data. One conceivable reason for this observation can be the extra coverage of semantics and correlation between the word vectors of English information, which can be utilized for code blended Hinglish information, hence serving as prior data for Hinglish embeddings information. The method works practically equivalent to a knowledge transfer step in which embeddings for English information are utilized as earlier information for embeddings of Hinglish information. Additionally, increased accuracies of all models in case of FastText embeddings, as compared to the Word2Vec embeddings, is observed. One possible reason for this could be the existence of code blended information where FastText enables the coverage of code-mixed vocabulary as against word2Vec which works only on the basis of overall context of word. The transformer based BERT model clearly outperforms both CNN and RNN based models, majorly because of its profound efficiency and its ability to process the input out of order.

The major obstacles in the task of detecting emotions in Hindi-English code-mixed data are handling the linguistic complexities associated with code-mixed data and absence of clean data. Thus, we require even more class-specific cleaner data, in order to reduce the effect of noise, which comes from spelling mistakes, stemming words and the presence of multiple contexts.

## 6 Conclusion

As recent years have seen the rise in usage of social media for open expression of stance and opinions, sentiment analysis and opinion mining have gained attention as problems and become primary areas of research.

In this paper, we present an openly available class-balanced dataset of Hindi-English code-mixed data, consisting of tweets belonging to 6 types of emotions, which are happiness, sadness, anger, surprise, fear and disgust. We contrast the performance of two types of word representations, both trained on relevant scraped tweets from scratch. We develop two different types of embeddings, one which is trained on solely Hinglish tweets, the other which is trained on a mix of Hinglish and English tweets, and present the performance in both cases. Also, we present deep learning based models including CNNs, RNNs, and transformers, where BERT performs the best

[4] `https://huggingface.co/transformers/`

among all.

As future scope, the problem can be solved to obtain even better results by carrying out a comparison of MUSE aligned vectors, pre-aligned FastText word embeddings and language specific transformer based word embeddings.

## References


2009. *The Cambridge Handbook of Linguistic Code-switching*. Cambridge Handbooks in Language and Linguistics. Cambridge University Press.

Cecilia Alm, Dan Roth, and Richard Sproat. 2005. Emotions from text: Machine learning for text-based emotion prediction. pages 579—-586.

Saima Aman and Stan Szpakowicz. 2007. Identifying expressions of emotion in text. In *Proceedings of the 10th International Conference on Text, Speech and Dialogue*, TSD'07, page 196–205, Berlin, Heidelberg. Springer-Verlag.

Peter Auer and Li Wei. 2007. *Handbook of Multilingualism and Multilingual Communication*. De Gruyter Mouton, Berlin, Boston.

Kalika Bali, Jatin Sharma, Monojit Choudhury, and Yogarshi Vyas. 2014. "I am borrowing ya mixing ?" an analysis of English-Hindi code mixing in Facebook. In *Proceedings of the First Workshop on Computational Approaches to Code Switching*, pages 116–126, Doha, Qatar. Association for Computational Linguistics.

Piotr Bojanowski, Edouard Grave, Armand Joulin, and Tomas Mikolov. 2017. Enriching word vectors with subword information. *Transactions of the Association for Computational Linguistics*, 5:135–146.

Lea Canales and Patricio Martínez-Barco. 2014. Emotion detection from text: A survey.

Ying Chen, Sophia Lee, Shoushan Li, and Chu-Ren Huang. 2010. Emotion cause detection with linguistic constructions. volume 2, pages 179–187.

Jacob Devlin, Ming-Wei Chang, Kenton Lee, and Kristina Toutanova. 2018. Bert: Pre-training of deep bidirectional transformers for language understanding.

Paul Ekman. 1992. An argument for basic emotions. *Cognition and Emotion*, 6(3-4):169–200.

Wael Ezat, Mohamed Dessouky, and Nabil Ismail. 2020. Multi-class image classification using deep learning algorithm. *Journal of Physics: Conference Series*, 1447:012021.

Jean Greaves, Travis Bradberry, and Patrick M. Lencioni. 2009. *Emotional Intelligence 2.0*. CA : TalentSmart, San Diego.

Sakshi Gupta, Piyush Bansal, and Radhika Mamidi. 2016. Resource creation for hindi-english code mixed social media text.

Sepp Hochreiter and Jürgen Schmidhuber. 1997. Long short-term memory. *Neural Comput.*, 9(8):1735–1780.

Aditya Joshi, Balamurali A R, and Pushpak Bhattacharyya. 2010. A fall-back strategy for sentiment analysis in hindi: a case study. In *Proceedings of the 8th ICON*.

Armand Joulin, Edouard Grave, Piotr Bojanowski, and Tomas Mikolov. 2017. Bag of tricks for efficient text classification. In *Proceedings of the 15th Conference of the European Chapter of the Association for Computational Linguistics: Volume 2, Short Papers*, pages 427–431, Valencia, Spain. Association for Computational Linguistics.

Byoung Chul Ko. 2018. A brief review of facial emotion recognition based on visual information. *Sensors*, 18(2):1–20.

Efthymios Kouloumpis, Theresa Wilson, and Johanna D. Moore. 2011. Twitter sentiment analysis: The good the bad and the omg! In *ICWSM*, pages 538–541.

Zhenzhong Lan, Mingda Chen, Sebastian Goodman, Kevin Gimpel, Piyush Sharma, and Radu Soricut. 2019. Albert: A lite bert for self-supervised learning of language representations.

Hugo Liu, Henry Lieberman, and Ted Selker. 2003. A model of textual affect sensing using real-world knowledge. In *Proceedings of the 8th International Conference on Intelligent User Interfaces*, IUI '03, page 125–132, New York, NY, USA. Association for Computing Machinery.

Yinhan Liu, Myle Ott, Naman Goyal, Jingfei Du, Mandar Joshi, Danqi Chen, Omer Levy, Mike Lewis, Luke Zettlemoyer, and Veselin Stoyanov. 2019. Roberta: A robustly optimized bert pretraining approach.

Amit Mandelbaum and Adi Shalev. 2016. Word embeddings and their use in sentence classification tasks.

Tomas Mikolov, Ilya Sutskever, Kai Chen, Greg Corrado, and Jeffrey Dean. 2013. Distributed representations of words and phrases and their compositionality. In *Proceedings of the 26th International Conference on Neural Information Processing Systems - Volume 2*, NIPS'13, page 3111–3119, Red Hook, NY, USA. Curran Associates Inc.

Stella Mónica, Mónica Cárdenas-Claros, and Neny Isharyanti. 2009. Code switching and code mixing in internet chating: betwen "yes", "ya", and "si" a case study. *The jaltcall Journal*, Vol 5:67–78.

Dong-Phuong Nguyen and A. Seza Dogruoz. 2013. Word level language identification in online multilingual communication. In *Proceedings of the 2013 Conference on Empirical Methods in Natural Language Processing*, pages 857–862, United States. Association for Computational Linguistics (ACL).

Alexander Pak and Patrick Paroubek. 2010. Twitter as a corpus for sentiment analysis and opinion mining. volume 10.

Rosalind W Picard. 2000. *Affective computing*. MIT press.

Shana Poplack and James Walker. 2003. Pieter muysken, bilingual speech: a typology of code-mixing. cambridge: Cambridge university press, 2000. pp. xvi+306. *Journal of Linguistics*, 39:678 – 683.

Ameya Prabhu, Aditya Joshi, Manish Shrivastava, and Vasudeva Varma. 2016. Towards sub-word level compositions for sentiment analysis of hindi-english code mixed text.

Maximilian Schmitt, Fabien Ringeval, and Björn W. Schuller. 2016. At the border of acoustics and linguistics: Bag-of-audio-words for the recognition of emotions in speech. In *INTERSPEECH*, pages 495–499.

Duc Tran, Hieu Mac, Van Tong, Hai-Anh Tran, and Giang Nguyen. 2017. A lstm based framework for handling multiclass imbalance in dga botnet detection. *Neurocomputing*, 275.

Deepanshu Vijay, Aditya Bohra, Vinay Singh, Syed Sarfaraz Akhtar, and Manish Shrivastava. 2018. Corpus creation and emotion prediction for Hindi-English code-mixed social media text. In *Proceedings of the 2018 Conference of the North American Chapter of the Association for Computational Linguistics: Student Research Workshop*, pages 128–135, New Orleans, Louisiana, USA. Association for Computational Linguistics.

Yequan Wang, Minlie Huang, Xiaoyan Zhu, and Li Zhao. 2016. Attention-based LSTM for aspect-level sentiment classification. In *Proceedings of the 2016 Conference on Empirical Methods in Natural Language Processing*, pages 606–615, Austin, Texas. Association for Computational Linguistics.

# Nearest neighbour approaches for Emotion Detection in Tweets

**Olha Kaminska**
Computational Web Intelligence
Department of Applied Mathematics,
Computer Science and Statistics
Ghent University

**Chris Cornelis**
Computational Web Intelligence
Department of Applied Mathematics,
Computer Science and Statistics
Ghent University

**Veronique Hoste**
LT3 Language and Translation Technology Team
Ghent University
{Olha.Kaminska,Chris.Cornelis,Veronique.Hoste}@UGent.be

## Abstract

Emotion detection is an important task that can be applied to social media data to discover new knowledge. While the use of deep learning methods for this task has been prevalent, they are black-box models, making their decisions hard to interpret for a human operator. Therefore, in this paper, we propose an approach using weighted $k$ Nearest Neighbours (kNN), a simple, easy to implement, and explainable machine learning model. These qualities can help to enhance results' reliability and guide error analysis.

In particular, we apply the weighted kNN model to the shared emotion detection task in tweets from SemEval-2018. Tweets are represented using different text embedding methods and emotion lexicon vocabulary scores, and classification is done by an ensemble of weighted kNN models. Our best approaches obtain results competitive with state-of-the-art solutions and open up a promising alternative path to neural network methods.

## 1 Introduction

In this paper, we consider SemEval-2018 Task 1 EI-oc: Affect in Tweets for English[1] (Mohammad et al., 2018). This is a classification problem in which data instances are raw tweets, labeled with scores expressing how much each of four considered emotions (anger, sadness, joy, and fear) are present.

Our target is to implement the weighted $k$ Nearest Neighbor (wkNN) algorithm to detect emotions in tweets. In doing so, we consider different ways of tweet embeddings and combine them with various emotional lexicons, which provide an emotional score for each word.

The motivation for using wkNN is to show the potential of a simple, interpretable machine learning approach compared to black-box techniques based on more complex models like neural networks (NNs). By contrast to the latter, wkNN's predictions for a test sample can be traced back easily to the training samples (the nearest neighbours) that triggered this decision.

We note that we still use NN-based methods for obtaining tweet embeddings. One could therefore argue that our method is not fully explainable; however, we feel that it is less important to understand how tweets are initially represented in an $n$-dimensional space, than to explain how they are used in making predictions for nearby instances.

The remainder of this paper is organized as follows: in Section 2 we discuss related work, mainly focusing on the winning approaches of SemEval-2018 Task 1. In Section 3, we describe the methodology behind our solution, including data cleaning, tweet representations through word embeddings, lexicon vocabularies, and their combinations; our proposed ensemble method for classification; and finally, evaluation measures. In Section 4, we report the observed performance on training and development data for the different setups of our proposal, while Section 5 lists the results of the best approach on the test data and compares them to the competition results. In Section 6, we examine some of the test samples with correct and wrong predictions to see how we can use our model's interpretability to explain the obtained results. Finally, in Section 7, we discuss our results and consider possible ways to improve them.

[1] https://competitions.codalab.org/competitions/17751



*Proceedings of the 11th Workshop on Computational Approaches to Subjectivity, Sentiment and Social Media Analysis*, pages 203–212
April 19, 2021. ©2021 Association for Computational Linguistics

## 2 Related work

First, we briefly recall the most successful proposals[2] to the SemEval-2018 task. The winning approach (Duppada et al., 2018) uses tweet embedding vectors in ensembles of XGBoost and Random Forest classification models. The runners-up (Gee and Wang, 2018) perform transfer learning with Long Short Term Memory (LSTM) neural networks. The third-place contestants (Rozental and Fleischer, 2018) train an ensemble of a complex model consisting of Gated-Recurrent-Units (GRU) using a convolution neural network (CNN) as an attention mechanism.

It is clear that the leaderboard is dominated by solutions that are neither simple nor interpretable. This comes as no surprise, given that the effectiveness of a solution is evaluated only using the Pearson Correlation Coefficient (see formula (3) in Section 3.5).

In general, machine learning models in the Natural Language Processing (NLP) field rarely explain their predicted labels. This inspires the need for explainable models, which concentrate on interpreting outputs and the connection of inputs with outputs. For example, Liu et al. (2019) present an explainable classification approach that solves NLP tasks with comparable accuracy to neural networks and also generates explanations for its solutions.

Recently, Danilevsky et al. (2020) presented an overview of explainable methods for NLP tasks. Apart from focusing on explanations of model predictions, they also discuss the most important techniques to generate and visualize explanations. The paper also discusses evaluation techniques to measure the quality of the obtained explanations, which could be useful in future work.

In this paper, we consider one of the simplest explainable models: the kNN method. In the context of NLP, kNN has recently been applied by (Fatema Rajani et al., 2020) as a backoff method for classifiers based on BERT and RoBERTa (see Section 3.2). In particular, when the latter NN methods are less confident about their predictions, the kNN solution is used instead. In this paper, we will only use such NN approaches at the data representation level and rely on weighted kNN only during classification.

[2]Competition results: `https://competitions.codalab.org/competitions/17751#results`

## 3 Methodology

In this section, we describe the different ingredients of our approach, more precisely, data preprocessing, embedding methods, emotional lexicon vocabularies, classification, and evaluation methods.

We focus on the emotion intensity ordinal classification task (EI-oc) (Mohammad et al., 2018). Given each of the four considered emotions (anger, fear, joy, sadness), the task is to classify a tweet in English into one of four ordinal classes of emotion intensity (0: no emotion can be inferred, 1: low amount of emotion can be inferred, 2: moderate amount of emotion can be inferred, 3: high amount of emotion can be inferred) which best represents the mental state of the tweeter.

Separate training, development, and test datasets were provided for each emotion. To train the classification model, we merge the training and development datasets to evaluate our results with the cross-validation method.

### 3.1 Data cleaning

Before starting the embedding process, we can clean tweets in several ways:

- General preprocessing. First, we delete account tags (starting with '@'), newline symbols ('\n'), extra white spaces, all punctuation marks, and numbers. Next, we replace '&' with the word 'and' and replace emojis with textual descriptions.

  We save hashtags as a potential source of useful information (Mohammad and Kiritchenko, 2015) but delete '#' symbols.

  We do not delete emojis because, following the observations from Wolny (2016), using emoji symbols could significantly improve precision in identifying various types of emotions. In the source data, emojis are present in two ways: combinations of punctuation marks and/or letters and small pictures decoded with Unicode. The first type of emojis is replaced with their descriptions taking from the list of emoticons on Wikipedia[3]. The second type of emojis are transformed using the Python package *"emoji"* [4].

[3]`https://en.wikipedia.org/wiki/List_of_emoticons`

[4]`https://pypi.org/project/emoji/`

- Stop-word removal: for this process, the list of stop-words from the NLTK package[5] is used.

We do not apply preprocessing or stop-word removal a priori, but rather examine whether they improve the classification during the experimental stage.

### 3.2 Tweet embedding

To perform classification, each tweet is represented by a vector or set of vectors, using the following word embedding techniques:

- Pre-trained Word2Vec from the Gensim package[6]. This model includes 300-dimension word vectors for a vocabulary with 3 million words and phrases trained on a Google News dataset. It is included here because of its popularity in NLP tasks.

- DeepMoji[7] is a state-of-the-art sentiment embedding model, pre-trained on millions of tweets with emojis to recognize emotions and sarcasm. We used its implementation on PyTorch by Huggingface[8], which provides for each sentence an embedding of size 2304 dimensions.

- The Universal Sentence Encoder (USE) (Cer et al., 2018) is a sentence-level embedding approach developed by the TensorFlow team[9]. It provides a 512-dimensional vector for a sentence or even a whole paragraph that can be used for different tasks such as text classification, sentence similarity, etc. USE was trained with a deep averaging network (DAN) encoder on several data sources.

  The model is available in two options: trained with a DAN and with a Transformer encoder. After basic experiments, we chose the second one for further experiments.

- Bidirectional Encoder Representations from Transformers (BERT) by Devlin et al. (2019). The used script[10] was developed by The Google AI Language Team and extracted pre-computed feature vectors from a PyTorch BERT model. The length of the output vector for a word is 768 features. Words that are not in the BERT vocabulary were split into tokens (for example, the word "*tokens*" will be resented as "*tok*", "*##en*", "*##s*"), and for each token, a vector was created.

- Sentence-BERT (SBERT) is a modified and tuned BERT model presented in Reimers and Gurevych (2019). It uses so-called siamese and triplet network structures, or a "twin network", that processes two sentences in the same way simultaneously. SBERT provides embeddings at a sentence level with the same size as the original BERT.

- Twitter-roBERTa-based model for Emotion Recognition, one of the seven fine-tuned roBERTa models presented by Barbieri et al. (2020). Each described model was trained for a specific task and provided an embedding at the token level similar to BERT. The model that we consider was trained for the emotion detection task (E-c) using a different collection of tweets from the same authors of SemEval 2018 Task 1 (Mohammad et al., 2018), in which the emotions anger, joy, sadness, and optimism are used.

Sentence-level embeddings are applied to each tweet as a whole, while for word (or token) level embeddings, we represent a tweet vector as the mean of its words' (tokens') vectors.

### 3.3 Emotional lexicon vocabularies

As an additional source of information to complement tweet embeddings, we also consider lexicon scores. Emotional lexicons are vocabularies that provide scores of different emotion intensity for a word. In our experiments, we use the following English lexicons:

- Valence Arousal Dominance (NRC VAD) lexicon (20,007 words) (Mohammad, 2018a) – each word has a score (float number between 0 and 1) for Valence, Arousal, and Dominance.

[5] http://www.nltk.org/nltk_data/

[6] https://radimrehurek.com/gensim/models/word2vec.html

[7] https://deepmoji.mit.edu/

[8] https://github.com/huggingface/torchMoji

[9] https://www.tensorflow.org/hub/tutorials/semantic_similarity_with_tf_hub_universal_encoder

[10] https://github.com/dnanhkhoa/pytorch-pretrained-BERT/blob/master/examples/extract_features.py

- Emotional Lexicon (EMOLEX) (14,182 words) lexicon (Mohammad and Turney, 2013) – each word has ten scores (0 or 1), one per emotion: anger, anticipation, disgust, fear, joy, negative, positive, sadness, surprise, and trust.

- Affect Intensity (AI) lexicon (nearly 6,000 terms) (Mohammad, 2018b) – each word has four scores (float number from 0 to 1), one per emotion: anger, fear, sadness, and joy.

- Affective norms for English words (ANEW) lexicon (1034 words) (Bradley and Lang, 1999) – each word has six scores (float number between 0 and 10): Mean and SD for Valence, Arousal and Dominance.

- Warriner's lexicon (13,915 lemmas) (Warriner et al., 2013) – each word has 63 scores (float number between 0 and 1000 ), reflecting different statistical characteristics of Valence, Arousal, and Dominance.

We consider the following two methods of combining word embeddings with lexicon vocabulary scores:

- For each word during the embedding process, lexicon scores are appended to the end of the tweet vector. The size of the obtained vector is the word embedding size plus the number of lexicon scores.

- We construct a separate feature for each lexicon. These models are then combined with the embedding vectors in an ensemble classifier, as described in Section 3.4.

We perform experiments for all emotion datasets with one or several lexicons. The results are presented in Section 4.

### 3.4 Classification methods

In this subsection, the weighted $k$ Nearest Neighbors (wkNN) classification method (Dudani, 1976) and its similarity relation are described.

The wkNN is a refinement of the regular kNN, where distances to the neighbors are taken into account as weights. This approach aims to assign more significant weight to the closest instances and a smaller weight to the ones that are further away. The wkNN has two main parameters: the used metric or similarity relation and the number $k$ of considered neighbours.

To choose an appropriate similarity relation, we follow Huang (2008), who compared metrics for the document clustering task. The cosine metric was shown to be one of the best:

$$cos(A,B) = \frac{A \cdot B}{||A|| \times ||B||}, \quad (1)$$

where $A$ and $B$ denote elements from the same vector space, $A \cdot B$ is their scalar product, $|| * ||$ - vector norm.

Values provided by this measure are between -1 (perfectly dissimilar vectors) and 1 (perfectly similar vectors). In order to obtain a [0,1]-similarity relation instead of a metric, we use the following formula:

$$cos\_similarity(A,B) = \frac{1 + cos(A,B)}{2}. \quad (2)$$

Formula (2) is used as the primary similarity relation throughout this paper.

Regarding the parameter $k$, there is no one-fits-all rule to determine it. As a general *"rule of thumb"*, we can put $k = \frac{\sqrt{N}}{2}$, where $N$ is the number of samples in the dataset. However, to examine the impact of $k$, we will use various numbers of neighbors for each emotion dataset for the best-performing methods in our experiments.

We use wKNN both as a standalone method as well as inside of a classification ensemble. For the latter, a separate model is trained for each information source (vectors containing tweet embeddings, lexicon scores, or their combination).

For each test sample, each model's outputs are combined using the standard average as a voting function, i.e., each model gets the same weight in this vote. The architecture of our approach is illustrated in Fig. 1.

Note that in this way, the predictions will be float values between 0 and 3, rather than integer labels (0, 1, 2 or 3); however, at the training stage, this does not represent a problem.

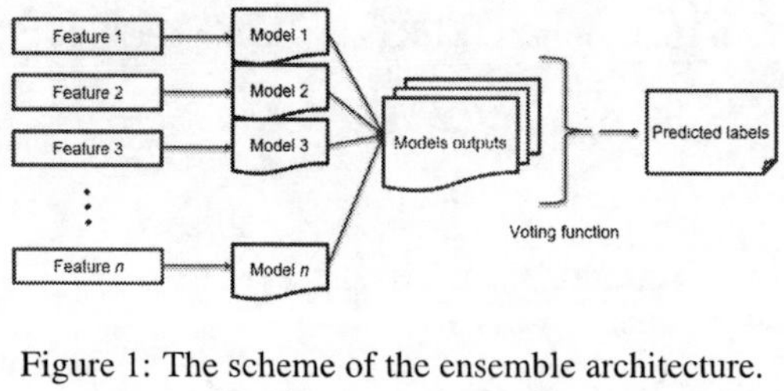


Figure 1: The scheme of the ensemble architecture.

Table 1: The best setup for each emotion for different embeddings.

| Setup | Anger | Joy | Sadness | Fear |
|---|---|---|---|---|
| **roBERTa-based** | | | | |
| Tweets preprocessing | No | No | No | Yes |
| Stop-words cleaning | No | No | No | No |
| Number of neighbors | 19 | 13 | 9 | 11 |
| PCC | **0.6651** | **0.6919** | **0.7055** | 0.5694 |
| **DeepMoji** | | | | |
| Tweets preprocessing | Yes | Yes | Yes | Yes |
| Stop-words cleaning | Yes | No | No | No |
| Number of neighbors | 11 | 21 | 13 | 13 |
| PCC | 0.6190 | 0.6426 | 0.6490 | **0.5737** |
| **USE** | | | | |
| Tweets preprocessing | Yes | Yes | Yes | No |
| Stop-words cleaning | No | No | No | No |
| Number of neighbors | 19 | 21 | 19 | 11 |
| PCC | 0.5174 | 0.5580 | 0.6067 | 0.5589 |
| **SBERT** | | | | |
| Tweets preprocessing | Yes | Yes | Yes | Yes |
| Stop-words cleaning | No | No | No | No |
| Number of neighbors | 21 | 9 | 21 | 13 |
| PCC | 0.4946 | 0.5413 | 0.5505 | 0.4608 |
| **Word2Vec** | | | | |
| Tweets preprocessing | Yes | Yes | Yes | Yes |
| Stop-words cleaning | Yes | Yes | Yes | Yes |
| The number of neighbors | 5 | 23 | 21 | 13 |
| PCC | 0.4824 | 0.4791 | 0.5136 | 0.4303 |

### 3.5 Evaluation method

To evaluate the performance of the implemented methods, 5-fold cross-validation is used, using as evaluation measure the Pearson Correlation Coefficient (PCC), as was also done for the competition.

Given the vectors of predicted values $y$ and correct values $x$, the PCC measure provides a value between $-1$ (a total negative linear correlation) and 1 (a total positive linear correlation), where 0 represents no linear correlation.

Hence, the best model should provide the highest value of PCC:

$$PCC = \frac{\sum_i (x_i - \bar{x})(y_i - \bar{y})}{\sqrt{\sum_i (x_i - \bar{x})^2 \sum_i (y_i - \bar{y})^2}}. \quad (3)$$

Here $x_i$ and $y_i$ refer to the $\text{i}^{\text{th}}$ component of vectors $x$ and $y$, while $\bar{x}$ and $\bar{y}$ represent their mean.

The correlation scores across all four emotions were averaged by the competition organizers to determine the bottom-line metric by which the submissions were ranked.

## 4 Experiments

Our experiments on the train and development are designed as follows: first, we compare the individual tweet embedding methods (Section 4.1) and examine which setup gives the best results. Then, in Section 4.2, we also involve the emotional lexicons, either independently, by appending them to tweet embedding vectors and in ensembles.

### 4.1 Detecting the best setup for embeddings

In this subsection, we describe the process of detecting the best data cleaning method and the best $k$ parameter value for each emotion dataset and each embedding. The results are shown in Table 1.

In the first step, for each emotion and each embedding, we calculate the PCC for different versions of the dataset: original raw tweets, preprocessed tweets, and preprocessed tweets with stop-words removed. To verify which approach works better, we perform statistical analysis using the two-sided $t$-test in Python's package $'stats'$.

In the second step, we repeat the experiments for the best preprocessing setups with different amounts of neighbours $(5, 7, 9, ..., 23)$ to detect the most appropriate $k$ value. These values and the resulting PCC for the optimal setup are shown in Table 1.

We can observe that stop-word cleaning only improved results for the Word2Vec embedding and that for the roBERTa-based model, it makes sense to use the raw tweets.

Also, among the different embeddings, roBERTa obtains the highest results on three out of four datasets, while for Fear, the best result is obtained by DeepMoji (with roBERTa a close second). This can be explained by the fact that these two embeddings are explicitly trained on emotion data. The three remaining embeddings lag considerably, with the notable exception of USE for Fear. We conjecture that this may have to do with the imbalanced nature of the fear dataset.

To measure the balance of the different datasets, we calculated the Imbalance Ratio (IR) of the combined train and development data, where IR is equal to the ratio of the sizes of the largest and smallest classes in the dataset. A value close to 1 represents balanced data.

With IR values of 1.677 and 1.47, respectively, the anger and joy datasets can be considered fairly balanced. While the imbalance is somewhat higher for the sadness dataset (IR = 2.2), the fear dataset is the most imbalanced dataset among with a IR value of 8.04.

### 4.2 Combining embeddings and lexicons

In this subsection, we discuss our experiments joining the previously identified best setups of the embedding methods with all emotional lexicons, using the different combination strategies outlined in Section 3.3.

#### 4.2.1 Lexicon-only based models

We first evaluate models based purely on lexicons. The goal here is to check the intrinsic classification strength of each lexicon and of the lexicon-based approach as a whole.

A lexicon works as a dictionary: if a word is present in the lexicon, it receives a particular score, in the other case, it is assigned a score of zero. For lexicons with several scores per word, we take all of them. To obtain the lexicon score for a full tweet, as usual, we compute the mean of its words' scores.

For each of the five lexicons, the output is saved as a separate vector. The sixth vector is constructed by combining all lexicons' scores and has a total length of 86 values (the sum of the number of scores for all five lexicons). For each of these vectors, a weighted kNN classification model is applied.

Initially, we use the same number of neighbours for all datasets, computed using the rule of thumb $k = \sqrt{N}/2$, where $N$ is the size of the dataset. The dataset sizes are mostly near to 2000 instances, so $k = 23$ is used. Results are presented in Table 2.

Table 2: Results for the lexicon-based approach.

| Lexicon | Anger | Joy | Sadness | Fear |
|---|---|---|---|---|
| VAD | 0.1983 | 0.2823 | 0.2043 | 0.0928 |
| EMOLEX | 0.3014 | 0.2893 | 0.3404 | 0.1943 |
| AI | **0.3284** | 0.2673 | **0.3723** | 0.1549 |
| ANEW | 0.1972 | 0.3050 | 0.3254 | **0.2278** |
| Warriner | 0.1901 | 0.2705 | 0.2970 | 0.1505 |
| Combined | 0.2133 | **0.3051** | 0.3151 | 0.1626 |

We can observe that the AI lexicon is the best performing lexicon, showing the highest results for two out of the four datasets.

Then, for each emotion dataset and its best performing lexicon, the best $k$ value is detected. These results are presented in Table 3.

Table 3: The best setup for each emotion for different lexicon-based feature vectors.

| Dataset | Lexicon | $k$ value | PCC |
|---|---|---|---|
| Anger | AI | 11 | 0.3359 |
| Joy | Combined | 19 | 0.3320 |
| Sadness | AI | 23 | 0.3723 |
| Fear | ANEW | 17 | 0.2412 |

As we can see, for different datasets, different values of $k$ perform better.

#### 4.2.2 Models appending lexicon scores to word embeddings

In this approach, embedding and lexicon scores are normalized to values between 0 and 1 to account for differences in ranges. To obtain the vector of a tweet, we take the average of all vectors of its words.

The results of these combination experiments are provided in Table 4. To check the appending strategy's added value, Table 4 also presents the previously obtained PCC score using none of the lexicons for each embedding method.

As can be seen, for half of the experiments, the use of lexicons does not improve the PCC value. The roBERTa-based model is the only model that

Table 4: Results for the first combination approach.

| Lexicon | Anger | Joy | Sadness | Fear |
|---|---|---|---|---|
| | **roBERTa-based model** | | | |
| VAD | 0.6536 | 0.6845 | 0.6986 | 0.5424 |
| EMOLEX | **0.6653** | 0.6819 | **0.7106** | **0.5712** |
| AI | 0.6636 | 0.6853 | 0.6996 | 0.5582 |
| ANEW | 0.6573 | **0.6927** | 0.6859 | 0.5505 |
| Warriner | 0.6519 | 0.6757 | 0.6969 | 0.5563 |
| None | 0.6651 | 0.6919 | 0.7055 | 0.5694 |
| | **DeepMoji** | | | |
| VAD | 0.6060 | 0.6292 | 0.6380 | 0.5557 |
| EMOLEX | 0.5923 | 0.6235 | 0.6449 | 0.5672 |
| AI | 0.6124 | 0.6269 | 0.6325 | 0.5754 |
| ANEW | 0.6046 | 0.6352 | 0.6356 | 0.5613 |
| Warriner | 0.6002 | 0.6215 | 0.6325 | **0.5795** |
| None | **0.6190** | **0.6426** | **0.6490** | 0.5737 |
| | **USE** | | | |
| VAD | 0.5079 | 0.5526 | 0.5881 | 0.5382 |
| EMOLEX | 0.5042 | 0.5509 | 0.5786 | 0.5451 |
| AI | 0.4932 | 0.5462 | 0.5961 | 0.5447 |
| ANEW | **0.5293** | 0.5484 | 0.5932 | 0.5297 |
| Warriner | 0.5071 | 0.5475 | 0.5829 | 0.5589 |
| None | 0.5174 | **0.5580** | **0.6067** | **0.5589** |
| | **SBERT** | | | |
| VAD | 0.4781 | 0.5247 | 0.5249 | 0.4506 |
| EMOLEX | 0.4808 | 0.5363 | 0.5303 | 0.4512 |
| AI | 0.4631 | 0.5439 | 0.5395 | 0.4273 |
| ANEW | 0.4835 | 0.5461 | **0.5576** | 0.4486 |
| Warriner | 0.4773 | **0.5481** | 0.5169 | 0.4591 |
| None | **0.4946** | 0.5413 | 0.5505 | **0.4608** |
| | **Word2Vec** | | | |
| VAD | 0.4463 | 0.4662 | 0.4887 | **0.4463** |
| EMOLEX | 0.4574 | 0.4749 | 0.5098 | 0.4215 |
| AI | 0.4527 | 0.4728 | 0.5108 | 0.4247 |
| ANEW | 0.4621 | 0.4779 | **0.5156** | 0.4382 |
| Warriner | 0.4574 | 0.4716 | 0.5039 | 0.4340 |
| None | **0.4824** | **0.4791** | 0.5136 | 0.4303 |

seems to benefit from the added lexicon information for each emotion dataset, although the improvement is marginal.

For three out of four datasets, for the roBERTa-based model, the EMOLEX lexicon was the best. For other embedding models, mostly approach with no lexicon benefited, and when some lexicons improved results, they were different for different datasets, with no noticeable pattern. If we compare the best lexicons from Table 4 with the best ones from Table 3, we can see that they are different for each dataset.

#### 4.2.3 Ensembles

The first ensemble that we tried combines the five classifiers based on embedding models from Section 4.1, i.e., the roBERTa-based, DeepMoji, USE, SBERT, and Word2Vec embeddings. We train the weighted kNN models for each vector separately with the best $k$ value and tweet preprocessing pipeline. Results are listed in the first line of Table 5 and indicate that these five embeddings already provide a good baseline, improving the best results from Table 1 by 8% on average. Especially for Fear, the improvement is notable (18% up).

Next, we consider the inclusion of lexicons into the ensembles. In a first setup, for each dataset, we take the best performing lexicon from Table 3 and add this is as a separate classifier to the baseline ensemble. For comparison, we also consider a setup where all five lexicons and their combination are added as six more classifiers, to check how each of them influences the output scores. The obtained results, shown in the second and third lines of Table 5, illustrate that, in general, the lexicons are unable to improve the baseline and that adding all lexicons takes the scores down considerably.

Given that the roBERTa-based method performs the best among all embeddings (Table 1), and that it is the only one that benefits from the lexicon appending strategy (Table 4), we also consider two additional setups. One that extends the baseline with the lexicon-appended roBERTa classifier and another one that adds the best lexicon to the previous ensemble.

The last two approaches results are presented in the second half of Table 5. We can see that these adjustments improve the scores noticeably. For three out of four emotion datasets, the last setup performs best, while for Sadness, the results are almost equal. Therefore, we consider this last ensemble as the best solution.

## 5 Results on the test data

To determine the generalization strength of the obtained best approach from Section 4, we evaluated it on the test data by submitting predicted labels in the required format to the competition page[11]. PCC scores were calculated for each emotion dataset, and obtained results were averaged. Because of the mean voting function in our model's ensemble, our predicted labels are in float format. Therefore, to match the requested format on the competition page, before submitting results, we rounded them to the nearest integer label.

[11] https://competitions.codalab.org/competitions/17751#learn_the_details-evaluation

Table 5: Results for the ensemble approach with different feature vectors, for all datasets.

| The vectors | Vector size | Anger | Joy | Sadness | Fear |
|---|---|---|---|---|---|
| The baseline (top-five embeddings vectors) | 5 | 0.6929 | 0.7420 | 0.7329 | 0.6783 |
| With the best lexicon | 6 | 0.6902 | 0.7336 | 0.7400 | 0.6773 |
| With all five lexicons and their combination | 11 | 0.6431 | 0.6796 | 0.6962 | 0.6585 |
| With roBERTa combined with the best lexicon | 6 | 0.7120 | 0.7496 | **0.7579** | 0.6719 |
| With the best lexicon and roBERTa combined with the best lexicon | 7 | **0.7190** | **0.7526** | 0.7566 | **0.6804** |

The obtained PCC scores are shown in Table 6, together with the results obtained on the training and development data for comparison.

Table 6: Pearson Coefficient of the best approach on the cross-validation and test data for the four emotion datasets.

| Dataset | Training and development data | Test data |
|---|---|---|
| Anger | 0.719 | 0.638 |
| Joy | 0.752 | 0.631 |
| Sadness | 0.756 | 0.670 |
| Fear | 0.680 | 0.601 |
| Averaged scores | 0.726 | 0.635 |

As expected, the average PCC for the test data drops several points compared to the training and development data, but, in general, our proposal appears to generalize well to new data.

We also mention that the first three contestants of the SemEval 2018 competition obtained a PCC equal to 0.695, 0.653 and 0.646, respectively[12], and that our proposal would therefore be just behind them in fourth position.

## 6 Discussion and error analysis

To illustrate our approach's explainability, in this section we explore some correctly and wrongly predicted test samples.

As an example of a correct prediction, we can take a look at an anger test tweet: *"I know you mean well, but I'm offended. Prick."* with real anger class "2". Our best model predicted label 2.4, which was rounded to 2, so our result is correct. To analyze how this label is obtained, we look at the predictions by all models separately. They are shown in Table 7 (sample (a)) with the number of neighbors of each class from the training data selected by each model. We can see that the roBERTa-based model was the most accurate, while most others were also close enough.

Next, we also examined the neighbours chosen by the models and their classes, especially those which are selected by different models. To find some patterns, we took the intersection of the neighbours closest to the test instance, chosen by the ensemble's models.

We should mention that those models are based on different embeddings, which may locate tweets in $n$-dimensional space differently. However, one tweet with class "2" from the train data was chosen by 4 models out of 7 and five more tweets (four of them with class "2" and one with class "1") by 3 models.

A closer examination of those tweets revealed that all of them contain the word "offended". From this, we could conclude that this word has a high emotional intensity that influences the sentence's tone.

Table 7: Predictions of models from the ensemble for some test tweets.

| Model in ensemble | k | Classes 0 | 1 | 2 | 3 | 0 | 1 | 2 | 3 |
|---|---|---|---|---|---|---|---|---|---|
| | | Sample (a) | | | | Sample (b) | | | |
| roBERTa | 19 | 0 | 4 | 11 | 4 | 5 | 3 | 11 | 0 |
| DeepMoji | 11 | 0 | 0 | 5 | 6 | 2 | 2 | 5 | 2 |
| USE | 19 | 2 | 5 | 7 | 5 | 5 | 2 | 7 | 5 |
| SBERT | 21 | 6 | 5 | 6 | 4 | 8 | 8 | 3 | 2 |
| Word2Vec | 5 | 1 | 1 | 0 | 3 | 0 | 0 | 3 | 2 |
| AI lexicon | 11 | 2 | 1 | 3 | 5 | 2 | 5 | 4 | 0 |
| roBERTa with AI | 11 | 0 | 2 | 8 | 1 | 0 | 4 | 7 | 0 |

[12] https://competitions.codalab.org/competitions/17751#results

The next sample we examined is another anger test tweet, with gold label "0": *"We've been broken up a while, both moved on, she's got a kid, I don't hold any animosity towards her anymore..."* Our solution predicted a score 1.5, which was rounded to 2, leading to a false prediction.

Similar to the previous sample, we took a look at the classes predicted by the different models in the ensemble (Table 7, sample (b)). Here, we can observe that only the SBERT-based model predicted the result correctly, so roBERTa does not always provide the best answer.

We also explored the most frequent neighbours, which were chosen by 3 models (one tweet with class "1") and by 2 models (nine tweets with different classes). We did not find any noticeable patterns; the misclassification is probably caused by words with high emotional intensity, like "animosity", which is used in combination with a negation in this specific context.

## 7 Conclusion and future work

In this paper, we evaluate an explainable machine learning method application for the emotion detection task. As the main conclusion, we can say that using simple optimizations and the weighted kNN method can perform nearly on par with more complex state-of-the-art neural network-based approaches. In the future, we plan to incorporate more elaborate nearest neighbour methodologies, which also take into account the inherently fuzzy nature of emotion data. Some initial experiments with ordered weighted average based fuzzy rough sets (Cornelis et al., 2010) show promising results.

Another observation that can be made from our results is that the most informative input to solving the emotion detection task is provided by the tweet embeddings, and that lexicons generally do not improve the results a lot. Meanwhile, adding the combined vector of roBERTa embedding and the best lexicon scores increased PCC scores noticeably. As a possible further improvement, we may refine the voting function by assigning different weights to the different members of the ensemble, which can be based, for example, on the confidence scores.

Furthermore, as another strategy to improve results, additional text preprocessing steps could be performed, for example, using exclamation marks or word lemmatization. Also, we can give more weight to the hashtag and emoji descriptions during the tweet embedding process.

Another important characteristic that influences the results is data imbalance. As observed, we obtained the lowest PCC scores on the Fear dataset, most likely because it is the most imbalanced one. For further experiments with Fear, we consider the usage of imbalanced machine learning classification methods. In particular, Vluymans (2019) discusses several approaches based on fuzzy rough set theory.

Finally, Danilevsky et al. (2020) provide several hints to investigate and improve solution explainability. For example, we can examine feature importance, measure the quality of explainability, etc.

## Acknowledgment

This work was supported by the Odysseus programme of the Research Foundation—Flanders (FWO).

## References

Francesco Barbieri, Jose Camacho-Collados, Luis Espinosa Anke, and Leonardo Neves. 2020. TweetEval: Unified benchmark and comparative evaluation for tweet classification. In *Findings of the Association for Computational Linguistics: EMNLP 2020*, pages 1644–1650, Online. Association for Computational Linguistics.

Margaret M Bradley and Peter J Lang. 1999. Affective norms for english words (anew): Instruction manual and affective ratings. Technical report, Technical report C-1, the center for research in psychophysiology.

Daniel Cer, Yinfei Yang, Sheng-yi Kong, Nan Hua, Nicole Limtiaco, Rhomni St. John, Noah Constant, Mario Guajardo-Cespedes, Steve Yuan, Chris Tar, Brian Strope, and Ray Kurzweil. 2018. Universal sentence encoder for English. In *Proceedings of the 2018 Conference on Empirical Methods in Natural Language Processing: System Demonstrations*, pages 169–174, Brussels, Belgium. Association for Computational Linguistics.

Chris Cornelis, Nele Verbiest, and Richard Jensen. 2010. Ordered weighted average based fuzzy rough sets. In *Proceedings of the 5th International Conference on Rough Sets and Knowledge Technology (RSKT 2010)*, pages 78–85.

Marina Danilevsky, Kun Qian, Ranit Aharonov, Yannis Katsis, Ban Kawas, and Prithviraj Sen. 2020. A survey of the state of explainable AI for natural language processing. In *Proceedings of the 1st Conference of the Asia-Pacific Chapter of the Association for Computational Linguistics and the 10th In-*

*ternational Joint Conference on Natural Language Processing*, pages 447–459, Suzhou, China. Association for Computational Linguistics.

Jacob Devlin, Ming-Wei Chang, Kenton Lee, and Kristina Toutanova. 2019. Bert: Pre-training of deep bidirectional transformers for language understanding. In *Proceedings of the 2019 Conference of the North American Chapter of the Association for Computational Linguistics: Human Language Technologies, Volume 1 (Long and Short Papers)*, pages 4171–4186.

Sahibsingh A Dudani. 1976. The distance-weighted k-nearest-neighbor rule. *IEEE Transactions on Systems, Man, and Cybernetics*, (4):325–327.

Venkatesh Duppada, Royal Jain, and Sushant Hiray. 2018. SeerNet at SemEval-2018 task 1: Domain adaptation for affect in tweets. In *Proceedings of The 12th International Workshop on Semantic Evaluation*, pages 18–23, New Orleans, Louisiana. Association for Computational Linguistics.

Nazneen Fatema Rajani, Ben Krause, Wengpeng Yin, Tong Niu, Richard Socher, and Caiming Xiong. 2020. Explaining and improving model behavior with k nearest neighbor representations. *arXiv e-prints*, pages arXiv–2010.

Grace Gee and Eugene Wang. 2018. psyML at SemEval-2018 task 1: Transfer learning for sentiment and emotion analysis. In *Proceedings of The 12th International Workshop on Semantic Evaluation*, pages 369–376, New Orleans, Louisiana. Association for Computational Linguistics.

Anna Huang. 2008. Similarity measures for text document clustering. In *Proceedings of the sixth new zealand computer science research student conference (NZCSRSC2008), Christchurch, New Zealand*, volume 4, pages 9–56.

Hui Liu, Qingyu Yin, and William Yang Wang. 2019. Towards explainable NLP: A generative explanation framework for text classification. In *Proceedings of the 57th Annual Meeting of the Association for Computational Linguistics*, pages 5570–5581, Florence, Italy. Association for Computational Linguistics.

Saif Mohammad. 2018a. Obtaining reliable human ratings of valence, arousal, and dominance for 20,000 English words. In *Proceedings of the 56th Annual Meeting of the Association for Computational Linguistics (Volume 1: Long Papers)*, pages 174–184, Melbourne, Australia. Association for Computational Linguistics.

Saif Mohammad, Felipe Bravo-Marquez, Mohammad Salameh, and Svetlana Kiritchenko. 2018. SemEval-2018 task 1: Affect in tweets. In *Proceedings of The 12th International Workshop on Semantic Evaluation*, pages 1–17, New Orleans, Louisiana. Association for Computational Linguistics.

Saif M. Mohammad. 2018b. Word affect intensities. In *Proceedings of the 11th Edition of the Language Resources and Evaluation Conference (LREC-2018)*, Miyazaki, Japan.

Saif M Mohammad and Svetlana Kiritchenko. 2015. Using hashtags to capture fine emotion categories from tweets. *Computational Intelligence*, 31(2):301–326.

Saif M. Mohammad and Peter D. Turney. 2013. Crowdsourcing a word-emotion association lexicon. 29(3):436–465.

Nils Reimers and Iryna Gurevych. 2019. Sentence-BERT: Sentence embeddings using Siamese BERT-networks. In *Proceedings of the 2019 Conference on Empirical Methods in Natural Language Processing and the 9th International Joint Conference on Natural Language Processing (EMNLP-IJCNLP)*, pages 3982–3992, Hong Kong, China. Association for Computational Linguistics.

Alon Rozental and Daniel Fleischer. 2018. Amobee at SemEval-2018 task 1: GRU neural network with a CNN attention mechanism for sentiment classification. In *Proceedings of The 12th International Workshop on Semantic Evaluation*, pages 218–225, New Orleans, Louisiana. Association for Computational Linguistics.

Sarah Vluymans. 2019. *Dealing with imbalanced and weakly labelled data in machine learning using fuzzy and rough set methods*. Springer.

Amy Beth Warriner, Victor Kuperman, and Marc Brysbaert. 2013. Norms of valence, arousal, and dominance for 13,915 english lemmas. *Behavior research methods*, 45(4):1191–1207.

Wiesław Wolny. 2016. Emotion analysis of twitter data that use emoticons and emoji ideograms.

# L3CubeMahaSent: A Marathi Tweet-based Sentiment Analysis Dataset

Atharva Kulkarni[1,3], Meet Mandhane[1,3], Manali Likhitkar[1,3], Gayatri Kshirsagar[1,3], and Raviraj Joshi[2,3]
[1]Pune Institute of Computer Technology, Pune
[2]Indian Institute of Technology Madras, Chennai
[3] L3Cube, Pune
{k.atharva4899,meetmandhanemnm,manalil1806,gayatrimohan7}@gmail.com
ravirajoshi@gmail.com

## Abstract

Sentiment analysis is one of the most fundamental tasks in Natural Language Processing. Popular languages like English, Arabic, Russian, Mandarin, and also Indian languages such as Hindi, Bengali, Tamil have seen a significant amount of work in this area. However, the Marathi language which is the third most popular language in India still lags behind due to the absence of proper datasets. In this paper, we present the first major publicly available Marathi Sentiment Analysis Dataset - L3CubeMahaSent. It is curated using tweets extracted from various Maharashtrian personalities' Twitter accounts. Our dataset consists of ~16,000 distinct tweets classified in three broad classes viz. positive, negative, and neutral. We also present the guidelines using which we annotated the tweets. Finally, we present the statistics of our dataset and baseline classification results using CNN, LSTM, ULMFiT, and BERT-based deep learning models.

## 1 Introduction

The use of social media has seen a sharp upward trend in recent years. It plays a big role in forming and shaping the views of people on various issues. From sharing facts and opinions to voicing dissent and grievances, the platform has gained popularity amongst many users (Nielsen and Schrøder, 2014). Twitter is a significant social media platform. It has been quite popular in India for the past few years. It has been used by many politicians, journalists, and activists to connect with people directly. These kinds of interactions are generally strong on emotions, and can be used for developing sentiment analysis systems (Pak and Paroubek, 2010; Mathew et al., 2019). Such systems have proven to be important for political analysis as well as identifying and curbing more complex issues such as fake news, harassment, hate speech, and bullying (Schmidt and Wiegand, 2017; Joshi et al., 2021; Wani et al., 2021). In this work, we consider basic sentiment analysis or polarity identification tasks.

Popular languages such as English, Arabic, Russian, Mandarin (Rogers et al., 2018; Nabil et al., 2015; Yu et al., 2020) as well as Indian languages such as Hindi, Bengali and Tamil have been explored on the sentiment task for a long time (Arora, 2013; Patra et al., 2015; Akhtar et al., 2016; Mukku and Mamidi, 2017; Ravishankar and Raghunathan, 2017). Many resources such as properly annotated datasets, SentiWordNets, annotation guidelines have been developed for these languages (Socher et al., 2013; Saif et al., 2013; Hu and Liu, 2004). Alternatively due to the low resource nature of many languages, translated versions of the English datasets were used for analysis (Joshi et al., 2019; Refaee and Rieser, 2015; Mohammad et al., 2016). However, such translated datasets are often noisy due to the limitation of current translation systems for low resource languages.

Marathi is an Indian language spoken by around 83 million people and ranks as the third most spoken language in India. But surprisingly, there is no significant work or resource for the task of sentiment analysis in Marathi (Kulkarni et al., 2021). A sentiment analysis dataset curated by IIT-Bombay is available, but it has a very small size consisting of only 150 samples (Balamurali et al., 2012). In this paper, we present L3CubeMahaSent[1] - the largest publicly available Marathi Sentiment Analysis dataset to date. This dataset is gathered using Twitter. Our work is summarized as follows:

1. We present a ~16,000 tweets strong Marathi Sentiment Analysis Dataset, manually tagged into three classes viz. positive, negative, and

[1]https://github.com/l3cube-pune/MarathiNLP



*Proceedings of the 11th Workshop on Computational Approaches to Subjectivity, Sentiment and Social Media Analysis*, pages 213–220
April 19, 2021. ©2021 Association for Computational Linguistics

neutral.

2. We provide a comprehensive annotation policy useful for tagging sentences by their sentiment. We also provide statistics for our dataset and a balanced split for experimentation.

3. We present the result of our experiments on this dataset on recent deep learning approaches to create a benchmark for future comparisons.

## 2 Related Work

Sentiment analysis is a fundamental task of Natural Language Processing (Medhat et al., 2014). The absence of a proper sentiment analysis dataset for the Marathi language has led to limited research in this area. In this section, we will review some of the works introducing data resources in Indian and other languages. Balamurali et al. (2012) presented an approach for cross-lingual sentiment analysis using linked wordnets for Marathi and Hindi languages. For this purpose, they used various blogs and travel editorials as a dataset which consisted of about 75 positive and 75 negative reviews. The WordNet approach showed an improvement of 14-15 percent over the approach using a bilingual dictionary. The Marathi dataset created in this work is very small and cannot be used to train existing deep learning algorithms.

Bhardwaj et al. (2020) presented a hostility detection dataset in Hindi. Data was collected from various online platforms like Twitter, Facebook, Whatsapp, etc., and was benchmarked using machine learning algorithms namely, support vector machine (SVM), decision tree, random forest, and logistic regression. They also labeled each hostile post as either fake, hateful, offensive, or defamation.

Patra et al. (2018) presented details of a shared task in a competition on sentiment analysis of code-mixed data pairs of Hindi-English and Bengali-English. The best performing team used SVM for sentence classification. The sentiment analysis of code-mixed English-Hindi and English-Marathi text is also studied in (Ansari and Govilkar, 2018).

Nabil et al. (2015) introduced Arabic sentiments tweets dataset consisting of 10,000 tweets classified as objective, subjective positive, subjective negative, and subjective mixed. They tried 4-class sentiment analysis as well as 3-class sentiment analysis on the dataset and found that the former was more challenging. They also concluded that SVM performed well on the dataset for the task.

Rogers et al. (2018) presented RuSentiment, a dataset for sentiment analysis in the Russian language. They performed experiments on their dataset using algorithms like logistic regression, linear SVM, and neural networks. The best performance was observed in the case of neural networks. They also released the fastText embeddings that they have used for experimentation.

Ikoro et al. (2018) presented results of analyzing sentiments of UK energy consumers on Twitter. They proposed a method in which they combined functions from two sentiment lexica. The first lexicon was used to extract the sentiment-bearing terms and the negative sentiments. The second lexicon was used to classify the rest of the data. This method improved the accuracy compared to the general method of using one lexicon.

## 3 Curation of Dataset

### 3.1 Dataset Collection

For creating our dataset, we first manually created a list of various famous personalities who actively tweet about current affairs. Twitter profiles were shortlisted based on their frequency, relevance of activity, and degree of the sentiment of the tweets. Hence a majority of the tweets are from political personalities' profiles and activists as they express a wide range of emotions and sentiments. We attempted to improve the diversity of the points of view contained in the dataset.

All tweets in this dataset are specifically in the Marathi language. All hashtags, mentions, special symbols, and the occasional English words are kept in the tweets in the publicly available version of the dataset. We think it is best to keep the original dataset unhampered for anyone to experiment on it. However, while performing experiments, we have removed the aforementioned tokens from the tweets during data pre-processing. Also, the dataset does not retain any context of the tweets such as the tweeting profile, time of posting, region, etc.

As far as scraping the tweets is concerned, there are multiple python libraries available. Some of them are Tweepy (the official open-source library provided by Twitter)[2], GetOldTweets3[3], Twint[4], and Snscrape[5]. We have used the Twint library to scrape tweets.

### 3.2 Dataset Annotation

We have manually labeled the entire dataset into three classes: positive, negative, and neutral. These three classes have been denoted by '1','-1', and '0' respectively. The dataset was split among the entire team to tag in parallel. In order to maintain consistency while tagging tweets, we developed an annotation policy.

To begin with, we ensured not to take into account the author of the tweet, thereby eliminating any bias towards any author. Tweets are tagged by a general assumption that they are posted by any random person. Positive emotions such as happiness, gratitude, respect, inspiration, support are tagged as positive. Negative emotions such as hate, disrespect, grief, insult, disagreement, the opposition are tagged as negative. Tweets that do not convey a strong feeling, such as simple facts, statistics, or statements are tagged as neutral.

Tweets containing sarcasm, irony which clearly depict a negative sentiment are tagged as negative. Congratulatory and thank-you tweets are tagged as positive. A tweet that criticizes something or someone, or which states a fact stating an adverse event or reaction is termed negative. However, if the criticism comes as constructive and healthy, mentioning possible solutions, then it is tagged as positive. Finally, tweets containing mixed sentiments are labeled by the more dominant emotion expressed.

Even though these rules were laid down, there were some tweets that simply were difficult to tag by a single individual and needed to be reviewed. In such cases, we took a vote amongst the team and tagged the tweet according to the majority votes. Tweets for which no consensus could be formed were removed.

Some examples of tagged tweets are mentioned for more clarity in Table 3 given in the Appendix.

### 3.3 Dataset Statistics

Initially, we annotated a total of 18,378 tweets. But, in order to ensure that the classes are balanced, we randomly selected an equal number of tweets for each class. Hence, the final version of L3CubeMahaSent consists of 15,864 tweets. Table 1 shows class-wise distribution and the train-test-validation split. The remaining 2,514 annotated tweets will also be published along with the dataset. It consists of 2,355 positive and 159 negative tweets. These extra tweets have not been used for model evaluation. Commonly occurring words in each class can be visualized in the form of word-clouds as shown in Figure 2.

| Split | Total Tweets | 1 | -1 | 0 |
|---|---|---|---|---|
| Train | 12114 | 4038 | 4038 | 4038 |
| Test | 2250 | 750 | 750 | 750 |
| Validation | 1500 | 500 | 500 | 500 |

Table 1: Dataset Statistics.

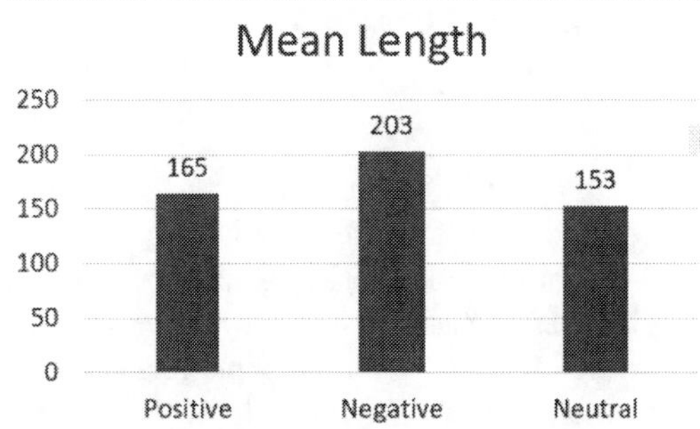


Figure 1: Mean length of records per class (in words)

## 4 Evaluation

### 4.1 Experimentations

We performed 2-class and 3-class sentiment analysis on our dataset. For conducting baseline experiments on our dataset, hashtags, mentions, and special symbols were removed during preprocessing. We used some of the widely used text classification architectures for sentiment classification (Kulkarni et al., 2021; Kowsari et al., 2019; Kim, 2014; Sun et al., 2019). The text is tokenized as words or sub-words and passed to the algorithms mentioned below:

- **CNN:** The initial embedding layer outputs word embeddings of size 300. These embeddings are passed to a Conv1D layer having 300 filters and kernel size 3. A global max-pooling is applied to the output sequences to get a sentence representation. This is then

[2]https://www.tweepy.org/
[3]https://pypi.org/project/GetOldTweets3/
[4]https://pypi.org/project/twint/
[5]https://github.com/JustAnotherArchivist/snscrape

Figure 2: Positive, Neutral and Negative wordclouds

passed on to a dense layer having size 100. A final dense layer having size equal to the number of classes is added to give classification results. We have experimented with various types of embedding layers having random initialization (word and subword), original Facebook fastText embeddings (trainable and non-trainable) (Mikolov et al., 2018), and Indic fastText embeddings (trainable and non-trainable) by IndicNLP (Kakwani et al., 2020).

- **BiLSTM+GlobalMaxPool:** This is similar to the CNN network with Conv1D layer replaced by a Bi-LSTM layer. Inputs are fed to an embedding layer which outputs word embeddings of size 300. These embeddings are given to a bi-directional LSTM layer with cell size 300 and then output is max pooled over time. A dense layer of size 100 and a subsequent dense layer of size equal to the number of classes complete the architecture. Embeddings same as those mentioned in the CNN section are also experimented with.

- **ULMFiT:** ULMFiT is also a LSTM based model (Howard and Ruder, 2018). It uses transfer learning which allows the model to be finetuned quickly on the target dataset using even a small sample set. We use a publicly available ULMFiT model for the Marathi language released by iNLTK and finetune it on our dataset (Arora, 2020).

- **BERT:** The BERT is a transformer based model pretrained on a huge text corpora, which can be finetuned for any target dataset (Devlin et al., 2019). Many publicly available flavours of BERT are available, and we use two specific multilingual models:
  - Multilingual-BERT (mBERT)
  - Indic-BERT by IndicNLP (Kakwani et al., 2020)

  For both of these models, we used the CLS token for sequence classification.

## 4.2 Results

We experimented with a variety of architectures such as CNN and BiLSTM for text classification on our dataset along with different embeddings. We have used random word and subword initializations, and also used pre-trained word embeddings made public by Facebook and IndicNLP. Both of these pre-trained embeddings were used in trainable and static modes. Along with these architectures, pre-trained models such as ULMFiT, mBERT, and IndicBERT were also used.

The results from our experiments were in line with previous works done in Marathi text classification. Pretrained word embeddings give a definite edge over random initializations. The CNN-based models have a slight advantage over BiLSTM based models. It was observed that though models using random initializations generally give good results, they tend to quickly overfit while training. The use of pre-trained embeddings significantly reduces overfitting. The results for 3-way and 2-way classification are shown in Table 2. The neutral class is dropped for 2-way classification.

The Marathi word embeddings provided by IndicNLP perform better than the original versions released by Facebook. Keeping word embeddings trainable further increases the accuracy. The ULMFiT gives results that are comparable with simple CNN and BiLSTM models. The CNN model combined with trainable Indic fastText word embeddings gives the best results in the 2-class classifi-

| Model | Variant | 3-class Accuracy | 2-class Accuracy |
|---|---|---|---|
| CNN | random-word | 79.47 | 90.00 |
| | random-subword | 81.56 | 91.73 |
| | FB fastText-Trainable | 81.02 | 92.67 |
| | FB fastText-Static | 80.18 | 90.93 |
| | Indic fastText-Trainable | **83.24** | **93.13** |
| | Indic fastText-Static | 83.00 | 92.47 |
| BiLSTM | random-word | 80.93 | 90.87 |
| | random-subword | 79.42 | 89.80 |
| | FB fastText-Trainable | 81.78 | 92.33 |
| | FB fastText-Static | 79.87 | 89.67 |
| | Indic fastText-Trainable | **82.89** | 91.8 |
| | Indic fastText-Static | 82.41 | **92.67** |
| ULMFiT | (iNLTK) | 80.80 | 91.40 |
| BERT | mBERT | 80.66 | 91.40 |
| | IndicBERT (INLP) | **84.13** | **92.93** |

Table 2: Classification accuracies over different architectures. The 2-class accuracy corresponds to positive and negative class only.

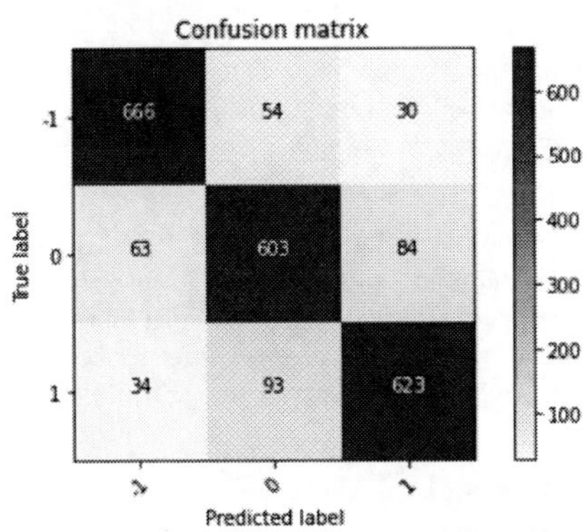


Figure 3: Confusion Matrix for IndicBERT - 3 class classification

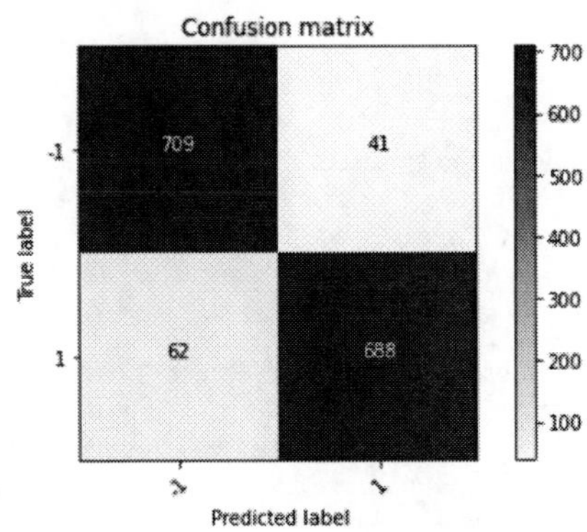


Figure 4: Confusion Matrix for CNN with Indic fastText (trainable) - 2 class classification

cation experiments, slightly outperforming the IndicBERT. The IndicBERT was the best performing model for the more difficult 3-class classification experiments. The respective confusion matrices are shown in Figure 4 and Figure 3.

## 5 Conclusion

In this paper, we have presented L3CubeMahaSent - the first major publicly available dataset for Marathi Sentiment Analysis which consists of ~16000 distinct tweets. We also describe the annotation policy which we used for manually labeling the entire dataset. We performed 2-class and 3-class sentiment classification to provide a benchmark for future studies. The deep learning models used for sentiment prediction were CNN, BiLSTM, ULMFiT, mBERT, and IndicBERT. The publicly available Marathi fastText embeddings were used with word-based models. We report the best accuracy using IndicBERT and CNN with Indic fastText word embeddings. We hope that our dataset will play a crucial role in advancing NLP research for the Marathi language.

## Acknowledgments

This work was done under the L3Cube Pune mentorship program. We would like to express our gratitude towards our mentors at L3Cube for their continuous support and encouragement.

## References


Md Shad Akhtar, Ayush Kumar, Asif Ekbal, and Pushpak Bhattacharyya. 2016. A hybrid deep learning architecture for sentiment analysis. In *Proceedings of COLING 2016, the 26th International Conference on Computational Linguistics: Technical Papers*, pages 482–493.

Mohammed Arshad Ansari and Sharvari Govilkar. 2018. Sentiment analysis of mixed code for the transliterated hindi and marathi texts. *International Journal on Natural Language Computing (IJNLC) Vol*, 7.

Gaurav Arora. 2020. inltk: Natural language toolkit for indic languages. *arXiv preprint arXiv:2009.12534*.

Piyush Arora. 2013. Sentiment analysis for hindi language. *MS by Research in Computer Science*.

AR Balamurali, Aditya Joshi, and Pushpak Bhattacharyya. 2012. Cross-lingual sentiment analysis for indian languages using linked wordnets. In *Proceedings of COLING 2012: Posters*, pages 73–82.

Mohit Bhardwaj, Md Shad Akhtar, Asif Ekbal, Amitava Das, and Tanmoy Chakraborty. 2020. Hostility detection dataset in hindi. *arXiv preprint arXiv:2011.03588*.

Jacob Devlin, Ming-Wei Chang, Kenton Lee, and Kristina Toutanova. 2019. Bert: Pre-training of deep bidirectional transformers for language understanding. In *Proceedings of the 2019 Conference of the North American Chapter of the Association for Computational Linguistics: Human Language Technologies, Volume 1 (Long and Short Papers)*, pages 4171–4186.

Jeremy Howard and Sebastian Ruder. 2018. Universal language model fine-tuning for text classification. In *Proceedings of the 56th Annual Meeting of the Association for Computational Linguistics (Volume 1: Long Papers)*, pages 328–339.

Minqing Hu and Bing Liu. 2004. Mining and summarizing customer reviews. In *Proceedings of the tenth ACM SIGKDD international conference on Knowledge discovery and data mining*, pages 168–177.

Victoria Ikoro, Maria Sharmina, Khaleel Malik, and Riza Batista-Navarro. 2018. Analyzing sentiments expressed on twitter by uk energy company consumers. In *2018 Fifth International Conference on Social Networks Analysis, Management and Security (SNAMS)*, pages 95–98. IEEE.

Ramchandra Joshi, Purvi Goel, and Raviraj Joshi. 2019. Deep learning for hindi text classification: A comparison. In *International Conference on Intelligent Human Computer Interaction*, pages 94–101. Springer.

Ramchandra Joshi, Rushabh Karnavat, Kaustubh Jirapure, and Raviraj Joshi. 2021. Evaluation of deep learning models for hostility detection in hindi text. *arXiv preprint arXiv:2101.04144*.

Divyanshu Kakwani, Anoop Kunchukuttan, Satish Golla, NC Gokul, Avik Bhattacharyya, Mitesh M Khapra, and Pratyush Kumar. 2020. inlpsuite: Monolingual corpora, evaluation benchmarks and pre-trained multilingual language models for indian languages. In *Proceedings of the 2020 Conference on Empirical Methods in Natural Language Processing: Findings*, pages 4948–4961.

Yoon Kim. 2014. Convolutional neural networks for sentence classification. In *Proceedings of the 2014 Conference on Empirical Methods in Natural Language Processing (EMNLP)*, pages 1746–1751, Doha, Qatar. Association for Computational Linguistics.

Kamran Kowsari, Kiana Jafari Meimandi, Mojtaba Heidarysafa, Sanjana Mendu, Laura Barnes, and Donald Brown. 2019. Text classification algorithms: A survey. *Information*, 10(4):150.

Atharva Kulkarni, Meet Mandhane, Manali Likhitkar, Gayatri Kshirsagar, Jayashree Jagdale, and Raviraj Joshi. 2021. Experimental evaluation of deep learning models for marathi text classification. *arXiv preprint arXiv:2101.04899*.

Binny Mathew, Ritam Dutt, Pawan Goyal, and Animesh Mukherjee. 2019. Spread of hate speech in online social media. In *Proceedings of the 10th ACM conference on web science*, pages 173–182.

Walaa Medhat, Ahmed Hassan, and Hoda Korashy. 2014. Sentiment analysis algorithms and applications: A survey. *Ain Shams engineering journal*, 5(4):1093–1113.

Tomáš Mikolov, Édouard Grave, Piotr Bojanowski, Christian Puhrsch, and Armand Joulin. 2018. Advances in pre-training distributed word representations. In *Proceedings of the Eleventh International Conference on Language Resources and Evaluation (LREC 2018)*.

Saif M Mohammad, Mohammad Salameh, and Svetlana Kiritchenko. 2016. How translation alters sentiment. *Journal of Artificial Intelligence Research*, 55:95–130.

Sandeep Sricharan Mukku and Radhika Mamidi. 2017. Actsa: Annotated corpus for telugu sentiment analysis. In *Proceedings of the First Workshop on Building Linguistically Generalizable NLP Systems*, pages 54–58.

Mahmoud Nabil, Mohamed Aly, and Amir Atiya. 2015. Astd: Arabic sentiment tweets dataset. In *Proceedings of the 2015 conference on empirical methods in natural language processing*, pages 2515–2519.

Rasmus Kleis Nielsen and Kim Christian Schrøder. 2014. The relative importance of social media for accessing, finding, and engaging with news: An eight-country cross-media comparison. *Digital journalism*, 2(4):472–489.

Alexander Pak and Patrick Paroubek. 2010. Twitter as a corpus for sentiment analysis and opinion mining. In *LREc*, volume 10, pages 1320–1326.

Braja Gopal Patra, Dipankar Das, and Amitava Das. 2018. Sentiment analysis of code-mixed indian languages: an overview of sail_code-mixed shared task@ icon-2017. *arXiv preprint arXiv:1803.06745*.

Braja Gopal Patra, Dipankar Das, Amitava Das, and Rajendra Prasath. 2015. Shared task on sentiment analysis in indian languages (sail) tweets-an overview. In *International Conference on Mining Intelligence and Knowledge Exploration*, pages 650–655. Springer.

Nadana Ravishankar and Shriram Raghunathan. 2017. Corpus based sentiment classification of tamil movie tweets using syntactic patterns. *IIOAB Journal: A Journal of Multidisciplinary Science and Technology*, 8(2):172–178.

Eshrag Refaee and Verena Rieser. 2015. Benchmarking machine translated sentiment analysis for arabic tweets. In *Proceedings of the 2015 Conference of the North American Chapter of the Association for Computational Linguistics: Student Research Workshop*, pages 71–78.

Anna Rogers, Alexey Romanov, Anna Rumshisky, Svitlana Volkova, Mikhail Gronas, and Alex Gribov. 2018. Rusentiment: An enriched sentiment analysis dataset for social media in russian. In *Proceedings of the 27th international conference on computational linguistics*, pages 755–763.

Hassan Saif, Miriam Fernandez, Yulan He, and Harith Alani. 2013. Evaluation datasets for twitter sentiment analysis: a survey and a new dataset, the sts-gold.

Anna Schmidt and Michael Wiegand. 2017. A survey on hate speech detection using natural language processing. In *Proceedings of the fifth international workshop on natural language processing for social media*, pages 1–10.

Richard Socher, Alex Perelygin, Jean Wu, Jason Chuang, Christopher D Manning, Andrew Y Ng, and Christopher Potts. 2013. Recursive deep models for semantic compositionality over a sentiment treebank. In *Proceedings of the 2013 conference on empirical methods in natural language processing*, pages 1631–1642.

Chi Sun, Xipeng Qiu, Yige Xu, and Xuanjing Huang. 2019. How to fine-tune bert for text classification? In *China National Conference on Chinese Computational Linguistics*, pages 194–206. Springer.

Apurva Wani, Isha Joshi, Snehal Khandve, Vedangi Wagh, and Raviraj Joshi. 2021. Evaluating deep learning approaches for covid19 fake news detection. *arXiv preprint arXiv:2101.04012*.

Wenmeng Yu, Hua Xu, Fanyang Meng, Yilin Zhu, Yixiao Ma, Jiele Wu, Jiyun Zou, and Kaicheng Yang. 2020. Ch-sims: A chinese multimodal sentiment analysis dataset with fine-grained annotation of modality. In *Proceedings of the 58th Annual Meeting of the Association for Computational Linguistics*, pages 3718–3727.

## 6 Appendix

This section lists some sample annotated tweets as shown in Table 3.

| S.No. | Tweet | English Translation | Tag |
|---|---|---|---|
| 1 | विधान परिषदेचे उपसभापती आणि प्रदेश कॉंग्रेस कमिटीचे माजी अध्यक्ष आमचे लाडके नेते आ.माणिकराव ठाकरे यांना वाढदिवसानिमित्त हार्दिक शुभेच्छा | A very happy birthday to the deputy chairman of the Assembly, former president of Regional Congress Committee and our beloved leader Mr. Manikrao Thackrey | 1 |
| 2 | ९ August ला मराठा काय असतो ते सरकारला कळेल. मराठा झुकता नहीं झुकाता है! खोट्या सरकारला झुकावेच लागेल.लढाई न्यायाची,हक्काची | Government will come to know the power of Maratha community. Marathas do not bend but make others bend. This fake Government will have to accept defeat. This is a battle of justice and our rights! | 1 |
| 3 | खा.अशोक चव्हाण यांच्या नेतृत्वाखाली @INCIndia चा जनसागर आज जनआक्रोश हल्ला बोल मोर्चात सहभागी झाला. बहुसंख्य कॉंग्रेस कार्यकर्त्यांनी मोर्चा यशस्वी करण्यासाठी सिंहांचा वाटा उचलल्याबाबत हार्दिक अभिनंदन!फडणवीस सरकारच्या पायाखालची जमीन हादरली. काउंट डाऊन सुरू. | Under the guidance of MP Ashok Chavan, the sea of @INCIndia supporters participated in a 'Halla Bol' demonstration. A very hearty congratulations to majority of the congress workers who gave their lion's share to make this demonstration successful. The ground under Fadanvis Government is shaken. Count down begins! | 1 |
| 4 | सलग तिस-या वर्षी महाराष्ट्र भ्रष्टाचारात पहिला का आहे ? याचे उत्तर चिक्की घोटाळ्याच्या चौकशीवरून लक्षात येत आहे. कॉंग्रेस पक्ष या भयंकर घोटाळ्याचा सतत पाठपुरावा करत राहून दोषींना शासन होत नाही तोपर्यंत स्वस्थ बसणार नाही. राज्यातले सरकार 'क्लीन-चीटर' सरकार आहे. | Why does Maharashtra rank first in corruption consecutively for the third year? The answer to this question unfolds from the chikki scam investigation. Congress will not remain calm until these people get punsihed. State government is a clean cheater government. | -1 |
| 5 | महाराष्ट्र विधानपरिषदेचे माजी उपसभापती वसंत डावखरे यांच्या निधनाने एक अतिशय हसतमुख , अजातशत्रू आणि कर्तबगार नेता आपल्यातून निघून गेला. त्यांच्या परीवारास हे दुःख सहन करण्याची शक्ती मिळो ही प्रार्थना! भावपूर्ण श्रद्धांजली! | With the demise of former leader of Maharashtra's Assembly Mr. Vasant Davkhare, an ever-smiling, friendly and capable leader has left us. I pray his family gets the strength to cope with this grief. My deepest condolences. | -1 |
| 6 | मातीयुक्त चिक्की खाण्यायोग्य असल्याचे लॅबचे प्रमाणपत्र दाखवले आता पोषण आहारातील शियात सापडलेला मृत बेडूक पौष्टीक म्हणून सरकारने सांगावे | Chikki containing soil has been deemed fit to eat by a lab certification. Now, the government should say that a dead frog found in food served at school lunch is nutritious. | -1 |
| 7 | मित्रा, यूपी मध्ये भाजपाचे 71 खासदार आहेत आणि त्यातले केंद्रात मंत्रीही आहेत | Dear friend, there are 71 MPs of BJP in UP and some of them are central ministers as well. | 0 |
| 8 | हा हा, स्टुडियोत वेगळे भाषण होते का? | Haha, was there a different speech at the studio? | 0 |
| 9 | सिंघम प्रवीण पोटे यांची शासनाने तात्काळ पोलिस दलात नियुक्ति करावी व पोलिसांना माशा मारण्याचे महत्वपूर्ण काम द्यावे | Singham Pravin Pote should be appointed in the police immediately and the police should be given the work of swatting flies. | -1 |

Table 3: Sample annotated tweets.

# Multi-Emotion Classification for Song Lyrics

**Darren Edmonds**
Donald Bren School of ICS
University of California, Irvine
dedmond1@uci.edu

**João Sedoc**
Stern School of Business
New York University
jsedoc@stern.nyu.edu

## Abstract

Song lyrics convey a multitude of emotions to the listener and powerfully portray the emotional state of the writer or singer. This paper examines a variety of modeling approaches to the multi-emotion classification problem for songs. We introduce the Edmonds Dance dataset, a novel emotion-annotated lyrics dataset from the reader's perspective, and annotate the dataset of Mihalcea and Strapparava (2012) at the song level. We find that models trained on relatively small song datasets achieve marginally better performance than BERT (Devlin et al., 2019) fine-tuned on large social media or dialog datasets.

## 1 Introduction

Text-based sentiment analysis has become increasingly popular in recent years, in part due to its numerous applications in fields such as marketing, politics, and psychology (Rambocas and Pacheco, 2018; Haselmayer and Jenny, 2017; Provoost et al., 2019). However, the vast majority of sentiment analysis models are built to identify net positive or negative sentiment rather than more complex, ambiguous emotions such as anticipation, surprise, or nostalgia (Jongeling et al., 2017). As a result, current models usually fail to portray the coexistence of multiple emotions within a text sample, resulting in limited characterization of a human's true emotions. Songs are often created to elicit complex emotional responses from listeners, and thus are an interesting area of study to understand nuanced emotions (Mihalcea and Strapparava, 2012).

This paper examines a variety of approaches to address the multi-emotion classification problem. We aim to build an emotion classification model that can detect the presence of multiple emotions in song lyrics with comparable accuracy to the typical inter-annotator agreement for text-based sentiment analysis (70-90%) (Diakopoulos and Shamma, 2010; Bobicev and Sokolova, 2017; Takala et al., 2014). Building such a model is especially challenging in practice as there often exists considerable disagreement regarding the perception and interpretation of the emotions of a song or ambiguity within the song itself (Kim et al., 2010).

There exist a variety of high-quality text datasets for emotion classification, from social media datasets such as CBET (Shahraki, 2015) and TEC (Mohammad, 2012) to large dialog corpora such as the DailyDialog dataset (Li et al., 2017). However, there remains a lack of comparable emotion-annotated song lyric datasets, and existing lyrical datasets are often annotated for valence-arousal affect rather than distinct emotions (Çano and Morisio, 2017). Consequently, we introduce the Edmonds Dance Dataset[1], a novel lyrical dataset that was crowdsourced through Amazon Mechanical Turk. Our dataset consists of scalar annotations for the 8 core emotions presented by Plutchik (2001), with annotations collected at the song level and from the reader's perspective.

We find that BERT models trained on out-of-domain data do not generalize well to song lyrics and have lower F1 scores than Naive Bayes classifiers for emotions such as disgust and fear. However, BERT models trained on small lyrical datasets achieve marginally better performance, despite in-domain datasets being orders of magnitude smaller than their counterparts. We also find that surprise has significantly lower inter-annotator agreement and test accuracy than other core emotions.

## 2 Related Work

A multitude of models and techniques have been explored for song emotion classification. Both He et al. (2008) and Wang et al. (2011) found that fea-

[1]The Edmonds Dance dataset is available by request from the authors of this paper.



*Proceedings of the 11th Workshop on Computational Approaches to Subjectivity, Sentiment and Social Media Analysis*, pages 221–235
April 19, 2021. ©2021 Association for Computational Linguistics

ture extraction from lyrics improves emotion classification performance. Researchers have trained Naive Bayes, HMM, SVM, clustering, and Random Forest models on lyrical and sometimes audio features to predict emotion in songs (Hu et al., 2009; Kim and Kwon, 2011; Jamdar et al., 2015; An et al., 2017; Rachman et al., 2018). Deep learning frameworks have also been widely utilized for song emotion classification, ranging from CNNs and LSTMs (Delbouys et al., 2018; Abdillah et al., 2020) to transformer-based models such as BERT and ELMo (Parisi et al., 2019; Liu and Tan, 2020).

Multiple researchers have taken a multi-modal approach to emotion prediction. Strapparava et al. (2012), introduced a novel corpus of both music and lyrics, and achieved promising results when using both musical and lyrical representations of songs in emotion classification. Similarly, Yang et al. (2008) found an increase in 4-class emotion prediction accuracy from 46.6 to 57.1 percent when incorporating lyrics into models trained on audio.

However, audio data can lead to problematic bias in emotion classification. Susino and Schubert (2019b) explored the presence of emotion stereotyping in certain genres, and found that heavy metal and hip-hop music were perceived to have more negative emotions than pop music with matched lyrics. Susino and Schubert (2019a) also found that emotional responses to an audio sample of a song could be predicted by stereotypes of the culture with which the song's genre was associated. Additionally, Fried (1999) found that violent lyrical passages were seen to be significantly more negative when represented as rap songs rather than country songs. Dunbar et al. (2016) validated Fried's findings through multiple studies in which participants believed that identical lyrics were more offensive when portrayed as rap rather than country music.

Lyrics are paramount for the accurate prediction of emotion in music. Yang and Lee (2009) transformed song lyrics into psychological feature vectors using a content analysis package and concluded that song lyrics alone can be used to generate promising, human-comprehensible classification models. Hu et al. (2009) found that audio features did not always outperform lyric features for mood prediction, and that combining lyric and audio features does not necessarily improve mood prediction over simply training on lyrics features. In later research, Hu and Downie (2010) found that lyrics features significantly outperformed audio features in 7 of 18 mood categories, while audio features outperformed lyrical features in only one.

Research is split regarding crowdsourced emotion annotation quality; while Mohammad and Bravo-Marquez (2017) achieved strong results through crowdsourcing labels, Hasan et al. (2014) found crowd labels to sometimes not even be in agreement with themselves. Surprise is an emotion that is especially difficult to model (Buechel and Hahn, 2017; Schuff et al., 2017), less frequent (Oberländer and Klinger, 2018), and is sometimes divided into positive and negative surprise (Alm et al., 2005).

## 3 Datasets

### 3.1 In-domain Datasets

Lyrics are valuable for song emotion prediction and decent classification models can be generated solely on song lyrics. However, many lyrical datasets for song emotion classification are based on valence-arousal and lack emotions such as surprise or fear, which are important components of mood (Ekman and Friesen, 2003). In addition, there is a lack of large, high quality datasets capturing complex emotion in music.

**A Novel Lyrics Dataset Annotated for Emotion** Consequently, we created the Edmonds Dance dataset, a novel corpus of English song lyrics annotated for emotion from the reader's perspective. By searching a Spotify playlist consisting of 800 songs, both lyrical and instrumental, and collecting available lyrics from LyricFind, Genius, and MusixMatch (Lyr; Gen; Mus), we retrieved lyrics for 524 songs. We then labeled our dataset based on Plutchik's 8 core emotions of Anger, Anticipation, Disgust, Fear, Joy, Sadness, Surprise, and Trust (Plutchik, 2001). Table 1 depicts a subsection of the Edmonds Dance dataset, while the Appendix has more information on our labeling methods.

**Mihalcea/Strapparava Dataset Reannotation** In addition to the Edmonds Dance dataset, we also reannotated the dataset introduced in Mihalcea and Strapparava (2012), a multimodal corpus of songs that includes scalar annotations of both audio and lyrics for Ekman's six core emotions: Anger, Disgust, Fear, Joy, Sadness, and Surprise (Ekman, 1993). The original dataset was annotated from the songwriter's perspective and at a line level. We averaged these line-level lyrical annotations to achieve classifications at higher levels, thus gen-

| Song | Artist | Lyrics | Emotion |
|---|---|---|---|
| I'm Done | MYNGA, Hechmann | You ruined my life<br>What you said in your message that night<br>Left me broken and bruised... | Anger, Disgust, Sadness |
| I Lived | OneRepublic | I'd like to teach the world to sing<br>Hope when you take that jump<br>You don't fear the fall... | Anticipation, Joy, Trust |
| Jubel | Klingande | Save me, save me, save me<br>You think I don't laugh, oh<br>Do things I can like, so<br>Why are we losing time... | Fear, Sadness, Surprise, Trust |

Table 1: Examples from the Edmonds Dance Dataset

| | Mihalcea/Strapparava | Edmonds Dance |
|---|---|---|
| Songs | 100 | 524 |
| Lines | 4976 | 22924 |
| Words | 109332 | 708985 |
| Vocabulary | 2233 | 6563 |

Table 2: Lyrical Dataset Basic Statistics

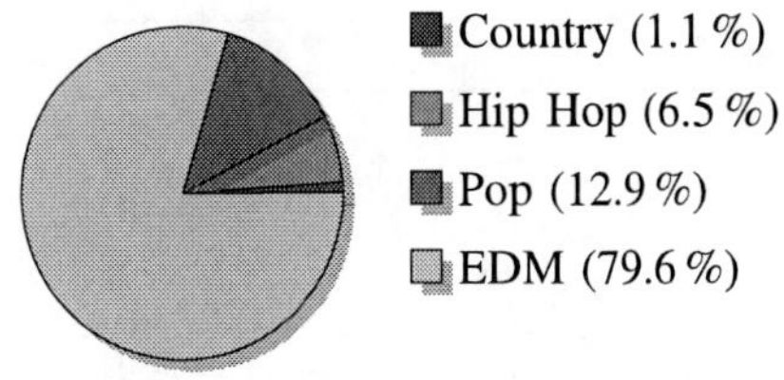


Figure 1: Genres within Edmonds Dance HITs

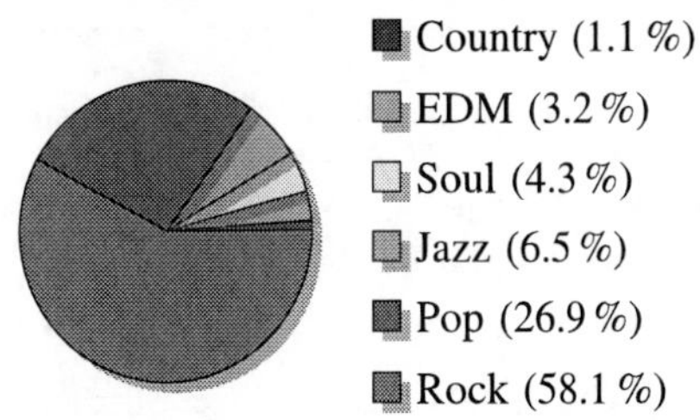


Figure 2: Genres within Mihalcea/Strapparava HITs

erating 452 verse-based and 100 song-based annotations. Table 2 provides some basic statistics for the lyrical datasets used in our research.

**Mechanical Turk** We submitted HITs on Mechanical Turk to validate lyric annotations. Each HIT contained three songs to be annotated from the reader's perspective for 8 emotions on a 6-point Likert scale. We also queried whether the annotator had heard of each song (yes/no), and whether they liked it (yes/no/unsure). Of the 186 songs annotated in total, 93 were from the Edmonds Dance dataset and 93 were from the Mihalcea/Strapparava dataset. HITs encompassed multiple genres, with the Edmonds Dance dataset mostly consisting of electronic music and the Mihalcea/Strapparava dataset mostly consisting of rock music. Figures 1 and 2 summarize HIT breakdowns by genre.

**Annotation Guidelines** To generate reliable annotations, our HIT included detailed annotation instructions. We organized these guidelines into four sections: initial instructions, important notes, definitions, and examples. The initial instructions section provided the annotator with basic task information, stating that he or she will be given a set of song lyrics, and is expected to record the degree to which the lyrics contain eight specific emotions. We also stated that emotions would be rated on a 6-point scale ranging from the complete absence of an emotion to the extreme presence of an emotion.

The important notes section emphasized that English speakers were required for the task, and that completion of all fields was required. The definitions section provided dictionary-level definitions for each of the eight emotions, while the examples section provided two annotated examples, along with general annotation guidelines (see Appendix A.2 for HIT images).

Each HIT contained the same two example songs. Each of the eight emotions was present in at least one of the songs, and emotions evoked by each song were apparent from the lyrics. Our HITs are available upon request.

**Error Analysis** We evaluated annotator reliability by calculating the average Cohen's Kappa of each annotator against others assigned to the same HIT, and discarding those below the threshold of 0.25. We then analyzed agreement across emotions by calculating Krippendorf's Alpha on the remaining annotators, and examined the agreement between original and Turker annotations using Pearson's correlation coefficient. Table 3 depicts our results, with more details available in the Appendix.

Surprise had significantly lower inter-annotator agreement than other emotions. Krippendorf's Alpha and Pearson's Correlation values were lowest for Surprise, with significant correlation differences compared to all other emotions except Anticipation. Meanwhile, Joy and Sadness had relatively higher alpha and correlation values, suggesting a hierarchy of difficulty in emotion classification.

| Emotion | Krippendorf's Alpha | Correlation±90 % CI |
|---|---|---|
| All | 0.625 | 0.276±0.029 |
| Anger | 0.571 | 0.249±0.083 |
| Anticipation* | 0.572 | 0.294±0.149 |
| Disgust | 0.563 | 0.302±0.081 |
| Fear | 0.564 | 0.421±0.072 |
| Joy | 0.641 | 0.407±0.074 |
| Sadness | 0.63 | 0.411±0.072 |
| Surprise | 0.532 | 0.078±0.087 |
| Trust* | 0.617 | 0.384±0.138 |

Table 3: Inter-annotator Agreement at Cohen's Kappa Threshold of 0.25, and Pearson's Correlation between Original and Turker labels. Starred emotions were not present in the original Mihalcea/Strapparava dataset.

**Analysis of Crowd Workers** To confirm the quality of our dataset, we analyzed differences in annotation patterns between included and discarded Turkers. Discarded annotators had lower median completion time across the Edmonds Dance and Mihalcea/Strapparava datasets (p<.005), were more likely to say that they disliked a song (p<.005), and were less likely to say that they were unfamiliar with a song (p<.001). We also found that discarded annotators spent less time than included annotators on labeling songs that they disliked (p<.001). Further details are in the Appendix.

### 3.2 Out of Domain Datasets

To explore the efficacy of out-of-domain model training, we used the CBET (Shahraki, 2015), TEC (Mohammad, 2012), and DailyDialog (Li et al., 2017) datasets, three large collections of text annotated for multiple emotions including 6 core emotions present in both the Edmonds Dance and Mihalcea/Strapparava datasets. The CBET and TEC datasets respectively consist of 81,163 and 21,048 tweets, while the DailyDialog dataset consists of 102,979 statements collected from 13,118 transcripts of two-person conversations. Emotion distributions of the CBET, TEC, Daily Dialog, Edmonds Dance, and Mihalcea/Strapparava datasets are depicted in Table 4.

| Emotion | CBET | TEC | DD | Dance | M/S |
|---|---|---|---|---|---|
| Anger | 11.2% | 7.4% | 1.0% | 13.7% | 9.1% |
| Disgust | 10.7% | 3.6% | 0.3% | 21.9% | 2.9% |
| Fear | 11.2% | 13.3% | 0.2% | 19.7% | 1.8% |
| Joy | 13.4% | 39.1% | 12.5% | 43.9% | 50.4% |
| Sadness | 11.4% | 18.2% | 1.1% | 35.3% | 33.0% |
| Surprise | 11.4% | 18.3% | 1.8% | 13.0% | 0.9% |

Table 4: Presence of Emotion by Dataset

To train more robust baseline models, we also created augmented and transformed versions of the datasets; details on this process are available in the Appendix. While no versions of the CBET, TEC, and DailyDialog datasets include music lyrics, they are large enough to train deep models which we hypothesized could accurately predict emotions in smaller, gold-standard test datasets of song lyrics.

## 4 Model Implementation

We chose Naive Bayes as our first baseline emotion classification model due to its widespread applications in text classification and sentiment analysis (Raschka, 2014). Given its robustness to outliers and ability to deal with imbalanced data (Chen et al., 2004), a Random Forest baseline model was also implemented. Lastly, we utilized a Most Frequent Sense (MFS) baseline model, given its strong performance in word sense disambiguation tasks and its applications to emotion classification (Preiss et al., 2009). We trained our Naive Bayes model on bag-of-words features and our Random Forest model on transformed feature vectors which were generated from our textual datasets using the NRC Hashtag Emotion Lexicon (Mohammad and Turney, 2013); see Appendix for further details.

To improve upon emotion classification quality, we also explored more complex models. Due to its ability to generate powerful contextualized word embeddings and its state-of-the-art results in numerous language understanding tasks (Devlin et al., 2019), the $\text{BERT}_{\text{BASE}}$ uncased architecture was fine-tuned for multi-emotion classification from the text of song lyrics. $\text{BERT}_{\text{BASE}}$ consists of 12 Transformer blocks, a hidden size of 768, 12 self-attention heads, and an additional output layer which we used for fine-tuning.[2]

## 5 Evaluation

We trained separate BERT models for each emotion on the original and augmented CBET datasets, and tested their performance on the Edmonds Dance and Mihalcea/Strapparava datasets. We then compared these results with those of our baseline Naive Bayes, Random Forest, and Most Frequent Sense models. To compare emotion prediction accuracy across multiple text corpora, we also trained BERT models on the TEC and DailyDialog datasets, and tested them on our lyrical datasets.

We found that BERT models trained on the CBET, TEC, and DailyDialog datasets did not generalize well to lyrical data. While models for joy and sadness improved upon the performance of baseline classifiers, models for disgust and fear performed worse than our Naive Bayes baseline. Furthermore, data augmentation techniques improved the performance of our baseline Naive Bayes model, but did not significantly increase BERT model accuracy.

To compare in-domain model accuracy with our out-of-domain results, we trained and tested BERT models on the Edmonds Dance and Mihalcea/Strapparava datasets, and vice versa. Models trained and tested on lyrical datasets had marginally better accuracy and F1 scores than out-of-domain models for anger, joy, and sadness. Given the much smaller sizes of lyrical datasets compared to their counterparts, as well as the differences in song genre and annotation perspective across lyrical datasets, our findings suggest a significant advantage in using in-domain data to train models for complex emotion classification of songs.

Finally, all models performed poorly when classifying surprise, and F1 scores for anger, disgust, and fear remained consistently low across models, suggesting a steep hierarchy of difficulty regarding emotion classification. Inter-annotator agreement was much lower for surprise than other emotions, and none of our models were able to accurately predict the presence of surprise in song lyrics. Our work implies that surprise is unique from the perspective of emotion classification.

Tables 5 and 6 highlight our model results. A complete version of our evaluation results is available in the Appendix.

[2]BERT$_{\textbf{BASE}}$ is available at `https://tfhub.dev/google/bert_uncased_L-12_H-768_A-12/1`.

| Emotion | MFS | Naive Bayes | CBET BERT | Lyrics BERT |
|---|---|---|---|---|
| Anger | 0.88 | 0.67 | 0.85 | **0.88** |
| Disgust | 0.88 | 0.79 | 0.88 | 0.88 |
| Fear | 0.89 | 0.77 | 0.89 | 0.89 |
| Joy | 0.47 | 0.53 | 0.58 | **0.7** |
| Sadness | 0.66 | 0.58 | 0.7 | **0.73** |
| Surprise | 0.92 | 0.92 | 0.92 | 0.92 |

Table 5: Model Accuracy on Lyrics By Emotion

| Emotion | Naive Bayes | CBET BERT | Lyrics BERT |
|---|---|---|---|
| Anger | 0.17 | 0.04 | **0.2** |
| Disgust | **0.21** | 0 | 0 |
| Fear | **0.18** | 0.14 | 0 |
| Joy | 0.03 | 0.24 | **0.69** |
| Sadness | **0.55** | 0.48 | 0.54 |
| Surprise | 0 | 0 | 0 |

Table 6: Model F1 Score on Lyrics By Emotion

## 6 Conclusion

In this paper we explore a variety of approaches to the multi-emotion classification problem for songs. We introduce the Edmonds Dance dataset, a novel lyrical dataset annotated for emotion at the song level and from the reader's perspective. We find that emotion classification of song lyrics using state-of-the-art methods is difficult to accomplish using out-of-domain data; BERT models trained on large corpora of tweets and dialogue do not generalize to lyrical data for emotions other than joy and sadness, and are outperformed by Naive Bayes classifiers on disgust and fear. On the other hand, models trained on song lyrics achieve comparable accuracy to models trained on out-of-domain data, even when lyrical datasets are orders of magnitude smaller than their counterparts, have been aggregated from line to song level, have been annotated from different perspectives, and are composed of different genres of music. Our findings underscore the importance of using in-domain data for song emotion classification.

## 7 Ethical Consideration

Our dataset was annotated by 184 Amazon Mechanical Turk crowdworkers. Annotators were paid \$0.15 per task or $\sim$ \$6.75 per hour, and reliable annotators (see Appendix A.2) were awarded a bonus of \$0.10 per task or $\sim$ \$11.25 per hour.

## References


Genius website. https://genius.com/.

Lyricfind website. https://www.lyricfind.com/.

Musixmatch website. https://www.musixmatch.com/.

Jiddy Abdillah, Ibnu Asror, Yanuar Firdaus Arie Wibowo, et al. 2020. Emotion classification of song lyrics using bidirectional lstm method with glove word representation weighting. *Jurnal RESTI (Rekayasa Sistem Dan Teknologi Informasi)*, 4(4):723–729.

Cecilia Ovesdotter Alm, Dan Roth, and Richard Sproat. 2005. Emotions from text: machine learning for text-based emotion prediction. In *Proceedings of human language technology conference and conference on empirical methods in natural language processing*, pages 579–586.

Yunjing An, Shutao Sun, and Shujuan Wang. 2017. Naive bayes classifiers for music emotion classification based on lyrics. In *2017 IEEE/ACIS 16th International Conference on Computer and Information Science (ICIS)*, pages 635–638. IEEE.

Victoria Bobicev and Marina Sokolova. 2017. Inter-annotator agreement in sentiment analysis: Machine learning perspective. In *RANLP*, pages 97–102.

Sven Buechel and Udo Hahn. 2017. Emobank: Studying the impact of annotation perspective and representation format on dimensional emotion analysis. In *Proceedings of the 15th Conference of the European Chapter of the Association for Computational Linguistics: Volume 2, Short Papers*, pages 578–585.

Erion Çano and Maurizio Morisio. 2017. Moodylyrics: A sentiment annotated lyrics dataset. In *Proceedings of the 2017 International Conference on Intelligent Systems, Metaheuristics & Swarm Intelligence*, pages 118–124.

Chao Chen, Andy Liaw, Leo Breiman, et al. 2004. Using random forest to learn imbalanced data. *University of California, Berkeley*, 110(1-12):24.

Rémi Delbouys, Romain Hennequin, Francesco Piccoli, Jimena Royo-Letelier, and Manuel Moussallam. 2018. Music mood detection based on audio and lyrics with deep neural net. In *Proceedings of the 19th International Society for Music Information Retrieval Conference, ISMIR 2018, Paris, France, September 23-27, 2018*, pages 370–375.

Jacob Devlin, Ming-Wei Chang, Kenton Lee, and Kristina Toutanova. 2019. BERT: Pre-training of deep bidirectional transformers for language understanding. In *Proceedings of the 2019 Conference of the North American Chapter of the Association for Computational Linguistics: Human Language Technologies, Volume 1 (Long and Short Papers)*, pages 4171–4186, Minneapolis, Minnesota. Association for Computational Linguistics.

Nicholas A Diakopoulos and David A Shamma. 2010. Characterizing debate performance via aggregated twitter sentiment. In *Proceedings of the SIGCHI conference on human factors in computing systems*, pages 1195–1198.

Adam Dunbar, Charis E Kubrin, and Nicholas Scurich. 2016. The threatening nature of "rap" music. *Psychology, Public Policy, and Law*, 22(3):280.

Paul Ekman. 1993. Facial expression and emotion. *American psychologist*, 48(4):384.

Paul Ekman and Wallace V Friesen. 2003. *Unmasking the face: A guide to recognizing emotions from facial clues*. ISHK.

Carrie B Fried. 1999. Who's afraid of rap: Differential reactions to music lyrics 1. *Journal of Applied Social Psychology*, 29(4):705–721.

Maryam Hasan, Emmanuel Agu, and Elke Rundensteiner. 2014. Using hashtags as labels for supervised learning of emotions in twitter messages. In *ACM SIGKDD workshop on health informatics, New York, USA*.

Martin Haselmayer and Marcelo Jenny. 2017. Sentiment analysis of political communication: combining a dictionary approach with crowdcoding. *Quality & quantity*, 51(6):2623–2646.

Hui He, Jianming Jin, Yuhong Xiong, Bo Chen, Wu Sun, and Ling Zhao. 2008. Language feature mining for music emotion classification via supervised learning from lyrics. In *International Symposium on Intelligence Computation and Applications*, pages 426–435. Springer.

Xiao Hu and J Stephen Downie. 2010. When lyrics outperform audio for music mood classification: A feature analysis. In *ISMIR*, pages 619–624.

Xiao Hu, J Stephen Downie, and Andreas F Ehmann. 2009. Lyric text mining in music mood classification. *American music*, 183(5,049):2–209.

Adit Jamdar, Jessica Abraham, Karishma Khanna, and Rahul Dubey. 2015. Emotion analysis of songs based on lyrical and audio features. *arXiv preprint arXiv:1506.05012*.

Robbert Jongeling, Proshanta Sarkar, Subhajit Datta, and Alexander Serebrenik. 2017. On negative results when using sentiment analysis tools for software engineering research. *Empirical Software Engineering*, 22(5):2543–2584.

Minho Kim and Hyuk-Chul Kwon. 2011. Lyrics-based emotion classification using feature selection by partial syntactic analysis. In *2011 IEEE 23rd International Conference on Tools with Artificial Intelligence*, pages 960–964. IEEE.

Youngmoo E Kim, Erik M Schmidt, Raymond Migneco, Brandon G Morton, Patrick Richardson, Jeffrey Scott, Jacquelin A Speck, and Douglas Turnbull. 2010. Music emotion recognition: A state of the art review. In *Proc. ismir*, volume 86, pages 937–952.

Yanran Li, Hui Su, Xiaoyu Shen, Wenjie Li, Ziqiang Cao, and Shuzi Niu. 2017. Dailydialog: A manually labelled multi-turn dialogue dataset. In *Proceedings of the Eighth International Joint Conference on Natural Language Processing (Volume 1: Long Papers)*, pages 986–995.

Gaojun Liu and Zhiyuan Tan. 2020. Research on multi-modal music emotion classification based on audio and lyirc. In *2020 IEEE 4th Information Technology, Networking, Electronic and Automation Control Conference (ITNEC)*, volume 1, pages 2331–2335. IEEE.

Rada Mihalcea and Carlo Strapparava. 2012. Lyrics, music, and emotions. In *Proceedings of the 2012 Joint Conference on Empirical Methods in Natural Language Processing and Computational Natural Language Learning*, pages 590–599.

Saif Mohammad. 2012. # emotional tweets. In ** SEM 2012: The First Joint Conference on Lexical and Computational Semantics–Volume 1: Proceedings of the main conference and the shared task, and Volume 2: Proceedings of the Sixth International Workshop on Semantic Evaluation (SemEval 2012)*, pages 246–255.

Saif Mohammad and Felipe Bravo-Marquez. 2017. Emotion intensities in tweets. In *Proceedings of the 6th Joint Conference on Lexical and Computational Semantics (*SEM 2017)*, pages 65–77, Vancouver, Canada. Association for Computational Linguistics.

Saif M Mohammad and Peter D Turney. 2013. Crowdsourcing a word–emotion association lexicon. *Computational Intelligence*, 29(3):436–465.

Laura Ana Maria Oberländer and Roman Klinger. 2018. An analysis of annotated corpora for emotion classification in text. In *Proceedings of the 27th International Conference on Computational Linguistics*, pages 2104–2119.

Loreto Parisi, Simone Francia, Silvio Olivastri, and Maria Stella Tavella. 2019. Exploiting synchronized lyrics and vocal features for music emotion detection. *arXiv preprint arXiv:1901.04831*.

Robert Plutchik. 2001. The nature of emotions: Human emotions have deep evolutionary roots, a fact that may explain their complexity and provide tools for clinical practice. *American scientist*, 89(4):344–350.

Judita Preiss, Jon Dehdari, Josh King, and Dennis Mehay. 2009. Refining the most frequent sense baseline. In *Proceedings of the Workshop on Semantic Evaluations: Recent Achievements and Future Directions (SEW-2009)*, pages 10–18.

Simon Provoost, Jeroen Ruwaard, Ward van Breda, Heleen Riper, and Tibor Bosse. 2019. Validating automated sentiment analysis of online cognitive behavioral therapy patient texts: An exploratory study. *Frontiers in psychology*, 10:1065.

Fika Hastarita Rachman, Riyanarto Sarno, and Chastine Fatichah. 2018. Music emotion classification based on lyrics-audio using corpus based emotion. *International Journal of Electrical & Computer Engineering (2088-8708)*, 8(3).

Meena Rambocas and Barney G Pacheco. 2018. Online sentiment analysis in marketing research: a review. *Journal of Research in Interactive Marketing*.

Sebastian Raschka. 2014. Naive bayes and text classification i-introduction and theory. *arXiv preprint arXiv:1410.5329*.

Hendrik Schuff, Jeremy Barnes, Julian Mohme, Sebastian Padó, and Roman Klinger. 2017. Annotation, modelling and analysis of fine-grained emotions on a stance and sentiment detection corpus. In *Proceedings of the 8th Workshop on Computational Approaches to Subjectivity, Sentiment and Social Media Analysis*, pages 13–23.

Ameneh Gholipour Shahraki. 2015. Emotion detection from text. Master's thesis, University of Alberta.

Carlo Strapparava, Rada Mihalcea, and Alberto Battocchi. 2012. A parallel corpus of music and lyrics annotated with emotions. In *Proceedings of the Eighth International Conference on Language Resources and Evaluation (LREC'12)*, pages 2343–2346, Istanbul, Turkey. European Language Resources Association (ELRA).

Marco Susino and Emery Schubert. 2019a. Cultural stereotyping of emotional responses to music genre. *Psychology of Music*, 47(3):342–357.

Marco Susino and Emery Schubert. 2019b. Negative emotion responses to heavy-metal and hip-hop music with positive lyrics. *Empirical Musicology Review*, 14(1-2):2–15.

Pyry Takala, Pekka Malo, Ankur Sinha, and Oskar Ahlgren. 2014. Gold-standard for topic-specific sentiment analysis of economic texts. In *Proceedings of the Ninth International Conference on Language Resources and Evaluation (LREC'14)*, pages 2152–2157, Reykjavik, Iceland. European Language Resources Association (ELRA).

Xing Wang, Xiaoou Chen, Deshun Yang, and Yuqian Wu. 2011. Music emotion classification of chinese songs based on lyrics using tf* idf and rhyme. In *ISMIR*, pages 765–770. Citeseer.

Dan Yang and Won-Sook Lee. 2009. Music emotion identification from lyrics. In *2009 11th IEEE International Symposium on Multimedia*, pages 624–629. IEEE.

Yi-Hsuan Yang, Yu-Ching Lin, Heng-Tze Cheng, I-Bin Liao, Yeh-Chin Ho, and Homer H Chen. 2008. Toward multi-modal music emotion classification. In *Pacific-Rim Conference on Multimedia*, pages 70–79. Springer.

# A Appendix

## A.1 Lyrical Datasets

The Mihalcea/Strapparava dataset initially consisted of 4976 lines across 100 songs which were annotated using a scale from 0 to 10, with 0 as the absence of emotion and 10 as the highest intensity of emotion. Annotations were based on Ekman's six core emotions: Anger, Disgust, Fear, Joy, Sadness, and Surprise (Ekman, 1993). As the dataset was annotated at a line level, we averaged emotion annotations on each line to achieve classifications at higher levels. Through averaging, we generated 452 verse-based and 100 song-based annotations.

With regards to the Edmonds Dance Dataset, the basis for label selection was provided by Plutchik's Theory of Emotion, which postulates that all emotions are combinations of the 8 core emotions present in our label (Plutchik, 2001). As a result, the label can lead to additional classification models for emotions which are theorized to be dyads of the core emotions (e.g, PLove = PJoy $*$ PTrust, or PAggressiveness = PAnger $*$ PAnticipation ). Our dataset was initially labeled using an array of size 8; each array index contained a binary value to indicate an emotion's presence.

| Dataset | Emotion | Krippendorf's Alpha |
|---|---|---|
| Dance | All | 0.717 |
| Dance | Anger | 0.704 |
| Dance | Anticipation | 0.706 |
| Dance | Disgust | 0.691 |
| Dance | Fear | 0.69 |
| Dance | Joy | 0.718 |
| Dance | Sadness | 0.73 |
| Dance | Surprise | 0.653 |
| Dance | Trust | 0.705 |
| M/S | All | 0.532 |
| M/S | Anger | 0.438 |
| M/S | Anticipation | 0.437 |
| M/S | Disgust | 0.435 |
| M/S | Fear | 0.437 |
| M/S | Joy | 0.564 |
| M/S | Sadness | 0.53 |
| M/S | Surprise | 0.411 |
| M/S | Trust | 0.528 |

Table A1: Interannotator Agreement at Cohen's Kappa Threshold of 0.25

| Dataset | Emotion | Pearson's Correlation | 90% CI |
|---|---|---|---|
| Dance | All | 0.396 | (0.343, 0.445) |
| Dance | Anger | 0.204 | (0.033, 0.363) |
| Dance | Anticipation | 0.294 | (0.129, 0.443) |
| Dance | Disgust | 0.429 | (0.278, 0.559) |
| Dance | Fear | 0.31 | (0.146, 0.457) |
| Dance | Joy | 0.362 | (0.203, 0.502) |
| Dance | Sadness | 0.316 | (0.154, 0.462) |
| Dance | Surprise | 0.175 | (0.003, 0.336) |
| Dance | Trust | 0.384 | (0.228, 0.522) |
| M/S | All | 0.183 | (0.124, 0.241) |
| M/S | Anger | 0.28 | (0.114, 0.431) |
| M/S | Disgust | 0.214 | (0.045, 0.371) |
| M/S | Fear | 0.499 | (0.358, 0.618) |
| M/S | Joy | 0.439 | (0.289, 0.568) |
| M/S | Sadness | 0.477 | (0.333, 0.6) |
| M/S | Surprise | 0.01 | (-0.161, 0.18) |

Table A2: Pearson's Correlation between Original and Turker annotations

## A.2 Annotator Error Analysis

To evaluate the reliability of our Mechanical Turk annotations, we first used Cohen's Kappa to calculate the average inter-annotator agreement of each Turker against others assigned to the same HIT. We then discarded all annotators who failed to meet a threshold of 0.25, and calculated average agreement for each emotion using Krippendorf's Alpha on the remaining annotators. Krippendorf's Alpha values were highest for the emotions of joy, sadness, and trust; additionally, alpha values were relatively consistent across emotions. 31.6% of annotations in Mihalcea and Strapparava's dataset failed to meet the Cohen's Kappa threshold, while 63.2% of annotations in the Edmonds Dance dataset failed to meet the threshold. Our results are summarized in Table A1, while Figures A1, A2, and A3 depict pictures of our HITs.

Next, we calculated the Pearson's correlation coefficient and related p-values between original annotations and the Turker annotations for both the Edmonds Dance and Mihalcea/Strapparava datasets. We were also unable to calculate correlation coefficients for Anticipation or Trust in the Rada dataset as the original dataset did not include annotations for these emotions. These results are summarized in Table A2.

While the relative strength of Pearson's Correlations across emotions was similar to that of our alpha values, correlation with fear was relatively higher than expected, and correlation with anger and surprise were lower than expected. Finally, we looked at Krippendorf's Alpha Values on an an-

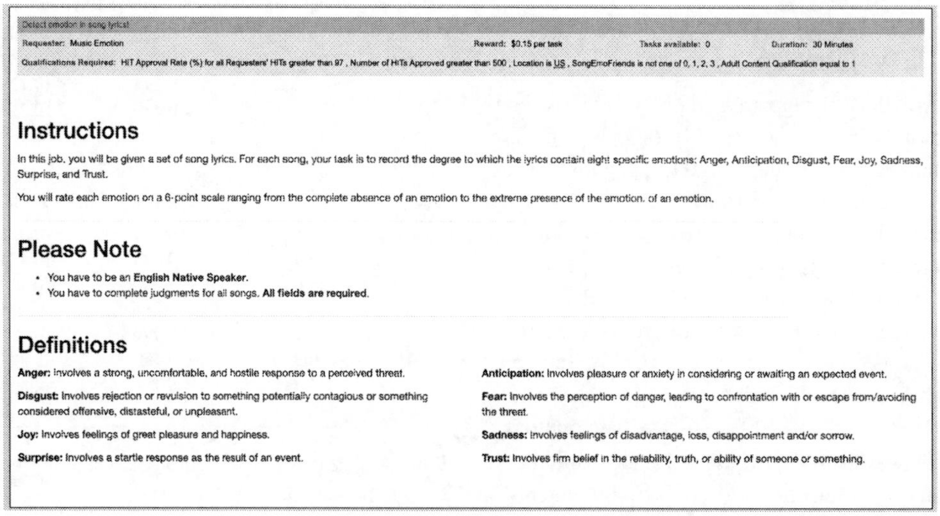


Figure A1: HIT Preliminary Instructions

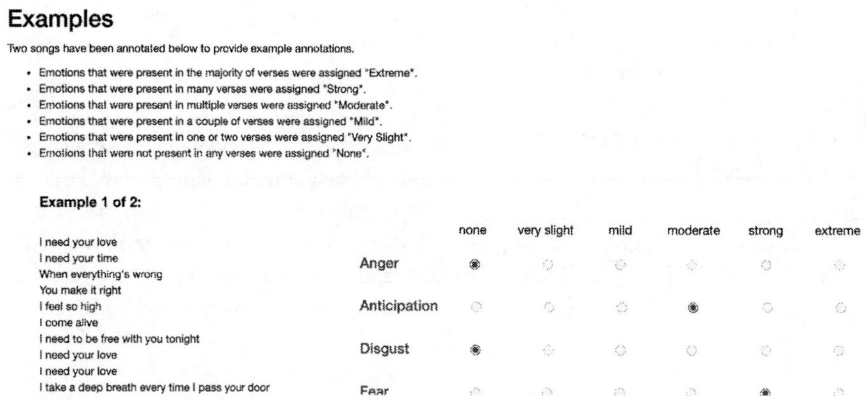


Figure A2: HIT Example Annotations

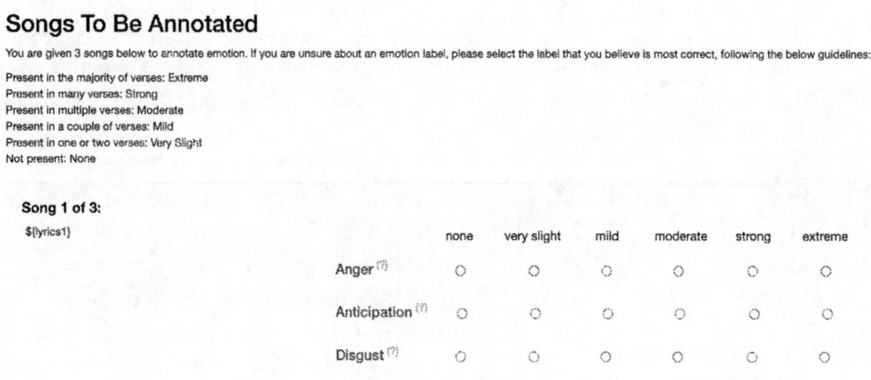


Figure A3: HIT Annotation Format

notation group level to better understand whether annotation agreement for specific emotions were consistently similar across songs. Our results, summarized in Table A3, provide evidence for a hierarchy of difficulty in emotion classification. Joy and Sadness have the most favorable distribution of alpha values with few low item-level alpha scores (<0.2), and greater numbers of medium (0.2-0.6) and high (>0.6) item-level alpha scores. Anger and Trust have the next most favorable distributions, while Anticipation, Disgust, and Fear have similar but lower agreement distributions. Finally, Surprise has the worst distribution, with almost all item-level Krippendorf's Alpha values being classified as low agreement.

| Emotion | Agreement | | |
|---|---|---|---|
| | Low | Moderate | High |
| Anger | 25 | 17 | 8 |
| Anticipation | 27 | 15 | 3 |
| Disgust | 26 | 21 | 3 |
| Fear | 30 | 18 | 2 |
| Joy | 12 | 24 | 14 |
| Sadness | 10 | 23 | 17 |
| Surprise | 48 | 2 | 0 |
| Trust | 17 | 25 | 8 |

Table A3: Krippendorf's Alpha Values By Emotion Over 50 Annotator Groups

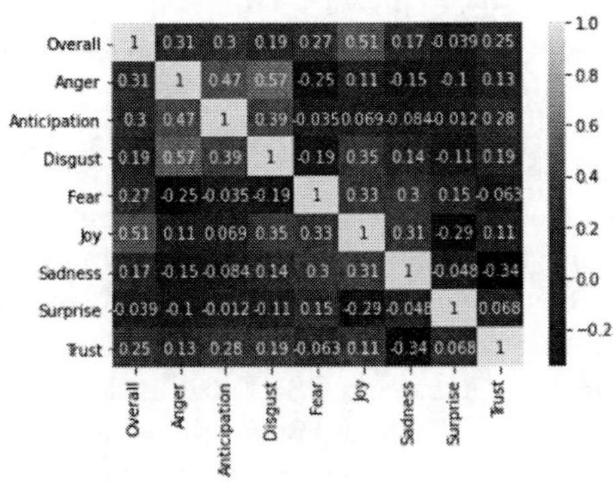


Figure A4: Correlation Heatmap of Krippendorf's Alphas

We then created a heat map of item-level Krippendorf's Alphas to explore correlation of interannotator agreement across emotions. Our results, visualized in Figure A4, reveal that alpha values are only slightly correlated across emotions. This implies that classification difficulty of a specific emotion varies depending on the song being annotated; indeed, the only emotions that have an inter-annotator agreement correlation above 0.4 are Anger/Disgust and Anger/Anticipation. We can also see that only joy has a moderate correlation with overall agreement across emotions, implying that songs with annotation agreement regarding joy may be easier to classify overall, but songs with annotation agreement regarding other emotions may not necessarily be easier to annotate. Consequently, the claim of a consistent hierarchy of difficulty is somewhat undermined and instead it seems that classification difficulty of a specific emotion varies depending on the song being annotated.

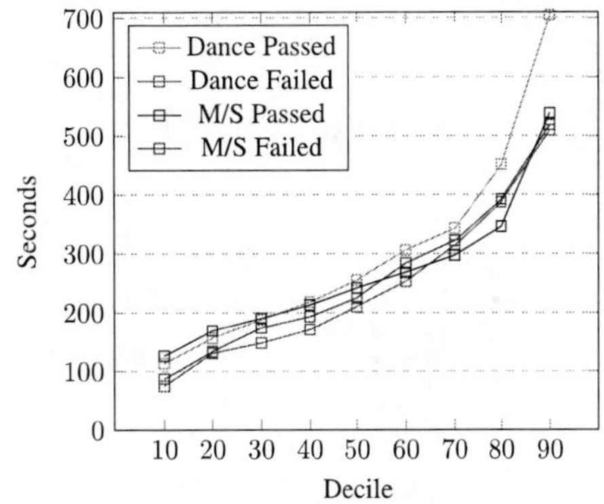


Figure A5: Annotation Completion Time by Quantile

### A.3 Analysis of Crowd Workers

We analyzed the completion time of annotations across good and bad annotators for the Edmonds Dance and Mihalcea/Strapparava datasets, summarized in Figure A5. We can see that the distributions of completion times were very similar for bad annotators, while the distributions for good annotators were skewed upwards at higher deciles. In addition, the median completion time for good annotators was 31 seconds greater than the median completion time for bad annotators, and the mean completion time for good annotators was 37 seconds greater than that of bad annotators.

Next, we looked at differences between good and bad annotator groups regarding annotator enjoyment and familiarity of labeled songs. We found that bad annotators were more likely than good annotators to say that they were familiar with a song ($p<.00001$), or that they disliked a song ($p<.005$). Bad annotators also spent significantly less time than good annotators on labeling songs that they said they disliked ($p<0.0001$). These results are summarized in Figures A6 and A7.

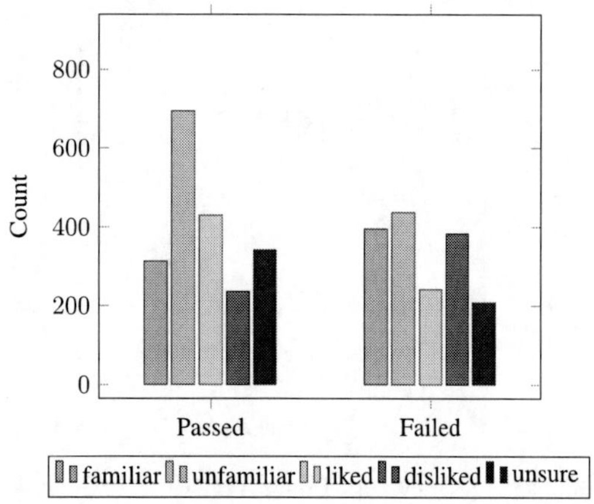


Figure A6: Annotator Enjoyment/Familiarity of Songs by Count and Annotation Quality

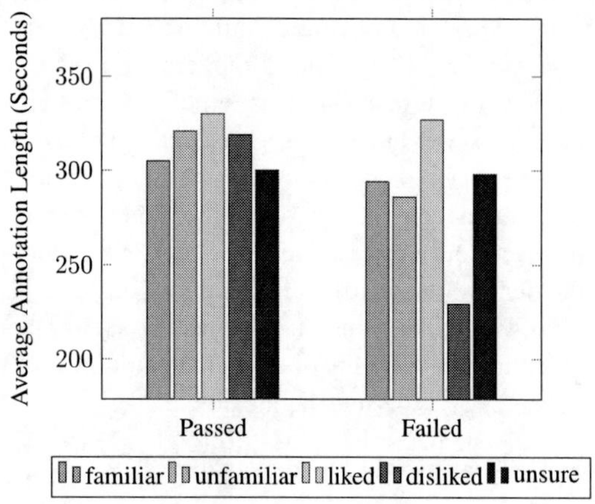


Figure A7: Annotator Enjoyment/Familiarity of Songs by Annotation Time and Quality

### A.4 Additional Dataset Information

#### A.4.1 Data Augmentation and Transformation

To address misclassification of the minority class, we implemented oversampling techniques so classes would be more balanced. For each emotion in the CBET dataset, we added copies of tweets suggesting the presence of the emotion such that the new number of tweets with presence of emotion was between 40-60 percent of the total number of tweets. We then trained two BERT models for each emotion, one using the augmented CBET dataset and the other using the original. To confirm the quality of the original CBET dataset, we also trained and tested BERT models on subsets of CBET data that were randomly sampled without replacement. These results are shown in Table A4.

To explore another approach to the multi-emotion classification problem, lyrical data was then transformed into a feature vector of length 9 using the NRC Hashtag Emotion Lexicon, which contains binary indicators regarding the presence or absence of Plutchik's 8 core emotions in 14182 common English words (Mohammad and Turney, 2013). This occurred by iterating through a song's lyrics, counting each word present in the NRC Emotion Lexicon as well as its emotional classification, and storing this information in the feature vector. For example, the feature vector [5, 10, 1, 9, 4, 2, 2, 3, 28] would correspond to a song's lyrics that contained 28 words (not necessarily all distinct) which were present in the NRC Emotion Lexicon. Of these words, 5 were associated with joy, 10 with trust, 1 with fear, etc. This transformed dataset was generated for the purpose of exploring Random Forest methods for song emotion classification.

### A.5 Evaluation

To gauge the quality of the CBET dataset, we first calculated the accuracies of BERT models trained and tested on randomly ordered subsets of CBET data, with an 80/20 train/test split. Emotion classification accuracies of these models were at least 90%, confirming the quality of the dataset. Next, we trained BERT models on the full CBET datasets, and evaluated them on the verse-based variation of Mihalcea and Strapparava's dataset, as well as the Edmonds Dance dataset. All BERT models were trained for 3 epochs, and used a sequence length of 128, batch size of 32, learning rate of $2e^{-5}$, and warmup proportion of 0.1. The performance of these models, depicted in Table A4, were then compared to the performance of baseline Naive Bayes and Random Forest models, shown in Tables A5 and A6. Only the baseline Naive Bayes model trained on augmented CBET data is depicted in Table A5, as the Naive Bayes model trained on normal CBET data had precision and recall of zero for each emotion.

It can be seen from Table A4 that BERT models trained on CBET did not generalize well to lyrical datasets. While models for joy and sadness improved on the performance of Naive Bayes and Random Forest classifiers, models for other emotions did not significantly improve on the baseline, and in some cases performed worse than baseline classifiers. BERT models for anger and fear had lower precision and recall than corresponding

| Emotion | Train | Test | Accuracy | AUC | Prec | Rec |
|---|---|---|---|---|---|---|
| Anger | CBET sub | CBET sub | 0.91 | 0.73 | 0.6 | 0.49 |
| Anger | CBET | Dance | 0.84 | 0.51 | 0.19 | 0.04 |
| Anger | CBET aug | Dance | 0.81 | 0.53 | 0.2 | 0.14 |
| Anger | CBET | Dance Turk | 0.81 | 0.5 | 0 | 0 |
| Anger | CBET | M/S | 0.85 | 0.05 | 0.1 | 0.07 |
| Anger | CBET aug | M/S | 0.90 | 0.55 | 0.42 | 0.12 |
| Anger | CBET | M/S Turk | 0.89 | 0.54 | 0.25 | 0.125 |
| Disgust | CBET sub | CBET sub | 0.93 | 0.79 | 0.7 | 0.61 |
| Disgust | CBET | Dance | 0.78 | 0.5 | 0 | 0 |
| Disgust | CBET aug | Dance | 0.78 | 0.5 | 0 | 0 |
| Disgust | CBET | Dance Turk | 0.94 | 0.49 | 0 | 0 |
| Disgust | CBET | M/S | 0.97 | 0.5 | 0 | 0 |
| Disgust | CBET aug | M/S | 0.97 | 0.5 | 0 | 0 |
| Disgust | CBET | M/S Turk | 0.96 | 0.5 | 0 | 0 |
| Fear | CBET sub | CBET sub | 0.95 | 0.86 | 0.82 | 0.74 |
| Fear | CBET | Dance | 0.77 | 0.55 | 0.34 | 0.19 |
| Fear | CBET aug | Dance | 0.8 | 0.52 | 0.5 | 0.06 |
| Fear | CBET | Dance Turk | 0.78 | 0.53 | 0.29 | 0.12 |
| Fear | CBET | M/S | 0.97 | 0.49 | 0 | 0 |
| Fear | CBET aug | M/S | 0.97 | 0.55 | 0.13 | 0.13 |
| Fear | CBET | M/S Turk | 0.87 | 0.53 | 0.33 | 0.09 |
| Joy | CBET sub | CBET sub | 0.9 | 0.76 | 0.67 | 0.57 |
| Joy | CBET | Dance | 0.61 | 0.56 | 0.82 | 0.16 |
| Joy | CBET aug | Dance | 0.58 | 0.53 | 0.74 | 0.07 |
| Joy | CBET | Dance Turk | 0.45 | 0.5 | 0 | 0 |
| Joy | CBET | M/S | 0.54 | 0.54 | 0.95 | 0.09 |
| Joy | CBET aug | M/S | 0.52 | 0.53 | 1 | 0.06 |
| Joy | CBET | M/S Turk | 0.56 | 0.52 | 1 | 0.05 |
| Sadness | CBET sub | CBET sub | 0.9 | 0.7 | 0.59 | 0.45 |
| Sadness | CBET | Dance | 0.7 | 0.64 | 0.6 | 0.45 |
| Sadness | CBET aug | Dance | 0.7 | 0.63 | 0.6 | 0.42 |
| Sadness | CBET | Dance Turk | 0.68 | 0.6 | 0.63 | 0.29 |
| Sadness | CBET | M/S | 0.69 | 0.59 | 0.57 | 0.03 |
| Sadness | CBET aug | M/S | 0.7 | 0.55 | 0.82 | 0.12 |
| Sadness | CBET | M/S Turk | 0.68 | 0.67 | 0.76 | 0.49 |
| Surprise | CBET sub | CBET sub | 0.92 | 0.78 | 0.66 | 0.6 |
| Surprise | CBET | Dance | 0.87 | 0.5 | 0 | 0 |
| Surprise | CBET aug | Dance | 0.87 | 0.5 | 0 | 0 |
| Surprise | CBET | Dance Turk | 0.88 | 0.5 | 0 | 0 |
| Surprise | CBET | M/S | 0.99 | 0.5 | 0 | 0 |
| Surprise | CBET aug | M/S | 0.99 | 0.5 | 0 | 0 |
| Surprise | CBET | M/S Turk | 0.9 | 0.49 | 0 | 0 |

Table A4: BERT Trained on CBET Variations

| Emotion | Test | Accuracy | Precision | Recall |
|---|---|---|---|---|
| Anger | Dance Original | 0.65 | 0.14 | 0.29 |
| Anger | Dance Turk | 0.63 | 0.14 | 0.31 |
| Anger | M/S Original | 0.7 | 0.12 | 0.34 |
| Anger | M/S Turk | 0.84 | 0.23 | 0.38 |
| Disgust | Dance Original | 0.77 | 0.43 | 0.2 |
| Disgust | Dance Turk | 0.84 | 0 | 0 |
| Disgust | M/S Original | 0.82 | 0.04 | 0.23 |
| Disgust | M/S Turk | 0.92 | 0.29 | 0.5 |
| Fear | Dance Original | 0.7 | 0.27 | 0.3 |
| Fear | Dance Turk | 0.73 | 0.35 | 0.53 |
| Fear | M/S Original | 0.84 | 0.03 | 0.25 |
| Fear | M/S Turk | 0.77 | 0.14 | 0.18 |
| Joy | Dance Original | 0.57 | 0.8 | 0.02 |
| Joy | Dance Turk | 0.45 | 0 | 0 |
| Joy | M/S Original | 0.5 | 0.67 | 0.02 |
| Joy | M/S Turk | 0.54 | 0 | 0 |
| Sadness | Dance Original | 0.61 | 0.47 | 0.77 |
| Sadness | Dance Turk | 0.53 | 0.42 | 0.79 |
| Sadness | M/S Original | 0.55 | 0.4 | 0.77 |
| Sadness | M/S Turk | 0.61 | 0.58 | 0.71 |
| Surprise | Dance Original | 0.86 | 0 | 0 |
| Surprise | Dance Turk | 0.87 | 0 | 0 |
| Surprise | M/S Original | 0.97 | 0 | 0 |
| Surprise | M/S Turk | 0.91 | 0 | 0 |

Table A5: Naive Bayes Trained on Augmented CBET

| Emotion | Test | Accuracy | Precision | Recall |
|---|---|---|---|---|
| Anger | Dance Original | 0.85 | 0.1 | 0.01 |
| Anger | Dance Turk | 0.84 | 0 | 0 |
| Anger | M/S Original | 0.86 | 0.04 | 0.02 |
| Anger | M/S Turk | 0.87 | 0 | 0 |
| Disgust | Dance Original | 0.78 | 0 | 0 |
| Disgust | Dance Turk | 0.95 | 0 | 0 |
| Disgust | M/S Original | 0.96 | 0 | 0 |
| Disgust | M/S Turk | 0.96 | 0 | 0 |
| Fear | Dance Original | 0.74 | 0.26 | 0.17 |
| Fear | Dance Turk | 0.76 | 0.27 | 0.18 |
| Fear | M/S Original | 0.93 | 0 | 0 |
| Fear | M/S Turk | 0.81 | 0.11 | 0.09 |
| Joy | Dance Original | 0.58 | 0.61 | 0.12 |
| Joy | Dance Turk | 0.48 | 0.71 | 0.1 |
| Joy | M/S Original | 0.53 | 0.73 | 0.11 |
| Joy | M/S Turk | 0.56 | 0.67 | 0.09 |
| Sadness | Dance Original | 0.6 | 0.36 | 0.18 |
| Sadness | Dance Turk | 0.65 | 0.54 | 0.21 |
| Sadness | M/S Original | 0.66 | 0.36 | 0.03 |
| Sadness | M/S Turk | 0.54 | 0.58 | 0.16 |
| Surprise | Dance Original | 0.87 | 0 | 0 |
| Surprise | Dance Turk | 0.86 | 0 | 0 |
| Surprise | M/S Original | 0.98 | 0 | 0 |
| Surprise | M/S Turk | 0.91 | 0 | 0 |

Table A6: Random Forest Trained on Transformed CBET

Naive Bayes and Random Forest models, while models for surprise were more or less equivalent

| Emotion | Train | Test | Accuracy | AUC | Prec | Rec |
|---|---|---|---|---|---|---|
| Anger | TEC | Dance | 0.85 | 0.58 | 0.39 | 0.22 |
| Anger | TEC | M/S | 0.89 | 0.55 | 0.29 | 0.15 |
| Anger | TEC | Dance Turk | 0.78 | 0.49 | 0.11 | 0.08 |
| Anger | TEC | M/S Turk | 0.92 | 0.56 | 1 | 0.13 |
| Disgust | TEC | Dance | 0.78 | 0.5 | 0 | 0 |
| Disgust | TEC | M/S | 0.97 | 0.5 | 0 | 0 |
| Disgust | TEC | Dance Turk | 0.95 | 0.5 | 0 | 0 |
| Disgust | TEC | M/S Turk | 0.96 | 0.5 | 0 | 0 |
| Fear | TEC | Dance | 0.74 | 0.58 | 0.33 | 0.32 |
| Fear | TEC | M/S | 0.9 | 0.76 | 0.1 | 0.63 |
| Fear | TEC | Dance Turk | 0.77 | 0.54 | 0.3 | 0.18 |
| Fear | TEC | M/S Turk | 0.8 | 0.61 | 0.27 | 0.36 |
| Joy | TEC | Dance | 0.67 | 0.66 | 0.65 | 0.54 |
| Joy | TEC | M/S | 0.66 | 0.66 | 0.68 | 0.62 |
| Joy | TEC | Dance Turk | 0.68 | 0.68 | 0.74 | 0.63 |
| Joy | TEC | M/S Turk | 0.66 | 0.66 | 0.62 | 0.65 |
| Sadness | TEC | Dance | 0.7 | 0.61 | 0.7 | 0.28 |
| Sadness | TEC | M/S | 0.73 | 0.6 | 0.83 | 0.23 |
| Sadness | TEC | Dance Turk | 0.75 | 0.69 | 0.76 | 0.47 |
| Sadness | TEC | M/S Turk | 0.51 | 0.49 | 0.46 | 0.13 |
| Surprise | TEC | Dance | 0.85 | 0.49 | 0 | 0 |
| Surprise | TEC | M/S | 0.97 | 0.49 | 0 | 0 |
| Surprise | TEC | Dance Turk | 0.88 | 0.5 | 0 | 0 |
| Surprise | TEC | M/S Turk | 0.9 | 0.49 | 0 | 0 |

Table A7: BERT Trained on TEC

| Emotion | Train | Test | Accuracy | AUC | Prec | Rec |
|---|---|---|---|---|---|---|
| Anger | DD | Dance | 0.76 | 0.65 | 0.28 | 0.51 |
| Anger | DD | M/S | 0.9 | 0.69 | 0.43 | 0.44 |
| Anger | DD | Dance Turk | 0.86 | 0.63 | 0.5 | 0.31 |
| Anger | DD | M/S Turk | 0.9 | 0.61 | 0.4 | 0.25 |
| Disgust | DD | Dance | 0.78 | 0.5 | 0 | 0 |
| Disgust | DD | M/S | 0.97 | 0.5 | 0 | 0 |
| Disgust | DD | Dance Turk | 0.95 | 0.5 | 0 | 0 |
| Disgust | DD | M/S Turk | 0.96 | 0.5 | 0 | 0 |
| Fear | DD | Dance | 0.8 | 0.5 | 0.5 | 0 |
| Fear | DD | M/S | 0.98 | 0.68 | 0.33 | 0.38 |
| Fear | DD | Dance Turk | 0.82 | 0.5 | 0 | 0 |
| Fear | DD | M/S Turk | 0.88 | 0.5 | 0 | 0 |
| Joy | DD | Dance | 0.61 | 0.57 | 0.72 | 0.2 |
| Joy | DD | M/S | 0.55 | 0.56 | 0.72 | 0.18 |
| Joy | DD | Dance Turk | 0.53 | 0.57 | 1 | 0.14 |
| Joy | DD | M/S Turk | 0.61 | 0.58 | 0.1 | 0.16 |
| Sadness | DD | Dance | 0.66 | 0.51 | 0.86 | 0.03 |
| Sadness | DD | M/S | 0.67 | 0.51 | 1 | 0.01 |
| Sadness | DD | Dance Turk | 0.66 | 0.53 | 1 | 0.06 |
| Sadness | DD | M/S Turk | 0.51 | 0.49 | 0 | 0 |
| Surprise | DD | Dance | 0.87 | 0.51 | 0.33 | 0.03 |
| Surprise | DD | M/S | 0.99 | 0.5 | 0 | 0 |
| Surprise | DD | Dance Turk | 0.88 | 0.5 | 0 | 0 |
| Surprise | DD | M/S Turk | 0.91 | 0.5 | 0 | 0 |

Table A8: BERT Trained on DailyDialog

to the baseline. Additionally, BERT and Random Forest models were unable to correctly identify disgust, while Naive Bayes models successfully identified multiple instances of disgust. As there was not a significant difference in balance between emotion classes within the CBET dataset, the fact that data augmentation did not significantly improve baseline precision and recall implies that class imbalance was not a main factor in discrepancies between classification accuracy of different emotions.

To compare emotion prediction accuracies across multiple text corpora, we then trained BERT models on the TEC and DailyDialog datasets, and tested them on the Edmonds Dance and Mihalcea/Strapparava datasets. The results are summarized in Tables A7 and A8. Both test accuracy for the TEC and the DailyDialog models were similar to those of the CBET models, implying that the dialog domain does not necessarily show more promise than the social media domain when considering the complex emotion classification problem in lyrics.

Finally, to compare in-domain model accuracy with our out of domain results, we trained and tested BERT models on the larger, original versions of the Edmonds Dance and Mihalcea/Strapparava datasets respectively, and vice versa. The results are summarized below in Table A9. We found that the accuracies of models trained and tested on the Edmonds Dance and Mihalcea/Strapparava datasets were on par with those of the out of domain models despite the much smaller training size and genre differences across the lyrical datasets, implying a significant advantage in using in-domain data to train models for complex emotion classification of songs.

It is important to note that precision and recall values for disgust, fear, and surprise remained very low, which could imply that certain emotions are generally more difficult than others to classify. This conclusion is supported by our Turker error analysis in Section 3.1.3, in which we found that emotions such as anticipation, disgust, fear and surprise had relatively lower inter-annotator agreement, while other emotions such as joy and sadness had relatively high agreement.

### A.6 Miscellaneous: Emotion Magnitudes by Line

Mihalcea and Strapparava included a table in their paper with the number of lines that each of their 6 core emotions was present in, as well as the average magnitude for each emotion across all annotated lines. We used this information to calculate the average magnitude for each emotion across lines in which they were present, shown in Table A10.

As emotions were annotated on a scale from 0

| Emotion | Train | Test | Accuracy | AUC | Prec | Rec |
|---|---|---|---|---|---|---|
| Anger | M/S | Dance | 0.86 | 0.51 | 0.5 | 0.01 |
| Anger | Dance | M/S | 0.89 | 0.58 | 0.31 | 0.2 |
| Disgust | M/S | Dance | 0.78 | 0.5 | 0 | 0 |
| Disgust | Dance | M/S | 0.97 | 0.5 | 0 | 0 |
| Fear | M/S | Dance | 0.8 | 0.5 | 0 | 0 |
| Fear | Dance | M/S | 0.98 | 0.5 | 0 | 0 |
| Joy | M/S | Dance | 0.7 | 0.69 | 0.67 | 0.62 |
| Joy | Dance | M/S | 0.7 | 0.7 | 0.74 | 0.62 |
| Sadness | M/S | Dance | 0.72 | 0.66 | 0.64 | 0.46 |
| Sadness | Dance | M/S | 0.73 | 0.65 | 0.66 | 0.4 |
| Surprise | M/S | Dance | 0.87 | 0.5 | 0 | 0 |
| Surprise | Dance | M/S | 0.99 | 0.5 | 0 | 0 |

Table A9: BERT Trained and Tested on Lyrical Datasets

| Emotion | Average Magnitude |
|---|---|
| Anger | 1.88 |
| Disgust | 1.44 |
| Fear | 1.41 |
| Joy | 4.14 |
| Sadness | 2.94 |
| Surprise | 1.39 |

Table A10: Average Emotion Magnitude per Line in Mihalcea/Strapparava Dataset

to 10, we found it worthwhile to note that annotations for the presence of negative emotions such as anger, disgust, and fear were more likely to be mild than strong. We also found it interesting that only joy had an average magnitude greater than 3, which represented the cutoff for the presence of an emotion (Mihalcea and Strapparava, 2012).

# ONE: Toward ONE model, ONE algorithm, ONE corpus dedicated to sentiment analysis of Arabic/Arabizi and its dialects

**Imane Guellil[1,2,3], Faical Azouaou[3], Fodil Benali[4],Ala-Eddine Hachani[5]**

1 SEA Research group, Aston university / Birmingham, UK
2 Microports.net Ltd / Birmingham, UK
3 Laboratoire des Méthodes de Conception des Systèmes (LMCS),
Ecole nationale Supérieure d'Informatique,BP 68M, 16309, Oued-Smar, Alger, Algérie
4 Capgemini / Paris, France
5 Legal doctrine / Algiers, Algeria
i.guellil@aston.ac.uk

## Abstract

Arabic is the official language of 22 countries, spoken by more than 400 million speakers. Each one of this country uses at least on dialect for daily life conversation. Then, Arabic has at least 22 dialects. Each dialect can be written in Arabic or Arabizi Scripts. The most recent researches focus on constructing a language model and a training corpus for each dialect, in each script. Following this technique means constructing 46 different resources (by including the Modern Standard Arabic, MSA) for handling only one language. In this paper, we extract ONE corpus, and we propose ONE algorithm to automatically construct ONE training corpus using ONE classification model architecture for sentiment analysis MSA and different dialects. After manually reviewing the training corpus, the obtained results outperform all the research literature results for the targeted test corpora.

## 1 Introduction

All the survey works in the literature (Habash, 2010; Farghaly and Shaalan, 2009; Harrat et al., 2017) classify Arabic in three main varieties: 1) Classical Arabic (CA), 2) Modern Standard Arabic (MSA) and 3) Dialectal Arabic (Boudad et al., 2017). Arabic Dialects are another form of Arabic used in daily life communication. Each dialect shares many features with MSA, but they globally differ in some aspects. Arabic and its dialects can be written either in Arabic Script or in Arabizi one. Arabizi is a form of writing Arabic text that relies on Latin letters, numerals and punctuation rather than Arabic letters (Guellil et al., 2019a,b). For example, the Arabic sentence: راني فرحانة, meaning "I am happy," is written in Arabizi as "rani fer7ana". Arabizi is generally used by Arab speakers in social media or chat and SMS applications. Almost all the work on Arabic sentiment analysis focus on constructing new resources (new lexicons(Abdul-Mageed and Diab, 2012; Mataoui et al., 2016; Mohammad et al., 2016a; Gilbert et al., 2018), new training corpora(Aly and Atiya, 2013; ElSahar and El-Beltagy, 2015; Mourad and Darwish, 2013; Rahab et al., 2019; Alahmary et al., 2019; Al-Twairesh et al., 2017), new language models(Baly et al., 2020)) for each dialect. More recently, particular attention has been given to Arabizi as well(Baert et al., 2020). However, constructing a unique resource for each dialect is time and effort consuming. Moreover, this resource will be exploitable only for the targeted dialect.

This paper proposes a general algorithm constructing a language model from a large corpus and a training corpus automatically to bridge the gap. It also proposes the transliteration of the Arabizi messages into Arabic. This approach was applied to Algerian dialect (a Maghrebi dialect), having a lack of resources. However, the constructed model was used for classifying the sentiment of messages written in MSA, Tunisian dialect or even Egyptian dialect. The results were very encouraging. However, the manual review of a small part of the training corpus constructed automatically leads to outperform all the research literature results for the testing corpora cited above.



*Proceedings of the 11th Workshop on Computational Approaches to Subjectivity, Sentiment and Social Media Analysis*, pages 236–249
April 19, 2021. ©2021 Association for Computational Linguistics

## 2 The research works inspiring the proposed work

The aim of the proposed model is to analyse the sentiment of Arabic message (written with both Arabic/Arabizi scripts). In this context, we need to focus on three categories of works: 1) Works on Arabizi transliteration. 2) Works on lexicon-based approach. 3) Works on corpus-based approach. In the following sections, we present the set of strengths/weaknesses of the research works inspiring our proposed approach.

### 2.1 The research works inspiring our transliteration approach

The transliteration approach is firstly inspired by the work presented by van et al. (van der Wees et al., 2016), where the authors used a table extracted from Wikipedia[1] for the passage from Arabizi to Arabic. We also present a passage table from Arabizi to Arabic. However, we also use a set of passage rules for handling the position of letters and some missed cases in the literature studied approaches. The proposed approach is also inspired by the works presented in (Al-Badrashiny et al., 2014; Darwish, 2013; May et al., 2014; van der Wees et al., 2016). All these authors generate a set of possible candidates for the transliteration of an Arabizi word into Arabic. The major issue of these approaches is the omission of some candidates because the vowels are not properly handled. Finally, This work is also inspired by the proposed approach in (Darwish, 2014; van der Wees et al., 2016) using a language model to determine the best possible candidate for a word in Arabizi. On the other hand, these works assimilate the task of transliteration to a translation task. The major drawback of these approaches is that they depend on a parallel corpus. The used corpus is usually constructed manually.

### 2.2 The research works inspiring our lexicon-based approach

The proposed sentiment lexicon construction approach is firstly inspired by the group of approaches using the automatic translation of an existing English lexicon (Mohammad et al., 2016a; Salameh et al., 2015; Mohammad et al., 2016b; Abdul-Mageed and Diab, 2012; Abdulla et al., 2014). The majority of these approaches are based on Google translate. However, Google translate deals with MSA only (i.e. Google translate is not adequate for translating dialects). Moreover, the Arabic/English dictionaries are covering MSA and some dialects such as Egyptian and Levantine. Limited resources are dedicated to Maghrebi dialects such as Tunisian, Moroccan or Algerian dialects. Hence, we opt to use Glosbe API [2], which is an online API offering the translation from/to MSA and almost all dialects. This API is open-source (i.e. no fees are required for using it). The proposed approach is also inspired by the work using a semi-automatic construction (El-Beltagy, 2016) where the authors manually review the constructed lexicon.

For handling morphological aspects of Arabic dialects, some works relying on stemming tools, dedicated to MSA. For example, the work of Mataoui et al. (Mataoui et al., 2016) used the Khoja stemmer (Khoja and Garside, 1999) for stemming the DALG, which is designed for MSA. In our work, we treat agglutination by employing an algorithm that supports the originality of the studied dialect (DALG), principally related to its prefixes, suffixes, and negative pronouns. The work of Al-Twairesh et al. (Al-Twairesh et al., 2017) also inspires the proposed approach. This work is relying on sentiments words for automatically annotating large corpus in Saudi dialects. However, in contrast to this work, our approach is not only concentrating on sentiment words, but it is also based on a sentiment algorithm for handling opposition, Arabic morphology and negation.

### 2.3 The research works inspiring our corpus-based approach

The works that firstly inspire our proposed (Pak and Paroubek, 2010; Hogenboom et al., 2013; Yadav and Pandya, 2017) are not dedicated to Arabic but other languages (English and Dutch) The main idea of these works is to use emoticons for automatically tag a large corpus. Hence, the proposed contribution also exploits the presence of emoticons to determine the sentiment of messages. However, it can be

[1] https://en.wikipedia.org/wiki/Arabic_chat_alphabet

[2] https://en.glosbe.com/

seen that all emoticons are not appropriate for determining sentiment. Hence, our proposed approach also considers emoticons for annotation but not all emoticons, only the emoticons with the strongest sentiment (either positive or negative). Our approach of constructing corpus is also inspired by the work of Gamal et al. (Gamal et al., 2019) that they relied on a sentiment lexicon to automatically annotate a sentiment corpus. However, their algorithm relies only on the positive and negative words count. For these authors, if the number of positives words is higher than or equal twice the number of negatives words than the message is considered as positive, and the same philosophy is applied for the negative messages. In contrast to these authors, we developed more sophisticated algorithms handling Arabic agglutination, opposition and negation. We also consider a set of heuristics, including the number of words.

Our contribution is also inspired by the work of Medhaffar et al. (Medhaffar et al., 2017), which is the unique work, to the best of our knowledge, focusing on Arabic and Arabizi at the same time. However, in contrast to this work, we used a more voluminous corpus (which was constructed automatically), and we propose a transliteration step. Finally, our contribution is also inspired by the approach proposed by Duwairi et al. (Duwairi et al., 2016). Hence, we firstly define and apply a transliteration step. However, in contrast to this work, our contribution is dealing with ambiguities treatment (especially vowels ambiguities), and our corpus sentiment is constructed automatically, so it is more voluminous than the corpora which the authors constructed manually.

## 3 Methodology

### 3.1 The proposed algorithm

The general algorithm proposed and developed in the context of this work is presented in Algorithm 1.

It can be seen from Algorithm 1 that the proposed steps are executed in the following order :

1. The first step is to manually construct some resources including the list of the identifiers of some famous Algerian pages, the list of positive/negative emoticons and expressions, the list of prefixes/suffixes and finally the list of negation/ opposition terms. This step is illustrated by the function MANUALRESCONSTRUCTION().

2. The second step is to automatically extract comments from Facebook pages (using the collected identifiers). This step is illustrated by the function COMMENTSEXTRACTION($Facebook_{key}$).

3. The third step is to automatically construct the Algerian sentiment lexicon by relying on an existing English sentiment lexicon. This step is illustrated by the function AUTOMATICARLEXCONSTRUCT($Eng_{lex}$).

4. The fourth step is to review the constructed lexicon manually. This step is illustrated by the function MANUALLEXREVIEW($Alg_{lexV1}$).

5. The fifth step is to automatically annotate each message from the corpus (extracted from Facebook). This step is illustrated by the function ANNOTATE($Alg_{lexV2}, m, L_{emp}, L_{emn}, L_{exp}, L_{exn}, L_{pr}, L_{sf}, L_{neg}, L_{op}, pos, neg$).

6. The sixth step is to transliterate each message in the used Arabizi corpus. This step is illustrated by the function ARABIZITRANSLITERATE(CORPUS). For transliteration we rely on the same algorithm proposed and used by Guellil et al. (Guellil et al., 2018c, 2020a, 2018a)

7. The last step is to classify the sentiment (written with Arabic script) in both corpora (the initially Arabic one and the transliterated one). This step is illustrated by the function SENTIMENTCLASS($corpus, Senti_{A}lg$).

### 3.2 The used models for classification

For classification, we use two kinds of algorithms, shallow and deep. For both classifications, we extract features with word embedding techniques. With shallow classification,

**Algorithm 1** Sentiment analysis of Arabic/ Arabizi messages

**Input:**
$Eng_{lex}$ : English lexicon,
$ArTest_{corp}[]$ : List of Arabic sentiment corpora,
$ArabiziTest_{corp}[]$ : List of Arabizi sentiment corpora,
$ArabiziTrTest_{corp}[]$ : List of Arabizi transliterated sentiment corpora,
$Facebook_{Key}$: A key for accessing RestFB API

**Output:**
$Alg_{lexV1}$ : Algerian Lexicon V1,
$Alg_{lexV2}$ : Algerian lexicon V2,
$Ar_{corp1}$ ,$Ar_{corp2}$ : Large Arabic corpora,
$Senti_{Alg}$ : Automatic annotated Algerian (Arabic) corpus
$L_f$: List identifiant of Facebook pages,
$L_{emp}$: List of positive emoticons,
$L_{emn}$: List of negative emoticons,
$L_{exp}$: List of positive expressions,
$L_{exn}$: List of negative expressions,
$L_{pr}$: List of prefixes, $L_{sf}$: List of suffixes,
$L_{neg}$: List of negation terms,
$L_{op}$: List of opposition terms[3]

$Senti_{Alg} \leftarrow \emptyset$
$L_f, L_{emp}, L_{emn}, L_{exp}, L_{exn}, L_{pr}, L_{sf}, L_{neg}, L_{op} \leftarrow$ MANUALRESCONSTRUCTION()
$Ar_{corp1}, Ar_{corp2} \leftarrow$ COMMENTSEXTRACTION($Facebook_{key}$)
$Alg_{lexV1} \leftarrow$ AUTOMATICARLEXCONSTRUCT($Eng_{lex}$)
$Alg_{lexV2} \leftarrow$ MANUALLEXREVIEW($Alg_{lexV1}$)
**for each** $m \in Ar_{corp2}$ **do**
  polarity$\leftarrow$ ANNOTATE($Alg_{lexV2}, m, L_{emp}, L_{emn}, L_{exp}, L_{exn}, L_{pr}, L_{sf}, L_{neg}, L_{op}$)
  add $m, polarity$ in $Senti_{Alg}$
**end for**
**for each** $corpus \in ArTest_{corp}$ **do**
  SENTIMENTCLASS($corpus, Senti_{Alg}$)
**end for**
**for each** $corpus \in ArabiziTest_{corp}$ **do**
  $Corpus_{tr} \leftarrow$ ARABIZITRANSLITERATE($corpus, Ar_{corp1}$)
  ADD($ArabiziTrTest_{corp}, Corpus_{tr}$)
  SENTIMENTCLASSIFICATION($Corpus_{tr}, Senti_{Alg}$)
**end for**

we use Word2vec algorithm. While we use fastText for deep classification. For Word2vec, we used a context of 10 words to produce representations for both CBOW and SG of length 300. For classification we use five Algorithms such as: GaussianNB (GNB), LogisticRegression (LR), RandomForset (RF), SGDClassifier (SGD, with loss='log' and penalty='l1') and LinearSVC (LSVC with C='1e1'). For deep learning classification, we first used the model presented by Attia et al. (Attia et al., 2018) with five layers using 300 filters and a width equal to 7. To enrich this model, our approach also uses the CBOW and SG of FastText for calculating the weights of embedding_matrix. Also, our approach used other deep learning algorithms, such as LSTM and Bi-LSTM. Table 1 gives more details about the configuration and architecture of the layers of our models on the training corpus. For all the models, we use an epoch equal to 100 with an early_stopping parameter. This parameter is used for stopping the iteration in the absence of improvements (for handling overfitting). This parameter allows stopping the models after 20 epochs (on average). Adam optimiser is used in all the deep learning experiments.

## 4 Evaluation and Discussion

### 4.1 Dataset

For the experiments part, the following dataset were used:

1) A large corpus (Ar_corpus2), extracted in November 2017, and containing 15,407,910 messages with 7,926,504 written in Arabic letters.

2) ALG_Senti(Guellil et al., 2018b, 2020a) is an annotated sentiment corpus which was automatically constructed based on ALGLex_V2(Guellil et al., 2020b) and on the sentiment algorithm that we proposed and implemented. The annotation process also considers other features such as the sentiment score of the message and the number of positives/negatives words recognised in the lexicon. The final corpus contains 127,004 positive messages and 127,004 negative ones.

3) TSAC[4] (Medhaffar et al., 2017) is a Tunisian sentiment corpus. This corpus is the unique corpus in the research literature, to the best of our knowledge, containing both Arabic and Arabizi. For testing our approach on other corpus presented in the research literature, we propose to transliterate the Arabizi part of TSAC into Arabic, using our transliteration approach.

4) SANA_Alg[5] (Rahab et al., 2019) is an Algerian annotated sentiment corpus. This corpus includes 513 messages that were manually annotated.

5) ASTD/QCRI/ARTwitter[6] (Altowayan and Tao, 2016) is an Arabic corpus including 1,589 tweets from astd(Nabil et al., 2015), 1, 951 tweets from ArTwitter (Abdulla et al., 2013) and 754 from QCRI(Mourad and Darwish, 2013)

[4]https://github.com/fbougares/TSAC

[5]http://rahab.e-monsite.com/medias/files/corpus.rar

[6]https://github.com/iamaziz/ar-embeddings/tree/master/datasets

### 4.2 Experimental results

The aim of this work is to classify an Arabic message into positive/negative automatically. More particularly to use a language model and the resources constructed for one dialect for classifying the sentiments of an another dialect (and MSA). Hence, for validating our approach , we applied it on four corpora annotated manually by natives speakers. Two of these corpora are in Algerian dialect (Senti_Alg(Guellil et al., 2018b,a) and Sana_Alg(Rahab et al., 2019)), one of them is in MSA (ASTD_QCRI_ArTwitter)(Altowayan and Tao, 2016) and the last one in Tunisian dialect (TSAC)(Medhaffar et al., 2017). Two of these corpora include both Arabic and Arabizi (Senti_Alg and TSAC) and the others are dedicated to Arabic script. Our purpose behind the different experiments is not only to validate our approach but to also highlight its adaptability to MSA and other dialects written with both scripts Arabic and Arabizi. For doing so, we apply the following steps:

1. For Senti_Alg, we focus on both sides, Arabic and Arabizi. For Arabizi part, we investigate the results using both automatic and manual transliteration.
2. As Sana_Alg and ASTD_QCRI_ARTwitter use only Arabic script, no need for the transliteration process.
3. As TSAC_Test represents a combination between Arabic and Arabizi messages, for each experiment on TSAC, we use both, the initial test (Initial_test) corpus and the test corpus obtained after applying the proposed translietration system (Transliterated_test).

The different experiments and the obtained results are presented in the following sections.

#### 4.2.1 Results on Algerian dialect

**Results on the Arabic side of Senti_Alg (Senti_Alg_test_Arabic)** The experiments done on `Senti_Alg_test_Arabic` show that the best results are obtained using CBOW of Word2vec model combined with GNB classifier (F1= 87.77). For deep learning classification, the combination of FastText, CBOW and MLP gives the best results (F1-score=

| Model | Layers | output shape | params |
|---|---|---|---|
| CNN | embedding_1(default/CBOW/SG) | (None,12,300) | 41789100 |
| | conv1d_d | (None,12,300) | 630300 |
| | global_max_pooling1d_1 | (None,300) | 0 |
| | dropout_1 | (None,300) | 0 |
| | dense_1 | (None,600) | 180600 |
| | dense_2 | (None,2) | 1202 |
| MLP | embedding_1(default/CBOW/SG) | (None,12,300) | 41789100 |
| | dense_1 | (None,12,64) | 19264 |
| | global_max_pooling1d_1 | (None,64) | 0 |
| | dropout_1 | (None,64) | 0 |
| | dense_3 | (None,600) | 39000 |
| | dense_4 | (None,2) | 1202 |
| LSTM | embedding_1(default/CBOW/SG) | (None,12,300) | 41789100 |
| | lstm_1 | (None,12,64) | 93440 |
| | global_max_pooling1d_1 | (None,64) | 0 |
| | dropout_1 | (None,64) | 0 |
| | dense_1 | (None,600) | 39000 |
| | dense_2 | (None,2) | 1202 |
| Bi-LSTM | embedding_1(default/CBOW/SG) | (None,12,300) | 41789100 |
| | bidirectional_1 | (None,12,128) | 186880 |
| | global_max_pooling1d_1 | (None,6128) | 0 |
| | dropout_1 | (None,128) | 0 |
| | dense_1 | (None,600) | 77400 |
| | dense_2 | (None,2) | 1202 |

Table 1: Deep learning models architecture

80.99). However, the results obtained using Word2vec model combined with shallow classifiers outperform those obtained using FastText model combined with deep learning classifiers. It can also be seen from this Table that CBOW model results generally outperform the results returned by using the SG model. More details are presented (in the Appendices, section 7) in the Table 1)

**Results on the Arabizi side of Senti_Alg (Senti_Alg_test_Arabizi)** obtained on the Arabizi side of Senti_Alg, that we named `Senti_Alg_test_Arabizi`. However, as our language model and training corpus is in Arabic script, the corpus `Senti_Alg_test_Arabizi` was firstly transliterated. For showing the efficiency of our transliteration system, we transliterate this corpus in both ways, automatically (for obtaining `Senti_Alg_test_trauto`) and manually (for obtaining `Senti_Alg_test_trmanu`). The best results for the corpus `Senti_Alg_test_trauto` were obtained using SG of Word2vec combined with SGD classifier (F1= 75.23). For deep learning classification, the combination of FastText, CBOW and CNN gives the best results for the corpus `Senti_Alg_test_trauto` (F1-score= 69.78). However, the results obtained using Word2vec model combined with shallow classifiers outperform those obtained using fastText model combined with deep learning classifiers. The results obtained by using the corpus transliterated manually (`Senti_Alg_test_trmanu`) are better than those obtained on the corpus transliterated automatically ((`Senti_Alg_test_trauto`). However, the improvement between both transliterations is non-consequential (0.9, less than 1 point For F1-score). This small improvement rate highlights the quality of the proposed transliteration system. More details are presented (in the Appendices, section 7) in the Table 2)

**Results on SANA_Alg** The experiments done on `SANA_Alg` show that the best results were obtained using CBOW of word2vec combined with GNB classifier (F1= 81.00). For

| Test_corpora | Metrics | Best_results | Embedding | Models | Classifier |
|---|---|---|---|---|---|
| Senti_Alg_test_Arabic | P | 93.50 | Word2vec | CBOW | GNB |
| | R | 90.40 | Word2vec | CBOW | SGD |
| | F1 | 87.77 | Word2vec | CBOW | SGD |
| Senti_Alg_test_trauto | P | 82.18 | Word2vec | CBOW | GNB |
| | R | 82.00 | Word2vec | SG | SGD |
| | F1 | 75.23 | Word2vec | SG | SGD |
| Senti_Alg_test_trmanu | P | 85.47 | Word2vec | CBOW | GNB |
| | R | 77.20 | Word2vec | SG | SGD |
| | F1 | 76.13 | Word2vec | SG | SGD |
| SANA_Alg | P | 82.74 | Word2vec | SG | SGD |
| | R | 96.67 | Word2vec | SG | GNB |
| | F1 | 81.00 | Word2vec | CBOW | GNB |
| TSAC_Test | P | 88.97 | Word2vec | CBOW | SGD |
| | R | 95.82 | Word2vec | SG | SGD |
| | F1 | 77.29 | Word2vec | SG | LSVC |
| TSAC_Test_Tr | P | 91.66 | FastText | CBOW | Bi-LSTM |
| | R | 91.65 | Word2vec | SG | SGD |
| | F1 | 91.59 | FastText | SG | MLP |
| ASTD/QCRI/ARTwitter | P | 77.65 | Word2vec | CBOW | SGD |
| | R | 85.61 | Word2vec | CBOW | GNB |
| | F1 | 80.58 | Word2vec | CBOW | GNB |

Table 2: Synthesis of the best obtained results

deep learning classification, the combination of FastText, CBOW and LSTM gives the best results (F1-score= 63.29). However, the results obtained using Word2vec model combined with shallow classifiers outperform those obtained using FastText model combined with deep learning classifiers. The CBOW model results generally outperform the results returned by using the SG model. More details are presented (in the Appendices, section 7) in the Table 3).

#### 4.2.2 Results on Tunisian dialect

For the experiments, we use both versions of the Tunisian corpus. We denote the version in its current state (before transliteration) as TSAC_test. We denote the version after proceeding to the transliteration as TSAC_Test_Tr. To compare the sentiment analysis results obtained before and after transliteration step, we divide Table 4 into two parts: the first one illustrates the sentiment classification results obtained on TSAC_test and the second one, the results obtained on TSAC_Test_Tr. For the experiments done on both corpora, it can be seen that the best results were obtained using SG of Word2vec combined with SGD classifier (F1= 73.69). For deep learning classification, the combination of FastText, CBOW/SG and CNN gives the best results for the corpus TSAC_Test (F1-score= 52.88). For the corpus TSAC_Test_Tr, the best results were obtained using SG of Word2vec combined with SGD classifier (F1= 75.24). For deep learning classification, the combination of FastText, CBOW and CNN gives the best results for the corpus TSAC_Test_Tr (F1-score= 62.98). More details are presented (in the Appendices, section 7) in the Table 4)

#### 4.2.3 Results on MSA

**Experiments using ASTD/QCRI/ARTwitter** The experiments done on `ASTD/QCRI/ARTwitter` show that the best results obtained using CBOW of word2vec combined with GNB classifier (F1= 80.58). For deep learning classification, the combination of FastText, CBOW and CNN gives the best results (F1-score= 64.03). However, the results obtained using Word2vec model combined with shallow classifiers outperform those obtained using FastText model combined with deep learning classifiers. More details are presented (in the Appendices, Section 7) in the Table 6)

## 5 Synthesis and corpus validation

### 5.1 Synthesis

The best results obtained from the different experiments and that we discussed in Section 4.2 are summarised in Table 2.

For Algerian dialect, the corpora that we used (i.e. `Senti_Alg_test_Arabic`, `Senti_Alg_test_trauto` and `Senti_Alg_test_trmanu`) were presented and used in many research papers (Guellil et al., 2017, 2018b,a; Imane et al., 2019). We based on the issues of each presented research work to improve the results presented in this paper (where the best F1= 87.77% for the Arabic side and F=76.13% for the Arabizi side, after transliteration). The best results obtained on SANA_Alg are up to 81.00% (for F1-score). This result outperforms the results presented in the research literature, where the F1-score presented by Rahab et al. .(Rahab et al., 2019) was up to 75%. Hence, our approach and corpus lead to an improvement of 6% on this corpus.

For Tunisian dialect, it can be seen that the results obtained by using the corpus transliterated `(TSAC_Test_Tr)` are relatively better than those obtained on the initial corpus `(TSAC_Test)` (without transliteration). Medhaffar et al. (Medhaffar et al., 2017) obtained an F1-score up to 78% for TSAC_Test corpus. Our best results by using our approach on the corpus (Senti_Alg) is up to 75.24% (F1-score). The results are then comparable to the results obtained by the authors (even with a corpus constructed automatically and dedicated to Algerian dialect). However, our transliteration system drastically improves the results. The results are up to 91.59% after transliterating both the training and the testing corpus (by using TSAC_train for the training). Hence an improvement of 14% was observed on this corpus. Another interesting observation is that, except for the training corpus, all the approach and corpora used for TSAC corpus are the same that we used for our other experiments. The vast corpus used for training Word2vec and fastText dedicated to Algerian dialect. The language model used for extracting the best candidate transliteration was also dedicated to Algerian dialect. Finally, concerning MSA, we opt for using the corpus ASTD/QCRI/ArTwitter (Altowayan and Tao, 2016). The best results obtained by Altowayen et al. (Altowayan and Tao, 2016) are up to 79.62% (for F1-score). It can be seen from Table 6 that the best results that we obtained are up to 80.58% (for F1-score). Moreover, This corpus is dedicated to MSA with a focus on Egyptian dialect (for ASTD). Hence, our approach and corpus, which are dedicated to Algerian dialect, outperforms the results presented for corpora dedicated to MSA and Egyptian dialect.

### 5.2 Manual corpus validation

To validate the constructed corpus automatically, we focus on a sample containing 3,048 messages (1,488 positives and 1,560 negatives). Afterwards, we manually review this sample. The messages that are correctly annotated were kept, and the messages which were wrongly annotated were corrected. Our first observation is that, among the 3,048 messages that are manually reviewed, 85.17% (2,596 messages) were correctly annotated. To the best of our knowledge, this corpus is the first manually checked annotated sentiment corpus that handles DALG as well as MSA. For showing the efficiency of the manually reviewed corpus, we present Table 3. Almost all the results were improved with the corpus, which was reviewed manually. The best F1 on Senti_Alg_test_Arabic is now up to 90.16 (it was up to 87.77 with Senti_Alg_auto). The best F1 on Senti_Alg_test_trauto is now up to 80.95 (it was up to 75.23 with Senti_Alg_auto). The best F1 on Senti_Alg_test_trmanu is now up to 83.10 (it was up to 76.13 with Senti_Alg_auto). The best F1 on ASTD/QCRI/ARTwitter is now up to 81.75 (it was up to 80.58 with Senti_Alg_auto). The decrease for SANA_Alg is insignificant, where the best F1 was up to 81.00, and now it is up to 80.97.

Concerning the experiments on Tunisian corpus (TSAC), It can be seen from Table 3 the reviewed corpus outperforms the results obtained by the Algerian corpus constructed automatically. For the corpus constructed auto-

| Test_corpora | Metrics | Best_results | Embedding | Models | Classifier |
|---|---|---|---|---|---|
| Senti_Alg_test_Arabic | P | 95.43 | Word2vec | SG | LR |
| | R | 91.60 | Word2vec | SG | SGD |
| | F1 | 90.16 | Word2vec | SG | SGD |
| Senti_Alg_test_trauto | P | 88.21 | Word2vec | SG | LR |
| | R | 78.40 | fastText | CBOW | Bi-LSTM |
| | F1 | 80.95 | Word2vec | SG | LR |
| Senti_Alg_test_trmanu | P | 90.73 | Word2vec | SG | LR |
| | R | 82.00 | Word2vec | SG | SVC |
| | F1 | 83.10 | Word2vec | SG | SGD |
| SANA_Alg | P | 91.36 | Word2vec | CBOW | SGD |
| | R | 93.75 | Word2vec | SG | GNB |
| | F1 | 80.97 | Word2vec | SG | LR |
| TSAC_Test | P | 88.94 | Word2vec | CBOW | SGD |
| | R | 92.82 | Word2vec | SG | SGD |
| | F1 | 75.61 | Word2vec | SG | SGD |
| TSAC_Test_Tr | P | 87.14 | Word2vec | SG | LR |
| | R | 87.41 | Word2vec | CBOW | SGD |
| | F1 | 80.69 | Word2vec | SG | SGD |
| ASTD/QCRI/ARTwitter | P | 89.29 | Word2vec | SG | SGD |
| | R | 88.36 | Word2vec | SG | GNB |
| | F1 | 81.75 | Word2vec | SG | LR |

Table 3: Synthesis of the best-obtained results on the manually reviewed corpus

matically, F1 was up to 73.69 (for TSAC_Test) and up to 75.24 (for TSAC_Test_TR). By using the manually reviewed corpus, F1 is up to 75.61 (for TSAC_Test) and up to 80.69 (for TSAC_Tr). These results outperform the results presented in the research literature ((Medhaffar et al., 2017)), where the best-presented F1 was up to 78.00. Hence, the manual reviewing of a corpus which was initially constructed automatically outperforms all the results presented in the research literature.

## 6 Conclusion

The major contribution in this paper is the new perspectives that it opens:

- Automatic training corpus construction.
- Using one language model trained for one dialect to MSA and either to other dialects.
- Moreover, using the training corpus of one dialect to others (which is a case of transfer learning).
- Stop handling Arabizi as it is. Translitertaion is crucial for improving the results.

Moreover, only simple word embedding models were used (word2vec and fastText). It was for showing the efficacy of the approach even with the fastest models. However, in the future, we are planning to improve this approach with the most recent models such as BERT(Devlin et al., 2018) or ELMO(Peters et al., 2018).

## References

Muhammad Abdul-Mageed and Mona Diab. 2012. Toward building a large-scale arabic sentiment lexicon. In *Proceedings of the 6th international global WordNet conference*, pages 18–22.

Nawaf Abdulla, Salwa Mohammed, Mahmoud Al-Ayyoub, Mohammed Al-Kabi, et al. 2014. Automatic lexicon construction for arabic sentiment analysis. In *Future Internet of Things and Cloud (FiCloud), 2014 International Conference on*, pages 547–552. IEEE.

Nawaf A Abdulla, Nizar A Ahmed, Mohammed A Shehab, and Mahmoud Al-Ayyoub. 2013. Arabic sentiment analysis: Lexicon-based and corpus-based. In *Applied Electrical Engineering and Computing Technologies (AEECT), 2013 IEEE Jordan Conference on*, pages 1–6. IEEE.

Mohamed Al-Badrashiny, Ramy Eskander, Nizar Habash, and Owen Rambow. 2014. Automatic transliteration of romanized dialectal arabic. In *Proceedings of the Eighteenth Conference on Computational Natural Language Learning*, pages 30–38.

Nora Al-Twairesh, Hend Al-Khalifa, AbdulMalik Al-Salman, and Yousef Al-Ohali. 2017. Arasenti-tweet: A corpus for arabic sentiment analysis of saudi tweets. *Procedia Computer Science*, 117:63–72.

Rahma M Alahmary, Hmood Z Al-Dossari, and Ahmed Z Emam. 2019. Sentiment analysis of saudi dialect using deep learning techniques. In *2019 International Conference on Electronics, Information, and Communication (ICEIC)*, pages 1–6. IEEE.

A Aziz Altowayan and Lixin Tao. 2016. Word embeddings for arabic sentiment analysis. In *Big Data (Big Data), 2016 IEEE International Conference on*, pages 3820–3825. IEEE.

Mohamed Aly and Amir Atiya. 2013. Labr: A large scale arabic book reviews dataset. In *Proceedings of the 51st Annual Meeting of the Association for Computational Linguistics (Volume 2: Short Papers)*, volume 2, pages 494–498.

Mohammed Attia, Younes Samih, Ali El-Kahky, and Laura Kallmeyer. 2018. Multilingual multi-class sentiment classification using convolutional neural networks. In *LREC*.

Gaétan Baert, Souhir Gahbiche, Guillaume Gadek, and Alexandre Pauchet. 2020. Arabizi language models for sentiment analysis. In *Proceedings of the 28th International Conference on Computational Linguistics*, pages 592–603.

Fady Baly, Hazem Hajj, et al. 2020. Arabert: Transformer-based model for arabic language understanding. In *Proceedings of the 4th Workshop on Open-Source Arabic Corpora and Processing Tools, with a Shared Task on Offensive Language Detection*, pages 9–15.

Naaima Boudad, Rdouan Faizi, Rachid Oulad Haj Thami, and Raddouane Chiheb. 2017. Sentiment analysis in arabic: A review of the literature. *Ain Shams Engineering Journal*.

Kareem Darwish. 2013. Arabizi detection and conversion to arabic. *arXiv preprint arXiv:1306.6755*.

Kareem Darwish. 2014. Arabizi detection and conversion to arabic. In *Proceedings of the EMNLP 2014 Workshop on Arabic Natural Language Processing (ANLP)*, pages 217–224.

Jacob Devlin, Ming-Wei Chang, Kenton Lee, and Kristina Toutanova. 2018. Bert: Pre-training of deep bidirectional transformers for language understanding. *arXiv preprint arXiv:1810.04805*.

Rehab M Duwairi, Mosab Alfaqeh, Mohammad Wardat, and Areen Alrabadi. 2016. Sentiment analysis for arabizi text. In *Information and Communication Systems (ICICS), 2016 7th International Conference on*, pages 127–132. IEEE.

Samhaa R El-Beltagy. 2016. Nileulex: A phrase and word level sentiment lexicon for egyptian and modern standard arabic. In *LREC*.

Hady ElSahar and Samhaa R El-Beltagy. 2015. Building large arabic multi-domain resources for sentiment analysis. In *International Conference on Intelligent Text Processing and Computational Linguistics*, pages 23–34. Springer.

Ali Farghaly and Khaled Shaalan. 2009. Arabic natural language processing: Challenges and solutions. *ACM Transactions on Asian Language Information Processing (TALIP)*, 8(4):14.

Donia Gamal, Marco Alfonse, El-Sayed M El-Horbaty, and Abdel-Badeeh M Salem. 2019. Twitter benchmark dataset for arabic sentiment analysis. *International Journal of Modern Education and Computer Science*, 11(1):33.

Badaroand Gilbert, Jundiand Hussein, Hajj Hazem, El-Hajj Wassim, and Habash Nizar. 2018. Arsel: A large scale arabic sentiment and emotion lexicon.

Imane Guellil, Ahsan Adeel, Faical Azouaou, Fodil Benali, Ala-eddine Hachani, and Amir Hussain. 2018a. Arabizi sentiment analysis based on transliteration and automatic corpus annotation. In *Proceedings of the 9th Workshop on Computational Approaches to Subjectivity, Sentiment and Social Media Analysis*, pages 335–341.

Imane Guellil, Ahsan Adeel, Faical Azouaou, and Amir Hussain. 2018b. Sentialg: Automated corpus annotation for algerian sentiment analysis. *arXiv preprint arXiv:1808.05079*.

Imane Guellil, Faical Azouaou, Fodil Benali, Ala Eddine Hachani, and Marcelo Mendoza. 2020a. The role of transliteration in the process of arabizi translation/sentiment analysis. In *Recent Advances in NLP: The Case of Arabic Language*, pages 101–128. Springer.

Imane Guellil, Faical Azouaou, Fodil Benali, ala-eddine Hachani, and Houda Saadane. 2018c. Approche hybride pour la translitération de l'arabizi algérien : une étude préliminaire. In *Conference: 25e conférence sur le Traitement Automatique des Langues Naturelles (TALN), May 2018, Rennes, FranceAt: Rennes, France*. `https://www.researchgate.net/publication/326354578_Approche_Hybride_pour_la_transliteration_de_l%27arabizi_algerien_une_etude_preliminaire`.

Imane Guellil, Faical Azouaou, and Francisco Chiclana. 2020b. Arautosenti: Automatic annotation and new tendencies for sentiment classification of arabic messages. *Social Network Analysis and Mining*, 10(1):1–20.

Imane Guellil, Faical Azouaou, Houda Saâdane, and Nasredine Semmar. 2017. Une approche fondée sur les lexiques d'analyse de sentiments du dialecte algérien.

Imane Guellil, Faical Azouaou, and Alessandro Valitutti. 2019a. English vs arabic sentiment analysis: A survey presenting 100 work studies, resources and tools. In *2019 IEEE/ACS 16th International Conference on Computer Systems and Applications (AICCSA)*, pages 1–8. IEEE.

Imane Guellil, Houda Saâdane, Faical Azouaou, Billel Gueni, and Damien Nouvel. 2019b. Arabic natural language processing: An overview. *Journal of King Saud University-Computer and Information Sciences*.

Nizar Y Habash. 2010. Introduction to arabic natural language processing. *Synthesis Lectures on Human Language Technologies*, 3(1):1–187.

Salima Harrat, Karima Meftouh, and Kamel Smaïli. 2017. Maghrebi arabic dialect processing: an overview. In *ICNLSSP 2017-International Conference on Natural Language, Signal and Speech Processing*.

Alexander Hogenboom, Daniella Bal, Flavius Frasincar, Malissa Bal, Franciska de Jong, and Uzay Kaymak. 2013. Exploiting emoticons in sentiment analysis. In *Proceedings of the 28th Annual ACM Symposium on Applied Computing*, pages 703–710. ACM.

Guellil Imane, Darwish Kareem, and Azouaou Faical. 2019. A set of parameters for automatically annotating a sentiment arabic corpus. *International Journal of Web Information Systems*.

Shereen Khoja and Roger Garside. 1999. Stemming arabic text. *Lancaster, UK, Computing Department, Lancaster University*.

M'hamed Mataoui, Omar Zelmati, and Madiha Boumechache. 2016. A proposed lexicon-based sentiment analysis approach for the vernacular algerian arabic. *Research in Computing Science*, 110:55–70.

Jonathan May, Yassine Benjira, and Abdessamad Echihabi. 2014. An arabizi-english social media statistical machine translation system. In *Proceedings of the 11th Conference of the Association for Machine Translation in the Americas*, pages 329–341.

Salima Medhaffar, Fethi Bougares, Yannick Esteve, and Lamia Hadrich-Belguith. 2017. Sentiment analysis of tunisian dialects: Linguistic ressources and experiments. In *Proceedings of the Third Arabic Natural Language Processing Workshop*, pages 55–61.

Saif Mohammad, Mohammad Salameh, and Svetlana Kiritchenko. 2016a. Sentiment lexicons for arabic social media. In *LREC*.

Saif M Mohammad, Mohammad Salameh, and Svetlana Kiritchenko. 2016b. How translation alters sentiment. *Journal of Artificial Intelligence Research*, 55:95–130.

Ahmed Mourad and Kareem Darwish. 2013. Subjectivity and sentiment analysis of modern standard arabic and arabic microblogs. In *Proceedings of the 4th workshop on computational approaches to subjectivity, sentiment and social media analysis*, pages 55–64.

Mahmoud Nabil, Mohamed Aly, and Amir Atiya. 2015. Astd: Arabic sentiment tweets dataset. In *Proceedings of the 2015 Conference on Empirical Methods in Natural Language Processing*, pages 2515–2519.

Alexander Pak and Patrick Paroubek. 2010. Twitter as a corpus for sentiment analysis and opinion mining.

Matthew E Peters, Mark Neumann, Mohit Iyyer, Matt Gardner, Christopher Clark, Kenton Lee, and Luke Zettlemoyer. 2018. Deep contextualized word representations. *arXiv preprint arXiv:1802.05365*.

Hichem Rahab, Abdelhafid Zitouni, and Mahieddine Djoudi. 2019. Sana: Sentiment analysis on newspapers comments in algeria. *Journal of King Saud University-Computer and Information Sciences*.

Mohammad Salameh, Saif Mohammad, and Svetlana Kiritchenko. 2015. Sentiment after translation: A case-study on arabic social media posts. In *Proceedings of the 2015 conference of the North American chapter of the association for computational linguistics: Human language technologies*, pages 767–777.

Marlies van der Wees, Arianna Bisazza, and Christof Monz. 2016. A simple but effective approach to improve arabizi-to-english statistical machine translation. In *Proceedings of the 2nd Workshop on Noisy User-generated Text (WNUT)*, pages 43–50.

Payal Yadav and Dhatri Pandya. 2017. Sentireview: Sentiment analysis based on text and emoticons. In *Innovative Mechanisms for Industry Applications (ICIMIA), 2017 International Conference on*, pages 467–472. IEEE.

## 7 Appendices

In this section, more details about the obtained results on each model, corpus are given.

| Model | Type | ML Algo | Arabic | | |
|---|---|---|---|---|---|
| | | | P | R | F1 |
| Word2vec | CBOW | GNB | **93.50** | 74.80 | 83.11 |
| | | LR | 82.09 | 88.00 | 84.94 |
| | | RF | 85.07 | 75.20 | 79.83 |
| | | SGD | 85.28 | **90.40** | **87.77** |
| | | LSVC | 82.71 | 88.00 | 85.27 |
| | SG | GNB | 90.34 | 74.80 | 81.84 |
| | | LR | 85.10 | 86.80 | 85.94 |
| | | RF | 85.59 | 76.00 | 80.51 |
| | | SGD | 84.62 | 88.00 | 86.27 |
| | | LSVC | 85.32 | 86.00 | 85.66 |
| FastText | CBOW | CNN | 80.03 | 80.00 | 79.99 |
| | | MLP | 81.04 | 81.00 | 80.99 |
| | | LSTM | 79.65 | 79.60 | 79.59 |
| | | Bi-LSTM | 79.92 | 79.60 | 79.54 |
| | SG | CNN | 78.44 | 78.20 | 78.15 |
| | | MLP | 79.63 | 79.60 | 79.59 |
| | | LSTM | 79.04 | 79.00 | 78.99 |
| | | Bi-LSTM | 76.84 | 76.80 | 76.79 |

Figure 1: Results on the Arabic side of Senti_Alg (Senti_Alg_test_Arabic)

| Model | Type | ML Algo | Senti_Alg_test_trauto | | | Senti_Alg_test_trmanu | | |
|---|---|---|---|---|---|---|---|---|
| | | | P | R | F1 | P | R | F1 |
| Word2vec | CBOW | GNB | **82.18** | 57.20 | 67.45 | **85.47** | 58.80 | 69.67 |
| | | LR | 69.81 | 74.00 | 71.84 | 75.00 | 76.80 | 75.89 |
| | | RF | 73.06 | 64.00 | 68.23 | 72.20 | 64.40 | 68.08 |
| | | SGD | 69.10 | 79.60 | 73.98 | 73.71 | 74.00 | 73.85 |
| | | LSVC | 70.04 | 72.00 | 71.01 | 75.70 | 76.00 | 75.85 |
| | SG | GNB | 79.50 | 63.60 | 70.67 | 85.41 | 63.20 | 72.64 |
| | | LR | 68.40 | 73.60 | 70.91 | 73.08 | 76.00 | 74.51 |
| | | RF | 72.29 | 66.80 | 69.44 | 76.47 | 67.60 | 71.76 |
| | | SGD | 69.49 | **82.00** | **75.23** | 75.10 | **77.20** | **76.13** |
| | | LSVC | 69.08 | 72.40 | 70.70 | 72.76 | 74.80 | 73.77 |
| FastText | CBOW | CNN | 69.85 | 69.80 | 69.78 | 73.65 | 73.60 | 73.58 |
| | | MLP | 67.64 | 67.60 | 67.58 | 71.81 | 71.80 | 71.80 |
| | | LSTM | 68.69 | 68.60 | 68.56 | 70.01 | 70.00 | 70.00 |
| | | Bi-LSTM | 68.95 | 68.80 | 68.74 | 71.93 | 71.40 | 71.22 |
| | SG | CNN | 68.52 | 68.20 | 68.06 | 73.29 | 72.60 | 72.40 |
| | | MLP | 68.25 | 68.20 | 68.18 | 71.37 | 71.20 | 71.14 |
| | | LSTM | 69.42 | 69.40 | 69.39 | 72.60 | 72.60 | 72.60 |
| | | Bi-LSTM | 68.84 | 68.80 | 68.78 | 70.60 | 70.60 | 70.60 |

Figure 2: Results on the Arabizi side of Senti_Alg (Senti_Alg_test_Arabizi) after transliteration

| Model | Type | ML Algo | SANA_Alg | | |
|---|---|---|---|---|---|
| | | | P | R | F1 |
| Word2vec | CBOW | GNB | 81.17 | 80.83 | **81.00** |
| | | LR | 76.23 | 70.83 | 73.43 |
| | | RF | 71.54 | 77.50 | 74.40 |
| | | SGD | 80.28 | 72.92 | 76.42 |
| | | LSVC | 74.44 | 69.17 | 71.71 |
| | SG | GNB | 62.37 | **96.67** | 75.82 |
| | | LR | 79.09 | 72.50 | 75.65 |
| | | RF | 72.05 | 76.25 | 74.09 |
| | | SGD | **82.74** | 67.92 | 74.60 |
| | | LSVC | 78.80 | 71.25 | 74.84 |
| FastText | CBOW | CNN | 62.26 | 62.30 | 62.28 |
| | | MLP | 59.65 | 60.00 | 59.64 |
| | | LSTM | 63.42 | 63.22 | 63.29 |
| | | Bi-LSTM | 62.08 | 62.07 | 60.29 |
| | SG | CNN | 60.76 | 61.15 | 60.22 |
| | | MLP | 57.57 | 57.93 | 57.62 |
| | | LSTM | 60.37 | 60.23 | 60.29 |
| | | Bi-LSTM | 59.28 | 59.77 | 58.87 |

Figure 3: Results on SANA_Alg

| Model | Type | ML Algo | TSAC_Test | | | TSAC_Test_Tr | | |
|---|---|---|---|---|---|---|---|---|
| | | | P | R | F1 | P | R | F1 |
| Word2vec | CBOW | GNB | **80.31** | 36.71 | 50.38 | **81.25** | 65.76 | 72.69 |
| | | LR | 61.38 | 88.82 | 72.60 | 70.06 | 77.35 | 73.53 |
| | | RF | 58.75 | 78.82 | 67.32 | 70.01 | 64.41 | 67.10 |
| | | SGD | 61.81 | 89.29 | 73.05 | 71.72 | 77.88 | 74.68 |
| | | LSVC | 61.38 | 87.88 | 72.28 | 70.27 | 76.76 | 73.38 |
| | SG | GNB | 60.92 | 89.76 | 72.58 | 71.51 | 76.76 | 74.04 |
| | | LR | 75.45 | 41.76 | 53.77 | 72.37 | 76.41 | 74.33 |
| | | RF | 59.15 | 77.59 | 67.12 | 67.28 | 60.35 | 63.63 |
| | | SGD | 62.02 | **90.76** | **73.69** | 71.44 | **79.47** | **75.24** |
| | | LSVC | 75.09 | 38.82 | 51.18 | 72.48 | 75.76 | 74.09 |
| FastText | CBOW | CNN | 59.69 | 56.62 | 52.88 | 63.84 | 63.32 | 62.98 |
| | | MLP | 58.86 | 55.97 | 52.06 | 62.65 | 62.50 | 62.39 |
| | | LSTM | 59.12 | 55.79 | 51.36 | 63.01 | 62.21 | 61.61 |
| | | Bi-LSTM | 57.36 | 55.29 | 51.93 | 62.08 | 61.91 | 61.78 |
| | SG | CNN | 57.70 | 55.79 | 52.88 | 61.45 | 61.38 | 61.33 |
| | | MLP | 55.87 | 54.21 | 50.71 | 62.21 | 62.15 | 62.10 |
| | | LSTM | 56.33 | 42.4 | 50.11 | 61.09 | 60.85 | 60.65 |
| | | Bi-LSTM | 57.25 | 54.88 | 50.87 | 61.36 | 61.15 | 60.96 |

Figure 4: Results on TSAC_Test by using Senti_Alg as training

| Model | Type | ML Algo | TSAC_Test | | | TSAC_Test_Tr | | |
|---|---|---|---|---|---|---|---|---|
| | | | P | R | F1 | P | R | F1 |
| Word2vec | CBOW | GNB | 78.65 | 32.29 | 45.79 | 82.39 | 57.24 | 67.55 |
| | | LR | 65.08 | 89.47 | 75.35 | 84.76 | 84.76 | 84.76 |
| | | RF | 62.51 | 83.76 | 71.59 | 87.13 | 78.82 | 82.77 |
| | | SGD | 64.34 | 92.12 | 75.76 | 82.55 | 89.06 | 85.68 |
| | | LSVC | 85.70 | 42.65 | 56.95 | 84.65 | 87.29 | 85.95 |
| | SG | GNB | 76.39 | 31.59 | 44.69 | 82.70 | 56.53 | 67.16 |
| | | LR | 65.66 | **89.88** | **75.89** | 87.26 | 87.41 | 87.33 |
| | | RF | 83.45 | 33.82 | 48.14 | 87.53 | 78.88 | 82.98 |
| | | SGD | 65.46 | 89.65 | 75.67 | 83.76 | **91.65** | 87.53 |
| | | LSVC | **88.10** | 43.53 | 58.27 | 86.64 | 88.12 | 87.37 |
| FastText | CBOW | CNN | 75.53 | 66.50 | 63.25 | 89.94 | 89.65 | 89.63 |
| | | MLP | 75.29 | 67.21 | 64.36 | 90.81 | 90.76 | 90.76 |
| | | LSTM | 75.71 | 67.41 | 64.55 | 91.52 | 91.41 | 91.41 |
| | | Bi-LSTM | 77.53 | 67.44 | 64.16 | **91.66** | 91.21 | 91.18 |
| | SG | CNN | 75.85 | 66.85 | 63.69 | 91.58 | 91.47 | 91.46 |
| | | MLP | 76.13 | 67.50 | 64.57 | 91.65 | 91.59 | **91.59** |
| | | LSTM | 75.78 | 66.91 | 63.80 | 90.85 | 90.71 | 90.70 |
| | | Bi-LSTM | 77.10 | 65.59 | 61.50 | 91.39 | 91.03 | 91.01 |

Figure 5: Results on TSAC_Test using TSAC_train_Tr

| Model | Type | ML Algo | Arabic | | |
|---|---|---|---|---|---|
| | | | P | R | F1 |
| Word2vec | CBOW | GNB | 76.11 | **85.61** | **80.58** |
| | | LR | 71.93 | 75.31 | 73.58 |
| | | RF | 69.79 | 68.00 | 69.28 |
| | | SGD | **77.65** | 73.45 | 75.49 |
| | | LSVC | 70.90 | 74.66 | 72.73 |
| | SG | GNB | 66.33 | 92.59 | 77.29 |
| | | LR | 71.67 | 77.64 | 74.54 |
| | | RF | 71.09 | 67.12 | 69.05 |
| | | SGD | 71.12 | 82.58 | 76.42 |
| | | LSVC | 71.40 | 77.08 | 74.13 |
| FastText | CBOW | CNN | 64.24 | 64.11 | 64.03 |
| | | MLP | 62.65 | 62.65 | 62.65 |
| | | LSTM | 61.40 | 61.09 | 60.81 |
| | | Bi-LSTM | 62.97 | 62.88 | 62.81 |
| | SG | CNN | 63.30 | 63.27 | 63.26 |
| | | MLP | 60.83 | 60.81 | 60.78 |
| | | LSTM | 60.58 | 60.43 | 60.30 |
| | | Bi-LSTM | 60.48 | 60.41 | 60.34 |

Figure 6: Results of ASTD/QCRI/ArTwitter

# Me, myself, and ire: Effects of automatic transcription quality on emotion, sarcasm, and personality detection

**John Culnan, Seongjin Park, Meghavarshini Krishnaswamy, Rebecca Sharp**
University of Arizona, Tucson, Arizona, USA
{jmculnan, seongjinpark, mkrishnaswamy, bsharp}@email.arizona.edu

## Abstract

In deployment, systems that use speech as input must make use of automated transcriptions. Yet, typically when these systems are evaluated, gold transcriptions are assumed. We explicitly examine the impact of transcription errors on the downstream performance of a multi-modal system on three related tasks from three datasets: emotion, sarcasm, and personality detection. We include three separate transcription tools and show that while all automated transcriptions propagate errors that substantially impact downstream performance, the open-source tools fair worse than the paid tool, though not always straightforwardly, and word error rates do not correlate well with downstream performance. We further find that the inclusion of audio features partially mitigates transcription errors, but that a naive usage of a multi-task setup does not. We make available all code and data splits needed to reproduce all of our experiments.[1]

## 1 Introduction

With the large amount of available speech data, multimodal approaches to classic natural language processing tasks are becoming increasingly prevalent. Many of these proposed systems, however, demonstrate their gains under the assumption of gold transcriptions (e.g., Poria et al., 2019; Ghosal et al., 2020; Castro et al., 2019), a condition which is highly unrealistic in real-world scenarios. In practice, deployed systems will need to utilize an automatic speech recognition (ASR) tool to obtain transcriptions. However, when selecting the best tool given the constraints of the use case, the results of an *intrinsic evaluation* such as the word error rate (WER) are not necessarily correlated with *extrinsic performance* on the downstream task of interest (Faruqui et al., 2016). This issue is exacerbated when considering that ASR tools may perform quite differently across different domains (Georgila et al., 2020).

In this initial work, we explore how much transcription errors affect performance of a multimodal system on several related but distinct downstream tasks and domains. We compare two open-source and one paid transcription tools and evaluate on three multimodal English-language tasks: emotion, sarcasm, and personality detection. We explicitly compare intrinsic and extrinsic evaluations, and discuss the utility of WER as an indicator of task-performance.

Our specific contributions are:

1. An exploration of the relationship between transcription WER and performance on downstream multimodal tasks. We show that overall, the transcriptions from the paid tool may be more useful than those of the open-source tools, but that they perform worse than gold. Further, we show that differences in WER do not describe well the differences in the downstream tasks.

2. We explore using multitask (MT) training for mitigating issues with transcription quality. We find that, in this setting, MT does not help model performance, suggesting that problems with transcription quality need a more thoughtful approach to overcome. On the other hand, we show that inclusion of the audio modality does improve performance for all datasets when using automatic transcriptions, indicating that additional modalities can be helpful to mitigate transcription errors.

## 2 Related Work

Multimodal language work frequently makes use of video, audio, and text modalities to examine emo-

[1] https://github.com/clulab/tomcat-speech



*Proceedings of the 11th Workshop on Computational Approaches to Subjectivity, Sentiment and Social Media Analysis*, pages 250–256
April 19, 2021. ©2021 Association for Computational Linguistics

tion (Zadeh et al., 2018), sentiment (Soleymani et al., 2017), and personality (Rissola et al., 2019). Previous work in emotion recognition has used speech features alone (Latif et al., 2020), speech and text (Atmaja and Akagi, 2020), and speech, text, and video (Tsai et al., 2018) to make predictions. Ghosal et al. (2020) use transformer-based models to establish a new state of the art on multiple multimodal datasets. Recent work in personality detection has often examined the OCEAN traits (openness, conscientiousness, extraversion, agreeableness, and neuroticism; Ponce-López et al., 2016), using either apparent (as perceived by others) (Yan et al., 2020) or self-reported traits (Celli et al., 2014).

ASR systems have also been emphasized in recent decades. Some can be custom trained or used with pretrained models (Povey et al., 2011; Lamere et al., 2003), while others are extensively trained but limited in their customization (Bano et al., 2020). Georgila et al. (2020) examine the performance of different ASR transcription tools on multiple ASR datasets, providing a strong reference for WERs; however, to the best of our knowledge, we are the first to compare this form of intrinsic performance to performance on the downstream tasks of emotion, personality, and sarcasm detection.

## 3 Approach

When multimodal data including speech is used in a deployed system, the related text features generally come from automatic transcriptions of the speech itself. Here, we compare how errors in these transcriptions affect the performance of a neural network model on three distinct tasks. Further, we compare results from both a single-task and a multitask (MT) network composed of data from two datasets, a common strategy for mitigating issues with limited or flawed data (Schulz et al., 2018).

As we are not trying to define a new state of the art, we use a simple model for our experiments. This model takes as input text and audio features from MELD and FirstImpr (Section 4), and feeds them through a late-fusion network (i.e., one which processes the modalities separately, then concatenates them before predicting). In the MT setting, the final layers are task specific, and the base layers share parameters.

We generate transcriptions for each dataset using three separate ASR systems (Section 4.3) and find the intrinsic performance (WER[2]; Section 6.1) as well as the extrinsic performance for each (i.e., performance on the downstream tasks of interest; Section 6).

## 4 Data

For our experiments we use three datasets covering distinct tasks. For each data point, we extract acoustic features and obtain three different transcriptions, in addition to the dataset-provided gold transcriptions, which form the basis for our comparative study. Dataset sizes are shown in Table 1.[3]

| Dataset | Train | Dev | Test |
|---|---|---|---|
| MELD | 8878 | 2220 | 2610 |
| MUStARD | 414 | 138 | 138 |
| FirstImpr | 6000 | 2000 | 2000 |

Table 1: Number of utterances in each data partition.

### 4.1 Datasets

Our selected datasets represent distinct tasks that may have different levels of reliance upon each modality for successful prediction. For example, while emotions and personality may be expressed through word choice as much as pronunciation, sarcasm detection should rely much more heavily upon acoustics.

**Multimodal Emotion Lines Dataset (MELD; Zahiri and Choi, 2017; Poria et al., 2019):** MELD provides 13708 annotated utterances (< 5 words, with an average length of 3.59s) from 1,433 dialogues from the TV series *Friends*. Utterances are annotated for emotion (anger, disgust, sadness, joy, neutral, surprise and fear) and sentiment.

**Multimodal Sarcasm Detection (MUStARD; Castro et al., 2019):** MUStARD is a collection of 690 utterances (average of 14 tokens and 5.22s) from *Friends, The Golden Girls, The Big Bang Theory*, and *Sarcasmaholics Anonymous*. Each is gold-annotated as sarcastic or non-sarcastic.

**First Impressions V2 dataset (FirstImpr; Ponce-López et al., 2016):** FirstImpr contains 10,000 English utterances (average length 15s) taken from 3,000 YouTube video blogs and annotated for the OCEAN personality traits.

[2]We use the JiWER Python library (`https://pypi.org/project/jiwer/`) and the dataset-provided transcriptions to calculate WER.

[3]Note that for MELD we redistributed the train and dev partitions to make dev closer in size to test (we did not modify test in any way).

### 4.2 Acoustic features

We extract acoustic features with the Open-source Speech and Music Interpretation by Large-space Extraction toolkit v2.3.0 (OpenSMILE; Eyben et al., 2010). We use the INTERSPEECH 2010 (IS10; Schuller et al., 2010) or 2013 Paralinguistics Challenges (IS13; Schuller et al., 2013) features, using the set that performed the best on a task's development partition. These sets contain low-level descriptors (such as MFCCs and fundamental frequency) and the associated functionals, extracted at 10ms intervals (total 76 for IS10, 141 for IS13). We capture features only from the middle 50 percent of each audio file, and calculate mean feature values per utterance for both feature sets, with minimum, maximum, and mean plus/minus standard deviation concatenated to this for IS10.

### 4.3 Text features

Our text features consist of tokens extracted directly from the transcripts using the basic english tokenizer in `torchtext`.[4] We compare the transcriptions from the following:

**CMU Sphinx Open Source Toolkit (Sphinx; Lamere et al., 2003):** We utilize the open-source, lightweight PocketSphinx[5] version of Sphinx for transcription, using the pretrained acoustic and language models provided by CMU.

**Google Cloud Speech-to-Text[6] (Google):** Google Cloud Speech-to-Text is a commercial tool trained on data collected by Google and provided by users who have used Speech-to-Text and agreed to share their data. We use synchronous speech recognition.

**Kaldi Speech Recognition Toolkit (Kaldi; Povey et al., 2011):** Kaldi is an open-source tool for speech recognition. We use the Librispeech ASR model,[7] which is trained on Librispeech (Panayotov et al., 2015), and the online-decoding function.

**Gold:** Each dataset also provides a gold transcription. For MELD this is extracted from subtitles, MUStARD's comes both from subtitles and manual transcription, and FirstImpr's comes from a professional transcription service. With these we calculate the WERs (Section 6.1) and a ceiling performance in our extrinsic evaluations (Section 6).

## 5 Models

To evaluate the impact of transcription on performance, we create (a) baseline models that use only text or only audio features, plus (b) a multimodal model that uses audio and text. Note that as our goal here is not to achieve a new state of the art, but rather to explore the impact of real-world options for transcriptions, we use straightforward models that are not particularly architecturally tuned.

**Text-only baseline:** The text baseline consists of a two-layer LSTM (Hochreiter and Schmidhuber, 1997). 300d GloVe embeddings trained on 42B words (Pennington et al., 2014) are concatenated with 30d trainable text embeddings and fed through the network. The 100d output vectors representing each utterance are then fed through a prediction layer with a cross-entropy loss function[8].

**Audio-only baseline** The audio baseline is a simple feedforward neural network, where extracted audio features are averaged over the course of the utterance,[9] and used as input into two fully connected layers. The first layer decreases the audio to a 50-dimensional vector, while the second increases it back to its original size. The vector is finally fed through a prediction layer. We use IS10 features for MUStARD and IS13 for MELD and FirstImpr, chosen based on dev performance.

**Multimodal model (MM)** For our multimodal model, we concatenate the 100d output from the text component to the 141d (IS13) or 380d (IS10) output of the acoustic layers. These vectors are then fed through two fully connected layers and a prediction layer. This model works in both single task and multitask settings. As a multitask network (MM-MT), the two final layers are distinct for each dataset.

## 6 Experiments and Results

We evaluate how the automated transcriptions from different ASR tools affect performance on three distinct downstream tasks. We show the intrinsic

[4] https://pytorch.org/text/stable/index.html

[5] https://github.com/cmusphinx/pocketsphinx

[6] https://cloud.google.com/speech-to-text

[7] https://kaldi-asr.org/models/m13

[8] used for this and all other models

[9] While we also experimented with a version that used an RNN over the acoustic features, we found that it did not affect performance and it was far slower to train.

performance of the tools (in terms of WERs) and compare it to the extrinsic performance.

| Dataset | Sphinx | Kaldi | Google |
|---|---|---|---|
| MELD | 114.9 | 104.4 | 82.6 |
| MUStARD | 96.8 | 73.0 | 54.3 |
| FirstImpr | 97.4 | 83.5 | 63.8 |

Table 2: WER of MELD, MUStARD, and FirstImpr; results show the difficulty of ASR tools with these datasets' speech.

### 6.1 Intrinsic Transcription Evaluation

We use the provided gold transcriptions to calculate WERs, shown in Table 2. We see that Google consistently has lower WERs than either of the open-source tools, and that Kaldi consistently outperforms Sphinx, though the difference is smaller in MELD than the other datasets.

### 6.2 Extrinsic Evaluation

The results of our models trained on each transcription type for each task is given in Table 3. We report all results as weighted average F1 scores over all classes and we evaluate statistical significance by calculating p-values with bootstrap resampling over 10,000 iterations on model predictions with Bonferroni correction applied.

We include the comparable[10] state of the art (SotA) performance for reference for MELD and MUStARD. As FirstImpr was previously evaluated as a regression task, and here we perform maximum-class prediction for consistency, there is no relevant SotA to include. For MELD, Poria et al. (2019), use a CNN over GloVe embeddings and an LSTM over audio features from OpenSMILE.[11] For MUStARD, Castro et al. (2019) employ SVMs trained over the BERT (Devlin et al., 2018) encoding of the utterance, combined with extracted audio features, averaged over the utterance. We include this result only to give context to what we report; recall that here we evaluate on a test split, whereas they used 5-fold cross validation.

For text-only results, ASR transcriptions show significantly lower performance than the gold transcriptions in MELD ($p<0.001$) and, to a smaller degree, MUStARD, although the Kaldi transcriptions are better in FirstImpr ($p<0.001$). With audio included, i.e., the multimodal systems, we again see that gold transcription models achieve higher performance than those with ASR transcriptions for MELD ($p<0.001$) and MUStARD. For FirstImpr, the Google transcriptions yield the best performance, although this difference is not significant.

|  | MELD (7cls) | MUStARD (2cls) | FirstImpr (5cls) |
|---|---|---|---|
| Poria et al. (2019) | 55.51 | – | — |
| Castro et al. (2019) | – | 71.80 | — |
| Aud | 37.38 | **75.42** | 32.99 |
| Txt (Kaldi) | 33.94 | 52.61 | 32.35 |
| Txt (Sphinx) | 32.68 | 57.12 | 30.11 |
| Txt (Google) | 37.60 | 58.11 | 31.66 |
| Txt (Gold) | **57.32** | 59.48 | 30.20 |
| MM (Kaldi) | 39.47 | 69.51 | 34.22 |
| MM (Sphinx) | 37.90 | 70.89 | 32.71 |
| MM (Google) | 40.94 | 70.12 | **35.98** |
| MM (Gold) | 56.28 | 73.98 | 35.05 |
| MM-MT (Kaldi) | 39.36 | — | 32.99 |
| MM-MT (Sphinx) | 39.30 | — | 32.81 |
| MM-MT (Google) | 40.17 | — | 34.75 |
| MM-MT (Gold) | 56.57 | — | 34.21 |

Table 3: Extrinsic task performance of our single-task system using acoustic features (Aud), text features (Txt), or multimodal (MM). We also show performance of the multimodal multitask system (MM-MT) that utilizes MELD and FirstImpr. All results presented are weighted average F1.

|  | MELD | MUStARD | FirstImpr |
|---|---|---|---|
| Gold | 139580<br>(95.7%) | 10991<br>(98.7%) | 523387<br>(98.4%) |
| Google | 88913<br>(99.8%) | 7315<br>(99.8%) | 436272<br>(100%) |
| Kaldi | 89082<br>(100%) | 7039<br>(99.9%) | 369201<br>(100%) |
| Sphinx | 103659<br>(100%) | 6891<br>(100%) | 419214<br>(100%) |

Table 4: GloVe coverage (in tokens) for each transcription type with each dataset. Percentage of all corpus tokens appearing in GloVe are shown in parentheses.

However, when only considering the ASR models (i.e., in the deployment scenario), the inclusion of audio features improves all models, indicating that these features *are* able to mitigate some of the noise arising from imperfect transcriptions. That said, it is worth noting that for MUStARD, the best performance is achieved by using audio features only, though again this difference is not significant.

Among the ASR systems, we see that despite the substantial differences in WERs (Table 2), on the extrinsic evaluation, the story is more nuanced. Google transcription models do the best on MELD and FirstImpr, but on MUStARD, Sphinx transcriptions have the best performance. Further, none of

[10] Since we do not use the surrounding context or external resources in this initial work, we provide the results of the previous best performing system that did likewise.

[11] We are reading between the lines on this, as the paper does not provide clear explanation of this model, which they call *cMKL*.

|  | Anger | Disgust | Fear | Joy | Sadness | Surprise | All Emotions |
|---|---|---|---|---|---|---|---|
| Gold | 934 / 207 | 747 / 159 | 1398 / 239 | 2306 / 198 | 1182 / 220 | 1080 / 138 | 4428 / 656 |
| Google | 805 / 208 | 612 / 158 | 1056 / 245 | 1919 / 198 | 978 / 202 | 863 / 135 | 3666 / 644 |
| Kaldi | 664 / 216 | 521 / 157 | 1282 / 270 | 2008 / 241 | 1054 / 260 | 978 / 143 | 3861 / 741 |
| Sphinx | 973 / 239 | 665 / 168 | 1126 / 279 | 1806 / 211 | 1070 / 249 | 1063 / 145 | 3704 / 712 |

Table 5: Number of tokens (left) and types (right) of words from the NRC Word-Emotion Association Lexicon (Mohammad and Turney, 2010, 2013) for each emotion type appearing in the MELD transcriptions. Each word may be associated with more than one emotion, so the overall count is lower than the sum of the individual emotions.

these differences are statistically significant. Thus, depending on the task of interest, there may be no large advantage to more expensive tools. We also experiment with using a multi-task (MT) setup to determine whether using MT can mitigate transcription errors. We use only MELD and FirstImpr, as they both did best with the IS13 features. Further, the majority of utterances in MUStARD appear in MELD and cannot be restricted to the training partition, so it cannot be used fairly in a multitask system with MELD. For all transcription types, the MT setup performs similarly to the corresponding multimodal single-task models, suggesting that a more thoughtful approach may be needed to leverage external data to mitigate transcription noise, which is beyond the scope of the current work.

### 6.3 Error analysis

While transcription WERs are not intrinsically linked to model performance on a global level, it is possible that additional factors are at play. As such, we analyze GloVe's coverage for each transcription of each dataset and examine emotion words present in each transcription for MELD.

Results of Table 4 reveal that gold transcriptions contain both a larger number of overall tokens and a smaller percentage of coverage by GloVe than all other datasets. This larger number of tokens may allow a system to make fine-grained distinction, indicating potential need for caution with automatic transcription selection depending upon the dataset of interest. Google has the second highest number of tokens covered in GloVe for FirstImpr and MUStARD, while Sphinx has the second most for MELD. As models using sphinx transcriptions perform numerically worst with MELD, this indicates that GloVe coverage alone does not always correspond to downstream task performance.

For more fine-grained detail, we examine transcription success in one particular domain: identification of emotion words. To do this, we determine the number of emotion words identified for each transcription using the NRC Word-Emotion Association Lexicon (EmoLex; Mohammad and Turney, 2010, 2013).

As shown in Table 5, between the gold and automatic transcriptions, we see different patterns between the *type* and *token* frequencies of emotion words. Overall, the token frequency of emotion words is lower in the automatic transcripts than in the gold transcriptions, largely due to the increase in tokens of words expressing joy and fear, but the *type* frequency is higher, particularly with Kaldi and Sphinx. That is, there are fewer distinct emotion words in the gold transcriptions but they have more mentions. These frequency patterns may be partially responsible for the worse performance of models using Kaldi and Sphinx transcriptions, as some data points contain spurious false positive mentions of emotion words, and other data points are missing mentions of emotion words, due to transcription error.

## 7 Conclusions

We demonstrated that selecting the appropriate transcription service for a task is dependent upon the task and models to be used. Paid transcriptions may result in better model performance, but differences in task performance may be much smaller than suggested by only considering WER. Further, depending on the task, the noise introduced from automatic transcriptions may be mitigated by including additional input modalities, such as audio.

## Acknowledgments

Research was sponsored by the Army Research Office, Grant Number W911NF2010002. The views and conclusions are those of the authors and should not be interpreted as representing official policies, expressed or implied, of the Army Research Office or U.S. Government. Rebecca Sharp declares a financial interest in lum.ai. This interest has been properly disclosed to the University of Arizona Institutional Review Committee and is managed in accordance with its conflict of interest policies.

## References


Bagus Tris Atmaja and Masato Akagi. 2020. Dimensional speech emotion recognition from speech features and word embeddings by using multitask learning. *APSIPA Transactions on Signal and Information Processing*, 9.

Shahana Bano, Pavuluri Jithendra, Gorsa Lakshmi Niharika, and Yalavarthi Sikhi. 2020. Speech to text translation enabling multilingualism. In *2020 IEEE International Conference for Innovation in Technology (INOCON)*, pages 1–4. IEEE.

Santiago Castro, Devamanyu Hazarika, Verónica Pérez-Rosas, Roger Zimmermann, Rada Mihalcea, and Soujanya Poria. 2019. Towards multimodal sarcasm detection (an _obviously_ perfect paper). In *Proceedings of the 57th Annual Meeting of the Association for Computational Linguistics (Volume 1: Long Papers)*, Florence, Italy. Association for Computational Linguistics.

Fabio Celli, Elia Bruni, and Bruno Lepri. 2014. Automatic personality and interaction style recognition from facebook profile pictures. In *Proceedings of the 22nd ACM international conference on Multimedia*, pages 1101–1104.

Jacob Devlin, Ming-Wei Chang, Kenton Lee, and Kristina Toutanova. 2018. Bert: Pre-training of deep bidirectional transformers for language understanding. In *Proceedings of the 2019 Conference ofthe North American Chapter of the Association for Computational Linguistics: Human LanguageTechnologies, Volume 1 (Long and Short Papers)*, pages 4171–4186, Minneapolis, Minnesota. Association for Computational Linguistics.

Florian Eyben, Martin Wöllmer, and Björn Schuller. 2010. Opensmile: the Munich versatile and fast open-source audio feature extractor. In *Proceedings of the 18th ACM international conference on Multimedia*, pages 1459–1462.

Manaal Faruqui, Yulia Tsvetkov, Pushpendre Rastogi, and Chris Dyer. 2016. Problems with evaluation of word embeddings using word similarity tasks. *arXiv preprint arXiv:1605.02276*.

Kallirroi Georgila, Anton Leuski, Volodymyr Yanov, and David Traum. 2020. Evaluation of off-the-shelf speech recognizers across diverse dialogue domains. In *Proceedings of The 12th Language Resources and Evaluation Conference*, pages 6469–6476.

Deepanway Ghosal, Navonil Majumder, Alexander Gelbukh, Rada Mihalcea, and Soujanya Poria. 2020. Cosmic: Commonsense knowledge for emotion identification in conversations. *arXiv preprint arXiv:2010.02795*.

Sepp Hochreiter and Jürgen Schmidhuber. 1997. Long short-term memory. *Neural computation*, 9(8):1735–1780.

Paul Lamere, Philip Kwok, Evandro Gouvea, Bhiksha Raj, Rita Singh, William Walker, Manfred Warmuth, and Peter Wolf. 2003. The cmu sphinx-4 speech recognition system.

Siddique Latif, Rajib Rana, Sara Khalifa, Raja Jurdak, Julien Epps, and Bjórn Wolfgang Schuller. 2020. Multi-task semi-supervised adversarial autoencoding for speech emotion recognition. *IEEE Transactions on Affective Computing*.

Saif Mohammad and Peter Turney. 2010. Emotions evoked by common words and phrases: Using mechanical turk to create an emotion lexicon. In *Proceedings of the NAACL HLT 2010 workshop on computational approaches to analysis and generation of emotion in text*, pages 26–34.

Saif M Mohammad and Peter D Turney. 2013. Crowdsourcing a word–emotion association lexicon. *Computational intelligence*, 29(3):436–465.

V. Panayotov, G. Chen, D. Povey, and S. Khudanpur. 2015. Librispeech: An asr corpus based on public domain audio books. In *2015 IEEE International Conference on Acoustics, Speech and Signal Processing (ICASSP)*, pages 5206–5210.

Jeffrey Pennington, Richard Socher, and Christopher D Manning. 2014. Glove: Global vectors for word representation. In *Proceedings of the 2014 conference on empirical methods in natural language processing (EMNLP)*, pages 1532–1543.

Víctor Ponce-López, Baiyu Chen, Marc Oliu, Ciprian Corneanu, Albert Clapés, Isabelle Guyon, Xavier Baró, Hugo Jair Escalante, and Sergio Escalera. 2016. Chalearn lap 2016: First round challenge on first impressions-dataset and results. In *European conference on computer vision*, pages 400–418. Springer.

Soujanya Poria, Devamanyu Hazarika, Navonil Majumder, Gautam Naik, Erik Cambria, and Rada Mihalcea. 2019. Meld: A multimodal multi-party dataset for emotion recognition in conversations. In *Proceedings of the 57th Annual Meeting of the Association for Computational Linguistics*, pages 527–536, Florence, Italy. Association for Computational Linguistics.

Daniel Povey, Arnab Ghoshal, Gilles Boulianne, Lukas Burget, Ondrej Glembek, Nagendra Goel, Mirko Hannemann, Petr Motlicek, Yanmin Qian, Petr Schwarz, Jan Silovsky, Georg Stemmer, and Karel Vesely. 2011. The kaldi speech recognition toolkit. In *IEEE 2011 Workshop on Automatic Speech Recognition and Understanding*. IEEE Signal Processing Society. IEEE Catalog No.: CFP11SRW-USB.

Esteban Andres Rissola, Seyed Ali Bahrainian, and Fabio Crestani. 2019. Personality recognition in conversations using capsule neural networks. In *IEEE/WIC/ACM International Conference on Web Intelligence*, pages 180–187.

Björn Schuller, Stefan Steidl, Anton Batliner, Felix Burkhardt, Laurence Devillers, Christian Müller, and Shrikanth S Narayanan. 2010. The interspeech 2010 paralinguistic challenge. In *Eleventh Annual Conference of the International Speech Communication Association*.

Björn Schuller, Stefan Steidl, Anton Batliner, Alessandro Vinciarelli, Klaus Scherer, Fabien Ringeval, Mohamed Chetouani, Felix Weninger, Florian Eyben, Erik Marchi, et al. 2013. The interspeech 2013 computational paralinguistics challenge: Social signals, conflict, emotion, autism. In *Proceedings INTERSPEECH 2013, 14th Annual Conference of the International Speech Communication Association, Lyon, France*.

Claudia Schulz, Steffen Eger, Johannes Daxenberger, Tobias Kahse, and Iryna Gurevych. 2018. Multi-task learning for argumentation mining in low-resource settings. In *Proceedings of the 16th Annual Conference of the North American Chapter of the Association for Computational Linguistics: Human Language Technologies*. Association for Computational Linguistics.

Mohammad Soleymani, David Garcia, Brendan Jou, Björn Schuller, Shih-Fu Chang, and Maja Pantic. 2017. A survey of multimodal sentiment analysis. *Image and Vision Computing*, 65:3–14.

Yao-Hung Hubert Tsai, Paul Pu Liang, Amir Zadeh, Louis-Philippe Morency, and Ruslan Salakhutdinov. 2018. Learning factorized multimodal representations. *ICLR*.

Shen Yan, Di Huang, and Mohammad Soleymani. 2020. Mitigating biases in multimodal personality assessment. In *Proceedings of the 2020 International Conference on Multimodal Interaction*, pages 361–369.

Amir Zadeh, Paul Pu Liang, Soujanya Poria, Prateek Vij, Erik Cambria, and Louis-Philippe Morency. 2018. Multi-attention recurrent network for human communication comprehension. *Proceedings of the AAAI Conference on Artificial Intelligence*, 32(1).

Sayyed M Zahiri and Jinho D Choi. 2017. Emotion detection on TV show transcripts with sequence-based convolutional neural networks. In *Proceedings ofthe AAAI Workshop on Affective Content Analysis*, pages 44–51, New Orleans, LA.

# Emotional RobBERT and Insensitive BERTje: Combining Transformers and Affect Lexica for Dutch Emotion Detection

**Luna De Bruyne, Orphée De Clercq and Véronique Hoste**
LT[3], Language and Translation Technology Team
Ghent University
{luna.debruyne, orphee.declercq, veronique.hoste}@ugent.be

## Abstract

In a first step towards improving Dutch emotion detection, we try to combine the Dutch transformer models BERTje and RobBERT with lexicon-based methods. We propose two architectures: one in which lexicon information is directly injected into the transformer model and a meta-learning approach where predictions from transformers are combined with lexicon features. The models are tested on 1,000 Dutch tweets and 1,000 captions from TV-shows which have been manually annotated with emotion categories and dimensions. We find that RobBERT clearly outperforms BERTje, but that directly adding lexicon information to transformers does not improve performance. In the meta-learning approach, lexicon information does have a positive effect on BERTje, but not on RobBERT. This suggests that more emotional information is already contained within this latter language model.

## 1 Introduction

Computational analysis of affect in Dutch texts is mostly restricted to polarity analysis (negative/positive/neutral), for which we know a tradition of lexicon-based approaches. Recently, a BERT-based model, BERTje (de Vries et al., 2019), and a RoBERTa-based model, RobBERT (Delobelle et al., 2020), have been created for Dutch, and they have achieved promising results on the task of sentiment analysis. For emotion detection, however, these models have not yet been evaluated.

In a first step towards improving emotion detection for Dutch, we will evaluate BERTje and RobBERT on the task of emotion detection. Instead of casting aside the many efforts that have been made in the creation of Dutch sentiment and emotion lexica, we will investigate whether transformers and affect lexica can complement each other. Attempts of combining BERT models with additional features have already been successful for tasks like abusive language and sarcasm detection (Koufakou et al., 2020; Kumar et al., 2021).

We consider two architectures. In the first one, we inject lexicon information in the transformer model before the prediction layer. We do this by concatenating the `[CLS]` token of the target sentence (which BERT and RoBERTa models use as input for prediction) with a lexicon vector obtained from seven Dutch affect lexica. In the second approach, we employ a meta-learning architecture and use a support vector machine (SVM) that learns from the transformer model's output. The predictions from the transformer are concatenated with the lexicon vector and used as input for the SVM.

We evaluate our models on 1,000 Dutch Tweets and 1,000 transcribed utterances from Flemish TV-shows. As multiple researchers have emphasized the need of studying emotions not only in terms of basic emotions, but based on dimensions like valence, arousal and dominance as well (Buechel and Hahn, 2016; Mohammad and Kiritchenko, 2018), the data has been annotated in a bi-representational design: both with categorical annotations for anger, joy, fear, love, sadness or neutral, and scores for the dimensions valence, arousal and dominance.

First we will discuss related work on Dutch emotion detection and other attempts on combining transformer models with additional features in Section 2. In Section 3, we will describe the methodology of our experiments and in Section 4, we report the results. We end with a conclusion in Section 5.

## 2 Related Work

Although most emotion detection research deals with the English language, recent studies have shown interest in other languages as well, e.g. the recent work of Ahmad et al. (2020) for Hindi or the



*Proceedings of the 11th Workshop on Computational Approaches to Subjectivity, Sentiment and Social Media Analysis*, pages 257–263
April 19, 2021. ©2021 Association for Computational Linguistics

| Corpus | Text example | categorical | dimensional | | |
|---|---|---|---|---|---|
| | | | V | A | D |
| Tweets | @transavia Jaaah volgende vakantie Barcelona en na het zomerseizoen naar de Algarve<br>*EN: @transavia Yeah next holiday Barcelona and after summer season to the Algarve* | joy | 0.689 | 0.491 | 0.622 |
| Captions | Ik zou liever sterven dan hier te wonen, denk ik.<br>*EN: I'd rather die than live here, I think.* | sadness | 0.156 | 0.384 | 0.301 |

Table 1: Text examples from the Tweets and Captions subcorpora with their assigned categorical and dimensional label (V = valence, A = arousal, D = dominance).

SemEval-2018 task on Affect in Tweets, for which in addition to English data, Arabic and Spanish datasets were released (Mohammad et al., 2018). Moreover, research on multilingual emotion detection (Buechel and Hahn, 2018; Öhman et al., 2018) and sentiment analysis (Lo et al., 2017; Vilares et al., 2018) is emerging.

Concerning the automatic modelling of affect in Dutch, the main focus still is on sentiment analysis instead of fine-grained emotions. Many studies have used sentiment lexica for this purpose (e.g. Van de Kauter et al., 2015; De Clercq et al., 2017; Wang et al., 2020). Recently, transformer models like BERTje (de Vries et al., 2019) and RobBERT (Delobelle et al., 2020) have been used to classify reviews from the Dutch Book Reviews dataset as either positive or negative, in which RobBERT came out as best (accuracy of 95% versus 93%).

The only publicly available dataset for Dutch emotion detection is deLearyous (Vaassen and Daelemans, 2011). It consists of 740 Dutch sentences from conversations, annotated according to Leary's Rose (Leary, 1957). Vaassen and Daelemans (2011) found that classifying sentences from deLearyous into the quadrants or octants of Leary's Rose was difficult for machine learners, most likely because of the sparseness of the data and low inter-annotator agreement. However, after this study, no further studies on Dutch emotion detection were published. This clearly shows the need of new data and methods for this task.

Some researchers already revealed that combining BERT models with handcrafted features can have a positive effect on performance, e.g. for the task of essay scoring (accuracy of 71% versus 80%) (Uto et al., 2020) and sarcasm detection (F1-score of 78% versus 80%) (Kumar et al., 2021). Lexicon features have been combined with BERT as well, e.g. for abusive language detection (Koufakou et al., 2020), for which the authors found an improvement on four out of six datasets compared to a plain BERT model (maximum improvement of 3%). In all of these studies, the handcrafted features or lexicon features were injected into the transformer architecture by concatenating them with the BERT representation before the prediction layer.

## 3 Method

### 3.1 Data

We collect data from two domains: Twitter posts (Tweets subcorpus) and utterances from reality TV-shows (Captions). For the Tweets subcorpus, a list of 72 emojis was used as query in the Dutch tweets database Twiqs.nl, with as search period 1-1-2017 to 31-12-2017. Based on this one-year datadump we sampled a random subset of 1,000 tweets, but made sure that no duplicates or non-Dutch tweets were present in the dataset.

For Captions, episodes of three emotionally loaded Flemish reality TV-shows (*Blind getrouwd*; *Bloed, zweet en luxeproblemen* and *Ooit vrij*) were used. Three episodes per show were transcribed using a literal transcription method (without correcting colloquial elements). 1,000 utterances (sentences or short sequences of sentences) were selected from these transcripts, based on a rough screening of emotional content and more or less equally distributed over the shows (335 instances from *Blind getrouwd*, 331 from *Bloed, zweet en luxeproblemen* and 334 from *Ooit vrij*).

All data was annotated with both categorical labels and dimensions. For the categorical annotation, the instances were labeled with one out of six labels: joy, love, anger, fear, sadness, or neutral. For annotating the dimensions valence, arousal and dominance, best-worst scaling was employed as this was shown to be a reliable annotation method (De Bruyne et al., 2021). Per subcorpus, the 1,000 instances were converted into 2,000 4-tuples and distributed among the annotators. For each trial, the annotator had to indicate the best and worst example for each dimension: highest and lowest valence,

|  | A | F | J | L | S | N |
|---|---|---|---|---|---|---|
| Tweets | 188 | 51 | 400 | 44 | 98 | 219 |
| Captions | 185 | 97 | 331 | 42 | 185 | 160 |

Table 2: Number of instances in each emotion category per subdataset. A = anger, F = fear, J = joy, L = love, S = sadness, N = neutral.

highest and lowest arousal, and highest and lowest dominance. Best-worst counts were then converted to scores from 0 to 1 with the Rescorla-Wagner update rule (Rescorla et al., 1972). See Table 1 for an annotated example of an instance in each domain.

Table 2 lists the number of instances per emotion category in each domain. For the valence, arousal and dominance annotations, the mean ranges between 0.46 and 0.52 for all dimensions in both subsets, the standard deviation ranges between 0.18 and 0.22, the minimum between 0.05 and 0.07 and the maximum between 0.96 and 0.97. For the experiments, both datasets were split in 800 instances for training, 100 for validating and 100 for testing (same splits for all models/tasks).

### 3.2 Lexicon information

We investigate whether lexicon information and transformer models can be complementary either by injecting lexicon information directly into the transformer architecture or by using a meta-learning approach in which predictions from transformer models are combined with lexicon features. Both models require the creation of a lexicon vector per target sentence.

For the creation of this vector, we combine seven existing open-source Dutch sentiment and emotion lexica, namely Pattern (De Smedt and Daelemans, 2012), Duoman (Jijkoun and Hofmann, 2009), LIWC (Boot et al., 2017), NRC Emotion (Mohammad and Turney, 2013), NRC VAD (Mohammad, 2018), Memolon (Buechel et al., 2020) and the VAD norms by Moors et al. (2013). For each word in the target sentence, lexicon values are obtained through a lookup in each affect lexicon. These values are then averaged over the words in the target sentence. The vector is 33-dimensional, as all lexica include values for multiple emotion categories or dimensions which add up to 33 in total. For lexica that do not have entries for any of the words in the sentence, the respective value in the lexicon vector is 0.

### 3.3 Transformer model

In this architecture, we inject the lexicon information into the transformer model while fine-tuning the model on the emotion detection tasks: emotion classification and emotion regression with the dimensions valence, arousal and dominance (VAD), and this in both domains. This injection occurs just before the prediction layer by concatenating the `[CLS]` token, which is normally used on its own as input for the classification, with the lexicon vector. This concatenated vector goes through a pre-classifier (linear layer with 2,048 nodes) and then to the prediction layer with Sigmoid activation function. The model architecture is shown in Figure 1.

Two Dutch transformer models are investigated: BERTje (de Vries et al., 2019), based on BERT by Devlin et al. (2019) and RobBERT (Delobelle et al., 2020), the Dutch version of the robustly optimized RoBERTa (Liu et al., 2019). RobBERT is trained on 39GB of common crawl data (Suárez et al., 2019), while BERTje is trained on only 12GB (including multiple genres).

Both models are implemented with HuggingFace's Transformers library (Wolf et al., 2019). We use AdamW optimizer (Loshchilov and Hutter, 2017) and the ReduceLROnPlateau learning rate scheduler with $l_r = 5e - 5$. The loss function is Binary Cross Entropy for the classification task and Mean Squared Error loss for regression. The maximum sequence length is 64 tokens, batch size is 16 for Tweets and 64 for Captions. We set dropout to 0.2 and use GELU as activation function in the implementation of Hendrycks and Gimpel (2016). The `[CLS]` token based on the concatenation of the last four layers of the model is used for prediction (and concatenated with the lexicon vector). The maximum number of epochs is set to 100 with a patience of 5 for early stopping.

### 3.4 Meta-learner

In the second approach, we use a support vector machine as meta-learner that learns from the predictions of a transformer model. We apply the transformer model on the training set and the test set to extract probabilities and predictions for sentences. For the classification task we use the probabilities of the emotion classes as features (6 features) and for the regression task the predicted scores (3 features). During training, the output on the training set is accompanied by lexicon features (33 features)

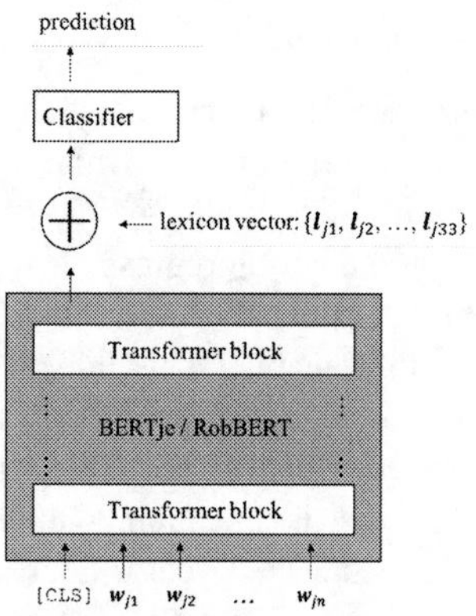


Figure 1: Transformer model with injection of lexicon features.

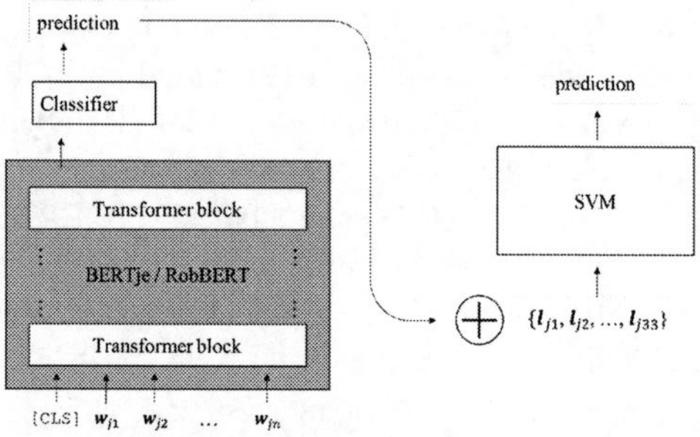


Figure 2: Meta-learner (SVM) with predictions from transformer and lexicon values as input features.

as input for the SVM. During testing, the output on the test set is combined with the lexicon features to feed the SVM. The model architecture is shown in Figure 2.

For all subtasks, we use a linear kernel and 1.0 as regularization parameter C. We use hinge loss and L2 penalty for classification and epsilon insensitive loss (L1 loss) for regression.

## 4 Results

### 4.1 Transformer model

We evaluate BERTje and RobBERT on the emotion classification (macro F1) and regression tasks (Pearson's $r$) for Tweets and Captions. We compare the results of the plain models and the models where the lexicon vector was injected.

Models are run ten times to account for variability and to be able to statistically compare the performance of different methods. The mean and standard deviation of these runs are reported in Table 3. Except for Captions classification, we observe that RobBERT is better for all datasets, with a notable margin: for Tweets classification and Captions regression there is an improvement of around 10% (from .16 to .26 and .60 to .68 respectively), and for Tweets regression the score almost doubled (from .36 to .70). This is in line with previous findings of RobBERT being more accurate in predicting sentiment (Delobelle et al., 2020), although our results are even more distinct. The robustly optimised RoBERTa framework and the larger corpus on which RobBERT was pre-trained clearly show their effect, although scores are in general still rather low. The results for the regression tasks seem more promising than for the classification task, although scores are difficult to compare as different metrics are used. We further notice that there is quite some variation between the runs, especially for the classification tasks.

Independent two-tailed t-tests were used for assessing whether the means of the models with and without lexicon vector are statistically different on a 5% significance level. For none of the datasets adding the lexicon vector was beneficial, as there was no significant difference in mean for any of the tasks (Tweets classification with BERTje: $t(9) = 1.3$, $p = 0.22$; Tweets classification with RobBERT: $t(9) = 0.6$, $p = 0.54$; Tweets regression with BERTje: $t(9) = 0.7$, $p = 0.50$; Tweets regression with RobBERT: $t(9) = -0.6$, $p = 0.52$; Captions classification with BERTje: $t(9) = 0.8$, $p = 0.42$; Captions classification with RobBERT: $t(9) = -1.0$, $p = 0.31$; Captions regression with BERTje: $t(9) = 0.5$, $p = 0.60$; Captions regression with RobBERT: $t(9) = -0.6$, $p = 0.58$). In contrast to previous studies regarding sarcasm and abusive language detection, we must thus conclude that this method of injecting lexicon information into the transformer model does not lead to higher performance on the task of emotion detection. We see two possible reasons for this: a) the lexica have no added value compared to the information that is already present in the language models, and/or b) the lexica do not have enough weight compared to the high-dimensional `CLS` token.

### 4.2 Meta-learner

In the meta-learning approach, we identify the best run (lowest loss on validation set) among the plain transformer models (i.e. without lexica), and apply that model on the training and test sets of the corresponding datasets. The probabilities (for classification) and predictions (for regression) are then

| Transformers | Tweets | | Captions | |
|---|---|---|---|---|
| Model | F1 (SD) | $r$ (SD) | F1 (SD) | $r$ (SD) |
| plain BERTje | .16 (.05) | .36 (.03) | .26 (.04) | .60 (.02) |
| BERTje + lex | .14 (.02) | .35 (.03) | .24 (.04) | .59 (.02) |
| plain RobBERT | .26 (.09) | .69 (.03) | .22 (.08) | .68 (.02) |
| RobBERT + lex | .23 (.07) | .70 (.01) | .25 (.04) | .68 (.02) |

Table 3: Results (macro F1-score and Pearson's $r$) of the plain transformer models (BERTje and RobBERT) versus the results with lexicon features added (BERTje/RobBERT + lex). F1-score and $r$ is the average of 10 runs, standard deviation is shown between brackets.

| | Tweets | | Captions | |
|---|---|---|---|---|
| Features | F1 | $r$ | F1 | $r$ |
| SVM lex | .16 | .32 | .12 | .28 |
| plain BERTje | .23 | .38 | **.28** | .61 |
| SVM lex + BERTje | ***.31*** | ***.41*** | .26 | ***.62*** |
| plain RobBERT | **.47** | .71 | .30 | .67 |
| SVM lex + RobBERT | .42 | .71 | .30 | ***.68*** |

Table 4: Results (macro F1-score and Pearson's $r$) of the plain transformer model versus the meta-learner. The results of an SVM model with only lexicon features are given in the first line as reference. The best result is shown in bold or bold italics if the best model is the meta-learner approach.

fed into an SVM together with the lexicon features. The results of the original plain transformer models and meta-learning models are shown in Table 4.

We see that a meta-learner using the output of a transformer model combined with lexicon features outperforms the plain transformer model in the case of BERTje for three out of four tasks (all but Captions classification). In the case of RobBERT, the meta-learner outperforms the plain transformer model for only one dataset (Captions regression), but only to a minor extent. In contrast to the previous approach, where lexicon information was injected directly into the transformer model, the meta-learner does seem to be able to improve performance. Where the previous approach might have failed because of the lexica not having enough weight, the meta-learner seems to be better in exploiting the lexicon information, however only for BERTje. Possibly, emotions are more contained in the RobBERT language model because of the improved training framework and notably larger training corpus, making RobBERT a more emotional language model. Therefore, RobBERT benefits less from the added lexicon information in contrast to BERTje.

## 5 Conclusion

As the recently developed transformer models for Dutch, BERTje and RobBERT, have not yet been tested on emotion detection tasks, we evaluated them on 1,000 Dutch Tweets and 1,000 captions for an emotion classification and regression task. We found that RobBERT outperformed BERTje in almost all cases. Further, we investigated whether these models could be enhanced with lexicon features and proposed two methods: one in which a lexicon vector was concatenated with the transformer's `[CLS]` token before prediction, and a meta-learning approach. In the first method, adding lexicon information did not seem beneficial. For the second approach, however, we found that the meta-learner had a positive effect in half of the cases, and especially on the models relying on BERTje, whereas the meta-learner had almost no impact on RobBERT. This is probably because more emotional information is already contained within this language model.


## Acknowledgements

This research was carried out with the support of the Research Foundation - Flanders under a Strategic Basic Research fellowship.


## References


Zishan Ahmad, Raghav Jindal, Asif Ekbal, and Pushpak Bhattachharyya. 2020. Borrow from rich cousin: transfer learning for emotion detection using cross lingual embedding. *Expert Systems with Applications*, 139:112851.

Peter Boot, Hanna Zijlstra, and Rinie Geenen. 2017. The dutch translation of the linguistic inquiry and word count (liwc) 2007 dictionary. *Dutch Journal of Applied Linguistics*, 6(1):65–76.

Sven Buechel and Udo Hahn. 2016. Emotion analysis as a regression problem - dimensional models and their implications on emotion representation and metrical evaluation. In *ECAI*.

Sven Buechel and Udo Hahn. 2018. Word emotion induction for multiple languages as a deep multi-task learning problem. In *Proceedings of the 2018 Conference of the North American Chapter of the Association for Computational Linguistics: Human Language Technologies, Volume 1 (Long Papers)*, pages 1907–1918, New Orleans, Louisiana. Association for Computational Linguistics.

Sven Buechel, Susanna Rücker, and Udo Hahn. 2020. Learning and evaluating emotion lexicons for 91 languages. In *Proceedings of the 58th Annual Meeting of the Association for Computational Linguistics*, pages 1202–1217, Online. Association for Computational Linguistics.

Luna De Bruyne, Orphée De Clercq, and Véronique Hoste. 2021. Annotating affective dimensions in user-generated content. *Language Resources and Evaluation*, pages 1–29.

Orphée De Clercq, Els Lefever, Gilles Jacobs, Tijl Carpels, and Véronique Hoste. 2017. Towards an integrated pipeline for aspect-based sentiment analysis in various domains. In *Proceedings of the 8th Workshop on Computational Approaches to Subjectivity, Sentiment and Social Media Analysis*, pages 136–142, Copenhagen, Denmark. Association for Computational Linguistics.

Tom De Smedt and Walter Daelemans. 2012. " vreselijk mooi!"(terribly beautiful): A subjectivity lexicon for dutch adjectives. In *LREC*, pages 3568–3572.

Pieter Delobelle, Thomas Winters, and Bettina Berendt. 2020. Robbert: a dutch roberta-based language model. *arXiv preprint arXiv:2001.06286*.

Jacob Devlin, Ming-Wei Chang, Kenton Lee, and Kristina Toutanova. 2019. BERT: Pre-training of deep bidirectional transformers for language understanding. In *Proceedings of the 2019 Conference of the North American Chapter of the Association for Computational Linguistics: Human Language Technologies, Volume 1 (Long and Short Papers)*, pages 4171–4186, Minneapolis, Minnesota. Association for Computational Linguistics.

Dan Hendrycks and Kevin Gimpel. 2016. Gaussian error linear units (gelus). *arXiv preprint arXiv:1606.08415*.

Valentin Jijkoun and Katja Hofmann. 2009. Generating a non-english subjectivity lexicon: Relations that matter. In *Proceedings of the 12th Conference of the European Chapter of the ACL (EACL 2009)*, pages 398–405.

Marjan Van de Kauter, Diane Breesch, and Veronique Hoste. 2015. Fine-grained analysis of explicit and implicit sentiment in financial news articles. *EXPERT SYSTEMS WITH APPLICATIONS*, 42(11):4999–5010.

Anna Koufakou, Endang Wahyu Pamungkas, Valerio Basile, and Viviana Patti. 2020. HurtBERT: Incorporating lexical features with BERT for the detection of abusive language. In *Proceedings of the Fourth Workshop on Online Abuse and Harms*, pages 34–43, Online. Association for Computational Linguistics.

Avinash Kumar, Vishnu Teja Narapareddy, Pranjal Gupta, Veerubhotla Aditya Srikanth, Lalita Bhanu Murthy Neti, and Aruna Malapati. 2021. Adversarial and auxiliary features-aware bert for sarcasm detection. In *8th ACM IKDD CODS and 26th COMAD*, CODS COMAD 2021, page 163–170, New York, NY, USA. Association for Computing Machinery.

Timothy Leary. 1957. *Interpersonal diagnosis of personality: A functional theory and methodology for personality evaluation*. Ronald Press Company.

Yinhan Liu, Myle Ott, Naman Goyal, Jingfei Du, Mandar Joshi, Danqi Chen, Omer Levy, Mike Lewis, Luke Zettlemoyer, and Veselin Stoyanov. 2019. Roberta: A robustly optimized bert pretraining approach. *arXiv preprint arXiv:1907.11692*.

Siaw Ling Lo, Erik Cambria, Raymond Chiong, and David Cornforth. 2017. Multilingual sentiment analysis: from formal to informal and scarce resource languages. *Artificial Intelligence Review*, 48(4):499–527.

I Loshchilov and F Hutter. 2017. Fixing weight decay regularization. *arXiv preprint arXiv:1711.05101*.

Saif Mohammad, Felipe Bravo-Marquez, Mohammad Salameh, and Svetlana Kiritchenko. 2018. SemEval-2018 task 1: Affect in tweets. In *Proceedings of The 12th International Workshop on Semantic Evaluation*, pages 1–17, New Orleans, Louisiana. Association for Computational Linguistics.

Saif Mohammad and Svetlana Kiritchenko. 2018. Understanding emotions: A dataset of tweets to study interactions between affect categories. In *Proceedings of the Eleventh International Conference on Language Resources and Evaluation (LREC 2018)*, Miyazaki, Japan. European Language Resources Association (ELRA).

Saif M. Mohammad. 2018. Obtaining reliable human ratings of valence, arousal, and dominance for 20,000 english words. In *Proceedings of The Annual Conference of the Association for Computational Linguistics (ACL)*, Melbourne, Australia.

Saif M. Mohammad and Peter D. Turney. 2013. Crowdsourcing a word-emotion association lexicon. *Computational Intelligence*, 29(3):436–465.

Agnes Moors, Jan De Houwer, Dirk Hermans, Sabine Wanmaker, Kevin Van Schie, Anne-Laura Van Harmelen, Maarten De Schryver, Jeffrey De Winne, and Marc Brysbaert. 2013. Norms of valence, arousal, dominance, and age of acquisition for 4,300 dutch words. *Behavior research methods*, 45(1):169–177.

Emily Öhman, Kaisla Kajava, Jörg Tiedemann, and Timo Honkela. 2018. Creating a dataset for multilingual fine-grained emotion-detection using gamification-based annotation. In *Proceedings of the 9th Workshop on Computational Approaches to Subjectivity, Sentiment and Social Media Analysis*, pages 24–30, Brussels, Belgium. Association for Computational Linguistics.

Robert A Rescorla, Allan R Wagner, et al. 1972. A theory of pavlovian conditioning: Variations in the effectiveness of reinforcement and nonreinforcement. *Classical conditioning II: Current research and theory*, 2:64–99.

Pedro Javier Ortiz Suárez, Benoît Sagot, and Laurent Romary. 2019. Asynchronous pipeline for processing huge corpora on medium to low resource infrastructures. In *7th Workshop on the Challenges in the*

*Management of Large Corpora (CMLC-7)*. Leibniz-Institut für Deutsche Sprache.

Masaki Uto, Yikuan Xie, and Maomi Ueno. 2020. Neural automated essay scoring incorporating handcrafted features. In *Proceedings of the 28th International Conference on Computational Linguistics*, Barcelona, Spain (Online). International Committee on Computational Linguistics.

Frederik Vaassen and Walter Daelemans. 2011. Automatic emotion classification for interpersonal communication. In *Proceedings of the 2nd Workshop on Computational Approaches to Subjectivity and Sentiment Analysis (WASSA 2.011)*, pages 104–110.

David Vilares, Haiyun Peng, Ranjan Satapathy, and Erik Cambria. 2018. Babelsenticnet: a commonsense reasoning framework for multilingual sentiment analysis. In *2018 IEEE Symposium Series on Computational Intelligence (SSCI)*, pages 1292–1298. IEEE.

Wietse de Vries, Andreas van Cranenburgh, Arianna Bisazza, Tommaso Caselli, Gertjan van Noord, and Malvina Nissim. 2019. Bertje: A dutch bert model. *arXiv preprint arXiv:1912.09582*.

Shihan Wang, Marijn Schraagen, Erik Tjong Kim Sang, and Mehdi Dastani. 2020. Dutch general public reaction on governmental covid-19 measures and announcements in twitter data. *arXiv preprint arXiv:2006.07283*.

Thomas Wolf, Lysandre Debut, Victor Sanh, Julien Chaumond, Clement Delangue, Anthony Moi, Pierric Cistac, Tim Rault, R'emi Louf, Morgan Funtowicz, and Jamie Brew. 2019. HuggingFace's Transformers: State-of-the-art Natural Language Processing. *ArXiv*, abs/1910.03771.

# EmpNa at WASSA 2021: A Lightweight Model for the Prediction of Empathy, Distress and Emotions from Reactions to News Stories

**Giuseppe Vettigli**
Centrica plc
giuseppe.vettigli@centrica.com

**Antonio Sorgente**
Institute of Applied Sciences
and Intelligent Systems
National Research Council
antonio.sorgente@isasi.cnr.it

**Abstract**

This paper describes our submission for the WASSA 2021 shared task regarding the prediction of empathy, distress and emotions from news stories. The solution is based on combining the frequency of words, lexicon-based information, demographics of the annotators and personality of the annotators into a linear model. The prediction of empathy and distress is performed using Linear Regression while the prediction of emotions is performed using Logistic Regression. Both tasks are performed using the same features. Our models rank 4th for the prediction of emotions and 2nd for the prediction of empathy and distress. These results are particularly interesting when considered that the computational requirements of the solution are minimal.

## 1 Introduction

In recent years the NLP community has put particular effort into the identification of emotions in natural language. Methodologies based on Deep Learning are driving these efforts as they are currently top-performing on all the tasks proposed until now. This is reflected by the results of the shared tasks at the recent editions of WASSA (Workshop on Computational Approaches to Subjectivity, Sentiment & Social Media Analysis). The shared task of WASSA 2017 (Mohammad and Bravo-Marquez, 2017) proposed to automatically identify the intensity of anger, fear, joy, and sadness from tweets. The task saw 21 participants and the winner used an ensemble model that combines three different types of Deep Neural Networks (Goel et al., 2017).

The Shared task EmoInt, hosted at WASSA 2018 (Klinger et al., 2018) proposed to identify emotions from tweets where words denoting emotions were removed. The winning solution (among 30 submissions) used an ensemble model consisting of language models together with a LSTM-based network containing a Convolutional Neural Network (CNN) as attention mechanism (Rozental et al., 2018).

The shared task at WASSA 2021 proposes to evaluate levels of empathy and distress and predict the emotion from news stories (Tafreshi et al., 2021). This new element around empathy and distress is of particular interest as it provides the community with a dataset where the annotations are supported by proper psychological theories regarding empathy and distress.

The same authors of the dataset have already shown that Deep Learning approaches can beat simpler methodologies, such as Ridge Regression, for the prediction of empathy and distress in (Buechel et al., 2018). More recently, a Mixed-Level Feed Forward Neural Network was also proven to be effective for the creation of lexicons for empathy and distress (Sedoc et al., 2020). Structures based on LSTM and CNN have also been proven to be effective on a separate dataset (Khanpour et al., 2017).

In a scenario where Deep Learning techniques have top performances but are also very demanding in regards to computational resources, we want to challenge the status quo by proposing a shallow model based on linear regression that has minimal computational requirements for both the tasks proposed at WASSA 2021. Thanks to specifically handcrafted features, the models that we propose have results comparable to much more sophisticated solutions already found in literature and, notably, can be trained on commodity hardware within seconds.

This paper is organized as follows. In Section 2 we will briefly introduce the dataset and the task. In Section 3 we will introduce the model used for the prediction. In Section 4 we will discuss the results. Finally, in Section 5 we will offer some conclusions regards our work and the directions of



*Proceedings of the 11th Workshop on Computational Approaches to Subjectivity, Sentiment and Social Media Analysis*, pages 264–268
April 19, 2021. ©2021 Association for Computational Linguistics

our future efforts.

## 2 Data and Task

The data includes 2130 essays, 270 released in a development set and 1860 released in the train set, annotated with an index between 1 and 7 for empathy and distress. Each essay is also associated with an emotion label among sadness, anger, neutral, fear, surprise, disgust, joy.

The task challenges the participant in predicting empathy, distress and emotion.

The essays are reactions to news articles and have length between 280 and 800 characters. This is an example of an essay from the dataset:

> "it is frightening to learn about all these shark attacks but these surfers should be aware of the risks associated with the sport. relocating the sharks should be a priority and it would be in the best interest to establish a moratorium on water sports until the shark epidemic is dealt with. closing beach in australia is a good precautionary method"

This essay is annotated with an empathy of 4.167 and a distress of 5.250 while the emotion is fear.

One of the most interesting features of this dataset is that, for each essay, it reports the following attributes regards the annotators: gender, education, race, age, income, personality conscientiousness, personality openness, personality extraversion, personality agreeableness, personality stability, interpersonal perspective taking, interpersonal personal distress, interpersonal fantasy, interpersonal empathetic concern.

The submissions to the challenge are evaluated on a test set of 525 samples. At the moment that we are writing the labels for the test set have not been released.

A restricted version of this dataset was initially introduced in (Buechel et al., 2018).

## 3 A Unified Model

The idea behind our approach is to achieve competitive results using well known tools that can be used on commodity hardware.

We build the features representing the text as n-grams and adding a set of characteristics extracted from a handcrafted set of lexicons. We decide to use Linear Regression for the prediction of empathy and distress and Logistic Regression for the prediction of emotions.

For the extraction of the lexical features and the creation of the prediction models, we use the scikit-learn library (Pedregosa et al., 2011).

### 3.1 Features

We combine features of three different types. Lexical features, extracted solely from the essays. Features reflecting the demographic and personality of the annotator that come along with the original data. Lexicon-based features extracted from a set of well known lexicons historically useful for the identification of emotions and Sentiment Analysis.

**Lexical.** Before extracting the lexical features we remove words with high frequency to avoid stop words, then normalize the remaining words using the Porter Stemmer via the NLTK implementation (Bird et al., 2009). Finally, we extract a set of n-grams from each essay and represent them using *tf-idf* (Salton and McGill, 1986).

**Demographics and Personality.** All the features regarding the demographics and the personality of the annotators. These features were normalized using standard scaling.

**Lexicon-based.** We consider a set of lexicons annotated with different psychological aspects. Each lexicon contains words annotated with a binary label or an intensity value. For each lexicon, we compute the average score for each word in the essay (binary labels are considered as 1 or -1). All the scores are considered as input features of the model.

This is the list of lexicons considered:

- Opinion Lexicon, words annotated as positive or negative towards opinion or sentiment (Hu and Liu, 2004).
- AFINN, list of words rated for valence with an integer between minus five (negative) and plus five (positive)(Nielsen, 2011).
- General Inquirer lexicon, list words classified as positive or negative according to the psychological Harvard-IV dictionary (Stone et al., 1966).
- Sentiment140 Lexicon, list of words annotated with a real-valued score from tweets with emoticons (Mohammad et al., 2013).

- +/-Effect Lexicon, list of words annotated as positive or negative with respect to the opinions expressed toward the effect that events have on entities (Choi and Wiebe, 2014).
- QWN, words annotated as positive or negative using the Q-WordNet PPV method (San Vicente et al., 2014).
- Twitter, list of words annotated using label propagation using the method described in (Speriosu et al., 2011).
- SenticNet, lexicon that contains a collection of concepts annotated with different values, in this work we consider only polarity, temper, attitude and sensitivity (Cambria et al., 2010).
- Affective rating, list of words annotated with affective norms (Warriner et al., 2013).

The scores extracted from the lexicons are also normalized using standard scaling.

### 3.2 Prediction of Empathy and Distress

The prediction of empathy and distress is done by combining all the features into a linear model. More specifically, the target variable is predicted as

$$\hat{y} = w^{(T)}x^{(T)} + w^{(D)}x^{(D)} + w^{(L)}x^{(L)} + w_0, \quad (1)$$

where $x^{(T)}$ contains the *tf-idf* representation of all the terms considered, $x^{(D)}$ the demographic and personality features and $x^{(L)}$ contains the features derived from the lexicons. The vectors $w^{(\cdot)}$ are weights to estimate while $w_0$ is a scalar representing a bias term. The system is trained computing the block vector of weights $\mathbf{w} = (w^{(T)}, w^{(D)}, w^{(L)}, w_0)$ as

$$\mathbf{w} = \arg\min_{\mathbf{w}} \|\mathbf{X}\mathbf{w} - \mathbf{y}\|_2^2,$$

where $\mathbf{X}$ is a matrix where each row contains all the features extracted from a given essay, plus a unit value to take into account the bias weight $w_0$, and $\mathbf{y}$ is the vector of targets. More formally each row of $\mathbf{X}$ is defined as $\mathbf{x} = (x^{(T)}, x^{(D)}, x^{(L)}, 1)$. Note that $\mathbf{w} \in \mathbb{R}^{F+1}$ and $\mathbf{X} \in \mathbb{R}^{N \times F+1}$ where $F$ is the total number of features and $N$ the number of essays available.

The training is done separately for empathy and distress.

The lexical features consider uni-grams, bi-grams and tri-grams. During pre-processing 20% of the most frequent words were removed for the model that predicts empathy and 30% of the most frequent words were removed for the model that predicts distress. These parameters have been selected using a Grid Search.

### 3.3 Prediction of Emotions

For the prediction of emotions we extend the model presented above to compute the probability of the essay presenting a specific emotion. We compute the probability of an emotion $e$ as

$$P_e = \frac{1}{1 + exp(-\gamma)},$$

where $\gamma$ is given by the linear combination in equation 1. The emotion related to the essay is predicted as the emotion with the highest probability.

The system this time is trained finding the vector $\mathbf{w}$ as

$$\mathbf{w} = \arg\min_{\mathbf{w}} \sum_{i=1}^{N} log(1 + e^{-y_i \mathbf{x}_i \mathbf{w}^\top}) + \lambda \|\mathbf{w}\|_2^2$$

Where $\lambda$ is a multiplier that allows us to regularize the model.

For this model we remove the 10% most frequent words and consider only uni-grams and bi-grams. We also truncate the number of terms extracted to 1000. The regularization parameter is set to $\lambda = \frac{1}{0.9}$. These parameters have also been selected using a Grid Search.

## 4 Results

To build the model for the identification of empathy and distress we used 10-fold cross-validation for an initial evaluation and comparison with the results available in the literature. We considered the Pearson correlation, metric adopted for the competition, as the main score but we also considered the Mean Absolute Error (MAE) and the Mean Squared Error (MSE).

In Table 1 we compare our model to the known state of the art, prior to the competition, given by the CNN-based solution introduced in (Buechel et al., 2018). In this comparison, it is important to keep in mind that the CNN model only uses textual data.

In the Table we note that our model restricted to n-grams has results that are already comparable to

| target | features | Pearson | MAE | MSE |
|---|---|---|---|---|
| empathy | CNN from (Buechel et al., 2018) | 0.404 | - | - |
| empathy | only n-grams | 0.390 | 2.908 | 1.413 |
| empathy | n-grams + lexicons | 0.460 | 2.623 | 1.320 |
| empathy | n-grams + demographics/personality | 0.493 | 2.596 | 1.322 |
| empathy | all | **0.496** | 2.606 | 1.335 |
| distress | CNN from (Buechel et al., 2018) | 0.444 | - | - |
| distress | n-grams | 0.424 | 2.529 | 1.307 |
| distress | n-grams + lexicons | **0.512** | 2.508 | 1.307 |
| distress | n-grams + demographics/personality | 0.494 | 2.491 | 1.294 |
| distress | all | 0.501 | 2.511 | 1.291 |

Table 1: Performances of the model with different set of features estimated using 10-fold cross-validation.

the CNN and that the CNN is outperformed when adding more features. We also note that demographics and personality features are particularly effective in predicting empathy while the lexicon-based features are able to give a major boost for the prediction of distress.

Considering the result on the final test set of the competition our model achieves a Pearson correlation of 0.516 for the prediction of empathy and 0.554 for the prediction of distress. The final score for the competition, computed averaging the results of both the predictions, is 0.554 and ranks 2nd in the final leader board with a difference of 0.009 from the highest score.

The results of the model for the prediction of emotions were less encouraging as we estimated a macro F1-Score of 0.330 and micro F1-Score of 0.413 using 10-fold cross-validation. While on the final test set the model achieves a Macro F1-Score of 0.313 and a Micro F1-Score of 0.396. These results are placed at the 4th position. Considering that the winning model achieved a macro F1-Score of 0.553 and a micro F1-Score of 0.623 we can conclude that our model is not competitive in the prediction of emotions.

## 5 Conclusions

Our submission demonstrated the effectiveness of using a shallow model with carefully handcrafted features for the prediction of empathy and distress. For this task we were able to beat the state of the art, previous to the competition, and achieve a highly ranked position on the leader board. An important result of our work is that our model demands only a fraction of the computational resources compared to the other models available.

We also showed that our model is too simplistic for the prediction of emotions and more sophisticated approaches are necessary to achieve good results.

From studying our models we realized that they have limited elements to be explained and we would like to improve this in our future efforts. In particular, we would like to study which lexical patterns and features drive the predictions of empathy and distress.

## References


Steven Bird, Ewan Klein, and Edward Loper. 2009. *Natural Language Processing with Python*. O'Reilly Media.

Sven Buechel, Anneke Buffone, Barry Slaff, Lyle Ungar, and João Sedoc. 2018. Modeling empathy and distress in reaction to news stories. In *Proceedings of the 2018 Conference on Empirical Methods in Natural Language Processing*, pages 4758–4765, Brussels, Belgium. Association for Computational Linguistics.

Erik Cambria, Robert Speer, Catherine Havasi, and Amir Hussain. 2010. Senticnet: A publicly available semantic resource for opinion mining. In *AAAI fall symposium: commonsense knowledge*, volume 10. Citeseer.

Yoonjung Choi and Janyce Wiebe. 2014. +/- effectwordnet: Sense-level lexicon acquisition for opinion inference. In *Proceedings of the 2014 Conference on Empirical Methods in Natural Language Processing (EMNLP)*, pages 1181–1191.

Pranav Goel, Devang Kulshreshtha, Prayas Jain, and Kaushal Kumar Shukla. 2017. Prayas at emoint 2017: An ensemble of deep neural architectures for emotion intensity prediction in tweets. In *Proceedings of the 8th Workshop on Computational Approaches to Subjectivity, Sentiment and Social Media Analysis*, pages 58–65.

Minqing Hu and Bing Liu. 2004. Mining and summarizing customer reviews. In *Proceedings of the tenth ACM SIGKDD international conference on Knowledge discovery and data mining*, pages 168–177.

Hamed Khanpour, Cornelia Caragea, and Prakhar Biyani. 2017. Identifying empathetic messages in online health communities. In *Proceedings of the Eighth International Joint Conference on Natural Language Processing (Volume 2: Short Papers)*, pages 246–251.

Roman Klinger, Orphee De Clercq, Saif Mohammad, and Alexandra Balahur. 2018. Iest: Wassa-2018 implicit emotions shared task. In *Proceedings of the 9th Workshop on Computational Approaches to Subjectivity, Sentiment and Social Media Analysis*, pages 31–42.

Saif Mohammad and Felipe Bravo-Marquez. 2017. Wassa-2017 shared task on emotion intensity. In *Proceedings of the 8th Workshop on Computational Approaches to Subjectivity, Sentiment and Social Media Analysis*, pages 34–49.

Saif M. Mohammad, Svetlana Kiritchenko, and Xiaodan Zhu. 2013. Nrccanada: Building the state-of-the-art in sentiment analysis of tweets. In *In Proceedings of the International Workshop on Semantic Evaluation, SemEval '13*.

Finn Årup Nielsen. 2011. A new anew: Evaluation of a word list for sentiment analysis in microblogs. In *Workshop on'Making Sense of Microposts: Big things come in small packages*, pages 93–98.

Fabian Pedregosa, Gaël Varoquaux, Alexandre Gramfort, Vincent Michel, Bertrand Thirion, Olivier Grisel, Mathieu Blondel, Peter Prettenhofer, Ron Weiss, Vincent Dubourg, et al. 2011. Scikit-learn: Machine learning in python. *the Journal of machine Learning research*, 12:2825–2830.

Alon Rozental, Daniel Fleischer, and Zohar Kelrich. 2018. Amobee at iest 2018: Transfer learning from language models. *arXiv preprint arXiv:1808.08782*.

Gerard Salton and Michael J McGill. 1986. Introduction to modern information retrieval.

Inaki San Vicente, Rodrigo Agerri, and German Rigau. 2014. Simple, robust and (almost) unsupervised generation of polarity lexicons for multiple languages. In *Proceedings of the 14th Conference of the European Chapter of the Association for Computational Linguistics*, pages 88–97.

João Sedoc, Sven Buechel, Yehonathan Nachmany, Anneke Buffone, and Lyle Ungar. 2020. Learning word ratings for empathy and distress from document-level user responses. In *Proceedings of The 12th Language Resources and Evaluation Conference*, pages 1664–1673.

Michael Speriosu, Nikita Sudan, Sid Upadhyay, and Jason Baldridge. 2011. Twitter polarity classification with label propagation over lexical links and the follower graph. In *Proceedings of the First workshop on Unsupervised Learning in NLP*, pages 53–63.

Philip J Stone, Dexter C Dunphy, and Marshall S Smith. 1966. The general inquirer: A computer approach to content analysis.

Shabnam Tafreshi, Orphée De Clercq, Valentin Barriere, Sven Buechel, João Sedoc, and Alexandra Balahur. 2021. WASSA2021 Shared Task: Predicting Empathy and Emotion in Reaction to News Stories. In *Proceedings of the Eleventh Workshop on Computational Approaches to Subjectivity, Sentiment and Social Media Analysis*. Association for Computational Linguistics.

Amy Beth Warriner, Victor Kuperman, and Marc Brysbaert. 2013. Norms of valence, arousal, and dominance for 13,915 english lemmas. *Behavior research methods*, 45(4):1191–1207.

# MilaNLP at WASSA 2021: Does BERT Feel Sad When You Cry?

**Tommaso Fornaciari**
Bocconi University
Via Sarfatti 25, 20136
Milan, Italy
tommaso.fornaciari@unibocconi.it

**Federico Bianchi**
Bocconi University
Via Sarfatti 25, 20136
Milan, Italy
f.bianchi@unibocconi.it

**Debora Nozza**
Bocconi University
Via Sarfatti 25, 20136
Milan, Italy
debora.nozza@unibocconi.it

**Dirk Hovy**
Bocconi University
Via Sarfatti 25, 20136
Milan, Italy
dirk.hovy@unibocconi.it

## Abstract

The paper describes the MilaNLP team's submission (Bocconi University, Milan) in the WASSA 2021 Shared Task on Empathy Detection and Emotion Classification. We focus on Track 2 – Emotion Classification – which consists of predicting the emotion of reactions to English news stories at the essay-level. We test different models based on multi-task and multi-input frameworks. The goal was to better exploit all the correlated information given in the data set. We find, though, that empathy as an auxiliary task in multi-task learning and demographic attributes as additional input provide worse performance with respect to single-task learning. While the result is competitive in terms of the competition, our results suggest that emotion and empathy are not related tasks – at least for the purpose of prediction.

## 1 Introduction

Different researchers have been exploring emotion prediction from text (Abdul-Mageed and Ungar, 2017; Nozza et al., 2017). The WASSA-2021 shared task (Tafreshi et al., 2021) tackles the prediction of empathy (Track 1 of the challenge) and emotion (Track 2 of the challenge) in text. We, the MilaNLP lab, participated in Track 2 of the challenge. Nozza et al. (2020) show that Bidirectional Encoder Representations from Transformers (BERT) (Devlin et al., 2019) can provide accurate results for many different languages in different tasks. Indeed, we contributed to this year's WASSA workshop with two papers (Lamprinidis et al., 2021; Bianchi et al., 2021) that show that BERT can obtain good results in the emotion prediction task.

This system paper describes our approach to the emotion prediction *shared* task. Based on our previous experience with text classification tasks (Rashid et al., 2020; Fornaciari and Hovy, 2019; Uma et al., 2020), our initial idea was to use BERT, and support emotion prediction by adding an auxiliary task with the empathy score provided in the training set. Using such a Multi-Task Learning (MTL) setup can significantly boost performance on the main task, by exploring complementary information in the tasks, and by acting as a regularizer (a model that has to be able to predict more than one task is less prone to overfitting to any one of them). However, we unexpectedly find evidence for the opposite: using empathy as an auxiliary task in multi-task learning in this setting does *not* work as expected. In fact, adding empathy prediction hurts performance compared to a single-task model.

This finding adds to the literature that auxiliary tasks in MTL setups need to be related to the main task to help performance (Martínez Alonso and Plank, 2017). It also indicates that empathy is not directly a contributing factor to emotions, i.e., that there is no strong correlation between the two tasks.

## 2 Data

In this paper, we focused on emotion prediction (Track 2) of reactions to English news stories. The data set is an extended version of the one presented in Buechel et al. (2018). Each instance corresponds to an empathic reaction to news stories extracted by popular online news platforms. A set of 1860 training documents annotated with seven emotions was given (see Table 2 for the data set size). With each text document, an empathy score that ranges from 1 to seven has been associated; in Table 1 we show some examples of text with the emotion and the empathy that come from the data set.



*Proceedings of the 11th Workshop on Computational Approaches to Subjectivity, Sentiment and Social Media Analysis*, pages 269–273
April 19, 2021. ©2021 Association for Computational Linguistics

| Text | Emotion | Empathy |
|---|---|---|
| it is really diheartening to read about these immigrants from this article who drowned. it makes me feel anxious and upset how the whole ordeal happened. it is a terrible occurrence that this had to happen at the mediterranean sea. thankfully there were some survivors. the fact that babies were lost makes it that much more emotional to read all of this | *sadness* | *5.667* |
| This is a crazy story with so many facets to it, omg. I mean on one hand, I don't support an eye for an eye. I don't support the death penalty and I don't support blinding someone. BUT on the other hand, this is a country where women really struggle and the justice system is not well developed. ALSO, he blinded a FOUR YEAR OLD GIRL. What the fuck is wrong with this guy. So if this was in America I would not support it, but I don't feel right condemning the actions of an entirely different country for doing what they felt needed to be done. | *anger* | *1* |

Table 1: Examples of documents with the emotion and the empathy that come from the data set. One document has relatively high empathy, while the second one has very low empathy.

| Emotion | sadness | neutral | fear | anger | disgust | surprise | joy |
|---|---|---|---|---|---|---|---|
| Training Set | 647 | 275 | 194 | 349 | 149 | 164 | 82 |
| Development Set | 98 | 31 | 76 | 25 | 12 | 14 | 14 |

Table 2: Training and Development set sizes

## 3 System Description

In this section, we describe the different configurations of the system we use for the emotion prediction task. We remind that we focused only on Track 2 of the WASSA Shared Task challenge.

### 3.1 Experimental Conditions

The data set allows building both Multi-Input (MI) and Multi-Task Learning (MTL) models. We tried both methods, separately and together, and we compare them with a single-input, single-task model. The single-input, single-output model uses text as input and predicts emotions.

We create three MI models. All of them take the texts as input: this is our Single-Task Learning (STL) model. We also build three Multi-Input (MI) models where, besides the text, we also include gender information (2-input model, MI1), gender and income (3-input model, MI2), and gender, income, and Interpersonal Reactivity Index (IRI) (4-input model, MI3).

Given the availability of further dependent variables, we create a Multi-Task Learning (MTL) model that takes the text as only input and jointly predicts emotions (classification task with categorical cross-entropy), empathy, and distress (regression task) (MTL2).

Lastly, we implement an MI-MTL model that exploits text, gender, income, and IRI as input and predicts emotions, empathy, and distress (MI3-MTL2).

### 3.2 Architectures of the Models

In all our models, we use the BERT language model (Devlin et al., 2019). In particular, we use the `bert-large-uncased` model for English, that is made of 336M parameters. The model comes with its own tokenizer that we use to extract a word $\times$ contextual embedding matrix for each text. We use such matrix as input for a single-layer, single-head Transformer, following Vaswani et al. (2017), that is in charge to detect specific patterns of emotion. Lastly, a fully connected layer provides the output prediction.

In the MTL models, we have a separate fully connected layer for each task. Even though the different tasks concern the prediction of values being in

| | Acc | P | R | F1 |
|---|---|---|---|---|
| STL | **58.48** | **54.64** | **47.05** | **48.65** |
| MI1 | 52.19 | 50.23 | 36.63 | 36.69 |
| MI2 | 44.76 | 32.34 | 29.11 | 26.09 |
| MI3 | 56.19 | 41.27 | 39.15 | 38.31 |
| MTL2 | 51.43 | 49.53 | 38.41 | 38.96 |
| MI3-MTL2 | 34.67 | 29.03 | 19.09 | 14.19 |

Table 3: Accuracy (Acc), Precision (P), Recall (R) and F1-score (F1) on the Development set. Significance levels over STL: $* : p \leq 0.05$

a similar scale, we also tried to add a normalization layer, with the aim of keeping such scale similar for all the tasks. We did not find performance improvements, therefore we show the results without normalization.

In the MI models, besides the BERT representation, we also use vectors of size 3, 1, and 4 for gender categories, income, and IRI values respectively. The gender vectors are one-hot encoded; income and IRI values are (column-wise) normalized float values.

As loss functions, we use cross-entropy for the classification, and mean squared error for the two regression tasks. We use Adam optimizer (Kingma and Ba, 2015). We select the models through an early-stopping that requires a decrement rate on the development set's loss lower than 12% for three consecutive epochs. Our learning rate is 0.002, drop-out probability 0.2, and batch size 64, manually tuned.

To test the significance of the possible improvements over the STL base model, we use a bootstrap sampling test (Søgaard et al., 2014), with 1000 loops and a sample size of 30%.

## 4 Discussion

Table 3 presents our results. In many cases (Ruder, 2017), using multi-task learning on related tasks can help performance, especially when labeled data is sparse or unbalanced. Intuitively, it would seem that empathy and emotion would make for good candidates. However, in our experiments with this combination, we found a negative effect of empathy on emotion prediction. Upon closer inspection, that makes sense: being empathetic towards someone does not necessarily entail a particular emotion.

Somewhat surprisingly, neither do demographic attributes. Various prior works have found those factors to help in classification settings (Volkova et al., 2013; Hovy, 2015; Lynn et al., 2017), especially with MTL (Ruder, 2017; Benton et al., 2017; Li et al., 2018). However, they do not seem to improve emotion classification here.

Therefore, for the shared task submission we choose the STL model, which showed the highest F-measure on the development set in our experimental conditions. On the test set, we obtained an F1-score equal to 48.6; with this score our team ranked third in the Track 2.

## 5 Conclusion

Our results seem to suggest that the combination between empathy and emotion is a difficult task. Given our low scores in the multi-task setting we also speculate on the fact that the two tasks might not be so easy to relate. Future work should consider better ways to aggregate the information coming from these two models.

## 6 Acknowledgments

The authors are members of the Data and Marketing Insights research unit in the Bocconi Institute for Data Science and Analysis.

## References

Muhammad Abdul-Mageed and Lyle Ungar. 2017. EmoNet: Fine-grained emotion detection with gated recurrent neural networks. In *Proceedings of the 55th Annual Meeting of the Association for Computational Linguistics (Volume 1: Long Papers)*, pages 718–728, Vancouver, Canada. Association for Computational Linguistics.

Adrian Benton, Margaret Mitchell, and Dirk Hovy. 2017. Multitask learning for mental health conditions with limited social media data. In *Proceedings of the 15th Conference of the European Chapter of the Association for Computational Linguistics: Volume 1, Long Papers*, pages 152–162, Valencia, Spain. Association for Computational Linguistics.

Federico Bianchi, Debora Nozza, and Dirk Hovy. 2021. Feel-it: Emotion and sentiment classification for the italian language. In *Proceedings of the Workshop on Computational Approaches to Subjectivity, Sentiment and Social Media Analysis*. Association for Computational Linguistics.

Sven Buechel, Anneke Buffone, Barry Slaff, Lyle Ungar, and João Sedoc. 2018. Modeling empathy and distress in reaction to news stories. In *Proceedings of the 2018 Conference on Empirical Methods in Natural Language Processing*, pages 4758–4765, Brussels, Belgium. Association for Computational Linguistics.

Jacob Devlin, Ming-Wei Chang, Kenton Lee, and Kristina Toutanova. 2019. BERT: Pre-training of deep bidirectional transformers for language understanding. In *Proceedings of the 2019 Conference of the North American Chapter of the Association for Computational Linguistics: Human Language Technologies, Volume 1 (Long and Short Papers)*, pages 4171–4186, Minneapolis, Minnesota. Association for Computational Linguistics.

Tommaso Fornaciari and Dirk Hovy. 2019. Geolocation with Attention-Based Multitask Learning Models. In *Proceedings of the 5th Workshop on Noisy User-generated Text (WNUT)*.

Dirk Hovy. 2015. Demographic factors improve classification performance. In *Proceedings of the 53rd Annual Meeting of the Association for Computational Linguistics and the 7th International Joint Conference on Natural Language Processing (Volume 1: Long Papers)*, pages 752–762, Beijing, China. Association for Computational Linguistics.

Diederik P. Kingma and Jimmy Ba. 2015. Adam: A method for stochastic optimization. In *Proceedings of the 3rd International Conference on Learning Representations, ICLR 2015, San Diego, CA, USA, May 7-9, 2015*.

Sotiris Lamprinidis, Federico Bianchi, Daniel Hardt, and Dirk Hovy. 2021. Universal joy a data set and results for classifying emotions across languages. In *Proceedings of the Workshop on Computational Approaches to Subjectivity, Sentiment and Social Media Analysis*. Association for Computational Linguistics.

Yitong Li, Timothy Baldwin, and Trevor Cohn. 2018. Towards robust and privacy-preserving text representations. In *Proceedings of the 56th Annual Meeting of the Association for Computational Linguistics (Volume 2: Short Papers)*, pages 25–30, Melbourne, Australia. Association for Computational Linguistics.

Veronica Lynn, Youngseo Son, Vivek Kulkarni, Niranjan Balasubramanian, and H. Andrew Schwartz. 2017. Human centered NLP with user-factor adaptation. In *Proceedings of the 2017 Conference on Empirical Methods in Natural Language Processing*, pages 1146–1155, Copenhagen, Denmark. Association for Computational Linguistics.

Héctor Martínez Alonso and Barbara Plank. 2017. When is multitask learning effective? semantic sequence prediction under varying data conditions. In *Proceedings of the 15th Conference of the European Chapter of the Association for Computational Linguistics: Volume 1, Long Papers*, pages 44–53, Valencia, Spain. Association for Computational Linguistics.

Debora Nozza, Federico Bianchi, and Dirk Hovy. 2020. What the [MASK]? making sense of language-specific bert models. *arXiv preprint arXiv:2003.02912*.

Debora Nozza, Elisabetta Fersini, and Enza Messina. 2017. A multi-view sentiment corpus. In *Proceedings of the 15th Conference of the European Chapter of the Association for Computational Linguistics: Volume 1, Long Papers*, pages 273–280, Valencia, Spain. Association for Computational Linguistics.

Farzana Rashid, Tommaso Fornaciari, Dirk Hovy, Eduardo Blanco, and Fernando Vega-Redondo. 2020. Helpful or hierarchical? predicting the communicative strategies of chat participants, and their impact on success. In *Proceedings of the 2020 Conference on Empirical Methods in Natural Language Processing: Findings*, pages 2366–2371.

Sebastian Ruder. 2017. An overview of multi-task learning in deep neural networks. *arXiv preprint arXiv:1706.05098*.

Anders Søgaard, Anders Johannsen, Barbara Plank, Dirk Hovy, and Héctor Martínez Alonso. 2014. What's in a p-value in nlp? In *Proceedings of the eighteenth conference on computational natural language learning*, pages 1–10.

Shabnam Tafreshi, Orphée De Clercq, Valentin Barriere, Sven Buechel, João Sedoc, and Alexandra Balahur. 2021. WASSA2021 Shared Task: Predicting Empathy and Emotion in Reaction to News Stories. In *Proceedings of the Eleventh Workshop on Computational Approaches to Subjectivity, Sentiment and Social Media Analysis*. Association for Computational Linguistics.

Alexandra Uma, Tommaso Fornaciari, Dirk Hovy, Silviu Paun, Barbara Plank, and Massimo Poesio. 2020. A case for soft loss functions. In *Proceedings of the AAAI Conference on Human Computation and Crowdsourcing*, volume 8, pages 173–177.

Ashish Vaswani, Noam Shazeer, Niki Parmar, Jakob Uszkoreit, Llion Jones, Aidan N Gomez, Łukasz Kaiser, and Illia Polosukhin. 2017. Attention is all you need. In *Advances in Neural Information Processing Systems 30: Annual Conference on Neural Information Processing Systems 2017, December 4-9, 2017, Long Beach, CA, USA*, pages 5998–6008.

Svitlana Volkova, Theresa Wilson, and David Yarowsky. 2013. Exploring demographic language variations to improve multilingual sentiment analysis in social media. In *Proceedings of the 2013 Conference on Empirical Methods in Natural Language Processing*, pages 1815–1827, Seattle, Washington, USA. Association for Computational Linguistics.

# Team Phoenix at WASSA 2021: Emotion Analysis on News Stories with Pre-Trained Language Models

**Yash Butala***, **Kanishk Singh***, **Adarsh Kumar*** **and Shrey Shrivastava**

Indian Institute of Technology Kharagpur, India
{yashbutala,kanishksingh,adarshkumar712}@iitkgp.ac.in
shrivastava.shrey@iitkgp.ac.in

## Abstract

Emotion is fundamental to humanity. The ability to perceive, understand and respond to social interactions in a human-like manner is one of the most desired capabilities in artificial agents, particularly in social-media bots. Over the past few years, computational understanding and detection of emotional aspects in language have been vital in advancing human-computer interaction. The WASSA Shared Task 2021 released a dataset of news-stories across two tracks, Track-1 for Empathy and Distress Prediction and Track-2 for Multi-Dimension Emotion prediction at the essay-level. We describe our system entry for the WASSA 2021 Shared Task (for both Track-1 and Track-2), where we leveraged the information from Pre-trained language models for Track specific Tasks. Our proposed models achieved an Average Pearson Score of **0.417**, and a Macro-F1 Score of **0.502** in Track 1 and Track 2, respectively. In the Shared Task leaderboard, we secured $\mathbf{4^{th}}$ rank in Track 1 and $\mathbf{2^{nd}}$ rank in Track 2.

## 1 Introduction

Sentiment analysis over texts has been a widely researched area in NLP. The number of papers published in sentiment analysis related domains has increased from 37 papers in 2000 to 6996 in 2016 (Mäntylä et al., 2016). Sentiment analysis is a trending research topic, possibly due to its applications that automatically collect and analyze a large corpus of opinions with text mining tools. From the conventional task of predicting polarity as positive, negative or neutral, the researchers are now increasingly focused on sophisticated tasks such as emotion recognition, aspect level sentiment analysis, intensity prediction, etc.

Recently, the researchers started exploring more sophisticated models of human emotion on a larger scale. Several datasets and corpora have been curated in this domain, such as (Mohammad et al., 2018), (Alm and Sproat, 2005), and larger datasets like (Demszky et al., 2020). (Buechel et al., 2018) presented an interesting computational work distinguishing between multiple forms of empathy, empathic concern, and personal distress. This data of empathic concern and personal distress along with Multi-dimension Emotions Labelling on news-stories across seven classes, namely: sadness, fear, neutral, anger, disgust, joy, surprise, has been released a Shared Task (Tafreshi et al., 2021) in WASSA-2021 Workshop as Two Tracks[1].

In this paper, we describe our system entry for both the tracks of WASSA 2021 Shared Task. The primary contributions of the paper are as follows:

**Track 1:**

- We demonstrate the efficacy of multi-tasking through parameter sharing which further strengthens the belief that empathic concern and personal distress are co-related.
- We amalgamate the information from sentence embeddings with normalized additional information to finally predict the empathic concern and personal distress using regression.

**Track 2:**

- We provide a comparative analysis of generation modelling against classification modelling for the task of Emotion Prediction.
- We illustrate the efficiency of Task Specific Incremental Fine-Tuning approach 4.2 on Pre-Trained Models for a small sized dataset.

## 2 Related Works

Pre-trained language models have proved to be a breakthrough in analyzing a person's emotional state. We now describe briefly some of these highly influential works.

* Equal Contribution

[1] refer Section 3 for more details



*Proceedings of the 11th Workshop on Computational Approaches to Subjectivity, Sentiment and Social Media Analysis*, pages 274–280
April 19, 2021. ©2021 Association for Computational Linguistics

### 2.1 Pre-trained Language Models

Over the past few years, pre-trained language models have progressed greatly in learning contextualized representations. Transformer (Vaswani et al., 2017), first proposed for machine translation, has enabled faster learning of complex representations of text. GPT (Radford et al., 2018), BERT (Devlin et al., 2018), RoBERTa (Liu et al., 2019), XLNet (Yang et al., 2019) all leverage transformer architecture along with statistical tokenizers. ELECTRA (Clark et al., 2020) a recent generator-discriminator-based pre-training approach offers a competitive performance despite requiring lesser compute. Domain specific language models also leads to a significant performance gain (Vaidhya and Kaushal, 2020; Lee et al., 2019; Beltagy et al., 2019).

### 2.2 Emotion Recognition

Emotion recognition through facial expressions and speech data has been the subject of extensive study in the past. (Tarnowski et al., 2017) presents an approach for recognition of seven emotional states based on facial expressions. (Yoon et al., 2018) utilizes a novel deep dual recurrent encoder model to obtain a better understanding of speech data using text data and audio signals simultaneously.

For text, various approaches have been proposed for emotion recognition. Deshmukh and Kirange (2012) proposed an SVM-based approach for predicting opinions on news headlines. Acheampong et al. (2020) paper analyses the efficacy of utilizing transformer encoders for detecting emotions. Kant et al. (2018) demonstrates the practical efficiency of large pre-trained language models for Multi-Emotion sentiment classification.

### 2.3 Computation of Empathy

Empathy and distress are core components of a person's emotional state, and there has been a growing interest in computational approaches to model them. Considering language variations across different regions, empathy and distress can also vary with demographics (Lin et al., 2018; Loveys et al., 2018), and recently (Guda et al., 2021) proposed a demographic-aware empathy modelling framework using BERT and demographics features.

Understanding empathy and distress are crucial for analyzing mental health and providing aid. Recently (Sharma et al., 2020) explored language models for identifying empathetic conversations in the mental health support system.

## 3 Task and Dataset Description

Our experiments' data consists of the emotion-labels to news stories released as part of the WASSA 2021 shared task. The dataset provided (Buechel et al., 2018) contained essays of 300-800 characters length, Batson empathetic concern, and personal distress scores along with other additional demographic and personality information.

The training corpus of WASSA-2021 shared task consists of 1860 training pairs containing seven emotion labels, namely: sadness, fear, neutral, anger, disgust, joy, surprise. The dataset also includes person-level demographic information (age, gender, ethnicity, income, education level) and personality information. We normalized these information before using in our model for Track 1. We excluded this information in Track 2 model.

| Emotion | Train | Dev |
|---|---|---|
| sadness | 647 | 96 |
| anger | 349 | 76 |
| neutral | 275 | 31 |
| fear | 194 | 25 |
| surprise | 164 | 14 |
| disgust | 149 | 14 |
| joy | 82 | 12 |
| **Total** | **1860** | **270** |

Table 1: Composition of Training and Development dataset

The objective of the Track-1 is to predict the Batson empathic concern and personal distress using the essay and any of the additional information to improve Pearson corelation between the predicted labels and gold standard labels. The task can formally be described as following:

**Empathic concern and personal distress prediction:** Given a paragraph $t$, additional information $i$, learn a model:
$g(t, I) \rightarrow (x, y)$ where $x \in R^{+}$ and $y \in R^{+}$.

The Track 2 is formulated as essay-level Multi-Dimension emotion prediction task. It is defined formally as:

**Emotion Prediction:** Given a paragraph $t$, the classification task aims to learn a model $g(t) \rightarrow \{l_1, l_2, .., l_k\}$ where $l_i$ is a label $\in \{sadness, anger, ..etc\}$.

# 4 Approach

## 4.1 Empathy and Distress Prediction Model

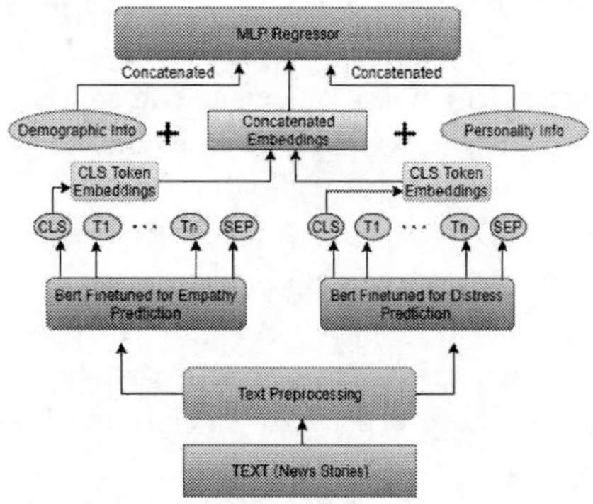


Figure 1

The system architecture for Empathy and Distress Prediction is shown in Figure 1. The approach is primarily based on fine-tuning pre-trained language models for down-stream tasks. We enforce the technique of hard-parameter sharing through concatenation of BERT-fine-tuned embeddings trained separately for Empathy and Distress Prediction. The final shared parameters are then concatenated with the scaled demographic and personality features given in the dataset. These separately fine-tuned BERT-embeddings for distress and empathy prediction are then concatenated with rest of the features before feeding them to the regression models. This parameter shared multi-task framework (Kaushal and Vaidhya, 2020) allows for the use of the same model, loss function, and hyper-parameters for the task of empathy prediction as well as Distress Prediction.

$$MSE(y_{true}, y_{pred}) = \sqrt{(\frac{1}{n})\sum_{i=1}^{n}(y_{true_i} - y_{pred_i})^2}$$

$$r = \frac{\sum_{i=1}^{n}(y_{true_i} - \bar{y_{true}})(y_{pred_i} - \bar{y_{pred}})}{\sqrt{\sum_{i=1}^{n}(y_{true_i} - \bar{y_{true}})^2}\sqrt{\sum_{i=1}^{n}(y_{pred_i} - \bar{y_{pred}})^2}}$$

where $y_{true}$ are the gold-standard and $y_{pred}$ being the predicted scores for empathy and distress. The final Pearson correlation score used for final evaluation was:

$$r_{avg} = \frac{r_{empathy} + r_{distress}}{2}$$

## 4.2 Emotion Label Generation Model

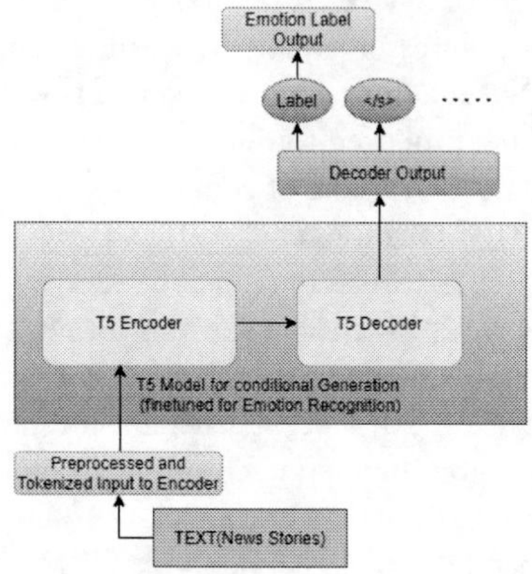


Figure 2

Our proposed approach for Emotion Prediction is shown in Figure 2. The approach is primarily based on T5 Model (Raffel et al., 2019) for conditional generation of emotion labels. Hence before feeding into the network, the emotion prediction task is cast as feeding the essay text as input and training it to generate target emotion labels as text. This allows for the use of the same model, loss function, and hyper-parameters for the task of emotion prediction as is done in other Text Generation tasks. More formally, the modeling of the task can be described as:

$$p(x|c) = \prod_{i=1}^{2} p(x_i|x_{<i}, c)$$

where *c* is the encoder input obtained after text tokenization and *x* is the target decoder output which is of length 2, with $x_1$ and $x_2$ as as *label_token* and *eos_token* respectively.

Here, the transformer network parameters $\theta$ are trained with negative log-likelihood over a dataset $D = \{(c^1, x^1), (c^2, x^2), ..., (c^D, x^D)\}$:

$$\mathcal{L}(\mathcal{D}) = -\sum_{k=1}^{|\mathcal{D}|} logp_\theta(x_i^k|x_{<i}^k, c^k)$$

**Task Specific Incremental Finetuning**: Along with the architecture proposed, instead of the T5 base model, we propose to use the T5 model finetuned on emotion recognition dataset (Saravia et al., 2018) for Emotion Recognition downstream task (Romero). This is done to leverage the task-specific knowledge beyond the available dataset of 1860 samples and to analyze the effect of task specific-incremental finetuning.

## 5 Experiments

The experiments were conducted using Pytorch (Paszke et al., 2019) and Hugging Face's transformers (Wolf et al., 2019). The experiments were performed on the Google Colab Laboratory tool, which provides a Tesla T4 GPU and 16 GB RAM. Adam's Optimizer (Kingma and Ba, 2017) with a learning rate of 2e-5 was used for optimization. The training batch provided in the WASSA-2021 Shared task consisted of 1860 examples. An 80-20 split on the training set was performed for the train-valid split. The development set consisted of 210 examples was used as a test set. As suggested in the WASSA-2021 Shared Task, the average value of the Pearson correlation score of distress and empathy was used for evaluation in Track 1 and Macro F1 score was used in Track 2.The code and trained models are available at https url[2]

**Models used in Experiment for Track 1:** For Empathy and Distress Prediction from the finally obtained parameter-rich concatenated vector, we experimented on a variety of Supervised Machine-Learning architectures along with our final system. Brief details on these architectures are given below:

- **SVR** is a Support vector machine that supports linear and non-linear regression. It tries to fit as many instances as possible between the lines while limiting the margin violations.
- **Ada-Boost** is a meta-estimator that begins by fitting a regressor on the original dataset and then fits additional copies of the regressor on the same dataset but where the weights of instances are adjusted according to the error of the current prediction.
- **XG-Boost** is an applied machine learning algorithm, decision-tree-based ensemble that uses a framework for gradient boosting. It is an implementation of gradient boosted decision trees designed for speed and performance.
- **MLP** is a class of feedforward artificial neural network (ANN). MLP utilizes a supervised learning technique called backpropagation for training.[3] Used the architecture described in the Section 4.1 for final prediction.

**Models used in Experiment for Track 2:** For Emotion Classification, we experimented on a variety of architectures along with our final system. Brief details on these architectures are given below:

- **BERT-base** (Devlin et al., 2018) and **ALBERT-base-v2** (Lan et al., 2019) are the text classification models, in which pooled output, (i.e. output from the first token or *[CLS]* token of last layer of the model) is used as the contextualized embeddings for the text which was then fed into a single feed-forward linear layer for Binary Classification (Kamal et al., 2021), trained with Binary Cross-Entropy Loss.
- **T5-base** (Raffel et al., 2019) and **T5-Finetuned** (Romero)[4] models use the architecture described in the Section 4.2 for conditional generation, the only difference being the pre-trained versions of T5 model used.
- **Pegasus-xsum** (Zhang et al., 2019) model also uses the same approach as used in T5 model for conditional generation, and performs better in several downstream tasks.

Links to pre-trained models used for experiment can be found in the Supplemental Section A.

## 6 Result

This section discusses the results from different approaches and architectures used in our experiments. While the train and development dataset were already available, the gold standard annotations of the test are withheld in the Shared Task of WASSA-2021. The experiments were performed considering Development set as our test dataset. Performance of only the final submissions are provided on the held-out test dataset.

### 6.1 Results for Track 1

Table 2 shows the model performance discussed in the development dataset section (used as validation set) for Track 1. Our final approach, which is described in Section 4.1 outperforms other approaches by an appreciable margin on development set but it failed on empathy prediction on the latest test set submission in the Codalab. It was due to an erroneous submission from us. Though during the post-evaluation phase, the model performed better

[2] https://github.com/yashbutala/WASSA

[3] Our final approach used for submission in WASSA-2021 Shared Task Track 1

[4] Our final approach used for submission in WASSA-2021 Shared Task Track 2

| Predictor | Distress | Empathy | Average |
|---|---|---|---|
| SVR | 0.400 | 0.406 | 0.403 |
| XG-Boost | 0.431 | 0.394 | 0.413 |
| Ada-Boost | 0.418 | 0.374 | 0.396 |
| **MLP*** | **0.462** | **0.473** | **0.468** |

Table 2: Performance of our system on the development datatset of Track 1. Our final submission approach for Track 1 is marked with *.

| Predictor | Distress | Empathy | Average |
|---|---|---|---|
| MLP | **0.476** | **0.358** | **0.417** |

Table 3: Performance of our final submission on the held-out Test datatset of Track 1. Our final submission secured **4th** rank on the Shared Task Leaderboard

on test set than the (Buechel et al., 2018). Table 3 shows the performance of our final submission for WASSA-2021 on the held-out test dataset

### 6.2 Results for Track 2

Table 4 shows the performance of the models discussed in section on the Development dataset (used as validation set) for Track 2. While its clear that our final approach described in Section 4.2 outperforms other approaches by an appreciable margin, there are two other important aspects to note from the table. First, the performance of Conditional Generation models, i.e. Pegasus-xsum and T5 models over Pre-trained Contextual Embedding based Classification model used for BERT and ALBERT models. Second, the improvement obtained by using already finetuned model[5] over T5-base model. As can be seen in Table 4, our approach of generation of emotion labels performs way better than Contextual Embeddings-based classification. Furthermore, the improvement obtained by using task-specific finetuned model over the base T5 model suggests that the model is able to exploit the benefit of task specific incremental finetuning and was able to extrapolate the knowledge features learned from previous finetuning on Emotion recognition onto the newly finetuned model. Table 5 shows the performance of our final submission for WASSA-2021 on the held-out test dataset.

## 7 Conclusion and Future Work

In this paper, we presented an approach for predicting empathic concern and personal distress by fine-tuning a pre-trained language model using parameter sharing. As empathy and distress are correlated, we observe that parameter sharing improves the performance on this task. We amalgamated the sentence embeddings and other additional data, which further used the regression model for prediction. The ablation studies show that on the validation set, the MLP works best.

Also, opposite to most text classification approaches, which use embeddings from the final layer of pre-trained language models, we illustrated the efficiency of formulating finetuning of language models as a label generation task for emotion prediction. Our ablation studies demonstrated usefulness of using task-specific incremental finetuning.

In the future, we plan to extend our multi-tasking based model to incorporate soft parameter sharing. Inclusion of personality related traits provided in the dataset used in this paper, while predicting emotion labels might also be a promising direction to work on.

| Model | Macro-F1 score |
|---|---|
| BERT-base | 0.38 |
| ALBERT-base-v2 | 0.4739 |
| Pegasus-xsum | 0.502 |
| T5-base | 0.5259 |
| T5-Finetuned* | **0.572** |

Table 4: Macro F1 score for Emotion Prediction on Development set. Model descriptions are provided in Section 6. Our final submission approach for Track 2 is marked with *.

| Metric | Result |
|---|---|
| Macro F1 Score | 0.502 |
| Micro F1 Score | 0.594 |
| Accuracy | 0.594 |
| Macro Precision | 0.550 |
| Micro Precision | 0.594 |
| Macro Recall | 0.483 |
| Micro Recall | 0.594 |

Table 5: Performance of our system on the held-out test datatset, for track 2. Our final submission secured **2nd** rank on the Shared Task Leaderboard

[5]https://huggingface.co/mrm8488/t5-base-finetuned-emotion

## References


Francisca Acheampong, Henry Nunoo-Mensah, Chen Wenyu, and Rubungo Andre Niyongabo. 2020. Recognizing emotions from texts using a bert-based approach.

Cecilia Alm and Richard Sproat. 2005. Emotional sequencing and development in fairy tales. pages 668–674.

Iz Beltagy, Kyle Lo, and Arman Cohan. 2019. Scibert: A pretrained language model for scientific text.

Sven Buechel, Anneke Buffone, Barry Slaff, Lyle Ungar, and João Sedoc. 2018. Modeling empathy and distress in reaction to news stories. In *Proceedings of the 2018 Conference on Empirical Methods in Natural Language Processing*, pages 4758–4765, Brussels, Belgium. Association for Computational Linguistics.

Kevin Clark, Minh-Thang Luong, Quoc V. Le, and Christopher D. Manning. 2020. Electra: Pre-training text encoders as discriminators rather than generators.

Dorottya Demszky, Dana Movshovitz-Attias, Jeongwoo Ko, Alan Cowen, Gaurav Nemade, and Sujith Ravi. 2020. GoEmotions: A dataset of fine-grained emotions. In *Proceedings of the 58th Annual Meeting of the Association for Computational Linguistics*, pages 4040–4054, Online. Association for Computational Linguistics.

Ratnadeep Deshmukh and D. Kirange. 2012. Emotion classification of news headlines using svm.

Jacob Devlin, Ming-Wei Chang, Kenton Lee, and Kristina Toutanova. 2018. BERT: pre-training of deep bidirectional transformers for language understanding. *CoRR*, abs/1810.04805.

Bhanu Prakash Reddy Guda, Aparna Garimella, and Niyati Chhaya. 2021. Empathbert: A bert-based framework for demographic-aware empathy prediction.

Ojasv Kamal, Adarsh Kumar, and Tejas Vaidhya. 2021. Hostility detection in hindi leveraging pre-trained language models.

Neel Kant, Raul Puri, Nikolai Yakovenko, and Bryan Catanzaro. 2018. Practical text classification with large pre-trained language models. *CoRR*, abs/1812.01207.

Ayush Kaushal and Tejas Vaidhya. 2020. Winners at W-NUT 2020 shared task-3: Leveraging event specific and chunk span information for extracting COVID entities from tweets. In *Proceedings of the Sixth Workshop on Noisy User-generated Text (W-NUT 2020)*, pages 522–529, Online. Association for Computational Linguistics.

Diederik P. Kingma and Jimmy Ba. 2017. Adam: A method for stochastic optimization.

Zhenzhong Lan, Mingda Chen, Sebastian Goodman, Kevin Gimpel, Piyush Sharma, and Radu Soricut. 2019. ALBERT: A lite BERT for self-supervised learning of language representations. *CoRR*, abs/1909.11942.

Jinhyuk Lee, Wonjin Yoon, Sungdong Kim, Donghyeon Kim, Sunkyu Kim, Chan Ho So, and Jaewoo Kang. 2019. Biobert: a pre-trained biomedical language representation model for biomedical text mining.

Bill Yuchen Lin, Frank F. Xu, Kenny Zhu, and Seung-won Hwang. 2018. Mining cross-cultural differences and similarities in social media. In *Proceedings of the 56th Annual Meeting of the Association for Computational Linguistics (Volume 1: Long Papers)*, pages 709–719, Melbourne, Australia. Association for Computational Linguistics.

Yinhan Liu, Myle Ott, Naman Goyal, Jingfei Du, Mandar Joshi, Danqi Chen, Omer Levy, Mike Lewis, Luke Zettlemoyer, and Veselin Stoyanov. 2019. Roberta: A robustly optimized BERT pretraining approach. *CoRR*, abs/1907.11692.

Kate Loveys, Jonathan Torrez, Alex Fine, Glen Moriarty, and Glen Coppersmith. 2018. Cross-cultural differences in language markers of depression online. In *Proceedings of the Fifth Workshop on Computational Linguistics and Clinical Psychology: From Keyboard to Clinic*, pages 78–87, New Orleans, LA. Association for Computational Linguistics.

Mika Viking Mäntylä, Daniel Graziotin, and Miikka Kuutila. 2016. The evolution of sentiment analysis - A review of research topics, venues, and top cited papers. *CoRR*, abs/1612.01556.

Saif M. Mohammad, Felipe Bravo-Marquez, Mohammad Salameh, and Svetlana Kiritchenko. 2018. Semeval-2018 Task 1: Affect in tweets. In *Proceedings of International Workshop on Semantic Evaluation (SemEval-2018)*, New Orleans, LA, USA.

Adam Paszke, Sam Gross, Francisco Massa, Adam Lerer, James Bradbury, Gregory Chanan, Trevor Killeen, Zeming Lin, Natalia Gimelshein, Luca Antiga, Alban Desmaison, Andreas Köpf, Edward Yang, Zach DeVito, Martin Raison, Alykhan Tejani, Sasank Chilamkurthy, Benoit Steiner, Lu Fang, Junjie Bai, and Soumith Chintala. 2019. Pytorch: An imperative style, high-performance deep learning library. *CoRR*, abs/1912.01703.

Alec Radford, Jeffrey Wu, Rewon Child, David Luan, Dario Amodei, and Ilya Sutskever. 2018. Language models are unsupervised multitask learners.

Colin Raffel, Noam Shazeer, Adam Roberts, Katherine Lee, Sharan Narang, Michael Matena, Yanqi Zhou, Wei Li, and Peter J. Liu. 2019. Exploring the limits of transfer learning with a unified text-to-text transformer. *CoRR*, abs/1910.10683.

Manuel Romero. T5 finetuned model for emotion recognition.

Elvis Saravia, Hsien-Chi Toby Liu, Yen-Hao Huang, Junlin Wu, and Yi-Shin Chen. 2018. CARER: Contextualized affect representations for emotion recognition. In *Proceedings of the 2018 Conference on Empirical Methods in Natural Language Processing*, pages 3687–3697, Brussels, Belgium. Association for Computational Linguistics.

Ashish Sharma, Adam Miner, David Atkins, and Tim Althoff. 2020. A computational approach to understanding empathy expressed in text-based mental health support. In *Proceedings of the 2020 Conference on Empirical Methods in Natural Language Processing (EMNLP)*, pages 5263–5276, Online. Association for Computational Linguistics.

Shabnam Tafreshi, Orphée De Clercq, Valentin Barriere, Sven Buechel, João Sedoc, and Alexandra Balahur. 2021. WASSA2021 Shared Task: Predicting Empathy and Emotion in Reaction to News Stories. In *Proceedings of the Eleventh Workshop on Computational Approaches to Subjectivity, Sentiment and Social Media Analysis*. Association for Computational Linguistics.

Paweł Tarnowski, Marcin Kołodziej, Andrzej Majkowski, and Remigiusz J. Rak. 2017. Emotion recognition using facial expressions. *Procedia Computer Science*, 108:1175–1184. International Conference on Computational Science, ICCS 2017, 12-14 June 2017, Zurich, Switzerland.

Tejas Vaidhya and Ayush Kaushal. 2020. IITKGP at W-NUT 2020 shared task-1: Domain specific BERT representation for named entity recognition of lab protocol. In *Proceedings of the Sixth Workshop on Noisy User-generated Text (W-NUT 2020)*, pages 268–272, Online. Association for Computational Linguistics.

Ashish Vaswani, Noam Shazeer, Niki Parmar, Jakob Uszkoreit, Llion Jones, Aidan N. Gomez, Lukasz Kaiser, and Illia Polosukhin. 2017. Attention is all you need. *CoRR*, abs/1706.03762.

Thomas Wolf, Lysandre Debut, Victor Sanh, Julien Chaumond, Clement Delangue, Anthony Moi, Pierric Cistac, Tim Rault, Rémi Louf, Morgan Funtowicz, and Jamie Brew. 2019. Huggingface's transformers: State-of-the-art natural language processing. *CoRR*, abs/1910.03771.

Zhilin Yang, Zihang Dai, Yiming Yang, Jaime Carbonell, Russ R Salakhutdinov, and Quoc V Le. 2019. Xlnet: Generalized autoregressive pretraining for language understanding. In *Advances in Neural Information Processing Systems*, volume 32. Curran Associates, Inc.

Seunghyun Yoon, Seokhyun Byun, and Kyomin Jung. 2018. Multimodal speech emotion recognition using audio and text. *CoRR*, abs/1810.04635.

Jingqing Zhang, Yao Zhao, Mohammad Saleh, and Peter J. Liu. 2019. PEGASUS: pre-training with extracted gap-sentences for abstractive summarization. *CoRR*, abs/1912.08777.

# A Supplemental Material

Links to the huggingface models used in the experiment:

- Bert-base: `https://huggingface.co/bert-base-uncased`
- Albert-base-v2: `https://huggingface.co/albert-base-v2`
- Pegasus-xsum: `https://huggingface.co/google/pegasus-xsum`
- T5-base: `https://huggingface.co/t5-base`
- T5-Finetuned: `https://huggingface.co/mrm8488/t5-base-finetuned-emotion`

**Association for Computational Linguistics**
209 N. Eighth Street
Stroudsburg, Pennsylvania 18360

ISBN 978-1-7138-2973-7

CURRAN ASSOCIATES INC.
proceedings
.com